Get Connected.

Presentation Capture Tool

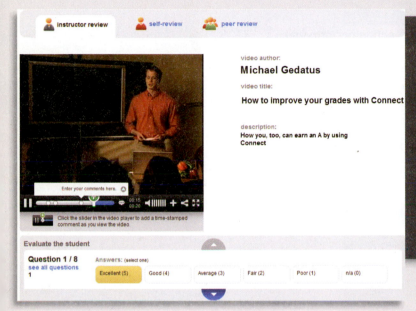

The presentation capture tool gives instructors the ability to evaluate presentations and students the freedom to practice their presentations anytime and anywhere. With its fully customizable rubrics, the tool allows instructors to measure students' uploaded presentations against course outcomes and to give students specific feedback on where improvement is needed.

Interactive Applications

Interactive Applications for each chapter of the textbook allow students to practice real business situations, stimulate critical thinking, and reinforce key concepts. Students receive immediate feedback and can track their progress in their own reports. Detailed results let instructors see at a glance how each student performs and easily track the progress of every student in their course.

Get Engaged.

Assessment

Connect's easy-to-use assessment tools allow instructors to focus on what's important and ensure there is less time spent on administration and grading, and more time spent on teaching and connecting with students.

The assignments in Connect are automatically graded, are tied to learning objectives and accreditation standards, and feed into instructor reports. This allows instructors to track student progress and view reports that assess specific learning outcomes. Instructors can easily generate complete, at-a-glance reports for individual students or the whole class.

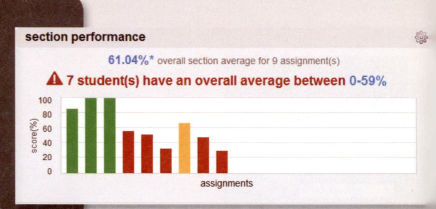

section performance

61.04%* overall section average for 9 assignment(s)

⚠ **7 student(s) have an overall average between 0-59%**

score(%) — assignments

Lecture Capture

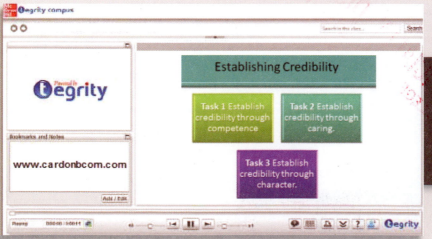

Make your classes available anytime anywhere. With simple, one-click recording, students can search for word or phrase and be taken to the exact place in your lecture that they need to review.

Business Communication
Developing Leaders for a Networked World

Peter W. Cardon

University of Southern California

McGraw-Hill Irwin

BUSINESS COMMUNICATION: DEVELOPING LEADERS FOR A NETWORKED WORLD
Published by McGraw-Hill/Irwin, a business unit of The McGraw-Hill Companies, Inc., 1221 Avenue of the
Americas, New York, NY, 10020. Copyright © 2014 by The McGraw-Hill Companies, Inc. All rights reserved. Printed in the United States of America. No part of this publication may be reproduced or distributed
in any form or by any means, or stored in a database or retrieval system, without the prior written consent of
The McGraw-Hill Companies, Inc., including, but not limited to, in any network or other electronic storage or
transmission, or broadcast for distance learning.

Some ancillaries, including electronic and print components, may not be available to customers outside the
United States.

This book is printed on acid-free paper.

1 2 3 4 5 6 7 8 9 0 DOW/DOW 1 0 9 8 7 6 5 4 3

ISBN 978-0-07-340319-9
MHID 0-07-340319-9

Senior Vice President, Products & Markets: *Kurt L. Strand*
Vice President, Content Production & Technology Services: *Kimberly Meriwether David*
Managing Director: *Paul Ducham*
Senior Brand Manager: *Anke Braun Weekes*
Executive Director of Development: *Ann Torbert*
Development Editor II: *Kelly I. Pekelder*
Executive Marketing Manager: *Michael Gedatus*
Marketing Specialist: *Elizabeth Steiner*
Lead Project Manager: *Lori Koetters*
Content Project Manager: *Katie Klochan*
Buyer II: *Debra R. Sylvester*
Lead Designer: *Matthew Baldwin*
Cover/Interior Designer: *Matthew Baldwin*
Cover Image: *© Shutterstock/Marish*
Senior Content Licensing Specialist: *Jeremy Cheshareck*
Photo Researcher: *Editorial Image, LLC*
Media Project Manager: *Joyce J. Chappetto*
Typeface: *10/12 Times Roman*
Compositor: *MPS Limited*
Printer: *R. R. Donnelley*

All credits appearing on page or at the end of the book are considered to be an extension of the copyright page.

Library of Congress Cataloging-in-Publication Data
Cardon, Peter W.
    Business communication: developing leaders for a networked world/Peter W. Cardon.
       p. cm.
    Includes bibliographical references and index.
    ISBN 978-0-07-340319-9 (alk. paper) — ISBN 0-07-340319-9 (alk. paper)
    1. Business communication. 2. Business enterprises—Computer networks. 3. Business
  communication—Computer network resources. I. Title.
  HF5718.C267 2014
  658.4'5—dc23
                                                                              2012040504

The Internet addresses listed in the text were accurate at the time of publication. The inclusion of a website
does not indicate an endorsement by the authors or McGraw-Hill, and McGraw-Hill does not guarantee the
accuracy of the information presented at these sites.

Dedication

To the women of my life: My wonderful wife, Natalie, and our two beautiful girls, Camilla and Audrey, have supported me during this entire project. My Mom has always been a model of curiosity, adventure, and determination. Thank you, ladies!

—Peter W. Cardon

About the Author

Peter W. Cardon, MBA, PhD, is an associate professor in the Center for Management Communication at the University of Southern California. He teaches a variety of courses in the MBA and undergraduate business programs, including management communication, intercultural communication, and social business. With nearly 40 refereed articles, Pete is an active contributor to the latest research in intercultural communication and social networking. He is proud to engage in a discipline that helps so many business professionals and students reach career and personal goals.

Pete is an active member of the Association for Business Communication (ABC). He currently serves in the presidency of ABC and as an Editorial Review Board member for *Business Communication Quarterly* (BCQ). He previously served on the ABC Board of Directors, the ABC Business Practices Committee, and as a BCQ section editor.

Prior to joining higher education, Pete worked as a marketing director at an international tourism company that focused on the markets of Brazil, South Korea, Japan, and Taiwan. Before that position, he was an account manager in a manufacturing company.

Pete is a strong advocate of global business ties. Having worked in China for three years and consulted in and traveled to nearly 40 countries, he has worked extensively with clients, customers, colleagues, and other partners across the world. To help students develop global leadership skills, he has led student groups on company tours and humanitarian projects to mainland China, Macao, Taiwan, South Korea, Mexico, and the Dominican Republic.

Pete is particularly interested in efforts to improve literacy. He currently serves as co-president of the Friends of Orchid Foundation and as a board member of the Orchid Foundation, both of which support orphanages and schools in the Dominican Republic. In his spare time, he is an avid hiker, surfer wannabe, and fossil collector.

Brief Contents

Developing Leaders for a Networked World

Welcome to the first edition of *Business Communication*. This textbook develops leaders for a networked world. Through the author's practitioner and case-based approach, students are more likely to read and reflect on the text. They are better positioned to understand why credibility is essential to efficient and effective business communication. Cardon's integrated solution, including the text and digital offering, provides a contemporary yet traditional view into the business communication field, allowing instructors to teach bedrock communication principles while also staying up to date with cultural and technological changes. Students are empowered to thoroughly master foundational concepts and practice their communication skills anytime and anywhere, transforming them into leaders for a networked world. This integrated solution is unique in its approach and content.

Approach

In many ways, the business communication field is at a crossroads, as communication technologies are rapidly reshaping how professionals communicate in the workplace. Many communication principles are enduring and remain relevant. Yet, many communication practices are evolving to match shifts in business culture and changes in communication tools. This textbook sticks to bedrock communication principles but also presents a forward-looking approach to adapting to changing technologies. It also effectively engages students so they are more likely to read and reflect on the text. In short, our text and digital integrated content engages and empowers students through the following central principles: credibility; forward-looking vision built on tradition; business focus; engagement; and mastery of interpersonal, writing, and business presentation skills.

Credibility

Since professional success depends on managing and working within professional relationships, this textbook uses credibility or trust as a central principle throughout. Principles of relationship-building such as personal credibility, emotional intelligence, and listening hold a prominent role throughout the book. Credibility is considered a key leadership attribute in today's networked world.

> " *I think it is refreshing and NECESSARY to begin a business communication textbook with a chapter on credibility. In today's business world, it is essential!* "
>
> Dr. Jorge Gaytan, North Carolina A&T University

Forward-looking vision built on tradition

The book stays true to core business communication principles established over many decades. Yet it also goes beyond traditional texts by its inclusion of the latest communication practices facilitated by communication technologies and its enhanced coverage of increasingly important business communication topics such as:

Interpersonal communication (Chapters 2-4), technology (Chapter 7), crisis communication and public relations (Chapter 11), oral communication (throughout the book), and business plan and business proposal (Chapter 13).

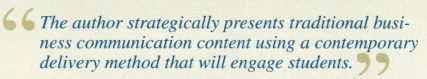

Technology Tips. Each chapter contains a one-page technology tip about applying the latest technologies to communication. These tips encourage students to experiment with new technologies, most of which are rarely used even by today's tech-savvy students. These tips provide a basis for expanded conversation in class.

See page 103

TECHNOLOGY TIPS

ONLINE CALLS

Business professionals frequently use online calls—voice and video—to communicate conveniently and inexpensively. Online calls use VoIP (Voice over IP) technology to allow people to speak with one another over Internet connections. Well-known software packages for online calls include Skype and Vonage.

Skype is the most commonly used online call system for businesses. Skype now has over one billion users, so it may be particularly important for your international dealings. It has caught on for business use for international calls because it is so inexpensive (free for PC-to-PC calls) and convenient. Furthermore, it is often more convenient than mobile phones because many business professionals have phones without international plans. Consider the following when making online calls.

Understand the limitations of online calls. Online calls often provide excellent audio and video quality. However, they are generally less predictable than landline calls. Network outages, heavy traffic creating bandwidth problems, and even power failures threaten call quality. Most software for online calls contains components of online-meeting software packages, such as videoconferencing, file transfer, and screen sharing. These additional features are useful but sometimes contribute to lower audio quality due to bandwidth limitations. Test your equipment and be aware of its limitations before making important calls.

Be sensitive to those who share work space with you. If you work in cubicles or an open office, you may inadvertently distract your colleagues from their work when making online calls. Online calls are typically louder for two reasons. First, you are broadcasting the voices of those with whom you are speaking. Second, you will find that you often project your voice more loudly on online calls than on phones.

Spend time setting up the camera, look professional, and tidy up your work area. Most online calls allow video. If possible, take advantage of this option to add nonverbal cues to your conversation. Take time to set up the camera so that it displays your image in an appealing manner rather than at an odd angle. Also, pay attention to your work space. During lengthy online video calls, the person you are talking with will certainly notice your surroundings. Some will make judgments about your professionalism based on how you maintain your desk and office space.

Business focus

The business case–based approach allows students to better learn how communications can build bridges between professionals. It helps students envision how they will communicate to accomplish workplace objectives and build rich and productive relationships. Each chapter opens with a short business case and, unlike any other book on the market, weaves examples from the case throughout the chapter and into the model documents, engaging readers in the story behind each business message. It offers a broad representation of business problems by discipline, including examples from finance, operations, marketing, human resources, and business information systems. Additionally, these problems are significant in scope, involving some time horizons of five to ten years and projects involving significant outlay of financial resources.

> **❝** *I like how the opening case was used throughout the remainder of the chapter to illustrate key points and bring the reader back to the 'problem' or focus at hand.* **❞**
>
> Lisa M. O'Laughlin, Delta College

See page 56

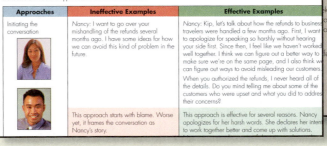

Chapter Case: Listening and Communicating in Teams at the Prestigio Hotel

Who's Involved

Andrea Garcia, general manager

Nancy Jeffreys, director of marketing

Barbara Brookshire, director of conventions

Kip Yamada, marketing associate

The Prestigio Marketing Team

Situation 1 Andrea and Barbara Hold Different Perspectives of Internet Pricing

Andrea and Barbara have disagreed for months about Internet pricing for group guests to the Prestigio, a four-star hotel. Andrea thinks the Internet pricing is appropriate and comparable to other high-end hotels. Barbara, as director of conventions and meetings, deals more closely with groups and often hears these guests complain about the high pricing. She believes an adjustment would increase overall satisfaction among group guests.

Task 1 How will Andrea and Barbara listen to one another effectively when they see things so differently?

ekly meeting. Team members intend to discuss plans for on an ongoing initiative to improve customer service, ove communication within the team, and finalize plans

fectively to implement a cohesive marketing approach?

See page 77

TABLE 3.9

Ineffective and Effective Approaches to Difficult Conversations

Approaches	Ineffective Examples	Effective Examples
Initiating the conversation	*Nancy:* I want to go over your mishandling of the refunds several months ago. I have some ideas for how we can avoid this kind of problem in the future.	*Nancy:* Kip, let's talk about how the refunds to business travelers were handled a few months ago. First, I want to apologize for speaking so harshly without hearing your side first. Since then, I feel like we haven't worked well together. I think we can figure out a better way to make sure we're on the same page, and I also think we can figure out ways to avoid misleading our customers. When you authorized the refunds, I never heard all of the details. Do you mind telling me about some of the customers who were upset and what you did to address their concerns?
	This approach starts with blame. Worse yet, it frames the conversation as Nancy's story.	This approach is effective for several reasons. Nancy apologizes for her harsh words. She declares her inten to work together better and come up with solutions.

Communication Q&A. Each chapter contains an interview with an accomplished business professional about specific types of communication related to a topic in the chapter. These profiles offer current perspectives on chapter content in the professionals' own words, in a question-and-answer format. These interviews can serve as effective platforms for class discussion and for written assignments.

> **❝** *[The author] did engage the reader with Q&A and sound wisdom from industry luminaries. This helps to substantiate the importance of strong communication skills.* **❞**
>
> Lisa D. Lenoir, Columbia College Chicago

COMMUNICATION Q&A

CONVERSATIONS WITH CURRENT BUSINESS PROFESSIONALS

Pete Cardon: How important is trust in the workplace?

Melvin Washington: When people trust you, they listen and respond. It really does not matter whether the communication is internal or external. When you have the reputation of being an honest and trustworthy manager, people will listen. They may not agree with every suggestion or policy you bring to the table, but they will respond with objectivity and honesty.

A business environment is analogous to a team sport. Each team member is trusted to do his or her part. At Anheuser-Busch, I was responsible for forecasting the sales of hundreds of products for an array of market segments. The distributorships trusted me to provide the correct information in order to provide an adequate supply of product to each region. Similarly, I depended on and trusted the sales team to provide me with accurate information, enabling me to forecast future sales correctly. Reliable information was the key to success. In other words, we depended on and, most of all, trusted each other to accomplish our corporate goals.

One aspect of trust is confidentiality. If a trust is betrayed, it may never be regained. It does not matter whether you're the best employee the company has ever hired, if you can't be trusted, you can't be tolerated. A manager at one of the past distributorships where I was employed was an extremely competent employee. She was what you would call a "go-to person." Her performance reviews were among the best in the company. However, she couldn't be trusted. She did not know how to keep matters confidential and constantly repeated information that was told to her in private. Hence, many of the employees ignored her, and it became increasingly difficult for her to function effectively on the job. Eventually, she became incompatible within the company climate and resigned from the job.

Melvin Washington has worked in senior manage ment positions for over 2 years at Anheuser-Busch and ARA Services. He has supervised hundreds of employees in opera tions and supply logistics roles. He currently is a professor of marketing at Howard University.

X

See page 16

Engagement

This case-based textbook tells a story of effective communication in a compelling, research-based, practical, and interesting way. The business communication terminology flows easily from one chapter to the next, creating a smooth flow between chapters. The text challenges and promotes excellence for business students of all levels—poor, average, and top performers. Chapters present lists and models for effective communications. Chapters also help students take into account the context of various business situations.

Why Does This Matter?

Each chapter begins with a section that states the compelling reasons the content is crucial to career success. These first few paragraphs are intended to gain buy-in among students. A QR code located at the beginning of these sections allows students to view a short video clip of the author reinforcing this message.

See page 55

> " *[The author] does an excellent job in engaging the student with real workplace cases carried throughout the chapter for in-class discussion purposes.* "
>
> Laura L. Alderson, University of Memphis

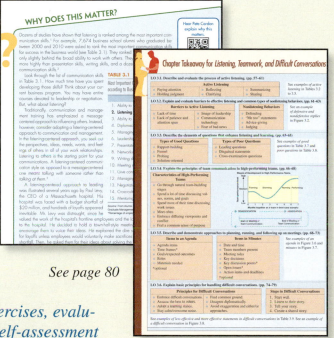

See page 80

Chapter Takeaways:

The chapter takeaway is provided in a visual format. With graphics and lists, it quickly engages students with key chapter content and serves as a reference for applying the principles to their oral and written communication.

> " *By having a graphical representation of the summary of the chapter, I believe it is much more reader-effective than a small paragraph(s) to get the main points of the chapter across to the reader.* "
>
> Susan E. Hall, PhD, University of West Georgia

> " *Such learning exercises, evaluation exercises, self-assessment exercises, and application exercises provide a competitive advantage in the learning experience because of their diverse approach to critical thinking.* "
>
> Michael Shaw, MA, Montana State University

Learning exercises. Each chapter contains between 15 and 25 engaging learning exercises. These exercises are organized into discussion exercises, evaluation exercises, and application exercises to help students develop expertise in business communication.

Mastery of interpersonal, writing, and business presentation skills

McGraw Hill **connect** | BUSINESS COMMUNICATION

In *Connect Business Communication*, students put responsible writing into practice through a personalized learning plan that develops and improves their grammar and editing skills in a pathway-oriented environment. Through an outcome-based assessment approach, students are empowered to develop their communication skills.

Content

The content of this textbook is organized around the traditional business communication topics such as routine messages, persuasive messages, bad-news messages, reports, and presentations Beyond the basics, it adds unique and modern topics that instructors want and need in their courses. The unique content includes the following:

A beginning chapter on credibility

Most business communication instructors recognize that credibility or trust is central to efficient and effective communication. This textbook begins with a discussion of credibility and refers to it throughout the book.

> *No comparision—this is the first time I've seen a BCom text start out with a chapter on credibility, well done.*
>
> Bennie J. Wilson III, University of Texas at San Antonio

Expanded focus on interpersonal communication

This book contains three chapters about interpersonal communication (Chapters 2, 3, and 4), fulfilling the wish of many business communication instructors for enhanced coverage of this material and arming students with skills that will be valued in the workplace. It also contains an entire chapter (Chapter 4), rather than a 5- to10-page section within a chapter, on intercultural communication. Many business communication instructors and students are drawn to this increasingly important topic in the business world.

> *This is a key differentiating factor from traditional texts and gives a clear advantage in terms of really focusing in on how interpersonal communications and relationships play an important role in the business world.*
>
> Melissa Hancock, Texas Tech University

Enhanced coverage of technology

This book adopts a more visionary and reliable view of the communication technologies of tomorrow. While nearly all textbooks refer to use of social media, they focus on a thin slice of social media activities that involve marketing and customer relations. This book, by contrast, takes a larger view of social media use that includes team communication and communication with external partners. It prepares students for communication in the evolving workplace that involves truly networked communication. It also addresses the need for students to develop an online professional persona that builds personal credibility.

The book devotes an entire chapter to electronic communication, including emails and internal social networking on corporate intranets. This book also includes a section (in the first interpersonal communication chapter, Chapter 2) about strategically choosing communication technologies. Furthermore, it contains a roughly one-page technology tip in each chapter that addresses a particular technology (e.g., online calls, videoconferences).

Since a textbook can never stay up to date with the technical features of communication technologies, the discussions about communication technology focus on principles that outlast the cycle of a textbook edition. Thus, the coverage of communication technologies is more extensive, more strategic, and more focused on business communication (not on marketing) than other business communication textbooks.

> **"** *This text is very contemporary with its analysis and recommended application of current technology.* **"**
>
> Daniel McRoberts, Northcentral Technical College

A chapter on public relations and crisis communication

In the era of social media and demand for transparency, business professionals are increasingly expected to understand principles of public relations, even from an early stage in their careers. Furthermore, these skills are career enhancers. This chapter (Chapter 11), contained in few business communication books, fills this need.

> **"** *This chapter [11] is a definite competitive advantage.... This is an excellent, interesting addition to traditional BC coverage.* **"**
>
> Cassie Rockwell, Santa Monica College

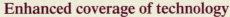

Mastery tools

Connect provides personalized learning plans to develop or improve editing skills and empowers students to put responsible writing into practice. This adaptive learning system helps students learn faster, study more efficiently, and retain more knowledge for greater success. It pinpoints concepts the student does not understand and maps a personalized study plan for success. With interactive documentation tools, it helps students master the foundations of writing. Developed through hours of ethnographic qualitative and quantitative research, it addresses the needs of today's classrooms, both online and traditional.

Connect's presentation capture tool gives instructors the ability to evaluate presentations and students the freedom to practice their presentations anytime and anywhere. With its fully customizable rubric, instructors can measure students' uploaded presentations against course outcome and give students specific feedback on where improvement is needed.

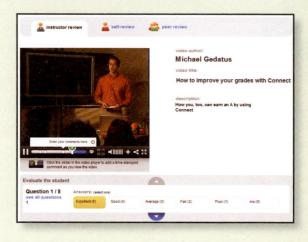

> " *A very useful tool for enhancing the educational experience for students and making it easier for faculty.* "
>
> Lon Doty, San Jose State University

Interactive Applications for each chapter of the textbook allow students to practice real business situations, stimulate critical thinking, and reinforce key concepts. Students receive immediate feedback and can track their progress in their own report. Detailed results let instructors see at a glance how each student performs and easily track the progress of every student in their course.

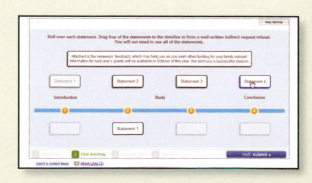

(Appreciation)

I extend my deepest thanks to the many business leaders and professionals, business communication scholars and instructors, and colleagues and friends who have contributed their valuable ideas. The business communication field is filled with professionals who possess unique insights and wisdom about best practices in communication, and I'm honored to affiliate with this community.

I deeply appreciate the efforts of the colleagues who have reviewed iterations of the chapters. With each round, reviewers provided excellent and influential feedback to improve and refine the content. I have made hundreds of changes to reflect the expert advice of these communication scholars and instructors.

Laura L. Alderson, University of Memphis

Melody Alexander, Ball State University

Delia Anderson-Osteen, Texas Tech University

Paula E. Brown, Northern Illinois University

Debra D. Burleson, Baylor University

Elizabeth Christensen, Sinclair Community College

G. Jay Christensen, California State University, Northridge

Anthony M. Corte, University of Illinois at Chicago

Anne Finestone, Santa Monica College

Marla Fowler, Albany Technical College

Jorge Gaytan, North Carolina A&T State University

Terri Gonzales-Kreisman, Delgado Community College

Douglas Gray, Columbus State Community College

Susan E. Hall, University of West Georgia

Melissa Hancock, Texas Tech University

Patricia L. Hanna-Garlitz, Bowling Green State University

Ronda G. Henderson, Middle Tennessee State University

Candy A. Henry, Westmoreland Community College

Susan M. Jones, Utah State University

Marguerite P. Joyce, Belhaven University

Ashley Keller Nelson, Tulane University

Mary Catherine Kiliany, Robert Morris University

Jack Kleban, Barry University, Miami Shores, Florida Atlantic University

Elizabeth A. Lariviere, University of Akron

Marianna Larsen, Utah State University

Newton Lassiter, Florida Atlantic University

Lisa D. Lenoir, Columbia College, Chicago

Jeffrey S. Lewis, Metropolitan State College of Denver

Jeré Littlejohn, University of Mississippi

Jennifer Loney, Portland State University

Kenneth R. Mayer, Cleveland State University

Sheryl McGough, Iowa State University

Daniel McRoberts, Northcentral Technical College

Julianne Michalenko, Robert Morris University

Joyce Monroe Simmons, Florida State University

Lisa M. O'Laughlin, Delta College

Ranu Paik, Santa Monica College

Melinda L. Phillabaum, Indiana University, Indianapolis

Betty Robbins, University of Oklahoma

Sherry J. Roberts, Middle Tennessee State University

Cassie Rockwell, Santa Monica College

Juliann C. Scholl, Texas Tech University

Nicola S. Scott, George Mason University

Michael Shaw, Montana State University

Patricia Smith, Northcentral Technical College

Rachel V. Smydra, Oakland University

Natalie Stillman-Webb, University of Utah

Allen D. Truell, Ball State University

Jie Wang, University of Illinois at Chicago

Tom Williams, University of Houston, Victoria

Bennie J. Wilson III, University of Texas at San Antonio

Caroline Yarbrough, Delgado Community College

This book has gone through McGraw-Hill/Irwin's thorough development process. It has benefited from numerous developmental and marketing focus groups with reviewers from across the country. The author and publisher wish to thank the following people who shared their insights, constructive criticisms, and valuable suggestions throughout the development of this project. Your contributions have improved this product.

Product Development Focus Groups
Spring 2011

Magdalena Berry, Missouri State University
Sheryl Broedel, University of North Dakota
Patrick Delana, Boise State University
Robert Goldberg, Prince Georges Community College
David Koehler, DePaul University
Anna Maheshwari, Schoolcraft College
Elizabeth Metzger, University of South Florida
Joyce Monroe Simmons, Florida State University
Gregory Morin, University of Nebraska at Omaha
Lisa M. O'Laughlin, Delta College
Jo Ann Oravec, University of Wisconsin – Whitewater

Rob Rector, Delaware Technical and Community College
Teeanna Rizkallah, California State University – Fullerton
Jo Ann Starkweather, Northeastern State University
Natalie Stillman-Webb, University of Utah
Bob Sprague, California State University, Chico
Jie Wang, University of Illinois at Chicago
Melvin Washington, Howard University
Kristin Watson, Metro State University of Denver
Diane Youngblood, Greenville Technical College

Spring 2012

Deborah Casanova, California State University – Dominguez Hills
Marilyn Chalupa, Ball State University
Lisa Kleiman, Boise State University
Jeré Littlejohn, University of Mississippi
Jennifer Loney, Portland State University
Cassie Rockwell, Santa Monica College
Sharon Rouse, The University of Southern Mississippi
Michael Shaw, Montana State University
Jeanetta Sims, University of Central Oklahoma
Bennie J. Wilson III, The University of Texas at San Antonio

Market Development Regional Focus Groups
Fall 2012

Carolyn Ashe, University of Houston – Downtown
Michael Buckman, The University of Texas at Arlington
Debra D. Burleson, Baylor University
Amy Burton, Northwest Vista College
Rosemarie Cramer, Community College of Baltimore
Linda Didesidero, University of Maryland – University College
Robert Goldberg, Prince Georges Community College
Kathy Hill, Sam Houston State University
Elaine Jansky, Northwest Vista College
Kayla Kelly, Tarleton State University
Cheryl Law, Tarrant County College
Jack Miao, Southern Methodist University
Chynette Nealy, University of Houston – Downtown
Ephraim Okoro, Howard University

Anita Pandey, Morgan State University
Delissa Perez, Northwest Vista College
Evelyn Pitre, University of North Texas
Lucia Sigmar, Sam Houston State University
Nelda Shelton, Tarrant County College
Kimberly Snyder, South Texas Community College
Melvin Washington, Howard University
McClain Watson, University of Texas at Dallas
Karin Wilking, Northwest Vista College
Kadi Wills, Northwest Vista College
Bennie J. Wilson III, The University of Texas at San Antonio
Robert Yale, University of Dallas
Lydia Yznaga, Northwest Vista College

Market Development Focus Groups
Fall 2012

Tena B. Crews, University of South Carolina
Patrick Delana, Boise State University
Joyce Ezrow, Anne Arundel Community College
Lynda Haas, University of California Irvine
Linda La Marca, Tarleton State University
Anna Maheshwari, Schoolcraft College
Lisa M. O'Laughlin, Delta College
Mary Padula, City University of NY BMCC
Beverly Payne, Missouri Western State University

I also recognize the entire editorial and marketing teams at McGraw-Hill that have made this book possible: Kelly Pekelder, Susan Messer, Ann Torbert, Anke Weekes, John Weimeister, Michael Gedatus, Dana Woo, Lori Koetters, Matthew Baldwin, Joni Thompson, and all of the talented McGraw-Hill publisher's representatives. It has been such a pleasure to work with these incredibly talented and skilled professionals who have shaped the content and design of this textbook. When I signed with McGraw-Hill, I was proud to be aligned with such a well-respected publisher. After working for three years with them, my respect has grown, as I can see the focus they place on producing learning materials that have real impact on the lives of students.

I also thank the teachers and mentors in my life. They have inspired me and influenced my philosophy of learning. In particular, I thank my English teachers Gayle Hawes and Pat Stoddart, my eighth-grade math teacher (and now mother-in-law) Nancy Drickey, my wrestling coach Ron McBride, my calculus teacher Roger Wilson, my chemistry teacher LaMar Anderson, and my German teacher Jane Nicholson.

My family has always been a great joy in my life, and each of my family members has left an indelible imprint on me. Thank you, Mom, Dad, Joe, Steve, David, and John.

Finally, I'd like to thank several people who have been instrumental in influencing my career direction and success. First, I recognize the influence of my dissertation advisor, James Calvert Scott. He contributed decades of research and teaching to the business communication field and selflessly devoted thousands of hours to my development. Without his influence, I would not have become part of the business communication community. Second, I recognize David Victor, author of the first textbook of its kind: *International Business Communication*. While considering returning to school for a doctorate degree about 15 years ago, I purchased a copy of this textbook at a university bookstore. The text inspired me and helped me decide to enter academia, focusing on intercultural business communication. It also led to a desire to write a textbook. Finally, I want to thank Pat Moody, former dean of the College of Hospitality, Retail, and Sport Management at the University of South Carolina. She hired me for my first position as a professor and showed faith in my abilities. She is the type of inspiring leader whom I would gladly work a lifetime for and who exemplifies effective leadership communication.

Peter W. Cardon
Associate Professor
Marshall School of Business
University of Southern California
Email: petercardon@gmail.com
Twitter: @petercardon
Facebook: facebook.com/cardonbcomm
Web: cardonbcom.com
LinkedIn: www.linkedin.com/in/petercardon

support materials

Business Communication, First Edition, includes a variety of supplemental materials to help instructors prepare and present the material in this textbook more effectively.

Instructor's Manual

Prepared by the author, the Instructor's Manual consists of a rich set of information to make teaching easier and more engaging. Within each chapter, the instructor's manual provides teaching notes for the chapter case, thumbnail images of the PowerPoint slides, and additional tips for discussion and learning exercises. It also contains answers and suggested responses to the end-of-chapter exercises.

Test Bank and EZ Test

The Test Bank includes more than 1,400 multiple-choice, true/false, and short-answer questions. Each question identifies the answer, difficulty level, and Bloom's Taxonomy level coding. Each test question is also tagged to the learning objective it covers in the chapter and the AACSB Learning Standard it falls under.

EZ Test Online

McGraw-Hill's *EZ Test Online* is a flexible and easy-to-use electronic testing program. The program allows instructors to create tests from book-specific items, accommodates a wide range of question types, and enables instructors to even add their own questions. Multiple versions of a test can be created, and any test can be exported for use with course management systems such as WebCT and Blackboard or with any other course management system. EZ Test Online is accessible to busy instructors virtually anywhere via the web, and the program eliminates the need for them to install test software. For more information about EZ Test Online, please see the website at www.eztestonline.com.

PowerPoint Presentation Slides

Each PowerPoint file has more than two dozen slides relating to the chapter, including two or more graphics from the textbook and notes offering tips for using the slides. The PowerPoint slides have been prepared by Professor Brad Cox of Midlands Technical College with the input of the author, allowing seamless integration between the slides and the Instructor's Manual.

McGraw-Hill *Connect® Business Communication*

 **Less Managing. More Teaching. Greater Learning.**

McGraw-Hill *Connect Business Communication* is an online assignment and assessment solution that connects students with the tools and resources they'll need to achieve success. McGraw-Hill *Connect Business Communication* helps prepare students for their future by enabling faster learning, more efficient studying, and higher retention of knowledge.

McGraw-Hill *Connect Business Communication* Features

Connect Business Communication offers a number of powerful tools and features to make managing assignments easier, so faculty can spend more time teaching. With *Connect Business Communication,* students can engage with their coursework anytime and anywhere, making the learning process more accessible and efficient. *Connect Business Communication* offers you the features described below.

Diagnostic and Adaptive Learning and Mastery of Concepts

Connect Business Communication provides personalized learning plans to develop or improve editing skills, and empowers students to put responsible writing into practice. This adaptive learning system helps students learn faster, study more efficiently, and retain more knowledge for greater success.

Practice of Presentation Skills Inside and Outside the Classroom

The presentation capture tool gives instructors the ability to evaluate presentations and gives students the freedom to practice their presentations anytime and anywhere.

Online Interactives

Online Interactives are engaging tools that teach students to apply key concepts in practice. These Interactives provide students with immersive, experiential learning opportunities. Students will engage in a variety of interactive scenarios to deepen critical knowledge on key course topics. They receive immediate feedback at intermediate steps throughout each exercise, as well as comprehensive feedback at the end of the assignment. All Interactives are automatically scored and entered into the instructor gradebook.

Student Progress Tracking

Connect Business Communication keeps instructors informed about how each student, section, and class is performing, allowing for more productive use of lecture and office hours. The progress-tracking function enables you to:

- View scored work immediately and track individual or group performance with assignment and grade reports.
- Access an instant view of student or class performance relative to learning objectives.
- Collect data and generate reports required by many accreditation organizations, such as AACSB.

Smart Grading

When it comes to studying, time is precious. *Connect Business Communication* helps students learn more efficiently by providing feedback and practice material when they need it, where they need it. When it comes to teaching, your time also is precious. The grading function enables you to:

- Have assignments scored automatically, giving students immediate feedback on their work and side-by-side comparisons with correct answers.
- Access and review each response; manually change grades or leave comments for students to review.
- Reinforce classroom concepts with practice tests and instant quizzes.

Simple Assignment Management

With *Connect Business Communication*, creating assignments is easier than ever, so you can spend more time teaching and less time managing. The assignment management function enables you to:

- Create and deliver assignments easily with selectable end-of-chapter questions and Test Bank items.
- Streamline lesson planning, student progress reporting, and assignment grading to make classroom management more efficient than ever.
- Go paperless with the e-Book and online submission and grading of student assignments.

Instructor Library

The *Connect Business Communication* Instructor Library is your repository for additional resources to improve student engagement in and out of class. You can select and use any asset that enhances your lecture. The *Connect Business Communication* Instructor Library includes:

- Instructor Manual
- PowerPoint files
- Test Bank
- Management Asset Gallery (which contains 23 Self-Assessments and Manager's Hot Seat videos)
- Self-contained detailed cases with accompanying learning exercises for each chapter in the book
- e-Book

Student Study Center

The *Connect Business Communication* Student Study Center is the place for students to access additional resources. The Student Study Center:

- Offers students quick access to lectures, practice materials, e-Books, and more.
- Provides instant practice material and study questions, easily accessible on the go.
- Gives students access to the Personalized Learning Plan, described above, model documents, a variety of innovative and current learning exercises, and more.

Lecture Capture via Tegrity Campus

Increase the attention paid to lecture discussion by decreasing the attention paid to note taking. For an additional charge, Lecture Capture offers new ways for students to focus on the in-class discussion, knowing they can revisit important topics later. See below for further information.

McGraw-Hill *Connect Plus Business Communication*

McGraw-Hill reinvents the textbook learning experience for the modern student with *Connect Plus Business Communication*. A seamless integration of an e-Book and *Connect Business Communication*, *Connect Plus Business Communication* provides all of the *Connect Business Communication* features plus the following:

- An integrated e-Book, allowing for anytime, anywhere access to the textbook.
- Dynamic links between the problems or questions you assign to your students and the location in the e-Book where that problem or question is covered.
- A powerful search function to pinpoint and connect key concepts in a snap.

In short, *Connect Business Communication* offers you and your students powerful tools and features that optimize your time and energies, enabling you to focus on course content, teaching, and student learning. *Connect Business Communication* also offers a wealth of content resources for both instructors and students. This state-of-the-art, thoroughly tested system supports you in preparing students for the world that awaits.

For more information about *Connect*, go to **www.mcgrawhillconnect.com**, or contact your local McGraw-Hill sales representative.

Tegrity Campus: Lectures 24/7

Tegrity Campus is a service that makes class time available 24/7 by automatically capturing every lecture in a searchable format for students to review when they study and complete assignments. With a simple one-click start-and-stop process, you capture all computer screens and corresponding audio. Students can replay any part of any class with easy-to-use browser-based viewing on a PC or Mac.

Educators know that the more students can see, hear, and experience class resources, the better they learn. In fact, studies prove it. With Tegrity Campus, students quickly recall key moments by using Tegrity Campus's unique search feature. This search helps students efficiently find what they need, when they need it, across an entire semester of class recordings. Help turn all your students' study time into learning moments immediately supported by your lecture. Lecture Capture enables you to:

- Record and distribute your lecture with a click of a button.
- Record and index PowerPoint presentations and anything shown on your computer so it is easily searchable, frame by frame.

- Offer access to lectures anytime and anywhere by computer, iPod, or mobile device.
- Increase intent listening and class participation by easing students' concerns about note taking. Lecture Capture will make it more likely you will see students' faces, not the tops of their heads.

To learn more about Tegrity, watch a 2-minute Flash demo at **http://tegritycampus.mhhe.com.**

Assurance of Learning Ready

Many educational institutions today are focused on the notion of *assurance of learning*, an important element of some accreditation standards. *Business Communication* is designed specifically to support your assurance-of-learning initiatives with a simple, yet powerful, solution.

Each Test Bank question for *Business Communication* maps to a specific chapter learning outcome/objective listed in the text. You can use our Test Bank software, EZ Test and EZ Test Online, or *Connect Business Communication* to easily query for learning outcomes/objectives that directly relate to the learning objectives for your course. You can then use the reporting features of EZ Test to aggregate student results in similar fashion, making the collection and presentation of assurance-of-learning data simple and easy.

AACSB Statement

The McGraw-Hill Companies is a proud corporate member of AACSB International. Understanding the importance and value of AACSB accreditation, the author of *Business Communication* recognizes the curricula guidelines detailed in the AACSB standards for business accreditation by connecting selected questions in the text and/or the Test Bank to the six general knowledge and skill guidelines in the AACSB standards.

The statements contained in *Business Communication* are provided only as a guide for the users of this textbook. The AACSB leaves content coverage and assessment within the purview of individual schools, the mission of the school, and the faculty. While *Business Communication* and the teaching package make no claim of any specific AACSB qualification or evaluation, we have within *Business Communication* labeled selected questions according to the six general knowledge and skill areas.

McGraw-Hill and Blackboard

McGraw-Hill Higher Education and Blackboard have teamed up. What does this mean for you?

1. **Your life, simplified.** Now you and your students can access McGraw-Hill's *Connect* and Create right from within your Blackboard course—all with one single sign-on. Say good-bye to the days of logging in to multiple applications.

2. **Deep integration of content and tools.** Not only do you get single sign-on with *Connect* and Create, but you also get deep integration of McGraw-Hill content and content engines right in Blackboard. Whether you're choosing a book for your course or building *Connect* assignments, all the tools you need are right where you want them—inside Blackboard.

3. **Seamless gradebooks.** Are you tired of keeping multiple gradebooks and manually synchronizing grades into Blackboard? We thought so. When a student completes an integrated *Connect* assignment, the grade for that assignment automatically (and instantly) feeds into your Blackboard grade center.

4. **A solution for everyone.** Whether your institution is already using Blackboard or you just want to try Blackboard on your own, we have a solution for you. McGraw-Hill and Blackboard can now offer you easy access to industry-leading technology and content, whether your campus hosts it or we do. Be sure to ask your local McGraw-Hill representative for details.

McGraw-Hill Campus

McGraw-Hill Campus™ is a new one-stop teaching and learning experience available to users of any learning management system. This institutional service allows faculty and students to enjoy single sign-on (SSO) access to all McGraw-Hill Higher Education materials, including the award-winning McGraw-Hill *Connect* platform, from directly within the institution's website. McGraw-Hill Campus™ provides faculty with instant access to all McGraw-Hill Higher Education teaching materials (e.g., e-textbooks, test banks, PowerPoint slides, animations and learning objects, etc.), allowing them to browse, search, and use any instructor ancillary content in our vast library at no additional cost to instructor or students. Students enjoy SSO access to a variety of free (e.g., quizzes, flash cards, narrated presentations, etc.) and subscription-based products (e.g., McGraw-Hill *Connect*). With this program enabled, faculty and students will never need to create another account to access McGraw-Hill products and services. Learn more at www.mhcampus.com.

McGraw-Hill Customer Care Contact Information

At McGraw-Hill, we understand that getting the most from new technology can be challenging. That's why our services don't stop after you purchase our products. You can email our Product Specialists 24 hours a day to get product training online. Or you can search our knowledge bank of Frequently Asked Questions on our support website. For Customer Support, call **800-331-5094**, email **hmsupport@mcgraw-hill.com**, or visit **www.mhhe.com/support**. One of our Technical Support Analysts will be able to assist you in a timely fashion.

McGraw-Hill's Expanded Management Asset Gallery!

McGraw-Hill/Irwin Management is excited to now provide a one-stop shop for our wealth of assets, making it quick and easy for instructors to locate specific materials to enhance their courses.

All of the following can be accessed within the Management Asset Gallery.

Manager's Hot Seat This interactive, video-based application puts students in the manager's hot seat, builds critical thinking and decision-making skills, and allows students to apply concepts to real managerial challenges. Students watch as 15 real managers apply their years of experience when confronting unscripted issues such as bullying in the workplace, cyber loafing, globalization, intergenerational work conflicts, workplace violence, and leadership versus management.

Self-Assessment Gallery Unique among publisher-provided self-assessments, our 23 self-assessments give students background information to ensure that they understand the purpose of the assessment. Students test their values, beliefs, skills, and interests in a wide variety of areas, allowing them to personally apply chapter content to their own lives and careers.

Every self-assessment is supported with PowerPoints and an instructor manual in the Management Asset Gallery, making it easy for the instructor to create an engaging classroom discussion surrounding the assessments.

Online Learning Center (OLC)
www.mhhe.com/cardonbcom

Find a variety of online teaching and learning tools that are designed to reinforce and build on the text content. Students will have direct access to the learning tools, while instructor materials are password-protected.

e-Book Options

e-Books are an innovative way for students to save money and to "go green." McGraw-Hill's e-Books are typically 40% off the bookstore price. Students have the choice between an online and a downloadable CourseSmart e-Book.

Through CourseSmart, students have the flexibility to access an exact replica of their textbook from any computer that has Internet service, without plug-ins or special software, via the online version or to create a library of books on their hard drive via the downloadable version. Access to the CourseSmart e-Books lasts for one year.

Features CourseSmart e-Books allow students to highlight, take notes, organize notes, and share the notes with other CourseSmart users. Students can also search for terms across all e-Books in their purchased CourseSmart library. CourseSmart e-Books can be printed (five pages at a time).

MORE INFO AND PURCHASE Please visit **www.coursesmart.com** for more information and to purchase access to our e-Books. CourseSmart allows students to try one chapter of the e-Book, free of charge, before purchase.

Binder-Ready Loose-Leaf Text

This full-featured text is provided as an option to the price-sensitive student. It is a four-color text that's three-hole punched and made available at a discount to students. It is also available in a package with *Connect Plus*.

Create

Craft your teaching resources to match the way you teach! With McGraw-Hill Create, **www.mcgrawhillcreate.com**, you can easily rearrange chapters, combine material from other content sources, and quickly upload content you have written, like your course syllabus or teaching notes. Find the content you need in Create by searching through thousands of leading McGraw-Hill textbooks. Arrange your book to fit your teaching style. Create even allows you to personalize your book's appearance by selecting the cover and adding your name, school, and course information. Order a Create book and you'll receive a complimentary print review copy in three to five business days or a complimentary electronic review copy (eComp) via email in about one hour. Go to **www.mcgrawhillcreate.com** today and register. Experience how McGraw-Hill Create empowers you to teach *your* students *your* way.

Contents

Dear Students,

You may wonder why you need to take a class in business communication skills. After all, you've been communicating all your life. And you've got plenty to do just to learn the technical business fundamentals—accounting, finance, operations, marketing, and so on. So why communication? How much are communication skills worth?

According to the most successful and well-known investor in history, Warren Buffett, *effective communication skills can add $500,000 to your lifetime earnings* and increase your earning power by 50 percent. How? The business world has many average communicators but few exceptional ones. Those few exceptional communicators are granted far more professional opportunities.

Warren Buffett is currently the chief executive officer (CEO) and primary shareholder of Berkshire Hathaway, a conglomerate holding company that owns subsidiary companies such as Geico, Fruit of the Loom, The Pampered Chef, See's Candies, and Dairy Queen. He manages businesses with over 233,000 employees across the world, and 88 CEOs report directly to him.

Buffett's extraordinary success can be traced to his passion for business from an early age. At age six, he started saving money. As a young boy, he delivered papers, sold popcorn and peanuts at baseball games, and started a used golf ball business and a pinball machine business. He regularly read financial publications such as *Barron's*. He filed his first income tax return, for $7, when he was 12 years old and was astute enough to deduct expenses associated with newspaper delivery—the $35 expense of his bicycle and his wristwatch. He purchased his first stock, for $120, at the age of 11.

Yet, despite his emerging business expertise, Buffett was, by his own admission, socially awkward and lacking in interpersonal communication skills. He didn't understand the importance of small talk and frequently offended those around him. A life-changing event occurred when he was denied entrance into Harvard Business School because of his poor interview performance. He knew his business knowledge and experience were far superior to those of his peers; however, his interpersonal communication skills were not adequate for exceptional performance in the business world.

As his daughter later stated, "Once upon a time there was a slightly nerdish young man by the name of Warren Buffett, who, at the age of 20, was frightened to death to stand up in front of people and speak to them. Then he discovered Dale Carnegie's course on public speaking and it changed his life. Not only did he develop the courage and skill to speak in front of groups of people, he learned to make friends and motivate people. Warren considers his Carnegie education a life-changing event and the most important diploma he has ever received."

In short, poor communication skills hindered Warren Buffett's early career. He turned this weakness into strength, however, and added excellent communication skills to his visionary knack for investing. Now, he is widely acclaimed as one of the best business leaders and managers in the world.

What do people in the business world say about the need for communication skills?

In one of the largest surveys of its kind (2,825 corporate recruiters in 2,092 companies in 63 countries), from a list of 18 tangible business skills, researchers identified *communication skills as the most important skill for business students.* Perhaps surprisingly, strong academic success ranked as number 11, sufficient years of experience ranked as number 13, and occupation in prior work experience ranked as number 14.

Along these same lines, in a recent *Wall Street Journal* survey, business school recruiters ranked 20 skills in terms of importance for business graduates. *Communication and interpersonal skills were ranked first with 89 percent of recruiters considering them extremely important.* Much lower on the list were qualities such as student years of work experience and content of core curriculum. The authors of the *Wall Street Journal* study came to the following conclusions:

> These days, the recruiter's ideal target is the student who shows promise as an articulate leader, but such [students] are proving to be all too rare. Of all the complaints recruiters register . . . inferior communication skills top the list. . . . Recruiters say they can count on students from any of the major business schools to bring solid knowledge of accounting, marketing, strategy and other business fundamentals. What distinguishes the most sought-after schools and [business] graduates are the "soft skills" of communication and leadership that happen to be among the hardest to teach.

Why do communication skills rank higher in importance than prior work experience, academic performance, and business knowledge?

I can offer several explanations: Excellent communication skills are rarer and thus more valuable; from a corporate perspective, communication skills are more difficult to teach than technical skills and business know-how; and business ideas are useful only when they can be communicated effectively.

Employers expect business students to have functional and technical skills related to their disciplines. Moreover, employers know that if business students lack some functional and technical skills and knowledge, they can acquire them through training and day-to-day business operations. In contrast, training employees to develop communication skills poses more of a challenge.

Understanding the value of communication skills does not necessarily translate into effective communication. Few professionals take strategic, concrete steps to improve their communication performance. In part, this is because improving business communication skills poses unique challenges. What are those challenges? Ironically, your lifetime of communication experiences may itself pose challenges. The most fundamental challenge is that you have deeply ingrained habits. Some are effective. Others are not. In either case, your communication habits feel natural and instinctive.

Adopting more-effective communication tactics may seem unnatural, so you may need to exert persistent and conscious effort to override your less-effective habits. Taking a course on business communication provides the laboratory in which to make that effort.

Also, communication in the business world has unique qualities. Young professionals must become adept at the language of business to project a professional and confident tone in communications and to adjust their communication to their audience (a boss, a peer, a client, a job candidate). They must learn the appropriate mix of formality and friendliness, especially when communicating from a leadership or management position.

A third challenge many business students have is that they have developed writing skills in the context of essay and report writing in the school environment. However, most essay writing focuses on societal-level issues or personal interests. Business writing, in contrast, focuses on corporate needs and logic—on customers, clients, and colleagues. It focuses on getting the job done. Also, a great deal of academic writing discusses subjects in an abstract way, but business writing generally focuses on specific actions and tasks. It is much more action-oriented.

What is the key message of this letter?

The message is that companies increasingly make communication and other soft skills the deciding factors in hiring and promotion decisions, even for highly technical business disciplines. The study and practice of communication skills will undoubtedly help you achieve your professional aspirations.

All my best wishes on this journey,

Pete

Peter W. Cardon
Associate Professor
Marshall School of Business
University of Southern California
Email: petercardon@gmail.com
Twitter: @petercardon
Facebook: facebook.com/cardonbcomm
Web: cardonbcom.com
LinkedIn: www.linkedin.com/in/petercardon

Warren Buffett, interview hosted by Becky Quick, "Warren Buffett and Bill Gates: Keeping America Great," CNBC Town Hall Event, CNBC, November 12, 2009, http://www.cnbc.com/id/33604479 (accessed November 19, 2009); Alex Crippen, "Warren Buffett's $100,000 Offer and $500,000 Advice for Columbia Business School Students," CNBC News, November 12, 2009, http://www.cnbc.com/id/33891448 (accessed November 19, 2009).

Sue Shellenbarger, "Before They Were Titans, Moguls and Newsmakers, These People Were. . . Rejected," The Wall Street Journal, March 24, 2010.

Mary Buffett and David Clark, Warren Buffett's Management Secrets: Proven Tools for Personal Success (New York: Scribner, 2009), p. xv.

Marina Murray, "2009 Corporate Recruiters Survey Report" (McLean, VA: Graduate Management Admission Council, 2009), http://www.gmac.com/NR/rdonlyres/E302D4F6-3781-4615-8D5A-932AA4A5D816/0/CorpRecruitersSurvey2009SR.pdf (accessed November 15, 2009).

Ronald Alsop, "How to Get Hired," The Wall Street Journal, September 22, 2004.

Ronald Alsop, "Poor Writing Skills Top M.B.A. Recruiter Gripes," The Wall Street Journal, January 17, 2006.

Stephen M. R. Covey and Rebecca R. Merrill, The Speed of Trust (New York: Free Press, 2006).

Jeanne M. Baugh, Gary A. Davis, Paul J. Kovacs, Johan Scarpino, and David Wood, "Employers and Educators Want Information Systems Graduates to Be Able to Communicate," Issues in Information Systems 10, no. 1 (2009): 198–207.

Introduction to Business Communication

Chapter 1   Establishing Credibility

PART ONE

Establishing Credibility

Learning Objectives

After studying this chapter, you should be able to do the following:

LO1.1 Explain the importance of establishing credibility for business communications.

LO1.2 Describe how competence, caring, and character affect your credibility as a communicator.

LO1.3 Define and explain business ethics, corporate values, and personal values.

LO1.4 Explain the *FAIR* approach to ethical business communications.

WHY DOES THIS MATTER?

Hear Pete Cardon explain why this matters.

Can't Scan? Try ScanLife at your app store or visit bit.ly.com/CardonWhy1

In most business situations, others make judgments about what you say, write, and do based on your credibility. **Credibility** is your reputation for being trustworthy—trustworthy to perform your work with excellence; to care about those you work with and for; to live by high ethical, corporate, and personal values; and to deliver on your promises. In short, your credibility is the degree to which others believe or trust in you. In this book, we often use the terms *trust* and *credibility* interchangeably.

Business communications occur in the context of working relationships, all of which depend on trust.[1] Credibility has always been important to business relationships, yet its importance has grown in recent years with an increasingly interdependent, knowledge-based workplace.[2] As one of the foremost thinkers on trust in the workplace, Stephen M. R. Covey made this observation:

> *Contrary to what most people believe, trust is not some soft, illusive quality that you either have or you don't; rather, trust is a pragmatic, tangible, actionable asset that you can create—much faster than you probably think possible. . . . It is the key leadership competency of the new global economy.*[3]

The importance of credibility as a basis for effective communication is universal. As Victor K. Fung, chairman of the Li and Fung Group centered in Hong Kong, China, stated, "A good leader is probably no different in any culture in the sense that a good leader must have credibility. That is something one establishes . . . based on the way one handles [oneself] . . . and by [an] established track record."[4] Fung's comments illustrate an important point that we will explore in detail: Credibility emerges from several sources, including abilities and achievements as well as interpersonal skills and traits.

In this chapter, we discuss the ways that business executives and the business community establish trust. Then, we focus on three components of credibility: competence, caring, and character.[5] First, however, we discuss the culture of trust at eBay. Throughout the chapter, we will return to the culture of trust at eBay with examples and comments from business executives.[6]

LO1.1 Explain the importance of establishing credibility for business communications.

Chapter Case: A Culture of Trust at eBay

Who's Involved

Pierre Omidyar
founder and chairman of eBay (1995–present)

Meg Whitman
former CEO (1998–2008)

John Donahoe
CEO of eBay (2008–present)

The Situation

Perhaps no company better exemplifies the importance of trust or credibility in business relationships than eBay. eBay's online auction and shopping website is built on the notion that buyers and purchasers can trust one another to accurately represent the quality and nature of products and ship them in a safe and timely manner—a business model based on the notion of *trusting a complete stranger*. In recent years, eBay has begun to post seller ratings, which are measures of seller credibility in terms of accuracy of item descriptions, honesty of communications, reliability in shipping time, and fairness of shipping and handling charges.

eBay started in 1995 when founder and computer programmer Pierre Omidyar's personal auction website sold its first item: a broken laser pointer for $14.83. Omidyar, a French-born American of Armenian-Iranian descent, is still chairman of eBay and now has a net worth of approximately $5.5 billion. Along with his wife, Pam, Omidyar also heads the Omidyar Network, a philanthropic investment firm "dedicated to harnessing the power of markets to create opportunity for people to improve their lives."

eBay grew rapidly in its first few years. By 1998, it had annual revenues of $4.7 million, half a million users, and 30 employees. Yet, its explosive growth really began when Omidyar asked Meg Whitman to take the CEO position. Whitman brought business credibility to the company. She had thrived in corporate leadership positions at Procter & Gamble, Bain & Company, The Walt Disney Company, and Hasbro, where she was in charge of global marketing for brands such as Playskool, Mr. Potato Head, and Teletubbies.

When Whitman first met Omidyar, she did not expect to take the position. After all, eBay was a small, unestablished, and relatively high-risk company. But she admired Omidyar's business model. As she explained in her memoir (*The Power of Many: Values for Success in Business and Life*), "Pierre carefully explained that he believed eBay was thriving because it was based on the idea that most people are basically good and that the users could be trusted to do the right thing most of the time. . . . Ultimately, eBay developed because millions of people bought into the idea that they could trust each other."

Task 1
Establish credibility through competence.

Task 2
Establish credibility through caring.

Task 3
Establish credibility through character.

The Role of Trust in the Post-Trust Era

Do you operate from a position of trust or credibility? That is one of the first things you should consider as you communicate. In the business world, you often start from a deficit of trust. As a result, one of your first goals should be to gain trust or credibility from colleagues, clients, customers, and other contacts.[7]

Given the major business scandals over the past decade (i.e., Enron, Adelphia Communications, WorldCom), trust in businesses and business executives has dropped to all-time lows. In a recent Gallup poll, just 12 percent of respondents considered business executives honest and ethical. For other business-related professions, trust ratings were also low: bankers, 19 percent; advertising practitioners, 11 percent; insurance salespeople, 10 percent; stockbrokers, 9 percent; and car salespeople, 6 percent.[8] As depicted in Figure 1.1, the trust extended by the general public to business executives is far lower than the trust extended to members of other selected professions.[9]

The public also increasingly views companies with less trust. Approximately 85 percent of senior executives surveyed believe that public trust in business has gone down. Approximately 62 percent of survey respondents across 20 countries said their trust in corporations had gone down following the economic crises of 2008 and 2009.[10]

A deficit of trust also exists within companies. Various surveys show that employees often do not trust their own business leaders. Just 51 percent of employees trust senior management, and only 36 percent of employees believe their company leaders act with honesty and integrity. Furthermore, approximately 76 percent of employees have seen

FIGURE 1.1

How Will You Overcome Public Perceptions to Build Credibility?

A Look at Trust in Professions over a Decade

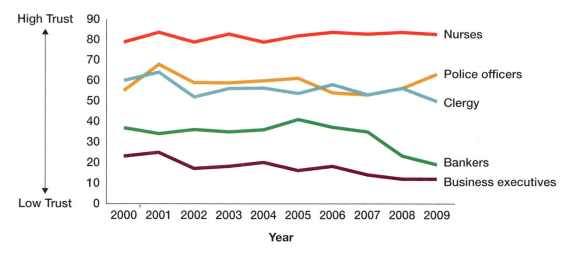

Note: Based on annual Gallup Poll surveys (Gallup Polls, "Honesty/Ethics in Professions," retrieved June 1, 2010, from www .gallup.com/poll/1654/honesty-ethics-professions.aspx). Percentages based on the number of respondents who responded "very high" or "high" to the following questions: *Please tell me how you would rate the honesty and ethical standards of people in these different fields—very high, high, average, low, or very low?*

illegal or unethical conduct in the past 12 months at their jobs.[11] As future business managers and leaders, you will often find yourself in charge of employees who are accustomed to not trusting those in leadership positions.

A strong predictor of cheating in the workplace is cheating in school. Sadly, recent research has found that cheating is so pervasive that some use the label a *global cheating culture.* Among high school students, 80 percent of high-performing students admit to having cheated, and 50 percent do not believe cheating is wrong. Other research about high school students found that more than 70 percent had engaged in serious cheating, and 50 percent had plagiarized assignments from the Internet. In a study of over 50,000 undergraduate students in the United States, more than 70 percent admitted to serious cheating. Nearly 80 percent stated that Internet plagiarism was not a serious offense.[12]

Perhaps most concerning is that business students are among the worst offenders. When asked in anonymous surveys if they had cheated to get into graduate school, many students admitted to having done so: 43 percent of liberal arts students, 52 percent of education students, 63 percent of medical students, 63 percent of law students, and 75 percent of business students. Think about that! Three-quarters of graduate-level business students admitted to some form of cheating to get into their programs. In another study involving hypothetical ethical dilemmas, convicts in minimum-security prisons scored as high on unethical behavior as MBA students.[13] In yet another study of 6,226 undergraduate business students in 36 countries, American business students viewed cheating no differently than did students from countries considered high in corruption.[14]

Michael Maslansky, a leading corporate communications expert, has labeled this the post-trust era. In the **post-trust era,** the public overwhelmingly views businesses as operating against the public's best interests, and the majority of employees view their leaders and colleagues skeptically. Regarding the post-trust era, Maslansky said, "Just a few years ago, salespeople, corporate leaders, marketing departments, and communicators like me had it pretty easy. We looked at communication as a relatively linear process. . . . But trust disappeared, things changed."[15]

Most of these perceptions about business leaders as untrustworthy are not necessarily fair. Daniel Janssen, former chairman of the board of directors of Solvay (a Belgian chemicals company operating in more than 50 countries), explained the dilemma:

> Executives of large companies today are generally perceived as efficient and competent, but also self-interested and ungenerous. However, I think that people who form this opinion are underestimating something of which they lack knowledge. Many executives, in top management and also at other levels, are incredibly generous and not at all self-interested. They do their job and they do it with respect for the common interest. But it is true that capitalism is too often marked by its dark and greedy side.[16]

You will often find yourself needing to establish credibility in this post-trust era. As a future manager and executive, you can control your reputation as a credible communicator by focusing on three well-established factors: competence, caring, and character.

The Role of Competence in Establishing Credibility

LO1.2 Describe how competence, caring, and character affect your credibility as a communicator.

Competence refers to the knowledge and skills needed to accomplish business tasks, approach business problems, and get a job done. Most people will judge your competence based on your track record of success and achievement.

In her memoir, Meg Whitman explains how as a young professional she gained credibility and displayed competence within her organization: "I just focused on delivering results," she said. "You have to excel at the tasks you're given and you have to add value to every single project, every conversation where someone seeks your input."[17]

People develop competence in many ways: through study, observation, and, most important, practice and real-world business experiences. Your entire business program is likely centered on developing competence in a certain business discipline and/or industry. You may already have significant business experience. If you're a novice, seeking internships and jobs related to your discipline will help you develop competence.

How you communicate directly affects the perceptions others have of your competence. Throughout this book, you will find an emphasis on two traits associated with competence: a focus on action and an emphasis on results.

A *focus on action* implies that you seize business opportunities. Meg Whitman emphasized this action-oriented approach to work: "The way I usually put it is, the price of inaction is far greater than the cost of making a mistake. You do not have to be perfect to be an effective leader, but you cannot be timid."[18] She also described the eBay *emphasis on results:*

> I don't believe that all a company needs to do is declare that it has values and then say, "Trust us, we know what's best." To be a success, you must identify a goal with a measurable outcome, and you must hit that goal—every day, every month, every year. Trying is important. But trying is not the same as achieving success. . . . [Some] people expect to advance in their careers regardless of results and are surprised when it doesn't happen. They feel entitled. Their attitude is: "Because I'm here, because I'm me, you owe me."[19]

In summary, you demonstrate competence by taking an active role in your business and by getting results. How you communicate your plan of action and the results of those actions will determine how others perceive your competence and your credibility.

The Role of Caring in Establishing Credibility

Your colleagues, clients, and even your customers will trust you far more if they know you care about them. As Mahatma Gandhi once stated, "The moment there is suspicion about a person's motives, everything he does becomes tainted." This statement applies in nearly all business circumstances: Once an individual is perceived as unconcerned about the interests of others or disinterested in causes above and beyond him- or herself, others distrust such a person. In the business world, **caring** implies understanding the interests of others, cultivating a sense of community, and demonstrating accountability.

Understanding the Interests of Others

Meg Whitman saw that the culture at eBay was committed to the best interests of buyers and sellers:

> Connecting with people's hopes and dreams is a dynamic I perceived in the eBay community. Both buyers and sellers so often loved eBay because it connected them to their aspirations—perhaps the desire of amassing a great collection, or the dream of financial stability from successfully building an online business.[20]

Your ability to gain credibility strongly depends on your ability to show that you care for the needs of others. Furthermore, your ability to show you care puts you in a rare position as a business leader. After all, less than half (42 percent) of employees believe their managers care about them. Even worse, less than one-third (29 percent) of employees believe their managers care about whether they develop skills.[21]

Effective communicators gain trust by connecting with others—that is, seeking to understand others' needs, wants, opinions, feelings, and aspirations. Virtually every aspect of communication you will focus on in this book relies on this other-orientation.

Cultivating a Sense of Community

The most effective business leaders in today's corporate environment have generally risen to their positions because of their sense of community and teamwork. Meredith Ashby and Stephen Miles recently interviewed hundreds of prominent and accomplished business leaders to answer questions such as *What are the burning issues for corporate leaders today?* and *How do companies identify, attract, develop, and retain the best and brightest people in the workplace?* Here is what they learned from these CEOs:

> Most defined their main responsibility as chief executive to be that of inspiring, influencing, setting the direction for, facilitating, coaching, mentoring, and developing their employees. The word "control" was rarely used; instead, they spoke emphatically about the importance of a strong team orientation. Their role was to identify and empower a team, not command it. Indeed, many of them characteristically used the term "we" rather than "I" in discussing success within the organization. Instead of thinking in terms of individual accomplishment, most tended to think in terms of what their management teams had achieved.[22]

Throughout this textbook, you will see techniques for communicating your "we" and "you" orientation rather than a "me" orientation. Speaking about "our needs" or "your needs" as opposed to "my needs" engenders trust and helps you come up with solutions that achieve mutual benefit.

Demonstrating Accountability

A sense of accountability implies an *obligation* to meet the needs and wants of others. It also involves an *enlarged vision* of those affected by your business activities. It takes a **stakeholder** view that includes all groups in society affected by your business.

In a commencement speech to business students at UCLA, Robert Eckert, CEO of Mattel, spoke about trust and, in particular, the sense of accountability that is needed among business executives and managers. He concluded his speech this way:

> You are the future leaders of business. And when it comes to trust, your leadership style affects those you are leading. . . . As you go to work, your top responsibility should be to

build trust. To perform every day at the highest standards. Not just for yourself, but for your team, for your supervisor, for the consumer, for the company's shareholders, for the rest of us in business. . . . It's day one of the next chapter of your life, and I'm putting my trust in each of you.[23]

Thus, a sense of accountability involves a feeling of responsibility to stakeholders and a duty to other employees and customers. By placing a rationale for accountability in your communications, you will generate substantial trust and goodwill from others.

The Role of Character in Establishing Credibility

Character refers to a reputation for staying true to commitments made to stakeholders and adhering to high moral and ethical values. Character has always been important in business relationships, especially long-term, collaborative relationships. It is becoming even more important—especially for leaders—in an increasingly open, transparent, connected, and interdependent workplace. David Pottruck, former president and co-CEO of the Charles Schwab Corporation, explained it this way:

> The twenty-first-century leader is surely different from the leaders of the last two decades. The Internet has placed real power in the hands of people around the world. It has increased the possibilities for millions to do the work that enlivens them. There will be little loyalty to people or to organizations that are not worthy. No longer do pension plans and benefits create chains that hold people in one spot. To create loyalty in such an environment, the new leader will understand how to create a compelling culture, one that will allow people to contribute their best. He or she will then communicate meaning and trustworthiness in every word and action. Culture, character, and communication are the cornerstones of today's new leadership.[24]

Character is central in creating trust. Consider the recent research, depicted in Figure 1.2.[25] Business executives were asked what the most important determinants of trust in workplace projects were. Overwhelmingly, character-based traits—that is, honesty, ethical behavior, and willingness to exchange information—ranked at the top.

In the following sections, we focus on four topics closely related to character: business ethics, corporate and personal values, open and honest communication, and fairness in business communication.

FIGURE 1.2

What Determines Trust in Individuals in the Workplace?

For Collaboration on Workplace Projects

Source: From Economist Intelligence Unit, *The Role of Trust in Business Collaboration.* Copyright © The Economist Newspaper Limited, London. Based on a survey of 453 business executives around the world who were considered expert collaborators.

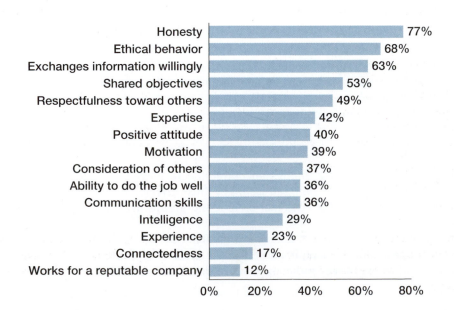

Honesty	77%
Ethical behavior	68%
Exchanges information willingly	63%
Shared objectives	53%
Respectfulness toward others	49%
Expertise	42%
Positive attitude	40%
Motivation	39%
Consideration of others	37%
Ability to do the job well	36%
Communication skills	36%
Intelligence	29%
Experience	23%
Connectedness	17%
Works for a reputable company	12%

Business Ethics

Ethics are "rules of conduct or moral principles that guide individual or group behavior."[26] **Business ethics** are the commonly accepted beliefs and principles in the business community for acceptable behavior. At a minimum, business ethics involve adhering to laws; safeguarding confidential or proprietary information; avoiding conflicts of interest and misuse of company assets; and refraining from accepting or providing inappropriate gifts, gratuities, and entertainment.[27]

As far as corporate communications, the dominant business ethic in recent years is transparency. **Transparency** involves sharing all relevant information with stakeholders. As defined by Transparency International, transparency "is a principle that allows those affected by administrative decisions, business transactions or charitable work to know not only the basic facts and figures but also the mechanisms and processes. It is the duty of civil servants, managers and trustees to act visibly, predictably and understandably."[28]

In recent years, perhaps in large part due to public scandals, employees of companies in the United States have observed higher ethical behavior within their companies and generally view their upper managers as ethical. For example, in a recent Ethics Resource Center survey of 3,010 employees across the United States, 80 percent of employees said they were satisfied with the information they received from top management about what was going on in the company; 74 percent trusted that top management would keep its promises and commitments; and 89 percent stated that top management actively encouraged employees to do the right thing. Furthermore, 82 percent of employees believed that top managers would be punished and held accountable if they were caught violating the organization's ethical standards.[29] For the foreseeable future, transparency is expected to remain the dominant business ethic related to communications.

You will soon be in leadership positions within your organization. You can create a transparent workplace by being accessible, acknowledging the concerns of others, and following through when you don't have immediate answers. Trust-building behaviors include extending trust, sharing information, telling it straight, providing opportunities, admitting mistakes, and setting a good example by following rules.[30]

You likely will need to analyze ethical dilemmas in your business program, while training for your job, and once you are on the job. You probably recognize that "making the right choice" is not always obvious. In such situations, where the law and ethical principles do not provide a clear answer, transparency is key: Decision making needs to be open, documented, and based on the collective conscience of your work team and affected stakeholders.

Often employees fail to speak up when they observe potentially unethical behavior. Business professionals remain silent for four basic reasons: (1) They assume it's standard practice, (2) they rationalize that it's not a big deal, (3) they say to themselves it's not their responsibility, or (4) they want to be loyal.

Prepare now to speak up constructively when you observe unethical behavior. It's part of your job. You can challenge rationalizations with questions such as these:

If this is standard, why is there a policy against it?

If it is expected, are we comfortable being public about it?

I may be new here, so I might not understand our policy clearly. But, shouldn't we . . .?[31]

When you frame your concerns in terms of benefits to your team or organization, your colleagues and other contacts will often respond appropriately. Over the long run, you will be rewarded for having a reputation of speaking up when ethical dilemmas arise.[32]

LO1.3 Define and explain business ethics, corporate values, and personal values.

Corporate and Personal Values

Corporate values are the stated and lived values of a company. The Society for Human Resource Management espouses corporate values as the essence of business ethics. It defines business ethics as "organizational values, guidelines, and codes," and it emphasizes "behaving within those boundaries when faced with dilemmas in business or professional work."[33]

Most organizations have created a written **code of conduct** or code of ethics. Publicly traded companies are required by the Sarbanes-Oxley Act of 2002 to have a code of ethics available to all employees and to ensure that it is enacted. eBay's culture of trust is embodied in its Code of Business Conduct (see Figure 1.3).

Aligning **personal values**—those values that individuals prioritize and adhere to—with corporate values is an important element of character. After all, if one is living corporate values that do not match one's personal values, then there is a lack of integrity. Paul Polman, CEO of Unilever, was recently interviewed about the importance of corporate values:

> One thing I've learned over the course of my career is that if your values—your personal values—are aligned with the company's values, you're probably going to be more successful in the long term than if they are not. Because if they aren't, it requires you to be an actor when you go to work or to have a split personality.[34]

FIGURE 1.3

eBay's Code of Business Conduct

Source: eBay's Code of Business Conduct, http://investor .ebayinc.com/documentdisplay .cfm?DocumentID=649.

We do business according to the highest ethical and legal standards. This Code of Business Conduct highlights some of the laws and policies you need to know in order to meet that test.

Ever since Pierre Omidyar founded eBay, we've stayed true to some core values:

- We believe people are basically good.
- We recognize and respect everyone as a unique individual.
- We believe everyone has something to contribute.
- We encourage people to treat others the way they want to be treated themselves.
- We believe that an honest, open environment can bring out the best in people.

These principles support our basic purpose:

We are pioneering new communities around the world built on commerce, sustained by trust, and inspired by opportunity. These values and this purpose help make eBay a special company. And the Code you're reading now helps us put them into practice. It's not just a set of rules, but an intentionally broad statement of principles. We've written it in a way that's meant to be easy to read. So please read it now, ask questions if you have them, and read it again and ask more questions down the line.

Of course, no code of conduct can cover every situation. All of us need to observe not just the letter, but also the spirit of this Code in all our dealings on behalf of the company.

We are an evolving company, and by our actions we continually shape our corporate culture. We want that culture to promote the reputation and reality of professional and ethical conduct. Please do everything you can to help us reach that goal.

— John Donahoe, President and CEO

Open and Honest Communication

In Tamar Frankel's excellent book on the role of honesty in American business culture, she chronicles the increasing abuses of honesty, including health care fraud, insurance fraud, check fraud, consumer fraud, identity theft, and student cheating, to name a few. She concludes her work with an appeal for more honesty:

> The goal of honesty is not to reduce competitive ardor but to channel it in less destructive ways. Honesty encourages competition on the merits and prohibits competition by cheating. Honesty brings better quality of products and services and less shoddy products and fake services. If businesses do not compete on fraud, they can be more successful in gaining and retaining customers.[35]

Frankel's point about honesty at an institutional level also applies on a personal level. By staying honest in all situations and avoiding cutting corners in any manner, you allow yourself to perform based solely on merit. Over the long run, complete honesty not only forges your character, it helps you develop and maximize your competencies.

Nothing short of complete honesty is demanded in business for several reasons. First, the price of dishonesty on financial performance can be devastating. Over her corporate career, Meg Whitman became adept at identifying when executives were avoiding reality: "At some companies, board meetings are mainly a mind-numbing series of *happy PowerPoints*. From the agenda and the demeanor of the CEO, you would think that all is sweetness, light, and ice cream."[36] Her comment points to three important issues. First, by avoiding open and honest communication of business problems, employees doom a business to poor financial performance. Second, dishonesty is among the primary reasons for lower employee morale. Nearly six in ten employees say that they've left an organization because of lack of trust—the key reasons being lack of communication and dishonesty.[37] Finally, dishonesty can be reason for dismissal. In some cases, dishonesty can destroy careers and even result in criminal charges.

Some business executives and managers view slight deviations from the truth in small matters as inconsequential. Often, they feel, these small lies are expressed with no ill will and without much impact on important business matters. Yet, experienced executives and management consultants have observed how damaging even minor dishonesty can be. Drs. Dennis S. Reina and Michelle L. Reina focus on this point in their book *Trust and Betrayal in the Workplace:*

> There was a time, many years ago, when we too assumed that what broke the delicate fiber of trust in relationships were large acts that had significant impact. However, our research and work over the last fifteen years have taught us differently. What gradually erodes trust and creates a climate of betrayal in our workplaces today are small, subtle acts that accumulate over time. When we don't do what we say we will do, when we gossip about others behind their backs, when we renege on decisions we agreed to, when we hide our agenda and work it behind the scenes, and when we spin the truth rather than tell it, we break trust and damage relationships.[38]

Today, most organizational cultures are moving to flatter, more open communication structures. However, you will also find yourself in many situations where confidentiality is mandated. Companies often direct employees to maintain confidentiality about information that can harm profitability, productivity, and employees within the organization if it is disclosed. In some cases, confidentiality is required by legal considerations, such as laws regarding medical records, disclosure of insider information, or copyrights. In other cases, you may need to protect intellectual property. When Apple rolled out the iPhone, employees underwent a code of silence for months when they could not even talk about their work to family members. In fact, until the release of the iPhone, many Apple employees could not even speak about certain iPhone features to Apple employees in other divisions.[39]

LO1.4 Explain the *FAIR* approach to ethical business communications.

Fairness in Business Communications

Generally, others' perceptions of your character—your unquestioned adherence to personal and corporate values—are largely determined by your communications. Moreover, your colleagues, clients, and customers will gauge your communications based on a judgment of how fair it is.

Thus, in all your communications, you should consider whether you are being fair to others. For routine communications, you make this calculation quickly. For important, less straightforward, and perhaps even controversial communications, you should spend a significant amount of time evaluating the best way to be fair. You might consider talking to your supervisor, peers, and other trusted individuals to appraise the situation. Meg Whitman explained this principle based on her experience at eBay:

> Ultimately the character of a company, like the character of a person, is an accumulation of many, many moments when the choices are not necessarily clear and we make the best decisions we can. But over time the logic and reasoning that we use to make those decisions, the moral compass to follow in making those decisions, is the essence of our authentic self, our character.[40]

One way to evaluate your communications is to use the *FAIR test* (see Figure 1.4). The FAIR test helps you examine how well you have provided the *facts*; how well you have granted *access* to your motives, reasoning, and information; how well you have examined *impacts* on stakeholders; and how well you have shown *respect*. As you

FIGURE 1.4

The FAIR Test of Ethical Business Communication

Are Your Communications FAIR?

Facts (How *factual* is your communication?)

- Have you presented the facts correctly?
- Have you presented all the relevant facts?
- Have you presented any information that would be considered misleading?
- Have you used the facts in a reasonable manner to arrive at your conclusions and recommendations? Would your audience agree with your reasoning?

Access (How *accessible* or *transparent* are your motives, reasoning, and information?)

- Are your motives clear, or will others perceive that you have a hidden agenda?
- Have you fully disclosed how you obtained the information and used it to make your case?
- Are you hiding any of the information or real reasons for making certain claims or recommendations?
- Have you given stakeholders the opportunity to provide input in the decision-making process?

Impacts (How does your communication *impact* stakeholders?)

- Have you considered how your communication impacts all stakeholders?
- Have you thought about how your communication will help or even hurt others?
- How could you learn more about these impacts?

Respect (How *respectful* is your communication?)

- Have you prepared your communication to recognize the inherent dignity and self-worth of others?
- Would those with whom you are communicating consider your communication respectful?
- Would a neutral observer consider your communication respectful?

respond to questions such as those posed in Figure 1.4, you ensure that your communications are fair to yourself and others.

High-Trust Relationships, Ease of Communication, and Improved Work Outcomes

Establishing credibility allows you to communicate more easily and more influentially. Extensive research has shown that high-trust relationships lead to more efficient and superior work outcomes.[41] In terms of ease of communication, credibility leads to less resistance from others, increased willingness to cooperate, and less likelihood of miscommunication:

> In low-trust work environments, people tend to assume the negative regarding others' actions. In higher-trust work environments, people tend to give others the benefit of the doubt and assume the positive, until proven otherwise.[42]

In high-trust relationships, since individuals willingly and freely give the benefit of the doubt, communication is simpler, easier, quicker, and more effective.[43] As Dr. Stephen R. Covey, among the most respected management writers of the past three decades, stated regarding trust:

> It simply makes no difference how good the rhetoric is or even how good the intentions are; if there is little or no trust, there is no foundation for permanent success. . . . What we are communicates far more eloquently than anything we say or do. We all know it. There are people we trust absolutely because we know their character. Whether they're eloquent or not, whether they have the human relations techniques or not, we trust them, and we work successfully with them.[44]

The level of trust in working relationships strongly impacts work outcomes and financial performance. In a recent survey of 453 executives across the globe, the executives were asked about recent collaborative projects. In projects where they had complete trust in a key individual, the projects were successful 92 percent of the time. By contrast, in projects where they had little trust, the projects were successful just 45 percent of the time.[45] These executives also described the impact of various breaches of trust on their projects. As you can see from Figure 1.5, in 88 percent of the cases, illegal acts both destroyed trust and halted the project. In only 7 percent of the projects involving illegal acts did the project continue, but even in these cases, trust was damaged, and the possibility of assigning new projects for the team was doubtful. Even a missed deadline (the lowest bar on the chart) had an impact on trust and current and future projects. Generally, issues of character (i.e., purposeful misleading or misrepresentation) had more serious impacts than issues of competence (i.e., accidental misstep, missed deadline).

An experience at eBay, related by Meg Whitman, also illustrates the relationship between trust and long-term workplace outcomes. In June 1999, eBay faced a daunting dilemma. The company was experiencing a system outage that had lasted 22 hours. Top managers discussed how to deal with the service agreements with eBay sellers. By contract, eBay was obligated to pay refunds to all sellers whose auctions were scheduled to close during the system downtime. However, top managers also recognized that the lengthy outage had severely disrupted other auctions as well. If eBay refunded all eBay sellers, not just those it was legally obligated to refund, it would cost an additional $5 million.

"What is the right thing to do?" Whitman asked her managers, and then she left them to discuss their course of action. The team quickly decided that they would refund all eBay sellers who had active auctions. Furthermore, they immediately established a policy that eBay sellers would be refunded the listing price for any auction that was disrupted for more than two hours. Meg Whitman explained her perspective on the experience:

> Now, this is a nice story, but it is not a story about the importance of always making the customer happy and worrying about the bottom line later. This . . . is about success

FIGURE 1.5

Consequences of Breaches in Trust

For Collaboration on Workplace Projects

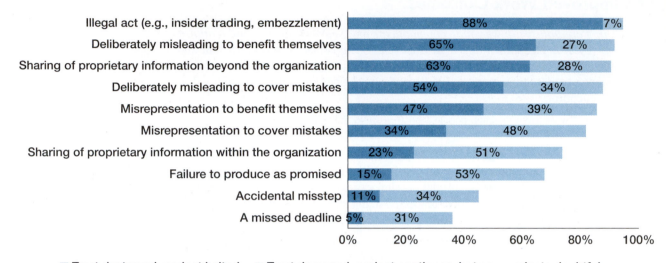

Source: From Economist Intelligence Unit, *The Role of Trust in Business Collaboration.* Copyright © The Economist Newspaper Limited, London. Based on a survey of 453 business executives around the world who were considered expert collaborators.

in both business and life. The reason I wanted to share this story is that while eBay's stock price was unstable during this crisis, Wall Street did not panic at the prospect of us missing our earnings targets as a result of the refund. Our users did not abandon us. Instead, . . . *we forged an even stronger bond of trust* with our users all over the world, and a better working relationship with our technology partners. We vowed to fix our computer system, and in short order we did that, too. I believe all this happened because we were a company that had made a clear and deliberate choice to behave according to a set of values.[46]

How You Can Improve Your Communication Skills

This textbook is designed to help you improve your skills in a variety of professional settings so that you can become a credible and trusted communicator. Overall, you may feel that you excel at some communication skills but not others. For example, you may feel more confident in your presentation skills than your writing skills, or vice versa. Regardless of your present skill level, this textbook gives you opportunities to deliberately and consciously elevate your communication skill set. It also gives you tools to continue developing your communication abilities over the course of your career.

Figure 1.6 provides an overview of the topics we will cover in this textbook. Chapter 1 focused on the credibility of the communicator, since at the core of all communication is the issue of trust (explored further in the Communication Q&A with Melvin Washington on page 16). The techniques and skills covered in the rest of this textbook are of little use if you are not considered credible.

Once you have established yourself as a credible communicator, the techniques and skills in other chapters can greatly increase your communication effectiveness and career opportunities. Thus, later chapters focus on core principles, such as the

FIGURE 1.6

Overview of Book

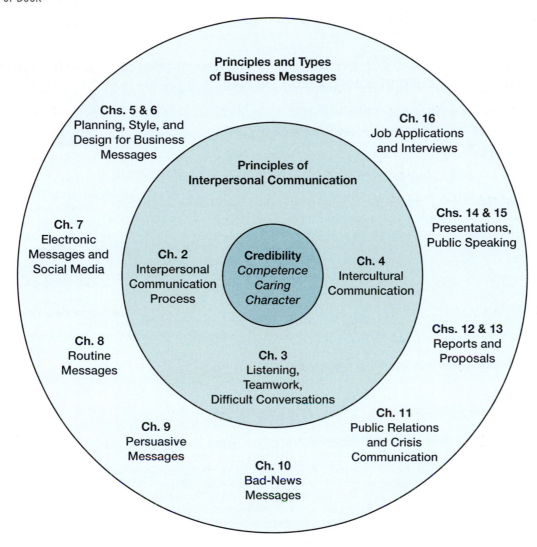

interpersonal communication process, emotional intelligence, active listening, team-work, and intercultural communication (the middle ring in Figure 1.6). These chapters lay out principles that also are important for written communication. For example, we discuss the listening-centered approach to communication, which is critical to effective writing.

You will also find chapters about planning and preparing written messages: routine messages, persuasive messages, email messages, bad-news messages, and public relations messages (the outer ring of the figure). And you will learn about conducting business research, writing business reports, and delivering presentations. You will work at developing résumés and preparing for job interviews.

As you read this book, you will be invited often to reflect about what you are reading. Try to apply what you read to your current challenges and your past experiences. Envision what you want to accomplish in your career. Imagine yourself communicating in business situations. Mentally evaluate your strengths and weaknesses. Turn off your phone and television. Reflect. You will be rewarded often during your career for staying aware of your communication skills and striving for consistent progress.[47]

COMMUNICATION Q&A

CONVERSATIONS WITH CURRENT BUSINESS PROFESSIONALS

Pete Cardon: How important is trust in the workplace?

Melvin Washington: When people trust you, they listen and respond. It really does not matter whether the communication is internal or external. When you have the reputation of being an honest and trustworthy manager, people will listen. They may not agree with every suggestion or policy you bring to the table, but they will respond with objectivity and honesty.

A business environment is analogous to a team sport. Each team member is trusted to do his or her part. At Anheuser-Busch, I was responsible for forecasting the sales of hundreds of products for an array of market segments. The distributorships trusted me to provide the correct information in order to provide an adequate supply of product to each region. Similarly, I depended on and trusted the sales team to provide me with accurate information, enabling me to forecast future sales correctly. Reliable information was the key to success. In other words, we depended on and, most of all, trusted each other to accomplish our corporate goals.

One aspect of trust is confidentiality. If a trust is betrayed, it may never be regained. It does not matter whether you're the best employee the company has ever hired, if you can't be trusted, you can't be tolerated. A manager at one of the past distributorships where I was employed was an extremely competent employee. She was what you would call a "go-to person." Her performance reviews were among the best in the company. However, she couldn't be trusted. She did not know how to keep matters confidential and constantly repeated information that was told to her in private. Hence, many of the employees ignored her, and it became increasingly difficult for her to function effectively on the job. Eventually, she became incompatible within the company climate and resigned from the job.

PC: How important is trust when working with customers and clients?

MW: In the business world, customers and clients are our lifeblood, and trust holds our business relationships together. Customers trust us to be competent and to look out for their interests. As business communicators, we must be careful to build and maintain that trust. In fact, if customers and clients do not trust us, many times they will not be honest with us.

During my tenure as a sales representative, I had a prospective customer who declined to speak with me. He did not carry any of our products in his establishment even though his store was in a market where the sale of our products had skyrocketed. After several attempts, however, he finally consented to a meeting. When I asked him why he did not want to do business with our company, he told me one of our past sales representatives had been untrustworthy. Apparently, this representative had promised him some incentives for promoting our product, which he never received. The merchant was willing to lose money by not selling our product because of a broken trust years before.

PC: How important is credibility for leaders?

MW: Credibility has to do with followers believing in their leaders. It is about leaders being trustworthy and following through on their promises. Also, employees are more willing to follow a leader who exhibits genuine care for them. Many managers are perceived as credible during the infancy of business relationships, but as the relationships continue, their honesty comes into question.

Melvin Washington *has worked in senior management positions for over 20 years at Anheuser-Busch and ARA Services. He has supervised hundreds of employees in operations and supply logistics roles. He currently is a professor of marketing at Howard University.*

Chapter Takeaway for *Establishing Credibility*

LO 1.1. Explain the importance of establishing credibility for business communications. (pp. 3–6)

You often operate from a deficit of trust when conducting business. In the **post-trust era,** skepticism is high. By establishing credibility, your colleagues, clients, customers, and other contacts will respond far more favorably to your communications.

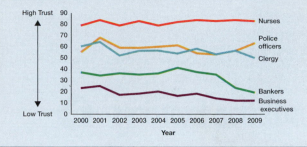

LO 1.2. Describe how competence, caring, and character affect your credibility as a communicator. (pp. 6–8)

At the heart of effective business communication is **credibility.** It is a reflection of your competence, caring, and character.

Competence relates to your proven set of skills and knowledge to accomplish business tasks. Others will judge you by your track record of success.	**Caring** shows that you will act in the interests of others, cultivate a sense of community, and demonstrate accountability to others.	**Character** shows that you will adhere to high personal, corporate, and business values. You can be counted on to do the right thing.

LO 1.3. Define and explain business ethics, corporate values, and personal values. (pp. 9–11)

Business ethics are the commonly accepted beliefs and principles in the business community for acceptable behavior. **Corporate values** are those values that are the stated and lived values of a company. They are often provided in a formal code of conduct. **Personal values** are those values prioritized and adhered to by individuals.

LO 1.4. Explain the *FAIR* approach to ethical business communications. (pp. 12–16)

FAIR TEST

Facts: How *factual* is your communication?
Access: How *accessible* or *transparent* are your motives, reasoning, and information?
Impacts: How does your communication *impact* stakeholders?
Respect: How *respectful* is your communication?

See *example questions for the FAIR test* in Figure 1.4.

Key Terms

business ethics (p. 9)

caring (p. 7)

character (p. 8)

code of conduct (p. 10)

competence (p. 6)

corporate values (p. 10)

credibility (p. 3)

ethics (p. 9)

personal values (p. 10)

post-trust era (p. 5)

stakeholder (p. 7)

transparency (p. 9)

Discussion Exercises

Note: Check with your instructor to see how she or he would like you to approach these exercises. Sometimes, you will work individually; other times, you'll work in teams.

1.1 Chapter Review Questions (LO 1.1, LO 1.2, LO 1.3, LO 1.4)

Answer each of the following questions with one to three paragraphs:

A. Explain the importance of establishing credibility in business communications.

B. Explain the three components of credibility: competence, caring, and character. How do they interrelate?

C. Define and explain business ethics, corporate values, and the relationship between them.

D. Explain the FAIR approach to evaluating ethical business communications.

E. Describe how credibility impacts communication efficiency and effectiveness.

1.2 Communication Q&A (LO 1.1, LO 1.2, LO 1.3, LO 1.4)

Read the Communication Q&A with Melvin Washington, and write a one- or two-paragraph response to each of the following questions:

A. What points does Melvin Washington make about the impact of competence in establishing credibility?

B. What points does he make about the impact of caring in establishing credibility?

C. What points does he make about the impact of character in establishing credibility?

D. Which of his comments or experiences do you view as particularly insightful or helpful? Why that one?

1.3 Character and Rules (LO 1.2)

As a former chairman of the United States Federal Reserve once said, "Rules cannot take the place of character." In two to three paragraphs, explain what you think he meant by this statement.

1.4 Transparency (LO 1.3)

As Drs. Dennis S. Reina and Michelle L. Reina explained in their book *Trust and Betrayal in the Workplace,* "Some leaders assume that . . . they are obligated to tell employees only what they specifically need to do their job. This couldn't be further from the truth."[48] In three to five paragraphs, explain the meaning of this statement. Why might leaders provide information about their activities and decision making, even when employees may not be directly affected?

1.5 Gather Information from Websites about Ethics in Business (LO 1.3)

Read at least three blogs or articles about trust and/or ethics from a reputable organization or other source. Choose an issue that interests you, and in four to five paragraphs, summarize key findings related to that issue. Consider the following options for gathering information:

- Ethics Resource Center (www.ethics.org)
- Ethics/Sustainability Resource Center for the Association to Advance Collegiate Schools of Business (www.aacsb.edu/resources/ethics-sustainability)
- Institute of Business Ethics (www.ibe.org.uk)
- Society of Corporate Compliance and Ethics (www.corporatecompliance.org)
- *Business Ethics* magazine (http://business-ethics.com)
- International Business Ethics institute (www.business-ethics.org)
- Edelman website about trust (www.edelman.com/trust)

1.6 Watch Interviews with Business Executives about Corporate Values (LO 1.2, LO 1.3)

Watch at least three videos of interviews with executives talking about corporate values. In four to five paragraphs, summarize what you learned. Consider the following options for gathering information:

- Go to CNBC's online video section (www.cnbc.com, select Video link) and search for CEO interviews about corporate values or corporate culture.
- Go to YouTube and search with terms such as *corporate values, core values,* and *corporate culture.* Select videos of business executives and managers speaking about corporate values. Choose videos that are five minutes or longer.
- See Meg Whitman and Rajiv Dutta talking about building corporate values at eBay: www.businessweek.com/managing/content/mar2009/ca20090327_626373.htm

1.7 Learn about Corporate Citizenship (LO 1.3)

In recent years, companies have increasingly focused on their social responsibility. Many companies refer to the actions they take to help or give back to society as *corporate citizenship.* Learn about corporate citizenship from at least three reliable organizations or sources. In four to five paragraphs, summarize what you've learned. Consider the following options for gathering information:

- Boston College Center for Corporate Citizenship (www.bcccc.net/index.cfm?pageId=2053)

- *Forbes* Special Section on Corporate Citizenship (www .forbes.com/leadership/citizenship/)
- World Economic Forum special section on Corporate Global Citizenship (www.weforum.org/en/initiatives/ corporatecitizenship/index.htm)
- Santa Clara University Markkula Center for Applied Ethics (www.scu.edu/ethics/)

1.8 Identify Specific Approaches to Corporate Citizenship (LO 1.3)

Choose a company and analyze its corporate citizenship measures. In four to five paragraphs, explain the company's major corporate citizenship initiatives and how they reflect its core values. Generally, you can find a corporate citizenship page at a company's website by navigating within sections with titles such as "About Us," "Company Overview," "Public Relations," "Media," and so on. If you are unsure which company you would like to learn about, consider the following:

- Boeing (www.boeing.com/companyoffices/aboutus/ community/)
- Citigroup (www.citigroup.com/citi/citizen/)
- Accenture (www.accenture.com/Global/About_Accenture/ Company_Overview/Corporate_Citizenship/default.htm)
- IBM (http://www.ibm.com/ibm/ibmgives/)

1.9 Business Ethics and Changing Values (LO 1.3)

David Pottruck, former president and co-CEO of the Charles Schwab Corporation, explained the following regarding ethics and law:

> At Schwab, we are constantly looking for new ways to express our values without compromising them. For example, we built the company on the principle of "no conflict of interest." For many years, we defined that principle as "we will not give investment advice," because we equated advice with the old-line practice of selling hot stocks to maximize brokerage commissions. When we found that our customers were demanding advice from us, we realized that our business model, one that did not compensate brokers for sales, made it possible for us to give advice and continue to avoid conflict. We changed our practice to give the customers what they wanted, expert advice that is "objective, uncomplicated and not driven by commission," and at the same time we strengthened our commitment to our values. We feel that was a highly responsible change.[49]

In three to five paragraphs, discuss whether you think corporate and personal values can and/or should change over time. Specifically discuss Pottruck's statements.

Evaluation Exercises

1.10 Compare Two Individuals' Credibility (LO 1.1, LO 1.2)

Think about two people—one whom you trust implicitly and another whom you do not trust. Ideally, these should be two people you currently work with or have worked with in the past. Compare them in the following ways: (a) competence; (b) caring; (c) character; (d) openness of communication; and (e) ease of communication. Write four to five paragraphs. Conclude with several general statements about the impact of credibility on communication efficiency and effectiveness.

1.11 Assess Credibility (LO 1.1, LO 1.2)

Think about four people: (a) a person who lacks complete credibility because he or she lacks competence; (b) a person who lacks credibility because he or she lacks caring; (c) a person who lacks credibility because he or she lacks character; and (d) a person with complete credibility. Compare and contrast these four individuals in terms of communication effectiveness in the workplace.

1.12 Evaluate a Communication Event (LO 1.1, LO 1.2)

Choose two communication events (conversations, email exchanges, and so on) that you were involved in—one in which you had credibility from the perspective of others and one in which you did not. If possible, choose communication events that occurred in the workplace. Respond to the following items about these two events:

A. Provide an overview of each communication event.
B. Explain the results of each event in terms of ease of communication and accomplishment of workplace objectives.

C. Explain why in one situation others granted you credibility but not in the other.
D. For the situation in which you had less perceived credibility, think about how you might have better established trust. Write down three ways you could have done so before the communication event occurred.

1.13 Examine Personal Credibility (LO 1.2)

Think about a specific professional context, and respond to each of the following questions. For the context, you can use a current or previous job. Or you could use a professional or student activity in which you participated. Ideally, you will select a context with challenging cooperation issues.

A. How much do/did others trust you in this situation?
B. How credible are/were you in terms of competency, caring, and character (from the perceptions of others)?
C. Do you think you are/were being perceived inaccurately in any ways? Why?
D. Have you done/did you do anything that may have broken trust in any way?
E. Have you kept/did you keep all your agreements? Explain.
F. List three things you need to do or should have done to better establish credibility.

1.14 Apply the FAIR Test (LO 1.4)

Choose a recent communication event (conversation, email exchange, and so on) that you were involved in, observed, or heard about. If possible, choose a communication event that occurred in the workplace and that involved a challenging ethical problem. Analyze the communication event with the FAIR test of ethical business communication. Devote at least one paragraph to each aspect of the test: (a) **facts** (how *factual* was the communication?);

(b) **access** (how *accessible* or *transparent* were the motives, reasoning, and information?); (c) **impacts** (how did the communication *impact* stakeholders?); (d) **respect** (how *respectful* was the communication?). See Figure 1.4 for more information about the FAIR test.

Application Exercises

1.15 Personal Mission Statement and Code of Conduct (LO 1.3)

Write your own mission statement, with a code of conduct included. Consider the following steps as you create the statement:

- Find several companies you admire. Use their code of conduct statements to help you craft your personal statement. Make sure you've personalized the statement to capture your deepest values and goals.
- Go to a career development website. These websites often contain articles and blogs about creating personal statements. For example, see the following:
  - "The Five-Step Plan for Creating Personal Mission Statements" by Randall S. Hansen (www.quintcareers .com/creating_personal_mission_statements.html)
  - "Writing a Personal Mission Statement" by Rodger Constandse (www.timethoughts.com/goalsetting/mission-statements.htm)
  - "Example Mission Statement," by Nightingale-Conant Sites (www.nightingale.com/tmission_examplestatement.aspx)
- Go to a consultant website specializing in mission statements. Usually, these websites provide free resources for developing your own statement. In some cases, you will be required to create a username and password, but the online assistance is free. For example, see FranklinCovey's step-by-step guide (www.franklincovey .com/msb/).

- Use resources companies use in developing their code of conduct statements:
  - www.ethics.org/resource/why-have-code-conduct
  - www.ibe.org.uk/codesofethics/codesofethics.html

1.16 Statement of Career Aspirations (LO 1.3)

When asked "What's your career advice for young people?" Vineet Nayar, CEO of HCL Technologies, a $5 billion IT services company centered in India, said the following:

> When you come out of college, you're raw. You have energy. You want to experiment. You want to learn. You have hopes. You have aspirations. You want to be Oprah Winfrey. You want to be Steve Jobs. You want to be Bill Gates. You want to be all that. Slowly, over time, you lose it. And by looking in the mirror every day as you get older, you fool yourself that you're OK. There has to be another way of looking in the mirror and revisiting what you really want to do. So I would say, maybe at the end of college, write it down honestly, in 100 words or whatever it is, and put it in a box. I call it the magic box. Revisit it once a year or once every two years and say, how honest are you to that? Don't let anybody run your life. That, in my mind, is very, very important. You should be in control of your life.[50]

Think about what Nayar's comments mean for you. In approximately 100 to 200 words, describe your deepest career aspirations. Include several statements about your guiding philosophy and the core personal values that drive your ambitions. Explain who you want to be in the future. Write the statement assuming that you will return to it in five, ten, or more years to see what progress you have made with your self-determined career aims.

Endnotes

1. Dennis S. Reina and Michelle L. Reina, *Trust and Betrayal in the Workplace* (San Francisco: Berrett-Koehler Publishers, 2006): 5.

2. Stephen R. Covey, "Foreword," Stephen M. R. Covey, *The Speed of Trust* (New York: Free Press, 2006).

3. Ibid: 2.

4. Ibid: 55.

5. These categories capture the dimensions of trust/credibility established by various scholars and experts. Various terms used in the scholarly literature include competence, benevolence, integrity, and intent. For sample works, see the following: Lisa C. Abrams, Rob Cross, Eric Lesser, and Daniel Z. Levin, "Nurturing Interpersonal Trust in Knowledge-Sharing Networks," *Academy of Management Executive* 17, no. 4 (2003): 64–77; Penelope Sue Greenberg, Ralph

H. Greenberg, and Yvonne Lederer Antonucci, "Creating and Sustaining Trust in Virtual Teams," *Business Horizons* 50 (2007): 325–333; Stephen M. R. Covey, *The Speed of Trust* (New York: Free Press, 2006); Dennis S. Reina and Michelle L. Reina, *Trust and Betrayal in the Workplace* (San Francisco: Berrett-Koehler Publishers, 2006).

6. Omidyar Network, "Evolution," retrieved June 28, 2010, from www.omidyar.com/about_us/evolution; "Meg Whitman," retrieved June 28, 2010, from wikipedia.org/wiki/Meg_Whitman; and Meg Whitman, *The Power of Many: Values for Success in Business and in Life* (New York: Crown Publishers, 2010): 8.

7. Reina and Reina, *Trust and Betrayal in the Workplace.*

8. Gallup Polls, "Honesty/Ethics in Professions," retrieved June 1, 2010, from www.gallup.com/poll/1654/honesty-ethics-professions.aspx.

9. Arthur W. Page Society, *The Dynamics of Public Trust in Business—Emerging Opportunities for Leaders: A Call to Action to Overcome the Present Crisis of Trust in Business* (New York: Business Roundtable Institute for Corporate Ethics, Arthur W. Page Society, 2009).

10. Sheila Bonini, David Court, and Alberto Marchi, "Rebuilding Corporate Reputations," *McKinsey Quarterly* no. 3 (2009).

11. Stephen M. R. Covey, *The Speed of Trust.*

12. Victoria L. Crittenden, Richard C. Hanna, and Robert A. Peterson, "The Cheating Culture: A Global Societal Phenomenon," *Business Horizons* 52 (2009): 337–346; D. McCabe, "Classroom Cheating among Natural Science and Engineering Majors," *Science and Engineering Ethics* 3 no. 4 (1996): 433–445; D. McCabe, *Levels of Cheating and Plagiarism Remain High* (Clemson, SC: Center for Academic Integrity, 2005); D. Callahan, *The Cheating Culture: Why More Americans Are Doing Wrong to Get Ahead* (New York: Harcourt, 2004).

13. Stephen M. R. Covey, *The Speed of Trust.*

14. Crittenden et al., "The Cheating Culture: A Global Societal Phenomenon"; McCabe, "Classroom Cheating among Natural Science and Engineering Majors"; McCabe, *Levels of Cheating and Plagiarism Remain High*; Callahan, *The Cheating Culture: Why More Americans Are Doing Wrong to Get Ahead.*

15. Michael Maslansky, *The Language of Trust* (New York: Prentice Hall, 2010): 6.

16. Patrick de Cambourg, *Corporate Accountability and Trust: Thoughts from 12 Top Managers* (Paris: Economica, 2006): 37.

17. Whitman, *The Power of Many: Values for Success in Business and in Life*: 81, 85.

18. Ibid: 45–46.

19. Ibid: 132.

20. Ibid: 179.

21. Stephen M. R. Covey, *The Speed of Trust.*

22. Meredith D. Ashby and Stephen A. Miles, *Leaders Talk Leadership: Top Executives Speak Their Minds* (New York: Oxford University Press, 2002): 5.

23. UCLA Anderson School of Management, "Robert Eckert of Mattel Shares Insight with Class of 2004 Commencement Address," June 18, 2004, retrieved June 5, 2010, from http://www.anderson.ucla.edu/x3704.xml.

24. Ashby and Miles, *Leaders Talk Leadership: Top Executives Speak Their Minds*: 55.

25. Economist Intelligence Unit, *The Role of Trust in Business Collaboration* (London: The Economist and Cisco Systems, 2008).

26. Ethics Resource Center, "Definitions of Values," retrieved June 24, 2010, from http://www.ethics.org/resource/definitions-values.

27. Peter J. Eide, "Introduction to the Human Resources Discipline of Ethics and Sustainability," retrieved June 25, 2010, from http://www.shrm.org/hrdisciplines/ethics/Pages/EthicsIntro.aspx.

28. Transparency International, "What Is 'Transparency'?" retrieved June 24, 2010, from http://www.transparency.org/news_room/faq/corruption_faq.

29. Patricia J. Harned and Michael G. Oxley, *2009 National Business Ethics Survey: Ethics in the Recession* (Arlington, VA: Ethics Resource Center, 2009).

30. Ken Blanchard Companies, *Building Trust* (Escondido, CA: Author, 2010).

31. Mary C. Gentile, "Keeping Your Colleagues Honest," *Harvard Business Review* (March 2010): 116.

32. Ibid: 114–117.

33. Eide, "Introduction to the Human Resources Discipline of Ethics and Sustainability."

34. Adam Bird, "McKinsey Conversations with Global Leaders: Paul Polman of Unilever," retrieved July 15, 2012, from http://www.mckinseyquarterly.com/McKinsey_conversations_with_global_leaders_Paul_Polman_of_Unilever_2456.

35. Tamar Frankel, *Trust and Honesty: America's Business Culture at a Crossroad* (Oxford: Oxford University Press, 2006): 206.

36. Whitman, *The Power of Many: Values for Success in Business and in Life*: 92.

37. Ken Blanchard Companies, *Building Trust.*

38. Reina and Reina, *Trust and Betrayal in the Workplace*: 7.

39. Lyle Sussman, "Disclosure, Leaks, and Slips: Issues and Strategies for Prohibiting Employee Communication," *Business Horizons* 51: 331–339.

40. Whitman, *The Power of Many: Values for Success in Business and in Life*: 99.

41. Stephen M. R. Covey, *The Speed of Trust.*

42. Reina and Reina, *Trust and Betrayal in the Workplace*: 36.

43. Stephen M. R. Covey, *The Speed of Trust.*

44. Stephen R. Covey, *The 7 Habits of Highly Effective People: Restoring the Character Ethic* (New York: Simon and Schuster, 1989): 22–23.

45. Economist Intelligence Unit, *The Role of Trust in Business Collaboration.*

46. Whitman, *The Power of Many: Values for Success in Business and in Life*: 3.

47. Stewart D. Friedman, "Be a Better Leader, Have a Richer Life," *Harvard Business Review* (April 2008): 1–13; Peter F. Drucker, "Managing Oneself," *Harvard Business Review* (January 2005): 16–28.

48. Reina and Reina, *Trust and Betrayal in the Workplace*: 37.

49. Ashby and Miles, *Leaders Talk Leadership: Top Executives Speak Their Minds*: 53.

50. New York Times Corner Office Blog, "Career Advice," retrieved June 15, 2010, at http://projects.nytimes.com/corner-office/Communication.

Principles of Interpersonal Communication

PART TWO

CHAPTER TWO

Introduction to Interpersonal Communication

Learning Objectives

After studying this chapter, you should be able to do the following:

LO2.1   Describe the interpersonal communication process and barriers to effective communication.

LO2.2   Explain how emotional hijacking can hinder effective interpersonal communication.

LO2.3   Describe the basic domains of emotional intelligence and related communication competencies and assess your own emotional intelligence.

LO2.4   Explain the trade-offs associated with richness, control, and constraints when choosing a communication channel.

LO2.5   Describe how forms of communication, level of formality, and communicator styles influence workplace communication.

LO2.6   Explain the role of civility in effective interpersonal communication and the common types of incivility in the workplace.

WHY DOES THIS MATTER?

In nearly any poll of skills needed for career success, employees identify interpersonal skills as the most important. For example, consider the results of a recent Gallup poll of working adults, depicted in Table 2.1.[1] More than any other item in the survey, respondents recognized "skill in dealing with people" as the most critical.

Consider also the remarks of Linda Hudson, president and CEO of BAE Systems:

I find new business school graduates come in here thinking that, first of all, they're going to run the company overnight. Many of them are convinced they've never made a mistake. They're not accustomed to encountering the kinds of roadblocks or disappointments that often come with the way decisions get made in a corporate environment, and they have almost no people skills. So I think an important part of teaching business ought to be focused more on realistic expectations and the people-skill part of business. . . . We give them all the book smarts, but we don't tend to give them the other skills that go along with business.[2]

In this chapter, we provide an overview of the interpersonal communication process, including an explanation of emotional intelligence, which is a foundation of effective interpersonal communication. We conclude with a discussion of civility in the workplace. In Chapters 3 and 4, we continue to focus on important forms of interpersonal communication, including listening, teamwork and meetings, managing difficult conversations, and intercultural communication.

Read the following short case about budget cuts at Eastmond Networking. Throughout the chapter, you'll find effective and ineffective examples of interpersonal communication that are based on this case.

TABLE 2.1

Skills That Determine Success

Skills	Percentage*
1. Skill in dealing with people	87
2. Critical-thinking skills	84
3. Basic use of computers	65
4. Writing ability	57
5. Basic mathematics	56
6. Advanced use of computers	44
7. Physical strength	33
8. Scientific knowledge	27
9. Advanced mathematics	23
10. Artistic skill	23
11. Knowledge of history	19

Source: From "Which Skills Hold the Secret to Success at Work?" by Linda Lyons, http://www.gallup.com/poll/9064/Which-Skills-Hold-Secret-Success-Work.aspx. Copyright © 2003 Gallup, Inc. All rights reserved. The content is used with permission; however, Gallup retains all rights of republication. *Percentage of American adults who rated skills as "critical" or "extremely important" to career success.

Chapter Case: Budget Cuts at Eastmond Networking

Who's Involved

Latisha Jackson, summer intern
- Hired for a summer internship to develop a corporate wellness program
- Double majoring in business administration and health education

Jeff Brody, personnel director
- Worked as the head of personnel at Eastmond Networking for the past five years

The Situation

Jeff Brody recently hired Latisha Jackson as a summer intern to help develop a corporate wellness program. During Latisha's interview, Jeff explained that he had seen a recent segment on a business network about how wellness programs could save companies money. He said, "Our company president is asking us to identify some low-cost options that can improve morale. So as far as I'm concerned, if we can provide a wellness program with little cost—maybe around $200 to $300 per year for each employee—and it improves morale, it would be worth it."

Typically, corporate wellness programs focus on nutrition, exercise, stress management, disease management, and even life enrichment. Since Latisha was a dual major in business administration and health education, this internship exactly matched her interests. Plus, she was passionate about physical fitness and even led a daily Zumba class.

She accepted the internship at minimum wage. She had been offered another summer internship in sales that offered $15 per hour plus commissions and bonuses. But she turned down the sales position to focus on her real passion: promoting health in the workplace. She thought she was making the right choice, but she had believed the same thing for an internship the previous summer. That internship turned out to be a disaster; the company was disorganized and provided her with few of the exciting professional opportunities that were promised.

During Latisha's first week of work, the company president informed Jeff that he would need to make 10 to 15 percent cuts in his department budget immediately. Furthermore, the company president told him to avoid any *nonessential* work functions or initiatives.

Just after receiving this news, Jeff saw Latisha enter her office down the hall. He knew how excited she was about developing the wellness program. Yet he knew that if anything could be classified as nonessential, it would be her project. He dreaded what he was about to do—tell her that they had to postpone any work on the wellness program and that she would be reassigned to other tasks.

Jeff went to Latisha's office and said, "Latisha, can I have a minute with you?"

"Sure," she responded. "Come on in." Jeff hoped the conversation would go well.

Task 1	**Task 2**	**Task 3**
Overcome barriers to communication.	Manage emotions to engage in constructive communication.	Select appropriate communication channels.

Understanding the Interpersonal Communication Process

LO2.1 Describe the interpersonal communication process and barriers to effective communication.

For the most part, we engage in interpersonal communication instinctively. By the time we are adults, we have engaged in hundreds of thousands of interpersonal interactions. We often take the interpersonal communication process for granted, rarely thinking about its building blocks and how they influence the quality of our communications. However, consciously becoming aware of these basic elements can help you improve your interpersonal communication skills and work more effectively with others. The **interpersonal communication process,** depicted in Figure 2.1, is the process of sending and receiving verbal and nonverbal messages between two or more people. It involves the exchange of simultaneous and mutual messages to share and negotiate meaning between those involved.[3]

Each person involved in interpersonal communication is both encoding and decoding meaning. **Meaning** refers to the thoughts and feelings that people *intend* to communicate to one another. **Encoding** is the process of converting meaning into messages

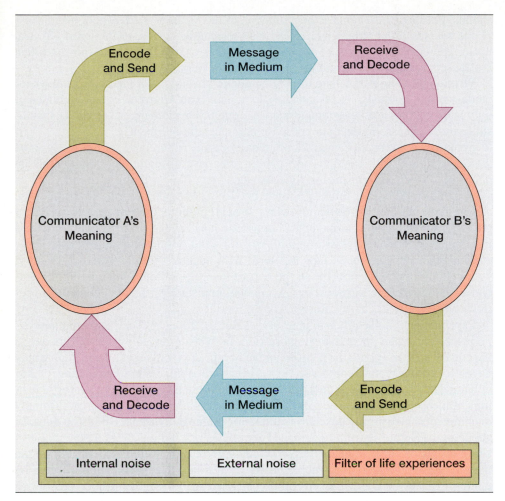

FIGURE 2.1

The Interpersonal
Communication Process

composed of words and nonverbal signals. **Decoding** is the process of interpreting messages from others into meaning.

In the interpersonal communication process, communicators encode and send messages at the same time that they also receive and decode messages. When Communicator A wants to express an idea, she encodes it as a verbal (i.e., language) and nonverbal (i.e., gestures, expressions) message. Communicator B simultaneously decodes the verbal and nonverbal message and ascribes meaning to it. Whereas the verbal communication process typically involves turn-taking, with Communicator A and Communicator B alternating between sending messages, the nonverbal communication in face-to-face communication is typically constant. Furthermore, the processing of messages in the form of encoding and decoding occurs continuously. One goal of interpersonal communication is to arrive at **shared meaning**—a situation in which people involved in interpersonal communication attain the same understanding about ideas, thoughts, and feelings. In practice, many barriers interfere with achieving shared meaning, including external noise, internal noise, and lifetime experiences.

Noise causes distortion to or interruption of messages. Four types of noise affect the quality of message delivery: physical noise, physiological noise, semantic noise, and psychological noise. **Physical noise** is external noise that makes a message difficult to hear or otherwise receive. Examples include loud sounds nearby that interrupt verbal signals or physical barriers that prevent communicators from observing nonverbal signals. Physical noise can also be a function of the medium used. A poor signal for a phone conversation or blurry video feed for a teleconference are examples of physical noise. The other three types of noise are distortions or interruptions of messages that are caused by *internal* characteristics of communicators.

Physiological noise refers to disruption due to physiological factors. Examples include hearing problems, illness, memory loss, and so on. Conversely, a communicator may have a difficult time sending a message due to physiological constraints such as stuttering, sickness, or other temporary or permanent impairments.

Semantic noise occurs when communicators apply different meanings to the same words or phrases. For example, two people may have different ideas about what an *acceptable profit margin* means. One manager may have a figure in mind, such as 10 percent. Another may think of a range between 20 and 30 percent. Semantic noise can be most difficult to overcome when strong emotions are attached to words or phrases. For example, a term such as *downsize* may invoke positive emotions for a manager who associates this term with frugality and wise cash management. However, another manager may view this term with negative emotions and associate it with callousness and disloyalty on the part of the corporation. In nearly all business conversations, people throw around words and phrases that they understand and interpret differently.

Psychological noise refers to interference due to attitudes, ideas, and emotions experienced during an interpersonal interaction. In many cases, this noise occurs due to the current conversation—the people involved or the content. For example, people may have preexisting feelings or stereotypes ("he's unreliable," "she's calculating," "they will not defend us in front of management") about those they are talking to. Those feelings influence how they encode and decode messages. People also may react strongly to comments made during the conversation. For example, a listener can't stop thinking about an inaccurate statistic mentioned by a speaker or the upside of a potential deal being discussed. In many cases, psychological noise comes from sources other than the interpersonal interaction. People nearly always begin a conversation affected by moods. Perhaps they are stressed and preoccupied with thoughts of upcoming deadlines. Perhaps a person is unhappy about a lost client and has a lingering sour mood. The demanding impacts of day-to-day business activities can create psychological noise for many reasons. In the next section about emotional intelligence, we focus on methods of managing psychological noise effectively.

All outgoing messages are encoded and all incoming messages are decoded through a **filter of lifetime experiences.** This filter is an accumulation of knowledge, values, expectations, and attitudes based on prior personal experiences. When people have more shared experiences, communication is easier.[4] For example, two business managers who grew up in the same community at the same time, got engineering degrees, and work in the same company likely share enough common background in the form of shared values and experiences that they can quite easily sort through noise as they speak with one another. However, people who grew up in different communities or cultures and at different times, who have far different educational backgrounds, and who have worked in different industries are far more likely to filter incoming messages differently. As a result, they are more likely to encounter noise and are less equipped to deal with the noise.

The short conversation between Jeff and Latisha in Figure 2.2 illustrates the interpersonal communication process. Notice the sender's intended messages and how they are encoded and decoded. Also notice the noise factors and filters and consider how they interfere with achieving shared meaning. Consider that this short conversation is between two well-meaning people who are both caught up in a frustrating but relatively straightforward situation. Both want to help the other. Yet, as you read the conversation, you will notice they do not understand one another completely and become agitated. Many business conversations are far more challenging than this one.

FIGURE 2.2

The Interpersonal Communication Process in a Short Conversation

Jeff Brody sat down, shifted uncomfortably, and sighed. Latisha Jackson turned down the radio volume, but Jeff could still hear the weather report.

"Latisha, you've done a great job for us." Shrugging his shoulders, he continued, "My hands are tied, though, and we need to abandon the wellness program initiative. I'm being forced to cut our budget immediately. There's simply no room for new projects that cost additional money."

Latisha looked stunned. "I thought we went through this already. We all know that this will help the employees and save money. Doesn't the company care about that?"

"Hey," Jeff said. "Don't overreact. Look, it's not about caring. It's about surviving so we can try not to lay anyone off."

"Are you saying I don't have an internship anymore?"

"Of course you have an internship," he said, exasperated. "We'll find some other great projects for you to work on. I'm going to schedule a time this afternoon with Jenn and you. We can all talk about some new tasks for you."

"OK," Latisha said, "well, whatever you want. I'll see you this afternoon then."

As Jeff got up, Latisha couldn't hide a look of displeasure. And, Jeff couldn't hide his frustration that Latisha didn't understand his predicament.

Jeff encodes: Thanks for your great work. Unfortunately, you will need to work on a different project.

Latisha decodes: Jeff thinks other projects are more important. This is an excuse.

Latisha encodes: The health initiative will help our employees and save money. Don't *you* care?

Jeff decodes: Latisha thinks I don't care about her project.

Jeff encodes: Of course I care. This is the reality of business. I'm doing my best to keep everyone's job.

Latisha decodes: Jeff thinks he has to fire people to save money.

Latisha encodes: Is my job safe?

Jeff decodes: She doesn't trust me.

Jeff encodes: You have great talents, and we want you to help on an important project.

Latisha decodes: Jeff probably wants to help but has no idea what I can do for the company.

Latisha encodes: I'll do whatever you want me to.

Jeff decodes: Latisha doesn't want to work on other projects.

Physical noise: Radio weather report is on.

Psychological noise: Jeff is worried about budget cuts in his department. He is also worried about disappointing Latisha. Latisha becomes disappointed and feels like she's in another dead-end internship.

Physiological noise: Jeff is physically tired from lack of sleep. He is also physically stressed from work.

Semantic noise: Jeff views the word *surviving* neutrally. He views it as a normal process that companies go through from time to time. Latisha perceives *surviving* as a panic word. She also views it as an excuse word to justify giving bad news.

Filter of lifetime experiences: Latisha has been disappointed by a lot of supervisors. For example, in her last internship, her supervisors repeatedly promised great opportunities and projects. She ended up doing menial database entry of personnel records. Jeff has been through ups and downs for companies. He has always tried to protect his employees during downturns and has always figured out how to do it. He has found that in each crisis, he is more effective when he avoids rash decisions.

Developing Emotional Intelligence

The ability to manage effective interpersonal communication depends on emotional intelligence. **Emotional intelligence** involves understanding emotions, managing emotions to serve goals, empathizing with others, and effectively handling relationships with others.[5] Business managers with high emotional intelligence are more effective at influencing others, overcoming conflict, showing leadership, collaborating in teams, and managing change.[6] Furthermore, research has shown emotional intelligence leads to better outcomes in business reasoning and strategic thinking.[7] You may see emotional intelligence referred to as **EQ,** which stands for *emotional quotient,* a play on the term IQ, *intelligence quotient*. We use both terms in this book.

Recently, EQ has been shown to be the single best predictor of workplace performance. About 90 percent of high performers in the workplace are high in EQ, whereas only 20 percent of low performers are high in EQ. On average, people with high EQs make $29,000 more per year than those with low EQs.[8]

Emotional intelligence comes into play in many business circumstances. It is especially important, however, during moments of stress, which are common in the world of business (see Table 2.2).[9] Emotional intelligence contributes to one's ability to communicate clearly and constructively, overcome nerves before a presentation, gain the courage to talk to someone about bad news, respond well to disappointment and failure, motivate team members to move toward a common goal, and many other situations. In short, emotional intelligence allows business managers and executives to think clearly about business objectives without letting their emotions get the best of them.

Business leaders increasingly emphasize the need for emotional intelligence in today's demanding business environment. Richard Anderson, CEO of Delta Air Lines, recently described the kind of qualities he's looking for in employees more so now than five or ten years ago:

> I think this communication point is getting more and more important. People really have to be able to handle the written and spoken word. . . . You've got to have not just the business skills, you've got to have the emotional intelligence. It's not just enough to be the best person operating an H-P calculator. You have to have the emotional intelligence to understand what's right culturally, both in your company and outside your company.[10]

In the upcoming pages, you will learn strategies for developing your emotional intelligence. In general, emotional intelligence is developed through conscious effort and attention to your feelings and interactions with others. Common approaches to improving emotional intelligence include reflecting on emotions and behavior, keeping a journal, and practicing interpersonal skills in social situations.[11]

In this section, we first focus on emotional hijacking. Then, we discuss four domains of emotional intelligence—self-awareness, self-management, empathy, and relationship management. Finally, we'll suggest strategies for improving your emotional intelligence in each of these domains to achieve more effective interpersonal communication in the workplace.

TABLE 2.2

Most Stressful Jobs

Five Most Stressful Jobs
1. Firefighter
2. **Business executive**
3. Taxi driver
4. Surgeon
5. Police officer

Source: From CareerCast.com, "America's Most Stressful Jobs 2010," www.cnbc.com/id/36715336/ America_s_Most_Stressful_Jobs_2010. Reprinted with permission.
Note: Stress measured for 200 jobs using 21 factors such as intensity and quantity of deadlines, quotas, win/lose situations, competitiveness, speed required, physical safety, and travel required.

LO2.2 Explain how emotional hijacking can hinder effective interpersonal communication.

Emotional Hijacking

Some people might wonder why emotional intelligence is so critical for business managers and executives, especially those in finance, accounting, and quantitatively driven disciplines and positions. After all, competence in many types of business decision making is primarily based on logic and reason. The primary reason that emotional intelligence is so critical is physiological: People are hardwired to experience emotions before reason. All signals to the brain first go through the limbic system, where emotions are produced, before going to the rational area of the brain (see Figure 2.3).[12]

In other words, you feel all your incoming messages before you reason about them. Furthermore, one function of the limbic system is protection. This part of the brain creates a fight-or-flight response when incoming messages appear as threats. For example, people may experience **emotional hijacking,** a situation in which emotions control our behavior, causing us to react without thinking. The impacts of emotions last long after they've subsided.[13]

Emotional hijacking prevents you from engaging in effective interpersonal communication. It can lead to unwanted behaviors: You may misrepresent your ideas, confuse the facts, say things to others that you later regret, display frustration or anger, remain silent when you would prefer to be heard, fail to listen to others, or disengage from working relationships that are in your best interest.

In the conversation between Jeff and Latisha (see Figure 2.2), both are in danger of emotional hijacking. Latisha is living the experience in the context of past disappointments with supervisors. She further panics when she perceives that her job may be in danger. All her thoughts are influenced by the emotions generated in the limbic system. Jeff similarly is at risk of emotional hijacking. He easily becomes agitated because he thinks Latisha does not trust him or understand his motives. Furthermore, he still has lingering stress from his conversation just minutes earlier with the company president, who informed him that he needed to cut nonessential work activities.

Domains of Emotional Intelligence

The most-used EQ test for business professionals shows that emotional intelligence can be divided into four domains: self-awareness, self-management, empathy, and relationship management. Throughout this section we refer to statistics based on this particular measure of EQ.[14]

Self-awareness is the foundation for emotional intelligence. It involves accurately understanding your emotions as they occur and how they affect you. One prominent researcher defines self-awareness as "ongoing attention to one's internal states."[15] People high in self-awareness understand their emotions well, what satisfies them, and what irritates them. Understanding your emotions as they occur is not always easy. In fact, research indicates that just 36 percent of people can accurately identify their emotions as they occur.[16]

Self-awareness is particularly important for stressful and unpleasant situations. People high in self-awareness have the ability to be self-reflective when they experience strong or even distressful emotions. Often, this involves the ability to explicitly identify feelings as they occur. For example, a person who becomes angry with a colleague can simultaneously think, "I'm feeling anger right now."[17]

High self-awareness includes the ability to manage events that stir strong—often fight-or-flight—responses. Events that cause strong emotional reactions are called **triggers.**[18] As you become more aware of your triggers or tendencies, you can adjust your interpersonal communication to avoid dysfunctional behaviors caused by emotional hijacking, such as blaming others as a defense mechanism or not speaking up when you're nervous.

Adele Lynne, one of the foremost experts on the role of emotional intelligence in workplace performance, explained the benefit of emotional intelligence.

> I'm sure you know people who go through life and never seem to learn from their mistakes, or they don't see how one experience is connected to another. Self-awareness will help prevent this from happening to you, but only if you keep building on your lessons. This linking of life experiences into ever-increasing lessons is the foundation of wisdom. It is the quintessential difference in living one year of experiences thirty times versus thirty years of experience.[19]

In the conversation between Jeff and Latisha, more self-awareness would help both of them manage their feelings and thoughts. If Jeff is self-aware, he says to himself,

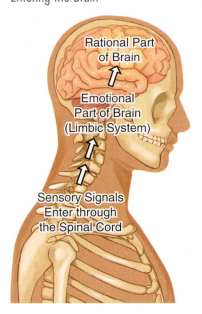

FIGURE 2.3

Neuropathways of Signals Entering the Brain

LO2.3 Describe the basic domains of emotional intelligence and related communication competencies and assess your own emotional intelligence.

TABLE 2.3

Low versus High Self-Awareness Thoughts

Low Self-Awareness Thoughts	High Self-Awareness Thoughts
Jeff: Latisha needs to learn how to trust people. She's not being fair to me and she needs to understand the constraints I'm facing.	*Jeff:* I'm bothered that she doesn't trust my motives. Typically, I feel disrespected when others don't trust my motives. Sometimes, I lash out in these circumstances.
Jeff ignores and deflects his feelings to focus on what he perceives as Latisha's misperceptions.	Jeff recognizes that he feels distrusted and disrespected by what Latisha said. He also recognizes that he often says things he later regrets in these situations.
Latisha: This is ridiculous. Jeff promised me that I'd be working on the health care initiative. How can he go back on his word so quickly?	*Latisha:* I feel afraid and confused. Jeff doesn't seem to care if I have challenging work. I've felt this way before at other jobs. I wonder how my past experiences are impacting how I'm judging Jeff.
Latisha overreacts to Jeff's words and actions because she is not aware of how past disappointments are affecting how she is judging Jeff.	Latisha notices that how she feels about Jeff is affected by previous, similar events. She knows she should be careful not to let those events make her rush to judgment.

"I'm feeling bothered that she doesn't trust me and thinks I don't care." Similarly, Latisha is self-aware if in the moment, she says to herself, "I feel afraid and confused. Jeff doesn't seem to care if I have challenging work. I've felt this way before at other jobs. I wonder how my past experiences are impacting how I'm judging Jeff." Table 2.3 shows differences in low versus high self-awareness in the encounter between Jeff and Latisha.

Self-management is the "ability to use awareness of your emotions to stay flexible and to direct your behavior positively."[20] It involves the discipline to hold off on current urges to meet long-term intentions. Excellent self-managers know how to use both positive and negative emotions to meet personal and business goals.[21]

Most strong emotions can impair rational communication and behavior. For example, anger is an intense emotion tied to a physical sense of endangerment. Most people have impulses to verbally attack or defend themselves during a rush of intense emotion. While intense emotions often last just moments, their impacts last far longer. For example, when you experience anger, the resulting adrenal and cortical excitation creates less-intense reactions to this sense of endangerment that can last hours and days. An individual may ignore this less-intense reaction yet still feel a sour mood for a period of time. Furthermore, research shows that anger builds on anger. Thus, people are more vulnerable to being provoked to anger during this period. Strong self-managers realize that they are still vulnerable for several days following feelings of anger and learn to heighten their levels of self-awareness during these time periods.[22]

People can quickly control moderate negative emotions. For example, an individual who tries to understand **mitigating information** can short-circuit moderate anger almost immediately. Mitigating information involves favorable explanations for why others have behaved in a certain way. See Table 2.4 for examples of low and high self-management and the use of mitigating information.

A common misperception of many business professionals is that venting negative feelings helps people cope with anger. Study after study has shown that venting is temporarily satisfying—but it rarely makes anger go away, especially when the venting is intended as retaliation. Physiologically, venting continues to arouse the brain with

TABLE 2.4

Low versus High Self-Management Thoughts and the Use of Mitigating Information

Low Self-Management Thoughts	High Self-Management Thoughts
Jeff: If Latisha is going to treat me like I'm the bad guy, then maybe I should just turn her over to someone else so I don't have to worry about her.	*Jeff:* Latisha is probably reacting this way because she cares so much about a health initiative, which helps the employees of this company. She is eager to contribute.
Jeff assumes the worst about Latisha's comments, thus allowing his frustration with her to grow. He considers an action that is extreme.	Jeff assumes a positive explanation for Latisha's actions *(mitigating information)*, thus short-circuiting his feelings of frustration and perhaps moderating anger.
Latisha: There's no way I can change anything. Jeff will assign me to another project and that's that. I'm stuck in another dead-end internship.	*Latisha:* I want to express to Jeff my desire to work on a meaningful project. We can discuss how my approach to the health initiative could be applied to another project. And we could discuss how I can still spend some time working on the health initiative in the planning process—in a way that does not require cash commitments during this budget crunch.
This thought process reflects *pessimism.* Latisha neither thinks of other options available to her for the health initiative nor assumes that other work tasks will provide her with rewarding challenges.	This thought process reflects *optimism.* Latisha considers how she can approach Jeff and constructively discuss options that are good for her and the company.

feelings of anger. Thus, venting is considered one of the least effective strategies for de-escalating anger.[23]

Typically, other strategies should be pursued to deal with intense anger. These strategies include removing oneself temporarily from the anger-inducing situation, going on a walk, breathing deeply, or enjoying some entertainment (e.g., TV, movies, reading). Also, writing about the feelings of frustration, anger, and hostility can help you articulate your feelings, review the events rationally, and challenge and reappraise the feelings. Typically, excellent self-managers experiment with ways of cooling down so that they find tried-and-true solutions to overcoming intense emotions. Generally, however, this cooling down is typically not effective when the time is used to relive the anger-inducing events.[24]

Self-management involves far more than corralling anger. It involves responding productively and creatively to feelings of self-doubt, worry, frustration, disappointment, and nervousness. It also includes tempering oneself when experiencing excitement and elation. In short, self-management helps you avoid knee-jerk reactions that may compromise your ability to meet your business and career objectives.[25]

A major distinction between those high in self-management and those low in self-management is **optimism** versus **pessimism.** Optimists view failures as events that can be changed in the future. They view these failures as temporary setbacks and learning experiences. Pessimists, by contrast, view failures as indications of their own incompetence or inability. They dwell on the past rather than looking to the future. Under duress or disappointment, optimists form a plan of action, whereas pessimists focus on the permanence of their situation and their inability to overcome the disappointment. One study showed that among insurance sales workers, optimists outperformed pessimists by 37 percent in sales. Furthermore, pessimists were twice as likely as optimists to quit.[26]

Whereas the first two dimensions of emotional intelligence primarily deal with identifying and managing one's own emotions, the final two dimensions—empathy and relationship management—involve understanding others and managing your interactions with them effectively. **Empathy** is the "ability to accurately pick up on emotions in other people and understand what is really going on with them."[27] Empathy also includes the desire to help others develop in their work responsibilities and career objectives.[28] **Relationship management** is the "ability to use your awareness of emotions and those of others to manage interactions successfully."[29] Table 2.5 displays each of the EQ dimensions and related communication skills and practices. Think about the abilities that would be most important for you to develop.

In the next chapter, we introduce the listening-centered approach to communication as one way of developing empathy and managing your work relationships effectively. In nearly each chapter thereafter, we discuss types of business communication with a constant focus on understanding and relating to the needs of others (empathy) and expressing your ideas to manage your work relationships effectively (relationship management).

TABLE 2.5

Emotional Intelligence Dimensions, Related Impacts on Interpersonal Communication, and Strategies for Improvement

EQ Dimension	Impact on Interpersonal Communication	Strategies for Improvement
Self-awareness	**Low self-awareness** • Unaware of own emotional states and related impacts on communication • Unaware of triggers that lead to emotional hijacking and making judgmental, rash, or unfair comments • Unaware of strengths and weaknesses of own communication abilities **High self-awareness** • Aware of own emotional states and related impacts on communication • Aware of triggers and related tendencies to say the wrong thing • Aware of strongest communication skills	• Constantly evaluate your feelings and moods; attempt to understand your feelings as they occur. • Think about your last reactions to the following experiences: joy, anger, self-doubt, frustration. • Ask yourself how certain emotions alter or distort your thinking. • Identify your triggers and make plans to handle them effectively. • Reflect on personal strengths, weaknesses, and values.
Self-management	**Low self-management** • Unable to control impulses • Frequently vent frustrations without a constructive work purpose • Spend a higher percentage of work conversations on small talk, gossip, and non-work-related issues • React defensively and with a me-first attitude when threats are perceived **High self-management** • Control emotional impulses that are not aligned with work and relationship goals • Discuss frustrations in the context of solving problems and improving relationships • Spend a higher percentage of work conversations on work-related topics with a focus on solutions • When threats are perceived, seek to de-escalate interpersonal tensions and resolve issues at hand	• Engage in relaxation techniques to clear your mind. • Examine strategies for overcoming impulses that compete with achieving your long-range goals. • Focus on how to improve for your next effort rather than dwelling on disappointments of the current failure. • Practice expressing positive emotions more frequently and in situations where you normally do not. • Talk to a trusted colleague who is an effective self-manager. • Sleep on it. • Practice self-talk and visualize yourself responding effectively to challenging interpersonal issues.

TABLE 2.5

(*Continued*)

EQ Dimension	Impact on Interpersonal Communication	Strategies for Improvement
Empathy	**Low empathy** • Fail to listen carefully to others • Direct conversations to topics that are important to self • Avoid volunteering to help others with their work assignments • Engage in a me-first approach to work with colleagues **High empathy** • Attempt to understand the feelings, perspectives, and needs of others • Direct conversations to topics that focus on the needs of others and self • Volunteer advice or help to others as appropriate • Show a sincere interest in others: their efforts, their ideas, and their successes	• Always attempt to place yourself in the position of others: think about the emotions and thoughts others are experiencing. • Anticipate how others will react during business conversations and meetings. • Listen to others, even when you disagree, without interrupting or judging. • Pay attention to nonverbal behavior. • Practice asking good questions. • Think about group dynamics and the related impacts on each team member. • Give others your undivided attention and time. • Get to know others.
Relationship management	**Low relationship management** • Focus exclusively on the task at hand without paying attention to rapport-building • Remain silent to avoid discussions about differences of opinions, or attempt to silence the dissenting opinions of others • Provide indirect and vague feedback and ideas to others • Disregard feedback and constructive criticism • Discourage dissent • Respond to others only when it's convenient **High relationship management** • Build rapport with others to focus on collaboration • Speak out constructively about differences of opinion • Provide direct and constructive feedback to others • Accept and even welcome feedback and constructive criticism • Encourage contrarian views • Respond to others when it's convenient for them	• Attend work-related social outings. • Keep records of people in your network and keep track of their skills, interests, hobbies, birthdays, and other important dates. • Maintain regular contact with colleagues and others in your work network. • Devote time to conversations on a range of topics. • Greet others by name. • Live up to your promises. • Collaborate more effectively with others. • Build up the courage to have a difficult conversation. • Speak up in meetings or work conversations when you ordinarily do not; or, encourage others who rarely speak up to voice their thoughts and feelings.

Strategically Selecting Channels for Communication

LO2.4 Explain the trade-offs associated with richness, control, and constraints when choosing a communication channel.

You have so many useful communication tools and technologies for getting in touch with your colleagues, your customers, and other contacts. Having so many options, however, also presents dilemmas about selecting an appropriate **communication channel**—the medium through which a message is transmitted. Examples of communication channels include emails, phone conversations, and face-to-face dialogue. Each communication channel has strengths and drawbacks, the topic we explore in this section.

In a recent study, company representatives were asked to state whether the amount of electronic communication, face-to-face communication, and print communication within their companies had increased, not changed, or decreased over the past two years (see Figure 2.4). Not surprisingly, use of print communication was on the decline (by nearly 50 percent) in the vast majority of companies. The use of interoffice memos and the like are slowly being replaced with other forms of electronic communication.

FIGURE 2.4

Change in the Use of
Communication Channels
during the Past Two Years

Source: Watson Wyatt Worldwide
Study, *Capitalizing on Effective
Communication: How Courage,
Innovation and Discipline Drive Busi-
ness Results in Challenging Times.*
Copyright © Towers Watson. Used
with permission.
Note: From a study of 328 organi-
zations in North America, Europe,
the Middle East, and Australia.

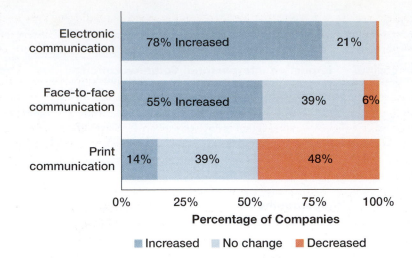

Also, not surprisingly, electronic communication had increased in nearly all companies (also nearly 80 percent). Interestingly, however, face-to-face communication had also increased in most companies (around 55 percent).[30] This study is reflective of today's business environment, which requires employees to collaborate through more communication channels—in person and with the aid of technology—than ever before.

Strategically selecting a communication channel means that you choose the one that is best able to meet your work objectives. Sometimes a quick phone call or text message is the most efficient way to figure out a meeting time. Other times you will need a face-to-face meeting to clarify misunderstandings about projects. In many of your working relationships, you'll use many communication channels—email, social media, calls, face-to-face conversations—on a daily or weekly basis. Strategically choosing a communication channel involves three basic considerations related to their limitations: richness, control, and constraints.

Richness involves two considerations: the level of immediacy and number of cues available. **Immediacy** relates to how quickly someone is able to respond and give feedback. In high-immediacy communication, people have immediate access to a variety of cues, including social cues (turn-taking), verbal cues (tone of voice), and nonverbal cues (gestures, facial expressions). Generally, face-to-face communications are considered the richest, since each person involved can get immediate verbal and nonverbal feedback. Richer communication typically leads to more trust-building, rapport, and commitment. It is generally the most efficient way to accomplish communication objectives quickly and is less likely to lead to misunderstandings.[31]

Control refers to the degree to which communications can be planned and recorded, thus allowing strategic message development. **Planning** implies that the communication can be tightly drafted, edited and revised, rehearsed, and otherwise strategically developed before delivery. **Permanence** refers to the extent to which the message can be stored, retrieved, and distributed to others. Control may be your primary concern for many important communications.

Constraints refer to the practical limitations of coordination and resources. **Coordination** deals with the effort and timing needed to allow all relevant people to participate in a communication. **Resources** deal with the financial, space, time, and other investments necessary to employ particular channels of communication. A meeting of ten corporate employees who fly in from different cities is a high-constraint communication that requires extensive coordination and resources.

At the most basic level, communication channels can be divided between the spoken and the written. Spoken messages in the workplace are generally high in richness but low in control. In other words, when people speak to one another face-to-face, they get immediate verbal and nonverbal feedback and respond accordingly. This leads to rapid understanding and bonding. However, they cannot prepare a set message (low planning) nor keep a permanent record that can be reviewed and distributed to others (low permanence).

In terms of constraints, spoken communication can range from low to high depending on a number of factors. For example, speaking to a colleague in the next office might require little scheduling (coordination) and few additional monetary and time resources. However, if colleagues are dispersed in various offices separated by time zones, scheduling could be challenging, and the company and the employees might invest a great deal of money and time on travel and related expenses to facilitate rich face-to-face conversation.

By contrast, written messages in the workplace are generally low in richness, since they typically do not allow immediate feedback and lack a variety of social, verbal, and nonverbal cues. Yet, they present a number of benefits. Individuals can carefully craft messages at their own pace and on their schedule (high in planning and low in coordination). Moreover, many business professionals consider writing conducive to deep thinking on business matters. Furthermore, writing creates a permanent record. Since written records are text-based, it is far easier to search for and retrieve relevant information. Generally, the constraints (resources and coordination) of writing are quite low.

Broadly speaking, the benefits of spoken versus written messages reflect an important point: Choosing between communication channels is generally a matter of trade-offs. There is no such thing as a perfect communication channel. Written business communication complements the weaknesses of spoken business communication and vice versa.

The distinctions between spoken and written business messages mirror the relative benefits and weaknesses of synchronous and asynchronous communications. **Synchronous communication** occurs in real time; the individuals involved give immediate responses to one another and engage in turn-taking. **Asynchronous communication** does not occur in real time. Individuals involved in such communication can pay attention to and respond to communications at a time of their choosing. Most successful working relationships depend on both synchronous and asynchronous communication. Scholars Arvind Malhotra, Ann Majchrzak, and Benson Rosen have studied hundreds of virtual teams over nearly a decade and concluded the following about successful communication between teams:[32]

> Most successful virtual team leaders establish a synchronous as well as an asynchronous collaboration rhythm. . . . Successful virtual teams use the time between meetings to asynchronously (through use of electronic discussion threads and annotation of documents in the repository) generate and evaluate ideas. By working asynchronously virtual team members can pick and choose when they can make their contributions. This allows team members with diverse backgrounds to have a different rhythm and pace of generating their own ideas and digesting others' ideas. Leaders also use asynchronous discussion threads to identify areas of disagreements because the discussion threads give members with different language capabilities time to share their thoughts in their non-native languages in ways that they find difficult in synchronous (fast-paced audio-conference) sessions.[33]

Table 2.6 summarizes the features of several communication channels in terms of richness, control, and constraints. Of course, the evolving nature of communication technologies impacts the richness, control, and constraints. For example, currently, most social networking websites primarily use text and pictures. When social networking platforms more easily accommodate and include real-time videoconferencing, they would be considered richer. However, adding these richer features would require additional constraints in terms of coordination and resources.

As ambiguity and sensitivity in your communications increase, you will generally seek richer forms of communication, such as face-to-face conversations, meetings, phone calls, and videoconferences. For less-ambiguous, highly detailed, and highly

TABLE 2.6

Richness, Control, and Constraints of Various Communication Channels*

Red indicates a major limitation in terms of effectiveness for the communication channel. Green indicates a major strength.

Communication Channel	Richness		Control		Constraints		When to Use†
	Immediacy	Cues	Planning	Permanence	Coordination	Resources	
Written messages	Low	Low	High	High	Low	Low	Ideal for asynchronous communication, matters that require documentation, and messages that need to be crafted with a lot of thought and precision.
Spoken communication	High	High	Low	Low‡	Low – High	Low – High	Ideal for matters that require rapport-building, discussion, brainstorming, clarification, and immediate feedback. Preferred for sensitive and emotion-packed situations.
Asynchronous Communication Channels							
Email	Low	Low	High	High	Low	Low	For one-to-one or one-to-many business messages. Email is the dominant communication tool for private, written business messages.
Texting	Low – Medium	Low	High	Medium	Low	Low	For short, one-to-one or one-to-many messages. Ideal for quick announcements and scheduling. Not well suited for important or complex business messages.
Blogs, wikis, and social networking	Low – High	Low – Medium	Medium – High	Medium – High	Low – Medium	Low – High	For team and networked communication. Facilitates a one-stop work space containing project and meeting information, shared files, and communication platforms.
Synchronous Communication Channels							
Phone conversations	High	Medium	Low – Medium	Low	Medium	Low	For one-to-one conversations between parties in different locations. A fairly rich communication channel to quickly discuss and clarify workplace issues.
Conference calls	High	Low – Medium	Low	Low – Medium‡	High	Medium	For team conversations. Typically less rich than one-to-one phone conversations because many participants do not provide cues continuously during the conversation.
Web conferences/ Webinars	High	Medium	Medium – High	Medium – High‡	High	Medium	For team meetings/sales presentations. A richer form of interacting than conference calls but typically requires more coordination due to technology requirements.
Videoconferences	High	High	Low	Low – Medium‡	High	High	For team meetings. A richer form of interacting than conference calls but typically requires more expensive equipment and careful scheduling and planning.

*Table is modified and adapted from Pearn Kandola's *The Psychology of Effective Business Communications in Geographically Dispersed Teams*.
†One of the chief considerations for when and when not to use various communication channels is based on the preferred communication channels of others.
‡The level of permanence depends on whether the communication is recorded and available after the event.

analytical messages, you will likely turn to higher-control channels. Thus, communicating with letters, emails, blogs, wikis, podcasts, and other asynchronous communication technologies may be particularly helpful.

Many work factors affect the communication channels you choose. In some cases, companies develop protocols for communicating. The stage of a project may be important, for instance. Generally, projects begin with face-to-face meetings because rich communication is particularly important to develop trust, establish work roles, and brainstorm in the early stages of a project. Later in the project, more control and fewer constraints may allow business professionals to work on their own schedules with less face-to-face meeting time. More of the communication may become mediated by communication technologies (i.e., email, wikis, phone calls, videoconferences).

Furthermore, some types of communication are considered more formal and appropriate for certain types of business activities. Typically, written communication is considered more formal. Proposals, agreements, contracts, and similar documents are written because that implies that the content is in certain and unambiguous terms. The formality of communication is further discussed in the next section about adapting your communication to the situation and style of others.

An essential component of developing expertise in business communication is staying up to date with the latest communication tools: their capabilities, limitations, strengths, and weaknesses. In each chapter you will find a Technology Tips box. As you read these tips, think about how you can use these tools effectively in the workplace. In this chapter you will find tips for mobile phone use on page 42.[34]

Let's assume that Latisha decides she wants to explore other ways to continue working on a health initiative. She thinks she could devote a portion of her work time to planning and justifying this project. The company would not have to make any investment other than her time. What would be the best communication channel for her to discuss this with Jeff? Ideally, a rich, face-to-face meeting would allow them to discuss this issue. One potential disadvantage of meeting in person is the lack of control. Latisha has far more control of her message if she writes it out and carefully thinks about her ideas before sending it to Jeff. If Jeff were out of the office for two weeks, would a phone conversation, online call, or email work best? Thinking about the trade-offs between richness, control, and constraints will help Latisha make a good selection.

Adapting Communication to the Situation and the Style of Others

LO2.5 Describe how forms of communication, level of formality, and communicator styles influence workplace communication.

Savvy communicators adjust their approaches to communication to match the situation and preferred communicator styles of others. As you adjust your approach, consider the following areas: forms of communication, level of formality, and communicator styles.

Forms of Communication

Workplace communication takes several broad forms. The most basic is one-to-one communication that involves just a few individuals about work matters. We refer to this type of communication as **private communication.** This does not necessarily imply that the communication is confidential. Rather, it means that the communication is relevant primarily for a select few individuals. For example, Jeff and Latisha discussing her internship is a private communication.

Many-to-many communication involves various professionals and/or clients communicating about shared projects or other business activities. The most common form of many-to-many communication is **team communication.** Team communication involves communication among team members that should be shared by and accessible to every team member. For example, a meeting is a type of team communication.

Another form of many-to-many communication that is growing in importance in the workplace is **networked communication.** It is similar to team communication in some regards but differs in several key ways. Whereas team communication occurs among people who know one another, networked communication allows people to contact, communicate with, and develop work relationships with people they do not know but who share work interests and goals. These people are often contacts of people you already know, or they are part of an organizational network (e.g., a company or a professional organization). Similarly, whereas team communication typically occurs in the context of formally created teams or units, networked communication allows groups to form and disband more informally and loosely.

In today's workplace, online social networking and corporate intranets increasingly facilitate team communication and networked communication. Certainly, younger employees are more adept at using online social networks since they are accustomed to public platforms such as Facebook. However, using social networking *for work purposes* requires new habits for old and young alike. We discuss these types of skills in Chapter 7 about electronic messages and social media in the workplace.

A final form of communication is called one-to-many, in which a single person broadcasts a message to many people. One of the most common types of one-to-many communications in the workplace is **leadership communication,** meaning that an executive, manager, or other organizational leader develops a message for all relevant employees. Leadership communication is often intended to announce big changes, inspire outstanding performance, boost morale, or create unity of vision for an organization.

Each form of communication—private, team, networked, and leadership—requires unique considerations about choosing a communication channel and tailoring the messages to meet the needs of others. Entry-level business professionals spend most of their time in private and team communication. Yet, networked communication is becoming more prominent in entry-level positions, and some business professionals rapidly gain leadership positions that involve sending leadership communications.

Level of Formality in Communication

In addition to adapting to the form of communication, you will constantly need to judge the level of formality to use in workplace communication. Typically, **formality** is associated with protocols, rules, structure, and politeness. **Informality** is associated with the absence of protocols and structure. During recent decades, business communication has become less formal. However, even in today's less-formal environment, very little business communication is informal. Even workplace social outings such as holiday parties involve expectations, boundaries, and unspoken rules for appropriate communication.

Many factors impact the level of formality in your communications, including the communication channel used, your relationship and familiarity with others, and the size of your organization (see Figure 2.5). Typically, written communication is more formal than spoken communication. Emails, letters, and speeches are considered formal communications with fairly standard expectations for format and tone. Presentations and meetings tend to be fairly formal communication channels, yet they allow for flexibility. Online social networking and phone conversations tend to be even less formal. Yet, compared to their use outside of the workplace, social networking and phone conversations are quite formal.

The size of the organization also strongly affects formality. In small, family-owned businesses, communication tends to be quiet informal. As the company size increases, however, formality typically increases. Rules and processes tend to be increasingly defined in larger companies.

Another factor that affects formality of communication is the nature of your work relationships. External communication (communication to people outside the company such as customers, clients, or suppliers) tends to be formal. Most internal communication (within a company) can be classified as upward (to superiors/bosses), downward

FIGURE 2.5

Factors Impacting the Formality of Business Communication

Communication Channel	Business socials, grapevine	Social networking, phone calls, IM, texting	Presentations, scheduled meetings	Emails, letters, speeches
Relationship	Lateral	Downward	Upward	External
Familiarity	Longtime friends	Longtime associates	Short-term associates	New acquaintances
Company Size	Family-owned	Small	Midsize	Large

Less Formal ←————————————————————————————————→ **More Formal**

(to subordinates), or lateral (with peers). Typically, upward communication is the most formal, and lateral communication is the least formal. Also, how well you know others (familiarity) has a strong impact on formality. As familiarity increases, formality typically decreases.

Communicator Styles

Communication scholars typically group people into four broad communicator styles. One of the classic distinctions of communication styles was developed by Paul P. Mok. He found that professionals could be grouped as shown in Table 2.7 and described below.[35]

- **Sensers** are pragmatic and results-oriented. When addressing sensers, be direct, brief, and to the point.

TABLE 2.7

Communicator Styles

Communicator Style	Attributes	Communication Preferences
Senser (44%)	• Pragmatic • Action-oriented • Focused on present • Results-oriented	• Wants only the relevant facts • To the point • Discusses immediate goal • Doesn't get off point
Feeler (30%)	• "People" person • Focuses on harmony, empathy • Needs personal security	• Enjoys small talk and begins conversations by warming up • Enjoys talking and frequently discusses feelings and stories
Thinker (14%)	• Focuses on logic and objectivity • Focuses on correct analysis	• Wants all the facts • Wants cautious, carefully crafted, and logical communication • Avoids exaggeration and big claims • Precise • Thoroughly discusses an idea before moving to the next idea
Intuitor (13%)	• Focuses on future • Focuses on big ideas, out-of-the-box thinking • Experimental	• Wants to feel approved and affirmed • Discusses concepts first and facts last • Moves from topic to topic

Sources: Paul P. Mok, *Interpretation Manual for CSS: A Survey of Communicating Styles* (Garland, TX: Training Associates Press, 1989); Anne Field, "Intuitor, Thinker, Feeler, Senser: Which One Are You Talking To?" *Harvard Management Communication Letter* 6, no. 7 (2003): 3–5.
Note: Percentages refer to approximate percentage of the general population.

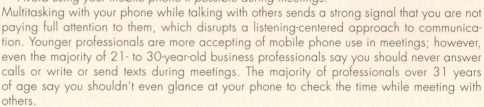

MOBILE PHONES

Mobile phones have transformed business communication: Most business professionals carry at least one phone at all times for calls, texting, Internet use, scheduling, and much more. In many ways, mobile phones increasingly serve as a communication center for many managers and executives. Keep in mind the following guidelines for mobile phone use:

Speak in person if possible. The advantage of using mobile phones for calls, texts, emails, and other messages is convenience. For important requests and other business matters, meet in person if possible. You can influence others more easily in a rich, face-to-face environment; they are far more likely to say "yes" in person.

Avoid using your mobile phone if possible during meetings. Multitasking with your phone while talking with others sends a strong signal that you are not paying full attention to them, which disrupts a listening-centered approach to communication. Younger professionals are more accepting of mobile phone use in meetings; however, even the majority of 21- to 30-year-old business professionals say you should never answer calls or write or send texts during meetings. The majority of professionals over 31 years of age say you shouldn't even glance at your phone to check the time while meeting with others.

If you need to use your phone during a meeting, do so discreetly and acknowledge your distracting behavior. If a must-answer call comes in during a meeting, quietly leave the room and make sure you apologize for any distraction. If appropriate, ask permission before taking the call.

Leave professional, brief but complete, and friendly voice mails. Make sure you keep voice mail messages to the point. Be brief about your requests but provide enough information for others to respond to your requests. If you must leave a lengthier message, make sure you leave your name and contact information at the beginning and the end of the message. Never leave an unfriendly voice mail message. Also, pay special attention to your greetings and leave pleasant closings. Finally, let people know your availability for a return call.

Speak with a pleasant, enthusiastic voice. Although others cannot see you, your nonverbal behaviors are often reflected in your voice. Consider sitting up straight or standing up, breathing deeply, intonating clearly, gesturing, and even smiling as you would if you were in person. These nonverbal actions will often carry through in a pleasant, professional voice and help you avoid a monotone. From time to time, consider listening to your recorded voice to pick up on ways in which you can speak more professionally and energetically.

Plan for your phone calls. Avoid simply winging calls. Like other forms of business communication, think ahead about your key discussion topics and points. Consider writing a few notes about these items or even plan an agenda. Also, let the person know how long you expect to take for the phone call.

Set expectations and boundaries about how you use your mobile phone. Talk to those you work with about how rapidly you hope for return calls, what you consider appropriate contact hours, and what types of messages you prefer to receive by phone as opposed to other communication channels (i.e., email, face-to-face). Conversely, ask others about their preferences.

Manage your incoming voice mail messages promptly and professionally. Always return calls within 24 hours. And make sure your voice mail box is never full; this sends the message that you are not responsive.

- **Feelers** tend to be more people-oriented and as a result, they focus heavily on harmony. When addressing feelers, include personal comments and explain the impacts of decisions on people.
- **Thinkers** are most focused on logic, objectivity, and correct analysis. When addressing thinkers, focus on well-organized, well-analyzed, dispassionate, and conclusive arguments.
- **Intuitors** are future-oriented, out-of-the-box thinkers. When communicating with intuitors, take more time for discussion and don't overemphasize the details.

Sensers make up the largest segment of the population and are particularly drawn to business disciplines. Many of the norms of written business communication come from the senser orientation: getting to the point quickly, staying on point, and presenting supporting facts in a logical order. Furthermore, most business communication is highly pragmatic, action-oriented, and results-oriented. Of course, written communication also adopts principles that feelers value. Typically, you will adapt more to various communicator styles in oral communication than you will in written communication.

Maintaining Civility

An outgrowth of emotional intelligence for interpersonal business communication is the notion of civility. Civility is a show of respect for the dignity and importance of others. It includes an orientation toward achieving honest, open, and respectful dialogues and validating the worth of others and their work efforts. In every instance, you should find ways to maintain civil communication in the workplace, especially for situations in which you disagree with others. Even when others treat you poorly—which will undoubtedly occur—responding civilly potentially de-escalates an ugly situation and shows your character and caring.

By contrast, incivility is "rudeness and disregard for others in a manner that violates norms for respect."[36] Unfortunately, incivility seems to be on the rise in the workplace.[37] In this section about civility, we first focus on the prominence and consequences of incivility. Then, we discuss common types and causes of incivility in the workplace. We conclude with strategies for maintaining civility.

LO2.6 Explain the role of civility in effective interpersonal communication and the common types of incivility in the workplace.

Incivility in Society and the Workplace

Many Americans perceive society as increasingly rude and disrespectful. A recent survey of over 2,000 people in the United States illustrated the extent to which they perceive rudeness in society.[38] Consider the following findings from this research:

- Seventy-nine percent of respondents felt that a lack of respect is a serious problem for our society and that we should try to address it.
- Eighty-eight percent of respondents said that they often or sometimes come across people who are rude and disrespectful.
- Seventy-three percent believe that Americans treated each other with more respect in the past.
- Thirty-seven percent say they are so affected by rudeness that they have thought about moving to another community.

One place respondents cite for lack of respect is retail stores. For example, 46 percent of respondents claim to have gotten such bad service sometime during the past year that they left the store. Among those making $75,000 or more (those from whom stores might lose the most business), 57 percent had received such bad service sometime during the past year that they left the store. Nearly four out of five respondents (77 percent) agreed that it is all too common to see employees act as if the customer is not even there. One danger for stores is that customers who feel disrespected may never say anything. Approximately 65 percent of respondents stated they hardly ever complained when getting bad service. On the other hand, 74 percent of respondents agreed that they often saw customers being rude or disrespectful to retail employees or customer service representatives.[39]

In the interactions among colleagues in the workplace, incivility is also common. Nearly four in ten respondents (39 percent) said they have colleagues who are rude or disrespectful. More than three in ten respondents (31 percent) said that their workplace supervisors are rude or disrespectful. About 30 percent of respondents said they *often* experienced rudeness at the workplace, and another 38 percent said they *sometimes* experienced rudeness in the workplace. The majority of respondents admitted that they are rude themselves; 61 percent agreed with the statement, "I'm so busy and pressed for time that I'm not as polite as I should be, and I feel sorry about it later on." As the researchers of this study concluded, "Few people can count on being consistently treated with respect and courtesy as they go about their daily lives. The cumulative social costs—in terms of mistrust, anger, and even rage—are all too real to ignore."[40]

Perhaps the foremost experts on workplace incivility are Christine Pearson and Christine Porath. They have examined the nature and consequences of incivility in hundreds of organizations in North America over the past decade, finding that roughly one-quarter to one-half of employees experience incivility on a *weekly* basis. Furthermore, the consequences are devastating to organizational performance. Incivility erodes organizational culture and can escalate into conflict. It lowers individuals' productivity, performance, motivation, creativity, and helping behaviors. It also leads to declines in job satisfaction, organizational loyalty, and leadership impact.[41] Employees who are targets of incivility respond in the following ways:

- Half lose work time worrying about future interactions with instigators of incivility.
- Half contemplate changing jobs.
- One-fourth intentionally cut back work efforts.
- Approximately 70 percent tell friends, family, and colleagues about their dissatisfaction.
- About one in eight leave their jobs: turnover expense per job is estimated at $50,000.

The cost to companies is not always easy to quantify. However, some companies have started civility initiatives that include cost estimates of incivility. For example, Cisco recently started a Global Civility Program. The company estimated its annual loss due to incivility was $71 million, based on lost productivity, turnover, and absenteeism.[42]

You will soon find yourself in business leadership positions. One primary cost of incivility is business leaders' time. By one estimate, business executives spend 13 percent of their time, or what amounts to seven weeks per year, managing the fallout of disputes among employees.[43]

Types and Causes of Workplace Incivility

People show disrespect and rudeness to others in almost limitless ways. Table 2.8 includes common types of workplace incivility.[44] This list is by no means exhaustive, but it does contain broad categories. Generally, incivility occurs when a person ignores others, fails to display basic courtesies, fails to recognize the efforts of others, fails to respect the time and privacy of others, and fails to recognize the basic worth and dignity of others. As you read through the list, think about whether you have witnessed or engaged in some of these types of incivility. These actions make people feel undervalued and unwelcome. They also lead to less collegiality and cooperation among co-workers.

The final category in Table 2.8—disrespecting the dignity and worth of others—is among the most serious types of incivility. Many of these actions involve direct

TABLE 2.8

Common Types of Incivility

Common Types of Incivility in the Workplace

Ignoring others

Not responding to calls or emails in a timely manner
Taking credit for the work of others
Not responding when others greet you
Withholding important information from colleagues
Not inviting colleagues to participate in important decisions
Overruling the decisions of others without providing any reasons
Not acknowledging the presence of others
Leaving some colleagues out of work social functions

Treating others without courtesy

Not using basic terms of courtesy such as *please* and *thank you*
Using a bossy or domineering tone, expression, or words
Copying the boss on emails as a power play
Interrupting others frequently
Not using titles such as *Mr.* and *Ms.* as appropriate

Disrespecting the efforts of others

Diminishing the ideas or efforts of others
Providing vague and ambiguous feedback
Blaming others unfairly

Disrespecting the time of others

Disrupting a meeting
Interrupting meetings or demanding an immediate meeting
Setting deadlines without sufficient notice
Sending too much email
Flagging all email as important
Calling colleagues on weekends or after work hours

Disrespecting the privacy of others

Taking up too much space or being messy in shared space
Being too noisy (especially in cubicles/shared work spaces)
Telling offensive jokes
Asking intrusive questions about the personal lives of others
Forwarding private or sensitive emails

Disrespecting the dignity and worth of others

Not greeting others warmly
Delivering bad news by email
Talking behind the backs of others and gossiping
Criticizing or reprimanding a person in front of others
Making condescending or demeaning comments to others
Attacking the character of others
Attacking others based on political, religious, or other beliefs
Giving others a dirty look or the silent treatment
Insulting or yelling at others
Insulting others due to gender, ethnicity, or sexual orientation
Harassing others

attacks on the identity and inherent worth of others. Verbal insults or even nonverbal expressions such as glares can send strong messages that show you do not value or respect others. Even without mean intentions, jokes about traits such as gender, ethnicity, or sexual orientation can create a hostile working environment for colleagues.

Of course, people of different personalities and cultures vary in their level of sensitivity to the behaviors listed in Table 2.8. Instigators of incivility are sometimes unaware of how much they impact others. Your responsibility, however, is to be sensitive to how others perceive your behaviors.

The world is increasingly interconnected. This is especially the case in the business world. Ironically, an increasingly interconnected world may be a force that removes many people from enduring, fairly permanent communities and creates a new kind of anonymity. P. M. Forni, founder of The Civility Initiative, highlighted the relationship between anonymity and incivility:

> Every day we encounter legions of strangers who will remain strangers. Soulless extras in our life stories, they hardly seem to warrant a nod of acknowledgment—let alone a kind word. In fact, we can easily get away with being rude to them. Gone are the days when the fear of being ostracized was an incentive to be civil: The cohesive social texture which allowed that motivation disappeared long ago. Anonymity gives us the feeling we can act with impunity.[45]

Maintaining Civil Communications

Forni, one of the leading voices on improving civility in society and the workplace, recommended eight guiding principles:[46]

1. Slow down and be present in life.
2. Listen to the voice of empathy.
3. Keep a positive attitude.
4. Respect others and grant them plenty of validation.
5. Disagree graciously and refrain from arguing.
6. Get to know people around you.
7. Pay attention to small things.
8. Ask, don't tell.

You may already use these strategies in your everyday life. The workplace, however, presents additional challenges. Intense competition and deadlines create pressures that make many of these strategies more difficult. Also, as you advance into higher leadership positions, these pressures can increase rapidly. Making a conscious effort to build emotional intelligence will help you maintain respectful communications even under moments of intense pressure.

One of the best ways of keeping your emotional intelligence high and maintaining the habit of communicating respectfully is to get to know people around you and humanize your work. While this approach may seem time-consuming, it will help you develop the types of work relationships that make communication easier, even for difficult conversations. Consider the comments of Joseph Plumeri, chairman and CEO of the insurance broker Willis Group:

> I spend 25 percent to 30 percent of my time calling my associates—whether they had a family problem or pulled off a great deal and brought in a new client, or saved a client. Two-minute phone call, or handwritten note. I can't begin to tell you how important that stuff is.[47]

In the opening case, Jeff and Latisha are each confronted with an uncomfortable situation. In the sections about the interpersonal process and emotional intelligence, you read examples of how they could have confronted this uncomfortable situation in less effective and more effective ways. If Jeff and Latisha make personal commitments to stay civil at all times, they are each more likely to communicate effectively and productively. Furthermore, a commitment to civility will help each of them build their emotional intelligence.

COMMUNICATION Q&A

CONVERSATIONS WITH CURRENT BUSINESS PROFESSIONALS

Pete Cardon: How important are interpersonal communication skills in terms of getting promoted?

Shane Stowell: To become a successful business executive, you must master a set of interpersonal communication skills early in your career. However, many business professionals believe this set of skills will take care of itself as they progress down their career path. In today's market, two individuals can have similar educational pedigrees and comparable business acumen, but the clear distinction used in the promotional decision is whether or not someone has exceptional interpersonal communication skills.

PC: How do employers assess interpersonal communication skills?

SS: In today's job market, human resources departments and hiring executives are using very sophisticated methods to better understand their candidates and maximize the value they receive for the investment they make in the hiring process. They often use multiple interviews to look for consistency of interaction styles. They look online to see if they can discern your judgment and character. They want to know how you might handle and react to stressful situations and solve real-world problems, so they create scenarios in the interview to test these skills. Finally, they rely on psychological measurement and assessment to help them understand personality style and how you will match the core values of the organization.

PC: Do employers pay attention to emotional intelligence? In what ways does emotional intelligence lead to better business performance?

SS: Successful organizations want to make sure you can help them move the business forward long term. The intangible leadership skills of wisdom, self-awareness, insight, integrity, executive maturity, fortitude, and a willingness to be vulnerable at the right time are critical leadership skills in today's global business climate. In its simplest form, emotional intelligence is at the core of all of these "softer" leadership skills. Awareness of how you impact others and how others impact you in an interaction should be a skill you actively develop.

PC: Businesspeople have so many choices of communication channels today. What are a few tips for how executives and managers should choose the right communication channel?

SS: Even in the midst of all of these options, the core components of clarity of message, respect for another person's time, openness to collaboration, and good listening skills are still the foundation of all communications. One word of advice would be to find a form of communication that allows for as much interpersonal interaction as possible. For instance, if given the choice between a conference call and a videoconference, I would select the videoconference in order to maximize your ability to use your core emotional intelligence skills.

Shane Stowell *is a principal with RHR International LLP, a business consulting firm that specializes in improving the assessment, selection, and development of senior-level executives. Before joining RHR, Stowell owned and ran a variety of businesses and earned a doctorate degree in psychology.*

Chapter Takeaway for *Interpersonal Communication Skills*

LO 2.1. Describe the interpersonal communication process and barriers to effective communication. (pp. 26–30)

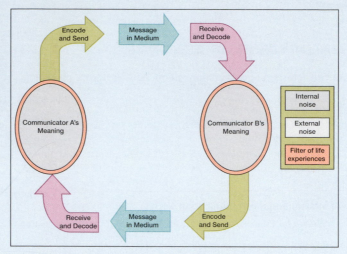

See an *example of the interpersonal communication process* in Figure 2.2.

LO 2.2. Explain how emotional hijacking can hinder effective interpersonal communication. (pp. 30–31)

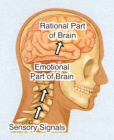

People are hardwired to experience emotions before reason. All signals to the brain first go through the limbic system, where emotions are produced, before going to the rational area of the brain. **Emotional hijacking** occurs when emotions control our behavior, causing us to react without thinking. During emotional hijacking, we often make statements that are rash, nonintentional, and nonanalytical.

LO 2.3. Describe the basic domains of emotional intelligence and related communication competencies and assess your own emotional intelligence. (pp. 31–35)

See *examples* of the following: *low versus high self-awareness thoughts* in Table 2.3, *low versus high self-management thoughts* in Table 2.4, a *summary of EQ impacts on communication* in Table 2.5, and *strategies for improving EQ* in Table 2.5.

LO 2.4. Explain the trade-offs associated with richness, control, and constraints when choosing a communication channel. (pp. 35–39)

See *summaries of trade-offs of communication channels* in Table 2.6.

LO 2.5. Describe how forms of communication, level of formality, and communicator styles influence workplace communication. (pp. 39–43)

See *factors impacting formality of communication* in Figure 2.5 and a *summary of communicator styles* in Table 2.7.

LO 2.6. Explain the role of civility in effective interpersonal communication and the common types of incivility in the workplace. (pp. 43–47)

Guiding principles: (1) Slow down and be present in life; (2) listen to the voice of empathy; (3) keep a positive attitude; (4) respect others and grant them plenty of validation; (5) disagree graciously and refrain from arguing; (6) get to know people around you; (7) pay attention to small things; (8) ask, don't tell. (*Source:* P. M. Forni's *The Civility Solution*)

See *examples of incivility* in Table 2.8.

Key Terms

asynchronous communication (p. 37)	informality (p. 40)	private communication (p. 39)
communication channel (p. 35)	interpersonal communication process (p. 26)	psychological noise (p. 28)
constraints (p. 36)	intuitors (p. 43)	relationship management (p. 34)
control (p. 36)	leadership communication (p. 40)	resources (p. 36)
coordination (p. 36)	meaning (p. 26)	richness (p. 36)
decoding (p. 27)	mitigating information (p. 32)	self-awareness (p. 31)
emotional hijacking (p. 31)	networked communication (p. 40)	self-management (p. 32)
emotional intelligence (EQ) (p. 30)	noise (p. 27)	semantic noise (p. 28)
empathy (p. 34)	optimism (p. 33)	sensers (p. 41)
encoding (p. 26)	permanence (p. 36)	shared meaning (p. 27)
feelers (p. 43)	pessimism (p. 33)	synchronous communication (p. 37)
filter of lifetime experiences (p. 28)	physical noise (p. 27)	team communication (p. 39)
formality (p. 40)	physiological noise (p. 28)	thinkers (p. 43)
immediacy (p. 36)	planning (p. 36)	triggers (p. 31)

Discussion Exercises

2.1 Chapter Review Questions (LO 2.1, LO 2.2, LO 2.3, LO 2.4, LO 2.5, LO 2.6)

A. What barriers are there to achieving shared meaning? Explain these barriers in terms of the interpersonal communication model.

B. List ten words that could easily be perceived differently. Choose words that create semantic noise because of generational differences, occupational differences, cultural differences, or other kinds of differences.

C. Why is emotional intelligence so important in logical business tasks?

D. What are the four domains of emotional intelligence? Describe three related communication competencies for each domain (see Table 2.5).

E. What do you think are the five best strategies for developing emotional intelligence? Explain your rationale. (See Table 2.5 for help.)

F. Explain how optimism and pessimism affect self-management.

G. Compare and contrast spoken versus written communication in terms of richness, control, and constraints.

H. Describe three communication channels and their strengths and weaknesses in terms of richness, control, and constraints.

I. Create a table similar to Table 2.6 that contains five communication channels that are different than or variations of those listed in the table.

J. Name the factors described in the book that affect the formality of a communication. What other factors might affect formality of communication in the workplace?

K. Consider the common types of incivility shown in Table 2.8. Which five types of incivility do you think are most common? Most serious? Name five other behaviors you view as common forms of incivility in the workplace, school, or society.

L. What are three things you can do to create a culture of civility and candor in the workplace? Explain.

2.2 Communication Q&A Discussion Questions (LO 2.2, LO 2.3, LO 2.4)

Read the Communication Q&A in this chapter. For each question, write a one- or two-paragraph answer.

A. What does Shane Stowell say about the role of emotional intelligence in determining career success and gaining promotions?

B. According to Stowell, what are the key benefits of strong interpersonal skills in the workplace?

C. What approaches do companies use to assess your interpersonal communication skills and emotional intelligence?

D. What principles does he describe as important in determining a choice of communication channel?

2.3 The Personal Part of Employees (LO 2.3, LO 2.5)

In response to the question "How do you hire?," Kasper Rorsted, CEO of Henkel, a consumer and industrial products company based in Düsseldorf, Germany, had this to say:

> I want to know who you are, who you've worked for, what kind of successes you've had, what are the failures or missteps in your career.

But what I try to spend a lot of time on is trying to understand the person I'm speaking to. Did you work in an ice cream parlor when you were young? Do you have sisters? Do you have brothers? Why are you now living here? I'm trying to figure out who's actually behind the person, and what are the value sets that drive you as a person.

Then I always ask the question, what would you do if you won 10 million bucks? Would you leave? Would you retire? Do you want to do charity work? Will you stay?

I never look at grades from university. I look at what they've done, but I look very much at what they've done outside work. How do they spend their time? Who do they relate to? Have they moved? Have they been put in situations in their personal and professional lives that were not very straightforward?

I'm concerned about people who have come through their career with "A" grades throughout their entire life, and have never really had any setbacks and have always been in environments where they knew the environment.

Also, do they say goodbye and hello to the person who stands in front of the building, and do they say hello to the person who sweeps the floor? How do they act as a person? The personal part is, for me, equally important to the professional part. Because I think you can get a lot of people who are professionally very

good, but I think the personal part and the value part are the difference between a good manager or leader and a great leader.[48]

Respond to the following questions:
A. When Rorsted says he is looking to find out about the *personal part,* not just the professional part, of a job applicant, what does he mean?
B. How does what Rorsted describes as the personal part of an employee relate to emotional intelligence? How about civility?
C. Rorsted explains that he wants to know how people have responded to setbacks. How does this relate to emotional intelligence?
D. He distinguishes between a good manager and a good leader. In two or three paragraphs, describe some characteristics that would distinguish a good leader from a good manager in terms of interpersonal communication, emotional intelligence, and/or civility.

2.4 Civility and Assertiveness (LO 2.3, LO 2.5)

Think of three business (or school) situations that require assertiveness. Describe how you can be assertive and also civil at the same time.

Evaluation Exercises

2.5 Describe a Miscommunication from a Movie or TV Episode (LO 2.1)

Think about a recent movie or TV episode you observed. Select a scene that involved a miscommunication. Ideally, it should include a conversation that might occur in a workplace. Based on this conversation, do the following:

A. Summarize the conversation in one paragraph.
B. Analyze the conversation in terms of the following components of the interpersonal communication process: encoding, decoding, physical noise, physiological noise, psychological noise, semantic noise, and filter of lifetime experiences.
C. Describe at least three strategies the characters in the conversation could have adopted to increase shared meaning and avoid miscommunication. Describe these strategies in terms of reducing noise and adapting to the filters of others.

2.6 Assess a Recent Miscommunication (LO 2.1)

Think about a recent miscommunication you had with someone. Ideally, select an in-depth conversation that occurred in the workplace or at school. Based on this conversation, do the following:

A. Summarize the conversation in one paragraph.
B. Analyze the conversation in terms of the following components of the interpersonal communication process: encoding, decoding, physical noise, physiological noise, psychological noise, semantic noise, and filter of lifetime experiences.
C. Describe at least three strategies you could have adopted to increase shared meaning and avoid miscommunication. Describe these strategies in terms of reducing noise and adapting to your and your counterpart's unique filters.

2.7 Analyze a Case of Emotional Hijacking at School or Work (LO 2.2)

Think about a recent situation at school or work in which you observed a serious instance of emotional hijacking. Based on this situation, do the following:

A. Briefly explain what happened. Who was involved and what were they doing? You can write about yourself and/or others.
B. Explain the cause and nature of the emotional hijacking. For example, explain what the emotions were and what caused them.
C. Explain the impacts of the emotional hijacking. How did it affect an interaction? How did it affect performance?
D. Describe how the emotional hijacking could have been avoided or lessened.
E. Write a set of self-awareness and self-management thoughts that would be considered effective and ineffective in this situation (see Tables 2.3 and 2.4).

2.8 Identify Your Triggers (LO 2.2)

In three to five paragraphs, describe three triggers that could lead to emotional hijacking for you. For each trigger, explain one or two strategies you can use to calm down and communicate constructively.

2.9 Assess Your Emotional Intelligence (LO 2.3)

Respond to the items below as you assess your emotional intelligence and develop a plan to raise your EQ. Ideally, choose situations from work or school. You may want to use Table 2.5 from the chapter as a guide.

A. Identify one strength and one weakness you have in terms of self-awareness. Describe a situation in which you showed low self-awareness and a situation in which you showed high self-awareness. Choose two strategies for improving your self-awareness.

B. Identify one strength and one weakness you have in terms of self-management. Describe a situation in which you showed low self-management and a situation in which you showed high self-management. Choose two strategies for improving your self-management.

C. Identify one strength and one weakness you have in terms of empathy. Describe a situation in which you showed low empathy and a situation in which you showed high empathy. Choose two strategies for improving your empathy.

D. Identify one strength and one weakness you have in terms of relationship management. Describe a situation in which you showed low relationship management and a situation in which you showed high relationship management. Choose two strategies for improving your relationship management skills.

2.10 Describe the Communication Skills of a Person with High EQ (LO 2.3)

Think of someone you have worked with extensively and who you think has high emotional intelligence. Describe at least two communication skills this person has that demonstrate each of the four EQ domains: self-awareness, self-management, empathy, and relationship management. Also, in two or three paragraphs, describe one challenging interpersonal situation this person handled effectively due to high EQ.

2.11 Evaluate Communicator Styles (LO 2.5)

Look at Table 2.7, which breaks communicators into four styles: senser, feeler, thinker, and intuitor. Based on these descriptions, respond to the following items:

A. What is your primary communicator style? Your secondary communicator style?

B. Which type of communicator style is most difficult for you to relate with? How can you accommodate people of this communicator style?

C. Describe one person you know for each communicator style. Describe how they do (or would) interact with one another.

2.12 Analyze an Episode of Incivility at Work (LO 2.6)

Think of a situation you have observed at work or at school that was uncivil. In one or two paragraphs, describe the event. Then, in two or three paragraphs, explain how each person involved in the encounter contributed to the uncivil event. Analyze the event in terms of noise, filter, and emotional intelligence. In two paragraphs, explain how the person who was most responsible for the incivility could have behaved to make the situation productive for everyone.

2.13 Assess Your Civility (LO 2.6)

Look at Table 2.8 in the chapter and think about various types of incivility: ignoring others, treating others without courtesy, disrespecting the time of others, disrespecting the privacy of others, and disrespecting the dignity and worth of others. Read through examples of behaviors associated with each type of incivility. In three or four paragraphs, describe three aspects of civility you will exemplify in your professional life and how you will avoid inadvertently communicating disrespectfully to others.

Application Exercises

2.14 Create a Presentation about Avoiding Miscommunication in the Workplace (LO 2.1)

Individually or in teams, develop a five- to ten-minute presentation about how to avoid miscommunication in the workplace. Use terms such as *noise, filter, encoding,* and *decoding* to explain miscommunication. Provide several specific scenarios that have happened or could happen in the workplace. Provide a simple set of recommendations that your audience will find compelling, insightful, and easy to remember.

2.15 Create a Presentation about EQ as a Basis for Effective Interpersonal Communication (LO 2.2, LO 2.3)

Individually or in teams, develop a five- to ten-minute presentation about the importance of EQ for effective communication in the workplace. Describe each of the four dimensions of emotional intelligence. Provide several specific scenarios that have happened or could happen in the workplace. Provide a simple set of recommendations that your audience will find compelling, insightful, and easy to remember.

2.16 Choose the Right Communication Channel (LO 2.4)

Assume the role of Latisha (from the chapter case). Latisha decides she wants to explore other ways to continue working on a health initiative. She thinks she could devote a portion of her work time to planning and justifying this project. It would not require expenditures on the part of the company, other than her time. She wants to communicate with Jeff about her ideas. What would be the best

communication channel for this discussion under each of the following circumstances? You may select more than one communication channel or even a combination of communication channels. Defend each answer with a discussion of richness, control, and constraints:

A. Jeff is in his office with the door open.

B. Jeff is in his office with the door closed, and he is not taking calls.

C. Jeff is out of town for two weeks.

D. Latisha is out of town for two weeks.

E. Latisha is nervous and uncomfortable about approaching Jeff.

F. Latisha thinks Jeff doesn't want to continue any work on the health initiative.

G. Latisha is a thinker and Jeff is a senser.

H. Latisha is a feeler and Jeff is a thinker.

2.17 Create a Presentation about Civility in Today's Workplace (LO 2.6)

Individually or in teams, develop a five- to ten-minute presentation about maintaining civil communications in the workplace. Provide several scenarios that have happened or could happen in the workplace. Provide a simple set of recommendations that your audience will find compelling, insightful, and easy to remember.

Endnotes

1.   Linda Lyons, "Which Skills Hold the Secret to Success at Work?" Gallup online (August 19, 2003), from http://www.gallup.com/poll/9064/Which-Skills-Hold-Secret-Success-Work.aspx.

2.   New York Times Corner Office Blog, "Career Advice," retrieved June 15, 2010, from http://projects.nytimes.com/corner-office/Career_advice.

3.   This model is based on the transactional model of communication: Paul Watzlawick, Janet H. Beavin, and Don D. Jackson, *Pragmatics of Human Communication: A Study of International Patterns, Pathologies, and Paradoxes* (New York: Norton, 1967); D. C. Barnland, "A Transactional Model of Communication," in K. K. Sereno and C. D. Mortensen, eds., *Foundations of Communication Theory* (New York: Harper & Row, 1970): 83–102; Uma Narula, *Handbook of Communication: Models, Perspectives, Strategies* (New Delhi, India: Atlantic Publishers, 2006); Richard West and Lynn H. Turner, *Understanding Interpersonal Communication: Making Choices in Changing Times,* 2nd ed. (Boston: Wadsworth Cengage Learning, 2009).

4.   West and Turner, *Understanding Interpersonal Communication: Making Choices in Changing Times.*

5.   Most discussion in this section, including this definition, comes from the following sources: Daniel Goleman, *Working with Emotional Intelligence* (New York: Bantam Dell, 2006); Daniel Goleman, *Emotional Intelligence: Why It Can Matter More Than IQ* (New York: Bantam Books, 1995); Adele B. Lynn, *The EQ Difference: A Powerful Plan for Putting Emotional Intelligence to Work* (New York: AMACOM, 2005); Travis Bradberry and Jean Greaves, *Emotional Intelligence 2.0* (San Diego: TalentSmart, 2009).

6.   Sue Campbell Clark, Ronda Callister, and Ray Wallace, "Undergraduate Management Skills Courses and Students' Emotional Intelligence," *Journal of Management Education* 27, no. 1 (2003): 3–23.

7.   Roderick Gilkey, Ricardo Caceda, and Clinton Kilts, "When Emotional Reasoning Trumps IQ," *Harvard Business Review* (September 2010): 27; Robert Kelley and Janet Caplan, "How Bell Labs Creates Star Performers," *Harvard Business Review* (July/August 1993): 128–139.

8.   Bradberry and Greaves, *Emotional Intelligence 2.0.*

9.   "America's Most Stressful Jobs 2010," retrieved April 14, 2011, from www.cnbc.com/id/36715336/America_s_Most_Stressful_Jobs_2010.

10.   New York Times Corner Office Blog, "Communication," retrieved June 15, 2010, from http://projects.nytimes.com/corner-office/Communication.

11.   Clark et al., "Undergraduate Management Skills Courses and Students' Emotional Intelligence."

12.   Bradberry and Greaves, *Emotional Intelligence 2.0.*

13.   Goleman, *Emotional Intelligence: Why It Can Matter More Than IQ*; Lynn, *The EQ Difference: A Powerful Plan for Putting Emotional Intelligence to Work*; Dan Ariely, "The Long-Term Effects of Short-Term Emotions," *Harvard Business Review* (January/February 2010): 38.

14.   Bradberry and Greaves, *Emotional Intelligence 2.0.*

15.   Goleman, *Emotional Intelligence: Why It Can Matter More Than IQ*: 46.

16.   Lynn, *The EQ Difference: A Powerful Plan for Putting Emotional Intelligence to Work*; Bradberry and Greaves, *Emotional Intelligence 2.0.*

17.   Goleman, *Emotional Intelligence: Why It Can Matter More Than IQ.*

18.   Bradberry and Greaves, *Emotional Intelligence 2.0.*

19.   Lynn, *The EQ Difference: A Powerful Plan for Putting Emotional Intelligence to Work*: 46.

20.   Bradberry and Greaves, *Emotional Intelligence 2.0*: 32.

21.   Lynn, *The EQ Difference: A Powerful Plan for Putting Emotional Intelligence to Work.*

22.   Goleman, *Emotional Intelligence: Why It Can Matter More Than IQ.*

23.   Ibid.

24.   Ibid.

25.   Lynn, *The EQ Difference: A Powerful Plan for Putting Emotional Intelligence to Work.*

26.   Goleman, *Emotional Intelligence: Why It Can Matter More Than IQ.*

27.   Bradberry and Greaves, *Emotional Intelligence 2.0*: 38.

28.   Goleman, *Emotional Intelligence: Why It Can Matter More Than IQ.*

29.   Bradberry and Greaves, *Emotional Intelligence 2.0*: 44.

30.   Watson Wyatt Worldwide, *Capitalizing on Effective Communication: How Courage, Innovation and Discipline Drive Business Results in Challenging Times, 2009/2010 Communication ROI Study Report* (New York: Watson Wyatt Worldwide, 2010).

31.   Pearn Kandola, *The Psychology of Effective Business Communications in Geographically Dispersed Teams* (San Jose: Cisco, 2006); Likoebe M. Maruping and Ritu Agarwal, "Managing Team Interpersonal Processes Through Technology: A Task-Technology Fit Perspective," *Journal of Applied Psychology* 89, no. 6 (2004): 975–990.

32.   Arvind Malhotra, Ann Majchrzak, and Benson Rosen, "Leading Virtual Teams," *Academy of Management Perspectives* 21 (2007): 64.

33.   Ibid: 60–70.

34.   Roy A. Cook and Gwen O. Cook, *Guide to Business Etiquette,* 2nd ed. (Upper Saddle River, NJ: Prentice Hall, 2011); Susan Bixler and Lisa Scherrer Dugan, *How to Project Confidence, Competence, and Credibility at Work: 5 Steps to Professional Presence* (Avon, MA: Adams Media, 2001); Beverly Langford, *The Etiquette Edge: The Unspoken Rules for Business Success* (New York: American Management Association, 2005); Dale Carnegie Training, *The 5 Essential People Skills: How to Assert Yourself, Listen to Others, and Resolve Conflicts* (New York: Simon & Schuster, 2009).

35.   Paul P. Mok, *Interpretation Manual for CSS: A Survey of Communicating Styles* (Garland, TX: Training Associates Press, 1989); Anne Field, "Intuitor, Thinker, Feeler, Senser: Which One Are You Talking To?" *Harvard Management Communication Letter* 6, no. 7 (2003): 3–5.

36.   Christine M. Pearson and Christine L. Porath, "On the Nature, Consequences and Remedies of Workplace Incivility: No Time for 'Nice'? Think Again," *Academy of Management Executive* 19, no. 1 (2005): 8.

37.   Ronald J. Alsop, "Social Disgraces," *Workforce Management* (January 2011): 34.

38.   Steve Farkas, Jean Johnson, Ann Duffett, and Kathleen Collins, *Aggravating Circumstances: A Status Report on Rudeness in America* (New York: Public Agenda), retrieved November 25, 2009, from http://www.publicagenda.org/files/pdf/aggravating_circumstances.pdf.

39.   Ibid.

40. Ibid, p. 24.

41. Pearson and Porath, "On the Nature, Consequences and Remedies of Workplace Incivility: No Time for 'Nice'? Think Again": 7–18.

42. Christine M. Pearson and Christine L. Porath, *The Cost of Bad Behavior: How Incivility Is Damaging Your Business and What to Do about It* (New York: Penguin Group, 2009).

43. Ibid.

44. These types of workplace incivility are adopted and modified from a variety of sources, including the following: Pearson and Porath, *The Cost of Bad Behavior: How Incivility Is Damaging Your Business and What to Do about It*; P. M. Forni, *The Civility Solution: What to Do When People Are Rude* (New York: St. Martin's Press, 2008);

Lorraine A. Krajewski, "Workplace Incivility: A Research Study," Presentation at the 2010 Annual Convention of the Association for Business Communication, October 27, 2010, Chicago.

45. Forni, *The Civility Solution: What to Do When People Are Rude*: 24.

46. Ibid: 29.

47. New York Times Corner Office Blog, "Managing by Walking Around," retrieved June 15, 2010, from http://projects.nytimes.com/corner-office/Management_by_walking_around.

48. New York Times Corner Office Blog, "No Need to Hit the 'Send' Key: Just Talk to Me," retrieved August 31, 2010, from www.nytimes.com/2010/08/29/business/29corner.html?src=me&ref=business.

CHAPTER THREE

Listening, Team Communication, and Difficult Conversations

Learning Objectives

After studying this chapter, you should be able to do the following:

LO3.1 Describe and evaluate the process of active listening.

LO3.2 Explain and evaluate barriers to effective listening and common types of nonlistening behaviors.

LO3.3 Describe the elements of questions that enhance listening and learning.

LO3.4 Explain the principles of team communication in high-performing teams.

LO3.5 Describe and demonstrate approaches to planning, running, and following up on meetings.

LO3.6 Explain basic principles for handling difficult conversations.

WHY DOES THIS MATTER?

Hear Pete Cardon explain why this matters.

bit.ly/com/CardonWhy3

Dozens of studies have shown that listening is ranked among the most important communication skills.[1] For example, 7,674 business school alumni who graduated between 2000 and 2010 were asked to rank the most important communication skills for success in the business world (see Table 3.1). They ranked listening skills second, only slightly behind the broad ability to work with others. They valued listening skills more highly than presentation skills, writing skills, and a dozen or so other types of communication skills.[2]

Look through the list of communication skills in Table 3.1. How much time have you spent developing those skills? Think about your current business program. You may have entire courses devoted to leadership or negotiation. But, what about listening?

Traditionally, communication and management training has emphasized a message-centered approach to influencing others. Instead, however, consider adopting a listening-centered approach to communication and management. In the listening-centered approach, you seek out the perspectives, ideas, needs, wants, and feelings of others in all of your work relationships. Listening to others is the starting point for your communications. A listening-centered communication style as opposed to a message-centered one *means talking with someone rather than talking at them.*[3]

A listening-centered approach to leading was illustrated several years ago by Paul Levy, the CEO of a Massachusetts hospital. His hospital was faced with a budget shortfall of $20 million, and hundreds of layoffs appeared inevitable. Mr. Levy was distraught, since he valued the work of the hospital's frontline employees and the loyalty they had shown to the hospital. He decided to hold a town-hall-style meeting for employees and encourage them to voice their ideas. He explained the dire situation and the need for layoffs unless employees would voluntarily make sacrifices to reduce the budget shortfall. Then, he asked them for their ideas about solving the problem.[4]

The reaction was overwhelming. Dozens of employees offered ideas at the meeting. Hundreds sent emails. Ultimately, the organization came up with solutions that saved the jobs of 450 employees. As one employee said, "It is not that it is such a brilliant idea to cut pay in order to reduce layoffs or any of the other ideas that were offered, but it is the fact that he has a policy of an open employee forum and an anonymous way to voice your opinion that is important."[5]

Listening is critical from day one in any entry-level business position. In fact, many successful executives point out that listening should be your primary focus. When asked, *What do you tell entry-level managers who come to work for you?* Niki Leondakis of the Kimpton Hotel & Restaurant Group said this:

> *Before you start telling people where you're coming from and what you're about and what you're going to do, listen first to what's going*

TABLE 3.1

Most Important Communication Skills according to Business Graduates (2000–2010)

Skills	Percentage*
1. Ability to work with others	93
2. Listening skills	**90**
3. Ability to influence others	89
4. Diplomacy and tact	87
5. Managing expectations	80
6. Leadership skills	78
7. Presentation skills	74
8. Networking skills	70
9. Writing skills	69
10. Meeting management	68
11. Give constructive feedback	65
12. Managing organizational politics	65
13. Negotiation skills	65
14. Cross-cultural sensitivity	52
15. Mentoring skills	45

Source: From Alumni Perspectives Survey 2009-2010. Reproduced with the permission of the Graduate Management Admission Council.

*Percentage of employees who rated this skill extremely or very important to their current job.

(continued)

on here, how do [others] feel about it, what are their views, what's their input, what are their personal goals, and take note of all they have to say, and then put together your version of "here's where I'm coming from." So, "listen and learn first" is a consistent piece of advice.[6]

After focusing on listening in this chapter, we also discuss team communication and difficult conversations. In today's increasingly collaborative work environment, you will spend thousands of hours working in teams. In one recent survey of more than 2,000 business professionals, over half (54 percent) stated they spent between 30 and 50 percent of their day in a team setting.[7] We will discuss various principles of effective team communication, all of which depend on effective listening. Working closely in teams and collaborating with others inevitably involves difficult conversations—those conversations that are uncomfortable or challenging due to strong disagreements or for other reasons. A listening-centered approach to these difficult conversations is necessary to achieve excellent business results and strong working relationships.

Read the following short case about listening and communicating in teams at the Prestigio Hotel. You will follow each of these individuals throughout the chapter.

Chapter Case: Listening and Communicating in Teams at the Prestigio Hotel

Who's Involved

Andrea Garcia, general manager

Nancy Jeffreys, director of marketing

Barbara Brookshire, director of conventions

Kip Yamada, marketing associate

The Prestig Marketing T

Situation 1   Andrea and Barbara Hold Different Perspectives of Internet Pricing

Andrea and Barbara have disagreed for months about Internet pricing for group guests to the Prestigio, a four-star hotel. Andrea thinks the Internet pricing is appropriate and comparable to other high-end hotels. Barbara, as director of conventions and meetings, deals more closely with groups and often hears these guests complain about the high pricing. She believes an adjustment would increase overall satisfaction among group guests.

Task 1   How will Andrea and Barbara listen to one another effectively when they see things so differently? (See the chapter section on listening.)

Situation 2   The Marketing Team Prepares for a Meeting

The marketing team is about to hold its biweekly meeting. Team members intend to discuss plans for upcoming market research, assess progress on an ongoing initiative to improve customer service, examine ways to use blogs and wikis to improve communication within the team, and finalize plans for a Valentine's Day marketing campaign.

Task 2   How will the marketing team work together effectively to implement a cohesive marketing approach? (See the team communication section.)

Situation 3   Nancy and Kip Hold Grudges from a Prior Disagreement

Nancy and Kip have ignored one another as much as possible in recent months. Problems started when Kip authorized refunds to ten business travelers totaling nearly $4,000. The business travelers complained that they were charged standard hotel rates over several months rather than at discounted rates as advertised on the hotel website. The travelers, however, were not incorrectly charged. Rather, they had not read the fine print on the website, which restricted discounts on weekends. Kip authorized the refunds because he felt the travelers were frequent guests who deserved special considerations.

Nancy was furious when she found out that Kip had given the refunds without first checking with her. She called him into her office and scolded him for not speaking to her first. Kip abruptly said, "So much for the famous Prestigio customer service," and left her office. Since then, Nancy had complained to co-workers that Kip didn't understand the business side of running a hotel. Kip complained that Nancy didn't relate to hotel guests and that the hotel was losing business because of it.

Task 3   How will Nancy and Kip discuss their differences and work productively together again? (See the chapter section on difficult conversations.)

Listening in the Workplace

Listening requires hard work. And it requires more than simply hearing. The traditional Chinese character for *listen* (displayed in Figure 3.1) captures the importance of listening with all of our senses and all of our efforts. The character includes components that represent the ears, the eyes, the heart, undivided attention, and king. The implication is that listening requires all one's senses and that you treat the speaker like royalty.[8]

Great listeners respond physically to others. Research indicates that brain activity in excellent listeners mimics that of the speakers. In some cases, the listener's brain shows activity before that of the speaker. In other words, the best listeners anticipate how a speaker thinks and feels.[9]

LO3.1   Describe and evaluate the process of active listening.

Engaging in Active Listening

The Chinese character for *listen* illustrates a comprehensive approach to listening. In recent years, management and communication scholars have increasingly emphasized this notion with the term *active listening*. Michael Hoppe of the Center for Creative Leadership has defined active listening as "a person's willingness and ability to hear and understand. At its core, active listening is a state of mind. . . . It involves bringing about and finding common ground, connecting to each other, and opening up new possibilities."[10] Hoppe breaks active listening down into six skills: (1) paying attention, (2) holding judgment, (3) reflecting, (4) clarifying, (5) summarizing, and (6) sharing.

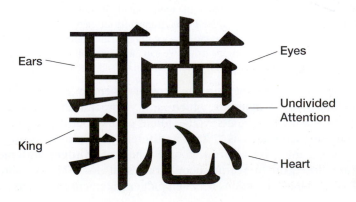

FIGURE 3.1

The Traditional Chinese Character for *Listen*

Excellent listeners use their ears, eyes, heart, and undivided attention to understand what others say. They treat others like royalty.

Paying Attention   This first step involves devoting your whole attention to others and allowing them enough comfort and time to express themselves completely. As others speak to you, try to understand everything they say from *their* perspective. Michael Mathieu, CEO of the video-advertising company YuMe, recently recommended that business managers pay better attention to those with whom they interact:

> Be connected, and have conversations with people. Don't be distracted, and the little nuances of life will show up, and you will hear things. I'm not immune. I have to do a lot of things, and I try to slow down sometimes. I try to be present so I can enjoy the richness and quality of interactions with people. Most people can't multitask without losing something in each of those tasks.[11]

Paying attention requires active nonverbal communication. Your body language, including appropriate eye contact, should show you are eager to understand the other person. Lean forward. Keep an open body position. Sit up straight. Nod to show you are listening. Smile as appropriate. Pay attention to the speaker's nonverbal behaviors. Avoid any distractions, such as taking calls or checking your phone. Become comfortable with silence. To hear people out inevitably requires a few breaks in the flow of the conversation.[12]

Holding Judgment   People will only share their ideas and feelings with you if they feel safe. Holding judgment is particularly important in tense and emotionally charged situations. One of the best ways to make others feel comfortable expressing themselves fully is to demonstrate a learner mind-set rather than a judger mind-set.

In a **learner mind-set,** you show eagerness to hear others' ideas and perspectives and listen with an open mind. You do not have your mind made up before listening fully. When you disagree, you stay open to the possibility of finding common ground and mutually beneficial solutions. Under the learner mind-set, difference of opinion is considered normal, even healthy, and potentially solution-producing.[13]

In a **judger mind-set,** people have their minds made up before listening carefully to others' ideas, perspective, and experiences. Judgers view disagreement rigidly, with little possibility of finding common ground unless the other person changes his or her views. Judging often involves punishing others for disagreement. At its extreme, the judger mind-set involves ascribing negative traits to others and labeling them in undesirable terms. For example, judgers often enter conversations with thoughts such as "she's not creative" or "he's unreliable." Not surprisingly, the judger mind-set stifles conversation.[14]

Holding judgment does not mean that you agree with everything you hear. It also does not mean you avoid critiquing the ideas of others. Rather, it's a commitment to hearing the entire version of others' ideas and experiences. It's a commitment to listen fully before reacting. And, it's a mind-set of rewarding others for opening up, especially when you disagree with them. Niki Leondakis, chief operating officer of the Kimpton Hotels, explained how she moved away from a judger mind-set to a learner mind-set over the course of her career:

> When I was a younger manager, my anxiety about what wasn't right drove me to confront things quickly. The faster I confronted it, the more quickly it could get fixed . . . and while that's a good thing, the manner in which I did it frequently left people feeling defensive. So by listening first and trying to understand how we got here and their story, I think it allows them to then hear my point of view. And then we can move into solutions. When people feel judged right out of the gate, it's hard for them to open up and listen and improve.[15]

You can create an environment in which others open up and you can listen more effectively with **learner statements,** which show your commitment to hearing people out. In effective learner statements, you explicitly state your desire to hear differing opinions with statements such as "I have a different perspective, so I want to understand how you see this." By contrast, people who make **judger statements,** which show they are closed off to hearing people out, shut down honest conversations.[16] Notice in Table 3.2 the distinctions between judger statements and learner statements

---

Active Listening Components

- Paying attention
- Holding judgment
- Reflecting
- Clarifying
- Summarizing
- Sharing

TABLE 3.2

Judger Statements versus Learner Statements

Judger Statements	Learner Statements
Barbara: You're overlooking the needs of our group guests. Why aren't you concerned about setting pricing to increase customer satisfaction?	*Barbara:* I think we're seeing this problem from different perspectives. I'd like to understand your view better.
This statement begins with an *I'm right, you're wrong* message. It directly calls into question the competence of the listener. Many listeners would become defensive.	This statement is neutral and shows a desire to learn about differences. The tone reflects a desire to understand the listener.
Andrea: I spend a lot of time comparing our pricing on various services with those of our competitors. Our pricing brings in good revenue and is completely consistent with the industry prices. You're paying too much attention to a few discontented customers.	*Andrea:* I spend a lot of time comparing our pricing on various services with those of our competitors, and our pricing seems to match industry pricing. But, maybe we need to examine more carefully how our pricing for group guests impacts revenues.
This statement demonstrates a belief that the speaker's position is well justified and the listener's position is not.	This statement reflects a learning stance and shows a cooperative approach moving forward.

that pick up from the opening case in which Barbara and Andrea disagree about Internet pricing for group guests.

Reflecting   Active listening requires that you reflect on the ideas and emotions of others. To make sure you really understand others, you should frequently paraphrase what you're hearing. As Table 3.3 shows, good reflecting statements begin with phrases such as "It sounds to me as though . . ."; "So, you're not happy with . . ."; or "Let me make sure I understand. . . ." [17]

Clarifying   Clarifying involves making sure you have a clear understanding of what others mean. It includes double-checking that you understand the perspectives of others *and* asking them to elaborate and qualify their thoughts. It is more than simply paraphrasing. It involves trying to connect the thoughts of others so you can better understand how they are making conclusions. As Table 3.4 shows, good clarifying

TABLE 3.3

Reflecting Statements

Types of Effective Reflecting Statements	Example
It sounds to me as though . . .	*Barbara:* It sounds to me as though you think our Internet pricing is appropriate since we are in line with our competitors.
So, you're not happy with . . .	*Andrea:* So, you're not happy with the pricing for groups because so many group guests express strong dissatisfaction.
Is it fair to say that you think . . .?	*Barbara:* Is it fair to say that you think we should consider changing our pricing just for group guests?
Let me make sure I understand . . .	*Andrea:* Let me make sure I understand your view. Are you saying that we should have one standard price for all guests?

TABLE 3.4

Clarifying Statements

Types of Effective Clarifying Statements	Example
What are your thoughts on . . .?	*Andrea:* What are your thoughts on adjusting the pricing model for groups?
Could you repeat that?	*Andrea:* Could you repeat what you just said about doing a survey of group guests? Could we get the information we need? Could we get enough responses?
I'm not sure I understand . . .	*Barbara:* I'm not sure I understand why we should follow our competitors on pricing. What are the advantages of setting our price right where the industry is?
Could you explain how . . .?	*Andrea:* Could you explain how you could use survey results to set better pricing levels? Are there other ways of identifying our best pricing points for group guests?
What might be your role in . . .?	*Andrea:* What roles do you think each of us should have in setting up a survey with our group guests?

questions are open-ended and start with learner-oriented phrases such as "What are your thoughts on . . .?" or "Could you explain how . . . ?"[18]

Summarizing   The goal of summarizing is to restate major themes so that you can make sense of the *big issues* from the perspective of the other person. Ideally, you can show that you understand the major direction of the conversation. You can summarize with statements that begin with phrases such as "So, your main concern is . . ." or "It sounds as though your key points are . . . ," as shown in Table 3.5.[19]

Sharing   Active listening also involves expressing your own perspectives and feelings. If you do not share your own ideas completely, your colleagues do not know what you really think. This is not fair to them or to you. It is even arguably dishonest. Michael Hoppe of the Center for Creative Leadership explains:

> Being an active listener doesn't mean being a sponge, passively soaking up the information coming your way. You are an active party to the conversation with your own thoughts and feelings. Yet active listening is first about understanding the other person, then about being understood.[20]

TABLE 3.5

Summarizing Statements

Types of Effective Summarizing Statements	Example
So, your main concern is . . .	*Andrea:* So, your main concern is that the prices for group guests are set so high that many of them are dissatisfied with their experiences. Many are not willing to pay the price and rely on the free service in the business center. They are further frustrated because of the limited capacity of the business center. Since you spend so much time listening to these complaints, you are often left with less time to focus on more important activities. Is that a fair summary?
It sounds as though your key points are . . .	*Barbara:* It sounds as though your key points are that this pricing reflects the industry best practices and that these best practices are based on maximizing revenue. Is that correct?

As a related point, business leaders often use the term *silence is agreement*. In other words, many organizational cultures expect all employees to state their ideas. If they don't say anything, they are presumed to agree. Because it can be so challenging to give others enough comfort and space to express themselves fully, some listeners avoid talking and inadvertently send signals that they agree. One key to active listening is allowing others to open up completely with their work-related ideas and then also to foster dialogue, which includes providing your respectful views.

Recognizing Barriers to Effective Listening

LO3.2 Explain and evaluate barriers to effective listening and common types of nonlistening behaviors.

Active listening is not easy, especially in certain corporate cultures and in the face of time constraints.[21] As you read about the following barriers to listening, consider which are most challenging to you.

Lack of Time   Not surprisingly, pressing deadlines give most managers the sense that they do not have time for listening. Furthermore, when talking to others, managers are often preoccupied with thoughts of other projects. In other words, managers may feel overwhelmed by internal noise. However, the best managers understand that listening pays strong dividends over time and that they need to schedule time for listening to others each day.

Lack of Patience and Attention Span   Some people simply do not have long attention spans or for other reasons feel impatient. Patience and attention span can be improved with conscious, consistent effort. Highly self-aware communicators frequently ask themselves questions such as the following: *Did I allow others enough time to express themselves? In which situations or with which people (triggers) do I feel most impatient? What strategies help me focus my attention when I'm feeling impatient?*

Image of Leadership   Some executives and managers think that listening too much shows indecisiveness and thus threatens their authority. To preserve a command-and-control approach to leading, they speak more and listen less. This view of listening is rarely effective, especially in today's increasingly flat organizations. Yet, some business professionals find it difficult to overcome the idea that strong leaders do most of the talking.

Communication Technology   Technology continues to create new and better opportunities for people to communicate with one another. However, most communication technologies make listening more difficult due to fewer and less-rich visual and nonverbal cues. Typically, using communication tools such as mobile phones and email can facilitate a listening-centered approach to communication, supplemented with significant face-to-face, rich communication. On the other hand, relying too heavily on communication technology can reduce effective listening.

Fear of Bad News or Uncomfortable Information   Once bad news and other forms of unpleasant information are out in the open, managers are generally responsible for creating solutions and responding to the morale needs of fellow employees. Listening fully to the feedback, concerns, and perspectives of colleagues and clients can make work more complicated. Astute business executives and managers recognize that they *need* information—even bad or unpleasant news—to lead an organization to its best potential performance. Conversely, when you do not listen, you may inadvertently encourage others to cover mistakes and weaknesses that harm the organization.[22]

In addition to barriers that prevent listening from occurring in the first place, other behaviors can disrupt a conversation and prevent real learning. **Nonlistening**

behaviors are those actions that prematurely deflect attention from speakers or prevent them from completely expressing their ideas and feelings. Such behaviors may display lack of caring and signal that the conversation is not equitable and reciprocal. Some common nonlistening behaviors in the workplace are defending, "me too" statements, advice-giving, and judging.[23]

Defending Instinctively, all of us engage in self-protective behaviors. Often, the comments of others in the workplace call into question our credibility, including our performance, competence, concern for others, or even ability to honor our commitments. When we feel threatened, we often become defensive. In other words, we are emotionally hijacked. Defensive comments end listening for several reasons. First, others often perceive them as threats or escalations. Thus, they may lead to self-protectiveness from all parties involved in a conversation and reduce trust and goodwill. These cycles of escalation close conversations off from complete and honest exchange of information. In some cases, people even attack others in an effort to protect themselves. Second, they shift attention away from the speaker to the listener—meaning the person who has made the defensive comment. This premature shift in focus is a *me-centered* maneuver that disrupts the listening process.

Figure 3.2 displays defensive and nondefensive replies to a potentially upsetting comment. Avoiding defensiveness requires a high level of self-awareness and self-management. It requires understanding the triggers that make you feel threatened in a professional environment. It also requires understanding how to manage these emotions so that you can maintain your roles as an active listener and a problem solver.

"Me Too" Statements As you listen to other people share their ideas and experiences—their stories—you often think about similar ideas and experiences of your own—your stories. This often leads to "me too" comments. We take the

FIGURE 3.2

Defensive and Nondefensive Replies

Original Statement

You're overlooking the needs of our group guests. Why aren't you concerned about setting pricing to increase customer satisfaction?

What the Listener Hears (Decodes)

You don't care about our customers. And, you're not competent enough to recognize the business consequences.

Defensive Reply (Judgmental Stance)

You can't take the comments of a few disgruntled customers and assume that you know a pricing policy that maximizes revenue. Look, I've been working in the industry a long time. When you've had more experience, you'll understand this.

Nondefensive Reply (Learning Stance)

I think you're right that we need to be aware of what our group guests are most concerned about. What do you think our options are?
or
I want to know how we can determine exactly how many of our group guests are purchasing the Internet services. Also, I want to know how many group guests are so dissatisfied that it impacts their overall satisfaction. How can we find answers to these questions?

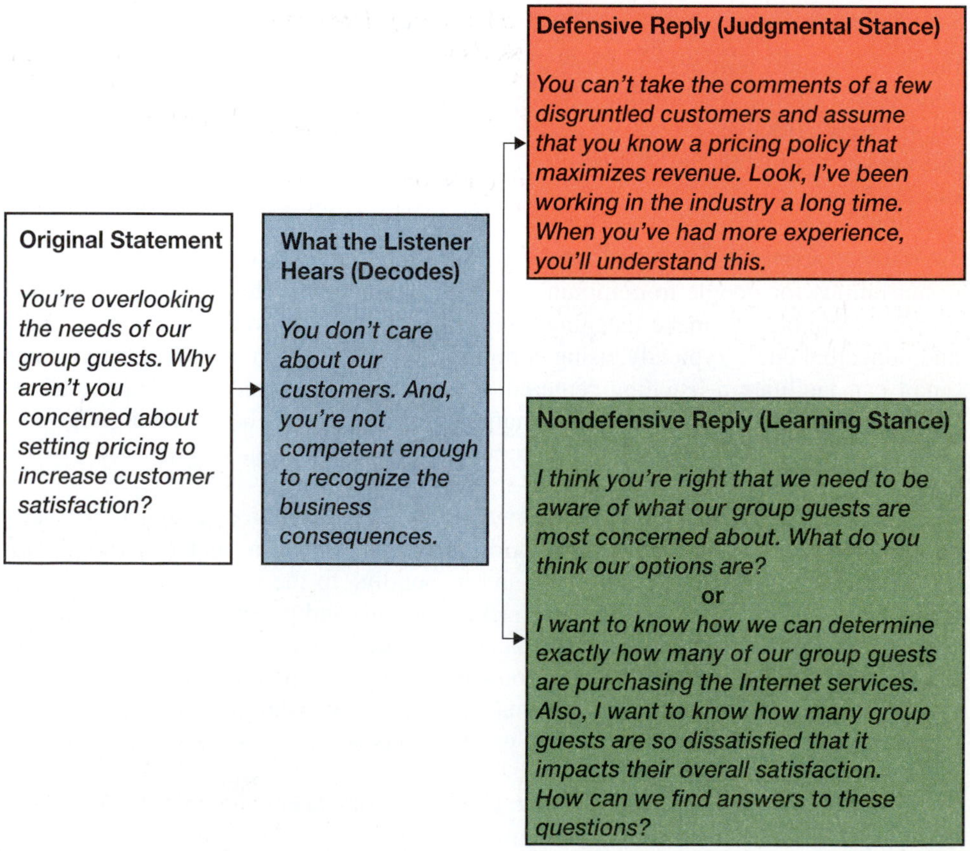

other person's story and respond with our story, in an effort to empathize and share. Sometimes, however, this shifts attention away from their story to your story. To listen effectively, be careful about prematurely drawing attention away from the stories of others.

Advice-Giving   In leadership roles, your job is often to tell others what to do and how to do it. Also, many of your bosses and colleagues will give you advice. Giving advice to others in a competitive work environment is inevitable and often desirable. However, during conversations, premature or heavy-handed advice can abruptly end dialogue and result in resistance. When you provide advice too soon, you give the impression of wanting to end the conversation. When you provide excessive advice, you challenge the autonomy and decision making of others and make them feel *micromanaged*. To avoid giving advice that cuts off listening, give others enough time to fully explain themselves. Once you talk about options and solutions, make sure that it is a "we" conversation rather than just your ideas for what others should do.

Judging   Judging is one of the worst nonlistening behaviors. It not only ends listening for the current conversation but also often leaves lingering animosity. Once people have displayed a judger mind-set, others may be unwilling to open up to them in the future. People who feel that their leaders are judgers might say, "He's really not interested in what I have to say," or "She's already made up her mind."[24]

Asking the Right Questions

Listening involves a cluster of communication skills. A crucial one is the ability to ask the right questions. In a recent survey of 2,181 accountants, the most sought-after interpersonal skill was *listening,* ranked 4.51 on a scale from 1 (not important) to 5 (essential). Following *listening* were closely related skills: *asks appropriate questions when talking with customers* (4.22) and *asks appropriate questions when talking with supervisors* (3.97). Next in the list of 14 skills was a cluster of presentation skills, such as *organizes presentations effectively* (3.86), *establishes rapport with audience* (3.59), and *maintains eye contact* (3.58). In other words, the ability to ask questions was valued more highly than presentation skills.[25]

On the most fundamental level, good questions reflect the learner mind-set, and poor questions reflect a judger mind-set. The ability to ask good questions creates a culture of learning. Good questions are not good in and of themselves, however. Unless you truly listen to the answers and even encourage other perspectives and dissent, you may not achieve learning. Notice examples of questions in Table 3.6 that reflect judger mind-sets and learner mind-sets.[26]

LO3.3 Describe the elements of questions that enhance listening and learning.

TABLE 3.6

Questions That Reflect the Judger Mind-Set and the Learner Mind-Set

Judger Mind-Set	Learner Mind-Set
How come this doesn't work?	How is this useful or beneficial?
Who is responsible for this mess?	What can we do about this?
Why can't you get it right?	Going forward, what can we learn from this?
Can't you try a better approach?	What are you trying to accomplish?
Why don't you focus on helping customers?	How will customers react?
Are you sure this approach will really meet your goals and objectives?	How well does this approach meet your goals and objectives?

TABLE 3.7

Types of Effective Questions

Types of Questions	Examples
Rapport-building	How was your trip to the green hotels expo? What did you learn about at the last Chamber of Commerce event?
	These questions, when asked sincerely, provide an opportunity for asker and listener to bond through understanding one another. They also break the ice for a substantive conversation about the business issues at hand.
Funnel	So, how do you think we should go about conducting surveys among group guests? → If we survey the last few groups, what can we find out about purchase behavior and pricing level? → What types of survey questions will help us understand appropriate pricing levels? → Could you give me a word-by-word example of how you'd capture that in a survey question?
	These questions progressively break down a problem into manageable pieces, starting with a large, open-ended question and moving to increasingly specific and tactical questions. Once broken into smaller pieces, the asker and listener are more likely to achieve shared meaning and move toward solution-making.
Probing	How often do you receive complaints from group guests about Internet pricing? Do you think you could estimate what percentage of group guests are fine with the current pricing? How much of your time is tied up in responding to complaints? How will this dissatisfaction with Internet pricing impact future purchase behavior at our hotel? How much would expansion of our business center reduce dissatisfaction with Internet pricing?
	These iterations of questions about the causes, consequences, and scope of group guest complaints attempt to look at the problem from every angle. This approach is effective at identifying root causes and best solutions.
Solution-oriented	How can we find out how Internet pricing impacts purchase of Internet service by group guests? How can we find out how Internet pricing impacts overall guest satisfaction during their stay? What can we do to improve the business center and add more capacity for less than $10,000?
	These questions form the basis for identifying options about how to move forward. Ideally, solution-oriented questions are open, we-oriented, and offer help to others.

To ask questions that facilitate the most learning, frame and structure your questions carefully. Generally, most good questions are open-ended. In contrast, closed questions require simple responses such as *yes* or *no*. Some basic types of learning-centered questions include rapport-building questions, funnel questions, probing questions, and solution-oriented questions. See Table 3.7 for examples of each type of question.[27]

Rapport-building questions are intended to create bonds between people. They can break the ice and gradually ease people into conversations about shared business interests. They tend to be casual and social and steer clear of divisive or offensive topics. Questions about current work projects, interests, and experiences are generally appropriate. As you will notice in the team communication section later, however, time devoted to building rapport should be limited. Too much time spent on this purpose can be counterproductive.

Funnel questions move from general to specific. They are intended to increasingly deconstruct a business issue so that a team can tackle or approach it in pieces. This approach involves starting with broad and open questions and moving to more specific and closed ones.

Probing questions are intended to analyze a business problem from every angle in order to uncover its root causes. Such questions can ensure that no explanation is overlooked, thus leading to a reliable understanding. The classic, institutionalized example of probing questions is the *Five Whys* approach at Toyota, in which employees were encouraged to ask at least five iterations of questions to understand manufacturing quality issues. Ultimately, this approach led to world-class quality standards that businesses around the world have studied.

Solution-oriented questions focus on how to overcome business problems. They focus on what *should* be done to accomplish business objectives. Solution-oriented questions are among the most difficult ones in which to maintain a learner mind-set. Nearly all of us have strong preconceptions about what *should* be done. Staying flexible and open to mutually developed solutions begins with open, solution-oriented questions.

Avoiding the Wrong Questions

Not all questions are good ones. Most poor questions fall into the category of the judgmental mind-set and can actually lead to less listening. Poor questions include leading questions, disguised statements, and cross-examination questions. Table 3.8 provides examples.

Leading questions are intended to guide people to your way of thinking. These questions are often perceived as dishonest or manipulative. Business professionals are notorious for leading questions in sales. In fact, some sales training programs even recommend using leading questions to build desire for products and services. However, recent research indicates that even for sales, the best questions are open ones that focus on learning customers' real wants and needs.[28]

Disguised statements are opinions presented in question form. Disguised statements almost always end a learning conversation when they are used to point out flaws.

Cross-examination questions are intended to find contradictions in what others have said or done. Like disguised statements, they can abruptly end learning conversations when they repeatedly call into question the credibility of others.

TABLE 3.8

Types of Counterproductive Questions

Types of Questions	Examples
Leading	Wouldn't you agree that we should adopt the pricing set by the market? I'm sure you think it's a good idea to improve guest satisfaction by providing fair Internet pricing, right?
	These questions are meant to lead the listener to agree with or adopt the perspective of the asker. Many listeners will resent feeling pressured to adopt the views of others. Also, this approach will not lead to a learning conversation.
Disguised statements	Why do you insist on not even considering a price change for our group guests? Don't you think you're jumping to conclusions by paying attention to the opinions of only a few disgruntled guests?
	These are not real questions. They are statements that say *you are close-minded on this issue.* This flaw-finding approach will cause many listeners to become defensive and/or avoid sharing their real thoughts. Many listeners will view disguised statements as underhanded and manipulative, since they are often attempts to get the listeners to acknowledge their own faults.
Cross-examination	You said you wanted us to focus on getting the pricing right for our group guests. Yet, you also said that some group guests will find any reason to be unhappy with our services. So, do you really believe price is the issue?
	This cross-examination question will put most listeners on the defensive. It may score points for the asker, but it will move the conversation away from learning and toward a battle of messages.

Principles of Effective Team Communication

LO3.4 Explain the principles of team communication in high-performing teams.

Teams can take many forms. Some teams are formally and permanently organized and titled (such as the *marketing team*). Other teams are temporarily formed for completing a project or an activity (i.e., project team, committee). The most common functions of teams are handling special projects, completing the work of particular departments, developing internal systems innovations, creating customer-service innovations, developing product innovations, engaging in employee development, and reducing time to market for products and services.[29]

In a recent survey, business professionals cited ineffective communication (66 percent) as the biggest barrier to team effectiveness. Other major barriers included lack of effective chartering and goal setting (56 percent), lack of clarity and understanding of roles (47 percent), low morale (44 percent), low productivity (42 percent), and lack of trust (36 percent). Similarly, when ranking the most frustrating aspects of being part of a team, business professionals cite the following: ineffective use of meeting time (54 percent), ineffective communication among team members (50 percent), lack of accountability (47 percent), individuals who don't complete assignments (44 percent), and lack of preparation in meetings (41 percent).[30] All of these factors in turn relate to communication competencies.

Your teams will perform far better if they follow the basic principles of team communication, all of which depend on a strong listening-centered approach. Work in teams is among the most researched aspects of work performance, and hundreds of studies have supported each of the following principles:

Teams go through four natural stages to reach high performance.[31] Nearly all high-performing teams go through four stages before they maximize their performance. In best-case scenarios, work teams take roughly six to seven months to reach this level (see Figure 3.3).[32] Typically, leaders become less directive and more consultative as the team progresses through the stages:

1. *Forming* (months 1 and 2). In the **forming** stage, team members focus on gaining acceptance and avoiding conflict. In some ways, this stage is a honeymoon period in which team members get to know one another.
2. *Storming* (months 2 and 3). In the **storming** stage, team members open up with their competing ideas about how the team should approach work. This stage is typically the least productive, since team members are attempting to make sense of uncertain roles, goals, and accountabilities.

FIGURE 3.3

Stages of Development in High-Performance Teams

Source: Adapted from Susan A. Wheelan, *Creating Effective Teams: A Guide for Members and Leaders* (Thousand Oaks, CA: Sage, 1999), which examines hundreds of scholarly studies on teamwork.

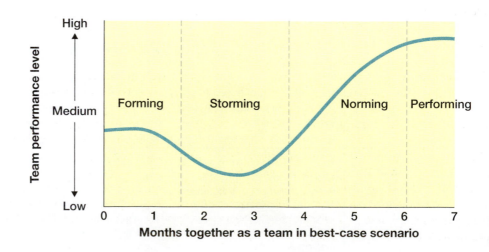

3. *Norming* (months 4 and 5). In the **norming** stage, the team arrives at a work plan, including the roles, goals, and accountabilities.

4. *Performing* (months 6 and 7). In the **performing** stage, teams operate efficiently toward accomplishing their goals. They have evolved to a level where they can transform disagreement and conflict into consensus for future action.

Effective teams build a work culture around values, norms, and goals. Organizations and teams constantly attempt to foster unity and high performance. **Team culture** refers to a set of shared perceptions and commitment to collective values, norms, roles, responsibilities, and goals.[33] Typically, teams rapidly develop such shared perceptions and commitment during the norming stage. Only at the performing stage do these shared perceptions and commitments lead to high productivity.

Effective teams spend a lot of time discussing values, norms, and goals. High-performing teams avoid simply going with the flow. Rather, they frequently, explicitly, and openly discuss the set of values, norms, and goals they share. This process is critical, since team members often attach different meanings to the same goals. Open discussion helps team members avoid misinterpreting each other's motivations and actions.

Effective teams spend most of their time discussing work issues. Out of every 100 comments team members in high-performing groups make, 60 to 70 directly relate to work—goals, coordination, roles, task clarification, and other project-related issues. Of the 100 comments, team members make about 15 to 20 supportive statements intended to show goodwill and encouragement. And, they make 10 to 15 statements that are primarily social.[34] By contrast, team members in lower-performing groups make far fewer work-related and supportive statements. They typically replace these statements with social statements that may help team members bond socially but not around work issues.

Effective teams meet often. Most groups underperform because they do not spend enough time meeting. Frequent meetings are necessary to establish shared perceptions of roles, goals, and accountabilities. (See the next section on managing meetings.) Also, meetings force team members to meet deadlines. Teams that do not meet often may never reach the performing stage. Or they regress from the performing stage to an even less-productive stage.

Effective teams embrace differing viewpoints and conflict. High-performing teams embrace conflict. They see differences of opinion as natural and as a path to creativity and innovation. So, they encourage one another to share their ideas, even when those ideas differ from their own.

In the next two sections of this chapter, we will discuss further principles for handling differences of opinion and even conflict. Here, we present two principles that team members use to embrace and respond to differing viewpoints: disassociation and association. **Disassociation** is a process by which professionals accept critique of their ideas without taking it personally and becoming defensive. On the other hand, **association** is the psychological bonding that occurs between people and their ideas. Since the purpose of most meetings and team communication is to increase agreement about roles, goals, and accountabilities and to increase the group's sense of purpose, team members should seek association by the end of a meeting or team communication. Generally, high-performing teams go through repeated cycles of disassociation and association. That is, they suspend attachment to ideas in the initial discussion phase and then attach themselves to ideas as they commit to mutually developed goals and related action items (see Figure 3.4).[35]

Effective teams feel a common sense of purpose. This sense of purpose feeds the team's morale, dedication, and ability to negotiate roles and accountabilities. Thus, high-performing teams frequently discuss their purposes. They also commit to bonding socially and showing concern for one another.[36]

FIGURE 3.4

The Cycle of Disassociation and Association in Team Communication

Managing Meetings

Meetings are one of the primary forums for teams to share and listen to one another's ideas. Because of the increasing importance of teams in the workplace, employees increasingly participate in project and interdepartmental teams. Meetings are an opportunity for teams to coordinate their efforts and increase productivity. Done well, they can be invigorating and produce new insights.[37]

At their best, problem-solving meetings provide incredible return on investment. For example, NorTel evaluated its return on investment on a series of 12 two-day meetings with the express purpose of reducing manufacturing costs. Altogether, the company invested $500,000, but calculations indicated that it saved $91 million due to solutions developed during the meetings.[38]

Yet, meetings have many trade-offs. The biggest drawback is that they take a lot of time. A survey of 150 financial executives found that, on average, they spent 7.8 hours per week in meetings. Over the course of a year, this amounted to 2.3 months of work. Ten years prior in this same survey, financial executives had averaged 6.0 hours per week in meetings, amounting to 1.8 months per year.[39]

Bad meetings are more than just a waste of time. They can create division, lower morale, and decrease productivity.[40] Thus, managers who run effective meetings help their teams work more productively and have better career opportunities.[41] As you prepare to lead and participate in meetings, consider all phases of successful meetings: preparing for them, running them, and following up afterward.

LO3.5 Describe and demonstrate approaches to planning, running, and following up on meetings.

Planning for Meetings

As with other communication responsibilities, running effective meetings starts with planning. For routine meetings, you should spend 30 to 60 minutes preparing.[42] For especially important and nonroutine meetings, you may need to spend at least several hours or days planning.

Essential Questions Planning for meetings requires strategy, scheduling, and coordination. At a minimum, you should answer the following questions in your preparations:[43]

- What is the purpose of the meeting? What outcomes do I expect?
- Who should attend?
- When should the meeting be scheduled?
- What roles and responsibilities should people at the meeting have?
- What will be the agenda?
- What materials should I distribute prior to the meeting?
- When and how should I invite others?
- What logistical issues do I need to take care of (reserving rooms, getting equipment, printing materials)?

As you answer these questions, keep in mind your purpose and ensure that your plans focus on productive outcomes. Also, think about how scheduling will impact productivity. Generally, you should avoid meetings, especially brainstorming meetings, during the least productive times of the day (usually the afternoon). Typically, most employees are at their best performance in the morning (see Figure 3.5).[44] As far

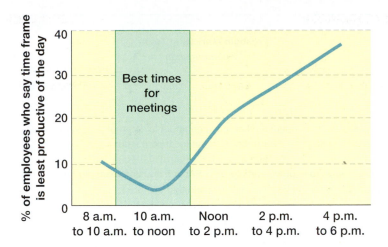

FIGURE 3.5

Least Productive Parts of the Workday

Source: Adapted from Accountemps, "Accountemps Survey: Employee Output Is Weakest Late in the Day," August, 17, 2010 (accessed November 20, 2010, at http://accountemps.rhi .mediaroom.com/least_productive).

as timing during the week, Tuesdays are overwhelmingly considered the most productive days (57 percent of employees think so). By contrast, Fridays are the least productive days (just 3 percent of employees think they are the most productive).[45]

In addition, think about the materials you should send ahead of time. Often, you will make requests of various meeting participants before the meeting to help them prepare. Plan to send materials sufficiently far in advance to give people enough time to do required preparation.

As you plan, consider the type of meeting you want. Meetings can be broadly categorized as coordination meetings or problem-solving meetings. **Coordination meetings** primarily focus on discussing roles, goals, and accountabilities. **Problem-solving meetings** typically involve brainstorming about how to address and solve a particular work problem. In actuality, nearly all meetings involve both coordination and problem solving. However, coordination meetings typically include many agenda items with a reasonable expectation of accomplishing each item in the allocated time. Problem-solving meetings, by contrast, involve more fluid issues that are less easily classified as discrete agenda items and that are less easily given time allotments. For especially difficult issues (i.e., periods of transition such as with mergers), some teams commit to meeting at the same time each day and without a preset agenda until they clearly define the issues at hand.[46]

Creating and Distributing the Agenda   Agendas provide structure for meetings. For most meetings, preparing and distributing an agenda ahead of time allows each meeting participant to form expectations and prepare.[47]

Most agendas should include items to be covered, time frames, goals and/or expected outcomes, roles, and materials needed. You can foster more effective meetings by getting others involved in the agenda-creation process. For example, at least several days in advance, ask meeting participants for agenda items they want included. Typically, you should send out the final agenda at least one day in advance. Sending the agenda out ahead of time and inviting team members to provide agenda items increases buy-in from meeting participants. You can also consider assigning roles. For example, you might assign someone as a facilitator, a note-taker (minutes), a timer, and so on.[48]

As you develop the agenda, pay attention to the ordering of items so that it flows much like you would expect other written communications to flow from point to point. Also, consider placing those agenda items of most importance near the beginning. This way, if items take longer than expected and you are forced to shelve some items, you have addressed the highest-priority items.[49] See Figure 3.6 for an agenda for the Prestigio marketing team.

Running Effective Meetings

If you've planned and prepared well for the meeting, you are in a great position to carry out your meeting objectives. Ideally, you've provided clear expectations for meeting participants—what they should have done before the meeting and what they can expect

Agenda Components

- Agenda items
- Time frames*
- Goals/expected outcomes
- Roles
- Materials needed

*optional

FIGURE 3.6

Sample Meeting Agenda

Prestigio Marketing Team
Meeting Agenda

Date: November 9   **Start Time:** 10 a.m.   **End Time:** 11 a.m.

Purposes:
1. Discuss plans to conduct market research about (a) Internet pricing for groups and (b) customer satisfaction levels relative to our local competitors.
2. Discuss progress on our Staff & Service Initiative started in January.
3. Examine ways to improve participation on our marketing team blogs and wikis.
4. Finalize plans for the Valentine's Day marketing campaign.

Desired Outcome:
Create action items to complete within the next month (by December 15). At our December 15 meeting, we will develop our annual marketing plan, which will include priorities for improving guest satisfaction and pricing.

Agenda Item 1: Internet Pricing for Groups (20 minutes)
- Summary of findings from Internet pricing survey for groups (Jeff)   5 min.
- Industry standards for Internet pricing for conference groups (Barbara)   5 min.
- Group discussion of findings and options   10 min.
- Develop action items   5 min.

Agenda Item 2: Improving Customer Satisfaction (20 minutes)
- Summary of findings from customer satisfaction research on external websites (Jeff)   5 min.
- Group discussion of findings and options   10 min.
- Develop action items   5 min.

Agenda Item 3: Enterprise Social Software
- Discuss goals for increased use of wikis and discussion forums (Andrea)   5 min.

Agenda Item 4: New Promotions
- Valentine's Day hotel promotions (Nancy)   5 min.

Summarize Action Items   3 min.

Participants: Andrea Garcia, Nancy Jeffreys, Barbara Brookshire, **Kip Yamada (note-taker)**, Jeff Anderton

---

in terms of content and length of the meeting. Once the meeting arrives, you have several options for achieving productive outcomes.

Create Tradition, Culture, and Variety
Most meetings at Starbucks Coffee start with a customer story.[50] Many manufacturing companies start meetings with safety stories. You can create traditions that take only moments or minutes but that reinforce the core values of your organization. These types of traditions create a common sense of purpose (one of the key ingredients of effective teamwork) and are a light way to open people up at the start of meetings.[51]

Set Expectations and Follow the Agenda
Take a few moments to explain the purpose of the meeting and what you hope to accomplish. You may also want to set some ground rules, such as your expectations for others to participate, how much time to take with comments, or how to deal with differences of opinion. Part of the ground rules may involve assigning the roles of facilitator, timer, and note-taker. They may also include protocol for use of mobile phones and other potentially disruptive

electronic equipment. You may also point out whether certain issues are considered confidential and shouldn't be discussed outside the meeting.[52]

For most meetings, keep the discussion focused on agenda items and stick to allotted times. Some meeting participants may become uninterested or annoyed if they perceive the meeting as unstructured or off schedule.[53]

Encourage Participation and Expression of Ideas

Each meeting should have a facilitator. The **facilitator** acts from a neutral position to get each person to participate in the conversation and ensure that each agenda item is properly discussed. Facilitators should acknowledge, check for understanding, paraphrase and summarize, not judge, ask for elaboration, and get everyone involved. Sometimes, this may require using explicit phrases such as "I'd like each person to take two minutes to. . . ." For routine meetings, the facilitator is often the organizer.[54]

The issue of neutrality for facilitating is critical. If others view the facilitator as predisposed toward certain positions or perspectives, they are less likely to express their real thoughts. This is especially the case when the facilitator is a person of higher authority.

Making your meetings "safe" for each team member requires conscious effort. After all, in surveys of nearly 2.5 million employees, just 15 percent of respondents agreed that *work teams function in a safe, "win-win" work environment,* and just 17 percent agreed that *work teams have mutual understanding and creative dialogue.*[55] As a meeting leader, encourage debate but defuse any comments that are perceived as noncollegial. The art of encouraging discussion but avoiding arguments takes time. In meetings, it requires that you initially foster disassociation but end with association. Research has shown that teams that have more dissent during meetings reach higher-quality decisions. By opening discussion to all available information and options, teams tend to adopt the best options more often and become more committed to the decisions.[56]

In problem-solving meetings, the leader must establish a pattern for discussion and debate. Generally, the first focus is getting agreement on the definition of the problem. Then, the focus switches to the history of the problem and its current impacts. Third, participants consider the causes and future consequences if the problem is not solved. Finally, the group is ready to brainstorm options for addressing the problem.[57]

Build Consensus and a Plan of Action

The primary purpose of meetings is to create a plan of action. When all the ideas have been stated, the team must evaluate the alternatives and create an action plan. For important decisions, the group should attempt to build consensus around a decision-making approach that prioritizes factors such as timelines, financial resources, and so on. You may find it difficult to build consensus on the bigger issues. Start by building consensus on smaller ones.[58]

Closing the Meeting

One priority should be to end the meeting on time. Before ending the meeting, summarize what you have accomplished. In just a few minutes, you can recap action items that the team has agreed on. Make sure the roles and assignments for each of these action items is clear, to establish accountabilities for follow-up.[59]

After a meeting ends (even for those you do not lead), you should mentally evaluate your performance. Consider these questions:[60]

- How much information, analysis, and interpretation did I provide?
- Did I communicate my ideas even if they conflicted with someone else's?
- Did I participate in the implementation of the timeline? Did I meet deadlines?
- Did I facilitate the decision-making process? Or did I just go with the flow?

Dealing with Difficult People

Inevitably, you will work on teams with disruptive members. They may consistently display a negative attitude, refuse to participate, interrupt others, make irrelevant comments, make condescending remarks about other participants or their ideas, or dominate with excessively lengthy comments. One

Meeting Follow-up/ Minutes Components

- Date and time
- Team members present
- Meeting roles
- Key decisions
- Key discussion points (optional)
- Open issues (optional)
- Action items and deadlines

of the best ways to prevent such behaviors is to provide strong leadership with a clear agenda, goals, and roles. If the problem persists, pull that team member aside. Talk about the disruptive behaviors, and explain how the behavior impacts group performance. Consider making specific and polite but firm requests such as the following: "At the next meeting, please give people more time to explain themselves."[61]

Following Up after Meetings

Follow up by distributing the minutes of the meeting (as a memo, in an email, in a meetings folder on the corporate intranet, or as part of a team blog or wiki). Minutes of the meeting should include the date and time, team members present, decisions, key discussion points, open issues, and action items and related deadlines. You can also include names of people who were invited but were absent and the assigned roles (i.e., note-taker). The minutes serve as a record of what your team accomplished. Figure 3.7 provides an example of meeting minutes.

FIGURE 3.7

Sample Meeting Minutes

Prestigio Marketing Team
November 9 Meeting Minutes

Date: November 9   **Start Time:** 10 a.m.   **End Time:** 11 a.m.

Agenda Item 1: Internet Pricing for Groups
Discussion: Jeff presented survey findings about conference attendees' purchases of Internet service while here. The group agreed that Internet-service purchases are far too low and that less use for lower-income groups suggests high price sensitivity.

Action Items	Responsibility	Completion Time
• Develop and conduct survey that identifies price points at which conference guests are willing to purchase Internet service	Barbara, Jeff	December 15
• Develop price sensitivity estimates and related revenue impacts	Barbara	December 15

Agenda Item 2: Improving Customer Satisfaction
Discussion: Jeff presented customer satisfaction ratings of Prestigio and three local competitors. The group agreed that our customer satisfaction ratings have improved, particularly in relation to competitors. We are most concerned about the areas of cleanliness, business center, and meeting rooms.

Action Items	Responsibility	Completion Time
• Develop plans to improve the equipment and furnishings of the business center	Andrea	December 15
• Develop plans for improving cleanliness and meeting rooms	Nancy, Andrea	January 15

Agenda Item 3: Enterprise Social Software
Discussion: Andrea encouraged the group to log on to the new enterprise social platform throughout the day, share documents, use wikis, and stay aware of progress on shared projects.

Action Item	Responsibility	Completion Time
• Use a wiki to collaborate on a joint project with another member of the marketing team	All members of marketing team	December 15

Agenda Item 4: New Promotions
Discussion: Nancy introduced her plans for Valentine's promotions, including a price special and advertising campaign designed to cater to local-area couples.

Action Item	Responsibility	Completion Time
• Negotiate TV and print ad campaign details with ad agency	Nancy, Kip	December 1

Participants: Andrea Garcia, Nancy Jeffreys, Barbara Brookshire, **Kip Yamada (note-taker)**, Jeff Anderton

TECHNOLOGY TIPS

ONLINE MEETINGS

Business professionals increasingly use online meetings for many purposes: to bring together work teams that have members in different locations, allow marketers and account representatives to show their products and services to customers and clients, provide training to employees, give manufacturers and suppliers a forum to work out quality issues from a distance, and deliver many other opportunities.

Online meetings allow you to conduct a meeting in a true, multimedia format. Typically, they are appropriate when people are far away, when the group is large (25 or more), when you feel too emotional or nervous for a face-to-face meeting, when you've already established trust with meeting participants, or when the agenda is fairly routine. Consider face-to-face meetings if possible when trust is not yet established or when discussing sensitive topics such as bad news or big changes.

Learn about the many functions of meeting software and its limitations. There are many software platforms for online meetings, including commercial options such as WebEx and GoToMeeting as well as platforms developed in-house. These software platforms include many functions, such as video calling, picture and drawing windows, screen sharing, virtual breakout rooms, instant polls, email, chats, slide shows, electronic whiteboards, discussion boards, shared folders, and a variety of online resources. Learn about each of these tools, experiment with them, and make sure you use them to accomplish the key objectives of your meetings.

Although online meetings provide an increasingly rich communication environment, they rarely attain the connection that face-to-face meetings do. You often encounter a lack of visual cues and thus are less able to develop trust and rapport. Also, participants can easily detach from the meeting and focus on other things going on in their own offices. So, you confront more difficulty directing or monitoring the behavior of meeting participants. Another limitation is that many meeting participants may not know how to use the meeting software well. Similarly, you may encounter technology failures. Most of these limitations can be overcome by using the many features of meeting software. Your job is to know how to use these features naturally so that you can employ them while orchestrating an effective meeting.

Prepare. Typically, you should follow roughly the same process for online meetings as face-to-face meetings: preparing an agenda, encouraging everyone to express their ideas, creating action items, and so on (see the discussion of effective meetings in the team communication section). However, since you are using meeting software with participants in many locations, you need extra time to plan how you will coordinate and keep people engaged. Consider assigning roles such as producer and moderator. Also, you should rehearse for important meetings and make sure technical details are functioning correctly before the meeting.

Discuss ways of documenting and distributing the discussion. Typically, face-to-face meetings are fairly straightforward to document: One person records the action items and/or minutes. This written document can be distributed to everyone on the team in a single format and serves as a reminder of important goals and action items and eventually a standard for follow-up. By contrast, online meetings generally involve many types of media. Plan how you will document the meeting and make it available to meeting participants later.

If you are the team leader, make sure your team members follow through on action items. Follow up as soon as possible on those issues you were not able to resolve during the meeting. If each participant knows you will follow up, they will perceive the meeting as important. If you do not follow up, team members are more likely to view the meeting as a waste of time.

Also, as a team leader, you will likely hold online meetings from time to time. Online meetings have become increasingly popular with improved technology and more dispersed teams. Principles of face-to-face meetings apply well to online meetings. However, online meetings present other challenges and benefits, the topic we discuss in the Technology Tips box above.

Managing Difficult Conversations

LO3.6 Explain basic principles for handling difficult conversations.

Business professionals routinely—often on a daily basis—encounter difficult conversations, especially when working in teams and collaborating with others. Difficult conversations are approached with apprehension, nervousness, anxiety, and even fear. Douglas Stone, Bruce Patton, and Sheila Heen of the Harvard Negotiation Project have spent three decades training business professionals to confront difficult conversations. They define difficult conversations as follows:

> Any time we feel vulnerable or our self-esteem is implicated, when the issues at stake are important and the outcome is uncertain, when we care deeply about what is being discussed or about the people with whom we are discussing it, there is potential for us to experience the conversation as difficult.[62]

Difficult conversations often center on disagreements, conflict, and bad news. Common types of difficult conversations for entry-level business professionals include receiving a bad performance review, having ideas rejected, critiquing a colleague, giving feedback to a boss, correcting someone, approaching rule-breakers about their behavior, talking to a slacker on a group project, and dealing with office politics.[63]

Many people prefer to avoid difficult conversations because they want to avoid hurting the feelings of others, want to avoid conflict, or for other reasons. Many business professionals believe that honesty during moments of conflict may backfire and hurt their careers. However, this is not necessarily the case. Those business managers and executives who approach difficult conversations in a timely, honest, and caring manner typically accomplish much more professionally. After working with corporate clients for nearly three decades, one research team concluded that the most influential people are those who can effectively handle difficult conversations:[64]

> As it turns out, you don't have to choose between being honest and being effective. You don't have to choose between candor and your career. People who routinely hold crucial conversations and hold them well are able to express controversial and even risky opinions in a way that gets heard. Their bosses, peers, and direct reports listen without becoming defensive or angry.[65]

In this section, we briefly present basic, tried-and-true principles for handling difficult conversations in the workplace. You will notice that these principles rely on active listening with a learner mind-set. You can see several examples of how to put these principles into practice (see Table 3.9 and Figure 3.8). These examples relate to Kip and Nancy from the opening case. Kip and Nancy hold strong grievances toward one other because of a past disagreement about issuing refunds to business travelers. They avoid one another when possible. Their poor working relationship hinders productivity and makes work less pleasant for them and their team.

Embrace Difficult Conversations and Assume the Best in Others

Most people back away from uncomfortable or unpleasant conversations. This is particularly the case when we feel we have a lot to gain but risk heavy losses if it doesn't go right. For these reasons, difficult conversations are often emotionally challenging.[66] Successful people in the workplace do not evade difficult conversations. Those who regularly tackle them with skill and tact improve work performance for themselves and others.

One way to embrace difficult conversations is to view conflict as an opportunity.[67] That is, the exchange of perspectives and competing ideas reflects open and honest communication. If there is no conflict, employees are likely not voicing their true perspectives. Generally, colleagues tend to respect one another more when they know they can safely disagree.

To make a difficult conversation safe, follow the advice of Jacqueline Kosecoff, CEO of Prescription Solutions:

> Assume positive intent. It's one of the ways to . . . keep communication on the high road. Perhaps somebody was misunderstood, or they misheard something. You have to go back and ask for the context, and it's very likely to be simply a misunderstanding. And if you listen, it can be resolved. And it tends to, I think, breed a lot more trust and respect among us.[68]

Adopt a Learning Stance and Commit to Hearing Everyone's Story

Earlier in the chapter, we distinguished between the judger and learner mind-sets. In emotionally charged, high-stakes conversations, approaching the conversation with a learner mind-set will often lead to productive outcomes. You can do this by avoiding the message-delivery stance.[69] Since difficult conversations typically involve unresolved problems, each person should participate in a joint process of understanding the problems and creating solutions. The message-delivery stance implies that you have nothing to learn from the other person involved in the conversation. In sensitive situations, others will resist your attempts to impose solutions.

The learning stance involves a commitment to understanding others' **stories**—their retrospective versions of interpersonal interactions or their explanations of business successes and failures. In difficult conversations, invite others to describe their views and feelings of disputed events. When people have the opportunity to share their stories, they are often less resistant to change and more accommodating of the views of others. Sharing stories with one another can lead to shared interpretations of events, empathy, and new ways of viewing workplace relationships and business possibilities.[70]

One major benefit of allowing all people involved in a difficult conversation to share their views is buy-in. Research has shown that when everyone involved shares their ideas, they tend to be more committed to the ultimate decision of the group, even when their ideas are not adopted. When they remain silent, they tend not to commit to the decision of the group.[71]

Stay Calm and Overcome Noise

Few business professionals prepare for difficult conversations. And since emotions run high during such conversations, they often do not go well. Participants face a lot of internal noise, and this muddies rational thinking: They are nervous about the outcome of the encounter for themselves and others, and they often feel incapable of constructively expressing all their thoughts and emotions.

During these difficult encounters, high emotional intelligence is crucial. Self-awareness is the foundation. When you feel angry or defensive, you need to ask yourself, "What do I really want?" and "How is what I'm feeling affecting how I'm responding?" By consciously asking yourself these questions, you are redirecting activity to the rational part of your brain. This de-escalates physical threats and allows you to respond more rationally.

While you should pay a lot of attention to your own emotions, intentions, and goals, you must also focus on those with whom you are speaking. They are likely experiencing similar emotions. Apply your active listening skills to feel and show empathy. If someone gets angry, view this as an opportunity. Do not return the anger, but rather help the other person channel the anger appropriately and rationally. Consider asking your conversational partner to sit down or offer a drink. As you summarize his or her thoughts and feelings, you defuse strong emotions and make the conversation constructive and rational.[72]

Find Common Ground

Finding common ground seems like obvious advice, but it's not easy to do during emotionally charged moments when you feel attacked. Finding common ground will

Principles of Difficult Conversations

- Embrace difficult conversations.
- Assume the best in others.
- Adopt a learning stance.
- Stay calm/ overcome noise.
- Find common ground.
- Disagree diplomatically.
- Avoid exaggeration and either/or approaches.

Components of Difficult Conversations

Steps
1. Start well/declare your intent.
2. Listen to their story.
3. Tell your story.
4. Create a shared story.

help you and others accomplish two things. Emotionally, it lessens the perceived distance between you, and it may even lead to bonding. Rationally, it helps you analyze the issues at hand in a way that will likely lead to mutually acceptable solutions. You can find common ground in a number of areas, including facts, conclusions, feelings, goals, and values.

Disagree Diplomatically

Difficult conversations involve different perspectives. To create a learning conversation rather than a defensive and judgmental one, find ways to disagree diplomatically. By disagreeing well, you lessen the resistance that others have to you and your views. Typically, you can disagree diplomatically by validating the views and feelings of others and using I-statements. **Validating** others means that you recognize their perspectives and feelings as credible or legitimate. It does not necessarily mean that you agree. **I-statements** begin with phrases such as *I think*, *I feel*, or *I believe*. During disagreements or difficult conversations, I-statements soften comments to sound more conciliatory and flexible and less blaming and accusatory (see examples in Table 3.9).

Avoid Exaggeration and Either/Or Approaches

As you navigate difficult conversations, avoid making them overly simplistic. Usually, you are encountering complex business and relationship issues. Also, by simplifying your story, you often inadvertently cause others to become defensive because you are in effect disputing their story or challenging their identity.

Two ways of oversimplifying your approach to difficult conversations is by exaggerating and by applying either/or approaches. If you find yourself using superlatives such as *always, never, most,* or *worst,* you might be exaggerating. By choosing other words, you're more likely to present your story accurately and also validate others. Applying an either/or approach to most business communication is ineffective. For difficult conversations, it usually translates into a right-versus-wrong approach. Approaching a difficult conversation with an *I'm right, you're wrong* approach inevitably dooms the conversation. See examples of exaggeration and either/or approaches in Table 3.9.

Initiate the Conversation, Share Stories, and Focus on Solutions

Initiating a difficult conversation is stressful. You may have avoided bringing up the issue because you are nervous about how the conversation will affect your working relationships with others, or you are worried about costs to your career. Starting well is crucial. The opening moments of a difficult conversation offer a great opportunity to frame or orient the conversation for problem solving. In the opening moments, consider declaring your intent—your sincere desire to understand and find a solution that works for each of you. One obstacle to holding difficult conversations is that one or more people involved tend to judge the motives of others unfairly. Declaring your intent can reduce the likelihood of unfairly judging motives. See Table 3.9 for examples of initiating a conversation.[73]

When you initiate a difficult conversation, a common learning stance is to listen to the story of others first, then share your story, and then create a shared story.[74] When you invite others to share their perspectives and versions of events first, they recognize your sincere interest in understanding and cooperating with them. By telling your story, you allow others to see another version of reality and empathize with you. Finally, together you create a shared story. A **shared story** involves combining yours and others' experiences, perspectives, and goals into a shared approach to work. The *their story–your story–shared story* process requires a substantial time commitment, but it is well worth it. Figure 3.8 presents a simplified example of this process.

TABLE 3.9

Ineffective and Effective Approaches to Difficult Conversations

Approaches	Ineffective Examples	Effective Examples
Initiating the conversation	*Nancy:* I want to go over your mishandling of the refunds several months ago. I have some ideas for how we can avoid this kind of problem in the future.	*Nancy:* Kip, let's talk about how the refunds to business travelers were handled a few months ago. First, I want to apologize for speaking so harshly without hearing your side first. Since then, I feel like we haven't worked well together. I think we can figure out a better way to make sure we're on the same page, and I also think we can figure out ways to avoid misleading our customers. When you authorized the refunds, I never heard all of the details. Do you mind telling me about some of the customers who were upset and what you did to address their concerns?
	This approach starts with blame. Worse yet, it frames the conversation as Nancy's story.	This approach is effective for several reasons. Nancy apologizes for her harsh words. She declares her intent: to work together better and come up with solutions. Nancy expresses her intent of discussing solutions that take into account both hers and Kip's perspectives (shared story). She invites Kip to tell his story.
Disagreeing diplomatically	*Nancy:* Look, you clearly overstepped your authority. You refunded $4,000, but you are authorized to refund $500. Simply because the computer system is set up on a per-customer basis doesn't mean you can authorize such large refunds. You definitely should have talked to me about these refunds prior to approval.	*Nancy:* Thanks for telling me how you felt. I can see that you were looking out for the interests of the guests and our long-term success here at the Prestigio. I do want to explain why I thought you should have consulted with me prior to making the refunds. We developed the weekend special together, so I think you were clear about the policies. In the reservation system, it's true that I've allowed you to refund up to $500 per traveler. However, I think you should have talked to me about these large refunds as soon as you started refunding more than one traveler for the same reason. I view you as overstepping your authority because you refunded nearly $4,000.
	Nancy does not recognize Kip's explanation or feelings as having any merit, which places Kip on the defensive and could lead him to resentment. Nancy projects a tone of blame by consistently using you-statements.	Nancy validates Kip's perspective by understanding how he *felt*. She explains why she thinks he overstepped his authority with a variety of I-statements.
Avoiding exaggeration and either/or approaches	*Kip:* I can never approach you with customer issues. You're always fixated on following the pricing policies to a tee, even when the guests have no way of knowing the costs they're incurring. You never try to understand the guest's perspective. Your approach is not working, and it's losing us money.	*Kip:* I'm hesitant to bring up customer issues with you. I think you sometimes take a tough approach to guests, even when they have legitimate complaints. I can think of several cases in which guests have stopped coming here after you denied their claims. In each case, I agreed with their reasoning and understood why they were not aware of costs they were incurring. In the end, I think we end up losing revenues when we deny refunds to our guests who feel unfairly charged.
	Kip repeatedly exaggerates the frequency of Nancy's actions with words such as *never* and *always*. He takes an either/or approach by saying Nancy's approach doesn't work.	Kip states his real feelings of frustration and explains his point of view. By using phrases such as *sometimes* and *I think*, he avoids a right-versus-wrong comparison between his and Nancy's approaches.

FIGURE 3.8

Sample Approach to a
Difficult Conversation

Nancy: Kip, let's talk about how the refunds to business travelers were handled a few months ago. First, I want to apologize for speaking so harshly without hearing your side first. Since then, I feel like we haven't worked as well together. I think we can figure out a better way to make sure we're on the same page, and I also think we can figure out ways to avoid misleading our customers.

When you authorized the refunds, I never heard all of the details. Do you mind telling me about some of the customers who were upset and what you did to address their concerns?

Kip: Well, I guess I think you overreacted. You were upset that I didn't get your permission before issuing the refunds. But I thought I was acting within my authority. In our reservation system, I'm cleared to authorize refunds of up to $500. So, I didn't see a need to get your permission when I'm already cleared in the system. And, I felt that you didn't even give me time to explain myself.

But that's not the whole story. I'm hesitant to bring up customer issues with you. I think you sometimes take a tough approach to guests, even when they have legitimate complaints. I can think of several cases in which guests have stopped coming here after you denied their claims. In each case, I agreed with their reasoning and understood why they were not aware of costs they were incurring. In the end, I think we end up losing revenue when we deny refunds to our guests who feel unfairly charged.

Nancy: Thanks for telling me how you felt. I agree that at the time I should not have snapped at you. I do want to explain why I thought you should have consulted with me prior to making the refunds. We developed the weekend special together, so I think you were clear about the policies. In the reservation system, it's true that I've allowed you to refund up to $500 per traveler. However, I think you should have talked to me about these large refunds as soon as you started refunding more than one traveler for the same reason. I view you as overstepping your authority because you refunded nearly $4,000. Now, I understand your perspective. I also know that you were acting with the best interests of our customers and the hotel in mind.

Kip: So, I think you're saying that you felt I overstepped my authority because, cumulatively, I was refunding far more than $500 for the same complaint, even though it was for different customers. Is that right?

Nancy: That's right. Now, I think the key is to figure out how we can work better together in the future. It sounds to me like there are several issues. First, we need to make sure we always hear one another out immediately instead of letting hard feelings fester. I think this issue would have been resolved right away if I had listened to you right away. Second, I think we should discuss the process for handling major guest complaints. Finally, but I think most importantly, we should reevaluate what we believe constitutes a reasonable complaint and under what circumstances we provide refunds. I think it's safe to say that we view this differently. Kip, do you have suggestions for how we should manage this situation in the future?

Kip: Well, I think there are several basic cases where we should refund our guests. For example . . .

——— *Nancy and Kip continue to talk about shared approaches and solutions.*———

Nancy initiates difficult conversation	
Kip's story	
Nancy's story	
Nancy and Kip's shared story	

COMMUNICATION Q&A

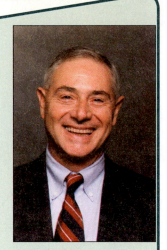

CONVERSATIONS WITH CURRENT BUSINESS PROFESSIONALS

Pete Cardon: What happens when people avoid difficult conversations about real or perceived differences they have with others?

Bob Mangone: It is part of most people's nature to avoid conflict and uncomfortable situations. In nonwork situations you can avoid conflict by merely not putting yourself in the situations that make you uncomfortable. However, in a work environment, short of finding another job, this is not always possible or practical.

When conflict and disagreements are not addressed in an open and honest way, the problem(s) that caused them will not go away. They may blend into the background as people try to get on with their daily activities, but they are always there. And they tend to pop back up at the most inopportune times. The person who feels he has been put upon will take every opportunity to bring the conflict into the discussion. This can only diminish the effectiveness of the enterprise and make it difficult, if not impossible, to create and maintain a cohesive and highly functioning team.

Bob Mangone *worked for more than 33 years with Pfizer, Inc., 27 of which were as a district sales manager. He currently consults and trains district sales managers in China and Japan.*

PC: What are some of the common reasons that employees fail to resolve their differences productively?

BM: In my opinion the most common reason is that one or both of the affected persons are not honest in their communications. They hide their feelings or emotions and internalize the perceived or actual grievances because they want to be liked by everyone. They say "it's OK" but don't believe it. Another reason is that some people feel they are victims. Rather than accept responsibility for their actions, they look for others to blame for their shortcomings or failure to perform at an acceptable level.

PC: What are a few approaches to helping employees resolve differences productively so that they work together more effectively and enjoy their work relationships more?

BM: I have found it effective to meet individually with each of the people to learn the answer to three questions: *WHAT is happening? WHY is it important? How does the individual FEEL about the issue?* In my experience you will have great difficulty in helping the individual resolve the conflict until you know how he or she feels. People make decisions based on emotions, not facts. Understanding how a person feels about an issue will guide you in the amount and type of advice you should offer.

After you have met individually and understand the answers to the WHAT, WHY, and FEEL questions, it is time to bring the individuals together to resolve their differences. Allow each of them to express their feelings, and ask them to state the other person's position and feelings about the conflict or disagreement. Ask them to identify common elements and common ground upon which they can build a solution. Finally, set a time in the near future for a follow-up meeting to see if their solutions have been implemented and if they have successfully lowered the stress level between them. They may never totally agree, but if they can find common ground, the conflict will go away.

PC: For young professionals, what concluding advice would you give for handling difficult conversations or even conflict in the workplace?

BM: Stephen Covey and St. Francis of Assisi both say, "First seek to understand before trying to be understood." Work to understand how a person FEELS about what is happening before trying to tell the other person how you feel. Whenever possible seek common ground, focusing on areas of agreement that will move the organization, and your career, forward. Don't be afraid to ask for help from co-workers, mentors, or managers when you cannot resolve the conflict on your own. Be open and honest in your communications with everyone. Finally, don't disagree with people and their ideas when it really isn't important. Choose what issues you can live with and which ones are important enough to challenge. This will help you avoid unnecessary conflicts that waste time, energy, and careers.

Chapter Takeaway for *Listening, Teamwork, and Difficult Conversations*

LO 3.1. Describe and evaluate the process of active listening. (pp. 57–61)

Active Listening		
• Paying attention	• Reflecting	• Summarizing
• Holding judgment	• Clarifying	• Sharing

See *examples of active listening* in Tables 3.2 to 3.5.

LO 3.2. Explain and evaluate barriers to effective listening and common types of nonlistening behaviors. (pp. 61–63)

Barriers to Active Listening		Nonlistening Behaviors
• Lack of time	• Image of leadership	• Defending
• Lack of patience and attention span	• Communication technology	• "Me too" statements
	• Fear of bad news	• Advice-giving
		• Judging

See an *example of defensive and nondefensive replies* in Figure 3.2.

LO 3.3. Describe the elements of questions that enhance listening and learning. (pp. 63–65)

Types of Good Questions	Types of Poor Questions
• Rapport-building	• Leading questions
• Funnel	• Disguised statements
• Probing	• Cross-examination questions
• Solution-oriented	

See *examples of good questions* in Table 3.7 and *poor questions* in Table 3.8.

LO 3.4. Explain the principles of team communication in high-performing teams. (pp. 66–68)

Characteristics of High-Performing Teams

- Go through natural team-building stages
- Spend a lot of time discussing values, norms, and goals
- Spend most of their time discussing work issues
- Meet often
- Embrace differing viewpoints and conflict
- Feel a common sense of purpose

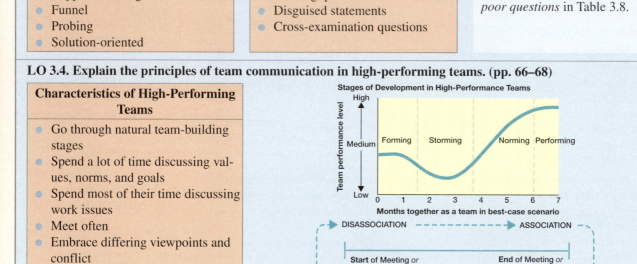

LO 3.5. Describe and demonstrate approaches to planning, running, and following up on meetings. (pp. 68–73)

Items in an Agenda	Items in Minutes
• Agenda items	• Date and time
• Time frames*	• Team members present
• Goals/expected outcomes	• Meeting roles
• Roles	• Key decisions
• Materials needed	• Key discussion points*
*optional	• Open issues*
	• Action items and deadlines
	*optional

See *examples of an agenda* in Figure 3.6 and *minutes* in Figure 3.7.

LO 3.6. Explain basic principles for handling difficult conversations. (pp. 74–79)

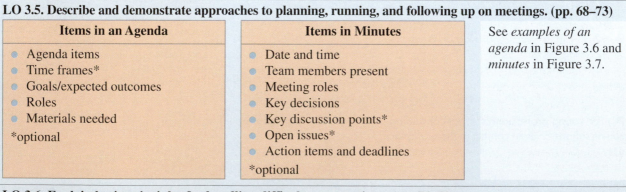

Principles for Difficult Conversations		Steps in Difficult Conversations
• Embrace difficult conversations.	• Find common ground.	1. Start well.
• Assume the best in others.	• Disagree diplomatically.	2. Listen to their story.
• Adopt a learning stance.	• Avoid exaggeration and either/or approaches.	3. Tell your story.
• Stay calm/overcome noise.		4. Create a shared story.

See *examples of less effective and more effective statements in difficult conversations* in Table 3.9. See an *example of a difficult conversation* in Figure 3.8.

Key Terms

association (p. 67)

coordination meetings (p. 69)

cross-examination questions (p. 65)

disassociation (p. 67)

disguised statements (p. 65)

facilitator (p. 71)

forming (p. 66)

funnel questions (p. 64)

I-statements (p. 76)

judger mind-set (p. 58)

judger statements (p. 58)

leading questions (p. 65)

learner mind-set (p. 58)

learner statements (p. 58)

nonlistening behaviors (p. 61)

norming (p. 67)

performing (p. 67)

probing questions (p. 64)

problem-solving meetings (p. 69)

rapport-building questions (p. 64)

shared story (p. 76)

solution-oriented questions (p. 65)

stories (p. 75)

storming (p. 66)

team culture (p. 67)

validating (p. 76)

Discussion Exercises

3.1 Chapter Review Questions (LO 3.1, LO 3.2, LO 3.3, LO 3.4, LO 3.5, LO 3.6)

A. What are some concrete examples of people with a message-centered approach to conversations compared to people with a listening-centered approach?

B. What are some signs of a judger mentality in conversations? How about a learner mentality?

C. The active listening process contains six steps. What steps do you think are most critical? Explain.

D. How can image of leadership be a barrier to active listening? Provide concrete examples.

E. Do you think fear of bad news is a common barrier to active listening among supervisors? Explain your viewpoint and provide some examples.

F. A common statement in classrooms is *there's no such thing as a bad question*. In the context of the workplace, in what ways would you agree and disagree with this statement? How would you qualify this statement?

G. Research shows that under ideal conditions, most teams reach high performance in six to seven months. How can a student team that must complete a project in a few weeks to a few months go through the stages of team development more quickly and reach peak performance?

H. In what ways can teams form a common sense of purpose? Provide examples from your experience.

I. Explain how creating and following an agenda is beneficial. Are there situations in which an agenda is not beneficial? Explain.

J. Explain what is meant by concluding a difficult conversation with a shared story.

3.2 Communication Q&A Discussion Questions (LO 3.3, LO 3.6)

Read the Communication Q&A section in this chapter and respond to the following questions:

A. According to Bob Mangone, what are common causes of conflict and disagreement in the workplace?

B. What are the negative consequences of avoiding conflicts?

C. What are common reasons that employees do not engage in honest conversation about their disagreements?

D. How does Mangone recommend resolving conflicts between employees?

E. What do you suppose Mangone means when he states, "Don't disagree with people and their ideas when it really isn't important"? Is this the same as not being honest?

3.3 Listening and Caring (LO 3.1, LO 3.2)

Tachi Yamada of the Bill & Melinda Gates Foundation recently described his thoughts on listening and caring:

> A second key lesson was from a doctor named Marcel Tuchman. He was the most compassionate person I have ever met in my life—I mean full of human kindness. And every time he met somebody, you had the sense that he cared more about them than anything else in the world. So what I learned from him is that when you actually are with somebody, you've got to make that person feel like nobody else in the world matters. I think that's critical. So, for example, I don't have a mobile phone turned on because I'm talking to you. I don't want the outside world to impinge on the conversation we're having. I don't carry a BlackBerry. I do my emails regularly, but I do it when I have the time on a computer. I don't want to be sitting here thinking that I've got an email message coming here and I'd better look at that while I'm talking to you. Every moment counts, and that moment is lost if you're not in that moment 100 percent.[75]

Based on Yamada's comments and your own experiences, answer the following questions:

A. What do you think Yamada means by the statement, "That moment is lost if you're not in that moment 100 percent"? How does this relate to listening? Do you think this is a reasonable expectation in the workplace?

B. What kinds of electronic gadgets and communication tools can take focus away from a conversation? What are some principles for making sure these gadgets and tools are not distracting?

C. Do you believe kindness is an important principle of listening and communicating in business? Can kindness be developed? How?

3.4 Speaking Up in Meetings (LO 3.4, LO 3.5, LO 3.6)

Barbara J. Krumsiek of the Calvert Group recently talked about the style of meetings that take place in her organization:

> I think it can be a little jarring actually for people who are used to perhaps a little more civility. I think we're civil, but we're direct. I don't like meetings if my direct reports leave the room and turn to somebody and say, "Can you believe someone said that?" And so I try to explain to them by example that if you find yourself doing that when you leave the room, or shaking your head, or kicking yourself for not having said something, or thinking that there were real problems with what somebody said, next time you have to say it in the room. You have to, or you will not be the most impactful member of this team. When I first got to Calvert, there was a lot of that. And I had one of my direct reports send me an email, complaining about something somebody else said. I just got back to them and said, "I'm not going to read this because I don't see the person you're talking about CC'd on it. So if you CC them on it and send it back to me, I will deal with it." Well, I never had to get it back, because once the person really dealt with it, it was fine.[76]

Based on Krumsiek's comments, answer the following:

A. What types of expectations are there for meetings at the Calvert Group?

B. What does Krumsiek say about the nature of directness and civility at meetings? Does this imply the meetings are not civil?

C. How does Krumsiek deal with complaints about other team members?

D. What are three principles from Krumsiek's comments that you can apply to how you approach team communication?

3.5 Brainstorming at Meetings (LO 3.4, LO 3.5)

Susan Docherty of General Motors recently described how she and her team communicate at meetings:

> I love to brainstorm with my team around the table in my office. I like to use a big whiteboard for ideas, because when you make things visual, you encourage the team to get up there at the whiteboard and put their thoughts out there. It's one thing to say that you're inclusive, but it's a whole other thing to be inclusive. And when people come into my office, they feel welcome. My door is open. They can bring ideas. They begin to understand that, as a leader, I want to be collaborative. I don't have all the answers or all the best ideas, nor do I want to. The whiteboard also keeps great ideas in front of us, not buried in an email and not buried in a stack of papers on our desks. And it enables everybody to own what we've got to get done. People will grab a marker and put up there that we're going to do a deep dive to

figure something out, and they put their name beside it. And there are lots of times where we put something on the board, and it requires a couple of people to get together to go work on it.[77]

Based on Docherty's comments and your own experiences, answer the following:

A. What strategies can you use for making meetings more visual? What are the benefits of making meetings visual?

B. What strategies can you use to make meetings more inclusive?

C. What does it mean for "everybody to own what we've got to get done"? What are a few approaches you can take to help make this happen for work teams?

3.6 *Being Friendly* versus *Being Friends* for Difficult Conversations (LO 3.6)

Kasper Rorsted, chief executive of Henkel, the consumer and industrial products company based in Düsseldorf, Germany, recently talked about the first time he had to be someone else's boss:

> [I first became someone else's boss] in 1989, right when I got promoted from being a sales rep in the Digital Equipment Corporation to being a sales manager at the age of 27. I had about 20 people at that point in time. All but two of them were older than I was. When you're 27, you're inexperienced, so you don't know what to fear. I didn't know what I probably should have known. The first time I realized it was serious was when, after about six months, I had to lay somebody off. And then suddenly you move from the sunny side of the deal to the real deal. I remember I was sleeping very poorly for almost a week. He had a family.
>
> So one of the lessons I learned from that, which I've been very aware of since, is to be friendly, but not a friend. I had grown up in the company and I knew everybody, so I was more a friend. But then I had to start having honest conversations with people about how they performed, and that taught me a lesson. I've always been friendly but never been friends anymore. When we have parties, I'm the one who will leave early.[78]

Based on Rorsted's comments, answer the following questions:

A. What do you think Rorsted means that he could "be friendly, but not a friend" once he became a boss and had to have difficult conversations with others?

B. Do you agree with his perspective about being friendly versus being friends? Do you think being friends makes having honest conversations in the workplace more difficult? Explain.

C. How can a person prepare for the difficult conversations necessary as one becomes a boss or supervisor?

Evaluation Exercises

3.7 Describe Nonverbal Behavior from a Movie or TV Episode (LO 3.2)

Think about a recent movie or TV episode you watched. Select a scene that involves interesting nonverbal communication—ideally, one that might occur in the workplace. Based on this scene, do the following:

A. Summarize the scene in approximately one paragraph.

B. Analyze the nonverbal communication. Explain how various body parts sent signals, including the eyes, mouth, shoulders, arms, and hands.

C. Describe how you can mimic or avoid three aspects of this nonverbal behavior in the workplace and why you would want to do so.

3.8 Describe the Listening Skills of an Excellent Listener and a Poor Listener (LO 3.1, LO 3.2)

Think of two people with whom you have worked at school or work—one an excellent listener and the other a poor listener. Describe and contrast these two individuals in terms of their ability to actively listen: paying attention, holding judgment, reflecting, clarifying, and sharing. Explain how each person made you feel as he or she listened, or didn't listen, to you. Explain two or three ways in which you want to emulate the excellent listener in the workplace.

3.9 Assess Your Active Listening Skills (LO 3.1, LO 3.2)

Think about how well you listen in high-pressure environments or when you're busy. Explain how well you do at each of the following active listening skills: paying attention, holding judgment, reflecting, clarifying, and sharing. For each skill, in two paragraphs explain how well you do these skills and think of strategies to help you improve.

3.10 Write a Listening Journal (LO 3.1, LO 3.2, LO 3.3)

For a length of time specified by your instructor (one week, two weeks, one month), write daily in a journal about your listening skills. Each day, describe one interaction you had and discuss whether you actively listened. Explain how well you did at each of the following active listening skills: paying attention, holding judgment, reflecting, clarifying, and sharing. For each of these interactions, describe the nonverbal behavior of others and the nonverbal behavior you exhibited to show your interest. Also, analyze how effectively you asked questions. Conclude your daily journal with a summary of lessons you have learned and five goals for improving your active listening.

3.11 Compare and Contrast an Excellent Meeting and a Poor Meeting (LO 3.5)

Think of two meetings you have attended at school or work—one excellent and the other poor. Compare and contrast these two meetings in the following areas: accomplishing team goals, setting expectations, participation and expression of ideas from all team members, open and honest communication, building consensus, and solving problems.

3.12 Describe a Difficult Conversation from a Movie or TV Episode (LO 3.6)

Think about a recent movie or TV episode you watched. Select a scene that involves an interesting but difficult conversation. Ideally, select one that might occur in the workplace. Based on this scene, do the following:

A. Summarize the scene in one paragraph.

B. Analyze the difficult conversation. Explain how well the characters involved applied effective principles for communicating.

C. Describe how you can apply two strategies from the scene as you approach difficult conversations in the workplace.

3.13 Assess a Recent Difficult Conversation (LO 3.3, LO 3.6)

Think about a recent difficult conversation you had. Ideally, select a conversation that occurred in the workplace or at school. Based on this conversation, do the following:

A. Summarize the conversation in one paragraph.

B. Evaluate your and others' performance in terms of assuming the best in one another, staying calm, finding common ground, disagreeing diplomatically, avoiding exaggeration and either/or approaches, and sharing all stories (including a shared story).

C. Describe three ways you would approach the conversation differently if you did it over again.

D. Assuming you had the conversation again, what are three questions you would ask to invite a learning stance?

Application Exercises

3.14 Listening Exercise (LO 3.1, LO 3.2, LO 3.3)

Form groups of three. You will complete this exercise three times, with each person rotating roles each time. The roles are asker, listener, and observer. Choose a time period (two minutes, three minutes, or five minutes) to complete the exercise. The asker will choose a topic to learn about from the listener (i.e., professional interests, reasons for choosing a major, challenges at work or in school right now). The asker will devote the time to learning about the other person through asking questions. The observer will take notes about how effective the asking, listening, and nonverbal

communication is of the asker. Once the exercise is complete, the observer will facilitate a three- to five-minute debriefing by explaining his/her observations and asking both the asker and the listener about their observations.

3.15 Creating an Agenda (LO 3.5)

Create an agenda for a recent meeting you had or a meeting that you will have soon (it could be a work or school agenda). Feel free to make up details if necessary. Prepare the agenda with agenda items, time frames, goals, roles, and materials needed.

Endnotes

1. Michael Purdy and Deborah Borisoff, *Listening in Everyday Life: A Personal and Professional Approach* (Lanham, MD: University Press of America, 1997).

2. Sabeen Sheikh, *2010 Graduate Management Admission Council Alumni Perspectives Survey* (McLean, VA: GMAC, 2010).

3. Judi Brownell, "The Skills of Listening-Centered Communication," in *Listening and Human Communication in the 21st Century,* ed. Andrew D. Wolvin (Hoboken, NJ: John Wiley & Sons, 2010): 141–156.

4. Michael Maslansky, *The Language of Trust* (New York: Prentice Hall, 2010).

5. Ibid: 68.

6. New York Times Corner Office Blog, "Communication," retrieved June 15, 2010, from http://projects.nytimes.com/corner-office/Communication.

7. The Ken Blanchard Companies, *The Critical Role of Teams* (Escondido, CA: Ken Blanchard Companies, 2006).

8. Melissa L. Beall, "Perspectives on Intercultural Listening," in *Listening and Human Communication in the 21st Century,* ed. Andrew D. Wolvin (Hoboken, NJ: John Wiley & Sons, 2010): 225–238; Sharon Ting and Peter Scisco, *The CCL Handbook of Coaching* (Hoboken, NJ: John Wiley & Sons, 2006). The Chinese character displayed in the text is a traditional Chinese character. Traditional Chinese characters are still used among Chinese populations in Taiwan, Hong Kong, Singapore, and various Chinatowns around the world. Chinese who live in mainland China now use simplified Chinese characters, which were created to increase literacy in China. The simplified character for *listen* is as follows: 听 (pronounced *tīng*). Originally, the Chinese character for *listen* was broken into two parts: ears (耳) and virtue (惪), implying the need to follow virtue. Later, people distinguished the components of eyes, heart (心), and undivided attention (一; this character for the number *one* implies complete and undivided). The components recognized as *eyes* include two characters: ten and eye. This implies that you should pay attention as if you had ten eyes. The character for king implies that you should listen to others as if they were royalty.

9. Uri Hasson, "I Can Make Your Brain Look Like Mine," *Harvard Business Review* (December 2010): 32–33.

10. Michael H. Hoppe, *Active Listening: Improve Your Ability to Listen and Lead* (Greensboro, NC: Center for Creative Leadership, 2006): 6, 12.

11. New York Times Corner Office Blog, "Communication."

12. Hoppe, *Active Listening: Improve Your Ability to Listen and Lead.*

13. Michael Marquardt, *Leading with Questions: How Leaders Find the Right Solutions by Knowing What to Ask* (San Francisco: Jossey-Bass, 2005): 77–78.

14. M. Adams, *Change Your Questions, Change Your Life: 7 Powerful Tools for Life and Work* (San Francisco: Berrett-Koehler, 2004); Marquardt, *Leading with Questions: How Leaders Find the Right Solutions by Knowing What to Ask*: 78.

15. New York Times Corner Office Blog, "Communication."

16. Hoppe, *Active Listening: Improve Your Ability to Listen and Lead.*

17. Ibid.

18. Ibid.

19. Ibid.

20. Ibid: 18.

21. Paul J. Donoghue and Mary E. Siegel, *Are You Really Listening? Keys to Successful Communication* (Notre Dame, IN: Ave Maria Press, 2005); Hoppe, *Active Listening: Improve Your Ability to Listen and Lead.*

22. Donoghue and Siegel, *Are You Really Listening? Keys to Successful Communication.*

23. Ibid.

24. Hoppe, *Active Listening: Improve Your Ability to Listen and Lead.*

25. David S. Christensen and David Rees, "An Analysis of the Business Communication Skills Needed by Entry-Level Accountants," *Proceedings of the 2002 Mountain Plains Management Conference.* Available at http://www.mountainplains.org/articles/2002/general/Communication%20Skills4_MPJ_.pdf.

26. John Baldoni, "Are You Asking the Right Questions?" *Harvard Management Communication Letter* (March 2003): 3–4.

27. Ibid; Douglas Stone, Bruce Patton, and Sheila Heen, *Difficult Conversations: How to Discuss What Matters Most* (New York: Penguin, 2000); Dale Carnegie Training, *The 5 Essential People Skills: How to Assert Yourself, Listen to Others, and Resolve Conflicts* (New York: Simon & Schuster, 2009); Adams, *Change Your Questions, Change Your Life: 7 Powerful Tools for Life and Work*; Marquardt, *Leading with Questions: How Leaders Find the Right Solutions by Knowing What to Ask.*

28. Maslansky, *The Language of Trust.*

29. The Ken Blanchard Companies, *The Critical Role of Teams.*

30. Ibid.

31. Susan A. Wheelan, *Creating Effective Teams: A Guide for Members and Leaders* (Thousand Oaks, CA: Sage, 1999); Bruce Tuckman, "Developmental Sequence in Small Groups," *Psychological Bulletin* 63, no. 6 (1965): 384–399. The terms *forming, storming, norming,* and *performing* are among the most commonly used terms for stages in team development. They are used in close approximation to Susan Wheelan's stages of dependency and inclusion, counterdependency and fight, trust and structure, and work.

32. Wheelan, *Creating Effective Teams: A Guide for Members and Leaders.*

33. Ibid.

34. Ibid.

35. Richard T. Watson and Cliff Saunders, "Managing Insight Velocity: The Design of Problem Solving Meetings," *Business Horizons* 48 (2005): 285–295.

36. Richard Benson-Armer and Tsun-Yan Hsieh, "Teamwork across Time and Space," *McKinsey Quarterly*, no. 4 (1997).

37. Tom Krattenmaker, "How to Make Every Meeting Matter," *Harvard Management Communication Letter* (May 2003): 3–5.

38. Watson and Saunders, "Managing Insight Velocity: The Design of Problem Solving Meetings": 285–295.

39. Accountemps, "Survey Finds Executives Waste More Than Two Months a Year in Unnecessary Business Discussion," June 8, 2000 (accessed January 10, 2010, at http://accountemps.rhi.mediaroom.com/index.php?s=189&item=336).

40. Barbara J. Streibel, *The Manager's Guide to Effective Meetings* (New York: McGraw-Hill, 2003).

41. Kim Ribbink, "Run a Meeting to Fast-Track Your Career," *Harvard Management Communication Letter* (October 2002): 3–4.

42. Krattenmaker, "How to Make Every Meeting Matter."

43. Ribbink, "Run a Meeting to Fast-Track Your Career."

44. Accountemps, "Accountemps Survey: Employee Output Is Weakest Late in the Day," August 17, 2010 (accessed November 20, 2010, at http://accountemps.rhi.mediaroom.com/least_productive).

45. Accountemps, "Second Day of the Week Remains Most Productive, Survey Shows," (February 7, 2008), retrieved January 10, 2010, from http://www.accountemps.com/PressRoom?id=2121.

46. Marty Linsky, "The Morning Meeting: Best-Practice Communication for Executive Teams," *Harvard Management Communication Letter* (Spring 2006): 3–5.

47. New York Times Corner Office Blog, "Meetings," retrieved June 15, 2010, from http://projects.nytimes.com/corner-office/Meetings.

48. Christina Bielaszka-DuVernay, "Is Your Company as Dull and Unproductive as Its Meetings?" *Harvard Management Communication Letter* (Summer 2004): 3–5.

49. Streibel, *The Manager's Guide to Effective Meetings*.

50. Terrence L. Gargiulo, *Stories at Work: Using Stories to Improve Communication and Build Relationships* (Westport, CT: Praeger, 2006).

51. Susan Bixler and Lisa Scherrer Dugan, *How to Project Confidence, Competence, and Credibility at Work: 5 Steps to Professional Presence* (Avon, MA: Adams Media, 2001).

52. Streibel, *The Manager's Guide to Effective Meetings*.

53. Bixler and Dugan, *How to Project Confidence, Competence, and Credibility at Work: 5 Steps to Professional Presence*.

54. Ribbink, "Run a Meeting to Fast-Track Your Career"; Streibel, *The Manager's Guide to Effective Meetings*; Bielaszka-DuVernay, "Is Your Company as Dull and Unproductive as Its Meetings?"; Janice Obuchowski, "Your Meeting: Who's in Charge?" *Harvard Management Communication Letter* (Spring 2005): 3–5.

55. Stephen R. Covey, *The 8th Habit: From Effectiveness to Greatness* (New York: Free Press, 2004).

56. S. Schulz-Hardt, F. C. Brodbeck, A. Mojzisch, R. Kerschreiter, and D. Frey, "Group Decision Making in Hidden Profile Situations: Dissent as a Facilitator for Decision Quality," *Journal of Personality and Social Psychology* 91, no. 6 (2006): 1080–1093.

57. Bielaszka-DuVernay, "Is Your Company as Dull and Unproductive as Its Meetings?": 3–5.

58. Ribbink, "Run a Meeting to Fast-Track Your Career"; Krattenmaker, "How to Make Every Meeting Matter": 3–5; Bielaszka-DuVernay, "Is Your Company as Dull and Unproductive as Its Meetings?"

59. Streibel, *The Manager's Guide to Effective Meetings*.

60. Lisa Gueldenzoph Snyder, "Teaching Teams about Teamwork: Preparation, Practice, and Performance Review," *Business Communication Quarterly* (March 2009): 77–78.

61. Obuchowski, "Your Meeting: Who's in Charge?"

62. Stone et al., *Difficult Conversations: How to Discuss What Matters Most*: xv.

63. Kerry Patterson, Joseph Grenny, Ron McMillan, and Al Switzler, *Crucial Conversations: Tools for Talking When Stakes Are High* (New York: McGraw-Hill, 2002); Laura L. Myers and R. Sam Larson, "Preparing Students for Early Work Conflicts," *Business Communication Quarterly* 68, no. 3 (2005): 306–317.

64. Patterson et al., *Crucial Conversations: Tools for Talking When Stakes Are High*.

65. Ibid: 9–10.

66. Ibid.

67. Renee Evenson, "Effective Solutions for Team Conflict," *Toastmasters* online (July 2009), www.toastmasters.org/ToastmastersMagazine/ToastmasterArchive/2009/July/EffectiveSolutions.aspx.

68. New York Times Corner Office Blog, "Teamwork," retrieved June 15, 2010, from http://projects.nytimes.com/corner-office/Teamwork.

69. Stone et al., *Difficult Conversations: How to Discuss What Matters Most*.

70. Ann C. Baker, *Catalytic Conversations: Organizational Communication and Innovation* (Armonk, NY: M. E. Sharpe, 2010).

71. Patterson, et al., *Crucial Conversations: Tools for Talking When Stakes Are High*.

72. Ibid.; Evenson, "Effective Solutions for Team Conflict"; Richard Bierck, "Managing Anger," *Harvard Management Communication Letter* (November 2001): 4–5.

73. Stephen M. R. Covey, *The Speed of Trust* (New York: Free Press, 2006).

74. Evenson, "Effective Solutions for Team Conflict."

75. New York Times Corner Office Blog, "Communication."

76. New York Times Corner Office Blog, "Meetings."

77. Ibid.

78. New York Times Corner Office Blog, "No Need to Hit the 'Send' Key: Just Talk to Me," retrieved August 31, 2010, from www.nytimes.com/2010/08/29/business/29corner.html?src=me&ref=business.

CHAPTER FOUR

Communicating across Cultures

Learning Objectives

After studying this chapter, you should be able to do the following:

LO4.1 Describe characteristics of cultural intelligence, its importance for global business leaders, and approaches to developing it.

LO4.2 Explain the major cultural dimensions and related communication practices.

LO4.3 Name and describe key categories of business etiquette in the intercultural communication process.

WHY DOES THIS MATTER?

Hear Pete Cardon explain why this matters.

bit.ly/CardonWhy4

You are living in one of the most exciting times because of opportunities to work and interact with people from across the globe. Only a few decades ago, few businesspeople worked closely with members of other cultures. Now, however, global business connections have increased rapidly, and you will undoubtedly work across cultures throughout your career. For example, you will probably have some chances to travel internationally for work assignments. More frequently, however, you are likely to work across cultures by collaborating with work teams in India, videoconferencing or emailing with customers or suppliers in China, or working in a culturally diverse office in your hometown. The possibilities are immense!

The rapid growth in intercultural business connections is driven by technological and cultural forces of globalization. Technology has allowed people to nearly instantaneously communicate with people around the world, transact business, and move capital. These technologies include the Internet, the digitization of work, ATMs, credit cards, smart cards, and GPS. Furthermore, convergence of many business standards and platforms has made conducting business easier and more predictable. These common standards and platforms include English as a global business language, trade agreements that specify rules for commerce (the World Trade Organization and North American

TABLE 4.1

Top Trading Partners with North America (United States and Canada)

Country	Total Trade (*in millions of dollars*)
1. China	$494,244
2. Mexico	326,802
3. Japan	167,520
4. United Kingdom	114,592
5. Germany	109,488
6. South Korea	77,247
7. France	69,009
8. Netherlands	52,952
9. Brazil	50,327
10. Italy	44,917

Note: China figure includes Hong Kong and Taiwan. Total trade combines total imports and exports with the United States and Canada. Based on 2009 trade figures.

Free Trade Agreement), and quality standards in manufacturing (e.g., supplier-customer relationships driven by ISO 9000 quality standards). Also, many non-Western executives are trained in business schools in the United States, Australia, and Western Europe, creating a more homogeneous business culture around the world.[1]

Throughout this chapter, you will see a variety of national cultures compared. The countries selected for this chapter are among the most important trading partners for the United States and Canada. In terms of trade volume, countries such as China (including Taiwan), Mexico, Japan, the United Kingdom, and Germany dominate. (See Table 4.1 for the most important trading partners of North America.) Of course, you will likely work with business professionals, clients, or customers from many other national backgrounds. Your business discipline, company, and industry will factor into the national cultures with which you most frequently interact. Carlos Ghosn, CEO of Nissan and Renault, explained the necessity of learning to work and communicate effectively across cultures:

> *Companies are going global, but the teams are being divided and scattered all over the planet. If you're head of engineering, you have to deal with divisions in Vietnam or China, and you have to work across cultures. You have to know how to motivate people who think very differently than you, who have different kinds of sensitivities, so I think the most important message is to get prepared to deal with teams who are multicultural, who do not think the same way.[2]*

Read the following case about Carlos Ghosn. Throughout the chapter, you will read more advice from him and other business executives.[3]

Chapter Case: Carlos Ghosn and Working across Cultures at Nissan

**Who's
Involved**

Carlos Ghosn, president and CEO of Nissan and Renault
- Held many international management positions: Michelin in France, 1978–1985; Michelin in Brazil, 1985–1989; Michelin in the United States, 1989–1996; Renault in France, 1996–present; Nissan in Japan, 1999–present.
- Speaks six languages: Arabic, Portuguese, Spanish, French, English, and Japanese.
- Born in Brazil, grew up in Lebanon, and moved to France for university studies.
- Industry analysts comment that Ghosn "epitomizes a new breed of borderless global managers. . . . These executives are multilingual, have worked around the world, and seem impervious to jet lag."[4]

**The
Situation**

In March 1999, Carlos Ghosn was asked to lead the turnaround at the struggling Japanese car-maker Nissan. The company was $23 billion in debt, had suffered declines in domestic market share for 27 straight years, was unprofitable on 43 of the 46 products it sold, and had lost money for seven of the prior eight years. Many viewed Ghosn, who was nicknamed *Le Cost-Killer* and renowned for his turnaround abilities, as the best hope to fix the crisis. Yet, many industry analysts thought the situation was impossible. They also wondered how a foreigner could succeed in the Japanese work environment.

Within 18 months, Nissan was restored to profitability and has sustained annual profitability for all but one year (during the recent worldwide recession) since then. Within five years of Ghosn's arrival in Japan to run Nissan, the debt of $23 billion had been turned into a $7 billion surplus. It now sells and markets cars in nearly every country in the world and runs manufacturing facilities in nearly 20 countries. Nissan is currently developing some of the most innovative cars, including the Nissan Leaf, the first zero-emissions car. Ghosn credits much of this turnaround at Nissan to his ability to work across cultures and to build on the best parts of each culture involved.

Questions to Consider as You Read

- What types of attitudes do business professionals need to communicate effectively across cultures?
- How can business students learn about and prepare to work with members of other cultures?
- How can understanding cultural dimensions help business professionals work cross-culturally?
- What advantages accrue to companies with a global mentality?
- What is the value of global leaders?

Developing Cultural Intelligence

LO4.1 Describe characteristics of cultural intelligence, its importance for global business leaders, and approaches to developing it.

Companies depend on business professionals who can manage across cultures. Companies such as Coca-Cola sell more products abroad than they do locally. In fact, Coca-Cola sells more drinks in Japan alone than in the United States. In Chapter 2, you read about emotional intelligence (EQ), your ability to manage emotions in interpersonal situations. Similarly, **cultural intelligence (CQ)** is a measure of your ability to work with and adapt to members of other cultures. Like EQ (but unlike IQ), CQ can be developed and improved over time with training, experience, and conscious effort.[5]

Business professionals with high CQ understand differences and similarities between and among cultures. **Culture** includes the shared values, norms, rules, and

TABLE 4.2

Cultural Intelligence in the Workplace

Characteristics of High Cultural Intelligence
• Respect, recognize, and appreciate cultural differences.
• Possess curiosity about and interest in other cultures.
• Avoid inappropriate stereotypes.
• Adjust conceptions of time and show patience.
• Manage language differences to achieve shared meaning.
• Understand cultural dimensions.
• Establish trust and show empathy across cultures.
• Approach cross-cultural work relationships with a learner mind-set.
• Build a co-culture of cooperation and innovation.

behaviors of an identifiable group of people who share a common history and communication system. There are many types of culture, such as national, organizational, and team. We discuss principles of intercultural communication in this chapter in the context of national cultures, which tend to be more permanent and enduring than other types of culture. The norms and values of national cultures are instilled in young members through a shared language, shared history and traditions, school systems, and political and economic systems.

When working with members of other cultures at the home office or abroad, business professionals with high CQ are skilled at forming goals, discussing and succeeding on joint projects, resolving differences, and negotiating mutually beneficial outcomes. They understand new markets and can develop global plans for marketing and supply chain management. When people with high CQ encounter unfamiliar situations, they implement a variety of the skills displayed in Table 4.2 and discussed throughout the chapter.[6]

Developing cultural intelligence is more than possessing favorable attitudes toward members of other groups. It also requires developing skills and knowledge. In this section, we focus briefly on several characteristics of cultural intelligence.

Respect, Recognize, and Appreciate Cultural Differences

Cultural intelligence is built on attitudes of respect and recognition of other cultures. This means that you view other cultures as holding legitimate and valid views of and approaches to managing business and workplace relationships. Ghosn, when first sent to Japan from France to turn around Nissan, demonstrated this view of cultures:

> People who try to impose one system onto another only wind up destroying it. This has never been our strategy. If Renault had wanted to do that, they would have picked anyone but me, because I'm completely convinced of the opposite course. Nissan had to be changed from the inside. If you're French and you come to Japan, you have no chance, zero, of budging the system an inch. I'm convinced of this. My conviction is both human and professional, and it's bolstered by the experience of having lived on several continents. Right from the beginning, I told them: "You're not missionaries. You've come here not to change Japan but to straighten out Nissan with the men and women of Nissan. We're the ones who have to assimilate with them—it's not up to them to adapt to us."[7]

In recent years, many public and educational campaigns have focused on embracing diversity. In this book, we refer to **diversity** as the presence of many cultural groups in the workplace. Business professionals with high cultural intelligence embrace diversity as a moral imperative and as a means to achieve higher performance. A great deal of research has examined the role of cultural diversity in the workplace. These studies have shown that a mix of cultural groups in terms of national culture, ethnicity, age, and gender leads to better decision making.[8] Nissan, like many companies, has recognized the moral and business value of diversity and explicitly states this on its website:

> At Nissan, we believe that diversity is a source of strength. . . . Nissan is committed to diversity to ensure that we meet the diverse needs of our customers and achieve sustainable growth for all stakeholders. Each and every employee will respect diversity and take full advantage of it. . . . We believe that embracing and leveraging this cultural diversity gives us a competitive advantage.[9]

Be Curious about Other Cultures

As a college student, you are in a stage of life that gives you unique opportunities to acquire cross-cultural experiences. Consider the following options: studying abroad, learning a language, developing friendships with international students on campus, and taking an interest in and learning about a particular culture.[10]

Study Abroad   Living in another culture is perhaps the best approach to learning about one. It allows you to immerse yourself in another way of living—to observe and experience up close how members of another cultural group communicate, work in groups, manage relationships, celebrate successes, and deal with disappointments. When asked, "What's your best career advice to young graduates?" Quintin E. Primo III, co-founder and chief executive of Capri Capital Partners, responded in the following way:

> Leave the country. Get out of here. That's what I tell everybody—just go. I don't care where you go, just go. Because the world is changing. It is no longer acceptable to speak only English if you are 25 and younger. . . . You have little chance of being successful if you speak only one language. If you don't understand Islam, you're in trouble because Islam comprises somewhere between 1.6 billion and 1.8 billion people, and there are markets that are untapped that need to be tapped. So you've got to get out of your front door, get out of the comfort and quiet of your home, and your safety zone, and step into a pool of risk where you have no idea what the outcome is going to be. Out of it all, you will have a much broader understanding of the world's cultures, and you will have a much clearer idea of how the world perceives our culture, and all the value, and the benefits, and the beauty of our culture. There is nothing more important. I don't care where you went to business school. I don't care whether your grades were good or bad. You have to leave the country."[11]

As freshmen, most university students express a desire to study abroad and even believe that they will have an opportunity to do so before they graduate. However, just 3 to 5 percent of university students actually do.[12] So, if you want to study abroad, make it a priority. Plan for it now. Furthermore, consider choosing locations and programs that are most important for your career. Typically, business recruiters value study-abroad programs that are at least one semester long, involve the development of business skills, and include language study. Also, business recruiters are more impressed with study-abroad programs located in countries that are considered strategically important business partners. Whereas most students choose locations in Western Europe and Australia, recruiters see more value in countries such as China, Japan, Brazil, Mexico, or India. Of course, this varies by discipline and industry. For example, if you are going into the fashion design industry, experience in Italy or France would be extremely valuable.

When you study abroad, learn all you can about adapting to the culture. However, avoid developing strong preconceptions and remain flexible. When you arrive in your chosen destination, open yourself completely to the experience. As Ghosn said about entering the Japanese culture, "I did not try to learn too much about Japan before coming, because I didn't want to have too many preconceived ideas. I wanted to discover Japan by being in Japan with the Japanese people."[13]

Learn a Language   Although English is considered the global business language and business managers in other parts of the world increasingly speak it well, you can benefit from learning another language for a variety of reasons. It gives you many insights into how people of other cultures think. It helps you appreciate the richness of other cultures. It fosters tremendous goodwill with others. And you may find yourself in situations where your language ability allows smoother communication than relying on English.

Ghosn, who now speaks six languages, commented on the reasons and the benefits: "Learning languages quickly became one of my passions. The study of language is the best way of understanding the connections between people and cultures."[14] Of course, learning languages takes a lot of time. Also, it requires forcing oneself into authentic and sometimes uncomfortable situations. Ghosn was determined to learn English while studying in Paris. So, twice each month, he invited Americans living in France to dinner to practice his English.[15]

Develop Friendships with International Students on Your Campus
Your university likely has hundreds or even thousands of international students. This presents you with a rare opportunity to experience the world. You can learn more about other cultures by befriending international students than you can by taking a group tour of another country. Also, you can help these students feel at home. One reason you can learn so much from international students is that they are experiencing the challenges of living in and adapting to a new culture. During your career, you are most likely to interact with business professionals who are the current generation of international students.

Take an Interest in a Culture and Routinely Learn about It   Each culture has its own complexity. Ideally, you should seek an in-depth understanding of one culture. Once you've done this, you can more quickly adapt to and learn other cultures. One of the best ways to gain an in-depth understanding is to take an inquisitive approach—asking questions and seeking the answers to how other cultures view knowledge; how they reason and approach problems; how they work, worship, and view the world; how they view time, and so on.[16] You can routinely learn about cultures of interest in some of the following ways:[17]

- *Watch films, television, documentaries, news, and other video of the culture*. It's increasingly easy to access video of other cultures. This allows you to observe many aspects of the culture in context with visual and auditory cues.
- *Follow the business culture of a country*. Many websites contain global business news sections with both text and videos. For example, consider the following: Bloomberg Businessweek, CNBC, Time, Foreign Exchange, and CIBERweb.
- *Take courses and attend events related to particular cultures*. Your university offers numerous opportunities, including taking courses about international and intercultural topics and attending symposia that feature international speakers.
- *Make friends with people who live in other cultures and communicate online*. You might try to make friends abroad and communicate frequently via email, chat, and online calls. One of the most common means of communicating internationally is via online call services such as Skype. Read the Technology Tips box on page 103 about online calls.

Avoid Inappropriate Stereotypes

When Ghosn moved to Japan, he selected a team of roughly 20 executives from Renault in France to join him. As he selected his team, he was adamant that each team member must be open to the Japanese:

> However competent a candidate may have been, however motivated, if I sensed that he or she was even slightly close-minded about cultural differences, that person was

excluded. . . . I wanted competent, enthusiastic, open-minded people capable of engaging in a real dialogue.[18]

We naturally develop stereotypes, or generalizations, to try to understand the attitudes and behavior of people we do not know, especially those of different cultures. It is an attempt by the brain to group and categorize in complex situations. Stereotypes can make interactions less complicated since they serve as a starting point for understanding the motives and values of others. For example, people may have a stereotype of tax accountants as credible, professional, competent, helpful, and detail-oriented. This stereotype allows people to go to a tax accountant's office with the assumption that the professional will help them and provide excellent service. Similarly, people who work across cultures often form stereotypes of how members of that culture communicate and approach work problems. These stereotypes can be productive as long as they are only a starting point, they are flexible, and they are primarily positive.[19]

Stereotyping about cultures can also be dysfunctional, counterproductive, and even hurtful. People tend to form two types of stereotypes when interacting with members of other cultures: *projected cognitive similarity* and *outgroup homogeneity effect*.[20] **Projected cognitive similarity** is the tendency to assume others have the same norms and values as your own cultural group. This occurs when people project their own cultural norms and values to explain the behaviors they see in others. Take the case of an American interviewing a Japanese man for a new position. The Japanese man might downplay his own achievements and give credit to the teams he has worked on. The American interviewer, based on the American cultural lens, may think the man lacks self-confidence and independence or initiative. The Japanese applicant, by contrast, is most likely displaying Japanese norms and values associated with modesty, politeness, and collectivism.

Outgroup homogeneity effect is the tendency to think members of other groups are all the same. Psychologically, this approach minimizes the mental effort needed to get to know people of other groups. Practically speaking, it is counterproductive to developing effective working relationships with members of other cultures. The reality is that all cultures contain a lot of diversity—individuals of many backgrounds, worldviews, interests, and approaches to life. In the "Individualism and Collectivism" section of this chapter, we will illustrate more about the nature of diversity.

Negative stereotyping can easily emerge from popular culture. Research has shown that television depictions of particular cultural groups as criminal, cruel, backward, or dishonest affect the stereotypes viewers have of those cultures.[21] Similarly, viewing members of other cultures through a political lens based on news stories about the political relations between countries often leads to unjustified negative stereotyping.

While you should be careful about forming negative or rigid stereotypes of members of other cultures, you should also be aware of stereotypes that others may have of you. Many people you interact with will have already formed some impressions of your cultural background and what to expect from you. Members of other cultures often form stereotypes of Americans based on news stories as well as popular culture (i.e., films, television shows, music). Typically, most people around the world hold mixed views of Americans (see Table 4.3). Even in countries where the majority of adults view Americans as dishonest or greedy, they also view Americans as hardworking and inventive.[22]

Adjust Your Conceptions of Time

One frustration that most people experience when communicating and working across cultures is dealing with time. This is because people have a lifetime of experiences, related to their particular culture, that form their expectations for when things should happen during any given process.

People high in CQ show patience. They understand that most tasks take longer when working across cultures because more time is needed to understand one another and cooperate effectively. Furthermore, many cross-cultural work projects are conducted

TABLE 4.3

Perceptions That Members of Various Cultures Have about Americans

	Hardworking	Inventive	Honest	Greedy	Rude
Canada	77%	76%	42%	62%	53%
China	44	70	35	57	44
France	89	76	57	31	36
Germany	67	56	52	49	12
India	81	86	58	43	27
Jordan	78	68	37	63	64
Netherlands	84	69	46	67	26
Russia	72	56	32	60	48
Spain	74	53	45	58	39
UK	76	64	57	62	35

Note: Red shading indicates a majority of adults in a country have a negative view. Green shading indicates a majority of adults in a country have a positive view.
Source: Pew Global Attitudes Project. Reprinted with permission.

across great distances. Naturally, this requires additional time due to the communication tools and organizational decision-making processes.

Guy McLeod, president of Airbus China, explained why business managers arriving in China need to adapt their pace: "When people have just arrived, they want to change things. But making quick moves in the wrong way isn't the right thing to do. You need to have patience, patience, patience. It is one of the clichés you hear in China, but it is true. You need to make a long-term strategy and stick to it."[23]

Also, people of various cultures conceptualize time differently. What seems *fast* in one culture may seem *slow* in another. One recent study ranked pace of life in various cultures by measuring walking speed over a distance of 60 feet, the average time for a postal worker to complete one request, and the accuracy of clocks in public. Countries such as Germany, Japan, and Italy were considered fast-paced cultures, whereas countries such as China, Brazil, and Mexico were considered slow-paced ones (see Figure 4.1).[24] The point is that cultures establish expectations about what is considered timely, late, rushed, and hectic. Cultures also differ in their priorities related to focusing on the present versus focusing on the future (as discussed in the "Future Orientation" section in the upcoming pages). As you can see, you will need to adjust your sense of time to coordinate effectively with members of other cultures.

A final time consideration relates to adjustment. You need time to get accustomed to and proficient in working with other cultures. When traveling to a new culture or taking an international assignment, you should allot time for adjusting. Ghosn noted the difficulties he and his family had when they moved to Japan:

> The language barrier was huge. When you first get to Japan, you're really constrained, because you feel dependent on other people for everything. . . . The culture's different. The customs are different. . . . As time passed, however, our family got its bearings.[25]

Manage Language Differences

English is increasingly considered the global business language. Many global companies such as Nissan, which are composed primarily of non-native English-speaking

FIGURE 4.1

Pace of Life across Cultures

Faster Pace of Life
↑
Germany
Japan
Italy
UK
Netherlands
Hong Kong
France
USA
Canada
S Korea
China
Brazil
Mexico
↓
Slower Pace of Life

business professionals, have adopted policies of conducting meetings in English. Yet, even with the strong push for English as a business language, many professionals around the business world speak limited English. Also, many forms of English exist— that of the United Kingdom, Australia, Singapore, and India, to name just a few places. Thus, standard English is a matter of interpretation. As you conduct business across cultures with those who have limited English ability, consider the following advice:[26]

- *Avoid quickly judging that others have limited communication proficiency.* Many non-native English speakers take time to warm up. The first moments—or in some cases days or weeks—of your interactions with them are not representative of their real language abilities. Many business professionals have studied English for years yet infrequently have opportunities to speak it in an authentic encounter.

- *Articulate clearly and slow down.* Many Americans inadvertently run their words together. Make sure you pronounce each word distinctly and slow your pace slightly.

- *Avoid slang and jargon.* Slang and jargon can be particularly confusing to members of other cultures. For example, Americans are well known for using sports slang in business (e.g., striking out, throwing a curve ball, hitting a home run). Use as much literal language as you can.

- *Give others time to express themselves.* Allow those with limited English ability enough time to process their thoughts into English. You will often find that non-native English speakers, given time, express their thoughts with a more precise, creative, and even accurate use of English words than native English speakers.

- *Use interpreters as necessary.* In some situations, you will rely on interpreters. Spend some time in advance getting to know the interpreter's abilities and preferences for facilitating an exchange. During interpretation, focus on the person you are communicating to rather than the interpreter. That is, focus on the person with whom you are trying to build rapport.

Ghosn made several excellent points about overcoming language barriers:

> Of course there are frustrations that always exist with language barriers: where you don't operate in an environment of spontaneous communication; where you have to go through a translator (you know that when you go through a translator, about 40 percent of your intended meaning is lost); where you're not sure that what you want to get across to people, on the shop floor or in meetings with customers, is actually being communicated the way you intended it. *These are what I consider small frustrations;* if you accept these and other things that perhaps are part of the fact that people don't think or act the same way in France or in Japan, it is easier to deal with such things as language barriers. When you have taken the time to understand that, and when you are really motivated and mobilized by a very strong objective, then the cultural differences can become seeds for innovation as opposed to seeds for dissention.[27]

Understanding Cultural Dimensions

LO4.2 Explain the major cultural dimensions and related communication practices.

In this section, we describe recent research on cultural norms and values among businesspeople throughout the world. This research, conducted by the GLOBE group (which includes dozens of business researchers around the world), is based on surveys and interviews of about 20,000 business leaders and managers in 62 countries.[28]

The GLOBE group found that cultures can be grouped into eight dimensions. **Cultural dimensions** are fairly permanent and enduring sets of related norms and values and are classified as (1) individualism and collectivism, (2) egalitarianism and hierarchy, (3) assertiveness, (4) performance orientation, (5) future orientation, (6) humane orientation, (7) uncertainty avoidance, and (8) gender egalitarianism. By understanding these eight dimensions, you can get a good sense of the underlying motivations and goals that impact acceptable behaviors within a culture.

Although cultures constantly evolve, usually over decades or generations, the cultural dimension that changes most rapidly is individualism and collectivism. As prosperity and economic development rise, individualism typically increases as well.

We describe each of the eight cultural dimensions, along with related communication practices, focusing on norms, meaning the range of expected and acceptable behaviors in each culture. You will notice that rankings are provided for each cultural dimension, and these rankings include the United States as well as the top ten trading partners of North America.[29] You can find rankings for other countries included in the GLOBE study in the online resources.

Individualism and Collectivism

Most intercultural communication scholars identify individualism and collectivism as the most influential cultural dimension. This dimension deals with the level of independence and interdependence that people in a society possess and encourage. **Individualism** refers to a mind-set that prioritizes independence more highly than interdependence, emphasizing individual goals over group goals, and valuing choice more than obligation. By contrast, **collectivism** refers to a mind-set that prioritizes interdependence more highly than independence, emphasizing group goals over individual goals, and valuing obligation more than choice.

Individualists view themselves as distinct and separate from their family members, friends, and colleagues. They pursue their own dreams and goals, even when it means spending less time with family members and friends. They enter friendships and relationships primarily based on common interests. They also leave relationships when they are no longer mutually satisfying, beneficial, or convenient. Decision making tends to be based on an individual's needs.[30]

On the other hand, collectivists view themselves as interdependent—forming an identity inseparable from that of their family members, friends, and other groups. They tend to follow the perceived dreams and goals of the group as a matter of duty and obligation, even when it means sacrificing their own hopes and ambitions. They form permanent and lifetime relationships. They also tend to stay in contact with and work through extended networks built on family relationships, schoolmates, and hometowns. Decisions are made by groups.[31] Figure 4.2 displays country rankings for individualism and collectivism in society. Of the countries we are considering here, China has the highest ranking for collectivism and the Netherlands has the lowest. Japan, which many people think of as highly collectivist, falls in the middle of this group. Table 4.4 shows communication practices normally associated with high individualism and high collectivism.

Traditionally, North American and Western countries have been far more individualist than Asian, Latin American, and other countries. However, some countries have

FIGURE 4.2

Individualism and Collectivism across Cultures

Collectivism in Society	
China	82
S Korea	77
Mexico	74
Taiwan	68
Hong Kong	64
Brazil	58
Italy	53
Japan	43
France	41
USA	26
Germany	24
UK	21
Netherlands	11
Individualism in Society	

TABLE 4.4

Communication Practices in High-Individualist and High-Collectivist Cultures

High Individualism	High Collectivism
• Discuss individual rewards and goals	• Discuss group rewards and goals
• Emphasize opportunities and choices	• Emphasize duties and obligations
• Spend less time in group decision making	• Spend more time in group decision making
• Socialize infrequently with colleagues outside of work	• Socialize frequently with colleagues outside of work
• Network in loosely tied and temporary social networks	• Network in tightly knit and permanent social networks
• Communicate directly to efficiently deal with work tasks and outcomes	• Communicate indirectly to preserve harmony in work relationships

FIGURE 4.3

Individualism and Collectivism within Companies

Collectivism in Organizations	
Japan	98
S Korea	97
China	68
Netherlands	65
UK	49
Taiwan	48
USA	43
France	43
Hong Kong	34
Germany	30
Mexico	29
Brazil	29
Italy	18
Individualism in Organizations	

increasingly become individualist, such as Japan. Generally, as countries increase the standard of living, they develop more individualist tendencies.

A major distinction in individualism and collectivism can be made between norms and values in *society* versus norms and values in *organizations*. All companies tend to promote both individualist and collectivist values. For example, encouraging self-initiative and individual accountability are individualist values. Encouraging teamwork and team incentives are collectivist values. In practice, many companies in individualist countries have attempted to adopt more team-oriented strategies in recent decades. Thus, highly individualist countries such as the United States exhibit many collectivist characteristics within organizations. Figure 4.3 displays country rankings for individualism and collectivism within companies. In many cases these rankings differ from norms and values in society at large.

One key to Ghosn's success with Nissan was his ability to work within the Japanese mind-set of collectivism.[32] He immediately formed cross-functional teams to develop solutions and goals. As Ghosn said, "One of the striking things about Japanese industry is the quality of teamwork. . . . In France, people aren't naturally inclined to teamwork. In Japan, on the other hand, people are quite comfortable working in teams."[33]

Cultures that exhibit extremely high collectivism within organizations tend to have a family-centered culture. Many Asian organizations adopt this family-oriented approach to running a company. As Ernst Behrens, president of Siemens China, explained, "The Chinese—and Asians generally—enter into employment with a different understanding than we have in Europe. For us, the company certainly is important, but mainly as an employment base. To the Chinese, the company is more like a family. The idea is, 'I am giving myself to Siemens. Now you have to take care of me.'"[34]

As you read through this section on cultural dimensions and view the continuums with rankings for each country, note that cultures are more than a spot on a scale. For example, Figure 4.4 shows how the United States, which is considered to have one of the most individualist cultures, and China, which is considered among the most collectivist cultures, overlap to some extent on this dimension (the triangular area enclosed by the intersection of the red and blue curves). In other words, some Chinese individuals behave in more individualist ways than some American individuals. However, by and large, most Chinese are more collectivist than most Americans. Furthermore, norms within a culture typically evolve to reflect what *most* people value. Even within cultures, there is great variety. Research in the United States has shown that individualism and collectivism vary significantly by region, with the Mountain West region the most individualist and the Deep South the most collectivist.[35] By constantly reminding yourself that variety exists within cultures, you are less likely to typecast people (outgroup homogeneity effect).

FIGURE 4.4

Variety in Individualist and Collectivist Norms in the United States, Japan, and China

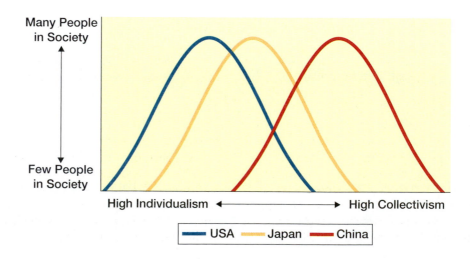

TABLE 4.5

Communication Practices in Egalitarian and Hierarchical Cultures

Egalitarianism	Hierarchy
• Decision making is more decentralized. • Protocol based on status is less important and is reserved for unusually formal business situations. • Subordinates speak more openly with leaders even during disagreements. • Subordinates do not take responsibility for the mistakes of leaders. • Leaders are approached directly.	• Decision making is more centralized. • Protocol (use of titles, seating arrangements) based on status is extremely important. • Subordinates defer to leaders during disagreements. • Subordinates take blame for and save face for leaders at all times. • Leaders are approached through intermediaries.

Egalitarianism and Hierarchy

All cultures develop norms for how power is distributed. In **egalitarian** cultures, people tend to distribute and share power evenly, minimize status differences, and minimize special privileges and opportunities for people just because they have higher authority. In **hierarchical** cultures, people expect power differences, follow leaders without questioning them, and feel comfortable with leaders receiving special privileges and opportunities. Power tends to be concentrated at the top.

In egalitarian organizations, leaders avoid command-and-control approaches and lead with participatory and open management styles. Competence is highly valued in positions of authority. People of all ranks are encouraged to voice their opinions. Status symbols for leaders are discouraged. Salary ranges between the top and the bottom of the organization are quite narrow. By contrast, in hierarchical organizations, leaders expect employees to fall in line with their policies and decisions by virtue of their authority. Employees are discouraged from openly challenging leaders. Status symbols are common. Salary differences between the top and the bottom of the organization are extreme.[36] Figure 4.5 displays country rankings for hierarchy and egalitarianism. Table 4.5 presents communication practices normally associated with hierarchy and egalitarianism.

Performance Orientation

Performance orientation (PO) is "the extent to which a community encourages and rewards innovation, high standards, and performance improvement."[37] Of all cultural dimensions, societies cherish this one the most, especially in business. Yet many cultures are still developing a performance orientation.[38] To some degree, the distinctions between high-PO and low-PO cultures are captured in the phrase *living to work versus working to live.*

The cultures of Far Eastern Asia, Western Europe, and North America are particularly high in performance orientation. For example, professionals in higher PO cultures often perceive members of lower PO cultures as not prioritizing results, accountability, and deadlines. By contrast, members of lower PO cultures often perceive members of higher PO cultures as impatient and even obsessed with short-term results.

Some cultures that are midrange PO cultures such as China and India are rapidly developing performance orientations in work culture. Each of these countries has implemented major economic reforms in recent decades and is achieving stunning economic growth. These countries increasingly have companies and workforces that adopt norms and policies promoting innovation, improvement, and accountability systems. Figure 4.6 displays country rankings for performance orientation. Table 4.6 presents communication practices normally associated with high- and low-performance orientation.

FIGURE 4.5

Hierarchy and Egalitarianism across Cultures

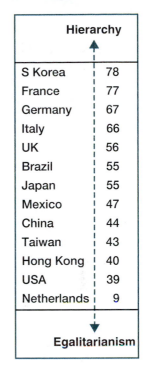

Hierarchy	
S Korea	78
France	77
Germany	67
Italy	66
UK	56
Brazil	55
Japan	55
Mexico	47
China	44
Taiwan	43
Hong Kong	40
USA	39
Netherlands	9

Egalitarianism

FIGURE 4.6

Performance Orientation across Cultures

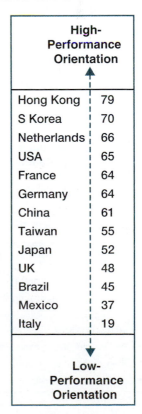

High-Performance Orientation	
Hong Kong	79
S Korea	70
Netherlands	66
USA	65
France	64
Germany	64
China	61
Taiwan	55
Japan	52
UK	48
Brazil	45
Mexico	37
Italy	19

Low-Performance Orientation

TABLE 4.6

Communication in High-Performance and Low-Performance Societies

High Performance	Low Performance
• Emphasize results more than relationships	• Emphasize relationships more than results
• Prioritize measurable goals and objectives in meetings and communications	• Discuss goals and objectives casually without mechanisms for measuring them
• View feedback as essential to improvement	• View feedback as judgmental and uncomfortable
• Explicitly talk about financial incentives	• De-emphasize financial incentives; consider this motivation inappropriate
• Value statements of individual accountability	• Value expressions of loyalty and sympathy
• Expect urgency in communications and emphasize deadlines	• Show a relaxed view of time and view overemphasis on deadlines as pushy

FIGURE 4.7

Time Orientation across Cultures

High Future Orientation	
Netherlands	91
Germany	74
UK	69
Japan	68
USA	59
Brazil	46
S Korea	46
Hong Kong	45
Mexico	38
France	37
China	34
Taiwan	32
Italy	15

Low Future Orientation

Hallmarks of high-performance orientation are competition and discipline. These attributes are often instilled through school systems, as Ghosn explained about his upbringing in the Jesuit education system:

> In their educational philosophy, discipline is very important, and competition equally so. There's a constant challenge, a grading system that encourages students to outdo one another. After all, the Jesuit order was the first multinational company in the world. . . . I learned a lot from the Jesuits, and by the time I graduated I had a firm sense of discipline and organization, along with a taste for competition and a job well done.[39]

Future Orientation

Future orientation (FO) involves the degree to which cultures are willing to sacrifice current wants to achieve future needs. Cultures with low FO (or present-oriented cultures) tend to enjoy being in the moment and spontaneity. They are less anxious about the future and often avoid the planning and sacrifices necessary to reach future goals. By contrast, cultures with high FO are imaginative about the future and have the discipline to carefully plan for and sacrifice current needs and wants to reach future goals.[40]

In future-oriented societies, many organizations create long-term strategies and business plans. Furthermore, they use these strategies and plans to guide their short-term business activities. By contrast, in present-oriented societies, organizations are less likely to develop clear long-term strategies and business plans. Moreover, they rarely focus short-term activities on long-term plans, even when they exist. Future orientation within organizations is a strong predictor of financial performance. High-FO cultures plan extensively for crises and unforeseen contingencies, whereas low-FO cultures take events as they occur.[41] Figure 4.7 displays country rankings for future orientation. Table 4.7 presents communication practices normally associated with high and low future orientation.

TABLE 4.7

Communication Practices in High and Low Future Orientation Cultures

High Future Orientation	Low Future Orientation
• Emphasize control and planning for the future	• Emphasize controlling current business problems
• Focus more on intrinsic motivation	• Focus more on extrinsic motivation
• Frequently discuss long-term strategies as part of business communications	• Rarely discuss long-term strategies as part of communications
• Use flexible and adaptive language	• Use inflexible and firm language
• Often mention long-term rewards and incentives	• Often mention short-term rewards and incentives
• Appreciate visionary approaches to business problems	• Prioritize proven and routine approaches to problems

Assertiveness

The level of directness in speech varies greatly across cultures, and this can lead to miscommunication, misinterpretation of motivations, and hard feelings. The cultural dimension of **assertiveness** deals with the level of confrontation and directness that is considered appropriate and productive.[42] Typically, North Americans and Western Europeans are the most assertive in business situations, whereas Asians tend to be less assertive. The mentality of "say it how it is," "cut to the chase," and "don't sugarcoat it" is emblematic of high assertiveness.

Members of highly assertive cultures often view members of less-assertive cultures as timid, unenthusiastic, uncommitted, and even dishonest, since they withhold or temper their comments. On the other hand, members of less-assertive cultures often view members of highly assertive cultures as rude, tactless, inconsiderate, and even uncivilized.[43]

In particular, businesspeople notice differences in levels of assertiveness when a yes or no answer is expected. In less-assertive cultures, the answer is sometimes vague; people are expected to read between the lines. As Guy McLeod, president of Airbus China, stated, "In Europe or the States, 'yes' means 'yes,' so we can work together toward a common goal. Here, 'yes' doesn't always mean 'yes,' and 'no' doesn't always mean 'no.' . . . One piece of advice I give people about China: Everything is difficult, but everything is possible."[44] Figure 4.8 displays country rankings for assertiveness. Table 4.8 presents communication practices normally associated with high and low assertiveness.

Humane Orientation

Humane orientation (HO) is "the degree to which an organization or society encourages and rewards individuals for being fair, altruistic, friendly, generous, caring, and kind."[45] In high-HO cultures, people demonstrate that others belong and are welcome. Concern extends to all people—friends and strangers—and nature. People provide social support to each other and are urged to be sensitive to all forms of unfairness, unkindness, and discrimination. Companies and shareholders emphasize social responsibility, and leaders are expected to be generous and compassionate.

In low-HO cultures, the values of pleasure, comfort, and self-enjoyment take precedence over displays of generosity and kindness. People extend material, financial, and social support to a close circle of friends and family. Society members are expected to solve personal problems on their own. Companies and shareholders focus primarily on financial profits, and leaders are not expected to be generous or compassionate.[46] Figure 4.9 displays country rankings for humane orientation. Table 4.9 presents communication practices normally associated with high and low humane orientation.

FIGURE 4.8

Assertiveness across Cultures

High Assertiveness	
Germany	92
Hong Kong	82
USA	80
Netherlands	77
France	76
S Korea	70
Mexico	66
Brazil	62
UK	60
Italy	52
China	26
Taiwan	21
Japan	21
Low Assertiveness	

TABLE 4.8

Communication Practices in High- and Low-Assertiveness Cultures

High-Assertiveness Cultures	Low-Assertiveness Cultures
• Emphasize direct and unambiguous language	• Emphasize indirect and subtle language
• Uncomfortable with silence and speak up quickly to fill the silence	• View silence as communicative and respectful
• Prioritize resolving issues over showing respect to others	• Prioritize showing respect over resolving issues
• Typically express more emotion	• Typically express less emotion
• Use tough, even dominant, language	• Use tender and pleasant language
• Stress equity and use competitive language	• Stress equality and use cooperative language
• Value unrestrained expression of thoughts and feelings	• Value measured and disciplined expression of thoughts and feelings

FIGURE 4.9

Humane Orientation across Cultures

TABLE 4.9

Communication Styles in High and Low Humane Orientation Cultures

High Humane Orientation	Low Humane Orientation
• Express greetings, welcome, concern, and appreciation in most interactions	• Express greetings and welcome in formal interactions
• Consider taking time to talk about feelings as critical	• Consider taking time to talk about feelings as inefficient
• Volunteer to help others	• Help others when asked
• Smile and display other nonverbal signs of welcome frequently	• Smile and display other nonverbal signs of welcome infrequently

Ghosn enjoyed the humane orientation encountered while working in the United States and Japan:

> Those were perhaps the most important years of my professional education. I had to learn how to be an American CEO, which is much different from being a Brazilian-style boss or a European CEO. . . . My education in America was extremely rich: the market, the competition, the mingling of cultures. . . . The United States is a very good training school for learning about customers, and about everything to do with marketing tools and communication.[47]

He similarly was grateful to the Japanese during his stay there:

> The Japanese are very courteous people, sensitive to the feelings of others. They'll never speak to you unpleasantly. When they don't think much of you, they keep quiet. But when they think a lot of you, they tell you. . . . But in any case, during those first months I was spared harsh criticism and negative comments. This was a big help. I didn't need anyone making my task more difficult.[48]

Uncertainty Avoidance

FIGURE 4.10

Uncertainty Avoidance across Cultures

Uncertainty avoidance (UA) refers to how cultures socialize members to feel in uncertain, novel, surprising, or extraordinary situations. In high-UA cultures, people feel uncomfortable with uncertainty and seek orderliness, consistency, structure, and formalized procedures. People in high-UA cultures often stress orderliness and consistency, even if it means sacrificing experimentation and innovation. They prefer that expectations are clear and spelled out precisely in the form of instructions and rules. People in high-UA cultures prefer tasks with sure outcomes and minimal risk. They also show more resistance to change and less tolerance for breaking rules.[49]

In low-UA cultures, people feel comfortable with uncertainty. In fact, they may even thrive, since they prefer tasks that involve uncertain outcomes, calculated risks, and problem solving and experimentation. They often view rules and procedures as hindering creativity and innovation. Members of low-UA cultures develop trust more quickly with people from other groups and tend to be more informal in their interactions. They also show less resistance to change, less desire to establish rules to dictate behavior, and more tolerance for breaking rules.[50] Figure 4.10 displays country rankings for uncertainty avoidance. Table 4.10 presents communication practices normally associated with high and low uncertainty avoidance.

Gender Egalitarianism

Gender egalitarianism deals with the division of roles between men and women in society. In high gender-egalitarianism cultures, men and women are encouraged to occupy the same professional roles and leadership positions. Women are

Table 4.10

Communication Styles in High and Low Uncertainty Avoidance Cultures

High Uncertainty Avoidance	Low Uncertainty Avoidance
• Document agreements in legal contracts • Expect orderly communication: keep meticulous records, document conclusions drawn in meetings • Refer to formalized policies, procedures, and rules as basis for decision making • Verify with written communication • Prefer formality in the majority of interpersonal business interactions	• Rely on the word of others they trust rather than contractual arrangements • Expect casual communication: less concerned with documentation and maintenance of meeting records • Feel unbound by formalized policies, procedures, and rules when discussing work decisions with others • Verify with oral communication • Expect informality in most interpersonal business interactions

included equally in decision making. In low gender-egalitarianism cultures, men and women are expected to occupy different roles in society. Typically, women have less influence in professional decision making. However, in societies where gender roles are highly distinct, women often have powerful roles in family decision making.[51]

Traditionally, nearly all cultures afforded low professional status to women. In recent decades, however, women have increasingly gained opportunity and status in many cultures. When Ghosn arrived at Nissan, only 1 percent of managers were women. He quickly made it a goal to increase the number of female managers. Now, 5 percent of the managers at Nissan are women, and the goal is to reach 10 percent in the near future.

Gender egalitarianism relates not only to equal professional opportunity for men and women, but also to expectations and customs about how men and women should communicate. Growing up, for example, Ghosn was accustomed to letting women walk through doors first. Yet, in Japan, the tradition is for men to enter doors and elevators first. Ghosn discussed how entering elevators in Japan before women remained uncomfortable for a long time due to his expectations about gender roles.[52] In Table 4.11 you will find communication practices normally associated with high and low gender-egalitarianism cultures.

Business Values around the World

To this point, we have discussed *norms,* or what cultures actually do. The GLOBE group also surveyed business professionals about *values,* or what they prefer for workplace culture. Refer to Table 4.12 to see which dimensions each culture prioritizes as their ideal work arrangements. Business cultures around the world show many convergences in terms of values—as a result of globalization and increased development. Business cultures, in particular, have converged more rapidly than other parts of society.

TABLE 4.11

Communication Practices in High and Low Gender-Egalitarianism Cultures

High Gender Egalitarianism	Low Gender Egalitarianism
• Provide equal professional opportunities to men and women • Expect men and women to have the same communication and management styles • Avoid protocol that draws attention to gender	• Provide more professional leadership opportunities to men • Expect men and women to communicate in distinct masculine and feminine ways • Prefer protocol that draws attention to gender

TABLE 4.12

Preferred Priorities for Work Cultures around the World

Brazil	China	France
1. Performance orientation	1. Performance orientation	1. Performance orientation
2. Future orientation	2. Assertiveness	2. Humane orientation
3. Organizational collectivism	3. Humane orientation	3. Collectivism
4. Humane orientation	4. Uncertainty avoidance	4. Future orientation
5. Collectivism	5. Collectivism	5. Organizational collectivism
6. Uncertainty avoidance	6. Future orientation	6. Uncertainty avoidance
7. Assertiveness	7. Organizational collectivism	7. Assertiveness
8. Hierarchy	8. Hierarchy	8. Hierarchy

Germany	Hong Kong	Italy
1. Performance orientation	1. Performance orientation	1. Performance orientation
2. Humane orientation	2. Future orientation	2. Future orientation
3. Collectivism	3. Humane orientation	3. Collectivism
4. Organizational collectivism	4. Collectivism	4. Humane orientation
5. Future orientation	5. Assertiveness	5. Organizational collectivism
6. Uncertainty avoidance	6. Uncertainty avoidance	6. Uncertainty avoidance
7. Assertiveness	7. Organizational collectivism	7. Assertiveness
8. Hierarchy	8. Hierarchy	8. Hierarchy

Japan	Mexico	Netherlands
1. Assertiveness	1. Performance orientation	1. Performance orientation
2. Humane orientation	2. Collectivism	2. Humane orientation
3. Collectivism	3. Future orientation	3. Collectivism
4. Future orientation	4. Uncertainty avoidance	4. Future orientation
5. Performance orientation	5. Humane orientation	5. Organizational collectivism
6. Uncertainty avoidance	6. Organizational collectivism	6. Uncertainty avoidance
7. Organizational collectivism	7. Assertiveness	7. Assertiveness
8. Hierarchy	8. Hierarchy	8. Hierarchy

South Korea	United Kingdom	United States
1. Future orientation	1. Performance orientation	1. Performance orientation
2. Humane orientation	2. Collectivism	2. Collectivism
3. Collectivism	3. Humane orientation	3. Humane orientation
4. Performance orientation	4. Future orientation	4. Future orientation
5. Uncertainty avoidance	5. Organizational collectivism	5. Assertiveness
6. Organizational collectivism	6. Uncertainty avoidance	6. Organizational collectivism
7. Assertiveness	7. Assertiveness	7. Uncertainty avoidance
8. Hierarchy	8. Hierarchy	8. Hierarchy

Source: Based on a GLOBE study of work values among business managers in 62 countries.
Notes: Performance orientation is the most valued dimension in nearly all work cultures (in green shade).
Hierarchy is the least valued dimension in all work cultures (in red shade).
Humane orientation is highly valued among most cultures (in light blue shade).

TECHNOLOGY TIPS

ONLINE CALLS

Business professionals frequently use online calls—voice and video—to communicate conveniently and inexpensively. Online calls use VoIP (Voice over IP) technology to allow people to speak with one another over Internet connections. Well-known software packages for online calls include Skype and Vonage.

Skype is the most commonly used online call system for businesses. Skype now has over one billion users, so it may be particularly important for your international dealings. It has caught on for business use for international calls because it is so inexpensive (free for PC-to-PC calls) and convenient. Furthermore, it is often more convenient than mobile phones because many business professionals have phones without international plans. Consider the following when making online calls.

Understand the limitations of online calls. Online calls often provide excellent audio and video quality. However, they are generally less predictable than landline calls. Network outages, heavy traffic creating bandwidth problems, and even power failures threaten call quality. Most software for online calls contains components of online-meeting software packages, such as videoconferencing, file transfer, and screen sharing. These additional features are useful but sometimes contribute to lower audio quality due to bandwidth limitations. Test your equipment and be aware of its limitations before making important calls.

Be sensitive to those who share work space with you. If you work in cubicles or an open office, you may inadvertently distract your colleagues from their work when making online calls. Online calls are typically louder for two reasons. First, you are broadcasting the voices of those with whom you are speaking. Second, you will find that you often project your voice more loudly on online calls than on phones.

Spend time setting up the camera, look professional, and tidy up your work area. Most online calls allow video. If possible, take advantage of this option to add nonverbal cues to your conversation. Take time to set up the camera so that it displays your image in an appealing manner rather than at an odd angle. Also, pay attention to your work space. During lengthy online video calls, the person you are talking with will certainly notice your surroundings. Some will make judgments about your professionalism based on how you maintain your desk and office space.

You will notice that nearly all cultures value performance orientation. Note also that all cultures place the lowest priority on hierarchy. In other words, business professionals across the world nearly universally want to focus on performance in an egalitarian, participatory work environment. Furthermore, nearly all cultures value a humane orientation, thus demonstrating that results-focused communication remains critical, but members of most cultures will increasingly expect this strong performance orientation to be framed in a caring manner. As you conduct business across cultures, stay aware of these trends.

Building and Maintaining Cross-Cultural Work Relationships

Thus far, we have focused on aspects of cultural intelligence primarily related to understanding other cultures. In this section, we focus on the process of building relationships and co-creating success with members of other cultures. This process may involve communicating and working in entirely new ways for you and those of other cultures.

Establish Trust and Show Empathy

As in any other business relationships, trust is critical in cross-cultural work relationships. And as in other relationships, you can establish your credibility through competence, caring, and character. These aspects of credibility take more time to demonstrate and convey when working across cultures. People from other cultures may interpret behavior differently, so consider how each aspect of credibility is earned in other cultures. Similarly, allow members of other cultures to show their credibility and learn to interpret how they display competence, caring, and character in their cultures.

Business managers often start relationships from a position of needing to earn the trust of others. This is further complicated when working across cultures, where the beliefs that *most people are fair* or *most people can be trusted* may be even less prominent than in North America (see Figures 4.11 and 4.12). China, Canada, the United States, the Netherlands, and Saudi Arabia are considered to be high-trust cultures, meaning that their citizens are more conditioned to trust. In contrast, Mexico, Brazil, and France are considered to be low-trust cultures.[53]

One way of establishing trust is to show empathy. After three decades of working across cultures and a full decade heading Nissan, Ghosn reflected on its importance: "I think one of the basics of transcultural leadership is empathy. I would say even though the term today is not very popular, love the country and love the culture you are in. And try to learn about its strengths, don't focus on the weaknesses, and make sure that all the people you are transferring with you are of the same opinion."[54]

FIGURE 4.11

Perceptions of Trust across Cultures

Note: % of adults who agree that *most people can be trusted.*

High-Trust Societies	
China	53
Netherlands	45
Japan	41
Canada	40
USA	38
Germany	34
UK	30
Italy	29
S Korea	29
Spain	27
Mexico	19
France	19
Brazil	9
Low-Trust Societies	

FIGURE 4.12

Expectations of Fair Play across Cultures

Note: % of adults who agree that *most people are fair.*

High Expectations of Fair Play	
Japan	57
China	55
USA	49
Netherlands	40
Mexico	30
Taiwan	29
Brazil	26
UK	25
S Korea	24
Hong Kong	23
Italy	20
France	17
Germany	1
Low Expectations of Fair Play	

Developing empathy is more than showing you care. It also involves understanding members of other cultures as individuals and in terms of business goals and competencies. As you read on, you will notice that trust and credibility across cultures are built on many levels, chief of which is a vision of shared business potential.

Adopt a Learner Mind-Set

Developing strong cross-cultural relationships requires a learner mind-set. With the learner mind-set, you expect that members of other cultures possess unique types of knowledge and unique approaches to problem solving that will be helpful for shared business interests. You expect that they will be full partners in the decision-making process. Ghosn exemplified this attitude when entering the Japanese environment: "I was bound and determined to become assimilated. When I signed on for this Japanese adventure, I told myself that Japan was going to be a part of me, just as Nissan was going to be a part of me. But assimilation doesn't mean that you lose your individuality or your originality."[55]

Although Ghosn did not know much about Japanese culture before he moved to Japan, he had a deep and profound respect for Japanese innovations in the car industry:

> The Japanese left an indelible mark on the automobile industry by extending the boundaries of the factory management system. . . . It was at Toyota that "lean production" was born. The system would be copied and adapted, more or less successfully, by the automobile industry worldwide, beginning with Toyota's competitors in Japan. . . . The Japanese aren't champions of theory. Their strong suit is to start from a simple, pragmatic observation and try to create a solution from that. I haven't seen very many theoretical solutions produced in Japan.[56]

The opposite of the learner mind-set when working with other cultures is the judger mind-set. In cross-cultural working relationships, the judger mind-set is often referred to as **ethnocentrism.** It is the belief that your own culture is superior—that it provides better approaches for solving work problems or dealing with work relationships and contains a better knowledge base to conceptualize work. In all interpersonal relationships, the judger mind-set is damaging. In cross-cultural relationships, it is particularly damaging because most people have a great deal of self-respect and self-esteem tied to their cultural identities.[57]

Build a Co-culture of Cooperation and Innovation

When working across cultures, people generally adopt a unique set of communication and collaboration practices. These practices combine aspects of each culture. Over time, these practices, norms, and values form a **co-culture** that combines elements of each culture. One of the best signs that your cross-cultural working relationships are going well is when you have become comfortable enough with one another to form a co-culture. Doing so requires a mind-set that you are creating something new—a belief that you will adopt the best practices of the other culture and vice versa, as Ghosn explained:

> In cross-border acquisitions or alliances, cultural differences can be viewed as either a handicap or a powerful seed for something new. From the beginning, I said that I viewed cultural differences as an opportunity to innovate in achieving the pragmatic business objectives we had before us. This is risky when you say it before you even start. It's been 15 months since I arrived at Nissan. And now, six months after the start of the revival plan, *I can tell you that today cultural differences are seen more as an object of cross-fertilization and innovation in the way we are doing things, than as a motive for frustration or reason to disagree.* This is because of one thing—the Nissan Revival Plan. When the Renault people came to Japan, the management of Nissan had from the beginning a very strong consciousness about the severity of the situation. There was no room for bickering

or fighting or infinite discussions about whose method or whose process we were going to adopt.[58]

Business managers high in cultural intelligence recognize that developing effective co-cultures requires creating something new. This is one reason that seasoned executives select people for international assignments who can handle uncertainty. As Ekkehard Rathgeber, president of Direct Group Asia, explained, "My belief is: If you pick the wrong person, no matter how much training you give, it won't work. You need to find a person who is very determined and can handle the ambiguity you find every day in China. . . . You must be very open to new things, excited by new things—not someone who wants to preserve his own culture and identity."[59]

Creating a co-culture involves abandoning some—not all—cultural norms and values from each culture. At Nissan, Ghosn replaced some elements of Japanese culture that were not serving the needs of the company. For example, he introduced merit pay increases rather than seniority pay increases and broke up the keiretsu supplier network (the traditional approach to Japanese partnerships between companies based on shared ownership and loyalty). As Ghosn explained, however, these changes were aligned with Nissan's business interests, implemented with the collectivist approach of cross-functional teams (CFTs), and accommodated various Japanese preferences for work:[60]

> I knew that if I had tried simply to impose the changes from the top, I would have failed. Instead, I decided to use as the centerpiece of the turnaround effort a set of cross-functional teams. I had used CFTs in my previous turnarounds and had found them a powerful tool for getting line managers to see beyond the functional or regional boundaries that define their direct responsibilities. . . . Inside Nissan, though, people recognized that we weren't trying to take the company over but rather were attempting to restore it to its former glory. We had the trust of employees for a simple reason: We had shown them respect. . . . We have been able to exploit the uniquely Japanese combination of keen competitiveness and sense of community that has driven the likes of Sony and Toyota—and Nissan itself in earlier times.[61]

Business leaders know that an effective co-culture has been built when corporate culture includes aspects of each culture and delivers results. Ghosn explained this sense of co-culture at Nissan:

> We spend all of our time collaborating. We're crossing cultures and experiences. In my opinion, that's an advantage for the future. Nissan is building a culture that's well adapted to this new world. At the top levels of the company, we can't think in specifically Japanese or French terms any longer. . . . I'm convinced that if General Motors and Ford are having difficulties today, it's because they haven't become truly global corporations. They have remained too American. They realize most of their profits are in the United States. . . . What we're on our way to understanding is that tomorrow's winners, at least those in the automobile industry, will be those that are truly global, capable of according importance to all markets. Tomorrow's company will be the one that assumes a global character without losing its identity.[62]

Learning the Etiquette of Another Culture

LO4.3 Name and describe key categories of business etiquette in the intercultural communication process.

Following the rules of etiquette in other cultures is one way of gaining favorable first impressions and showing respect. This is especially the case as you get to know potential partners or clients. On exploratory trips, you will participate in meetings and social engagements—banquets and meals, refreshments during meetings, and plenty of small talk. These are opportunities for members of each culture to get to know one another in a nonthreatening, casual environment.

COMMUNICATION Q&A

CONVERSATIONS WITH CURRENT BUSINESS PROFESSIONALS

Pete Cardon: How important is it for business leaders to understand other cultures?

Nipul Patel: It is extremely important. We live in a connected society. Social media (Facebook, Twitter, LinkedIn, etc.) are increasingly connecting cultures across the globe. Successful business leaders must understand the needs, wants, and desires of people in the cultures they want to conduct business with.

PC: What are a few of the major differences in how people communicate to conduct business in India and the United States?

NP: Some differences have gotten smaller over time. However, there are still big differences. The American business climate has a contract-based business approach. Even a simple rental contract requires many pages and goes through many revisions by many legal professionals. From the Indian perspective this contract-based approach shows distrust. In my opinion, it hinders the openness that must exist in conducting business transactions. In India, the majority of transactions are still conducted on a handshake basis. The value of one's word is still a major aspect of doing business overseas. We are in the process of establishing a business venture in Thailand and Bangladesh. I see many similarities in conducting business in India and those countries. Although the formalities involved in doing business in the United States protect both buyer and seller, trust is an ingredient for a successful recipe. In India if you don't get this trust, you have no chance of getting any deals with anyone.

PC: What can business students do right now to increase their knowledge of other cultures?

NP: Business students should learn as much about other cultures as possible. I would encourage every aspiring business student to study in another country for at least a semester, if not more. Studying abroad allows you to experience the culture firsthand. It is significantly different than just taking a course or two in foreign language. Although it is extremely important to learn the language, it is more important to learn the culture, traditions, and overall business climate of another country.

Nipul Patel *spends about nine months each year in the United States running the restaurants and convenience stores that he owns in Indiana. He lives in India for about three months per year to manage his real estate company and focus on various venture capital interests.*

You have many sources for learning about the appropriate customs and etiquette of other cultures. In Table 4.13, you will find examples from Brazil, Russia, India, and China (often called the *BRIC* countries because of their expected strategic importance for business during the 21st century).[63] This table includes the types of customs and etiquette you should become aware of before traveling to another country for business, including appropriate versus taboo topics of conversation, conversation style, punctuality and meetings, dining, touching and proximity, business dress, and gift giving.

TABLE 4.13

Etiquette and Customs in the BRIC Countries

	Brazil	Russia	India	China
Appropriate Topics of Conversation	Personal topics, soccer, weather, traffic, cultural events	Politics, Russian culture and history, art (if you know a lot about it), current events, books, films	Family and personal life, politics, cricket, films, economic reforms	Chinese history, art, calligraphy, Chinese food
Private or Taboo Topics of Conversation	Politics, poverty, crime, security, deforestation, corruption	Personal life, religion, comparing Moscow and St. Petersburg, comparing Russia to developing countries	Religion, Pakistan, poverty, slums, caste system	Taiwan, Tibet, Tiananmen Square, human rights
Punctuality and Meetings	Meeting times are relaxed and often start 10 to 15 minutes late.	Meetings are scheduled far in advance. Time is viewed flexibly.	Meetings are scheduled far in advance. Time is viewed flexibly.	Meetings begin on time; arrive at social events on time
Dining	Meals (lunch and dinner) are an important part of building relationships. Careful attention to etiquette: Food is never touched with the hands. Begin meal with the toast: "Saúde."	Meals (dinners) are often used to finish a deal. Seating arrangements follow protocol. Continental style of using utensils. Hands should always stay above the table. Drinking alcohol is an important part of socializing.	Meals are important to show hospitality to visitors.	Extravagant meals and banquets are an essential part of building relationships. Toasting is an important part of meals. Individual meals rarely served; rather, dishes for the group are provided on a Lazy Susan (rotating tray).
Touching and Proximity	Frequent and extended touching: handshakes, embraces between friends, kissing on cheeks between women as a greeting, touching arms, standing close to one another during conversation	Touching reserved for greetings and handshakes	People stand closer (2 to 2½ feet apart) to one another than in North America.	Handshakes and slight bows during greetings. Touching is rare. People commonly sit side by side rather than facing one another during meetings.
Conversation Style	Animated, lively, expressive, lots of interruptions, loud, spontaneous	Calm, deliberate, careful, metaphorical and symbolic, philosophical, frank	Agreeable, friendly, conflict-avoiding	Modest, reserved, cautious display of emotion, indirect about disagreements
Business Dress	Formal business attire is important. Should be stylish, fashionable. For women, dress should be feminine.	Brand-name, expensive suits	Men: suit and tie except in warmer climates where more casual. Women: salwar suit. Conservative dress is important.	Conservative suits. Bright colors are avoided. High heels are avoided.
Titles	Titles are used only in formal situations.	First names are appropriate only after a relationship is well established.	Titles are typically used unless directed otherwise.	Titles are generally used in the workplace.
Gift Giving	Gifts generally are not expected on first meeting. A better alternative is to buy a meal.	Gifts are appreciated. Cheap gifts should be avoided. Good gifts include chocolates, dessert items, fine wine.	Gift giving is a sign of friendship. Expensive and leather gifts should be avoided.	Gift giving is common in first meetings. Gifts should be presented with two hands. Expensive gifts are avoided.

Chapter Takeaway for *Communicating across Cultures*

LO 4.1. Describe characteristics of cultural intelligence, its importance for global business leaders, and approaches to developing it. (pp. 88–94)

Principles of High Cultural Intelligence

- Respect, recognize, and appreciate cultural differences.
- Possess curiosity about and interest in other cultures.
- Avoid inappropriate stereotypes.
- Adjust conceptions of time and show patience.
- Manage language differences to achieve shared meaning.

- Understand cultural dimensions.
- Establish trust and show empathy across cultures.
- Approach cross-cultural work relationships with a learner mind-set.
- Build a co-culture of cooperation and innovation.

LO 4.2. Explain the major cultural dimensions and related communication practices. (pp. 94–106)

Cultural Dimensions

Individualism refers to a mind-set that prioritizes independence more highly than interdependence, emphasizing individual goals over group goals, and valuing choice more than obligation.

Collectivism refers to a mind-set that prioritizes interdependence more highly than independence, emphasizing group goals over individual goals, and valuing obligation more than choice.

Egalitarianism refers to cultures that distribute and share power evenly, minimize status differences, and minimize special privileges and opportunities for people just because they have higher authority.

Hierarchy refers to cultures that expect power differences, follow leaders without questioning them, and feel comfortable with leaders receiving special privileges and opportunities.

Performance orientation refers to cultures that encourage and reward innovation and set high standards of performance.

Future orientation involves the degree to which cultures are willing to sacrifice current wants to achieve future needs.

Assertiveness deals with the level of confrontation and directness that is considered appropriate and productive within a culture.

Humane orientation refers to cultures that encourage and reward individuals for being fair, friendly, generous, and kind.

Uncertainty avoidance refers to how cultures socialize members to feel in uncertain, novel, surprising, or extraordinary situations.

Gender egalitarianism deals with the division of roles between men and women in society.

See *rankings of countries along these cultural dimensions* in Figures 4.2 through 4.10. See *related communication practices* in Tables 4.4 through 4.12. See a *comprehensive set of rankings* for 62 cultures in the online resources.

LO 4.3. Name and describe key categories of business etiquette in the intercultural communication process. (pp. 106–108)

Etiquette and Customs

- Appropriate topics of conversation
- Private or taboo topics
- Punctuality and meetings
- Dining
- Touching and proximity

- Conversation style
- Business dress
- Titles
- Gift giving

See *examples of etiquette and customs across the BRIC countries* in Table 4.13.

Key Terms

assertiveness (p. 99)

co-culture (p. 105)

collectivism (p. 95)

cultural dimensions (p. 94)

cultural intelligence (CQ) (p. 88)

culture (p. 88)

diversity (p. 89)

egalitarian (p. 97)

ethnocentrism (p. 105)

future orientation (p. 98)

gender egalitarianism (p. 100)

hierarchical (p. 97)

humane orientation (p. 99)

individualism (p. 95)

outgroup homogeneity effect (p. 92)

performance orientation (p. 97)

projected cognitive similarity (p. 92)

uncertainty avoidance (p. 100)

Discussion Exercises

4.1 Chapter Review Questions (LO 4.1, LO 4.2, LO 4.3)

A. As you choose a culture or cultures to learn about, which do you think would be most helpful for your career? Why?

B. Explain what cultural intelligence is. How is it similar to and different from emotional intelligence?

C. What does it mean to embrace diversity in the context of conducting business across cultures?

D. How can you learn about another culture? Map out a plan for learning about a culture of interest.

E. How can stereotypes be productive and counterproductive? How does popular culture impact stereotypes of cultures?

F. What strategies can you use to overcome language barriers?

G. Describe each of the cultural dimensions and related communication practices.

H. Explain what is meant by a co-culture. Explain how a co-culture of communication practices might take form in a business setting.

I. Based on what you've learned from Carlos Ghosn's comments and your own experiences, how can you show respect for other cultures while also attempting to change some aspect of the culture?

J. Think of a culture of interest to you. Describe several things you could learn from that culture to enrich your life, deepen your business expertise, and improve your communication skills.

4.2 Communication Q&A Discussion Questions (LO 4.1, LO 4.2, LO 4.3)

Read the Communication Q&A section in this chapter. Based on Nipul Patel's comments and your own experiences, respond to the following questions:

A. Patel speaks about the importance of trust in doing business in India. Based on his comments, how might you feel about doing business in India? Would you be able to adapt your level of trust and distrust?

B. What does Patel recommend for business students who want to learn about other cultures?

C. If you had the chance to speak with Patel before a trip to India for business, what five questions would you ask him?

4.3 Leadership Lessons Learned through International Experiences (LO 4.1)

Recently, Robert W. Selander of MasterCard was asked, "What are the most important leadership lessons you have learned?" He responded by describing his international experience:

> I spent a reasonable amount of time living overseas. So relatively early in my career I moved first to San Juan, then to Rio, then to London, then to Belgium, running businesses in those markets. Pretty early on, I recognized that more is the same than is different—fundamental values, wanting to give your children more opportunity or at least as much as you had in life, etc. It's present all around the world, and that happens to be true in a lot of aspects of business as well. More is the same than is different, but we tend to focus on differences, and perhaps exaggerate or accentuate those beyond the reality of what we have to worry about. I can remember when I moved to Brazil and I had spent two years learning Spanish. I was out visiting branches. I was working for Citibank at the time and had responsibility for consumer businesses there. Brazil is a big country. I was living in Rio and it's like living in Miami. I was out visiting a branch in the equivalent of Denver. Not everybody spoke great English and I hadn't gotten very far in Portuguese. As I was sitting there trying to discern and understand what this branch manager was saying to me, and he was struggling with his English, the coin sort of dropped that this guy really knows what he's talking about. He's having a hard time getting it out. As I thought about the places I'd been on that trip, I realized this was probably the best branch manager I'd seen, but it would have been very easy for me to think he wasn't, because he couldn't communicate as well as some of the others who were fluent in English. I think that was an important lesson. It is too easy to let the person with great presentation or language skills buffalo you into thinking that they are better or more knowledgeable than someone else who might not necessarily have that particular set of skills. So that was something that sounds obvious in hindsight, but as I was sitting there, boy, for me this was a thunderbolt. I think that's another thing that sort of served me well, not letting the veneer distract you from the substance.[64]

Based on Selander's comments and your own experiences, respond to the following questions:

A. In what ways might you misjudge the competence of others based on language skills?

B. What are several strategies to overcoming language barriers?

C. How can you improve your ability to be a good listener for those with limited English abilities?

Evaluation Exercises

4.4 Evaluate Your Cross-Cultural Stereotypes (LO 4.1)

Think about a culture of interest to you. Do the following:

A. Describe five preconceptions or stereotypes you have about the culture.

B. Conduct some research and find out how correct you are. Use books or articles written by experts on the culture. Or find a friend from that country or someone with a lot of experience working there and ask about the accuracy of your preconceptions and stereotypes.

C. Report your findings. For each preconception, describe causes and accuracy. Explain what this might mean about the way one develops impressions, holds preconceptions, and thinks in stereotypes of other cultures.

Application Exercises

4.5 Analyze, Explain, and Make a Presentation about Your Own Business Culture (LO 4.2)

Review the GLOBE rankings for the eight cultural dimensions for your culture. Also, go to a website that describes business etiquette in your country (e.g., www.executiveplanet.com). Assume you are going to train a group of business professionals from another country about doing business in your country. Also, assume the business professionals have read about the GLOBE rankings and learned about etiquette in your country. Create a presentation that includes the following:

A. Explain the five key norms and values that drive business culture in your country. Give at least one example of related communication behavior for each of the five key norms and values.

B. Describe the accuracy of the GLOBE rankings and information about business etiquette.

C. Explain three cases that involve exceptions to the rule. For example, if you say that performance orientation is one of the key norms and values, you could explain a few cases where views toward performance are more relaxed.

D. Provide three final tips for working effectively with members of your own culture that you won't find in books.

4.6 Analyze the Cultural Dimensions of a Country (LO 4.2)

Choose a country of interest to you. (The GLOBE study rankings for 62 countries are provided in the online resources that accompany this book.) Analyze the country in terms of the following cultural dimensions:

- Individualism and collectivism
- Egalitarianism and hierarchy
- Assertiveness
- Performance orientation
- Future orientation
- Humane orientation
- Uncertainty avoidance
- Gender egalitarianism

In conclusion, describe five communication practices you think may be key when working with members from this country.

4.7 Analyze the Etiquette of a Business Culture (LO 4.3)

Choose a country of interest to you. Go to the Executive Planet website (www.executiveplanet.com) or other website with cross-cultural comparisons of business etiquette. Read all the information about this country's business culture and then do the following:

A. Write about the five most intriguing aspects of the culture.

B. Write about the five aspects of etiquette you would observe when interacting with members of this culture.

C. Choose three relevant cultural dimensions (underlying sets of norms and values) and explain how they impact business etiquette in this country.

D. Write five questions about business etiquette you would like to ask a person from the country you chose.

4.8 Read News Stories Written by and for Members of Another Culture (LO 4.1, LO 4.2)

Read three online newspaper articles from a country of interest. You should be able to find an online English-language newspaper for your chosen country fairly easily. Go to these websites:

- www.world-newspapers.com
- www.onlinenewspapers.com
- www.refdesk.com/paper.html

After reading the three newspaper articles, write the following for each article:

A. *Article information:* article name, source (magazine name), date/edition, pages, web address if available.

B. *Summary:* a short summary of the article.

C. *Cultural lessons:* one paragraph that describes one or two aspects of culture that are illustrated by the article.

D. *Implications for business communication:* Explain how these aspects of the culture would impact conducting business with members of this culture.

4.9 Read a Magazine Article about Global Business
(LO 4.1, LO 4.2)

Read a magazine article about global business that includes issues about cross-cultural differences. Consider the following online sources for an article:

- www.businessweek.com/globalbiz/
- www.time.com/time/global_business
- edition.cnn.com/BUSINESS/

After reading the three articles, write the following for each:

A. *Article information:* article name, source (magazine name), date/edition, pages, web address if available.

B. *Summary:* a short summary of the article.

C. *Cultural lessons:* one paragraph that describes one or two aspects of culture that are illustrated by the article.

D. *Implications for business communication:* Explain how these aspects of the culture would impact conducting business with members of this culture.

4.10 Interview a Professional with International Experience
(LO 4.1, LO 4.2, LO 4.3)

Interview someone you know who has worked extensively with members of other cultures. Spend an hour or two asking this person about his/her experiences. Report what this person had to say about five of the following ten areas:

- Etiquette.
- Preferred communication channels.
- Working in teams.
- Conducting meetings.
- Approaches to resolving differences of opinion.
- Negotiation style.
- Cultural values and norms.
- Adjusting to living in another country.
- Approaching conflicts or disagreements.
- Persuasion.

4.11 Interview an International Student (LO 4.1, LO 4.2)

Interview an international student at your university. Report about the interview in five of the following ten areas:

- Business in the student's country.
- Popular entertainment in the country.
- Changes occurring in the culture.
- Challenges in adapting to the food.
- Challenges in adapting to housing.
- Challenges in adapting to transportation.
- Experiences making friendships with Americans.
- Experiences working in teams with American students.
- Experiences working with American professors.
- Observations about American culture.

Conclude your report with three recommendations you have for people doing business with members of that culture.

Endnotes

1. K. Ohmae, *The Next Global Stage: Challenges and Opportunities in Our Borderless World* (Upper Saddle River, NJ: Wharton School, 2005); Thomas L. Friedman, *The World Is Flat: A Brief History of the Twenty-First Century* (New York: Farrar, Straus, and Giroux, 2005); Peter W. Cardon, "The Importance of Teaching about Globalization in Business Education," *Journal for Global Business Education* 7 (2007): 1–20.

2. Richard M. Smith, "In the Driver's Seat," *Newsweek* (June 20, 2008).

3. John P. Millikin and Dean Fu, "The Global Leadership of Carlos Ghosn at Nissan," *Thunderbird International Business Review* 47, no. 1 (2005): 121–137; Carlos Ghosn, "Saving the Business without Losing the Company," *Harvard Business Review* (January 2002); Renault Nissan, "Alliance Facts & Figures 2009," retrieved April 26, 2011, from www.nissan-global.com/EN/DOCUMENT/PDF/ALLIANCE/HANDBOOK/2009/Alliance_FactsAndFigures_2009.pdf; Carlos Ghosn, "How I Work," *Fortune* (March 20, 2006); Alex Taylor III, "The Nissan Leaf Battery-Powered Car," *Fortune* (March 1, 2010): 90–98; Alex Taylor III, "The Man Who Vows to Change Japan Inc.," *Fortune* (December 20, 1999).

4. Alex Taylor III, "The Man Who Vows to Change Japan Inc.," *Fortune* (December 20, 1999).

5. P. Christopher Earley and Elaine Mosakowski, "Cultural Intelligence," *Harvard Business Review* (November 2004): 139–146; David Livermore, "CQ: The Test of Your Potential for Cross-Cultural Success," Forbes Leadership Blog, retrieved April 9, 2011, from www.forbes.com/2010/01/06/cq-cultural-intelligence-leadership-managing-globalization.html (January 10, 2010).

6. M. Javidan, R. M. Steers, and M. A. Hitt, "Putting It All Together: So What Is a Global Mindset and Why Is It Important?" in *The Global Mindset,* ed. M. Javidan, R. M. Steers, and M. A. Hitts (Oxford: Elsevier, 2007); Lillian H. Chaney and Jeanette S. Martin, *Intercultural Business Communication* (Upper Saddle River, NJ: Prentice Hall, 2011); Livermore, "CQ: The Test of Your Potential for Cross-Cultural Success"; Earley and Mosakowski, "Cultural Intelligence."

7. Carlos Ghosn and Philippe Riés (translated from French by John Cullen), *Shift: Inside Nissan's Historic Revival* (New York: Currency Doubleday, 2005): 90.

8. Susan A. Wheelan, *Creating Effective Teams: A Guide for Members and Leaders* (Thousand Oaks, CA: Sage, 1999); Kim Ribbink, "Seven Ways to Better Communicate in Today's Diverse Workplace," *Harvard Management Communication Letter* (November 2002): 3–5.

9. "Diversity," Nissan Global website (April 25, 2011), retrieved April 25, 2011, from www.nissan-global.com/EN/COMPANY/DIVERSITY/.

10. Peter W. Cardon and Bryan Marshall, "International Opportunities for Business Students," *National Business Education Yearbook*, 48 (2010): 223–235.

11. New York Times Corner Office Blog, "Get a Diploma, but Then Get a Passport," retrieved February 20, 2011, from http://www.nytimes.com/2010/08/01/business/01corner.html.

12. Peter W. Cardon, Bryan A. Marshall, Nipul Patel, Natalya Goreva, and Renée J. Fontenot, "A Comparison of Study Abroad and Globalization Attitudes among Information Systems, Computer Science, and Business Students: Recommendations for IS Curriculum Design," *Issues in Information Systems* 10, no. 1 (2009): 28–39.

13. Millikin and Fu, "The Global Leadership of Carlos Ghosn at Nissan": 121.

14. Ghosn and Riés, *Shift: Inside Nissan's Historic Revival*: 8.

15. Ibid.

16. Iris Varner and Linda Beamer, *Intercultural Communication in the Global Workplace* (3rd ed.) (Boston: McGraw-Hill, 2005).

17. Carol Briam, "Outsourced: Using a Comedy Film to Teach Intercultural Communication," *Business Communication Quarterly* 73, no. 4 (2010): 383–398; Peter W. Cardon, "Using Films to Learn about the Nature of Cross-Cultural Stereotypes in Intercultural Business Communication Courses," *Business Communication Quarterly* 73, no. 2 (2010): 150–165.

18. Ghosn and Riés, *Shift: Inside Nissan's Historic Revival*: 88.

19. S. P. Verluyten, *Cultures: From Observation to Understanding* (Leuven, Belgium: ACCO, 2007); S. P. Verluyten, *The Use of Video Excerpts in Intercultural Training,* paper presented at the 73rd Annual Convention of the Association for Business Communication, April 15, 2008.

20. I. Varner and L. Beamer, *Intercultural Communication in the Global Workplace*; J. W. Neuliep, *Intercultural Communication: A Contextual Approach* (Thousand Oaks, CA: Sage, 2009): 168–169; Cardon, "Using Films to Learn about the Nature of Cross-Cultural Stereotypes in Intercultural Business Communication Courses"; T. Dimnik and S. Felton, "Accountant Stereotypes in Movies Distributed in North America in the Twentieth Century," *Accounting, Organizations and Society* 31: 130.

21. C. R. Berg, *Latino Images in Film: Stereotypes, Subversion, Resistance* (Austin: University of Texas, 2002); M. Wingfield and B. Karaman, "Arab Stereotypes and American Educators," *Social Studies and the Young Learner* 7, no. 4 (March/April 1995): 7–10; D. E. Mastro, "A Social Identity Approach to Understanding the Impact of Television Messages," *Communication Monographs* 70, no. 2 (2003): 98–113.

22. Andrew Kohut, Richard Wike, Juliana Menasce Horowitz, Erin Carriere-Kretschemer, Jacob Poushter, Mattie Ressler, and Bruce Stokes, *Obama More Popular Abroad Than at Home, Global Image of U.S. Continues to Benefit* (Washington, DC: Pew Research Center, 2010).

23. Juan Antonio Fernandez and Laurie Underwood, *China CEO: Voices of Experience from 20 International Business Leaders* (Singapore: John Wiley & Sons, 2006): 265.

24. Robert V. Levine and Ara Norenzayan, "The Pace of Life in 31 Countries," *Journal of Cross-Cultural Psychology*, no. 2 (March 20, 1999): 178–205.

25. Ghosn and Riés, *Shift: Inside Nissan's Historic Revival*: 79.

26. Ribbink, "Seven Ways to Better Communicate in Today's Diverse Workplace."

27. Victoria Emerson, "An Interview with Carlos Ghosn, President of Nissan Motors, Ltd. and Industry Leader of the Year," *Journal of World Business* 36, no. 1 (Spring 2001).

28. R. J. House, P. J. Hanges, M. Javidan, P. W. Dorfman, and V. Gupta, eds., *Culture, Leadership, and Organizations: The GLOBE Study of 62 Societies* (Thousand Oaks, CA: Sage, 2004).

29. The scores in these rankings have been converted to a scale from 0 to 100 from the 7-point Likert scales provided in the GLOBE study. These conversions are similar in approach to how Geert Hofstede classified cultures to allow easier comprehension for readers.

30. M. J. Gelfand, D. P. S. Bhawuk, L. H. Nishii, and D. J. Bechtold, "Individualism and Collectivism," in R. J. House, P. J. Hanges, M. Javidan, P. W. Dorfman, and V. Gupta, eds., *Culture, Leadership, and Organizations: The GLOBE Study of 62 Societies* (Thousand Oaks, CA: Sage, 2004): 437–512; Geert Hofstede, *Culture's Consequences: Comparing Values, Behaviors, Institutions, and Organizations across Nations,* 2nd ed. (Thousand Oaks, CA: Sage, 2001); James W. Neuliep, *Intercultural Communication: A Contextual Approach,* 4th ed. (Thousand Oaks, CA: Sage, 2009).

31. Ibid.

32. Keith Jackson and Miyuki Tomioka, *The Changing Face of Japanese Management* (New York: Routledge, 2004).

33. Ghosn and Riés, *Shift: Inside Nissan's Historic Revival*.

34. Fernandez and Underwood, *China CEO: Voices of Experience from 20 International Business Leaders*: 268.

35. Joseph A. Vandello and Dov Cohen, "Patterns of Individualism and Collectivism across the United States," *Journal of Personality and Social Psychology* 77, no. 2: 279–292.

36. Geert Hofstede, *Culture's Consequences: Comparing Values, Behaviors, Institutions and Organizations across Nations* (Thousand Oaks, CA: Sage, 2001).

37. M. Javidan, "Performance Orientation," in R. J. House, P. J. Hanges, M. Javidan, P. W. Dorfman, and V. Gupta, eds., *Culture, Leadership, and Organizations: The GLOBE Study of 62 Societies* (Thousand Oaks, CA: Sage, 2004): 239.

38. Ibid: 239–281.

39. Ghosn and Riés, *Shift: Inside Nissan's Historic Revival*: 7.

40. N. Ashikanasy, V. Gupta, M. S. Mayfield, and E. Trevor-Roberts, "Future Orientation," in R. J. House, P. J. Hanges, M. Javidan, P. W. Dorfman, and V. Gupta, eds., *Culture, Leadership, and Organizations: The GLOBE Study of 62 Societies* (Thousand Oaks, CA: Sage, 2004): 282–342.

41. Ibid.

42. D. N. den Hartog, "Assertiveness," in R. J. House, P. J. Hanges, M. Javidan, P. W. Dorfman, and V. Gupta, eds., *Culture, Leadership, and Organizations: The GLOBE Study of 62 Societies* (Thousand Oaks, CA: Sage, 2004): 395.

43. Ibid: 395–436.

44. Fernandez and Underwood, *China CEO: Voices of Experience from 20 International Business Leaders*: 275.

45. H. Kabasakal and M. Bodur "Humane Orientation in Societies, Organizations, and Leader Attributes" in R. J. House, P. J. Hanges, M. Javidan, P. W. Dorfman, and V. Gupta, eds., *Culture, Leadership, and Organizations: The GLOBE Study of 62 Societies* (Thousand Oaks, CA: Sage, 2004): 569.

46. Ibid: 564–601.

47. Ghosn and Riés, *Shift: Inside Nissan's Historic Revival*: 44.

48. Ibid: 83.

49. M. S. De Luque and M. Javidan, "Uncertainty Avoidance," in R. J. House, P. J. Hanges, M. Javidan, P. W. Dorfman, and V. Gupta, eds., *Culture, Leadership, and Organizations: The GLOBE Study of 62 Societies* (Thousand Oaks, CA: Sage, 2004): 602–653; Hofstede, *Culture's Consequences*.

50. Ibid.

51. C. G. Emrich, F. L. Denmark, and D. N. den Hartog, "Cross-Cultural Differences in Gender Egalitarianism," in R. J. House, P. J. Hanges, M. Javidan, P. W. Dorfman, and V. Gupta, eds., *Culture, Leadership, and Organizations: The GLOBE Study of 62 Societies* (Thousand Oaks, CA: Sage, 2004): 343–394.

52. "The Transcultural Leader: Carlos Ghosn, CEO of Renault, Nissan," retrieved April 30, 2011, from INSEAD, http://knowledge .insead.edu/ILSTransculturalLeaderGhosn080501.cfm?vid=45.

53. Calculations from the *World Values Survey* data set. Data available for download at worldvaluessurvey.org.

54. "The Transcultural Leader: Carlos Ghosn, CEO of Renault, Nissan."

55. Ghosn and Riés, *Shift: Inside Nissan's Historic Revival*: 82.

56. Ibid: 81.

57. Neuliep, *Intercultural Communication: A Contextual Approach*: 29.

58. Emerson, "An Interview with Carlos Ghosn, President of Nissan Motors, Ltd. and Industry Leader of the Year."

59. Fernandez and Underwood, *China CEO: Voices of Experience from 20 International Business Leaders*: 265.

60. Millikin and Fu, "The Global Leadership of Carlos Ghosn at Nissan": 121–137.

61. Ghosn, "Saving the Business without Losing the Company."

62. Ghosn and Riés, *Shift: Inside Nissan's Historic Revival*: 167–168.

63. Chryscia Cunha, Mariana Barros, and Kelly Franca, "Brazil," retrieved April 30, 2011, from Executive Planet (http://www .executiveplanet.com/index.php?title=Brazil); Sergei Ivanchuk, "Russia," retrieved April 30, 2011, from Executive Planet (http://www.executiveplanet.com/index.php?title=Russia); Madhukar Shukla, "India," retrieved April 30, 2011, from Executive Planet (http://www.executiveplanet.com/index.php?title=India); "China," retrieved April 30, 2011, from Executive Planet (http://www .executiveplanet.com/index.php?title=China); Terri Morrison and Wayne A. Conaway, *Kiss, Bow, or Shake Hands,* 2nd ed. (Avon, MA: Adams Media, 2006).

64. New York Times Corner Office Blog, "Communication," retrieved May 2, 2011, from http://projects.nytimes.com/corner-office/ Communication.

Principles for Business Messages

PART THREE

CHAPTER FIVE

Creating Effective Business Messages

Learning Objectives

After studying this chapter, you should be able to do the following:

LO5.1 Explain the goals of effective business messages and the process for creating them.

LO5.2 Identify the needs of your audience in the AIM planning process.

LO5.3 Develop and refine business ideas in the AIM planning process.

LO5.4 Develop your primary message and key points in the AIM planning process.

LO5.5 Explain and apply positive and other-oriented tone in business messages.

You will have countless opportunities over your career to communicate important messages. Every situation will be unique and involve an array of business problems and recipients. In all your communications, however, this principle will remain constant: Effective messages emerge from a consistent planning process and a positive and other-oriented tone.

This chapter first explains the process of developing business messages. Then, we focus on the most critical stage—planning—followed by a discussion of tone. Although the chapter is concerned particularly with writing, the principles transfer effectively to any type of communication.

Throughout, we will provide examples from the chapter case about a challenging communication task. Not all communication tasks demand such rigorous planning and preparation. In fact, the majority will be fairly routine, meaning they will require less time and encounter little resistance from your readers. However, even routine messages require a strategic focus on planning and tone. As you apply these principles to your communications, you will find that you are far more effective and influential.

Chapter Case: Justifying a Wellness Program at Eastmond Networking

Who's Involved

Latisha Jackson, summer intern
- Working as a summer intern in the human resource department
- Assigned to research options for a wellness program

Jeff Brody, personnel director
- Has held current position for five years
- Trying to develop initiatives that improve employee well-being and morale amid steep budget cuts

Lisa Johnson, finance manager
- Has held current position for three years
- Specializes in developing budgets and financial forecasts

The Situation

Jeff recently asked Latisha to spend around ten hours per week to develop a wellness program as an effort to improve employee morale and productivity. However, since the company is facing major budget constraints, executives are skeptical of resource-intensive initiatives. Jeff wants Latisha to focus her attention on the financial implications of a wellness program first. He wants her to present her preliminary findings within one month.

Latisha was excited about the opportunity to keep working on the wellness program initiative, even on this limited basis. She was also slightly nervous—one month was a short time to analyze how a wellness center would impact the financial well-being of the company, and she wanted to prove she was up to the task. Each week, she gathered information. She talked to HR directors at several local businesses of roughly the same size that had implemented wellness programs in the past few years and also met with several wellness program vendors.

One of the trickiest parts of the project was estimating the financial impact of a wellness program. Latisha had taken a few classes in finance but had no real experience. So, she met with the finance manager, Lisa Johnson, and showed her the information she had collected. Lisa agreed to spend some time estimating the potential return on investment from a wellness program. Later, Lisa emailed the following:

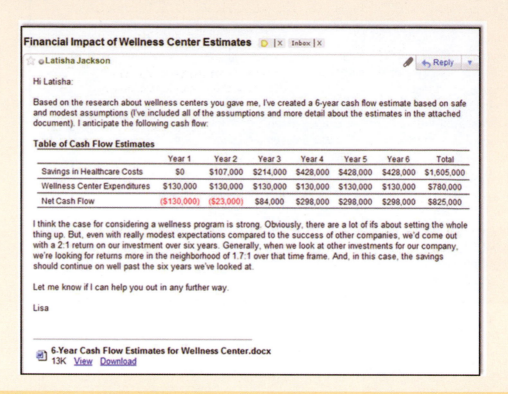

Financial Impact of Wellness Center Estimates   ⬜ | ✕   Inbox | ✕

⭐ ○ Latisha Jackson   ✏   ↩ Reply   ▼

Hi Latisha:

Based on the research about wellness centers you gave me, I've created a 6-year cash flow estimate based on safe and modest assumptions (I've included all of the assumptions and more detail about the estimates in the attached document). I anticipate the following cash flow:

Table of Cash Flow Estimates

	Year 1	Year 2	Year 3	Year 4	Year 5	Year 6	Total
Savings in Healthcare Costs	$0	$107,000	$214,000	$428,000	$428,000	$428,000	$1,605,000
Wellness Center Expenditures	$130,000	$130,000	$130,000	$130,000	$130,000	$130,000	$780,000
Net Cash Flow	($130,000)	($23,000)	$84,000	$298,000	$298,000	$298,000	$825,000

I think the case for considering a wellness program is strong. Obviously, there are a lot of ifs about setting the whole thing up. But, even with really modest expectations compared to the success of other companies, we'd come out with a 2:1 return on our investment over six years. Generally, when we look at other investments for our company, we're looking for returns more in the neighborhood of 1.7:1 over that time frame. And, in this case, the savings should continue on well past the six years we've looked at.

Let me know if I can help you out in any further way.

Lisa

📄 **6-Year Cash Flow Estimates for Wellness Center.docx**
   13K View Download

Task 1
How can Latisha address Jeff's and other key decision makers' needs and concerns? (See the "Audience Analysis" section.)

Task 2
How should Latisha organize the information she has found? (See the "Idea Development" section.)

Task 3
How should Latisha organize her message? (See the "Message Structuring" section.)

Task 4
How can Latisha strike the right tone? (See the section on setting the right tone.)

The Process for Creating Business Messages

LO5.1 Explain the goals of effective business messages and the process for creating them.

Writing effective business messages involves a process—one that involves examining, developing, and refining business ideas in a way that provides business value to your audience. The very process that we explain in this section drives excellence in business thinking. Furthermore, it drives collaboration and productivity in your work relationships.

The process of developing business messages is fairly straightforward: *plan, draft, and review.* You've likely been trained and coached in a similar process many times during your education. Nearly all business professionals have been trained in this

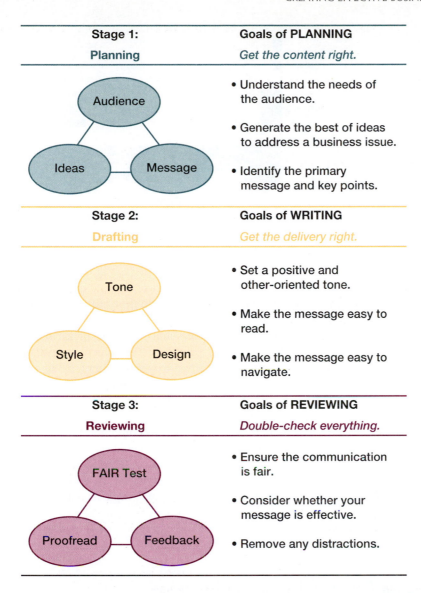

Stage 1:

Planning

Goals of PLANNING

Get the content right.

- Understand the needs of the audience.

- Generate the best of ideas to address a business issue.

- Identify the primary message and key points.

Stage 2:

Drafting

Goals of WRITING

Get the delivery right.

- Set a positive and other-oriented tone.

- Make the message easy to read.

- Make the message easy to navigate.

Stage 3:

Reviewing

Goals of REVIEWING

Double-check everything.

- Ensure the communication is fair.

- Consider whether your message is effective.

- Remove any distractions.

FIGURE 5.1

The Stages and Goals of Effective Message Creation

process. Yet few business professionals excel at it and, consequently, few business professionals produce excellent written communication. Making this process a habit requires discipline and scheduling.

Notice Figure 5.1, which depicts the stages and goals for creating effective messages. We will focus on each of the three stages (planning, drafting, and reviewing) in this chapter and the following one. It's worth noting that these stages are not necessarily linear and often overlap one another. Business writers frequently move back and forth between the stages.

Expert writers, however, more carefully and consciously break these stages apart. For example, they are more likely to analyze the needs of the audience, generate the best ideas to tackle a problem, and identify the primary message and key points before starting a formal draft of a business message. On the other hand, poor and average writers are more likely to begin drafting or writing right away. They often address planning issues—audience analysis, ideas for solving a problem, and message organization—as they go. Consequently, they tend to write in a less organized, perhaps even haphazard, manner. They generally produce less strategic and influential messages.

Developing expertise in this process makes you more effective, plus it makes you more efficient. In Figure 5.2, you'll see a chart that contrasts the time that poor, average, and expert business writers commit to planning, drafting, and reviewing. Not

FIGURE 5.2

Time Spent by Poor, Average, and Expert Writers Developing a Complete Business Message

Source: Time estimates based on author's observation of thousands of business students and consistent with decades of research about expertise as described in Michael Pressley and Christine B. McCormick, *Advanced Educational Psychology for Educators, Researchers, and Policymakers* (New York: HarperCollins, 1995).

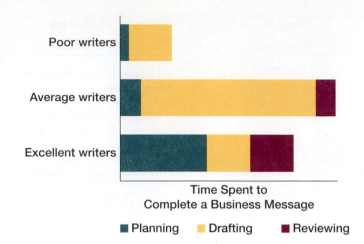

surprisingly, poor writers spend less overall time than average and expert writers. They are aimless and sloppy. They generally spend little or no time planning and usually do not review their messages before sending them.[1]

The contrast between average business writers and expert business writers is most intriguing. Expert business writers not only produce more-effective written communications, but they also do so more quickly than average writers. Their secret is to devote a much higher percentage of their time to the planning and reviewing stages. In particular, they spend far more time planning than average or poor writers. They take the time to understand the business issues well, piece together great ideas, make sure the ideas meet the needs of their audiences, and structure their messages for greatest clarity and impact. Once they start drafting, the content is essentially in place.

As you craft business messages, maintain a listener-centered approach (as opposed to a message-centered approach as described in Chapter 3). In the listener-centered approach to writing business messages, you seek as much input as reasonably possible from colleagues, clients, and customers. You ask them about their opinions, preferences, and areas of expertise. You find out what those to whom you are writing really want and expect. You adopt a learning, other-oriented approach to writing.

The AIM Planning Process for Effective Business Messages

LO5.2 Identify the needs of your audience in the AIM planning process.

The most important stage of creating effective business messages is planning. Throughout the remainder of the book, we will refer to the three-component AIM planning process for developing influential messages. It focuses on three areas: (1) *A*udience analysis; (2) *I*dea development; and (3) *M*essage structuring (see Figure 5.3). In short, the planning process should include analyzing the needs of your audience, developing sound ideas that meet those needs, and then structuring your message. The *AIM* planning process unleashes your best thinking and allows you to deliver influential messages.

Audience Analysis

Effective business communicators possess an uncanny ability to step into the shoes of their audience members. They think about their audience's needs, priorities, and values. They envision how their readers will respond when getting the message—in thought, feeling, and action. They also consider how the message will impact their working relationships. Effective business communicators regularly take the following actions to tailor their messages to others: identify reader benefits and constraints, consider reader values and priorities, estimate personal credibility, anticipate reactions, and consider secondary audiences.

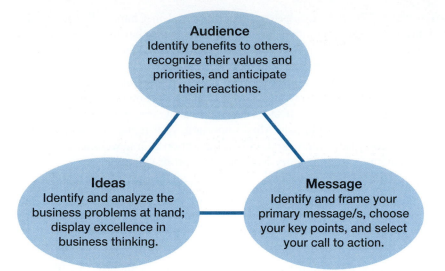

FIGURE 5.3

The AIM Planning Process for Business Messages

Identifying Reader Benefits and Constraints   For many messages, this is the single most important planning step. Simply put, your readers respond when you provide them with something that they value. When you communicate no apparent benefits, your readers are unlikely to engage.

Similarly, think about the constraints your audience faces. Your readers will often see value in your messages but may not be able to respond as you hope because they don't have enough time, resources, or authority to make certain decisions.

In Latisha's case, she can point out to Jeff many potential benefits of the wellness program. Presumably, Jeff cares about the employees and would like them to have better health. Jeff would also like to save money for the company. And, like most employees, Jeff would likely want to be associated with any successful work initiative. In this regard, Latisha's challenge is choosing which reader benefits appeal most to Jeff in this situation.

Latisha should keep in mind that no matter how much Jeff views the wellness program as beneficial, he likely faces a number of constraints. He would certainly need to get agreement for a project of this size from other members of the leadership team. So, he would need to persuade others and risk his own credibility. In addition, since the company faces a financial crisis, any initiative may be viewed with higher-than-usual scrutiny and even skepticism. Latisha should anticipate these constraints and develop her message accordingly.

Considering Reader Values and Priorities   Being an effective business communicator requires that you learn about other people—what they value, prioritize, and prefer. **Values** refer to enduring beliefs and ideals that individuals hold. Since values are at the core of belief systems, appeals to an individual's values can have strong influence. Generally, people hold workplace values—beliefs and ideals about the appropriate way to approach business problems, resolve issues, and choose goals. **Priorities** involve ranking or assigning importance to things, such as projects, goals, and tasks. Priorities tend to shift more often than values.

Latisha has not known Jeff for long, but she can attempt to understand some of his values and priorities. She believes that he is fundamentally invested in the wellness program initiative because of his strong commitment to employees. He seems to value detailed analysis and careful decision making (he leans toward a thinker communicator style). Based on his comments, he seems to prioritize efficiency and cost-cutting. This may be due to the current financial situation or it may be due to deeper, long-held values. He also refers frequently to the "company president," which suggests a respect for the chain of command. Jeff's frequent mention of the company president may mean that Jeff is under a great deal of pressure to perform according to the president's expectations.

Audience Analysis Components

- Identify reader benefits and constraints.
- Consider reader values and priorities.
- Estimate your credibility.
- Anticipate reactions.
- Consider secondary audiences.

Estimating Your Credibility As discussed in Chapter 1, your readers will inevitably judge your recommendations, requests, and other messages based on their view of your credibility. If your credibility is low, consider how to strengthen your message in ways that overcome your lack of credibility.

Many entry-level professionals face this situation; they have relatively low professional credibility because they are viewed as the newcomers. Establishing a professional reputation takes time. It takes less time, however, if you stay aware of your strengths, weaknesses, and goals. Most important, your reputation depends on adding value in the workplace. Yet, overcoming a reputation as a newcomer isn't easy. Consider this statement from an entry-level business professional:

> When my bosses first hired me, I was a novice with misguided ideas. They often ignored my suggestions with just cause. As I have learned more about our industry, and gained experience, my ideas have matured. Yet, my bosses continue to ignore my suggestions even when they have proven to be correct and insightful. How can I get my bosses to listen to my opinions and ideas when they still think of me as the young novice?[2]

Changing your reputation will likely take at least six months. To break out of a reputation as an inexperienced newcomer, consider the following options:[3]

- Set up a time to talk with your boss. Explain your growth in various areas and ask for his/her ideas about improving your professional reputation.
- Ask your boss if you can take on any higher-responsibility projects.
- Make sure you fit in with the corporate culture in terms of professional dress and communication style.
- Attend a lot of meetings to get to know as many colleagues as possible. Participate appropriately.
- Create a professional blog about a niche area.

As a newcomer, Latisha recognizes that Jeff has many reasons to doubt her credibility. She is an undergraduate business student without a degree or significant business experience. She has worked for Jeff for only a short time, so he can't make a good judgment about her ability to get things done. But he obviously saw promise in her or he wouldn't have hired her to develop a work initiative that was so important to him. Latisha felt that her credibility would be enhanced by including a trusted, competent voice in her memo. As a result, she sought the opinion of Lisa Johnson. By highlighting Lisa's estimate and opinions, Latisha elevates her own credibility. Lisa is competent in her area (finance) and reliable (she has a track record at Eastmond). Jeff will likely give more credence to Latisha's message because it references Lisa's cash flow estimate.

Anticipating Reactions In the planning stage, envision how others will respond to your message. Imagine how your readers will think, feel, and act as they read it. Always think about what you want to achieve in terms of workplace relationships. Most business activities cannot be separated from the web of working relationships involved. Sometimes your positions or ideas may displease others. In these instances, consider how you can articulate your views most constructively.

Latisha believes that Jeff will respond sensibly to a clearly articulated, logical justification of the wellness center. Based on the strength of the cash flow estimates, Latisha thinks he will respond favorably. Even if he disagrees, she assumes he will respect her hard work and reward her with challenging assignments.

Keeping Secondary Audiences in Mind In most situations, you should anticipate that individuals other than your primary recipient will view your messages. In some cases, you will distribute your message to additional individuals whom it will affect. For example, you might copy team members on a correspondence between you and a client so that they are aware of project progress. In other cases, your primary recipient will forward your message or otherwise share the information with others. You should consider which secondary audiences will view your messages and, if necessary, modify them accordingly.

Latisha recognizes that her proposal for developing a wellness program would impact everyone in the organization and would require significant resources. If Jeff finds merit in the proposal, he will undoubtedly share the message with a variety of individuals involved in the decision-making process.

Idea Development

Developing great business ideas involves sorting out the business issues and objectives, collecting as many relevant facts as possible, and making sound judgments about what the facts mean and imply. You are making sense out of often complex and confusing pieces of business information.

Excellent business thinkers possess a number of characteristics. First, they clearly and precisely identify and articulate key questions and problems. Second, they gather information from a variety of sources. Third, they make well-reasoned conclusions and solutions. Fourth, they remain open to alternatives to approaching and reasoning about the business problem—that is, they are mentally flexible. They can hold opposing views, avoid either/or thinking, avoid one-way linear thinking, and are open to nonconventional solutions. Finally, they are skilled at communicating with others to figure out and solve complex problems.[4]

Business professionals use many methods of bringing out their best thinking. Some write notes, some draw diagrams, some brainstorm with colleagues, some write ideas in outline form, and some just examine the ideas in their minds. Generally, for complex problems, such as the opening case, writing ideas down in some form is an important part of developing sound ideas. In this section, we focus on three broad areas: (1) identifying the business problem/s; (2) analyzing the business problem/s; and (3) clarifying objectives.

Identifying the Business Problem/s   To remain competitive and profitable, businesses constantly need to identify and overcome problems. One of the best reputations you can gain as a business professional is that of a problem solver. The first step in problem solving is identifying business problems. This involves understanding an organization's business objectives and related challenges. It involves asking many questions from a lot of angles.

In Latisha's case, she has been given a charge: Find out how a wellness program would impact Eastmond. This is a classic business problem. Latisha can break the problem down by asking a variety of questions: How do wellness programs impact health care costs? What benefits do health care programs deliver to employees? How do other businesses measure return on investment for wellness programs? How do wellness programs impact productivity, absenteeism, morale, retention, and recruiting?

Analyzing the Business Problem/s   Analyzing the business problem typically involves uncovering relevant facts, making conclusions, and taking positions. **Facts** are statements that can be relied on with a fair amount of certainty (most things are not absolutely certain in the business world) and can be observed objectively. **Conclusions** are statements that are reasoned or deduced based on facts. **Positions** are stances that you take based on a set of conclusions. In the workplace, you will often make recommendations, which are a type of position.

Latisha analyzed the business problem by collecting a variety of facts and making five or six broad conclusions about corporate wellness programs based on those facts (see Figure 5.4). For example, she concluded that the return on investment for wellness programs is substantial (her second-to-last conclusion) based on findings from several academic and corporate studies, listed with bullet points. This form of outlining facts and conclusions can be particularly helpful once Latisha begins writing.

Idea Development Components

- Identify the business problems.
- Analyze the business problems.
- Clarify objectives.

LO5.3 Develop and refine business ideas in the AIM planning process.

FIGURE 5.4

Analysis of Facts and Conclusions during Idea Development[5]

Analysis of Wellness Programs

Most Americans suffer poor health due to lifestyle-related issues.

- The U.S. Surgeon General has stated that about 75% of all illnesses are due to lifestyle. (American Institute for Preventive Medicine, 2008)

- 68% of Americans are overweight (BMI of 25 or greater); 34% of American adults are obese (A body mass index [BMI] of 30 or greater). (American Institute for Preventive Medicine, 2008)

- Overweight and obesity raise the risk for type 2 diabetes, high blood pressure, high cholesterol, coronary heart disease, stroke, asthma, cancers, and many other illnesses. (American Institute for Preventive Medicine, 2008)

Employees with poor health raise health care costs to employers.

- For example, compared to employees with low health risks, employees with the following conditions are associated with costs to the employer that are significantly higher: depression (70.2% higher cost); stress (46.3%); glucose (34.8%); weight (21.4%); tobacco (19.7%); blood pressure (11.7%); exercise (10.4%). (American Institute for Preventive Medicine, 2008)

Most employers make wellness programs available to their employees.

- Most companies have created wellness programs. About 73% of large companies, 56% of medium-sized companies, and 44% of small companies currently have wellness programs available to their employees. (American Institute for Preventive Medicine, 2008)

- Companies implement wellness programs for a variety of reasons. In a survey of business, the top reasons were to (1) increase employee morale; (2) improve employee health; (3) reduce health care costs; (4) reduce accidents on the job; (5) reduce absenteeism; and (6) increase productivity (8%). (American Institute for Preventive Medicine, 2008)

- Mid- to large-sized companies spend on average about 2% of their health care claim costs on wellness programs. (National Business Group on Health, 2010)

Employers benefit significantly from providing wellness programs to their employees, including lower health care costs, lower absenteeism, higher productivity, and higher morale.

- A review of 56 scientific studies about the impact of corporate wellness programs found the following average benefits:
  - % change in sick leave absenteeism: average: −26.8%
  - % change in health costs: −26.1%
  - % change in workers' compensation/disability management costs: −32.0%
- Reduced presenteeism losses. (Chapman, 2005)
- Increased productivity by 2% to 52%. (Chapman, 2005)
- A recent study of 200 people at three major corporations revealed that an employee's quality of life, mental performance, and time management were 15% better on days when they exercised. (Chapman, 2005)
- A Johnson & Johnson study showed that employees who participated in a corporate wellness program reported more positive attitudes in organizational commitment, supervision, working conditions, job competence/security, and pay/benefits. (Chapman, 2005)

The return on investment (ROI) for corporate wellness programs is substantial.

- Studies generally indicate a $4–$6:$1 ROI for wellness programs. In terms of just medical costs: $3.93 (28 studies); absenteeism: $5.07 (18 studies); medical costs, absenteeism, and workers' comp: $5.93 (42 studies); and medical costs and absenteeism: $5.81 (56 studies). (George, 2008)

- Many companies and organizations have reported the impact of their wellness programs. For example, the following companies reported the following ROIs: Northeast Utilities: 6:1; Motorola: 3.93:1; Wisconsin Education Insurance Group: 4.75:1.; DuPont: 1.42:1 due to reduced absenteeism; Citibank: 4.56:1; Bank of America: 5.96:1; General Mills: 3.50:1; Washoe County School District: 15.6:1; Pfizer: 4.29:1 for fitness centers. (George, 2008)

- For employees who participate in wellness programs, significant savings occur. Just by enrolling in fitness programs, companies can save hundreds of dollars. Coca-Cola reported saving $500 per person who enrolled in a corporate fitness program. Pacific Bell reported $300 in savings. Prudential Insurance reported $262. (George, 2008)

- Savings reach optimal point in years 3 or 4. (George, 2008)
- Reduced health care costs by 20% to 55%. (George, 2008)

FIGURE 5.4

(Continued)

Companies have many decisions to make when implementing wellness programs.

- Corporate wellness programs are diverse. Hundreds of national and local companies specialize in providing corporate wellness programs. Many companies, especially large companies, develop in-house wellness programs. The range of services offered is immense. Among mid- to large-sized companies, the average number of wellness programs offered is 21.

- For companies with wellness programs, the most common incentives are: premium reductions (34%); cash/bonuses (20%); merchandise (19%); gift cards (17%); other incentives (17%); and health account contributions (13%). (Capps, 2007)

- For wellness programs, about 45% of corporate expenses are devoted to prevention and lifestyle wellness and about 43% to disease/illness management (after onset of illness). The most common prevention and lifestyle programs include employee assistance programs (92%), on-site flu shots (90%), stress management (68%), preventive-care reminders related to screenings or annual exams (68%), and smoking cessation (66%). The most common condition-management programs include nurse hotlines, diabetes disease management, coronary artery disease management, congestive heart failure management, and asthma disease management. (American Institute for Preventive Medicine, 2008)

Latisha also relied on insiders for information. She asked Lisa Johnson, the company's finance manager, to estimate the financial impact a wellness program would have on health care costs and revenues (see details in the opening chapter case). In many cases, you conduct data gathering and analysis within your networks of colleagues and other business partners.

Clarifying Objectives As you develop the ideas for your message, also clearly identify your goals. You are essentially asking yourself, "Now that I understand the problem, what exactly do I want to accomplish?" Knowing how committed you are to various work outcomes will help you decide how hard to push certain positions. It will also help you balance your preferred work outcomes with your work relationships.

Latisha has carefully thought about her attitudes toward developing a wellness program. She is certain she wants the chance to work on the initiative. She is passionate about this issue and wants to gain experience combining her interests in management and health. Latisha has thought about whether her self-interests are too strong. But, she feels confident that this initiative is good for the company: It will benefit the employees and it will save the company money. She is committed to taking a strong position.

Message Structuring

Once you have analyzed the needs of your audience and developed your ideas for the message, you plan the basic message structure. This includes identifying and framing the primary message and setting up the logic with supporting points and a call to action. The set of questions you will address include the following:

1. *Framing the primary message.*
   a. What is the primary message?
   b. What simple, vivid statement (15 words or less) captures the essence of your message?
2. *Setting up the logic of your message.*
   a. What are your supporting points?
   b. What do you want to explicitly ask your readers to do (call to action)?
   c. How will you order the logic of your message?

Framing the Primary Message Framing involves showcasing a message from an overarching theme. It focuses a reader or listener on a certain key idea or argument and highlights the premises and support for this key idea or argument. As one

LO5.4 Develop your primary message and key points in the AIM planning process.

Message Structuring Components

- Frame the primary message.
- Set up the structure and logic of the message.

management communication expert said, "No communication skill . . . is more critical to the manager than the ability to frame an issue effectively."[6] Your job in framing the message is to help your reader see the issue from a strategic perspective. Just as a frame draws out particular aspects of a painting, the frame you apply to your message can create a unique prism through which your audience will read.

Strategic communicators consider alternative frames before they settle on the one that will be most compelling. Ideally, it should be a vivid statement with rational and emotional appeal. One standard you'll encounter frequently in this book is whether a reader would remember the frame later. Regarding your frame, ask questions such as the following: Will readers remember my primary message two hours from now? What about in two days or two weeks? Will this frame make readers more likely to support my call to action?[7]

The art of creating effective frames involves capturing your primary message in a short, memorable statement of 15 words or less. Eduardo Castro-Wright, president and CEO of Wal-Mart Stores USA, discussed this strategy in the context of organizational communication:

> I've worked 30 years now in management roles, and a number of times I've seen a new CEO come in, and the first act is typically to get the leadership team to an offsite. And you get a consultant—because you can't do it without a consultant—and the consultant then helps the team design a vision. And then you've got all these words, and several thousand dollars and a couple of days of golf later, you go back to the company to actually try to communicate that vision throughout the organization. So you hire another consultant to do that. It shouldn't be like that. We have a very clear view of what we do for consumers around the world. And we can describe our complete strategy in 10 words. And that makes it very easy to get everybody energized and aligned.[8]

As Latisha was thinking about how to justify the wellness program, she came up with three options for framing the message:

Frame A—creating a wellness program is the right thing to do. We are responsible for our employees.

Frame B—creating a wellness program will cut costs and improve morale at the same time.

Frame C—wellness programs will increase our profitability.

She thinks each frame is powerful. She personally relates to Frame A with her passion for physical fitness and personal health. However, she thinks this case is weakest in the current financial situation and with Jeff's apparent budgetary limitations. She believes that Frame B is strong. The company needs to cut costs, and Jeff has explicitly noted the company president's interest in improving morale. She also believes that Frame C is strong. The emphasis on profitability is a broader concept; it is the ultimate measure of strong financial performance and encompasses not just lower expenses but also increased revenues.

The choice between Frame B and Frame C is difficult. Ultimately, Latisha selects Frame C for several reasons. First, Frame C has stronger external (from other companies) and internal evidence (from Lisa's cash flow estimate). With Jeff's preference for brief, to-the-point, result-oriented, and well-reasoned positions, she believes this frame is best suited for this communication approach. Second, she believes the concept of profitability emphasizes the return on investment for this project more so than any other frame. She wants to emphasize that a wellness program is an asset—not a liability of any sort.

Setting Up the Message Framework

Most business arguments employ a **direct** or **deductive** approach. In other words, they begin by stating the primary message, which is typically a position or recommendation. Then they lay out the supporting reasons. Most business messages conclude with a call to action. The call to action in many cases is a more detailed and elaborate version of the initial position or recommendation.

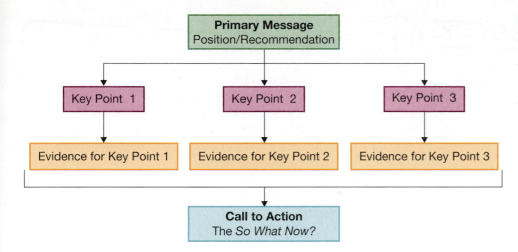

FIGURE 5.5

Typical Deductive Framework
for a Business Argument and
Related Paragraph Structure

Typical Paragraph Organization in a Deductive Business Message	Deductive Business Message Components
Primary message as topic sentence. xx xxxxxxxxxxxxxxxxxxxxxxxxxxxxxxxxxxxx xxxxxxxxxxxxxxxxxxxxxxxxxxxxxxx. *Preview sentence.* *Key Point 1* as topic sentence. xxxxxxxxxx xxxxxxxxxxxxxxxxxxxxxxxxxxxxxxxxxxxx xxxxxxxxxxxxxxxxxxxxxxxxxxxxxxxxxxxxx xxxx. *Key Point 2* as topic sentence. xxxxxxxxxx xxxxxxxxxxxxxxxxxxxxxxxxxxxxxxxxxxxx xxxxxxxxxx. *Key Point 3* as topic sentence. xxxxxxxxxx xxxxxxxxxxxxxxxxxxxxxxxxxxxxxxxxxxxx xxxxxxxxxx. *Call to action* as topic sentence. xxxxxxxxxx xxxxxxxxxxxxxxxxxxxxxxxxxxxxxxxxxxxx xxxxxxxxxxxxxxxxxxxxxxxxxxxxxxxxxxxxxx.	**Opening Paragraph** • *Primary message* as topic sentence. • *Preview sentence* as concluding sentence: We should do [position] because of Key Point 1, Key Point 2, and Key Point 3. **Body** • *Supporting paragraphs* for each key point. • *Key points* as topic sentences. • Most paragraphs are three to five sentences and 40 to 100 words. **Concluding Paragraph** • *Restates* primary message. • Contains a *call to action*—specific steps to be taken.

Figure 5.5 illustrates the framework of most deductive business arguments. Generally, a reader could get the gist of your message—the primary message, rationale, and call to action—simply by reading the opening paragraph, the first sentence of each supporting paragraph, and the final paragraph. In fact, many of your readers, who are generally busy, will do exactly that. They will skim the communication to understand the main ideas and implications. If they see merit in your ideas, they will go back and read the entire message more carefully.

In upcoming chapters, we will focus on many types of messages for common business situations. The framework for these various messages may differ slightly from the one illustrated in Figure 5.5. For some messages such as when delivering bad news (see Chapter 10), you may adopt a more **indirect** or **inductive** approach, in which you will provide supporting reasons first followed by the primary message. In all messages, however, the importance of framing and arranging supporting ideas to accentuate the main idea remains the same.

One option for setting up the structure and appearance of various documents is to use templates. For ideas on enhancing the structure and appearance of various types of business messages, see the Technology Tips feature on page 128.

When you are setting up the logic of your message, you may find that sketching out or diagramming it is helpful. Latisha's logic for Frame C involves the claim that

TECHNOLOGY TIPS

USING TEMPLATES

You will set up many types of business messages. One way to help you create a framework and format for some types of business messages is to use templates. Templates can help you organize your messages and make them visually appealing. You can search through hundreds of templates at Microsoft's website as well as other online sources for memos, business reports, cover letters, résumés, and other types of business messages.

As you use templates, consider the following advice:

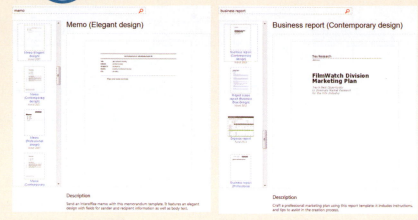

- Choose templates that help you accentuate your primary message and key points.

- Avoid templates with too much formatting. Ironically, templates that are too heavy in visual design may draw attention away from your message.

- Modify template formatting to make your own unique design. Many templates are used so frequently that they are unoriginal (this is especially the case for PowerPoint templates).

a wellness program will increase profitability. It will do so directly through reducing health care costs and indirectly through increasing revenues. To support this frame, she is making the case that a wellness program will directly decrease absenteeism and increase productivity, which will then increase revenues. By diagramming her logic, she tightens her thinking about the problem and transfers her ideas more effectively into written form (Figure 5.6).

FIGURE 5.6

Message Structure for Latisha's Justification of a Wellness Program

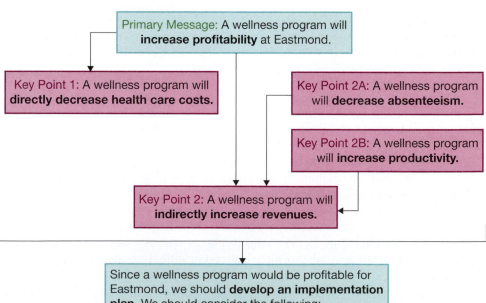

TABLE 5.1

Avoiding Unsupported Generalizations

Less Effective	More Effective
A wellness program would reduce absenteeism because our employees would be sick less and feel more energetic.	We can expect that a wellness program will reduce absenteeism. A recent review of 56 scientific studies of corporate wellness programs showed that once the program was in place, sick leave absenteeism was an average of 27 percent lower. In our case, the average employee takes seven sick leave days per year. Assuming a similar reduction in sick leave absenteeism for our 200 full-time employees, we could gain approximately 380 additional work days per year from our employees.
Without any supporting facts, this broad generalization will be viewed skeptically by many readers.	This statement confidently states an expectation based on research and shows how findings from the research could apply to this situation.

As you set up the structure of the message, carefully test its logic. Business decisions are consequential. Seasoned businesspeople expect solid business logic to support important decisions, and they dismiss ideas that are based on flimsy reasoning. If you ensure that your messages are built on strong reasoning, you will be far more influential because your company will benefit and you will gain credibility.[9] To build well-reasoned business positions, avoid the following types of logical inconsistencies: unsupported generalizations, faulty cause/effect claims, weak analogies, either/or logic, slanting the facts, and exaggeration.

Avoiding Unsupported Generalizations This issue boils down to providing supporting facts for your claims. As you look at the examples in Table 5.1, notice that the less-effective example is a blanket claim without support. The more-effective example provides a variety of supporting facts.

Avoiding Faulty Cause/Effect Claims As you analyze business issues, you are often trying to identify causes and effects. For example, when proposing new initiatives, you will generally claim that your actions will *cause* a certain result. The ability to precisely predict effects is always tricky, so choose your language and reasoning carefully. If readers are troubled by one of your cause/effect claims, they will become increasingly picky about your reasoning throughout the message (see Table 5.2).

Avoiding Weak Analogies As you make sense of business issues, you will often try to identify analogies with other organizations, people, or things. Strong analogies serve to bolster your arguments. However, weak analogies may lead to inaccurate conclusions and recommendations. Be sure that the analogies you make are based on close and relevant similarities (see Table 5.3).

Avoiding Either/Or Logic One of the main characteristics of critical thinking is to remain flexible and open to alternative explanations and options. In business, you will always want to stay aware of alternative ways of solving the same problem. Furthermore, most of your readers will respond better to you when they view you as flexible and open to other ideas (including their own). In the less-effective example in

TABLE 5.2

Avoiding Faulty Cause/Effect Claims

Less Effective	More Effective
Lisa Johnson's calculations show that Eastmond will definitely save at least $820,000 over the next six years by implementing a wellness program.	Lisa Johnson's initial estimates show that Eastmond could achieve net savings of about $820,000 over the next six years by implementing a wellness program. She emphasized that her estimates are "safe" and "modest." In other words, she used assumptions that projected low-end savings and high-end expenses. She estimated that Eastmond would save approximately $1.6 million in health care costs over six years. It would cost approximately $780,000 to run and manage the wellness program over this time period (see Lisa's attached estimate for assumptions and other details).
This statement assumes that a wellness program will result in a definite result: at least $820,000 in savings. The certainty of this claim would raise skepticism among many readers.	This statement provides facts, assumptions, and calculations to make a confident estimate. The statements are carefully crafted to avoid stating absolute outcomes.
Last year we turned down two major contracts worth nearly $100,000 due to a lack of personnel. This was in large part due to low employee productivity on other projects, which occurs because our employees do not have access to a wellness program.	Last year we turned down two major contracts worth nearly $100,000 due to a lack of personnel. Were we to have our employees working at their highest levels of performance, perhaps we would be able to accept profitable projects such as those. Implementing a wellness program is one approach to improving productivity and potentially gaining more contracts.
This statement casually states several causes that are nearly impossible to demonstrate convincingly. The most unconvincing claim—without strong evidence—is that the lack of a wellness program caused the company to turn down two contracts.	This statement does not attribute low productivity in the past as the single cause of turned-down projects. Rather, it focuses on wellness programs as a possible contributor to increased productivity, which could result in more business opportunities for the company. The language is measured and objective.

TABLE 5.3

Avoiding Weak Analogies

Less Effective	More Effective
Since many companies such as Coca-Cola and Prudential have lowered health care costs by up to 55 percent after implementing wellness programs, we can assume similar savings when we start our program.	In studies of wellness programs, small companies such as ours typically achieve savings of 20 to 35 percent within three years. Therefore, in her estimate, Lisa assumed that Eastmond will achieve 20 percent savings by the fourth year of implementation.
This statement is a weaker analogy because it compares a smaller organization, Eastmond, with large organizations that can take a different approach in terms of personnel, resources, and program options. Readers in smaller organizations would consider this a weak analogy.	This statement is a stronger analogy because it makes an analogy to similar-sized organizations with similar resources and constraints. Readers are far more likely to consider this a credible analogy.

Table 5.4, the claim is that wellness programs are the only way to increase employee morale—that is, *either we provide a wellness program and improve employee morale, or we don't provide a wellness program and continue to have low morale.* In the more-effective claim, providing a wellness program is still identified as a way of increasing employee morale. However, this claim does not eliminate other options for improving employee morale.

Avoiding Slanting the Facts Slanting means only presenting those facts that are favorable to your position. To maintain your credibility, avoid slanting in all cases. While slanting may provide short-term benefits, many executives and managers have lost a lifetime of credibility when their gross misrepresentation was exposed. At a minimum, when readers notice that you have slanted the facts, they will be skeptical of the logic and reasoning of your entire message (see Table 5.5).

Avoiding Exaggeration As with slanting, exaggeration impacts readers' perceptions of your overall credibility as well as the credibility of the message. Be careful not to make exaggerated claims, as illustrated in Table 5.6.

TABLE 5.4

Avoiding Either/Or Logic

Less Effective	More Effective
Without providing a wellness program, employees will continue to suffer from low morale.	Providing a wellness program is one option for improving employee morale.
This logic is either/or: without a wellness program, employees will have low morale; with a wellness program, they will have high morale.	This statement does not imply that a wellness program is the only option for improving employee morale. Readers will perceive this statement as confident but grounded and measured.

TABLE 5.5

Avoiding Slanting the Facts

Less Accurate	More Accurate
Many studies have been conducted about improved productivity due to wellness programs, with productivity increases of up to 52 percent.	Many studies have been conducted about improved productivity due to wellness programs, with productivity increases ranging between 2 and 52 percent.
This statement leaves out the bottom of the range to imply higher productivity increases.	This statement provides the bottom of the range and thus provides complete information.

TABLE 5.6

Avoiding Exaggeration

Less Effective	More Effective
A wellness program would completely change our work environment for the better, allowing us to reach levels of performance previously unimagined.	A wellness program could significantly improve morale, an issue that our company president is particularly interested in.
Many readers would view this statement with skepticism since the language seems exaggerated and unbelievable. This would lead some readers to call into question the credibility of the writer and the entire message.	This statement projects confidence but does not contain exaggerated, unrealistic, or overly ambitious language.

Setting the Tone of the Message

Principles for Setting the Right Tone

- Demonstrate positivity.
- Show concern for others.

LO5.5 Explain and apply positive and other-oriented tone in business messages.

How many times have you heard phrases such as these? "It's not what he said, but how he said it," or "She said one thing but meant another." People often build resistance not to the content of a message but to the way it is delivered. One of your primary goals as a communicator is to express your messages in ways that respect and inspire others. Readers judge a message partially by its **tone**—the overall evaluation the reader perceives the writer to have toward the reader and the message content. Readers will judge your message based on how positive and concerned they think you are.

Business communicators generally aim to project positivity and concern for others in all business messages. By following the suggestions in this section, you will more effectively project messages with these tones. Many of the examples provided focus on the sentence level (primarily due to space constraints). However, tone is generally perceived across an entire message. Applying these principles across an entire message will dramatically alter the overall tone of the message.

Positivity

A positive attitude in the workplace improves work performance, allows more creativity, provides more motivation to excel, facilitates more helpfulness between coworkers, and gains more influence on clients and customers.[10] Bottom line, your ability to remain positive and exude optimism in your communications can strongly influence others. You can adopt a number of techniques to make your messages more positive.

Display a Can-Do, Confident Attitude Focus on actions you can accomplish, and demonstrate a realistic optimism, as illustrated in Table 5.7. At the same time, be careful not to exaggerate or set unrealistic expectations.

Focus on the Positive Rather Than Negative Traits of Products and Services Emphasize what products and services are rather than what they are not (see Table 5.8).

Use Diplomatic, Constructive Terms Related to Your Relationships and Interactions Find ways to avoid terms that unnecessarily focus on differences and may imply opposing or even adversarial relationships or positions (see Table 5.9).

TABLE 5.7

Displaying a Can-Do, Confident Attitude

Less Effective	More Effective
Let me know if you want me to keep working on the implementation plan.	I look forward to putting together a detailed implementation plan.
This statement is weak—it expresses little enthusiasm or passion for pursuing this project.	This statement is strong. It expresses an enthusiasm for putting together a successful plan.
Based on the information I have access to, and if everything goes according to Lisa's analysis, I think that a wellness program might increase profitability at Eastmond.	Based on a cash flow estimate from Lisa Johnson in Finance and other studies about corporate wellness programs, we can be confident that a wellness program here at Eastmond would increase profitability.
This statement is qualified with too many weak words—*based on . . ., if, think, might.* Collectively, these words display a lack of confidence in the program.	This statement expresses confidence that the program will be profitable based on well-developed estimates. It does not seem exaggerated.

TABLE 5.8

Focusing on Positive Traits

Less Effective	More Effective
A wellness program is not just an exercise program.	A wellness program is a comprehensive approach to preventive health care.
Without any additional elaboration, this sentence does not provide any positive information about a wellness program.	This sentence effectively frames the positive and total impacts of a wellness program. It is a strategic statement.
A wellness program is not a perk.	A wellness program would be an asset to our company, bringing in a strong return on investment.
Without any follow-up sentences, this statement falls short of what it could accomplish with positive phrasing.	This positive statement effectively frames the wellness program as an asset.

TABLE 5.9

Using Diplomatic, Constructive Terms

Less Effective	More Effective
I would like to present my argument for why we should continue with the wellness program initiative.	Thank you for giving me a few weeks to provide you with some additional information about how wellness programs could benefit Eastmond.
The term *argument* unnecessarily implies contention and difference of opinion.	This statement prefaces the goal of the communication with a compliment, which is a show of solidarity.
Your characterization of the wellness program as a perk is inaccurate since the wellness program would actually save the company money.	The wellness program would feel like a perk to employees, which could boost morale. Yet, unlike most perks, it would actually save us money.
The phrase *your characterization* immediately creates a me-versus-you tone.	By stating the perception of the wellness program being a perk in neutral terms, the statement would not be perceived as confrontational or divisive.

Concern for Others

In every facet of business communication, focusing on others is important. It is a basic component of your credibility (caring). In content and form, your message should show that you have the interests of your audience in mind. Therefore, avoid any sense of self-centeredness. Also aim for a tone that is inviting—that implies your interest in your readers' opinions, feelings, needs, and wants. The following guidelines will help you demonstrate concern for others (also referred to as *other-oriented language* in some parts of the book).

Avoid Relying Too Heavily on the I-Voice The subject of a sentence almost always becomes the focus or emphasis. Generally, place the focus on your reader (you-voice), your shared interests with the reader (we-voice), or simply the business issue at hand (impersonal voice). Table 5.10 provides guidelines for selecting appropriate subjects for sentences.

Typically, readers sense tone over an entire message. The guidelines for choosing appropriate subjects for your sentences influence tone—for good or bad—over the entirety of a paragraph or message. Notice in Table 5.11 how the repeated use of the

TABLE 5.10

Using You-Voice, We-Voice, Impersonal Voice, and I-Voice Appropriately

	Appropriate Situations	**Examples**
You-Voice	*Use when focus is solely on the reader.* It is particularly well suited to describing how products and services benefit customers, clients, and colleagues. *Avoid* when pointing out the mistakes of others or when the statement may be presumptuous.	**Effective:** You will receive regular updates about preventive health care workshops and other opportunities after you enroll in the wellness program. **Effective:** You may be interested in Lisa's cash flow analysis. She found that a wellness center would save approximately $825,000 over six years.
We-Voice	*Use when focus is on shared efforts, interests, and problems.* It is particularly well suited to messages within a company (i.e., work team).	**Effective:** Were we to have our employees available more often and working at their highest levels of performance, we might not be forced to turn down lucrative projects such as those. **Effective:** We could further discuss the estimates for how a wellness program could impact Eastmond.
Impersonal Voice	*Use when rational and neutral analysis is expected.* It is well suited for explaining business ideas, plans, and reports.	**Effective:** A wellness program would directly reduce health care costs and indirectly increase revenue through lower absenteeism and higher productivity. **Effective:** The implementation plan would include five components.
I-Voice	*Use with nonthreatening verbs (i.e., think, feel) when there is bad news, difference of opinion, or even blame involved.* It is well suited for situations that could result in personal disappointments. Used most often in oral communication.	**Effective:** I think right now is not the right time to focus on a wellness program. **Effective:** I think your ideas about the wellness program make a lot of sense, but the company is not in a position to make the initial investments to get it started.

TABLE 5.11

Ineffective Use of I-Voice

Less Effective	**More Effective**
I would like to know as soon as possible when you could meet. I want to go over the estimates with you to show you how strong the case is for pursuing this option. Also, I have developed a timeline for writing the implementation plan that I want to show you right away.	Please let me know when there is a convenient time to meet. We could further discuss the estimates for how a wellness program could impact Eastmond. Also, if you think we should pursue the wellness program initiative, we could discuss the timeline for developing an implementation plan.
The repeated use of I-voice may be perceived as self-centered, inconsiderate, or pushy.	The repeated use of we-voice will likely be perceived as team-oriented and flexible.
I've set up the wellness program so that you will have access to exercise programs, health workshops, immunization shots, preventive care checkups, and disease management options. I'm especially proud of the exercise programs that I have set up. In my experience, I always work better when I've gotten exercise. I'm more productive and worry-free. I also want you to know that there are incentives to participate in the wellness program. For example, I've made sure that you will get $200 taken off your annual deductible if you enroll in the wellness program.	The wellness program will provide you with many options for managing your personal health, including exercise programs, health workshops, immunization shots, preventive care checkups, and disease management options. Ideally, participation in the various exercise programs will take some of your stress and worries away. You will have a variety of incentives available for enrolling in the program. For example, you will get $200 taken off of your annual deductible as soon as you enroll.
The repeated use of I-voice may come off as self-absorbed or insincere.	The repeated use of you-voice frames everything in terms of reader benefits.

I-voice amplifies the self-centered tone, whereas the repeated use of we-voice and you-voice amplifies a tone that reflects other-orientation.

Respect the Time and Autonomy of Your Readers The business world can be a hectic, deadline-filled environment. In many situations you will want fast responses. If you show consideration for others' time as well as for their sense of autonomy, you will often achieve your intended results more effectively than if your words sound bossy and demanding (see Table 5.12). Keep in mind that statements you can say with a nonpushy tone may be decoded as pushy when in written form.

Give Credit to Others *What comes around goes around* is a maxim that holds true in many situations in the business world. Show your genuine appreciation and sincere recognition for the efforts of others (see Table 5.13), and it will pay off in many ways, including through improved camaraderie and willingness of others to give you ample and deserved credit in other situations. In short, make sure not to take credit for the work of others.

TABLE 5.12

Showing Respect for Time and Autonomy

Less Effective	More Effective
Call me as soon as you get out of your meeting.	Please give me a call when it's convenient.
This abrupt and demanding sentence would sound bossy to some people.	Using the courteous term *please* and focusing on the message recipient's convenience (rather than your own) shows respect.
We need to meet before Monday to go over the proposal. Have your administrative assistant set up a time for us and get back to me as soon as you know a time.	I think discussing the proposal with you before Monday would give us a chance to include your ideas in the proposal before we submit it on Wednesday. I'm available anytime before noon on Thursday or Friday. Is there a time that works for you? We could meet at your office or talk by phone.
These sentences will be interpreted as overly demanding to some readers. In written form, these statements can easily be misinterpreted.	These statements focus on achieving results together by a deadline while still respecting the time of the message recipient.

TABLE 5.13

Giving Credit to Others

Less Effective	More Effective
The wellness program could also impact revenues at Eastmond.	Lisa also helped me understand how a wellness program could impact revenues at Eastmond.
This statement implies that the writer is responsible for this analysis.	This statement implies that Lisa was instrumental in the analysis.
I gave Lisa information about wellness programs so she could plug the numbers in and see what it meant for Eastmond. As I anticipated, the estimate showed that Eastmond would save about $825,000 over six years.	Lisa Johnson's initial estimates of potential savings due to a wellness program show that Eastmond could save about $825,000 over the next six years by implementing a wellness program.
These statements give credit to Lisa yet imply that the *real* analysis was conducted by the writer.	This sentence gives full credit to Lisa for her time-consuming, thorough, and insightful work.

FIGURE 5.7

Latisha's Memo to Justify a Wellness Program

Underlining is added to distinguish between facts, conclusions, and positions. Refer to Figure 5.6 to see how the planned message structure matches the final document.

To:	Jeff Brody, Personnel Director
From:	Latisha Jackson, Intern
Date:	June 14, 2013
Subject:	Increasing Profitability with a Corporate Wellness Program

> Primary message as subject line and topic sentence.

Thank you for giving me a few weeks to provide you with some additional information about how wellness programs could benefit Eastmond.

Based on a cash flow estimate from Lisa Johnson in Finance and other studies about corporate wellness programs, we can be confident that a wellness program here at Eastmond would increase profitability. A wellness program would directly reduce health care costs and indirectly increase revenue through lower absenteeism and higher productivity.

Reduced Expenses Due to Wellness Program

> **Key Point 1.** Most important key point placed first for emphasis.

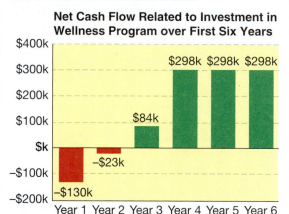

Net Cash Flow Related to Investment in Wellness Program over First Six Years

$400k
$300k $298k $298k $298k
$200k
$100k $84k
$k
–$100k   –$23k
–$200k –$130k
Year 1 Year 2 Year 3 Year 4 Year 5 Year 6

Assumptions: 1. Per-employee savings are 0% of health care costs ($10,700 annually) at Year 1; 5% at Year 2; 10% at Year 3; 20% at Year 4 and after; 2. Per-employee costs to run a wellness program are $650 per year.

> **Key Point 2A.**

Lisa Johnson's initial estimates show that Eastmond could *achieve net savings of about $820,000 over the next six years by implementing a wellness program*. She emphasized that her estimates are "safe" and "modest." In other words, she used assumptions that projected low-end savings and high-end expenses. She estimated that Eastmond would save approximately $1.6 million in health care costs over six years. It would cost approximately $780,000 to run and manage the wellness program over this time period (see Lisa's attached estimate for assumptions and other details).

Increased Revenue Due to Wellness Program

We can expect that a wellness program will reduce absenteeism. A recent review of 56 scientific studies about corporate wellness programs showed that sick leave absenteeism was lowered by an average of 27 percent. In our case, the average employee takes seven sick leave days per year. Assuming a similar reduction in sick leave absenteeism for our 200 full-time employees, we would gain approximately 380 work days per year from our employees.

Sending the Right Meta Messages

A related notion to tone is that of meta messages. Whereas tone relates to the overall attitudes or feelings that writers convey toward a message and its recipients, **meta messages** are the overall but often underlying messages people take away from a communication or group of communications. Meta messages are encoded and decoded as a combination of content, tone, and other signals.

In your written and oral communications, think about the lasting meta messages you send. Over the course of many communications—conversations, email exchanges, content on user profiles, comments on social networking websites, discussions during meetings—you send meta messages that become the basis for your reputation. These meta messages form others' impressions of your credibility: your

FIGURE 5.7

(*Continued*)

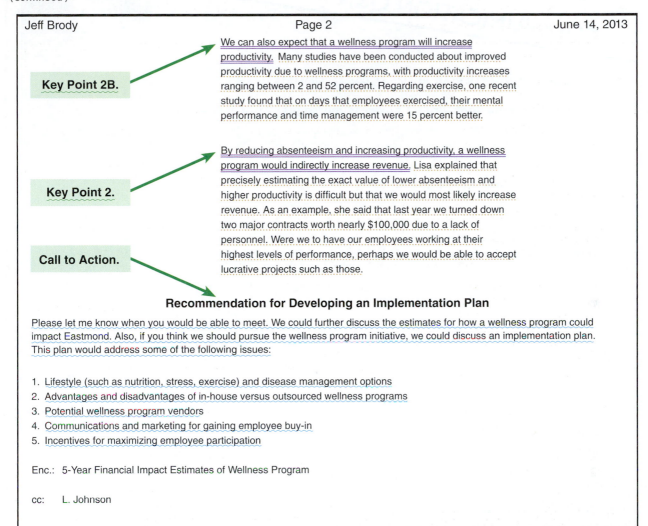

Jeff Brody   Page 2   June 14, 2013

Key Point 2B.

We can also expect that a wellness program will increase productivity. Many studies have been conducted about improved productivity due to wellness programs, with productivity increases ranging between 2 and 52 percent. Regarding exercise, one recent study found that on days that employees exercised, their mental performance and time management were 15 percent better.

Key Point 2.

By reducing absenteeism and increasing productivity, a wellness program would indirectly increase revenue. Lisa explained that precisely estimating the exact value of lower absenteeism and higher productivity is difficult but that we would most likely increase revenue. As an example, she said that last year we turned down two major contracts worth nearly $100,000 due to a lack of personnel. Were we to have our employees working at their highest levels of performance, perhaps we would be able to accept lucrative projects such as those.

Call to Action.

Recommendation for Developing an Implementation Plan

Please let me know when you would be able to meet. We could further discuss the estimates for how a wellness program could impact Eastmond. Also, if you think we should pursue the wellness program initiative, we could discuss an implementation plan. This plan would address some of the following issues:

1. Lifestyle (such as nutrition, stress, exercise) and disease management options
2. Advantages and disadvantages of in-house versus outsourced wellness programs
3. Potential wellness program vendors
4. Communications and marketing for gaining employee buy-in
5. Incentives for maximizing employee participation

Enc.: 5-Year Financial Impact Estimates of Wellness Program

cc: L. Johnson

---

competence, caring, and character. Some positive meta messages that business professionals might hope to send include "I'm skilled in my area" (competence), "I want you to succeed on this project" (caring), and "I will follow our corporate code of conduct" (character).

Mixed signals occur when the content of a message conflicts with the tone, nonverbal communication, or other signals. Sending mixed signals is not only confusing, but it also frequently results in negative meta messages. Even if a business message is well reasoned and justified, if readers perceive a selfish or manipulative tone, they may decode meta messages such as "I'm not being straight with you" or "I'm opportunistic." In a job interview, an applicant may say the right things but because of unprofessional dress send meta messages such as "I'm not serious about this job" or "I don't understand the culture of this company."

Notice Latisha's final memo in Figure 5.7. It is well analyzed, positive, and other-oriented. She intends the memo to appeal logically and emotionally to Jeff and others

COMMUNICATION Q&A

CONVERSATIONS WITH CURRENT BUSINESS PROFESSIONALS

Pete Cardon: For important written business messages, what process do you go through?

Kim Asbill: First, I listen. I also ask a lot of questions. The more, the better! Sometimes I brainstorm and come to a meeting prepared with a list of questions. Some clients communicate better verbally, and they tell you their business message. That's when you take really good notes and try to repeat and rephrase what they are saying to demonstrate understanding. Other clients respond best to written information. In that case, I often craft a message on my own based on my knowledge of the situation and use the written document to communicate back and forth until the message is correct.

Kim Asbill *is the owner of Asbill Public Relations and a public relations manager at SCANA. She has worked in public relations for various businesses and organizations for over two decades.*

PC: What strategies do you use to get the right tone in your writing?

KA: You have to know your audience to get the right tone. When I worked at an ad agency, one of our clients was Nickelodeon cable TV network. We worked on a campaign called "The Big Help" designed to encourage kids to volunteer in their communities. For that client, the tone was very informal and fun. You weren't allowed to use the word *child*. You had to use *kid*. You can imagine, writing for a bank or an electric utility would be much more formal. You have to know what your goal is too. Are you trying to get more customers to eat at a local restaurant? Maybe you are using a persuasive tone. Are you informing young mothers about how to install a car seat properly? Maybe your tone is focused on a step-by-step process.

PC: How do you think business writing is changing?

KA: I think the digital media age has changed business writing profoundly. Email was the first thing to change the way people communicate in business. The need for good writers in the workplace is more important than ever. The ability for these writers to communicate correctly for different audiences in a variety of mediums, traditional and digital, is what will set them apart in this new age of technology.

PC: What advice would you give young professionals about writing effective messages in the business world?

KA: Write. Write all the time! Think before you write. Use outlines. Remember your audience. Less is more. Read good writing. Attend workshops on writing; even webinars are great. Volunteer your writing skills to organizations you care about. Don't be shy about asking someone to proof your work. And never stop learning!

who read it. Ideally, it will send meta messages such as "I can be trusted with important projects" or "A wellness program makes financial sense for this company, and I'm the right person to continue working on it."

In addition to reviewing the final memo for its tone and meta messages, take a few moments to notice its logic and structure. It contains color-coded underlining to distinguish between facts, conclusions, and positions. Immediately following the final memo, you'll find the Communication Q&A, which offers additional insights as it provides one business professional's ideas and approaches to crafting effective messages.

Chapter Takeaway for *Creating Effective Messages*

LO 5.1. Explain the goals of effective business messages and the process for creating them. (pp. 118–120)

The Stages and Goals of Effective Message Creation

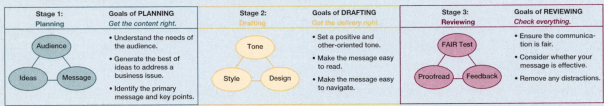

Stage 1: Planning	Goals of PLANNING *Get the content right.*	Stage 2: Drafting	Goals of DRAFTING *Get the delivery right.*	Stage 3: Reviewing	Goals of REVIEWING *Check everything.*
Audience, Ideas, Message	• Understand the needs of the audience. • Generate the best of ideas to address a business issue. • Identify the primary message and key points.	Tone, Style, Design	• Set a positive and other-oriented tone. • Make the message easy to read. • Make the message easy to navigate.	FAIR Test, Proofread, Feedback	• Ensure the communication is fair. • Consider whether your message is effective. • Remove any distractions.

LO 5.2. Identify the needs of your audience in the AIM planning process. (pp. 120–123)

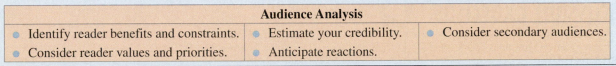

Audience Analysis		
• Identify reader benefits and constraints.	• Estimate your credibility.	• Consider secondary audiences.
• Consider reader values and priorities.	• Anticipate reactions.	

LO 5.3. Develop and refine business ideas in the AIM planning process. (pp. 123–125)

Idea Development		
• Identify the business problems.	• Analyze the business problems.	• Clarify objectives.

See an *example of idea development* in Figure 5.4.

LO 5.4. Develop your primary message and key points in the AIM planning process. (pp. 125–132)

Message Structuring	Testing Logic	
• Frame the main point. • Set up the structure/logic of the message.	**Avoid** the following: • Unsupported generalizations • Faulty cause/effect claims • Weak analogies	• Either/or logic • Slanting of facts • Exaggeration

See an *example of a deductive framework* in Figure 5.5.
See *typical paragraph structure* in a deductive business message in Figure 5.6.

LO 5.5. Explain and apply positive and other-oriented tone in business messages. (pp. 132–138)

Setting the Right Tone	
Demonstrate positivity	**Show concern for others**
• Display a can-do, confident attitude.	• Avoid relying too heavily on I-voice.
• Focus on positive rather than negative traits.	• Respect the time and autonomy of your readers.
• Use diplomatic, constructive terms.	• Give credit to others.

Key Terms

conclusions (p. 123)
deductive (p. 126)
direct (p. 126)
facts (p. 123)

indirect (p. 127)
inductive (p. 127)
meta messages (p. 136)
positions (p. 123)

priorities (p. 121)
tone (p. 132)
values (p. 121)

Discussion Exercises

5.1 Chapter Review Questions (LO 5.1, LO 5.2, LO 5.3, LO 5.4, LO 5.5)

A. Describe each of the three components in the AIM planning process for business messages: audience analysis, idea development, and message structuring.

B. Explain the general nature of excellence in business thinking and how it applies to the idea development stage of planning messages.

C. Discuss basic considerations in the audience analysis stage of planning messages.

D. Describe the nature of framing for business messages.

E. Explain common types of logical inconsistencies in business messages.

F. Discuss the importance of achieving positive and other-oriented tone in business messages.

5.2 Communication Q&A Discussion Questions (LO 5.1, LO 5.2, LO 5.3, LO 5.4, LO 5.5)

Read the comments and advice of Kim Asbill in the Communication Q&A section. Respond to the following questions:

A. What does Asbill say about the process of writing messages? What two strategies will you better incorporate into your approach to writing?

B. She also mentions tone several times. According to her, what is the importance of tone? What type of tone does she try to project?

C. In what ways does she say that business writing is changing? How will you adapt to some of these changes?

D. What pieces of advice that she gives are most relevant for your writing? Explain.

5.3 Worst Words to Use at Work? Displaying Confidence with Words (LO 5.5)

In a recent *Forbes* magazine article called "Worst Words to Say at Work," business consultant and psychotherapist Linnda Durre listed nine words or phrases that show someone is not confident.[11] These phrases, according to Durre, cause others to perceive you as undependable and untrustworthy. To read the article, go

to www.forbes.com/2010/04/26/words-work-communication-forbes-woman-leadership-career.html. Then respond to each of the following, which are excerpted from her article, with four to five sentences about whether you agree or disagree with her point of view:

A. *Try* is a weasel word. "Well, I'll try," some people say. It's a cop-out. They're just giving you lip service when they probably have no real intention of doing what you ask.

B. *Whatever*—this word is a trusted favorite of people who want to dismiss you, diminish what you say, or get rid of you quickly. . . . It's an insult and a verbal slap in the face. It's a way to respond to a person without actually responding.

C. *Maybe* and *I don't know*—People will sometimes avoid making a decision and hide behind these words. Sometimes during a confrontation people will claim not to know something or offer the noncommittal response "maybe," just to avoid being put on the spot.

D. *I'll get back to you*—When people need to buy time or avoid revealing a project's status, they will say, "I'll get back to you," and they usually never do.

E. *If*—Projects depend on everyone doing his or her part. People who use *if* are usually playing the blame game and betting against themselves. They like to set conditions rather than assuming a successful outcome.

F. *Yes, but . . .*—This is another excuse. You might give your team members suggestions or solutions and they come back to you with "Yes, but . . ." as a response. They don't really want answers, help, or solutions.

G. *I guess . . .*—This is usually said in a weak, soft-spoken, shoulder-shrugging manner. It's another attempt to shirk responsibility—a phrase is only muttered when people half agree with you, but want to leave enough leeway to say, "Well, I didn't really know. . . . I was only guessing."

H. *We'll see . . .*—How many times did we hear our parents say this? We knew they were buying time, avoiding a fight or confrontation, or really saying no.

Evaluation Exercises

5.4 Evaluating Latisha's Proposal for an Implementation Plan of a Wellness Program (LO 5.2, LO 5.3, LO 5.4, LO 5.5)

Based on the completed message from Latisha in Figure 5.7, answer the following questions:

A. How effectively is this message framed? Would you suggest any changes?

B. How effective is the business logic? Would you suggest any changes?

C. How effective is the tone? Would you suggest any changes?

D. What adjustments would you make if Jeff had a different preferred communication style? For example, what adjustments might you make if he was primarily a feeler, thinker, and/or intuitor?

5.5 Evaluating a Business Message (LO 5.2, LO 5.3, LO 5.4, LO 5.5)

Choose a business message to evaluate. You could find a recent letter you have received from a business, go to a website and choose a message for customers or stockholders, or use a message specified by your instructor. Select a message that contains at least three or four paragraphs. Evaluate the message in the following ways:

A. How effectively are facts and conclusions written?

B. How effectively is the message targeted to its audience? Do you have any suggestions for how it could have been better adapted for the audience?

C. Does it have any logical inconsistencies? Explain.

D. Does the message portray a tone of positivity? Other-orientation? Describe your viewpoint with examples.

5.6 Self-Assessment of Approach to Writing (LO 5.2, LO 5.3, LO 5.4, LO 5.5)

Evaluate yourself with regard to each of the practices listed in the table below. Circle the appropriate number for each.

Before sending important written messages, I . . .	1 – Rarely/Never	2 – Sometimes	3 – Usually	4 – Always
Make sure I gather all the facts.	1	2	3	4
Think carefully about what the facts mean.	1	2	3	4
Take time to think about what my audience wants and needs.	1	2	3	4
Spend time envisioning how my audience will respond.	1	2	3	4
Think about how the gist of my message could be captured in one short statement.	1	2	3	4
Map out the main supporting ideas for my primary message.	1	2	3	4
Check the message for logical consistency.	1	2	3	4
Make certain the tone is positive (as appropriate).	1	2	3	4
Ensure that the tone is other-oriented.	1	2	3	4
Reread the message to make sure everything is correct.	1	2	3	4

Add up your score and consider the following advice:

35–40: You are a strategic writer. You nearly always think carefully about the strength of your message and its intended influence on your audience. Keep up the great work.

30–34: You are a careful writer. You have many good habits in writing preparation. Identify the areas where you need to improve. By preparing slightly more in these areas, you will become a powerful, strategic writer in the workplace.

25–29: You are a somewhat careful writer. Sometimes and in some ways you are careful about your writing. You occasionally ask the right questions about getting your message right for your audience. You are inconsistent, however. Focus on preparing carefully for all important messages.

Under 25: You are a casual writer. You rarely take enough time to think carefully about your written messages. Even if you are a gifted and savvy writer, at some point, your lack of preparation will harm your work achievements. Make a habit of spending more time in the preparation stage asking questions about how to construct your message to appropriately influence your audience.

Once you've completed the short assessment, write about three areas of writing preparation in which you intend to improve. Describe specific steps you will take to improve and benchmarks for checking your progress.

Application Exercises

5.7 Avoiding Logical Errors (LO 5.4)

For each of the following sentences, identify what you consider to be logical inconsistencies. Explain whether these inconsistencies relate to unsupported generalizations, faulty cause/effect claims, either/or logic, slanting the facts, or exaggeration. Then revise the sentences to eliminate the logical inconsistencies.

A. Jim's Old Fashioned Burgers provides the best management training program in the industry.

B. The training consists of five stages: manager-in-training, second assistant manager, first assistant manager, restaurant manager, and regional director. The training places you on the fast track to success; advancing from one stage to the next takes from as few as three months up to just two years.

C. Many trainees eventually become upper-level executives, showing that hands-on training is better than getting a business degree.

D. Eventually, approximately 10 percent of trainees become regional directors. Employees from this elite group are those who show perseverance and determination to reach their professional goals.

E. Since just 5 percent of Jim's employees are selected for the training program, your acceptance in the program shows that you have great leadership potential.

F. We encourage you to apply for the training program so that you avoid staying in the same position without making career progress.

G. Restaurant managers make approximately $35,000 to $40,000 per year. The annual salary has grown at approximately 5 percent per year during the past three years, far outpacing income growth for restaurant managers at McDonald's or Burger King. So reaching the restaurant manager stage places you in a better economic position than you would be in at competing restaurants.

5.8 Displaying a Can-Do, Confident Tone (LO 5.5)

For each of the following items, rewrite the sentences to achieve a better can-do, confident tone.

A. Even though I do not have any supervisory experience, I think I have excellent leadership skills.

B. I have excellent leadership skills and will certainly increase profitability as I am promoted through the ranks of the training program.

C. I might be a good candidate for the training program since I work so hard.

D. We feel that next year's annual profits could increase if the economy picks up and if we are able to fill all of our management positions.

E. We believe that improving customer service is one way of driving increased revenues.

5.9 Focusing on Positive Traits (LO 5.5)

For each of the following items, rewrite the sentences to achieve a more positive tone.

A. All employees who show commitment and strong leadership skills are eligible for the management training program, even if they lack any higher education.

B. None of the training requires you to go through a traditional, business-like educational program.

C. You will begin as a manager-in-training and will do far more than flip burgers.

D. Those employees who do not show exceptional leadership skills at the manager-in-training stage do not advance to the next stage of training.

E. We are seeking individuals who do not settle for average customer service.

F. You will lose your opportunity to be considered for the program unless we receive your application by July 1.

G. Employees who have not done poorly on their performance reviews are eligible to apply for the program.

5.10 Using Diplomatic, Constructive Terms (LO 5.5)

For each of the following items, rewrite the sentences to achieve a more positive, constructive tone.

A. You probably won't be accepted into the management training program because you haven't worked here long enough to show any commitment.

B. Your contention that you have enough supervisory experience to make you qualified is questionable.

C. I think you must reconsider your views on the management training program if you expect it to succeed. You're just not in touch with reality if you expect to get quality managers without paying them higher salaries sooner in the program.

5.11 Using Appropriate Voice (LO 5.5)

For each of the following items, rewrite the sentences in you-voice, we-voice, or I-voice to achieve a more effective tone.

A. I'm happy to offer you a spot in the manager-in-training program.

B. I'm positive that this opportunity will help your career.

C. You must turn in the application before July 1.

D. I will lead the first orientation session for the program, and then I'll turn the remainder of the afternoon meetings over to my colleague.

E. I've come up with some ideas for the training program, and I'd like to meet as soon as possible to get some discussion going. I want us to focus on a conversation about the salaries and benefits that would motivate more employees to apply for the program.

5.12 Respecting the Time and Autonomy of Others (LO 5.5)

Rewrite each of the following items twice. Rewrite the first time assuming that you are writing to a peer. Rewrite the second time assuming that you are writing to a subordinate.

   A. Get back to me before Friday afternoon about your availability for an interview.

   B. I think we should review the manager-in-training applicants. Please come to my office on Tuesday at 9:30 a.m.

   C. I have chosen the five applicants who are most strongly suited for the training program. Could you send me an email confirming that you agree with my selections?

   D. I'm swamped with other projects, and we need to make the selections for the training program. Please take care of it yourself before this Friday at noon. You can count on me agreeing with your selections.

Case for Problems 5.13 through 5.15: Learning about Stress Management Programs for Eastmond Networking

When Jeff arrived back at the office, he spent 15 minutes reading Latisha's proposal to work on a wellness program. He found the work impressive and insightful. If only more of his employees had the same drive, initiative, and analytical skills as Latisha, thought Jeff, Eastmond would be far more successful. If Latisha kept up this level of analysis in her work, Jeff would definitely find a way to employ her full-time at Eastmond. Her thorough and thoughtful approach to this business problem showed she could excel in many of the entry-level management positions at the company.[12]

However, Jeff wasn't quite ready to move forward on implementing her plan. He was concerned about the expense. Although he trusted the estimates on returns, he was worried about the cash investments needed in the first few years before Eastmond would see returns. Before Latisha worked on a plan, he wanted her to do some more background work and investigate a more modest investment. He was especially interested in learning more about how a disease-management program could impact the company.

Jeff approached Latisha and explained what he wanted, and he asked her to write a brief report similar to the one she had already done.

He said, "I'd like you to focus on just the biggest problems. You know, programs to help with diabetes or heart health. Maybe we could help employees lower their cholesterol levels and their blood pressure. I'm thinking that we should learn how we can get the biggest bang for our buck—focus on say four or five of the costliest health problems and go from there. Also, I'd like to get a sense of the best way to prioritize our limited dollars to invest in disease management."

"If you're looking for some specific interventions that can make the biggest difference," Latisha answered, "we should start with stress. Stress costs us more in terms of health care costs and lower productivity than any other health care risk covered in a wellness or disease management program. Stress management programs are fairly inexpensive and deliver results pretty quickly."

"Really?" he said. "Stress costs more than heart disease or diabetes? OK, then how about you focus on stress management programs for the next week or two and write up what you find out. We'll go forward from there."

Latisha spent the next week learning about corporate stress management programs. She learned the following:

- Health care costs of people suffering chronic, extreme stress are 46% higher than those who are not.

- According to the American Medical Association, stress is as bad for your heart as smoking and high cholesterol.

- Forty percent of job turnover is due to stress.

- Stress reduction programs can have major impacts. In one company, 42% of 5,900 employees suffered moderate to severe stress. In fact, 80 percent of doctor visits for these employees were related to stress. After a stress reduction program, employee physician services dropped from $7.4 million annually to $5.3 million annually.

- Employees with various health risks directly increase health care costs to employers. For example, compared to employees with low health risks, employees with the following conditions significantly increase costs to the employer: depression (70.2% higher cost); stress (46.3%); glucose (34.8%); weight (21.4%); tobacco (19.7%); blood pressure (11.7%); exercise (10.4%).

- According to the Department of Health and Human Services, employees suffer the following risk factors: stress, 44%; overweight, 38%; use alcohol excessively, 31%; high cholesterol, 30%; have cardiovascular disease, 25%; don't exercise, 24%; smoke, 21%; don't wear seatbelts, 20%; are asthmatic, 12%; are diabetic, 6%.

- One study showed the annual per-employee absenteeism costs for the following conditions as follows: stress, $136; weight issues, $70; tobacco use, $44; glucose problems, $29.

- The Canadian Institute of Stress showed the following results for corporate stress management programs: work stress: 32% improvement; work satisfaction: 38% improvement; absenteeism: 18% reduction; disability days: 52% reduction; grievances: 32% reduction; productivity: 7% improvement; quality measures: 13% improvement; work engagement: 62% improvement.

- Stress management programs are most effective when offered in conjunction with broad wellness programs.

- Setting up stress management programs is challenging. Other disease management programs are more easily defined in terms of who has conditions and how to treat them (i.e., diabetes, heart disease).

- Most employees do not enroll in stress management programs unless there are incentives.

- Stress management can be achieved through workplace policies that alleviate work and personal stress. Some companies have tried flextime, allowing work at home, child care initiatives, sick child care, and other incentives to help employees reduce stress and be more productive.

- Stress management can also involve training through workshops and professional coaching.

• Lisa estimates that hiring a full-time professional coach for the workplace would cost approximately $60,000 per year (salary plus benefits and other related costs). The coach would run workshops, distribute educational materials, and also offer one-to-one coaching in stress relief. The coach would be qualified to work on other wellness areas such as weight loss, exercise, and dietary improvements. Assuming that Eastmond offered $150 reductions on health care premiums per year, Lisa estimates the company could achieve 90 percent participation (about 175 employees) in a basic stress management program. She thinks it's reasonable to assume that Eastmond could save about $500 per enrolled employee between health care and absenteeism costs.

5.13 Idea Development by Organizing Facts into Conclusions and Recommendations (LO 5.2)

Assume you are Latisha and you will write a proposal to Jeff asking that Eastmond develop a stress management program. You can use any of the facts she has discovered and even search for some online (there's lots of information about stress management), but your task is to make sense of the facts you've gathered. Organize them into groups that support three or four major conclusions (in a format similar to Figure 5.4). Then write three or four recommendations you would make based on your conclusions.

5.14 Writing a Proposal in Support of Developing a Stress Management Program (LO 5.2, LO 5.3, LO 5.4, LO 5.5)

Assume the role of Latisha. Write a proposal to develop a stress management program. Use well-justified logic to support your conclusions and recommendations.

5.15 Writing a Proposal to Broaden the Focus of a Wellness Program (LO 5.2, LO 5.3, LO 5.4, LO 5.5)

Assume the role of Latisha. You have concluded that although a stress management program would be beneficial, focusing on stress management without a comprehensive wellness program is shortsighted and less cost-effective. Use well-justified logic to support your conclusions and recommendations.

Endnotes

1. These time estimates are based on observing thousands of business students and are consistent with decades of research about expertise as described in Michael Pressley and Christine B. McCormick, *Advanced Educational Psychology for Educators, Researchers, and Policymakers* (New York: HarperCollins, 1995).

2. Elizabeth Garone, "How to Escape a Reputation as a Novice," *The Wall Street Journal* (October 8, 2008).

3. Ibid.

4. Roger Martin, "How Successful Leaders Think," *Harvard Business Review* (June 2007): 72–83; Richard Paul and Linda Elder, *The Miniature Guide to Critical Thinking Concepts and Tools* (Dillon Park, CA: Foundation for Critical Thinking Press, 2008); David Carrithers and John C. Bean, "Using a Client Memo to Assess Critical Thinking of Finance Majors," *Business Communication Quarterly* 71, no. 1 (2008): 10–26.

5. Statistics and other information came from a variety of sources, including the following: American Institute for Preventive Medicine, *The Health & Economic Implications of Worksite Wellness Programs* (Farmington Hills, MI: Author, 2008); Elizabeth Mendes, "Americans Exercise Less in 2009 Than in 2008; Having a Safe Place to Exercise Contributes to Exercise Frequency," *Gallup Poll Briefing,* January 15, 2010; Katherine Capps, *Employee Health & Productivity Management Programs: The Use of Incentives* (Lyndhurst, NJ: IncentOne, 2007); Pamela Kufahl, "America's Obesity Rate at a 10-Year Plateau, Study Finds," *Club Industry,* February 1, 2010; Larry Chapman,

"Meta-evaluation of Worksite Health Promotion Economic Return Studies: 2005 Update," *The Art of Health Promotion* (July/August 2005): 1–15; Michael George, *Corporate Fitness and the Bottom Line* (Petaluma, CA: Inspired Fitness, 2008); U.S. Department of Health and Human Services, *Prevention Makes Common "Cents"* (Washington, DC: U.S. Department of Health and Human Services, September 2003); American College of Sports Medicine, *ACSM's Worksite Health Promotion Manual* (Champaign, IL: American College of Sports Medicine, 2003); Buck Consultants, *Working Well: A Global Survey of Health Promotion and Workplace Wellness Strategies* (San Francisco: Buck Consultants, 2008); National Business Group on Health, "New Study Finds Most Employers Spend Nearly 2% of Health Care Claims Budget on Wellness Programs," January 25, 2010, retrieved April 21, 2010, from http://www.businessgrouphealth.org/pressrelease.cfm?ID=149.

6. Melissa Raffoni, "Framing for Leadership," *Harvard Management Communication Letter* 5, no. 12 (2002): 3–4.

7. Lyle Sussman, "How to Frame a Message: The Art of Persuasion and Negotiation," *Business Horizons* 42, no. 4 (1999): 2–6; Raffoni, "Framing for Leadership."

8. New York Times Corner Office Blog, "Simplicity," retrieved June 15, 2010, from http://projects.nytimes.com/corner-office/Communication.

9. Jane Thomas, *Guide to Managerial Persuasion and Influence* (Upper Saddle River, NJ: Pearson Education, 2004).

10. Timothy A. Judge and Remus Ilies, "Is Positiveness in Organizations Always Desirable?" *Academy of Management Executive* 18, no. 4 (2004): 151–155.

11. Linnda Durre, "Worst Words to Say at Work," *Forbes* online (April 26, 2010), retrieved August 5, 2010, from www.forbes.com/2010/04/26/words-work-communication-forbes-woman-leadership-career.html.

12. This case problem uses information from several additional resources, including the following: American Institute for Preventive Medicine, *A Worksite Wellness White Paper* (Farmington Hills, MI: American Institute for Preventive Medicine, 2009), retrieved August 5, 2010, from www.healthylife.com/template.asp?pageID=75; Catherine Calarco and Bruce Cryer, *Return on Investment Paper* (Boulder Creek, CA: HeartMath, 2009); HealthAdvocate, *Setting Up a Stress Management Program: A Checklist for Success* (Plymouth Meeting, PA: HealthAdvocate, 2010).

CHAPTER SIX

Improving Readability with Style and Design

Learning Objectives

After studying this chapter, you should be able to do the following:

LO6.1 Describe and apply the following principles of writing style that improve ease of reading: completeness, conciseness, and natural processing.

LO6.2 Explain and use navigational design to improve ease of reading.

LO6.3 Describe and apply the components of the reviewing stage, including a FAIR test, proofreading, and feedback.

WHY DOES THIS MATTER?

In Chapter 5, we focused on getting your message right with the AIM planning process. Then we introduced the importance of tone as you begin formally drafting your message. In this chapter, we focus on style and design—the next considerations as you draft your message. At this point, *your entire focus should be making your message easy to read.*

In short, your audience members—whether executives, managers, other professionals, or clients and customers—are typically preoccupied with many projects and overwhelmed with messages and information. When you make your messages easy to read, your audience is more likely to read them carefully and understand them as you intended.[1]

Many of the principles in this chapter focus on simplifying your words and sentences. This should not be confused with oversimplifying and minimizing your message. Your messages should contain the best of ideas with strong support. If your message is difficult to read, however, your ideas may not even be considered.

In this chapter, we discuss four broad goals. The first three goals relate to writing style and include being complete, concise, and natural. The final goal is to design your document for rapid navigation. Throughout the chapter, you will find less-effective and more-effective examples of each of these style and design elements. These examples come directly from the chapter case. Make sure to skim Stephanie's original difficult-to-read brochure draft (see Figure 6.1) so you understand the context for the chapter examples. By the end of the chapter, you will see the revisions that result in the final version of the brochure (see Figure 6.3).

Chapter Case: Promoting Franchises at Sunrise Greeting Cards and Flowers

Who's Involved

Stephanie Jorgenson, owner and founder
- Started her greeting card business 20 years ago
- Has expanded to 32 stores
- Wants to set up franchises

The Situation

Over the past 20 years, Sunrise Greeting Cards and Flowers has succeeded far beyond Stephanie Jorgenson's original expectations. Her model of high-end greeting cards, flower arrangements, and other special-occasion gifts appealed to a growing customer base. In fact, even with increasing accessibility to low-end greeting cards at department stores and free e-cards, she found that her customers had grown more loyal and purchased more than ever.

In recent years, Stephanie has received many requests from people to open franchises. Since she was not in a position to expand as quickly as the market seemed to dictate, she thought franchising would be a good option.

Six months ago, she hired a franchising consultant, who provided her with a basic strategy and action plan to make franchising possible. With her top management team, she set up the basic terms for franchises.

One of Stephanie's immediate goals was to produce a brochure to explain opportunities for franchisee opportunities. Stephanie had thought carefully about the audience for the brochure. She wanted financially strong and ambitious individuals. She also wanted people with a strong sense of optimism and customer orientation. She felt that success in her business was strongly related to genuine delight in helping others celebrate their special moments.

In terms of message structure, she had seen a number of brochures that she felt could be good models. Generally, they included an introductory message from the company president. Then, they typically contained information about financial qualifications and application procedures. She wanted a brochure that would be upbeat but also clear about the strong financial position needed to qualify for a franchise.

Her plan was to distribute the brochure personally to contacts at industry expos she attended throughout the year. She also envisioned mailing it, placing it on the company website, and sending it by email.

Stephanie drafted a document (see Figure 6.1) for the brochure. She asked several of her colleagues for input on the content. They all told her the same thing: "This is hard to read."

Task 1

How can Stephanie improve the writing style of the document so that potential franchisees will easily read it? (See the "Improving Ease of Reading with Completeness," "Improving Ease of Reading with Conciseness," and "Improving Ease of Reading with Natural Style" sections.)

Task 2

How can Stephanie improve her document's navigational design so that potential franchises can find important pieces of information rapidly? (See the "Improving Ease of Reading with Navigational Design" section.)

Improving Ease of Reading with Completeness

LO6.1 Describe and apply the following principles of writing style that improve ease of reading: completeness, conciseness, and natural processing.

Most of your messages in the workplace have a clear goal: to update your team members, to promote a service to a client, to give an assignment, and so on. Your goal of completeness means that your message provides all the information necessary to meet that purpose. Your colleagues, clients, and other contacts expect complete information so they can act on your message immediately. Otherwise, they will need to contact you to get additional information or, worse yet, ignore your message altogether. You can achieve completeness with three basic strategies: (1) providing all relevant information; (2) being accurate; and (3) being specific.

Provide All Relevant Information

One challenge is to judge which information is relevant for your message. After all, providing too much information can distract your readers and weigh your document down. On the other hand, not providing enough information can leave your reader wondering how to respond. The key to providing *all but only* relevant information is to plan, write, and review your message strategically. Repeatedly asking yourself what information is necessary for the purpose of your message will help you accomplish this.

In Stephanie's case, her basic purpose is to attract qualified individuals to apply for franchises. In the limited space of a two-page brochure, she wants to accomplish

FIGURE 6.1

Stephanie's Original, Difficult-to-Read Brochure

This document is difficult to read. It contains long paragraphs and long sentences. It flows poorly. It is not designed to help a reader navigate it for information. Most readers would get frustrated as they attempt to learn how to purchase a franchise.

Hello Potential *Sunrise Greeting Cards and Flowers* Shop Owner! Would you like to be part one of the most exciting businesses – providing those special somethings for those special someones on those special occasions and do you want to make your wildest dreams come true? There are many reasons for owning a Sunrise store, and it is wonderful to see happy customers day in and day out and be in a line of business where there are such great loyal customers. They are refined and appreciative of excellent craftsmanship and expect creative, original, and upscale greeting cards and flower arrangements. Our brand is one of the most strongly recognized among our customers and is associated with positive characteristics such as quality and reliability, and our customers associate these qualities with the special occasions in their lives. By owning a Sunrise store, you automatically tap into a brand that will provide profitability and join the Sunrise family. To help you reach your goals, we provide you with the products and resources to succeed. We also create a tight knit group of store owners and managers who share tricks of the trade with one another, and to this end, we organize an annual retreat for store owners and managers that provides synergistic solutions and proactive approaches to managing our stores.

We have made an estimate that you will need an initial investment of between $290,000 and $605,000. The initial investment costs include the following: fixtures ($60,000–$90,000); inventory ($80,000–$190,000); store improvements ($20,000–$130,000); retail equipment ($20,000–$35,000); miscellaneous expenses ($10,000–$30,000); and an initial franchise fee ($50,000). Fixtures include product displays, stock room components, and signing. Inventory includes greeting cards, gifts, flowers, and non-Sunrise items. Store Improvements include carpeting, electrical, plumbing, lighting, etc. Retail Equipment includes point-of-sale cash registers and software, pricing machines, accounting software, etc. Miscellaneous Expenses include various deposits, license fees, promotional costs, etc. You can pick possible locations for your new store.

Sunrise will make the final approval about your proposed sites and may suggest alternate locations based on our marketing formula, which has worked successfully in the past. As far as financial requirements, you must have a minimum net worth of $350,000, and you also will need minimum unencumbered assets of between $120,000 and $265,000. You may not finance more than two-thirds of the initial investment to open the store. You must also have access to financing in the range of $170,000 to $340,000 (assuming that you finance two thirds of the initial investment costs). Confirmation of loan, terms, and collateral is required. You will need to show that you can maintain an outside income of at least 80 percent of your present income for a period of at least two years to show that you have adequate financial stability as you get your business started. You will need to show that your liquid assets are available for investment and operations of your new Sunrise Gift Cards and Flowers shop, and the capital must be from your personal assets; capital in a current business will not be recognized as available to a new store. Sunrise does not provide loans.

Sunrise will assist in the business planning, such as helping in the development of a marketing plan, budgeting plan, and a break-even analysis consultation will be provided with your active participation. The budgeting plan that will be provided includes initial investments (building, fixtures, products, etc.), marketing costs, personnel expenditures, insurance and other potential expenses needed to run a Sunrise store, and an analysis of your chosen location will also be provided that includes demographics, traffic patterns, competitors, and a related analysis will be given to you that contains estimates of retail sales and revenue.

Stephanie Jorgenson, President and Owner
Sunrise Greeting Cards and Flowers, LLC
Stephanie@Sunrisegiftcards.com, 1-800-SUN-SET9

TABLE 6.1

Most Important Elements of Writing Style and Design according to Employers

Skills	Percentage of Employers Who Think Skill Is Extremely Important
1. **Accuracy**	**95**
2. **Clarity**	**75**
3. Language mechanics	59
4. Conciseness	41
5. Scientific precision	37
6. Visual appeal	11

Source: College Board survey of 2,825 corporate recruiters in 2,092 companies in 63 countries about needed skills for graduating college students. From *Writing: A Ticket to Work ...Or a Ticket Out: A Survey of Business Leaders.* Report of the National Commission on Writing in America's Schools and Colleges. Copyright © 2004 The College Board, www.collegeboard.org. Reproduced with permission.

several objectives to encourage applications of qualified individuals: show that she is committed to their success, describe the basic business model, and explain the financial qualifications for franchisees. As long as she keeps these objectives in mind, she can ensure that the brochure contains only relevant information.

Be Accurate

Accuracy is a basic objective of all business communications because your colleagues, customers, and clients base important decisions on your communications (see Table 6.1).[2] In short, accurate information is true, correct, and exact. You should aim for accuracy in facts, figures, statistics, and word choice. Inaccuracies may result from miscalculations, misinformation, poor word choice, or simply typos (see Table 6.2 for examples). Accuracy, like specificity, strongly impacts your readers' perceptions of your credibility. Just one inaccurate statement can lead readers to dismiss your entire message and lower their trust in your future communications as well.

TABLE 6.2

Being Accurate

Less Effective	More Effective
Your store should spend roughly 30 percent of annual sales on local advertising.	Your store should spend roughly 3 percent of annual sales on local advertising.
A typo (30 percent instead of 3 percent) implies an expense commitment that is ten times higher than the actual recommendation.	The revised version contains the corrected figure.
We estimate that you will need an initial investment of between $240,000 and $425,000. The initial investment costs include the following: fixtures ($60,000–$90,000); inventory ($80,000–$190,000); store improvements ($20,000–$130,000); retail equipment ($20,000–$35,000); miscellaneous expenses ($10,000–$30,000); and an initial franchise fee ($50,000).	We estimate that you will need an initial investment of between $240,000 and $525,000. The initial investment costs include the following: fixtures ($60,000–$90,000); inventory ($80,000–$190,000); store improvements ($20,000–$130,000); retail equipment ($20,000–$35,000); miscellaneous expenses ($10,000–$30,000); and an initial franchise fee ($50,000).
Incorrect calculation leads to one of the figures being off by $100,000.	The revised version contains the corrected figure.

TABLE 6.3

Being Specific

Less Effective	More Effective
Once approved, new Sunrise stores can be opened <u>quickly.</u>	Once approved, new Sunrise stores can typically be opened in <u>between 3 and 12 months.</u>
The term *quickly* is not specific.	The phrase *between 3 and 12 months* is specific and avoids ambiguity.
The minimum store size is based on location. Typically, the minimum size is <u>larger</u> in strip shopping centers than in shopping malls.	The minimum store size is based on location. In shopping malls, the minimum size should be approximately <u>2,500 square feet.</u> In strip shopping centers, the minimum size should be approximately <u>3,400 square feet.</u>
The term *larger* is not specific.	By stating specific figures for square feet, the difference is not open to interpretation.

Be Specific

Your readers expect you to be precise and avoid vagueness in nearly all business situations. The more specific you are, the more likely your readers are to have their questions answered. If you are not specific, your readers may become impatient and begin scanning and skimming for the information they want. If they can't find that information, they are unlikely to respond to your message as you intend.

Being specific also affects the judgments your readers make about your credibility. Specific statements lead your readers to believe that you know what you're talking about (competence); that you are not hiding anything (character); and that you want your readers to be informed (caring). Being vague, on the other hand, detracts from your credibility. See Table 6.3 for examples of less-specific and more-specific writing.

Improving Ease of Reading with Conciseness

When you write concisely, your message is far easier to read. Conciseness does not imply removing relevant information. Rather, it implies omitting needless words so that readers can rapidly process your main ideas. In response to the question "[Do you have] any thoughts on how language is used in the business world?" Clarence Otis Jr., CEO of Darden Restaurants, responded this way:

> I think writing in the business world is more functional than elegant. I felt that way making the transition from law to business. Lawyers write much better. They spend a lot more time on it. In the business world, it's less about how well you say it and more about how efficiently you say it.[3]

Otis's primary point is that your language should be efficient. You should say as much as you can in as few words as possible. His distinction between functionality and elegance means that your primary focus is not impressing with words, but rather impressing with ideas. In this section, we describe strategies for writing concisely, including controlling paragraph length, using shorter sentences, avoiding redundancy, avoiding empty phrases, and avoiding wordy phrases.

Control Paragraph Length

Before they even begin to read, readers form impressions about ease of reading by looking at paragraph length. When they see long paragraphs, they often enter skim mode—searching for certain words and ideas rather than reading. Long paragraphs can signal disorganization and even disrespect for the reader's time.

Improving Ease of Reading with Writing Style

Completeness
- Provide all relevant information.
- Be accurate.
- Be specific.

Conciseness
- Control paragraph length.
- Use short sentences.
- Avoid redundancy.
- Avoid empty phrases.
- Avoid wordy prepositional phrases.

Natural Style
- Use action verbs when possible.
- Use active voice.
- Use short and familiar words and phrases.
- Use parallel language.
- Avoid buzz words and figures of speech.
- Avoid it is/there are.

Typically, paragraphs should contain 40 to 80 words. For routine messages, paragraphs as short as 20 to 30 words are common and appropriate. As the level of information and analysis grows deeper, some paragraphs will be longer. Rarely should paragraphs exceed 150 words. In a matter of seconds, you can easily check how many words are in your paragraphs with nearly all word processing software.

One primary cause of overly lengthy paragraphs is placing more than one main idea or topic in the paragraph. Your readers can process the information in your message far more easily if you create unified paragraphs in which each paragraph focuses on one idea or topic. Paragraphs with more than one idea often confuse readers. Even worse, readers may miss some ideas altogether. The process of unifying helps you control paragraph length and even tighten your business reasoning (see Table 6.4).

TABLE 6.4

Controlling Paragraph Length

Less Effective	More Effective
As far as financial requirements, you must have a minimum net worth of $350,000. Also, you will need minimum unencumbered assets of between $120,000 and $265,000. You may not finance more than two-thirds of the initial investment to open the store. You must also have access to financing in the range of $170,000 to $340,000 (assuming that you finance two-thirds of the initial investment costs). Confirmation of loan, terms, and collateral is required. You will need to show that you can maintain an outside income of at least 80 percent of your present income for a period of at least two years. This allows you to have adequate financial stability as you get your business started. You will need to show that your liquid assets are available for investment and operations of your new Sunrise Greeting Cards and Flowers shop. Capital must be from your personal assets; capital in a current business will not be recognized as available to a new store. Sunrise does not provide loans.	Minimum financial requirements include a net worth of $350,000 with unencumbered liquid assets of between $120,000 and $265,000 (these financial requirements must be from personal assets, not from capital in a current business). You will need to show that these liquid assets are available for investment in your Sunrise store. You will also need to show that you can maintain an outside income of at least 80 percent of your present income for a period of at least two years.

You are required to finance less than two-thirds of the initial investment costs. Assuming that you can, you will need access to financing in the range of $170,000 to $340,000. Confirmation of loan, terms, and collateral is required. Sunrise does not provide loans. |
| This paragraph contains 168 words. It also contains excessive numerical figures. | This paragraph contains the same information but has been edited for conciseness and divided into two paragraphs. It contains one paragraph of 80 words and one paragraph of 44 words. Altogether, the information has been presented in 30 fewer words. |
| The right to open a new Sunrise store will be awarded based on the business plan, market potential in your chosen area, personal interviews, and financial criteria. Running a Sunrise store can be extremely profitable. Once approved, new Sunrise stores can typically be opened in 3 to 12 months. The minimum store size is based on location. In shopping malls, the minimum size should be approximately 2,500 square feet. In strip shopping centers, the minimum size should be approximately 3,400 square feet. Currently, average annual profit per Sunrise store is $153,000, with ranges between $49,000 and $215,000. Profit level depends on many factors, including choosing the right location, market demand, square footage, and managing the store effectively. Typically, profits become relatively stable after the first three years of operation. | The right to open a new Sunrise store will be awarded based on the business plan, market potential in your chosen area, personal interviews, and financial criteria. Once approved, new Sunrise stores can typically be opened in 3 to 12 months.

Currently, average annual profit per Sunrise store is $153,000, with ranges between $49,000 and $215,000. Profit level depends on many factors, including location, market demand, square footage, and management. Typically, profits become relatively stable after the first three years of operation. |
| This paragraph has two ideas or topics: (a) awarding the right to open a store and (b) average annual profit per store. This paragraph contains 130 words. | The revised paragraph is broken into two separate, unified paragraphs with 42 and 41 words, respectively. |

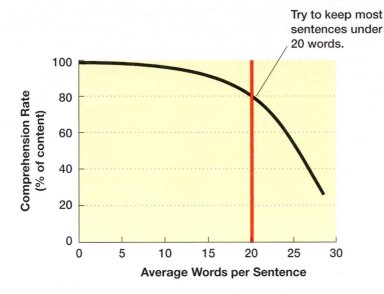

Try to keep most sentences under 20 words.

FIGURE 6.2

Comprehension Rate and Sentence Length

Source: Figure adapted from Ann Wylie, "How to Make Your Copy More Readable: Make Sentences Shorter," *Comprehension* (January 14, 2009), retrieved March 3, 2012, from http://comprehension .prsa.org/?p=217.

Use Short Sentences in Most Cases

Like relatively short paragraphs, short sentences allow your readers to comprehend your ideas more easily. Consider Figure 6.2, which depicts the data from a study conducted by the American Press Institute.[4] Readers were tested on their overall comprehension based on the length of sentences. When sentences had 10 words or fewer, readers had nearly 100 percent comprehension. Once sentence lengths reached around 20 words, comprehension dropped to about 80 percent. Thereafter, comprehension dropped rapidly. Sentence lengths of 28 words resulted in just 30 percent comprehension.

As a rule of thumb, then, for routine messages, aim for average sentence length of 15 or fewer words. For more analytical and complex business messages, you may have an average sentence length of 20 or fewer words. Of course, you will often deal with complex ideas and need to go above 20 words in some of your sentences. Use your judgment to minimize sentence length (see Table 6.5).

TABLE 6.5

Using Short Sentences

Less Effective	More Effective
Our brand is strongly recognized among our customers and is associated with positive characteristics such as quality and reliability, and our customers associate these qualities with the special occasions in their lives.	To our customers, our brand represents quality products that help them celebrate special occasions.
This sentence contains 32 words.	This sentence contains the same ideas in just 14 words.
Our team of experienced managers will apply our well-developed formula for analyzing the demographics, traffic patterns, local competitors, and other factors of your chosen location to provide you with estimates of retail sales and revenue.	Our team of experienced managers will apply our well-developed formula for analyzing the demographics, traffic patterns, local competitors, and other factors of your chosen location. From this analysis, we will provide you with estimates of retail sales and revenue.
This sentence contains 35 words.	The less-effective sentence has been split into one 25-word sentence and one 14-word sentence.

(continued)

TABLE 6.5

(Continued)

Less Effective	More Effective
Sunrise has aggressively advertised in print and radio in regional markets in recent years, and Sunrise has developed excellent brand recognition with its various advertising and promotional materials that will directly benefit your store, which, of course, depends and varies on your chosen store location.	In recent years, Sunrise has aggressively advertised in print and radio in regional markets. As a result, Sunrise brand recognition is strong. Your store will benefit from Sunrise regional advertising and promotional campaigns.
This sentence contains 45 words.	The less-effective sentence has been split into three sentences with 14, 8, and 11 words, respectively.

Avoid Redundancy

One way to reduce word count and make your messages easier to read is to avoid redundancies, which are words or phrases that repeat the same meaning. For example, consider the phrase *past history;* history can only be past, so there's no need to use both words. By eliminating redundancies, you can reduce overall word count (see Table 6.6).

Avoid Empty Phrases

Many phrases simply fill space without adding additional meaning. Many of these phrases are common in conversations but are not needed for written messages (see Table 6.7).

TABLE 6.6

Avoiding Redundancy

Less Effective	More Effective
To help you reach your goals, we provide you with the products and resources to succeed.	We provide you with the products and resources to succeed.
This sentence has 16 words. *To help you reach your goals* and *to succeed* are redundant phrases.	This sentence has 10 words. It removes redundancy.
We organize a fun-filled annual retreat each year for store owners and managers to share and discuss problems, solutions, and opportunities with one another.	We organize a fun-filled annual retreat for store owners and managers to share and discuss problems, solutions, and opportunities.
This sentence has 24 words. *Annual* and *each year* are redundant. *Share and discuss* implies *with one another,* making *with one another* redundant.	This sentence has 19 words. It removes redundancies.

TABLE 6.7

Avoiding Empty Phrases

Less Effective	More Effective
Needless to say, the profitability of a store depends on many factors.	The profitability of a store depends on many factors.
This sentence contains 12 words.	This revision contains 9 words.
With all due respect, Sunrise suggests other locations for your store based on our marketing formula.	Sunrise suggests other locations for your store based on our marketing formula.
This sentence contains 16 words.	This revision contains 12 words.

Table 6.8

Avoiding Wordy Prepositional Phrases

Less Effective	More Effective
In an effort to maximize your profitability as a Sunrise owner, you should be in attendance at each annual retreat.	Attending the annual Sunrise retreats helps you maximize profitability.
This sentence contains 20 words.	This revision of the less-effective sentence contains 9 words.
In the business planning process, please keep in mind that at Sunrise, we are here for you.	Please remember that we will help you in business planning.
This sentence contains 17 words.	This revision of the less-effective sentence contains 10 words.

Avoid Wordy Prepositional Phrases

Eliminating extra words allows you to get your ideas across as efficiently as possible. You will often find that you can reduce word count by 30 to 40 percent simply by converting many of your prepositional phrases into single-word verbs. Like other elements of style we have discussed already, prepositional phrases are not bad in themselves. In many cases, they are perfectly appropriate. Rather, their overuse leads to wordiness and less clarity (see Table 6.8).

Improving Ease of Reading with Natural Style

The closer you match your writing style to the way your readers think and talk, the easier it is for them to process the information you present. Ease of processing means your readers need less mental effort to understand your message, which is especially important for readers who are busy and preoccupied with other work challenges.

Several broad principles support the strategies in this section. First, people can generally process information more quickly when writers use action verbs. Second, people tend to think in a doer-action-object pattern, so using this pattern in your writing enhances comprehension. Furthermore, when the subject or doer is missing from the sentence, readers may become confused. Third, people generally process simple, short words more quickly than long, complex ones.

Use Action Verbs When Possible

As a business writer, you want to project a positive, can-do, action-oriented tone whenever possible. Indeed, fostering action is the basic purpose of most workplace communication. Using action verbs focuses on the goal of coordinating action in the workplace and livens up your writing. Also, it usually reduces word count.

Typically, then, you can focus on two types of revisions to achieve more effective action verbs. First, find nouns that you can convert to action verbs. For example, *have a meeting* becomes *meet* or *have a discussion* becomes *discuss*. Second, find forms of the verb *to be* (e.g., be verbs such as *is, are, am*) and convert them to action verbs (see Table 6.9). For example, *Sunrise is a great place to open a franchise with* becomes *Sunrise provides great opportunities for franchises*.

Use Active Voice

One way to immediately improve your writing is use active rather than passive voice in most sentences. Active voice and passive voice contain the following grammatical patterns:

Active voice: Doer as Subject + Verb + Object

Passive voice: Object as Subject + Be Verb + Verb + Doer (Optional)

TABLE 6.9

Using Action Verbs

Less Effective	More Effective
We have made an estimate that you will need an initial investment of between $290,000 and $605,000.	We estimate that you will initially invest between $290,000 and $605,000.
This sentence contains 17 words.	This revision contains 11 words.
Sunrise is a company with excellent customer service.	Sunrise provides excellent customer service.
This sentence contains 8 words.	This revision contains 5 words.

Consider the following examples:

Active voice: Sunrise provides free training for up to three people for each new store.

Passive voice: Free training is provided for up to three people for each new store.

In active voice, this sentence immediately identifies the doer (Sunrise). It then uses a strong verb (provides) and proceeds to the object (free training). In passive voice, this sentence begins with the object of the action (free training), proceeds to a weak verb (is), then employs a strong verb (provided), and leaves out the doer, thus lacking the clarity of active voice.

Using active voice in writing includes many benefits. The doer-action-object allows for faster processing because most people's natural thinking occurs in this way. It also emphasizes the business orientation of action. Perhaps most important, it specifies the doer. Since business activities depend on accountability and coordination, knowing the identity of the doer of an action is usually important. Furthermore, writing in the active voice usually results in fewer words (see Table 6.10).

While active voice is the preferred writing style for most business writing, passive voice is sometimes better when attempting to avoid blaming others or sounding

Table 6.10

Using Active Voice Appropriately

Less Effective (Passive Voice)	More Effective (Active Voice)
A marketing plan, budgeting plan, and break-even analysis will be provided to you with your active participation.	Sunrise will work directly with you to create a marketing plan, budgeting plan, and break-even analysis.
This passive sentence de-emphasizes who will create the plan and lacks an action-oriented tone.	The active verb construction in this sentence helps achieve a more engaging, action-oriented tone.
An analysis of your chosen location will also be provided that includes demographics, traffic patterns, competitors, and a related analysis will be given to you that contains estimates of retail sales and revenue.	Sunrise will use its well-developed formula for analyzing the demographics, traffic patterns, local competitors, and other factors of your chosen location. Sunrise will also provide you with estimates of retail sales and revenue.
This sentence contains two sets of passive verbs. Again, it de-emphasizes who will create the plan and lacks an action-oriented tone. It is also wordy. It contains 33 words.	These sentences clearly identifies that Sunrise will conduct the analyses. It is action-oriented. It is also easier to read. It breaks the thoughts into two sentences of 21 and 12 words, respectively.

TABLE 6.11

Using Passive Voice Appropriately

Less Effective (Active Voice)	More Effective (Passive Voice)
Since you did not meet the financial criteria, we have denied your application for a Sunrise franchise.	Since financial criteria were not met, your application for a Sunrise franchise was not accepted at this time.
This active verb construction emphasizes the reader's failures.	This passive verb construction provides the bad news without assigning blame or directly pointing out failure.
You need to complete the application forms carefully for us to seriously consider your application.	Application forms that are completed carefully allow us to better determine the merit of your application.
This active verb construction might be perceived as bossy (sounds like an order) or demeaning (implies the reader is not smart enough to understand basic procedures).	This passive verb construction emphasizes the importance of carefully completing the forms without directly implying the reader is likely to make elementary mistakes.

bossy. Some research reports also use passive voice to emphasize neutrality (see Table 6.11).

Use Short and Familiar Words and Phrases

Whenever possible, choose short, conversational, and familiar words. Using longer, less common ones to "sound smart" rarely pays off. They slow processing and distract from your message. They may even inadvertently send the signal that you are out of touch, quirky, or even arrogant (see Table 6.12).

TABLE 6.12

Using Short, Familiar Words and Phrases

Less Effective	More Effective
Sunrise advocates that you seek consultation with us during the application process.	Sunrise suggests that you seek our advice during the application process.
Advocates is a word that is less familiar to many readers. Furthermore, *advocates* and *consultation* are words that may suggest the need for legal counsel to some readers.	This sentence contains short, familiar words that allow for ease of reading.
Sunrise bestows you with many opulent greeting cards and singular flower arrangements that can only be found in Sunrise stores.	Sunrise provides you with many upscale greeting cards and unique flower arrangements that can only be found in Sunrise stores.
This sentence contains infrequently used adjectives (*opulent, singular*). These terms sound overblown and will confuse many readers.	This sentence contains shorter, more familiar terms that capture the intended meaning.
To facilitate this course of action, we organize a convivial annual retreat for store owners and managers where we collectively discuss our mutual challenges, solutions, and opportunities.	To help make this happen, we organize a fun-filled annual retreat where store owners and managers can discuss our shared problems, solutions, and opportunities.
This sentence contains rarely used or stuffy words (*course of action, convivial, collectively, mutual*) that will frustrate many readers.	This sentence avoids stuffy, formal-business-sounding words (*course of action, collectively, mutual*) and replaces them with shorter, more conversational words.

Use Parallel Language

Using parallel language means that you apply a consistent grammatical pattern across a sentence or paragraph. Parallelism is most important when you use series or lists. For example, when you describe a product with three characteristics, use the same grammatical pattern for each—that is, for example, choose adjectives or nouns or verbs for all of them. When you use consistent grammatical patterns for items in lists and series, readers can process the information far more naturally and quickly (see Table 6.13).

TABLE 6.13

Using Parallel Language

Less Effective	More Effective
Our customers are <u>refined</u> and <u>purchase high-end products</u>.	Our customers are <u>refined</u> and <u>upscale</u>.
The two characteristics of customers are not parallel. They are in the following pattern: adjective and verb-object.	The two characteristics of customers are parallel. They are both adjectives.
	OR
	Our customers <u>appreciate refined craftsmanship</u> and <u>purchase high-end products</u>.
	The two characteristics of customers are parallel. They both follow verb-object patterns.
Sunrise will work directly with you to <u>create a marketing plan, develop a budgeting plan, and break-even analysis</u>.	Sunrise will work directly with you to create a <u>marketing plan, budgeting plan, and break-even analysis</u>.
The three items in the list are not parallel. They are in the following pattern: verb-object, verb-object, noun.	The three items in the list are parallel. They are each nouns (each are objects of the verb *create*).
	OR
	Sunrise will work directly with you to <u>create a marketing plan, develop a budgeting plan, and set up a break-even analysis</u>.
	The three items in the list are parallel. They each follow verb-object patterns.
Profit level depends on many factors, including <u>choosing the right location, market demand, square footage, and managing the store effectively</u>.	Profit level depends on many factors, including <u>location, market demand, square footage, and management</u>.
The four factors do not have matching grammatical patterns. They are in the following pattern: verb-object, noun, noun, verb-object.	The four factors are parallel. They are each nouns.
	OR
	Profit level depends on many factors, including <u>choosing the right location, meeting market demands, leasing adequate store space, and managing the store effectively</u>.
	The four factors are parallel. They each follow a verb-object pattern.

Table 6.14

The Most Annoying Buzzwords

At the end of the day	Redeployed people
Synergy	On the runway
Solution	Win-win
Think outside the box	Value-added
Customer-centric	Get on the same page
Do more with less	Generation X
Paradigm	Accountability management
Incremental	Core competency
Metrics	Alignment
Take it offline	

Source: Accountemps surveys of financial executives, "What's the Buzz? Survey Reveals Most Overused Workplace Terms," retrieved March 3, 2012, from http://accountemps.rhi.mediaroom.com/index.php?s-189&item=255. Reprinted with permission of Robert Half International.

Avoid Buzzwords and Figures of Speech

To keep your writing natural and engaging, make sure you don't distract your readers with overused or out-of-place words or phrases. Buzzwords, which are workplace terms that become trite because of overuse, can stir negative feelings among some readers. In Table 6.14, you can see one list of annoying buzzwords cited in a recent survey of executives.[5] (Dozens of such lists exist because business professionals become so agitated by these overused words.)

Figures of speech, such as idioms and metaphors, which contain nonliteral meanings, are generally out of place or inappropriate in business writing. Since they are nonliteral, they lack the precise meanings needed in business. Also, some idioms and metaphors have become so clichéd that they have lost almost all meaning (see Table 6.15).

Avoid *It Is/There Are*

Readers naturally want to know precisely *who* or *what* the subject of a sentence is, particularly in business writing, where specificity is so important. Most sentences that begin with *it is* or *there are* fail to provide a specific subject and generally contain more words than necessary. A message can be particularly awkward when many of the sentences begin with *it is* or *there are*. By rewording *it is/there are* statements, you generally liven up your writing.

One way of recognizing when to reword *it is* statements is to ask the question *what does it refer to?* If you don't know the answer, your readers won't either. Consider the second sentence in Table 6.16: *It is wonderful to see happy customers day in and day out.* What does *it* refer to? Recognizing what *it* is requires you to think for a few seconds. By rewording the sentence, you can provide a more descriptive, concise, and natural statement: *Seeing happy customers day in and day out is wonderful.* After considering the examples in Table 6.16, read the Technology Tips on page 161 for ways that you can use your word processing program to further improve your writing.

TABLE 6.15

Avoiding Buzzwords and Figures of Speech

Less Effective	More Effective
Do you want to <u>make your wildest dreams come true</u>? There are many reasons for owning a Sunrise store.	Owning a Sunrise store can help you <u>reach your financial dreams</u> and satisfy your wish to be your own boss.
Making your wildest dreams come true is a figure of speech that sounds unbelievable to most readers.	This sentence is more believable. It avoids exaggerated figures of speech but remains extremely positive and future-oriented.
We also create a tight-knit group of store owners and managers who share <u>tricks of the trade</u> with one another.	We create a tight-knit group of store owners and managers who <u>share ideas about improving our brand and sales performance.</u>
Tricks of the trade is a figure of speech that is more appropriate in oral communication. Some readers may be unfamiliar with the phrase. In any case, it could create confusion.	This sentence is more specific. It explains what expertise is shared and discussed among owners and managers.
To this end, we organize an annual retreat that is a <u>total blast</u> for store owners and managers and that provides <u>synergistic</u>, <u>win-win</u> solutions and <u>proactive</u> approaches to managing our stores.	To help make this happen, we organize a <u>fun-filled</u> annual retreat for store owners and managers where they can <u>share and discuss problems, solutions, and opportunities.</u>
These sentences contain various figures of speech that readers may not receive well. A *total blast* is slang. Not only can slang be misunderstood, but it can also serve as a generation marker. Slang goes out of style and can make you look out of date. Other slang will highlight how young you are. The combination of buzzwords (*synergistic, win-win, proactive*) in the second sentence will annoy some readers.	This sentence, without the excessive slang and buzzwords, is easy to read. Readers can rapidly process this sentence and relate to its tone.

Table 6.16

Avoiding *It Is* and *There Are*

Less Effective	More Effective
<u>There are</u> many reasons for owning a Sunrise store.	Owning a Sunrise store has many benefits.
This sentence contains 9 words.	This sentence contains 7 words.
<u>It is</u> wonderful to see happy customers day in and day out.	Seeing happy customers day in and day out is wonderful.
This sentence contains 12 words.	This sentence contains 10 words.
<u>It is</u> great to be in a line of business where <u>there are</u> such extremely loyal customers.	In this line of business, customers are extremely loyal.
This sentence contains 17 words.	This sentence contains 9 words.

TECHNOLOGY TIPS

USING SPELLING AND GRAMMAR CHECKS

Most word processing software programs contain spelling and grammar checks to help you avoid misspellings and grammatical mistakes. Many of these programs, such as Microsoft Word, also have tools to evaluate writing style and ease of reading. Typically, these tools are not set by default. You will need to manually select them. (In Microsoft Word, you can access these additional tools by changing settings in the *Proofing* area of *Word Options*.)

When you run spelling and grammar checks, you can review your document sentence by sentence for passive voice, noun clusters, and other elements. Once you finish the check, you will see a final calculation of readability statistics. Keep in mind that the software is not perfect. Generally, however, it will help you improve your writing style.

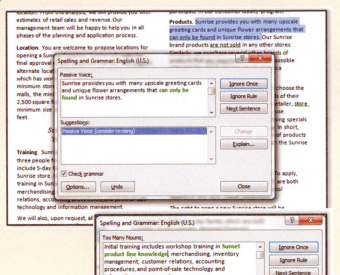

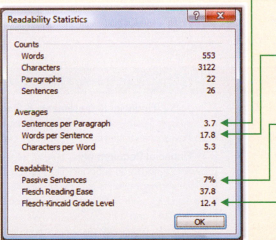

Should aim for 3 to 5 sentences in analytical business messages; 1 to 3 sentences in routine emails and digital communications.

Should aim for fewer than 20 words per sentence in analytical business messages and fewer than 15 words per sentence in routine, straight-forward business messages.

Should generally aim for less than 15 percent of all sentences to be passive sentences.

The Flesch Reading Ease and Flesch-Kincaid Grade Level scores are calculated based on word length and sentence length. Typically, you should aim for Flesch-Kincaid Grade Level scores of 10 or less for routine messages and 12 or less for more analytical business messages.

Improving Ease of Reading with Navigational Design

LO6.2 Explain and use navigational design to improve ease of reading.

Your primary goal for document design is making your message easy to navigate. Ask yourself these questions: How can I get my readers to see my main ideas and messages quickly? How can I make sure my readers can find the information they are most interested in? Several features will help you improve navigational design, including headings, highlighting, lists, white space, and simplicity. Later in the book, we will focus on additional ways of enhancing the appearance of your document with charts, figures, and graphics.

Improving Ease of Reading with Navigational Design

- Headings
- Highlighting
- Lists
- White space
- Simplicity

Use Headings

In information-rich and complex messages, headings can help your readers identify key ideas and navigate the document to areas of interest. As you create headings and subheadings, be consistent in font style and formatting throughout your document. One way to be consistent with your headings is to apply formatting features available in most word processing programs. For example, in Microsoft Word, you can assign heading levels for major heads and subheads (Heading 1, Heading 2, and so on). You have many options for the formatting styles you apply, and the software ensures that the formatting remains consistent throughout the document.

As you develop your headings, make sure you concisely and accurately convey the contents of a section. For example, notice the heading "Financial Requirements & Financing" in the more-effective example in Table 6.17. In contrast, the heading "Minimum Financial Requirements to Apply for a Franchise and Financing Stipulations" is likely too long for most documents. On the other hand, a subheading such as "Minimum Requirements" may not give readers accurate information about the contents of the section. Readers skimming the document for *financial* requirements might miss the section on the first pass. You can find more information about headings in Chapters 12 and 13 about reports.

Highlight Key Words and Phrases

When you want to highlight ideas or phrases, consider using **bold**, *italics*, or underlining to draw and keep your readers' attention. Typically, you will apply this type of formatting sparingly; if you use too much special formatting, your main ideas will not stand out. In general, apply only one type of formatting to a highlighted word/s (i.e., only bold or italics, not bold and italics) (see Table 6.18).

TABLE 6.17

Using Headings

Less Effective	More Effective
Sunrise will make the final approval about your proposed sites and may suggest alternate locations based on our marketing formula, which has worked successfully in the past. As far as financial requirements, you must have a minimum net worth of $350,000, and you also will need minimum unencumbered assets of between $120,000 and $265,000. You may not finance more than two-thirds of the initial investment to open the store. You must also have access to financing in the range of $170,000 to $340,000 (assuming that you finance two-thirds of the initial investment costs). Confirmation of loan, terms, and collateral is required. You will need to show that you can maintain an outside income of at least 80 percent of your present income for a period of at least two years to show that you have adequate financial stability as you get your business started. You will need to show that your liquid assets are available for investment and operations of your new Sunrise Greeting Cards and Flowers shop, and the capital must be from your personal assets; capital in a current business will not be recognized as available to a new store. Sunrise does not provide loans.	**Financial Requirements & Financing** Owning a Sunrise shop requires a strong financial position and evidence of the ability to finance a new business. **Financial Requirements.** Sunrise seeks franchise owners who are in a financially sound position. The minimum requirements include a total net worth of $350,000, with unencumbered liquid assets of between $120,000 and $265,000. You will need to show that these liquid assets are personal rather than capital in a current business and available for investment in your Sunrise store. You will also need to show that you can maintain an outside income of at least 80 percent of your present income for at least two years. **Financing.** You are required to finance less than two-thirds of the initial investment costs. Assuming that you finance up to two-thirds of the initial investment costs, you will need access to financing in the range of $170,000 to $340,000. Confirmation of loan, terms, and collateral is required. Sunrise does not provide loans.
This paragraph is 198 words with far too many numbers. Many readers would have a hard time locating the key information.	Visually, these paragraphs are far more appealing and inviting. The headings immediately orient the reader to the content.

TABLE 6.18

Applying Formatting to Key Words and Phrases

Less Effective	More Effective
Sunrise will work directly with you to create a marketing plan, budgeting plan, and break-even analysis.	*Sunrise will work directly with you* to create a marketing plan, budgeting plan, and break-even analysis.
By italicizing everything, nothing is highlighted.	By italicizing one short phrase, you emphasize it.
Sunrise will provide **free training** for up to three people for each new store.	Sunrise will provide **free training** for up to three people for each new store.
Applying two formatting features (bold and underlining) may appear overbearing.	Applying one formatting feature (bold) is sufficient to highlight the phrase.

Use Bulleted and Numbered Lists

You will often use lists in business writing. When you set these items apart with bullets or numbers, your readers notice and remember the items more easily (see Table 6.19).

Use White Space Generously

Your readers will form an immediate impression about your document based on how much white space (areas without text) it has. Documents with too much text and not enough white look daunting or cluttered. On the other hand, documents with too much white space may look insufficient. Many students are trained in the university setting to double-space documents. In the workplace, double-spaced documents are rare, however.

Keep It Simple

Visual appeal is not the first consideration for most written business communications (see Table 6.1 at the beginning of the chapter). Rather, the goal is to get your message across in an easy-to-read manner. As you design your document, focus first on easy navigation for your reader. Avoid formatting features that distract from the main message. See Figure 6.3 for effective use of navigational features and white space.

TABLE 6.19

Using Bulleted and Numbered Lists

Less Effective	More Effective
The brochure for prospective franchisees should first and foremost show how committed we are to the success of the franchisee. We can do this by providing a warm and inviting message from Stephanie on the front of the brochure. Then we should provide basic information that all prospective franchisees would be interested in, such as information about initial investment costs and profit potential, financial requirements and financing, our involvement in opening a new franchise store, and the application process. We should also have a section about our commitment to their success after they open a store.	The brochure for prospective franchisees should accomplish two main goals: (1) show our commitment to the success of franchisees and (2) provide basic information about becoming a franchisee. The brochure should contain the following sections: • Opening letter from Stephanie. • Initial investment costs and profit potential. • Financial requirements and financing. • Sunrise involvement in opening a new franchise store. • Sunrise support after opening a store. • Application process.
Without bullets, this paragraph contains a lot of items that are difficult for the reader to remember. Furthermore, it takes longer for the reader to visualize the components of the brochure.	With bullets, this paragraph allows the reader to rapidly process the information and visualize the components of the brochure. Furthermore, the use of enumeration and bullets more clearly distinguishes the overarching goals of the brochure and the components of the brochure.

FIGURE 6.3

Stephanie's Final, Easier-to-Read Brochure (Compare to Original Version in Figure 6.1)

Statistical Comparison of Original and Final Versions of Brochure

	Original Version	Revised Version
Paragraphs (#)	8	21
Longest Paragraph	216 words	95 words
Average Paragraph Length	143 words	55 words
Average Sentence Length	23 words	15 words

Owning a Franchise

Sunrise Greeting Cards and Flowers

Hello Potential *Sunrise* Shop Owner!

Would you like to own and run one of the most exciting businesses—providing happy customers with cards and flowers for those special occasions?

As a Sunrise store owner, you would be in a business with loyal customers who appreciate refined and excellent craftsmanship. They expect creative, original, and upscale greeting cards and flower arrangements, and Sunrise delivers. To our customers, our brand represents quality products that help them celebrate special occasions.

When you own a Sunrise store, you tap into a brand that provides profitability, and you also become part of the Sunrise family. We provide you with the products and resources to succeed. We create a tight-knit group of store owners and managers who share ideas about improving our brand and sales performance. To help make this happen, we organize a fun-filled annual retreat where store owners and managers can discuss our shared problems, solutions, and opportunities. We build success together.

In this brochure, you'll find basic answers to your questions about investment costs and profit potential; financial requirements and financing; Sunrise involvement in opening your store; Sunrise commitment to your success after you open your store; and the application process.

I will always be willing to personally answer your questions and explain the wonderful benefits of running a Sunrise business. Please call me or email me anytime to chat about your future with Sunrise!

Stephanie

Stephanie Jorgenson, President and Owner
Sunrise Greeting Cards and Flowers, LLC
Stephanie@sunrisegiftcards.com
1-800-SUN-SET9

Initial Investment Costs & Profit Potential

Initial investment costs for Sunrise shops are comparable to other franchises in the industry, yet average profits from our shops exceed industry averages by 20 to 50 percent.

Initial Investment Costs.* The initial investment typically ranges from $290,000 to $605,000. The table below shows ranges for the initial investment costs.

	Low	High
Fixtures	$ 60,000	$ 90,000
Inventory	80,000	190,000
Store Improvements	20,000	130,000
Retail Equipment	20,000	35,000
Miscellaneous	10,000	30,000
Initial Franchise Fee	50,000	50,000
Total Initial Costs	**$240,000**	**$525,000**
Plus Working Capital	$ 50,000	$ 80,000
Total Required Capital	**$290,000**	**$605,000**

*See our website, sunrisegiftcards.com/franchisees, for detailed information about these expenses.

Profit Potential. Currently, average annual profit per Sunrise store is $153,000, with ranges between $49,000 and $215,000. Profit level depends on many factors, including location, market demand, square footage, and management. Typically, profits become relatively stable after the first three years of operation.

Financial Requirements & Financing

Owning a Sunrise shop requires a strong financial position and evidence of the ability to finance a new business.

Financial Requirements. Sunrise seeks franchise owners who are in a financially sound position. The minimum requirements include a total net worth of $350,000, with unencumbered liquid assets of between $120,000 and $265,000. You will need to show that these liquid assets are personal rather than capital in a current business and available for investment in your Sunrise store. You will also need to show that you can maintain an outside income of at least 80 percent of your present income for at least two years.

FIGURE 6.3

(Continued)

Financing. You are required to finance less than two-thirds of the initial investment costs. Assuming that you finance up to two-thirds of the initial investment costs, you will need access to financing in the range of $170,000 to $340,000. Confirmation of loan, terms, and collateral is required. Sunrise does not provide loans.

Sunrise Involvement in
Opening a New Franchise Store

Sunrise will help plan your Sunrise business and find a location that best supports your goals.

Business Planning. Sunrise will work directly with you to create a marketing plan, budgeting plan, and break-even analysis. Our team of experienced managers will apply our well-developed formula for analyzing the demographics, traffic patterns, local competitors, and other factors of your chosen location. From this analysis, we will provide you with estimates of retail sales and revenue. Our management team will be happy to help you in all phases of the planning and application process.

Location. You are welcome to propose locations for opening a Sunrise franchise. Sunrise will make the final approval of your proposed site but may suggest alternate locations based on our marketing formula, which has worked successfully in the past. The minimum store size is based on location. In shopping malls, the minimum size should be approximately 2,500 square feet. In strip shopping centers, the minimum size should be approximately 3,400 square feet.

Sunrise Commitment to
Your Ongoing Success

After you open your shop, Sunrise will provide the training, marketing, customer support, and products to help you succeed.

Training. Sunrise will provide free training for up to three people for each new store. The training will include 5-day formal workshops about running a Sunrise store. Initial training includes workshop training in Sunrise product line knowledge, merchandising, inventory management, customer relations, accounting procedures, and point-of-sale technology and information management.

We will also, upon request, allow shadowing of a current store manager for up to one week. All travel expenses for the training are the responsibility of new owners.

Advertising/Marketing. Sunrise has aggressively advertised in print and radio in regional markets in recent years. As a result, Sunrise brand recognition is strong. Your store will benefit from Sunrise regional advertising and promotional campaigns (depending on your location). In addition, you will have access to all advertising materials developed by Sunrise for your own use. Your store should spend roughly 3 percent of annual sales on local advertising.

Customer Service/Website Support. Sunrise provides centralized customer service for all product lines at a toll-free number. We also provide a customizable website for your shop with built-in capabilities for your customers to make orders and purchase products. Your customers will also be able to participate in our consumer loyalty program.

Products. Sunrise provides you with many upscale greeting cards and unique flower arrangements that can only be found in Sunrise stores. Similarly, we purchase several other brands of products that we negotiate at the best possible rates and for which we have North America exclusivity rights.

Store owners make their own orders and choose the mix of products that best meets the needs of their customers. To retain status as a Sunrise retailer, store owners must carry certain product lines, use appropriate signs, and abide by advertising specials and offers in Sunrise regional advertising. In short, store owners are expected to carry a mix of products and marketing that match and strengthen the Sunrise brand.

Application Process

Please consider applying for a franchise. To apply, complete the following two forms, which are both available on our website: *Personal Financial Disclosure* and *Store Owner Application*.

The right to open a new Sunrise store will be awarded based on the business plan, market potential in your chosen area, personal interviews, and financial criteria. Once approved, new Sunrise stores can typically be opened in three to twelve months.

Reviewing Your Message

LO6.3 Describe and apply the components of the reviewing stage, including a FAIR test, proofreading, and feedback.

You will recall from Chapter 5 that expert business writers use their time differently than do average business writers (see Figure 5.2 in Chapter 5). They devote more time to planning and reviewing and proportionately less time to drafting. They spend most of their time—before and after drafting—carefully thinking about how the message will influence and affect others.

Many business professionals get anxious to send their messages as soon as they finish drafting them. It is human nature to want to move on to the next task. Resist the urge to move on without carefully reviewing your messages. During the reviewing stage, you will improve your message, making it far more successful. You will also minimize the possibility of embarrassing and damaging mistakes.

The reviewing process includes three interrelated components: conducting the FAIR test, proofreading, and getting feedback (not generally needed for routine messages). These reviewing components ensure that you show fairness, get the message right, avoid errors, and get perspectives from trusted colleagues. For short, routine messages (one to four paragraphs), expert business writers can often check for fairness and proofread in just a few minutes. For long, important messages, such as business proposals or business plans, the reviewing stage may take weeks or months.

Conduct a FAIR Test

In Chapter 1, we introduced the FAIR test as a way of ensuring ethical business communication. Of course, you will consider such issues during the planning and writing stages. Also, during the review process you can also take the time to think about the degree to which your entire message conforms to standards for facts, access, impacts, and respect. For important messages—particularly those that involve complicated business issues—apply the FAIR test:

- *Facts:* Are you confident in your facts? Are your assumptions clear? Have you avoided slanting the facts or made other logical errors?
- *Access:* Have you granted enough access to message recipients about decision making and information? Have you granted enough access to the message recipients to provide input? Are you open about your motives, or do you have a hidden agenda?
- *Impacts:* Have you thought about how the message will impact various stakeholders? Have you evaluated impacts on others from ethical, corporate, and legal perspectives?
- *Respect:* Have you demonstrated respect for the inherent worth of others: their aspirations, thoughts, feelings, and well-being? Have you shown that you value others?

Proofread

Proofreading involves rereading your entire document to make sure it is influential and accurate. You might consider rereading each sentence several times, each time with a different focus. On your first pass, place yourself in the position of your audience members. Imagine how they will respond. On your second pass, check for problems with writing style and language mechanics.

Get Feedback

As one business writing expert stated, one of the best ways to ensure that your communication is effective and fair is to get feedback from others:

> Ask some people whose judgment you respect to give it a test read and get their reaction. Do they think it's too energetic or hyperbolic for the audience and the occasion? Or is it too frosty? Similarly, do they think the writing is too distant or too familiar? What are the offending words or phrases? How can they be changed to do the job at hand? Using test readers is hardly rocket science, but those willing to go through this trouble invariably produce more effective writing.[6]

COMMUNICATION Q&A

CONVERSATIONS WITH CURRENT BUSINESS PROFESSIONALS

Pete Cardon: How important are writing skills in the workplace?

Ronald Scott: They are vital. Members of my staff are regularly required to take complex and technical ordinance language and explain it in plain terms to citizens or customers. This requires the ability to capture the essence and translate it into simple language that the customer can understand and act on. In today's workplace, having good writing skills is an asset that will distinguish an employee from his or her peers. One of the first opportunities an employer has to assess writing skills is when he or she reviews an application for employment or a résumé. A basic review of these two documents can either thoroughly impress or completely horrify a potential employer.

PC: How much time do you spend writing? What types of writing?

RS: I spend approximately half my time writing. Examples include writing emails; drafting letters to customers, citizens, and businesses; drafting letters to local, state, and federal officials; reviewing and correcting written documents and reports prepared by staff; creating policy and procedure manuals; creating form letters; creating grant application and grant documents; and creating budget documents and periodic budget reports.

PC: How formal is business writing?

RS: Typically, business writing is a formal means of communication. Recently, one of my employees wrote a letter to a customer he knew quite well. After his salutation he wrote, "How are you doing today? I hope you are doing well and that you are feeling better." While this language may have been acceptable for an in-person exchange, it seemed too casual and inappropriate for a business letter.

PC: What kinds of writing mistakes do you see most often in the workplace? How damaging are these mistakes? Could you give a recent example?

RS: In my profession we often communicate with large businesses about the cost of development permits for large projects. Some permit fees can be in excess of $50,000. A missing zero in a letter estimating permit fees can make a big difference when a business is preparing its budget. Recently, an employee addressed a letter to a customer about a code violation. He wrote, "You will not need a building permit to complete this work." He intended to write, "You will need a building permit to complete this work." What a difference one word made. Some delicate negotiations were necessary to make the situation right with that customer.

PC: How is writing in the workplace different from writing for school projects?

RS: Business writing requires you to maintain business relationships (even when giving bad news), build and maintain company loyalty and morale, retain customers/clients, and portray a positive image for yourself and your company. Academic writing focuses more on its subject than on the reader's reactions or on the goal of cultivating a long relationship with the reader. When writing for business purposes, we need to make sure we do not hamper business transactions and workflow due to misuse of language, inappropriate expressions and emotions, or lack of empathy.

Ronald Scott is the director of community development for Lexington County in South Carolina. He oversees all development ordinances in his community and administers approximately $2 million annually in federal block grant programs that serve low-income and moderate-income citizens and communities.

This advice reveals an important point: Your trusted colleagues are giving your message a trial run—trying to simulate how the intended message recipient will respond. As they review your message, they can provide insights about making it better. Before they begin to read, ask them to consider whether you have framed the idea correctly, whether the business logic holds up, whether the message has the intended effects, whether the tone is appropriate, and so on. Effective business communicators make a habit of getting this advance feedback for important messages. In the Communication Q&A with Ronald Scott, you can learn more about the importance of clarity, tone, and accuracy in business writing.

Chapter Takeaway for *Improving Readability with Style and Design*

LO 6.1. Describe and apply the following principles of writing style that improve ease of reading: completeness, conciseness, and natural processing. (pp. 148–161)

Improving Ease of Reading with Writing Style		
Completeness	**Conciseness**	**Natural Style**
• Provide all relevant information.	• Control paragraph length.	• Use action verbs when possible.
• Be accurate.	• Use short sentences.	• Use active voice.
• Be specific.	• Avoid redundancy.	• Use short and familiar words and phrases.
	• Avoid empty phrases.	• Use parallel language.
	• Avoid wordy prepositional phrases.	• Avoid buzzwords and figures of speech.
		• Avoid *it is/there are.*

See *examples of writing style improvements* in Tables 6.2 through 6.16.

LO 6.2. Explain and use navigational design to improve ease of reading. (pp. 161–165)

Improving Ease of Reading with Navigational Design		
• Headings	• Lists	• Simplicity
• Highlighting	• White space	

See *examples of navigational design* in Tables 6.17 through 6.19.

LO 6.3. Describe and apply the components of the reviewing stage, including a FAIR test, proofreading, and feedback. (pp. 166–167)

FAIR Test: Evaluate your message in terms of facts, access, impacts, and respect.
Proofreading: Ask trusted colleagues to review your message for effectiveness and accuracy.
Feedback: For important messages, ask trusted colleagues to give input about effectiveness and fairness.

Discussion Exercises

6.1 Chapter Review Questions (LO 6.1, LO 6.2, LO 6.3)

Answer the following questions:

A. How does complete writing improve ease of reading?

B. How does concise writing improve ease of reading?

C. How does natural writing improve ease of reading?

D. How does document design improve ease of reading?

E. Do you think that complete and concise writing are competing goals? Explain.

6.2 Communication Q&A Discussion Questions (LO 6.1)

Answer the following questions based on the comments from Ronald Scott in the Communication Q&A:

A. What does Scott say about the importance of writing? What are several examples he provides to illustrate his points?

B. Based on his statements, what are a few guidelines for determining if your writing is formal enough but not too formal?

C. What does he say about the importance of accuracy in writing?

D. What are some distinctions he makes between academic and business writing?

E. Scott advises young professionals to take writing seriously. What are a few ways you can do that?

Evaluation Exercises

6.3 Analyzing a Corporate Message (LO 6.1, LO 6.2)

In the early months of 2010, Apple and Adobe, two of the largest computer companies, engaged in a high-profile dispute. Adobe officials complained publicly that Apple was not allowing one of Adobe's most successful products, Flash, to run on Apple's new iPad. They even accused Apple of attempting to monopolize the market and engaging in noncompetitive practices. Apple officials claimed that Flash was outdated. In April, Steve Jobs, CEO of Apple, wrote a long statement defending Apple's actions. Read the message at www.apple.com/hotnews/thoughts-on-flash/.

Analyze this message for ease of reading in the following ways:

A. Identify and revise five sentences that are not complete.

B. Identify and revise five sentences that are not concise.

C. Identify and revise five sentences that are not natural.

D. Explain three strategies for designing the document for faster navigation.

E. Revise the document. Attempt to cut the length in half. Use headings and other design features to improve navigation.

6.4 Identifying Areas for Personal Improvement (LO 6.1, LO 6.2)

Identify three writing principles from this chapter that you most need to work on. For each principle, write a paragraph about why you want to improve in this area and how you will go about doing it. Choose from the following writing principles: be specific; be accurate; control paragraph length; use short sentences in most cases; avoid redundancy; avoid empty phrases; avoid wordy phrases; use action verbs when possible; use active voice; use short and familiar words and phrases; use parallel language; avoid buzzwords and figures of speech; avoid *it is* and *there are*; use headings; apply formatting to key words and phrases; use bulleted and numbered lists; use white space generously.

Application Exercises

Case for Exercises 6.5 through 6.18: Promoting the Supply Chain Management Club

Your roommate is the president of the Supply Chain Management Club. She wants you to help her revise a flyer that she has drafted to attract more members. Here is her draft.

Joining a Student Club

Have you thought about joining a student club? If so, we are organizing an information session to orient you to our club.

The purpose of the Supply Chain Management Club (SCMC) that we have here on campus is to support Supply Chain and Operations Management (SCOM) majors as well as other interested majors if they choose to gain a broader and balanced understanding of the opportunities, career paths, trends, and current burning issues in global supply chain management. Each and every semester, SCMC has facility tours, discussion panels, faculty interactions, and resume workshops in order for our members to gain a glimpse into the real world of global supply chain management and the nature of this constantly evolving and developing business field.

There are many, many reasons for being an SCMC member. It goes without saying that many of you want financial aid, and SCMC has received boatloads of generous donations to offer scholarships for qualifying SCMC students. All SCMC club members learn to market themselves more effectively by joining the club. There is a SCMC Placement Coordinator specifically directed to search for every possible job that you could apply for, and these jobs are placed on the SCMC website where you can view them anytime and anywhere. These jobs are in a plethora of industries, like Business Services, Consumer Products and Services, Food and Beverage, Health, Industrial, Public Sector, and Technology and Communications. Also, through SCMC and by also gaining a membership in ISM, certification opportunities will be at your fingertips. The sky's the limit in this club. SCMC board members are currently looking for new opportunities and are researching the potential of funding future group workshops and certification programs that we haven't had access to in the past.

The most popular part of the club that students like the most are the abundant events that are scheduled. Plant tours and speeches by supply-chain professionals are constantly being scheduled for SCMC club members to attend. These events create a big impact on your future career by giving you the opportunities to gain exposure to real-world professionals. One of the great opportunities you have as a member in the club is the opportunity to be in touch with the SCMC alumni group, which gives you a networking chance with people already working in supply chain management.

There are many opportunities to learn special skills since there are special-interest groups within the club. For example, there is a special-interest group devoted to learning about various software tools for global supply chain management. In the software group, you can learn statistical software programs such as POM for Windows, Excel Solver, ProcessModel, and SPSS as well as learning mapping software such as MapPoint. Skills acquired in these special-interest groups can be placed on your resume in conjunction with other skills developed in your studies from the SCOM major. It can't be stated enough how much these extra skills can enhance your qualifications to be a supply-chain manager.

The Supply Chain Management Club (SCMC) is designed to help club members understand the critical and essential organizational function of global supply chain and operations management that creates and distributes products and services; measures their quality and instigates the processes whereby quality improvement occurs; and simultaneously creates nimble, streamlined, and efficient business processes and supply chains. This critical business function is responsible for short-term survival and long-term profitability and growth of the organization in all types of businesses, such as large or small, manufacturing or service, or even for-profit or non-profit. In today's globally interconnected economy, prowess in global supply chain and operations management is the benchmark of the great manufacturers, retailers, and major companies, such as Dell, Wal-Mart, Southwest Airlines, Toyota, and Bank of America. Supply chain management is the fundamental competency that determines success in today's business world, and by joining the SCMC club, you literally have success in your hands since so many major businesses will need your services.

The Supply Chain Management Club (SCMC) is extremely practical with many career options in global manufacturing firms in production, purchasing, quality control, distribution and supply chain management; in service firms as general operations management and logistics/supply chain management; in consulting firms as business process and quality improvement consultants. In fact, even if you are pursuing other professions as primary careers, SCOM skills and competencies make one a better accountant, better at financial analysis, better as marketing manager, or even better at managing human resources or managing information technology for a company.

The club is affiliated with the Institute for Supply Chain Management (ISM), which was founded in the year 1915 and the biggest supply chain management association in the world and is recognized by supply chain professionals far and wide as the repository of best practices in the field. The ISM website can be visited at the following website: http://www.ism.ws/.

A pizza party will be held in the business building on January 29 to introduce you to the club. This meeting will provide a lot of information about reasons for joining the club.

All of our regular meetings are at the Marriot next to the business school. A speech is always given by an important industry professional. Dinner is served at just $10.

Rewrite each of the following sentences from her draft to be complete, concise, and natural. The sentences are organized by principles from the chapter; however, note that many sentences contain additional style issues for you to correct. Make reasonable embellishments as necessary.

6.5 Be Specific (LO 6.1)

A. Have you thought about joining a student club? If so, we are organizing an information session to orient you to our club.

B. A pizza party will be held in the business building on January 29 to introduce you to the club.

C. This meeting will provide a lot of information about reasons for joining the club.

D. All of our regular meetings are at the Marriot next to the business school.

6.6 Be Accurate (LO 6.1)

A. Supply chain management is the fundamental competency that determines success in today's business world, and by joining the SCMC club, you literally have success in your hands so all major businesses will need your services.

B. All SCMC club members learn to market themselves more effectively by joining the club.

6.7 Use Short Sentences in Most Cases (LO 6.1)

Cut these sentences by more than 50 percent. Use more than one sentence if necessary.

A. The purpose of the Supply Chain Management Club (SCMC) that we have here on campus is to support Supply Chain and Operations Management (SCOM) majors as well as other interested majors if they choose to gain a broader and balanced understanding of the opportunities, career paths, trends, and current burning issues in global supply chain management.

B. The Supply Chain Management Club (SCMC) is designed to help club members understand the critical and essential organizational function of global supply chain and operations management that creates and distributes products and services; measures their quality and instigates the processes whereby quality improvement occurs; and simultaneously creates nimble, streamlined, and efficient business processes and supply chains.

C. This critical business function is responsible for short-term survival and long-term profitability and growth of the organization in all types of businesses, such as large or small, manufacturing or service, or even for-profit or non-profit.

6.8 Avoid Redundancy (LO 6.1)

Remove redundancies and shorten these sentences.

A. Each and every semester, SCMC has facility tours, discussion panels, faculty interactions, and resume workshops in order for our members to gain a glimpse into the real world of global supply chain management and the nature of this constantly evolving and developing business field.

B. There is a SCMC Placement Coordinator specifically directed to search for every possible job that you could apply for, and these jobs are placed on the SCMC website where you can view them anytime and anywhere.

C. The most popular part of the club that students like the most are the abundant events that are scheduled.

6.9 Avoid Empty Phrases (LO 6.1)

Remove empty phrases and shorten these sentences.

A. It goes without saying that many of you want financial aid.

B. It can't be stated enough how much these extra skills can enhance your qualifications to be a supply-chain manager.

6.10 Avoid Wordy Prepositional Phrases (LO 6.1)

Rewrite these sentences to reduce wordy prepositional phrases.

A. Skills acquired in these special-interest groups can be placed on your resume in conjunction with other skills developed in your studies from the SCOM major.

B. One of the great opportunities you have as a member in the club is the opportunity to be in touch with the SCMC alumni group, which gives you a networking chance with people already working in supply chain management.

6.11 Use Action Verbs When Possible (LO 6.1)

Rewrite these sentences to include action verbs.

A. The Supply Chain Management Club (SCMC) is extremely practical with many career options.

B. These events create a big impact on your future career by giving you the opportunities to gain exposure to real-world professionals.

6.12 Use Active Voice (LO 6.1)

Rewrite these sentences to use active voice instead of passive.

A. Plant tours and speeches by supply-chain professionals are constantly being scheduled for SCMC club members to attend.

B. A speech is always given by an important industry professional.

6.13 Use Short and Familiar Words and Phrases (LO 6.1)

Replace uncommon words with familiar words and phrases.

A. These jobs are in a plethora of industries.

B. In today's globally interconnected economy, prowess in global supply chain and operations management is the benchmark of the great manufacturers, retailers, and major companies, such as Dell, Wal-Mart, Southwest Airlines, Toyota, and Bank of America.

6.14 Use Parallel Language (LO 6.1)

Rewrite these sentences so the language is parallel.

A. SCOM skills and competencies make one a better accountant, better at financial analysis, better as marketing manager, or even better at managing human resources or managing information technology for a company.

B. In the software group, you can learn statistical software programs such as POM for Windows, Excel Solver, ProcessModel, and SPSS as well as learning mapping software such as MapPoint.

6.15 Avoid Buzzwords and Figures of Speech (LO 6.1)

Rewrite these sentences to eliminate buzzwords and figures of speech.

A. Also, through SCMC and by also gaining a membership in ISM, certification opportunities will be at your fingertips.

B. The sky's the limit in this club.

C. SCMC has received boatloads of generous donations to offer scholarships for qualifying SCMC students.

6.16 Avoid *It Is* and *There Is/Are* (LO 6.1)

Rewrite these sentences to improve clarity.

A. There are many opportunities to learn special skills since there are special-interest groups within the club.

B. There is a special-interest group devoted to learning about various software tools for global supply chain management.

6.17 Setting Up Effective Navigational Design (LO 6.2)

A. If you were going to use headings in this document, how would you group sections? What headings would you use?

B. Which parts of the document would you consider converting to bulleted or numbered lists?

C. What other strategies would you consider for making the document easy to navigate?

6.18 Revising the Supply Chain Management Club Flyer (LO 6.1, LO 6.2)

Revise the entire student club flyer. Create an effective flyer to help promote the Supply Chain Management Club. Make sure the document is as easy to read as possible while retaining all relevant information.

6.19 Converting the Sunrise Brochure into a Frequently Asked Questions Document (LO 6.1, LO 6.2)

Convert the Sunrise brochure into a Frequently Asked Questions document. Assume that you will place it on the Sunrise website.

Case for Problems 6.20 and 6.21: Expressing Interest as a Prospective Sunrise Franchise Owner

Stephanie recently gave Jenny Li one of the franchise brochures while at an industry exhibition. Jenny Li was eager to learn more about franchise opportunities with Sunrise. She wrote the following letter to introduce herself and describe her qualifications.

Dear Stephanie,

It was an honor to meet you at the Flower Exhibition. It is with great interest that I write this letter to describe my genuine hopes to be a franchisee. There are many reasons why I am interested in this opportunity, and there are many reasons why I am qualified to be a franchisee for you. I have been in the flower industry for over twelve years in various capacities such as starting as a flower deliverer, then I acted as a flower arranger, and finally for the last eight years I was the shop manager for a flower shop in the mall. In my time as a shop manager, I was told by the shop owner and dozens of employees that I was the right person to lead the shop and that sales were higher at my location than any other shop in that chain (which has 18 shops at malls in my state and the three surrounding states). In fact, sales at my shop have increased every quarter that I have been the shop manager with the exception of just two quarters in the eight years of my stewardship. I am very proactive in my approach to sales and think that my approach of keeping repeat customers happy is the key to success at my shop and which I seek to continue as a franchisee. I have used so many marketing techniques to gain our customers' attention. Such as, I have created a Facebook group and I send specials to the people in that group. Not to mention I send targeted coupons by mail and email that are sent to the customers with specific types of interests. There is no substitute for knowing your customers. I also do many great special events at seasonal periods and have won prizes for flower arrangements many times that bring the shop good press. My flower arrangements were even featured in some TV commercials for the flower shops across our region. There are not any Sunrise stores near here and I believe from the bottom of my heart that this is the right time to invest in this area. I know without any doubt that you will be impressed with my work ethic and my focus on the customer. Needless to say, the customer is king, and we need to treat them that way. I am capable of meeting all of the financial obligations. Thank you and hope to hear from you soon. Most of all, is I love people, and if you are caring for your customers, you will achieve your goals and reach the pinnacle of success.

Regards,

Jenny

6.20 Revising a Message for Readability (LO 6.1, LO 6.2)

Analyze this message for ease of reading in the following ways:

A. Identify and revise five sentences that are not complete.

B. Identify and revise five sentences that are not concise.

C. Identify and revise five sentences that are not natural.

D. Explain three strategies for designing the document for faster navigation.

6.21 Rewriting a Message for Readability and Effectiveness (LO 6.1, LO 6.2, LO 6.3)

Rewrite the entire document. Ensure that the message is easy to read and effectively highlights Jenny's potential for owning and running a Sunrise franchise.

Use the following table with statistics about the cereal industry[7] for problems 6.22 through 6.33. In some cases, you will need to carefully review the information in the table to get the correct answers.

Comparisons between Kellogg Company and General Mills

	Kellogg Company (K)	**General Mills (GM)**
Top-Selling Cereal	Special K	Cheerios
Market Share in Cereal Industry	34%	31%
Number of Employees	30,900	33,000
Headquarters	Battle Creek, Michigan	Minneapolis, Minnesota
CEO Annual Salary	$11.5 million	$11.1 million
Main Products	Ready-to-eat cereals, cookies, toaster pastries, cereal bars, frozen waffles, and meat alternatives	Ready-to-eat cereals, yogurt, ready-to-serve soup, dry dinners, frozen vegetables, dough products, baking mixes, frozen pizza, snacks
Newly Introduced Products	Special K crackers, fruit crisps, and chocolate pretzel bars. New Special K flavors such as cinnamon pecan, fruit and nut clusters, and blueberry	Chocolate Cheerios, Yoplait Delights yogurt parfaits, Wanchai Ferry frozen foods, Betty Crocker gluten free dessert mixes, new Häagen-Dazs ice cream flavors
North American Revenues	67.7% of total revenues	81.6% of total revenues
Worldwide Revenues	$12.5 billion	$14.8 billion
Worldwide Advertising Expenses	$1.1 billion	$908 million
Net Sales Percentage to Wal-Mart	44%	30%
Negative Media Attention	Product recalls due to potential salmonella contamination	Ammonia leaks at its manufacturing facilities
Least Nutritious Children's Cereals (NPI is a nutritional ranking for cereals ranging from 34 [worst] to 72 [best] and issued by the Rudd Center.)	Corn Pops (NPI: 35.8); Froot Loops (NPI: 38.0); Apple Jacks (NPI: 40.0)	Reese's Puffs (34.0); Golden Grahams (36.0); Lucky Charms (36.0); Cinnamon Toast Crunch (36.6); Trix (38.0); Count Chocula (38.0)
Yogurt Sales	N/A	General Mills yogurt brands include Yoplait, Trix, Yoplait Kids, Go-GURT, Fiber One, YoPlus, and Whips! Approximately $1.5 billion in yogurt sales

Other statistics about the breakfast cereal industry:

- Approximately two-thirds of all cereals are sold with a deal (discounts, coupons).
- The total cereal market in the United States is approximately $9 billion.
- Gross profit margins in the breakfast cereal industry average between 40 and 45 percent.
- The global cereal market is approximately $28.7 billion.
- The ten cereals most marketed on TV to children are the following (company and percentage of sugar content displayed in parentheses): 1. Cinnamon Toast Crunch (GM; 33%); 2. Honey Nut Cheerios (GM; 32%); 3. Lucky Charms (GM; 41%); 4. Cocoa Puffs (GM; 44%); 5. Trix (GM; 38%); 6. Frosted Flakes (K; 37%); 7. Fruity and Cocoa Pebbles (Post; 37%); 8. Reese's Puffs (GM; 41%); 9. Corn Pops (K; 41%); 10. Froot Loops (K; 41%).

6.22 Being Accurate (LO 6.1)

Use the table above to proofread the following items and correct them as needed.

A. Please address correspondence to the following address: General Mills, PO Box 1493, Minneapolis, MI.

B. The annually salary for General Mills' CEO is higher than that of Kellogg Company's CEO by approximately $400 thousand.

C. With nearly half of their net sales to Wal-Mart, General Mills and Kellogg Company are extremely dependent on a single retailer.

D. General Mills has six children's cereals with NPI rankings below 40, whereas Kellogg's has just three.

E. General Mills spends approximately 8.1 percent of its total revenues on advertising, whereas Kellogg Company spends roughly 8.8 percent of its total revenues on advertising.

F. Kellogg's children's cereals are the least nutritious cereals in the industry.

G. Since only about one in four boxes of cereal is sold without deals of some kind, cereal producers must constantly market new and exciting discounts and coupons.

H. General Mills reached $1.5 million in yogurt sales last year.

I. One of Kellogg Company's worst negative publicity resulted from ammonia leaks at some its manufacturing facilities.

J. The United States cereal market accounts for approximately 35.1 percent of the world market.

6.23 Being Specific (LO 6.1)

Use information from the table above to revise the following sentences and make them more specific.

A. General Mills markets through television to children far more than other cereal makers.

B. Gross profit margins in the breakfast cereal industry are quite high.

C. Kellogg's Company and General Mills have each experienced negative media attention recently.

D. General Mills is more dependent on the North American market than Kellogg Company.

E. While General Mills and Kellogg Company have similar product mixes, they each market several products not offered by the other.

F. Kellogg Company and General Mills are the top two cereal makers.

G. Kellogg Company and General Mills have each introduced new flavors for their products in recent years.

H. General Mills offers the least nutritious children's cereal on the market.

I. Kellogg's cereals include three children's cereals with NPI scores at 40 or below: Corn Pops, Froot Loops, and Apple Jack's.

6.24 Using Short Sentences in Most Cases (LO 6.1)

Revise each of the following items to make the sentences shorter and more readable.

A. General Mills is a dominant player in the American yogurt industry with $1.5 billion in sales, and it sells yogurts under a variety of brands, including Yoplait, Trix, Yoplait Kids, Go-GURT, Fiber One, Whips!, and YoPlus.

B. The two cereal giants, Kellogg Company and General Mills, do not remain complacent with their existing products lines but rather routinely develop and market new products—after all, Kellogg Company has recently introduced new products such as Special K crackers, fruit crisps, and chocolate pretzel bars, and General Mills has recently added new products such as Chocolate Cheerios, Yoplait Delights yogurt parfaits, Wanchai Ferry frozen foods, and Betty Crocker gluten free dessert mixes.

C. The total cereal market in the United States is $9 billion, which is just a small and decreasing portion—31.4 percent—of the worldwide market, which is seeing robust growth in the BRIC countries of Brazil, Russia, India, and China.

6.25 Avoid Redundancy (LO 6.1)

Revise each of the following sentences to eliminate redundancy.

A. Discount coupons for select Kellogg's cereals contain rebates of between 10 and 20 percent that can save you money.

B. Kellogg Company definitely needs to view crisis communications for the salmonella outbreak as absolutely necessary.

C. Please make advance reservations for the bloggers conference hosted at General Mills to see how you can connect and cooperate together with other corporate bloggers.

6.26 Avoid Empty Phrases (LO 6.1)

Revise each of the following items to eliminate empty phrases.

A. Needless to say, General Mills is by all accounts among the worst offenders of marketing less healthy cereals to children.

B. In my personal opinion, Kellogg's children's cereals are in a very real sense superior to General Mills in terms of nutritional value.

C. The point I am trying to make is that parents, for all intents and purposes, are usually unaware of how unhealthy most children's cereals are.

6.27 Avoid Wordy Prepositional Phrases (LO 6.1)

Revise each of the following items to eliminate wordy prepositional phrases.

A. In view of the recent rankings about nutritional values for cereals, I think we should focus for the next product development cycle on a reduction in sugar content and an increase in fiber content.

B. For companies in the food industry, a heavy proportion of sales to Wal-Mart provides advantages in terms of higher revenues and a boost in name recognition but disadvantages in terms of lower margins on sales and reduction in customer perceptions of quality.

C. In light of the product recalls in recent times, Kellogg Company is in no position to tout a reputation for food safety.

6.28 Use Action Verbs When Possible (LO 6.1)

Improve each of the following sentences by using action verbs.

A. Kellogg Company has new product developments and marketing efforts as part of its re-branding strategy that demonstrates a healthy-food focus.

B. General Mills is a company with strong yogurt brand, and it is in a position of leverage in this regard to achieve higher visibility for healthy foods.

C. The CEO of Kellogg will provide an announcement about new corporate strategy, give his explanation for how the company will reach its goals, and do a presentation about the current financial situation.

6.29 Use Active Voice (LO 6.1)

Revise each of the following sentences to switch them from passive to active voice.

A. The NPI rankings were widely publicized in media outlets and were a cause for concern among many cereal executives.

B. The new Special K flavors—cinnamon pecan, fruit and nut clusters, and blueberry—were introduced last year, and Kellogg reports that they have been a huge success.

C. Market strategies to promote healthier cereals were the focus of discussions among industry insiders.

D. Your inaction in confronting the potential salmonella contamination lost us millions of dollars in revenues.

E. Quick crisis communications were the key to General Mills quickly eliminating negative press about the ammonia leaks.

6.30 Use Short and Familiar Words and Phrases (LO 6.1)

Revise the following sentences to eliminate unnecessarily long and/or unfamiliar words and phrases.

A. General Mills has abated the public's denouncements of its high-sugar children's cereals by curtailing sugar content by 8 percent on average.

B. The preeminent cereal brands for the dominant duo of cereal-makers, Kellogg Company and General Mills, are Special K and Cheerios, respectively.

C. By incentivizing discount programs with multi-purchase point allocations and associated rewards, cereal-makers could develop enhanced affinity to brands.

6.31 Use Parallel Language (LO 6.1)

Revise the following sentences for parallelism.

A. Kellogg Company and General Mills produce ready-to-eat cereals and also are selling cereal bars.

B. At the bloggers conference hosted by General Mills, the sessions will include the following: (a) reaching a business audience; (b) best practices in tagging; and (c) how to partner with companies.

C. Special K is Kellogg's leading cereal and is continuing to match sales targets.

D. Wanchai Ferry frozen foods are named after the famous tourist spot in Hong Kong, which is known for excitement, attracting boisterous crowds, and creates an exotic atmosphere.

E. Make sure to sign up for RSS feeds from the General Mills Investor Relations page to stay updated with stock prices and for gaining the latest news about the company.

6.32 Avoid Buzzwords and Figures of Speech (LO 6.1)

Revise the following sentences to eliminate buzzwords and clichéd figures of speech.

A. The latest hot news for the industry is that Kellogg's and General Mills will develop synergistic working relationships with international partners to get a piece of the pie in the BRIC countries.

B. General Mills' latest strategy is nothing more than a swing for the fence.

C. Just as an FYI, I want everyone to come ready to our next meeting to think outside of the box.

6.33 Avoid *It Is/There Are* (LO 6.1)

Revise the following sentences to eliminate the phrases *it is* and *there are*.

A. It is gratifying that General Mills has reduced sugar content in its children's cereals so that there are fewer children who face obesity.

B. There are several new product lines for Kellogg Company that it hopes will show that there is still plenty of innovation and creativity at the company.

C. It is critical for Kellogg Company to tell the public that there is a risk of salmonella contamination in some of its products and that there will be full rebates for products purchased with peanuts as ingredients.

Endnotes

1. Granville N. Toogood, *The Articulate Executive: Learn to Look, Act, and Sound Like a Leader* (New York: McGraw-Hill, 1996).

2. The National Commission on Writing for America's Families, Schools, and Colleges, *Writing: A Ticket to Work . . . Or a Ticket Out: A Survey of Business Leaders* (New York: CollegeBoard, September 2004).

3. New York Times Corner Office Blog, "Communication," retrieved June 15, 2010, from http://projects.nytimes.com/corner-office/Communication.

4. Figure adapted from Ann Wylie, "How to Make Your Copy More Readable: Make Sentences Shorter," *Comprehension* (January 14,

2009), retrieved March 3, 2012, from http://comprehension.prsa.org/?p=217.

5. Accountemps, "What's the Buzz? Survey Reveals Most Overused Workplace Terms," retrieved March 3, 2012, from http://accountemps.rhi.mediaroom.com/Buzzwords.

6. Richard Bierck, "Find the Right Tone for Your Business Writing," *Harvard Management Communication Letter* 4, no. 9 (2001): 10–11.

7. Cereal nutrition facts are based on 2009 figures from the Rudd Center: www.cerealfacts.org/media/Marketing_Rankings/Brand_Nutrition.pdf.

CHAPTER SEVEN

Email and Social Media for Business Communication

Learning Objectives

After studying this chapter, you should be able to do the following:

LO7.1   Apply principles for writing effective emails.

LO7.2   Explain how to handle emotion effectively in online communications.

LO7.3   Describe strategies for managing digital message overload.

LO7.4   Explain characteristics of the emerging Social Age.

LO7.5   Apply principles of effective social media use in professional settings.

LO7.6   Build a credible online reputation.

LO7.7   Describe the ethical use of social media for work.

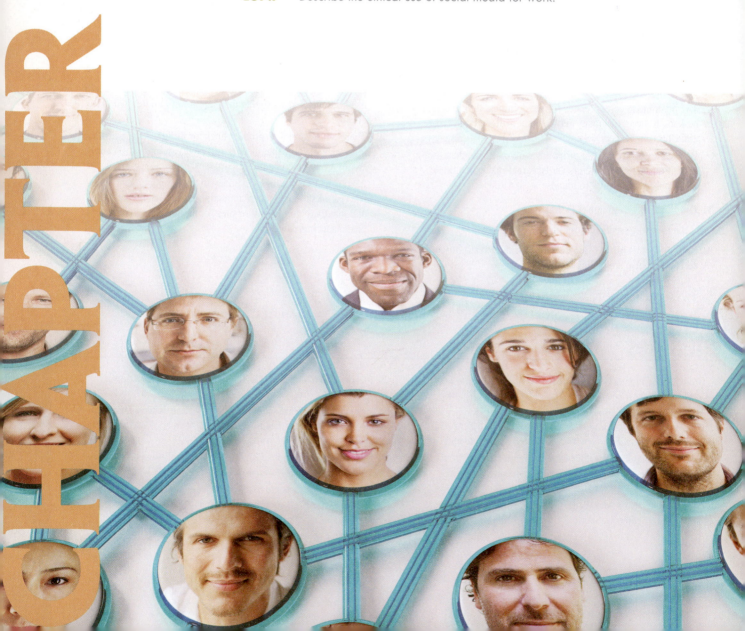

WHY DOES THIS MATTER?

Hear Pete Cardon explain why this matters.

bit.ly/CardonWhy7

For nearly two decades, email has been the primary written business communication tool. In Table 7.1, you can see that in a recent study, it ranked second in effectiveness among communication channels for coordinating work.[1] Even with so many emerging communication tools, *email remains the channel of choice.*[2]

Writing emails will likely consume much of your time early in your career. One study showed that corporate employees spend 25 percent of their days on email-related tasks. By comparison, they spend 14 percent of their time in personal meetings and 9 percent of their time in phone conversations.[3] Another study found that corporate workers average 14.5 hours per week reading and responding to email.[4] The number of emails that business professionals deal with is astounding; the average business professional receives 58 legitimate (non-spam) emails per day and writes 33. By 2015, business professionals are projected to receive 71 emails per day and write 41.[5]

Emails, however, are not efficient for all types of written communication. Typically, email is most appropriate for private communication. For team and networked communication, social media tools such as blogs and wikis are generally more efficient (see Chapter 2 for distinctions between private, team, and networked communication). Many businesses are now adopting social media (often used nearly synonymously with terms such as *Web 2.0, Enterprise 2.0, social networking, social software,* and a variety of other terms) for internal use; however, these tools still account for a small percentage of business communication. This will change rapidly over the next decade. Some analysts project that social media tools will dominate business communication by the year 2020.[6]

In this chapter we first focus on email in the workplace. Then, we discuss the evolving adoption of social media tools, which is transforming work culture into the Social Age. Next, we describe how blogs, wikis, and other social media tools are being used. We conclude with sections about managing your online reputation and using social media ethically. Examples throughout the chapter come from the chapter case about the Prestigio Hotel. Take a few minutes to familiarize yourself with this case prior to reading the remainder of the chapter.

TABLE 7.1

Most Effective Communication Channels for Coordinating Work

Skills	Percentage of Business Professionals
1. Scheduled meetings	89
2. Email	**84**
3. Landline phone	75
4. Cell phone	72
5. File sharing	57
6. Informal conversations	45
7. Texting	41
8. Instant messaging	29
9. Private messages on social networking platforms	15
10. Group messages on social networking platforms	12

Source: Peter W. Cardon, Melvin Washington, Ephraim A. Okoro, Bryan Marshall, and Nipul Patel, "Cross-Generational Perspectives on How Mobile Phone Use for Texting and Calling Influences Work Outcomes and Work Relationships," presented at the Association for Business Communication Southeast Conference, Charleston, South Carolina, April 1, 2011. *Note:* Percentages based on the number of business professionals who rated communication channel as *effective* or *extremely effective* in their current jobs.

Chapter Case: Communicating with Emails and Social Media at the Prestigio Hotel

Who's Involved

Andrea Garcia,
general manager

Nancy Jeffreys,
director of marketing

Barbara Brookshire,
director of conventions

Jeff Anderton,
marketing assistant

Kip Yamada,
marketing associate

The **Prestigio**
Marketing Team

Situation 1   Barbara Uses Emails with Clients to Establish Terms

Barbara leads efforts to negotiate contract terms for conferences. Generally, representatives of businesses and other organizations contact Barbara by phone or email. After an initial phone consultation and an on-site visit with potential clients, Barbara handles most of the marketing and negotiation by email. Before a deal is done, she typically sends and receives 20 emails with any given client to respond to questions and concerns and to finalize terms of the agreement.

Situation 2   Nancy and Kip Handle a Delicate Situation by Email

Nancy, the director of marketing, and Kip, a marketing associate, recently had a conflict that generated hard feelings. Nancy harshly criticized Kip for making what she believed were unauthorized refunds to some business travelers. Kip thought Nancy was unjustified. After several months of not working well together, they aired their grievances to one another. Nevertheless, Kip still had some unresolved issues and decided to send a quick email to Nancy expressing his feelings about the conversation.

Situation 3   The Marketing Team Adopts Social Media for Team Communication

The entire marketing team has recently started using enterprise social software (which functions in many ways like Facebook but is customized for use within an organization). The team is using blogs, wikis, and other tools to follow up with one another related to action items agreed on in meetings, discuss ongoing projects and campaigns, and update one another about their accomplishments.

Task 1
How will Barbara manage emails to show professionalism and increase her likelihood of success with prospects? (See the section on creating effective emails.)

Task 2
How will Kip compose an email in an emotionally charged situation? How will Nancy respond? (See the "Manage Emotion and Maintain Civility" section.)

Task 3
How will the marketing team use social media to work more efficiently together? (See "Internal Communication Tools for the Social Age.")

Creating Effective Emails

Email communication is the primary form of written business communication. Most analysts expect it to be the primary tool for at least the next five to ten years in most companies.[7] Some forward-thinking companies are increasingly adopting social networking platforms (SNPs) for employee communication (discussed later); however, even in companies that adopt these SNPs, employees will continue to use private electronic messages within these platforms, which function nearly identically to emails. Furthermore, many of your colleagues, clients, and other contacts will likely prefer to use email systems for many years to come.

LO7.1 Apply principles for writing effective emails.

Writing effective emails involves applying the principles of writing style that we discussed in Chapters 5 and 6. It also involves adapting to the unique characteristics of email. In this section, we explain basic principles for using emails effectively, including the basic components that ensure ease of reading. Then, we focus on managing emotion and maintaining civility in electronic communications.

Use Email for the Right Purposes

Email is easy and convenient. Before quickly sending out an email, however, consider whether it is the best communication channel for your work purposes.

Since emails are not rich—meaning lacking in virtually all verbal and nonverbal cues associated with face-to-face communication and lacking immediate feedback—they are best suited for routine, task-oriented, fact-based, and nonsensitive messages.[8] Communication specialist Alan Murray, in a *Wall Street Journal* article called "Should I Use Email?" explained:

> To avoid miscommunication, we suggest a simple rule: Email can be used effectively as a means to pass on straight facts, or to provide praise and encouragement. But it shouldn't be used to chastise, scold, or deliver bad news. If the message you are delivering is a discouraging one, it's best to deliver it in person.[9]

Email communication has few constraints (low cost, little coordination) and high control (the writer can think them out carefully, and they provide a permanent record). Yet because it is not a rich form of communication, it is rarely appropriate for sensitive or emotional communication tasks. It is also inefficient for facilitating discussions.

Principles of Effective Emails

- Use for the right purposes.
- Ensure ease of reading.
- Show respect for time.
- Protect privacy and confidentiality.
- Respond promptly.
- Maintain professionalism and appropriate formality.
- Manage emotion effectively.
- Avoid distractions.

Ensure Ease of Reading

In all written communication, ensuring ease of reading is critical. It is even more critical in emails and other digital messages. Simply put, your readers are unlikely to read your message unless you make it easy for them. Compare the ease of reading in the less-effective and more-effective examples of emails in Figures 7.1 and 7.2. Think about how quickly a reader can process the information. Also, use the following tips to ensure ease of reading in your emails.

Provide a Short, Descriptive Subject Line   Message recipients make immediate judgments about the importance of a message based on the subject line. If it is not clear and compelling, recipients may not open the message right away. Furthermore, when business professionals search for prior email messages, they often scan the subject lines in their in-boxes. Without a descriptive subject line, they may miss the message. Good subject lines are generally five to ten words long. By contrast, poor subjects are either too short (1 or 2 words) and thus nondescriptive or too long (12 words or longer) and thus difficult to process. Fundamentally, subject lines frame your entire message; they serve the same role that headlines do in newspapers and magazines.

Keep Your Message Brief Yet Complete   Get to the point within three or four sentences, and keep your paragraphs about half the size of those in business

Components of Effective Emails

- Subject line
- Greeting*
- Message
- Closing*
- Signature block*
- Attachments*

*optional

FIGURE 7.1

Less-Effective Email

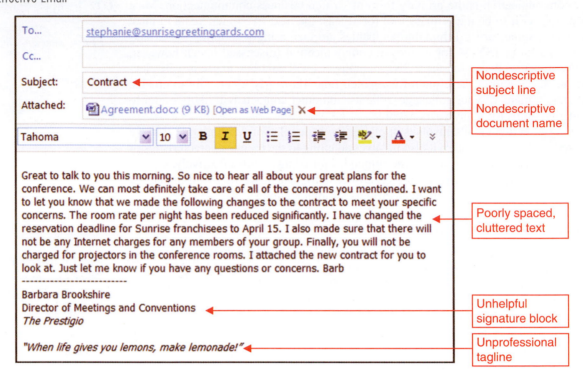

documents—ideally 30 to 50 words long. Consider placing the most critical information at the beginning so readers gather the most relevant information immediately. This is an important strategy, since most people are so inundated with messages that they often pay more attention to the beginning, skimming or skipping latter portions. This is especially important as business professionals increasingly use mobile devices.

Clearly Identify Expected Actions   Most emails are intended to spur action. Effective emails contain specific and clear requests so that recipients know exactly how to respond. In many cases, you can place these directions in the subject line for greatest clarity.

Provide a Descriptive Signature Block   Signature blocks should provide clear contact information. This allows recipients to easily contact you through richer communication channels if needed. It also enhances your professional image.

Use Attachments Wisely   Attachments allow business professionals to share files that do not display effectively in an email window. Messages that are more than several paragraphs long are typically appropriate as attachments. Also, pictures and other graphics, spreadsheets, databases, and many other types of files are nearly always more appropriate as attachments. However, be careful about sending attachments that are too large, since they may fill others' email boxes.

Show Respect for Others' Time

Since email communication is so convenient, some people overuse and even abuse it. With business professionals sending and receiving hundreds of emails each week, they often experience information overload and email fatigue. Every time you write an email, you might want to envision your colleagues and clients who are receiving them. Imagine their time pressures and the line of emails awaiting their response. Assume they will likely have low tolerance for poorly written, sloppy, unclear emails.

FIGURE 7.2

More-Effective Email

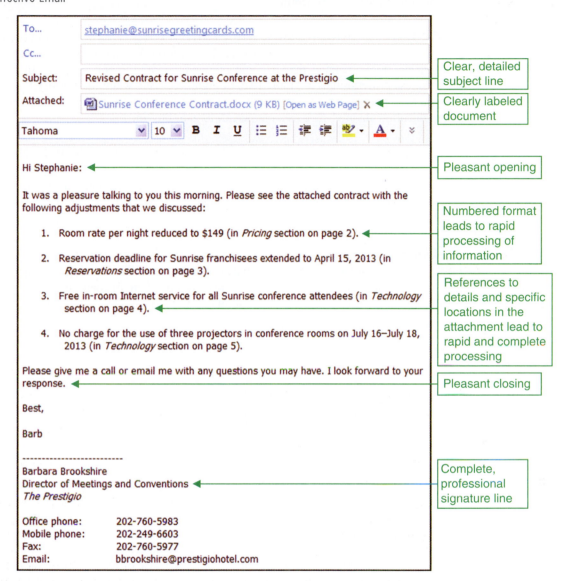

In the business world, where time pressures can be overwhelming, you can engender goodwill by writing emails that are professional, relevant, easy to read, and other-oriented. To show your respect for others when sending email, consider the following advice.

Select Message Recipients Carefully   Before sending an email, think about the workload you are creating for your colleagues or other message recipients. Not only do they commit time to reading your email, but they also often interrupt another work task to do so. If you are requesting information or action, your colleagues are further committed in terms of time. So, make sure the email is necessary and relevant for each of your message recipients.

Provide Timelines and Options   If you use email to coordinate tasks with deadlines, provide detailed information about time frames and your availabilities. If you are setting up appointments, make sure you have provided several options. By clearly providing timelines and schedules, you minimize the number of emails needed to coordinate your efforts, thus saving time. By providing options, you show respect for your colleagues' schedules.

Be Careful about Using the Priority Flag   You will routinely make requests of others that are time-sensitive. If you too often set the priority flag on such emails, your colleagues may become annoyed, perceiving you as pushy. In fact, some business professionals are more likely to ignore emails when the priority flag is set. If you need something urgently, mention it politely in the subject line or use a rich communication channel such as a phone call to gain buy-in.

Let Others Know When You Will Take Longer Than Anticipated to Respond or Take Action   If you can't respond to a request made in an email, reply immediately and explain how soon you can respond in full. You might use phrases such as "I will respond to your email by next Tuesday," or "I can take care of this by the end of next week."

Avoid Contributing to Confusing and Repetitive Email Chains
Email chains are groups of emails that are sent back and forth among a group of people. As the number of messages and people involved in an email chain increases, confusion can build. Consider the following complaint of a business professional:

> One of my biggest pet peeves has to do with forwards. My company will often send out a corporate email to the all-hands list, then a program manager will forward that email to the same all-hands list "in case you didn't get this," then the department head will forward the same email back to the same all-hands list "in case you didn't get this." Often another layer or two of management feels compelled to forward the same email down to their organizational levels for the same reason. I'm not exaggerating when I say that I often have to delete the same email five or six times! Please, if you're in the habit of forwarding announcements for "FYI" reasons, pay attention to which lists you're forwarding to and which people are already on those lists.[10]

Three features contribute to email chains: *forward, copy,* and *reply to all.* The forward feature allows you to send any message you receive to others with the click of the mouse. As always, make sure that those you are forwarding the message to *need* to see the email. Also, consider whether the original sender would consider it appropriate for you to forward the email to others; after all, he or she did not place those people on the original email. Similarly, many business professionals consider use of the *blind carbon copy* feature a breach of privacy. Furthermore, the ease of forwarding and copying can create other problems. Once you send an email, you have no control over whether others will forward it, and to whom, which leads to a good standard articulated by Tony DiRomualdo, strategy and IT researcher: "Don't say anything you would not want the entire planet to read at some point."[11]

Many business professionals use the *copy* feature liberally to let everyone in a department or work unit in on the conversation. Of course, one of your goals is transparency, allowing others in your relevant work group to know how decisions are being made. But copying too many people can lead to information overload. Furthermore, copying too many people on an email can dilute responsibility. When five or six people receive an email about accomplishing a specific task, uncertainty may arise about exactly who is supposed to do what. The more people you copy, the less likely you will get a response. Also, some people perceive copying a direct supervisor or boss on emails between peers as a subtle power play.[12]

The *reply to all* feature can contribute to confusing email chains in many of the same ways as the *forward* and *copy* features. In an email conversation of more than four or five people, various message recipients can lose track of the sequence of messages or miss some messages altogether. Reply email chains become especially confusing when some colleagues are using just the *reply* feature whereas others are using the *reply to all* feature. One advantage of team blogs and wikis in the workplaces is that they remove some of the inefficiencies and confusion of email chains by placing messages and shared content in a central location rather than in various, separate email boxes.

Protect Privacy and Confidentiality

Be careful about not spreading—purposely or inadvertently—sensitive or confidential information. Since emails are so convenient to send, even the rare mistake in an address line can result in damaging professional consequences. Consider, for example, that eight out of ten marketing and advertising executives say they have made mistakes via email, such as sending job offers to the wrong people or revealing confidential salary information to the entire company.[13] Double-checking that you have placed the correct people in the address line before you hit the send button is a worthwhile habit that requires just a few extra moments.

Respond Promptly

Most business professionals expect fast responses to emails. Of course, what seems like a quick response to one person seems like a delayed response to another. One recent study of business professionals found that nearly all business professionals expect an email response within one day (see Figure 7.3).[14] Younger professionals are more likely to expect a response immediately. The majority of business professionals in all age groups expect a response within one to two hours. If you choose not to check your email more than a few times a day (a strategy recommended later in the chapter), let others know how soon to expect replies.

Maintain Professionalism and Appropriate Formality

Email communication is typically considered fairly formal. Many business professionals are particularly sensitive to "sloppy" email. Management consultant Beverly Langford reported what thousands of business leaders have observed about an overly casual attitude toward email use:

> Many people seem to forget that email is, in fact, written communication, and, consequently, treat it much less carefully. Workplace email messages often contain terse and offhand remarks and project a flippant attitude that is sometimes excessive, even bordering on the unprofessional. Those who write the emails often seem to be overlooking how their

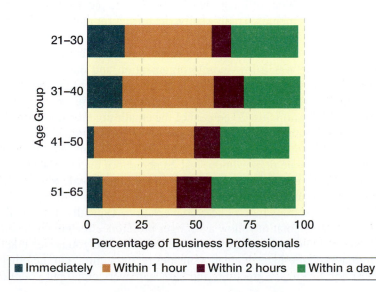

FIGURE 7.3

Appropriate Response Time to Emails

Source: Peter W. Cardon, Melvin Washington, Ephraim A. Okoro, Bryan Marshall, and Nipul Patel, "Cross-Generational Perspectives on How Mobile Phone Use for Texting and Calling Influences Work Outcomes and Work Relationships," presented at the Association for Business Communication Southeast Conference, Charleston, South Carolina, April 1, 2011.

message is coming across to the receiver. Further, when composing emails, many people don't seem to be nearly as concerned with structure and correctness as they would be when putting something on paper. This . . . is ironic because often many more people see an email than would ever see a hard copy of a memo or letter because it's so easy for the recipient to forward an email to anyone he or she chooses.[15]

Unfortunately, since so many more people can potentially see an email than would ever see a hard copy of a message, having high standards is even more important. In the past few years, a preference has emerged for less formal, stuffy writing. Still, you'll want to achieve a balance between formality and the friendliness associated with casual writing. Generally, you are better off erring on the side of too much formality as opposed to too much casualness. Consider the following recommendations.

Avoid Indications That You View Email as Casual Communication

Certain casual ways of writing and formatting appear unprofessional—for example, using all lowercase letters or nonstandard spelling (i.e., *hey barbara, how r u*), using excessive formatting (i.e., flashy background colors, unusual fonts), providing extraneous information in the signature line (i.e., favorite quotations), and typing in all caps (IMPLIES ANGER). Humor and sarcasm, too, can be misinterpreted in digital communications, even among close colleagues. Furthermore, even when considered funny, it can draw attention away from your central message.

Apply the Same Standards of Spelling, Punctuation, and Formatting You Would for Other Written Documents

Carefully review your message for typos, spelling, punctuation, or grammatical problems before sending it. For important messages, consider first composing with word processing software. This will help you apply a higher level of seriousness. In addition, you'll be able to use spell-check and grammar-check features that are more reliable than those within email systems. Finally, you can ensure that you do not inadvertently send the message without making sure it is polished and complete.

Use Greetings and Names

Although not technically required, consider using short greetings and the names of your message recipients. As one of Dale Carnegie's most famous pieces of networking advice goes, "A person's name is to that person the sweetest most important sound in any language."[16] This advice applies to most communication situations, including emails. People leave out names in emails for several reasons. Some professionals view the use of greetings and names as excessively formal, resembling letters. Other professionals view emails as the equivalent of memos. In fact, the layout of most emails—with a recipient line, sender line, and subject line—resembles memos. Traditionally, the format for memos calls for omitting a personal greeting and name.

In a recent study, a communication researcher was given access to the emails in two organizations. One was a low-morale organization and one was a high-morale organization. She found that the presence or absence of greetings and names at the beginning of emails was a strong indicator of company climate (see Figure 7.4).[17] In the low-morale organization, just 20 percent of the emails contained greetings, and just 36 percent contained names. By contrast, in the high-morale organization, 58 percent contained greetings, and 78 percent contained names. The same trend was shown in closings. In the low-morale organization, just 23 percent of the emails contained a polite closing and a name compared to 73 percent in the high-morale organization.

The conventions of using greetings and names are sometimes dropped as an email chain emerges and functions much like a conversation. Typically, feelers (those with the strongest people-orientation) show a stronger preference for greetings and names. If you're having an ongoing email exchange with a feeler and you notice that he or she is using a formal greeting in each email, consider reciprocating. On the other hand, if you're a feeler and like to see greetings and names in every email but your colleagues

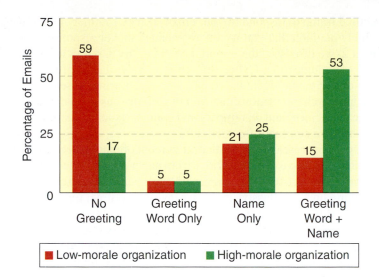

FIGURE 7.4

Use of Email Greetings and Names in a Low-Morale and a High-Morale Organization

Source: Data from Joan Waldvogel, "Greetings and Closings in Workplace Email," *Journal of Computer-Mediated Communication* 12, no. 2 (2007).

are not doing so, avoid getting hung up on it. Assume that they view emails much like memos or that they view excessive use of greetings and names in back-and-forth email chains as repetitive and unnecessary.

Manage Emotion and Maintain Civility

Many managers cite the lack of emotion in emails as positive. They see email as a channel that allows the exchange of messages in minimal form—objective, task-based, and straightforward. As one manager explained, "With email I find myself answering without all the kindness necessary to keep people happy with their job."[18]

Yet, avoiding emotion entirely, even for task-based messages, is nearly impossible. Business professionals often want to invoke some emotion—perhaps enthusiasm or a sense of urgency. Even when senders intend to convey a relatively nonemotional message, recipients may experience an emotional reaction.

In the absence of face-to-face communications, emails tend to elicit either the neutrality effect or the negativity effect. The **neutrality effect** means that recipients are more likely to perceive messages with an intended positive emotion as neutral. That is, the sender may wish to express enthusiasm about an event, but the receiver decodes the information without "hearing" the enthusiasm.[19] The **negativity effect** means that recipients are more likely to perceive messages that are intended as neutral as negative.[20] The effects of emotional inaccuracy due to the neutrality and negativity effects can lead to conflict escalation, confusion, and anxiety.[21] Expert business communicators remain aware of these tendencies.

Two characteristics of asynchronous electronic communications can lead to feelings of anger and frustration more so than in face-to-face communications. First, people often feel comfortable writing things they would not say in person. In some cases, this sense of online freedom leads to **flames,** which are emails or other digital communications with "hostile intentions characterized by words of profanity, obscenity, and insults that inflict harm to a person or an organization."[22]

The second aspect of asynchronous electronic communications that can lead to anger and frustration is **cyber silence,** which is nonresponse to emails and other communications. During the nonresponse stage, message senders often misattribute explanations for the silence. They sometimes wonder if message recipients are purposely avoiding or even ignoring them.[23] As the length of time between messages increases, they often experience more frustration and anger.[24]

As a message sender, grant the benefit of the doubt to your recipients when responses take longer than you expected. Instead of getting frustrated, consider giving them a phone call. Keep in mind that they may have different expectations about a

LO7.2 Explain how to handle emotion effectively in online communications.

reasonable time frame to respond to your email. If they routinely take longer than you expect, politely mention that you would appreciate quicker responses.

In Chapter 2, we discussed the importance of civility. Civility is likewise important in electronic communication. **Cyber incivility** is the violation of respect and consideration in an online environment based on workplace norms. Research has shown that "fast-paced, high-tech interactions may add to incivility, as people believe that they do not have time to be 'nice' and that impersonal contacts [such as electronic communications] do not require courteous interaction."[25]

Shockingly, recent research shows that 91 percent of employees reported experiencing either active or passive cyber incivility from supervisors in the workplace.[26] **Active incivility** involves direct forms of disrespect (i.e., being condescending, demeaning, saying something hurtful). **Passive incivility** involves indirect forms of disrespect (i.e., using emails for time-sensitive messages, not acknowledging receipt of emails, not replying to emails). Cyber incivility has been shown to lead to lower job satisfaction and organizational commitment. Active incivility was the most damaging. In Figure 7.5, you can see a summary of this research. One interesting finding was that male and female supervisors engaged in different types of incivility. Male supervisors were far more likely to engage in active incivility, whereas female supervisors were far more likely to engage in passive incivility.

FIGURE 7.5

Active and Passive Incivility from Supervisors

Source: Vivien K.G. Lim and Thompson S.H. Teo, "Mind Your E-manners: Impact of Cyber Incivility on Employees' Work Attitude and Behavior," *Information & Management* 46 (2009): 419–425. Copyright © 2009, with permission from Elsevier.

Active and Passive Incivility through Emails of Supervisors
(Percentage of Employees Who Stated Their Current Supervisor Had Engaged in Email Incivility)

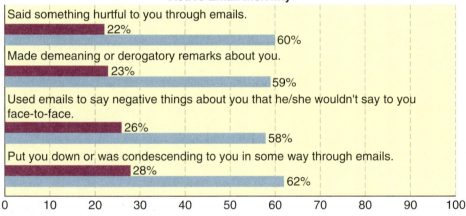

Active Email Incivility

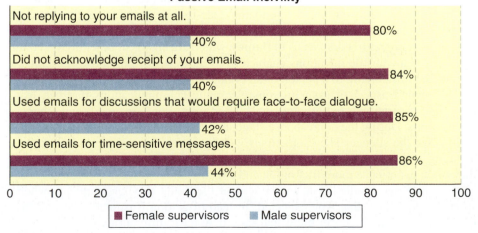

Passive Email Incivility

Inevitably, you will be the target of what you consider uncivil electronic communications. In nearly all situations, your goal should be to avoid escalation. You can take several steps to constructively address uncivil emails: reinterpretation, relaxation, and defusing. **Reinterpretation** involves adjusting your initial perceptions by making more objective, more fact-based, and less personal judgments and evaluations. When people are distressed, they often make extreme, subjective, and overly personal judgments. By reinterpreting the event, you allow yourself to take the communication less personally. This is easier said than done. Many people engage in relaxation techniques to help constructively reinterpret the event. **Relaxation** involves releasing and overcoming anger and frustration so that you can make a more rational and less emotional response. People use a variety of methods to alleviate the physiological impact of anger, including counting to ten, taking time-outs, engaging in deep breathing, and looking for the humor in the situation.[27]

In the opening case, you learned that Kip was frustrated with his direct supervisor, Nancy. Kip, perhaps unwisely, fired off an angry email (see the bottom message in Figure 7.6), and Nancy responded (the top message in Figure 7.6). Whether he was correct or not about Nancy's approach to guest service is somewhat beside the point. Email is rarely an effective communication channel to air complaints or to discuss emotionally charged issues. Figure 7.7 presents a more-effective response from Nancy to this exchange.

Defusing involves avoiding escalation and removing tension to focus on work objectives. You can take several steps to defuse the situation when you receive an uncivil email. First, focus on task-related facts and issues in your reply. Second, focus on shared objectives and agreements. Third, express interest in arranging a time to meet in person. If this is not possible, attempt a richer channel of communication such as a phone call or web meeting with video. Defusing the situation with an immediate email is only part of the process in restoring or perhaps even strengthening a working relationship. A follow-up meeting is nearly always essential to renew cooperation on shared work efforts.

You will often need to respond to electronic messages that you feel are unfair or inappropriate. Notice how Nancy escalates the problem in the less-effective response by writing in an impersonal, defensive, and confrontational manner. By contrast, notice how she defuses the situation in the more-effective response by avoiding defensiveness, focusing on shared interests, and arranging for a time to meet face-to-face. Your ability to defuse uncivil electronic communications during your career will pay off in many ways: It will help your colleagues and teams stay on task and perform better; it will help you develop a reputation for constructively resolving differences; and it will lead to more satisfying work experiences. The ability to defuse such situations requires high emotional intelligence, especially in self-awareness and self-management.

Manage Your Emails to Avoid Distractions

LO7.3 Describe strategies for managing digital message overload.

Constantly checking incoming messages—emails, texts, IMs, and various messages through social networking platforms—or simply hearing message alerts distracts business professionals from concentrating on the tasks at hand. As you are bombarded with incoming messages, your productivity decreases for two reasons: You are distracted from your immediate tasks and you try to multitask.

Interruptions from digital messages, or *e-interruptions,* are extremely costly to your performance. One recent study found that the average worker loses 2.1 hours per day due to interruptions. Many of these distractions are email and other incoming messages. Many business professionals check their email every five minutes, which amounts to 96 e-interruptions in an eight-hour day. Distractions impact your performance for much longer than the few moments you take to acknowledge and respond to incoming messages. A Microsoft study found that it takes 15 minutes

FIGURE 7.6

Less-Effective Response to an Angry Email

Re: Issues

Jeffreys, Nancy

To: Kip Yamada

Cc: Barbara Brookshire

We need to talk about this email when I get back in a week after Thanksgiving. I thought we had a productive conversation but you obviously were not candid. How can we make any progress if you're not honest? Also, please empty your voice mail. I tried reaching you several times only to get your full voice mail box.

From: Kip Yamada [kipyamada@prestigiohotels.com]
Sent: Saturday, November 23 9:54 PM
To: Nancy Jeffreys [njeffreys@prestigiohotels.com]
Cc: Barbara Brookshire [bbrookshire@prestigiohotels.com]

Subject: Issues

Nancy, our conversation really wasn't fair. I appreciate you striking up the conversation but you caught me off guard. I know your goal was good – to get us working together more effectively. But, in the spirit of compromise, I was not as forthright as I should have been. You are really hurting our business because you're not focusing on our customers. Our guests come to me all the time and complain about your unfair treatment. Even some of the employees mention how you are not really listening to our guests when they make complaints. I think the big issue we need to focus on is customer service, not whether I have authorization to make refunds. Kip

Impersonal. Leaves out greeting and name.

Confrontational. Immediately creates a *me-versus-you* approach with the phrase "we need to talk."

Defensive/attacking. Focuses on defending rather than understanding Kip's point of view.

Accusatory. Kip lays blame on Nancy in every regard. The repeated use of *you-voice* increases the accusatory tone.

on average to refocus after an interruption. Furthermore, these disruptions have been shown to reduce attention spans, increase stress, and even reduce creativity. The cost to companies is enormous. Intel estimates that large companies lose about $1 billion per year because of email overload. Not surprisingly, many major companies such as Google, Microsoft, IBM, and Intel have joined the Information Overload Research Group (iorgforum.org), which is devoted to finding solutions to such problems.[28]

Many business professionals erroneously assume they can respond immediately to all incoming messages *and* focus sufficiently on work tasks. This is simply not the case. A University of Michigan study found that productivity drops by up to 40 percent when people try to do two or more things at once. A variety of research about the brain shows that it is not hardwired to multitask effectively.[29]

In most business positions, however, you need to respond to others as soon as possible. This places you in a delicate balancing act; how can you stay responsive to others

FIGURE 7.7

More-Effective Response to Defuse an Angry Email

Reply   Reply All   Forward

Meeting to Improve Our Response to Guest Complaints

Jeffreys, Nancy

To: Kip Yamada

Cc: Barbara Brookshire

Hello Kip,

I'm sorry to hear that you did not think our conversation was fair. You're right – I didn't give you any chance ahead of time to gather your thoughts. I do appreciate your enthusiasm for treating our guests fairly.

When we're both back in the office, let's set up a time to discuss how to manage guest complaints. Would you be willing to come up with your ideas for managing what you consider the three most common guest complaints?

When we meet, I'd also like to discuss how we track our responses to guest complaints and whether our responses make business sense.

Would you like to include anyone else in our meeting? Do you think the entire marketing team should participate in this discussion?

Happy Thanksgiving!

Nancy

Cordial and personal. Uses Kip's name and extends warm wishes.

Validating. Compliments Kip on his attention to guest satisfaction.

Inviting. Asks for Kip's input in terms of ideas and people who should be included in a decision-making process.

Nondefensive. Nancy makes it clear that making "business sense" is an important part of the discussion. She does so without sounding defensive or intimidating (she is in the position of a superior).

Focus on rich communication. Nancy temporarily defuses the situation by email but realizes these issues require rich communication. She identifies a meeting as the next step in the process.

yet focus enough to achieve peak performance in your work tasks? Consider the following guidelines:[30]

- *Check digital messages just two to four times each day at designated times.* Unless your job calls for it (or your boss demands it!), you should never check your messages more than every 45 minutes. Consider taking interruption-free periods during the day exclusively devoted to email. For example, you might schedule 30 minutes to an hour at 11 a.m. and 3 p.m. each day to communicate via email and other online tools.

- *Turn off message alerts.* Over the course of a day, these alerts can distract you and reduce your focus.

- *Use rich channels such as face-to-face and phone conversations to accomplish a task completely.* Back-and-forth email chains and other sets of asynchronous digital messages may repeatedly draw attention away from tasks at hand. As appropriate, use rich, synchronous communication to take care of the matter immediately so that distractions do not compound themselves.

- *Reply immediately only to urgent messages.* When you reply immediately to non-urgent messages, you set a precedent. Others form an expectation that you can be interrupted at any time for any matter.

- *Avoid unnecessarily lengthening an email chain.* You can shorten email chains by placing statements such as "no reply necessary" in the subject line. You can also shorten email chains by not sending messages such as "got it" or "thanks." At the same time, make sure you don't abruptly end an email chain when others would appreciate a reply. For example, some business professionals appreciate short notes of gratitude and confirmation.

- *Use automatic messages to help people know when you're unavailable.* Set up automatic messages to let people know when you are out of the office for more than one day.

Communicating in the Workplace in the Social Age

LO7.4 Explain characteristics of the emerging Social Age.

Many relatively inexpensive, Internet-based communication tools used in business—social networking, blogs, wikis, discussion forums—are driving profound changes in how people connect and collaborate in the workplace. These changes are so profound that workplace culture is moving into a new era: from the Information Age to the Social Age (see Figure 7.8). The **Social Age** is an era in which people engage in networked communication, collaborate across boundaries, and solve problems communally.[31] However, even though the communication technologies that have paved the way for the Social Age are changing rapidly (in months and years), workplace culture is relatively slow to change (in years and decades). So, as you read this section, keep in mind that cultural norms and values more significantly influence the impact of social media in the workplace than do its technical capabilities.

FIGURE 7.8

The Evolving Workplace

Industrial Age	Information Age	Social Age
Command-and-control (Little communication between teams and units)	Mass two-way communication (Extensive communication between teams and units)	Networked communication (Extensive communication between individuals with shared interests)
Respect for position	Respect for expertise and position	Respect for expertise and contributions to the network
Holding authority is power	Holding knowledge is power	Sharing knowledge is power
Efficiency, competitiveness, and authority are key values	Autonomy, innovation, and achievement are key values	Transparency, honesty, and camaraderie are key values

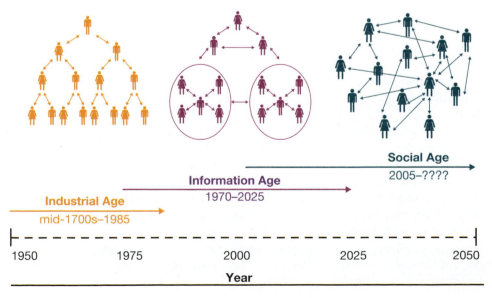

Social Age
2005–????

Information Age
1970–2025

Industrial Age
mid-1700s–1985

1950   1975   2000   2025   2050

Year

Characteristics of the Social Age

The evolution of the Internet during the past 15 years from Web 1.0 to Web 2.0 platforms is the primary driver of the Social Age. In the original Internet, referred to as **Web 1.0,** most web pages were read-only and static. As the Internet evolved, referred to as **Web 2.0,** what emerged was the read-write web, where users interact extensively with web pages—authoring content, expressing opinions, and customizing and editing web content among other things. Web 2.0 communication tools, often referred to as **social media,** include social networks, blogs, wikis, gaming, podcasts, and information tagging. In simple terms, Web 1.0 communication tools are primarily passive and static. By contrast, Web 2.0 communication tools are interactive, customizable, and *social.*[32] **User 1.0** refers to an individual who primarily uses and prefers Web 1.0 tools, whereas **User 2.0** refers to an individual who primarily uses and prefers Web 2.0 tools (see Table 7.2).[33] The emerging Social Age is adopting many workplace norms and values from users of Web 2.0 tools.

Increasingly, companies are adopting social networking platforms that contain Web 2.0 communication tools (also called *enterprise social software* and *Enterprise 2.0*) in the workplace. These platforms contain many of the features available on social networking websites: user profiles, microblogs, blogs, wikis, and file uploading. They often include a variety of other communication and collaboration tools as well, including online audio and video calls, shared work spaces, calendars, and private messaging (or email) systems. Thus, most companies—especially medium- to large-sized businesses—are increasingly moving toward corporate intranets that contain both Web 1.0 and Web 2.0 tools. One of the earliest organization-wide adopters of social media was Lockheed Martin, an employer of more than 140,000 worldwide. Lockheed Martin created an internal social networking platform called Unity over a decade ago to meet the challenges of its complex collaborations. Unity includes blogs, wikis, file sharing, tags, discussion forums, social bookmarking, and updates through RSS. Rather than using emails, managers use blogs to provide project updates and due dates.[34]

The emerging work culture associated with the Social Age presents many benefits to companies and business professionals in the context of team and networked communication (see Table 7.3).[35] When social media are used for professional purposes, teams can communicate more efficiently; companies can interface more responsively to customers, clients, and suppliers; customers and other interested individuals can be directly involved in the development of products and services; and anyone with shared professional interests can communicate easily, not needing to travel to see one another.

TABLE 7.2

Comparisons between User 1.0 and User 2.0

User 1.0	User 2.0
Passively reading and searching for content	Actively creating and sharing content online
Depends on content creator; does not express own opinion	Can express opinions and even change the content presented
Getting the web as is	Customizing web pages and content
Email is the main communication tool	Peer-to-peer programs are the main communication tools
The computer is the main access point	Connects from various devices
Connected online for time-limited sessions	Connected online all the time

TABLE 7.3

Benefits and Challenges of Social Media in the Workplace

Benefits of Social Media	Challenges and Risks of Social Media
To companies: • Team communication and collaboration • Succession planning • Recruitment and on-boarding • Idea sharing/knowledge management • Skills development and training • Interfacing with customers, suppliers, and partners • Decreased time to market for new products and services • More innovative, creative, effective, and profitable approaches to work problems • Less time and fewer resources needed for business travel	*To companies:* • Lack of adoption and penetration • Lack of permanence • Confusion over which communication channels to use • Distraction from work, too much socializing • Lack of control of information provided externally and internally • Lack of systems for rewarding networked and team communication and collaboration
To business professionals: • Build professional networks internally and externally • Access business expertise and knowledge more rapidly • Enhance camaraderie with peers	*To business professionals:* • Lack of boundaries between professional and private lives • Lower productivity due to multitasking • Excessive opportunism and self-promotion • Mistakes and incompetence broadcast to larger audiences

Major Components of Social Networking Platforms

- User profiles*
- Blogs/microblogs*
- Wikis*
- Private messaging systems**
- Discussion forums
- RSS feeds
- Social bookmarking
- Rating and tagging
- Video sharing
- Podcasts
- Mashups

*Given more attention in this section because they are writing-intensive
**Nearly identical to email in function and form

Social media also present many challenges and risks. The primary challenges are cultural. Some of them are age-based: older employees are more accustomed to the communication tools they have used for years and decades. Typically, the Web 1.0 tools reinforce many of older employees' work values, such as privacy and autonomy. The use of social media creates a free flow of information that, in many cases, runs counter to traditional business approaches to decision making, lines of authority, team formation, performance incentives, and so on.

One basic challenge of using social media internally is getting employees to participate. In most companies, participation in blogs and wikis is fairly low. The case of Wikipedia is instructive. Although millions of Internet users consider Wikipedia to be a reliable source of information, only a small fraction of users are also Wikipedia authors and contributors. Wikipedia is consistently among the ten most visited websites. Yet, less than 1 percent of users ever contribute to its entries.[36]

Social media use also presents a variety of risks. For companies, social media can lead to lower productivity when employees use it for social and entertainment purposes, release confidential and proprietary information, post inappropriate comments that lead to reputation loss for companies, and go around lines of authority. On an individual level, social media can lead to major credibility loss (discussed further in "Manage Your Online Reputation").

Internal Communication Tools for the Social Age

In this section, we briefly touch on several of the social software tools you can expect to use in the workplace: user profiles, blogs, and wikis. We focus on these tools for a few reasons. They are among the most widely used and most effective social tools, and they involve significant written communication. In Table 7.4, you can see results of a study by IBM about returns on investment from social media.[37] You will notice that social networking (with user profiles as the foundation for establishing connections), blogs, and wikis are among the most valuable social tools in terms of productivity gains, reduction in IT costs, and increase in revenues.

LO7.5 Apply principles of effective social media use in professional settings.

Organize Your Dashboard to Control Your Communication and Information Flow   Nearly all social software systems contain a *dashboard*, your

TABLE 7.4

Return on Investment for Internal Social Media

Social Tool	Improves Productivity	Reduces IT Costs	Increases Revenue
Wikis	29%	18%	16%
Tagging	20%	6%	6%
Blogs	12%	5%	6%
Social networking	12%	4%	6%
Syndication/RSS	12%	4%	4%
Podcast	8%	6%	N/A
Mashups	8%	6%	6%

Source: From Maria Azua, *The Social Factor: Innovate, Ignite, and Win Through Mass Collaboration and Social Networking,* 1st Edition, Copyright © 2010. Reprinted by permission of Pearson Education, Inc., Upper Saddle River, NJ.

front page when you log in to the system, which operates as your communication hub. In most cases, you can customize the dashboard to display the features that most interest you. For example, notice Figure 7.9, which shows Andrea Garcia's dashboard. She displays status updates of other team members so she can see what they are working on. She also wants to know how often other team members are using the social software (upper-right panel), and she subscribes to a business news service (lower-right panel). Think about setting up your dashboard to access messages and information that will help you work efficiently and avoid distractions.

FIGURE 7.9

Sample Dashboard with Enterprise Social Software

Create a Complete and Professional Profile

In your profile, you provide information about yourself, such as your position, contact information, professional interests, and current projects. You can usually provide a picture and list personal interests outside of work. One key benefit of social networking platforms is that as people view profiles of others, they feel more connected to them, more so than with Web 1.0 communication tools such as email. Furthermore, profiles are an excellent way of finding people within an organization with needed expertise or shared professional interests. Profiles as part of enterprise social software systems appear much like those in Facebook and LinkedIn. In Figures 7.12 and 7.13, you can see examples of less-effective and more-effective Facebook profiles for Kip Yamada. In Figure 7.14, you'll notice Kip's LinkedIn profile.

In your profiles, make sure you provide complete information. This is a chance for colleagues and clients who do not know you well to learn about your professional background, abilities, and interests. People within your organization who do not know you well may be more likely to follow your blogs and collaborate on wikis and other projects based on what they learn about you on your profiles. Keep in mind that the purpose of your business profile is typically different from the one you post on social networking websites such as Facebook. Your primary goals are professional collaborating and networking rather than socializing or entertaining.

Use Blogs for Team Communication

Blogs are posts that are arranged chronologically, similar to a journal format. Traditionally, most blogs have included entries by just one or a few individuals, although many provide the option for reader comments. Increasingly, teams and other professional groups write blogs. In the workplace, they allow business professionals to share their ideas and experiences. By focusing on specific topics and areas of expertise, bloggers can attract and connect with other employees with similar professional interests.[38] A variety of blog types have emerged in the workplace, including individual expert blogs, company executive blogs, company team blogs, company update blogs, company crisis blogs, and internal company blogs.[39]

Microblogs (such as Twitter), shorter blogs that contain just a few sentences, are part of most enterprise social networking platforms. Microblogs are tools for broadcasting announcements and urgent information. Members of a network can also use them to ask questions that need immediate responses.

For most business professionals, individual blogs have not caught on yet. A recent survey of corporate intranet use showed that most organizations (53 percent) have blogs on their intranets. Up to 87 percent of large companies (over 50,000 employees) make blogs available. However, senior-level executives write most blogs, and most employees view them as leadership communications. In a 2010 study at IBM, an ambitious adopter of enterprise social media, just 900 employees (less than .0025 percent of the company total) had blogged in the previous three months.[40] However, individual blogs are expected to grow in importance. Many business professionals have found that blogging gives them a unique forum to network inside and outside of their organizations (discussed further in "Manage Your Online Reputation").

Organizations are increasingly using team blogs and project blogs (many-to-many communication). **Team blogs** are typically organized around formal work teams, and **project blogs** are organized around particular projects that generally involve temporary teams. Team and project blogs are excellent ways to place all of the team's communications in a single place, such as updates, progress reports, problem-solving discussions, project timelines and goals, announcements, and a variety of other coordination tasks. These team and project blogs are also excellent for sharing success stories to build and shape organizational and team culture. A short example of a team blog is provided in Figure 7.10, where the Prestigio marketing team is describing and coordinating activities.

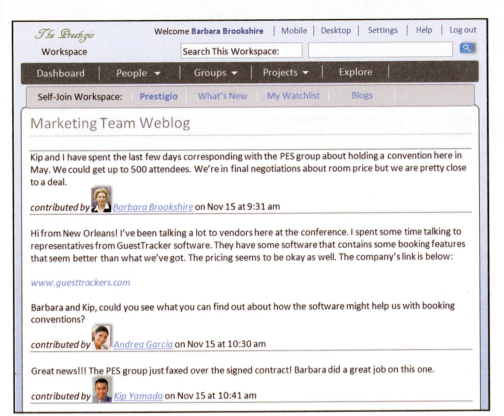

FIGURE 7.10

Sample Team Blog

Use Wikis for Team Communication

Wikis are collections of pages that anyone with approved access can edit, thus lending themselves to collaborative writing. Users can add, remove, and change content. Wikis allow employees to collaborate and participate in decision making more easily, creatively, and effectively. They create a culture of transparency, simplicity, and openness. The collaborative potential of wikis is stronger than any of the other social media tools (see Table 7.4). Particularly progressive companies, such as Finnish mobile phone manufacturer Nokia, use internal wikis for project updates and exchange of ideas. Nokia has also attempted to make wikis a primary communication channel for its teams. About 20 percent of Nokia's 68,000 staff members use wikis regularly.[41]

Wikis create an excellent knowledge management system. Since they are located on the corporate intranet or accessible online, employees can access information far more easily and efficiently than information tucked away in email boxes or on an individual user's computer. Wikis make the organization less dependent on single employees. Many organizations allow employees to constantly update wikis devoted to projects, reports, policies, and reference materials.[42] An example of a wiki in editing mode is provided in Figure 7.11, where Kip Yamada is directly editing a survey report that Jeff Anderton originally set up and posted.

Some organizations are exploring ways of using wikis for meetings. Wiki meetings can cut down on costs and accommodate people at many locations. For example, in September 2006, IBM held a global wiki meeting that lasted three days. Nearly 100,000 people in 160 countries participated in the brainstorming session.[43]

Other Social Media Tools

Many other communication tools exist on social networking platforms. Furthermore, Enterprise 2.0 platforms are constantly evolving and adding additional communication tools. You would be wise to experiment with all the communication tools available on these platforms so you can identify and use the channels best suited for your audiences.

FIGURE 7.11

Sample Wiki in Edit Mode

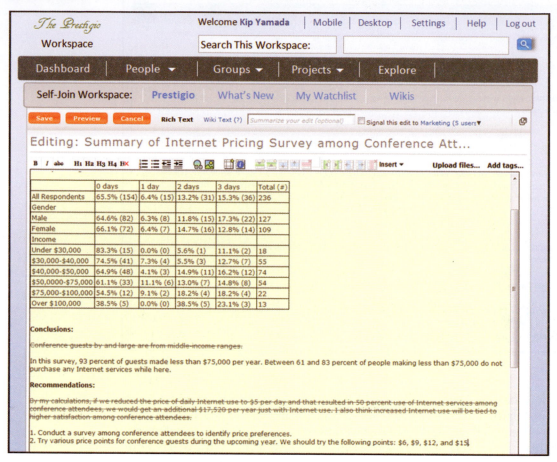

Guidelines for Using Social Media in the Workplace

Many communication tools fall under the social media platform. Generally, you can apply the following advice to any of them:

Be an Active Contributor and Participate Often   If your company or professional group has committed to using social networking platforms, make sure you contribute regularly and respond to the comments and work of others. As an example, for individual blogs, those employees who gain the largest followings (and thus a reputation for thought leadership) make blog entries two to three times per week.

Also, venture out from your formal work teams to establish work relationships with other members of your company or professional network. Voluntarily joining teams built around common interests—often called *communities of practice*—allows you to share and learn from other professionals in your area. This helps you grow professionally and increases organizational knowledge. Doing so also allows you to become involved in some of the long-term issues facing your organization, since communities of practice often focus on an organization's long-term issues, whereas teams tend to focus on short-term projects.[44]

Listen and Learn   Social media offer an ideal means of continuously learning about your company, your industry, and your discipline. In Chapter 3, we focused on the importance of approaching communication from a listening-centered approach. Used wisely, social media give you many ways to listen. As you follow the blogs of others in your company or industry, you gain insights into best practices. If you write an individual blog, you can float ideas and get responses. You can set up RSS feeds to get notices whenever people you follow update their blogs.

Focus on Content   Blogs and wikis are collaborative tools. In other words, they are intended to help you work more effectively with your team members, other colleagues, and clients. The goal is not to entertain others; it is to provide value to others and increase your professional, not social, credibility (as discussed in "Manage Your Online Reputation").[45] Blog content should focus on your work projects, meetings, shared goals, experiences, and expertise and knowledge.

Of course, social media are called *social* for a reason. They provide professionals with rich and exciting communication tools. Including social content is good to a point. In high-performing teams, 60 to 70 percent of all comments are directly related to work, about 15 to 20 percent of comments are supportive, and about 10 to 15 percent are primarily social. This is also the case for business communication via social media. As a good rule of thumb to achieve your professional goals, roughly 70 percent of your social media content should be directly related to work, roughly 20 percent should be supportive, and roughly 10 percent should be social.

Make Your Content Accessible   Contributing to blogs and wikis increases your organization's knowledge. However, if other people can't find and use your contributions, you have not accomplished your purpose. By naming, labeling, indexing, and tagging (applying keywords to your blogs or wikis) well, you help others find your information (see the Technology Tips about tagging on page 198). Also consider using links to your files to help others open them immediately.

Make Your Messages Authentic and Friendly   Authenticity is key to effective social media messages. Social media readers expect sincerity and the raw truth. Your messages should not come off as spin and should not contradict who you really are. Be clear about your intentions. Your messages should also have a friendly tone. However, authenticity and friendliness do not mean sloppy writing or rudeness. When engaging in collaborative writing, keep a friendly tone even when you disagree with others. Avoid any urges to delete the comments of others or engage in edit wars.[46]

Be Responsive and Help Others   One expectation of social networks is that you are a good member of the community. As a good member, you respond positively to the requests of others and help when possible. As you gain a reputation for responding and helping others, you can expect that other community members will respond and help you.

Respect Boundaries   The many communication tools available in the emerging Social Age allow people to communicate with nearly anyone at nearly anytime from nearly any location about nearly anything. In other words, the division between professional and private lives is becoming increasingly blurred. Stay observant about where your colleagues draw lines to preserve their lives away from work.

Manage Your Online Reputation

LO7.6 Build a credible online reputation.

Although nearly all business professionals are aware of social networking and the importance of strong online reputations, most are still learning to manage their online presences strategically. And although younger people are often expert at developing an online social persona, they are less skilled at developing an online professional presence.[47] As you read this section, think about the opportunities and risks for you as you develop your online reputation.

First, think carefully about developing a **personal brand** in a professional sense—a unique set of professional skills and attributes that others associate with you.[48] In the

TECHNOLOGY TIPS

USING TAGGING FOR KNOWLEDGE MANAGEMENT

One of the strongest benefits of enterprise social software is the ability to tag and index documents so you and your colleagues can find information rapidly. In some organizations, the intranet may contain millions of web pages and files with the collective knowledge of the organization. By providing tags and other information in your posts and files, you make it possible for any colleague in your organization to find your messages. Similarly, if you are writing online business messages for external audiences, your tags can lead customers, clients, and other contacts to your messages with simple Internet searches.

In the image at right, you can see an example of how information can be labeled and tagged for a word processing file. You can take similar actions for any type of business message in enterprise social software platforms to allow others to quickly find your files.

Internet Pricing Survey among Conference Attendees ...	
General / Summary / Statistics / Contents / Custom	
Title:	Internet Pricing Survey among Conference Attendees
Subject:	Internet Pricing
Author:	Jeff Anderton
Manager:	Barbara Brookshire
Company:	The Prestigio
Category:	Guest Surveys, Pricing
Keywords:	Internet pricing, Internet services, conferences, mark
Comments:	Shows results of a survey administered to recent conference guests regarding their satisfaction with Internet services and pricing.

final chapter of this book, when we turn to job applications, we discuss the notion of promoting your personal brand in more detail. Here, we introduce the idea of building your personal brand and using it as an asset in your career progression. Increasingly, you will express your personal brand through social media tools. One major goal, then, for your online activities is to build a reputation that showcases your credibility and personal brand.

Whether or not you have intentionally created an online presence, potential and current employers, colleagues, and clients will judge your credibility based on online information about you. Thus, you need to take as much control as you can of your online reputation. As portrayed in Table 7.5, one helpful approach is to consider the meta messages, or overall and underlying messages that others decode from your online communications.[49] These meta messages become one basis for your online reputation.

For example, consider two students, Jenny and Regina, who create blogs about their study-abroad experiences in Spain. Jenny's blog describes her observations of her homestay family, the people in the community, and her efforts to learn Spanish. She frequently talks about the generosity they extend to her. She posts pictures of cultural and historical sites as well as many of the people she meets. Her blog sends a meta message, "I'm grateful to the people in Spain for providing me with such a rich learning experience." This meta message feeds into a reputation for open-mindedness, flexibility, curiosity, and appreciation of others.

Regina, on the other hand, mostly posts pictures of herself at pubs. She describes the many friends she has made who are also American study-abroad students. Her longest entry explains how glad she was to go to the Hard Rock Café and get a hamburger "just like back at home." To many readers, the meta message Regina sends is, "I'm having a great time with my American friends in Spain." This meta message may feed into a reputation for complacency and closed-mindedness.

Take a few minutes to think about Table 7.5. You will notice a variety of positive meta messages and related reputations. You can see that these meta messages and reputations are grouped into four areas: personal and private; professional and private; personal and public; and professional and public. In each domain of your online communications, you should think about the meta messages you would like to send

TABLE 7.5

Developing a Credible Online Reputation

	Positive Meta Messages	**Sought-After Reputations**
Personal and Private (for family and friends) *Example:* a family blog	I'm a good listener (competence) I can take care of you (competence) I hope the best for you (caring) You can always count on me (caring) You can trust me (character) I'm a fun person (character)	Communicative, interpersonal skills Dependable, reliable, capable Considerate, caring, concerned Loyal, committed Honest, trustworthy Fun-loving, exciting
Professional and Private (for work colleagues) *Examples:* a corporate blog or wiki	I will get the job done (competence) I am a good team member (competence) I want you to succeed (caring) I want to work with you (caring) I will do what I say (character) I abide by the rules (character)	Competent, skilled, dependable Bring out the best in others Supportive, caring Team-oriented, collaborative Sincere, genuine, integrity Moral, ethical, fair
Personal and Public (for society) *Example:* social networking website such as Facebook	I have certain abilities (competence) I have certain interests (competence) I want to share my experiences and ideas (caring) I want to learn about you (caring) I have certain social values and priorities (character) I live my life according to certain beliefs (character)	Talented, skilled, capable Determined, focused, driven Open, networked, independent Inquisitive, curious, considerate Activist, cause-driven, passionate Moral, understanding
Professional and Public (for professional peers) *Example:* professional social networking website such as LinkedIn	I am an expert (competent) I want to lead a professional discussion (competent) I want to share my ideas with you (caring) I want to understand your experiences (caring) I am committed to my industry (character) I think my profession should maintain high standards (character)	Thought leader, forward-thinking Initiative, leadership, open-minded Generous, giving, collaborative Learning, inquisitive, curious Professional, passionate, committed Ethical, disciplined, consistent

so that you build a credible reputation. Also, because many of your online communications are accessible to personal friends as well as professional contacts, you need to consider whether you are prioritizing your professional or your social reputation.

Many business professionals have gained professional opportunities by developing personal brands online. For example, Scott Monty landed a senior-level marketing position at Ford after three years of blog writing about the convergence of marketing, advertising, and public relations. When Ford brought him in, he had 3,500 Twitter followers. Now he has 41,000.[50]

Social media tools make developing a personal brand easier than ever. You can broadcast your expertise and business interests to an ever-growing network of business professionals. However, social media tools also make it easier than ever to damage your personal brand and online reputation. When you make inaccurate or unprofessional posts, your incompetency, unprofessionalism, and other mistakes are broadcast to a much larger network. In fact, one mistake can undermine your reputation.[51]

Some business professionals damage their reputations because their social media use sends meta messages that they are self-promoters and careerists. Other employees view their online communications as opportunistic and self-centered, believing the self-promoters place their personal career interests ahead of the organization's interests.[52] Generally, the reputation as a self-promoter comes from excessively drawing attention to one's own professional skills and interests. As you adopt other-oriented, listening-centered approaches to social media use, you can highlight your

FIGURE 7.12

Less-Effective Personal Social Networking Profile

Nonstrategic. Does not draw attention to professional interests.

Nonflattering. Some people who do not know Kip will form their first impressions of him based on his interest in vulgar and violent movies and games.

Nonpersonal. Most business professionals are eager to see a picture in profiles.

own professional skills and interests without reaching what others consider excessive self-promotion.

Compare Kip's online profiles for Facebook, LinkedIn, and Twitter (in Figures 7.12, 7.13, and 7.14). In particular, compare his less-effective and more-effective Facebook profiles. The evaluations of the examples are based on professional standards, not social standards. Think about the meta messages these profiles may send. At the same time, think about your own online profiles and social networking activity. What meta messages are you sending? What type of reputation are you building?

Social media use is particularly well suited for networked communication. As we have discussed, working in networks is an increasingly important skill and integral to success in the emerging Social Age. As part of large professional networks, seek a reputation as a giver, not a taker. Similarly, always honor your commitments. In networked communication, word gets around quickly about which members are considered givers, which honor commitments, and which do not.

LO7.7 Describe the ethical use of social media for work.

Use Social Media Ethically

The use of social media, even for private use, complicates your relationship with your employer. Consider the following cases:[53]

> An employee who works in research and development updates his Facebook status, bemoaning the fact that he has to cancel his weekend golf plans due to yet another project delay. Other Facebook users connect this with a highly anticipated product launch, and the company's stock price declines.

> A salesperson posts a derogatory comment on Twitter about a prospective client's headquarters city as he lands there the day before a critical presentation. Someone forwards the tweet to the CEO, who cancels the meeting.

Strategic. Draws attention to professional interests in a variety of locations.

Nondistracting. Kip provides personal information that does not distract attention away from his professional interests.

Warm and personal. The profile picture displays Kip as a professional, friendly person.

FIGURE 7.13

More-Effective Personal Social Networking Profile

FIGURE 7.14

Using Social Media for Work Purposes

FIGURE 7.15

Example of Social Media Guidelines

Coca-Cola's Social Media Guidelines

The Company respects the rights of its associates and its authorized agencies' associates to use blogs and other social media tools not only as a form of self-expression, but also as a means to further the Company's business. It is important that all associates are aware of the implications of engaging in forms of social media and online conversations that reference the Company and/or the associate's relationship with the Company and its brands, and that associates recognize when the Company might be held responsible for their behavior.

Our Expectations for Associates' Personal Behavior in Online Social Media

There's a big difference in speaking "on behalf of the Company" and speaking "about" the Company. This set of 5 principles refers to those personal or unofficial online activities where you might refer to Coca-Cola.

1. Adhere to the Code of Business Conduct and other applicable policies. All Company associates, from the Chairman to every intern, are subject to the Company's Code of Business Conduct in every public setting. In addition, other policies, including the Information Protection Policy and the Insider Trading Policy, govern associates' behavior with respect to the disclosure of information; these policies are applicable to your personal activities online.

2. You are responsible for your actions. Anything you post that can potentially tarnish the Company's image will ultimately be your responsibility. We do encourage you to participate in the online social media space, but urge you to do so properly, exercising sound judgment and common sense.

3. Be a "scout" for compliments and criticism. Even if you are not an official online spokesperson for the Company, you are one of our most vital assets for monitoring the social media landscape. If you come across positive or negative remarks about the Company or its brands online that you believe are important, consider sharing them by forwarding them to [public relations].

4. Let the subject matter experts respond to negative posts. You may come across negative or disparaging posts about the Company or its brands, or see third parties trying to spark negative conversations. Unless you are a certified online spokesperson, avoid the temptation to react yourself. Pass the post(s) along to our official in-market spokespersons who are trained to address such comments.

5. Be conscious when mixing your business and personal lives. Online, your personal and business personas are likely to intersect. The Company respects the free speech rights of all of its associates, but you must remember that customers, colleagues, and supervisors often have access to the online content you post. Keep this in mind when publishing information online that can be seen by more than friends and family, and know that information originally intended just for friends and family can be forwarded on. Remember NEVER to disclose nonpublic information of the Company (including confidential information), and be aware that taking public positions online that are counter to the Company's interests might cause conflict.

Source: Example of Coca-Cola's Social Media Guidelines.

An employee is terminated for cause. A few weeks later, she asks a former colleague to recommend her on LinkedIn. The former colleague writes a glowing recommendation. The terminated employee later uses this recommendation as evidence in a discrimination suit, claiming she was terminated unfairly.

As these various examples illustrate, much more than your online reputation is at stake with social media use; the reputation and performance of your company is at stake as well. The line between what you believe is private use of social media and your role as an employee can be murky, since your private actions can damage your employer and hurt your career.

In short, constantly try to understand evolving norms for social media use in a professional context. For your own protection and that of your company, become familiar with your company's acceptable-use policies for social networking websites.[54] Coca-Cola recently compiled a set of social media guidelines (see Figure 7.15). Notice the principles of appropriate social media use. Then read the Communication Q&A with Catherine Norris (page 203) for her thoughts on workplace collaboration through face-to-face communication and through communication technologies.

COMMUNICATION Q&A

CONVERSATIONS WITH CURRENT BUSINESS PROFESSIONALS

Pete Cardon: What's an example of a project you have worked on recently that involves extensive collaboration and coordination? What are the communication challenges you faced on this project?

Catherine Norris: One of the major challenges of the project I am coordinating is communicating the need for change and how that change can improve performance in cost and quality. If the stakeholders are convinced that they need to make changes, then they are more likely to achieve quality and cost goals. Simply put, if I do not effectively communicate why change is needed, then the project fails.

Catherine Norris, *project manager, has worked in the health care industry for 25 years in a variety of capacities, including management and nursing.*

PC: How do you use communication technologies?

CN: The persons I work with on a daily basis have a broad range of familiarity with communication technologies such as social networking, blogs, and wikis. Some people are very comfortable with these methods, and others have never used them. Therefore, I use the technology communication tool that best fits the situation and is easiest. After all, if the project team and stakeholders do not use a given technology, then there is no point in forcing it.

The project team relies heavily on the use of email, the corporate intranet, and the Internet to communicate. For example, we use email to send routine messages and document attachments back and forth for review and approval. The advantage of using email is that the messages can be tracked. Furthermore, email communication is precise and efficient. You can access your email when you have the time as opposed to waiting to schedule a live face-to-face meeting. Many people today carry smartphones and have email access anywhere. Work gets done efficiently without wasting time.

The project team uses the corporate intranet to schedule meetings and access intranet links to our progress documents for projects. This is a place where internal users can review shared documents, update project assignments, and view project news and webcast links online. Conference phone calls and webcasts for product training and remote meetings have been a very effective means of communicating too.

PC: How do you choose when to use various communication technologies?

CN: Although I find email very effective for routine messages, face-to-face communication is crucial when the message needs emphasis. That is why our project team has conducted one-on-one, face-to-face meetings to communicate quality and cost performance data to our stakeholders. By doing so, we emphasize why we should focus on these goals now. In addition, it allows for a two-way dialogue with a personal touch. If we used an impersonal communication method like email or a written report delivered to a mailbox, we would miss a valuable opportunity to develop a personal relationship and dialogue around performance improvement.

Chapter Takeaway for *Email and Social Media for Business Communication*

LO 7.1. Apply principles for writing effective emails. (pp. 179–185)

Principles of Effective Emails

- Use for the right purposes.
- Ensure ease of reading.
- Show respect for time.
- Protect privacy confidentiality.
- Respond promptly.
- Maintain professionalism and appropriate formality.
- Manage emotion effectively.
- Avoid distractions.

Components of Effective Emails

- Subject line
- Greeting*
- Message
- Closing*
- Signature block*
- Attachments

*optional

See *examples of ineffective and effective emails* in Figures 7.1 and 7.2.

LO 7.2. Explain how to handle emotion effectively in online communications. (pp. 185–187)

Responding to Uncivil Communications

- Reinterpret
- Relax
- Defuse

See *examples of ineffective and effective responses to uncivil emails* in Figures 7.6 and 7.7.

LO 7.3. Describe strategies for managing digital message overload. (pp. 187–190)

Principles for Managing Emails to Avoid Distractions

- Check digital messages just two to four times each day at designated times.
- Turn off message alerts.
- Use rich channels such as face-to-face and phone conversations to accomplish a task completely.
- Reply immediately only to urgent messages.
- Avoid unnecessarily lengthening an email chain.
- Use automatic messages to help people know when you're unavailable.

LO 7.4. Explain characteristics of the emerging Social Age. (pp. 190–192)

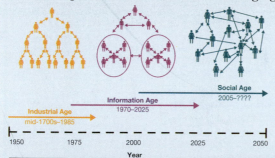

Characteristics of the Social Age

- Networked communication
- Respect for expertise and contributions to the network
- Sharing knowledge
- Transparency, honesty, and camaraderie

LO 7.5. Apply principles of effective social media use in professional settings. (pp. 192–197)

Principles for Using Internal Communication Tools in the Social Age

- Organize your dashboard to control your communication and information flow.
- Create a complete and professional profile.
- Use blogs for team communication.
- Use wikis for team communication.
- Participate and contribute often.
- Listen and learn.
- Focus on content.
- Make your content accessible.
- Make your messages authentic and friendly.
- Be responsive and help others.
- Respect boundaries.

See *examples of a social networking dashboard* in Figure 7.9, *a team blog* in Figure 7.10, and *a wiki* in Figure 7.11.

LO 7.6. Build a credible online reputation. (pp. 197–200)

See Table 7.5 for *types of positive meta messages you seek to establish your online reputation.* See *examples of ineffective and effective social networking profiles* in Figures 7.12 through 7.14.

LO 7.7. Describe the ethical use of social media for work. (pp. 200–203)

See *an example of corporate social media guidelines* in Figure 7.15.

Key Terms

active incivility (p. 186)

blogs (p. 194)

cyber incivility (p. 186)

cyber silence (p. 185)

defusing (p. 187)

flames (p. 185)

microblogs (p. 194)

negativity effect (p. 185)

neutrality effect (p. 185)

passive incivility (p. 186)

personal brand (p. 197)

project blogs (p. 194)

reinterpretation (p. 187)

relaxation (p. 187)

Social Age (p. 190)

social media (p. 191)

team blogs (p. 194)

User 1.0 (p. 191)

User 2.0 (p. 191)

Web 1.0 (p. 191)

Web 2.0 (p. 191)

wikis (p. 195)

Discussion Exercises

7.1 Chapter Review Questions (LO 7.1, LO 7.2, LO 7.3, LO 7.4, LO 7.5, LO 7.6, LO 7.7)

A. What strategies can you use to ensure ease of reading in your emails and other digital communications?

B. What strategies can you use to show respect for the time of others?

C. Explain the neutrality effect and negativity effect in digital communications. What do they imply for how you write digital messages?

D. What strategies can you use to avoid email overload and, as a result, increase your productivity?

E. Explain the following components of constructively responding to uncivil digital messages: reinterpretation, relaxation, and defusing.

F. What are some characteristics of the Social Age?

G. What elements of tone are most important for social media messages?

H. What strategies can you use to build a credible online reputation?

I. How can you use social media ethically from the perspective of your employer?

7.2 Questions about Communication Q&A with Catherine Norris (LO 7.1, LO 7.2, LO 7.5)

Read the Communication Q&A featuring Catherine Norris. Answer the following questions:

A. What principles does Norris use when deciding which communication technologies to use? In what ways do you agree and/or disagree?

B. In her view, how is the corporate intranet useful?

C. According to her, what are the main benefits and drawbacks of email? What future role does it have in business communications? In what ways do you agree and/or disagree?

D. According to her, what are the benefits and drawbacks of face-to-face communication? In what ways do you agree and/or disagree?

E. What was the most valuable information from this interview for you?

7.3 Information Overload Due to Digital Messages (LO 7.3)

Go to the Information Overload Research Group's website (iorgforum.org). Read a research article, blog entry, or other content about a topic of interest. In three to five paragraphs, explain the following: (a) main points in the article; (b) your views of the main points; and (c) three strategies you will adopt to avoid information overload in the workplace.

7.4 Social Media, Online Expression, and Collaboration (LO 7.4, LO 7.5)

Vineet Nayar, CEO of HCL Technologies, recently commented about the use of new communication channels. He specifically mentioned the use of social networking and the growing importance of Web 2.0 tools:

> As my kids became teenagers, I started looking at Facebook a little more closely. It was a significant amount of collaboration. There was open understanding. They didn't have a problem sharing their status. Nothing seemed to be secret, and they were living their lives very openly, and friends were commenting on each other and it was working. Here is my generation, which is very security-conscious and privacy-conscious, and I thought, what are the differences? This is the generation coming to work for us. It's not my generation. So we started having people make their presentations and record them for our internal website. We open that for review to a 360-degree workshop, which means your subordinates will review it. Your managers will read it. Your peers will read it, and everybody will comment on it. I will be, or your manager will be, one of the many who read it. So, every presentation was reviewed by 300, 400 people. What happened? There were two very interesting lessons that I learned. One, because your subordinates are going to see the plan, you cannot lie. You have to be honest. Two, because your peers are going to see it, you are going to put your best work into it. Third, you didn't learn from me. You learned by reviewing somebody else's presentation. You learned from the comments somebody else gave you. For the 8,000 people who participated, there was a massive collaborative learning that took place.[55]

Based on Nayar's comments and your own experiences, answer the following questions:

A. What are the potential personal and group benefits from using Web 2.0 communication channels?

B. What are some of the differing attitudes between generations about online expression? What impact might these differences have on workplace communication?

C. In what ways do online communications lead to more honesty and higher-quality work?

D. In what ways might online communications lead to less honesty and lower-quality work?

7.5 Challenges to Adopting Social Media for Professional Use (LO 7.4, LO 7.5)

Andrew McAfee, one of the premier experts on Enterprise 2.0 systems, commented about the challenges of adopting such systems and the shift in orientation needed by management to unleash a culture of User 2.0.

> I thought these technologies [such as Facebook, Wikipedia, Flickr, and YouTube] were essentially so cool that when you dropped them in an organization, people flocked to them. That was the assumption I carried around in my research. I very quickly had that overturned. This is not an overnight phenomenon at all. And while there are pockets of energy, getting mass adoption remains a pretty serious challenge for a lot of organizations.
>
> If you're a middle manager who essentially views your job as one of gatekeeping or refereeing information flows, you should be pretty frightened by these technologies, because they're going to greatly reduce your ability to do that. If you're someone who sees your job as managing people and fundamentally getting the human elements right that will lead your part of the organization to succeed, these technologies are not at all harmful to you. One of the things that we've learned is that there's no technology—even these great new social technologies—that's a substitute for face time. If you have another view of yourself, which is that you're someone who's responsible for output, these tools should be your best friend. Because all the evidence we have suggests that Enterprise 2.0 helps you turn out more and better products and actually is not a vehicle for time wasting or for chipping away at what you're supposed to be doing throughout the day.[56]

Based on McAfee's comments, contents of the chapter, and your own experiences, respond to the following questions:

A. What are the major obstacles to adopting Web 2.0 communication tools in the workplace?

B. McAfee distinguishes between information gatekeepers and managers of people. Explain what you think he means by this distinction and its relevance to the adoption of social software.

C. When are Web 2.0 communication tools more efficient than Web 1.0 communication tools such as email?

D. When are Web 1.0 communication tools such as email better choices than Web 2.0 communication tools?

E. Place yourself in the position of a middle or upper manager. Describe two ways in which the use of social media tools by your subordinates would benefit you and two ways in which they would threaten you.

7.6 Social Media Use and Interpersonal Skills (LO 7.4, LO 7.5)

Jeffrey Zaslow, in a November 5, 2009, article called "The Greatest Generation of Networkers" in *The Wall Street Journal*, examined attitudes about Millennials in the workplace. Consider a few of the comments:

> Because so many people in their teens and early 20s are in this constant whir of socializing—accessible to each other every minute of the day via cell phone, instant messaging and social-networking websites—there are a host of new questions that need to be addressed in schools, in the workplace, and at home. Chief among them: How

much work can "hyper-socializing" students or employees really accomplish if they are holding multiple conversations with friends via text messaging, or are obsessively checking Facebook?

> Some argue they can accomplish a great deal: This generation has a gift for multitasking, and because they've integrated technology into their lives, their ability to remain connected to each other will serve them and their employers well. Others contend that these hyper-socializers are serial time-wasters, that the bonds between them are shallow, and that their face-to-face interpersonal skills are poor.
>
> Does text messaging prepare one to interact in the workplace? "The unspoken attitude is, 'I don't need you. I have the Internet,'" says P.M. Forni, the 58-year-old director of the Civility Initiative at Johns Hopkins University, which studies politeness and manners. "The Net provides an opportunity to play hide-and-seek, to say and not say, to be truthful and to pretend. There is a lot of communication going on that is futile and trivial."
>
> That's far too harsh an assessment, says Ben Bajarin, 32, a technology analyst at Creative Strategies, a consulting firm in Campbell, California. He argues that because young people are so adept at multimedia socializing, their social skills are actually strengthened. They're good at "managing conversations" and getting to the pithy essence of an issue, he says, which will help them in the workplace.
>
> While their older colleagues waste time holding meetings or engaging in long phone conversations, young people have an ability to sum things up in one-sentence text messages, Bajarin says. "They know how to optimize and prioritize. They will call or set up a meeting if it's needed. If not, they text." And given their vast network of online acquaintances, they discover people who can become true friends or valued business colleagues—people they wouldn't have been able to find in the pre-Internet era.

Answer the following questions related to this passage from Zaslow:

A. In what ways do communication tools enhance the effective development of interpersonal skills needed in the workplace?

B. In what ways do communication tools hamper the effective development of interpersonal skills needed in the workplace?

C. What are some of the most valuable communication skills that Millennials bring to the workplace?

D. What are communication skills that you think Millennials most need to develop?

E. It's safe to assume that some non-Millennial workers hold a viewpoint similar to that of P. M. Forni in the passage above. What does this imply for you as you enter the workplace?

7.7 Blogs on Communication Technology (LO 7.5, LO 7.6, LO 7.7)

Select a blog entry about the impact of communication technologies on corporate culture from a well-known thinker. Search for a blog that interests you or choose from the following:

- Andrew McAfee's blog: http://andrewmcafee.org/blog/
- Jonathan Zittrain's blog: http://futureoftheinternet.org/

Based on the blog entry, respond to the following items:

A. Briefly summarize the topic of the blog entry.

B. According to the entry, what is the impact of communication technology on corporate culture?

C. Describe your feelings and attitudes regarding the entry. Do you agree or disagree with certain points? Are you enthusiastic or pessimistic about various parts of the entry?

D. Explain how the topic will impact you in the workplace.

7.8 Internet Communication Taking Over (LO 7.1, LO 7.4, LO 7.5, LO 7.6)

As researchers Simon Wright and Juraj Zdinak recently stated, "Internet communication is slowly taking over traditional phone-based voice communication and face-to-face communication. Restrictions to local or regional communities no longer apply: The Internet has enabled easy global communication."[57] Think about your future career and answer the following questions:

A. Is the prospect of communicating primarily via the Internet liberating? Explain.

B. Do you view the possibility of less face-to-face communication as disappointing? Explain.

C. What personal characteristics and skills are particularly well suited to success for predominantly Internet-based communication?

7.9 Setting Boundaries (LO 7.5, LO 7.6, LO 7.7)

In a recent survey of corporate employees, 76 percent thought it was OK to friend another employee who was a peer. Only 35 percent thought it was OK to friend a supervisor, and only 30 percent thought it was OK to friend a supervisee.[58] Answer the following related questions:

A. Do you think it is appropriate to friend a supervisor or supervisee on Facebook or another social networking website? What problems could arise by doing so? What work benefits might you achieve? What social boundaries should exist between supervisors and supervisees?

B. Do you think the boundaries between private life and work life are blurred by communication technologies such as social networking? What standards or principles do you want to use to keep parts of your private life separate from your colleagues?

C. Have you ever talked to your colleagues or classmates about your communication preferences? For example, have you discussed preferences for certain communication channels or expected response times? Describe your experiences.

7.10 Ethical Use of Social Media (LO 7.7)

Reread the three examples of personal social media use that hurt employers (p. 200). For each item, do the following:

A. Explain why the social media use was unethical.

B. Describe a similar behavior you have observed.

C. Recommend how employees can avoid such problems.

7.11 Corporate Social Media Guidelines (LO 7.7)

Reread Coca-Cola's social media guidelines in Figure 7.15. Respond to the following items:

A. Generally, what is the difference between speaking "on behalf of the Company" and speaking "about" the Company?

B. The policy states that employees are responsible for following the Code of Business Conduct in all public settings. Do you think your online activities on public social networking websites constitute a public setting? Explain.

C. The policy states that employees are responsible for any post that can "potentially tarnish the Company's image." Give five examples of posts that many people might consider private but that could damage a company's image.

D. What does it mean to be a scout?

E. What types of online conversations about the company are appropriate? Inappropriate?

F. What are some public positions employees might take that would be considered "counter to the Company's interests"?

Evaluation Exercises

7.12 Evaluating Email Messages (LO 7.1)

Compare the less-effective and more-effective emails in Figures 7.1 and 7.2 in the following ways:

A. Analyze the writing for each email based on tone, style, or design.

B. Evaluate them based on three principles for effective emails from this chapter.

C. Make two recommendations for improving the more-effective email.

7.13 Description of Past Work or School-Related Emails (LO 7.1)

Think of recent emails you have received related to work and school. Describe three effective email practices and three ineffective email practices you have observed. Describe each of these practices in detail (a paragraph each) and provide specific examples from emails you have received. You don't need to reveal who sent the emails.

7.14 Self-Assessment for Email Practices (LO 7.1)

Evaluate your typical practices with regard to email for school or work by circling the appropriate number for each item below.

	1 – Disagree	2 – Somewhat Disagree	3 – Somewhat Agree	4 – Agree
I almost always reread my email message in entirety before sending it.	1	2	3	4
I write emails in a professional and sufficiently formal manner.	1	2	3	4
I think carefully about what to write in the subject line.	1	2	3	4
I use a spell-checker for important email messages.	1	2	3	4

(continued)

	1 – Disagree	2 – Somewhat Disagree	3 – Somewhat Agree	4 – Agree
I envision how the recipient of my email message will respond when she/he receives it.	1	2	3	4
I think about the preferred communication channel of my message recipient before writing an email.	1	2	3	4
I read emails from others carefully and in their entirety before responding.	1	2	3	4
Before sending a reply email, I make one last check to see that I have responded to everything requested.	1	2	3	4
I regularly schedule uninterrupted time to focus on reading and responding to emails.	1	2	3	4
I set up an automatic email response or in other ways let others know when I will not be responsive to emails for an extended period (e.g., during vacation time).	1	2	3	4

Add up your score and consider the following advice:

35–40:   You are a *strategic* communicator by email. You carefully plan your emails and make sure that you send a professional communication. Notice the items you did not place a 4 next to and focus on improving in these areas.

30–34:   You are a *careful* communicator by email. You generally plan your emails well. However, you sometimes send them without enough thought or without reviewing them sufficiently. Focus on spending slightly more time in the planning stage.

25–29:   You are an *above average* communicator by email. Sometimes you plan your emails well. Make sure to spend more time before sending an email. Always make sure your content is completely professional before sending it.

Under 25:   You *need to improve* your approach to writing emails. You are too casual. Consider altering your orientation so that you view email as an important, formal business communication tool in which slight mistakes can damage your career.

Write three goals you have for becoming a more effective communicator by email. Go through the items in the survey one by one to help you think of areas where you most need to improve.

7.15 Assessment of Prior Email or Other Electronic Communication (LO 7.1, LO 7.2)

Think of an important email or other electronic communication you have sent in which others misunderstood your emotions and/or intent. How did the other person respond? Did you think the response was fair? Why did this person misunderstand? Did the lack of richness of the communication channel have an impact? How could you have written or approached your message differently to avoid misunderstandings?

7.16 Choosing the Right Type of Digital Message (LO 7.1, LO 7.5)

For each of the following communication tasks, identify which communication channel you think would work best: email, blogs, or wikis. Write several sentences explaining why you would

choose that communication channel. Assume you are a manager sending these messages to your subordinates:

A. Giving updates about an ongoing project.

B. Providing feedback on individual performance.

C. Sending a note of appreciation to one of your subordinates for excellent work.

D. Providing meeting minutes.

E. Setting up a working document about ground rules for participation in meetings.

F. Extending birthday wishes.

G. Sharing ideas with a few but not all of your subordinates.

H. Announcing a meeting for the whole team.

I. Announcing a meeting with two of the team members.

J. Working on a joint marketing proposal.

7.17 Responding to Cyber Incivility (LO 7.2)

Respond to the following questions:

A. What types of cyber incivility have you observed or heard about?

B. Based on your own experiences or those of your friends or colleagues, describe a situation in which someone was the target of cyber incivility. Describe the cyber incivility. How well did the target respond? How well did the target reinterpret, relax, and/or defuse the situation?

C. Compare the less-effective and more-effective responses to an angry email depicted in Figures 7.6 and 7.7. Explain three specific ways in which the more-effective response defuses the situation. Also, suggest two improvements you would make to the more-effective response in Figure 7.7.

7.18 Responding to Digital Messages and Managing Your Time (LO 7.3)

Answer the following questions about appropriately responding to digital messages:

A. What do you think is an appropriate response time to the following types of digital messages: texts, microblog messages (such as tweets), and emails?

B. Have others ever found your response time surprisingly fast? Have others ever found your response time to be slow enough to be considered impolite or uncivil? How can you influence the expectations of others regarding how quickly you respond to their digital messages?

C. Explain cyber silence. Provide three examples that you have observed.

D. What is the best way to respond to cyber silence when you need a response from someone else?

E. What three strategies do you or will you use in the upcoming five years to avoid e-interruptions in the workplace?

7.19 Evaluating Business Blogs (LO 7.5, LO 7.6)

Identify three individual business blogs in an area of interest to you. Analyze each blog in the following ways:

A. How does the blog provide value to readers?

B. What is the niche (unique offering) of this blog? What sets it apart from other blogs?

C. What tone does the writing convey? What are the meta messages from the blog?

D. How does the blog contribute to a personal brand for the author?

Conclude with five recommendations you have for how business professionals can create valuable blogs.

7.20 Evaluating Meta Messages (LO 7.6)

Based on the less-effective and more-effective social networking profiles depicted in Figures 7.12 and 7.13, respond to the following items:

A. What meta messages does each profile send to professionals who do not know Kip? Choose two primary meta messages for each profile.

B. What meta messages does each profile send to colleagues who do know Kip? Choose two primary meta messages for each profile.

C. What meta messages does each profile send to family members and friends? Choose two primary meta messages for each profile.

D. What three recommendations would you make to Kip to improve his Facebook profile (Figure 7.12) and his LinkedIn profile (Figure 7.14) to enhance his professional credibility?

7.21 Evaluating Your Online Reputation (LO 7.6)

A. Currently, what type of online reputation do you have in a professional sense?

B. In four or five sentences, explain the personal brand you would like to develop over the next five years.

C. Explain three strategies you will employ to develop your personal brand in your online communications. Devote at least one paragraph to each strategy.

7.22 Sending the Right Meta Messages with Your Online Communications (LO 7.5, LO 7.6)

Using Table 7.5 as a guide, do the following for each domain of your online reputation: personal and private; professional and private; personal and public; and professional and public:

A. What are the online communication channels you will use for each domain?

B. Will you use the same channels for more than one domain? If you share any of the communication channels for more than one domain, how will you prioritize which audiences to choose content for?

C. What are the primary meta messages you want to send? Choose two meta messages for each domain and explain how you intend to send these meta messages.

Endnotes

1. Peter W. Cardon, Melvin Washington, Ephraim A. Okoro, Bryan Marshall, and Nipul Patel, "Cross-Generational Perspectives on How Mobile Phone Use for Texting and Calling Influences Work Outcomes and Work Relationships," presented at the Association for Business Communication Southeast Conference, Charleston, South Carolina, April 1, 2011.

2. "Corporate Intranets 'Useless' to Business," *Concentra* website (March 2, 2010), retrieved July 6, 2010, from http://live.lewispr.com/concentra/2010/03/02/corporate-intranets-%E2%80%98useless%E2%80%99-to-business-598.

3. Sara Radicati, ed., and Masha Khmartseva, *Email Statistics Report, 2009–2013* (Palo Alto, CA: Radicati Group, April 2009).

4. "Email Has Made Slaves of Us," *The Daily Telegraph*, June 16, 2008.

5. Sara Radicati and Quoc Hoang, *Email Statistics Report, 2011–2015* (Palo Alto, CA: Radicati Group, 2011).

6. Jeanne C. Meister and Karie Willyerd, *The 2020 Workplace: How Innovative Companies Attract, Develop, and Keep Tomorrow's Employees Today* (New York: HarperCollins, 2010).

7. Ibid.

8. Beverly Langford, *The Etiquette Advantage: The Unspoken Rules for Business Success* (New York: American Management Association, 2005).

9. Alan Murray, "Should I Use Email?" *The Wall Street Journal* website, retrieved July 15, 2010, from http://guides.wsj.com/management/managing-your-people/should-i-use-email/.

10. Michael Hyatt, "Email Etiquette 101," retrieved July 15, 2010, from http://michaelhyatt.com/2007/07/email-etiquette-101.html.

11. Nick Morgan, "Don't Push That Send Button!" *Harvard Management Communication Letter* (August 2002): 4.

12. Susan Bixler and Lisa Scherrer Dugan, *How to Project Confidence, Competence, and Credibility at Work: 5 Steps to Professional Presence* (Avon, MA: Adams Media, 2001): 116.

13. Greg Wright, "Twitter with Care: Web 2.0 Usage Offers Few Second Chances," *Society for Human Resource Management* website, July 30, 2009, retrieved June 28, 2010, from http://www.shrm.org/hrdisciplines/technology/Articles/Pages/TwitterCarefully.aspx.

14. Peter W. Cardon, Melvin Washington, Ephraim A. Okoro, Bryan Marshall, and Nipul Patel, "Emotional Intelligence and Norms of Civility for Mobile Phone Use in Meetings," presentation at the Association of Business Communication 75th Annual Convention, Chicago, October 28, 2010.

15. Beverly Langford, *The Etiquette Advantage: The Unspoken Rules for Business Success*.

16. Dale Carnegie, *How to Win Friends and Influence People* (New York: Simon & Schuster, 1981): 83.

17. Joan Waldvogel, "Greetings and Closings in Workplace Email," *Journal of Computer-Mediated Communication* online 12, no. 2 (2007), from http://jcmc.indiana.edu/vol12/issue2/waldvogel.html.

18. Kristin Byron, "Carry Too Heavy a Load? The Communication and Miscommunication of Emotion by Email," *Academy of Management Review* 33, no. 2 (2008): 313.

19. Ibid.

20. Ibid.

21. Ibid.

22. Mei Alonzo and Milam Aiken, "Flaming in Electronic Communication," *Decision Support Systems* 36 (2004): 205.

23. Pearn Kandola, *The Psychology of Effective Business Communications in Geographically Dispersed Teams* (San Jose, CA: Cisco, 2006): 5.

24. Norman A. Johnson, Randolph B. Cooper, and Wynne W. Chin, "Anger and Flaming in Computer-Mediated Negotiation among Strangers," *Decision Support Systems* 46 (2009): 663.

25. Vivien K. G. Lim and Thompson S. H. Teo, "Mind Your E-manners: Impact of Cyber Incivility on Employees' Work Attitude and Behavior," *Information & Management* 46 (2009): 419.

26. Ibid: 419–425.

27. Johnson et al. "Anger and Flaming in Computer-Mediated Negotiation among Strangers": 660–672.

28. Joe Robinson, "Email Is Making You Stupid," *Entrepreneur* (March 2010): 61–63.

29. Ibid.

30. Ibid; Sally McGhee, "4 Ways to Take Control of Your Email Inbox," Microsoft At Work website, retrieved July 15, 2010, from www.microsoft.com/atwork/productivity/email.aspx.

31. Maria Azua, *The Social Factor: Innovate, Ignite, and Win through Mass Collaboration and Social Networking* (Upper Saddle River, NJ: IBM Press, 2010).

32. Michael Chui, Andy Miller, and Roger P. Roberts, "Six Ways to Make Web 2.0 Work," *McKinsey Quarterly* [online version] no. 1 (2010).

33. Simon Wright and Juraj Zdinak, *New Communication Behaviors in a Web 2.0 World—Changes, Challenges and Opportunities in the Era of the Information Revolution* (Paris: Alcatel-Lucent, 2008): 10.

34. Todd Henneman, "At Lockheed Martin, Social Networking Fills Key Workforce Needs While Improving Efficiency and Lowering Costs," *Workforce Management* online (March 2010), retrieved November 20, 2010, from www.workforce.com/section/software-technology/feature-lockheed-martin-social-networking-fills-key-workforce/index.html.

35. Wright and Zdinak, *New Communication Behaviors in a Web 2.0 World*; Andreas M. Kaplan and Michael Haenlein, "Users of the World, Unite! The Challenges and Opportunities of Social Media," *Business Horizons* 53, no. 1 (2010): 59–68; AON Consulting, *Web 2.0 and Employee Communications: Summary of Survey Findings* (Chicago: AON Consulting, March 2009); Jacques Bughin, Michael Chui, and Andy Miller, "How Companies Are Benefiting from Web 2.0," *McKinsey Quarterly* 17, no. 9 (2009); Andrew McAfee, *Enterprise 2.0: New Collaborative Tools for Your Organization's Toughest Challenges* (Boston: Harvard Business Press, 2009); Avanade, *CRM and Social Media: Maximizing Deeper Customer Relationships* (Seattle, WA: Avanade, 2008); Jennifer Taylor Arnold, "Twittering and Facebooking While They Work," *HR Magazine* 54, no. 12 (December 1, 2009); Soumitra Dutta, "What's Your Personal Social Media Strategy?" *Harvard Business Review* (November 2010): 127–130.

36. McAfee, *Enterprise 2.0: New Collaborative Tools for Your Organization's Toughest Challenges*.

37. Maria Azua, *The Social Factor: Innovate, Ignite, and Win through Mass Collaboration and Social Networking*.

38. Wright and Zdinak, *New Communication Behaviors in a Web 2.0 World*.

39. Andy Beal and Judy Straus, *Radically Transparent: Monitoring and Managing Reputations Online* (Indianapolis, IN: Wiley Publishing, 2008).

40. "Intranet Blogs Hit Critical Mass: Most Employees Don't Like to Blog, but They Like to Read Them," retrieved November 20, 2010, from www.prescientdigital.com/articles/intranet-articles/intranet-blogs-hit-critical-mass.

41. Kaplan and Haenlein, "Users of the World, Unite! The Challenges and Opportunities of Social Media": 62.

42. Wright and Zdinak, *New Communication Behaviors in a Web 2.0 World*; Sebastian Paquet, "Wikis in Business," in Jane Klobas, *Wikis: Tools for Information Work and Collaboration* (Oxford: Chandos Publishing, 2006): 99–117; Jane Klobas, *Wikis: Tools for Information Work and Collaboration* (Oxford: Chandos Publishing, 2006).

43. Daniel Nations, "The Business Wiki," retrieved November 20, 2010, from http://webtrends.about.com/od/wiki/a/business-wiki.htm.

44. Richard McDermott and Douglas Archibald, "Harnessing Your Staff's Informal Networks," *Harvard Business Review* (March 2010): 83–89.

45. Paquet, "Wikis in Business."

46. Goetz Boue, *Don't Say Web 2.0, Say Intranet 2.0* (London: Concentra, 2009); Dutta, "What's Your Personal Social Media Strategy?"; Beal and Straus, *Radically Transparent: Monitoring and Managing Reputations Online*.

47. Dutta, "What's Your Personal Social Media Strategy?"

48. Josh Hyatt, "Building Your Brand and Keeping Your Job," *Fortune* (August 16, 2010): 74.

49. Adapted from Dutta, "What's Your Personal Social Media Strategy?": 129.

50. Hyatt, "Building Your Brand and Keeping Your Job": 71–76.

51. Greg Wright, "Twitter with Care: Web 2.0 Usage Offers Few Second Chances," *Society for Human Resource Management* online.

52. Hyatt, "Building Your Brand and Keeping Your Job."

53. Arnold, "Twittering and Facebooking While They Work."

54. Ibid.

55. New York Times Corner Office Blog, "Communication," retrieved June 15, 2010, from http://projects.nytimes.com/corner-office/Communication.

56. Roger P. Roberts, "An Interview with MIT's Andrew McAfee," *McKinsey Quarterly*, no. 1 (2010).

57. Wright and Zdinak, *New Communication Behaviors in a Web 2.0 World*: 6.

58. "Online Etiquette & the Workplace," Liberty Mutual The Responsibility Project website, retrieved July 6, 2010, from http://www.responsibilityproject.com/infographics/rp-survey-online-etiquette-the-workplace#fbid=67LBedVyvn7.

Types of Business Messages

PART FOUR

CHAPTER EIGHT

Routine Messages

Learning Objectives

After studying this chapter, you should be able to do the following:

LO8.1   Describe how delivering routine messages impacts credibility.

LO8.2   Describe the process for developing routine business messages.

LO8.3   Construct routine business requests.

LO8.4   Compose routine sets of expectations.

LO8.5   Construct routine sets of directions.

LO8.6   Compose routine responses to inquiries.

LO8.7   Construct routine announcements.

LO8.8   Compose routine claims.

LO8.9   Construct routine appreciation messages.

LO8.10   Compose apologies.

LO8.11   Construct expressions of sympathy.

WHY DOES THIS MATTER?

The vast majority of business messages are routine. In routine messages, you are dealing with straightforward information that does not require in-depth analysis, so you generally expect your readers to react positively, and you do not anticipate resistance.

Most routine messages are simple. Yet, routine messages should not be treated as unimportant or inconsequential. They are the glue that holds together most coordinated business actions. In this chapter, we discuss common types of routine messages. Many of them primarily focus on work tasks, such as making requests, setting expectations, providing directions, making inquiries, providing announcements, and making claims. Other routine messages focus on maintaining and improving workplace relationships, such as showing appreciation, offering apologies, and expressing sympathy. The final two types of messages, apologies and expressions of sympathy, are unlike other messages in this chapter in that they occur far less frequently. However, like other messages in this chapter, they are fairly straightforward and require you to compose them fairly quickly.

The day-in-and-day-out routine messages you send may be among the most important for establishing your credibility in the workplace, especially early in your business career. Your approach to routine business messages strongly influences how others evaluate your responsiveness, reliability, attention to detail, commitment, and professionalism.

Read the chapter case about a typical morning at work for Bryan Atkins, an account executive at an advertising firm. Throughout the chapter, you'll see the routine messages Bryan completes before 11 a.m. While Bryan can answer most routine messages with emails of less than one paragraph, we focus on those examples that require slightly more effort. As a result, the examples are generally three to five paragraphs long.

Hear Pete Cardon explain why this matters.

bit.ly.com/CardonWhy8

LO8.1 Describe how delivering routine messages impacts credibility.

Chapter Case: Routine Emails at Smith & Smith Advertising

Who's Involved

Bryan Atkins, account executive at Smith & Smith Advertising
- Works extensively with clients to ensure they are satisfied with various advertising campaigns
- Leads and coordinates work with the creative teams working on these campaigns

Situation 1 (8 a.m.)

Bryan Requests a New Server

Bryan arrived with a minute to spare for the weekly morning meeting with the executive management team. His one agenda item was to purchase a replacement for a soon-to-be-outdated server. One of the partners, Andrea Johansen, thought this was a straightforward matter but asked Bryan to put his suggestions in writing with details about the needed purchases.

Situation 2
(9 a.m.)

Bryan Responds to Messages in His In-Box from Employees and Prospects

After the meeting, Bryan sat down at his computer to find 37 new messages from colleagues, clients, and prospects. Bryan thought all of the messages were important enough that he needed to respond to them within two to three hours. Several were most urgent:

- A member of the creative team, Barry Evermore, said he and his partner, John Anderson, had just finished an account and were waiting for new assignments.
- A new member of the creative team, John Anderson (Barry Evermore's partner), was scheduled to take a company trip, but he was unfamiliar with travel procedures at Smith & Smith. He was asking Bryan how to set up his trip.
- A potential client emailed Bryan about services offered by Smith & Smith.

Situation 3
(9:30 a.m.)

Bryan Makes an Announcement

As the chair of the social activities committee, Bryan wanted to send out an announcement.

Situation 4
(9:40 a.m.)

Bryan Takes Care of Overcharges from a Vendor

This morning he noticed that a hotel had overcharged Smith & Smith by not applying a negotiated rate to several hotel stays for members of his creative teams. Bryan wanted to resolve the matter immediately.

Situation 5
(10:05 a.m.)

Bryan Shows Appreciation to His Creative Team

During the morning, Bryan took a call from a recent client, Ana Galleraga, director of the local zoo. "Hey, Bryan," she said. "Just wanted to let you know what a great success we're having with the ad campaign you developed. Since we started putting up billboard ads and running the radio spots last month, we've increased participation in all of our community educational programs. We're also getting lots of comments about how beautiful the billboards are. Please let everyone over there know what a great job they've done. And, we'd like to figure out how to use the campaign concept in our online marketing." Of course, Bryan told her that the agency could help her out in that regard.

Situation 6
(10:20 a.m.)

Bryan Issues a Brief Apology

Over the weekend, he worried about insensitive comments he made in last Friday's leadership team meeting. Bryan had accused his colleagues of caring more about one of their clients than about their own employees. This particular client frequently made unreasonable requests, but Bryan and other members of the executive management team never pushed back because the client accounted for nearly one-quarter of Smith & Smith's total revenues.

Situation 7
(10:45 a.m.)

Bryan Expresses Sympathy to a Longtime Client

He wanted to write a sympathy card to his close client Felipe Bravo. Over the weekend, Felipe's wife, Rosa, passed away after a long battle with cancer. Bryan and Felipe have worked together for nearly a decade, and Bryan wanted to express his genuine sympathy to Felipe.

Task 1

How will Bryan write a routine request for a new server? (See the "Making Requests" section.)

Task 2

- How can Bryan best set expectations for Barry and John's upcoming work schedule? (See "Setting Expectations.")
- How can Bryan most efficiently help John make travel plans? (See "Providing Directions.")
- How can Bryan respond in a way that best answers the potential client's questions and maximizes the likelihood that he will become a client? (See "Responding to Inquiries.")

Task 3
How should Bryan announce a social outing so that his colleagues will get all the key information rapidly? (See the "Creating Announcements" section.)

Task 4
How should Bryan make sure the excessive charges are refunded or credited? (See "Making Claims.")

Task 5
How should Bryan go about congratulating his creative team on its excellent work? (See "Showing Appreciation.")

Task 6
How can Bryan make amends for his inappropriate comments? (See the "Making Apologies" section.)

Task 7
How should Bryan express condolences to his client? (See "Expressing Sympathy.")

Developing Routine Messages

LO8.2 Describe the process for developing routine business messages.

Since you will send and receive so many routine messages in any given business day, one of your primary goals is efficiency: You need to produce credible messages quickly. Excellent business communicators can develop routine written messages—even those that require several paragraphs—in a matter of minutes. The examples in this chapter should generally take 5 to 15 minutes to complete.

Typically, completing routine messages requires less time than other types of business messages. Also, compared to other types of business messages, routine messages require proportionately less time for planning and reviewing. *Developing routine messages quickly, however, does not mean abandoning the writing process of planning, drafting, and reviewing.*

For most routine messages, you can accomplish the AIM planning process fairly quickly (see Figure 8.1). Because you generally are working with straightforward matters and your audience is likely to respond positively, you will generally not need much time for *audience analysis*. Since you are typically dealing with straightforward matters, you don't need much time for *idea development*. Developing your ideas is mostly a matter of identifying and gathering relevant, accurate, and up-to-date information. However, avoid the impulse to skip this step. Ask yourself questions such as the following: *How would my audience want to receive this information? How much detail do my audience members expect?*

The most important planning step is *message structuring*. Since routine messages are so common and your readers are likely overloaded with so many other messages and tasks, your primary challenge is to make sure your readers pay attention. Therefore, your message should be direct and front-loaded. The primary message should have ten words or fewer, and you should typically place it in the subject line of your email to immediately capture attention. Furthermore, the primary message should appear in the first sentence or two of the message and again in the closing if your message is several paragraphs long.

In the body of the routine message, you should provide short paragraphs with related details. To make sure your message receiver will comply, include all needed information. Not only are readers less likely to comply when you don't provide enough information, but you also lose credibility. Once you establish a reputation for providing

Components of Routine Messages

- State the *primary message* (ten words or fewer).
- Provide *details* in paragraphs of 20 to 80 words.
- *Restate* the request or key message in more specific terms.
- State *goodwill*.

FIGURE 8.1

The Writing Process for
Routine Messages

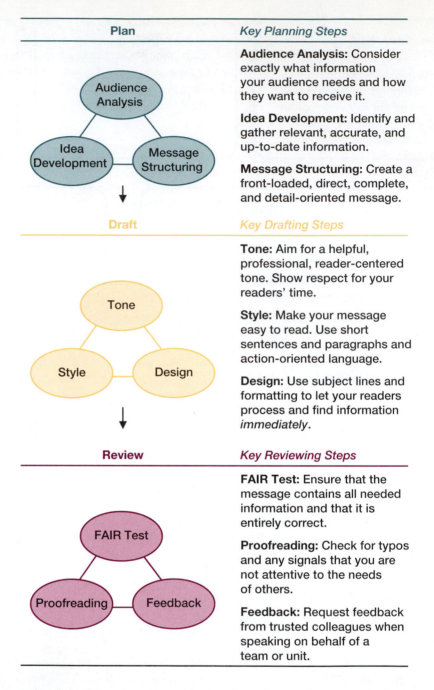

Plan	*Key Planning Steps*
	Audience Analysis: Consider exactly what information your audience needs and how they want to receive it.
	Idea Development: Identify and gather relevant, accurate, and up-to-date information.
	Message Structuring: Create a front-loaded, direct, complete, and detail-oriented message.
Draft	*Key Drafting Steps*
	Tone: Aim for a helpful, professional, reader-centered tone. Show respect for your readers' time.
	Style: Make your message easy to read. Use short sentences and paragraphs and action-oriented language.
	Design: Use subject lines and formatting to let your readers process and find information *immediately*.
Review	*Key Reviewing Steps*
	FAIR Test: Ensure that the message contains all needed information and that it is entirely correct.
	Proofreading: Check for typos and any signals that you are not attentive to the needs of others.
	Feedback: Request feedback from trusted colleagues when speaking on behalf of a team or unit.

incomplete, overly general messages, your readers are less likely to pay close attention to your future messages.

As you *draft* the message, aim for a helpful, professional, and reader-centered tone. Focus on making the message easy to read. Readers expect to understand your primary message in under 10 to 15 seconds, so use short sentences and paragraphs. Design your message so readers can find information in just moments. Use bullets, numbering, special formatting, and external links to relevant information to highlight key ideas.

Your proofreading in the *reviewing* stage should take a minute or two. Since business professionals send so many routine messages each day and their content can be repetitive, they often do not take time to reread them. Avoid this impulse to hit "send" without rereading your messages. By rereading, you will make sure the content is complete and without errors. Even minor typos can distract your readers from complying with your messages.

Since routine messages are straightforward and rarely sensitive, you generally do not need to ask for feedback from trusted colleagues. However, when you speak on behalf of your team, you might check with other team members to ensure they agree about the content. The most important aspect of the FAIR test is checking for accuracy—that is, making certain your information is accurate and reliable.

Making Requests

LO8.3 Construct routine business requests.

You will make thousands of requests of others during your career, and others will make thousands of requests of you. Requests are the essence of people coordinating work efforts, buying and selling products and services, and maintaining work relationships.

Routine requests involve cases where you expect little or no resistance from message recipients. Like all routine messages, routine requests should contain clear and specific subject lines, often stating the entire *request*. As you reread the message before sending it, one question you'll ask yourself is whether the message recipient will understand exactly what to do.

For most requests, you will often use a portion of the message to provide the *rationale* for the request. Since you expect a favorable response, you typically do not need to be particularly persuasive. However, justifying the request shows your professionalism and attention to detail. It also helps a company maintain transparency by keeping written records of why certain decisions were made.

One primary goal for routine requests is to retain *goodwill* with the recipient. No one wants to feel bossed around, so make sure you achieve a positive, other-oriented tone. Also, when working with superiors, be careful about setting deadlines. Even in today's flatter organizations, being bossy to the boss can be counterproductive. Finally, when making requests, showing respect for the recipient's time goes a long way in maintaining goodwill.

In Bryan's request memo to Andrea for a new computer server (see Figures 8.2 and 8.3), the request is routine because Andrea has already verbally committed to making the purchase. The primary goal is to convey the information in an easy-to-read, complete format. In the more-effective memo, Bryan asks for the purchase authorization within a specific time frame (within two weeks; preferably before the end of the week). He justifies the request with sufficient detail. Finally, he is direct but not bossy or domineering, which is important since he is writing to his boss.

> **Components of Requests**
>
> - Make request.
> - Provide rationale.
> - Call to action.*
> - State goodwill.
>
> *Optional—appropriate at the end of lengthy messages

Setting Expectations

LO8.4 Compose routine sets of expectations.

Working with others involves setting expectations, especially when you are in management and supervisory roles. Many young business professionals—especially first-time managers—are not comfortable with telling others what to do. They are nervous about overstepping their authority and disrupting a friendly feeling with subordinates. Yet, setting expectations is directly tied to your credibility and ability to foster interpersonal trust in the workplace. Dennis S. Reina and Michelle L. Reina have examined the nature of trust in hundreds of companies over the past few decades and say this about setting clear expectations:

> A lack of clarity regarding expectations causes misperceptions and misconstrued intentions. When people's expectations are not met, they may feel a range of emotions. They may feel disappointed, discounted, taken advantage of, angry, or hurt. The result may be distrust and feelings of betrayal. . . . When people don't find out what is expected of them until they run into a wall, go down the wrong road, or fail to get a promotion or pay raise, it's too late. In these kinds of situations, people may experience a range of emotions from disappointment to betrayal.[1]

So, although setting expectations is often a routine matter, failure to do it can lead to lasting professional disappointments and breakdowns in working relationships.

FIGURE 8.2

Less-Effective Routine Request

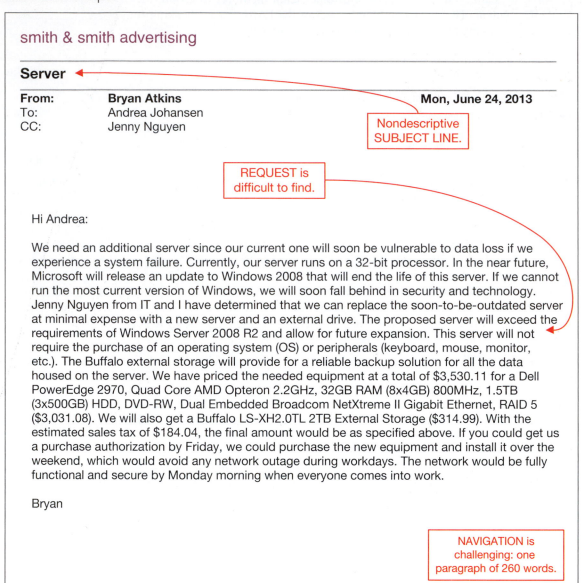

smith & smith advertising

Server

From:	**Bryan Atkins**	**Mon, June 24, 2013**
To:	Andrea Johansen	
CC:	Jenny Nguyen	

Nondescriptive
SUBJECT LINE.

REQUEST is
difficult to find.

Hi Andrea:

We need an additional server since our current one will soon be vulnerable to data loss if we experience a system failure. Currently, our server runs on a 32-bit processor. In the near future, Microsoft will release an update to Windows 2008 that will end the life of this server. If we cannot run the most current version of Windows, we will soon fall behind in security and technology. Jenny Nguyen from IT and I have determined that we can replace the soon-to-be-outdated server at minimal expense with a new server and an external drive. The proposed server will exceed the requirements of Windows Server 2008 R2 and allow for future expansion. This server will not require the purchase of an operating system (OS) or peripherals (keyboard, mouse, monitor, etc.). The Buffalo external storage will provide for a reliable backup solution for all the data housed on the server. We have priced the needed equipment at a total of $3,530.11 for a Dell PowerEdge 2970, Quad Core AMD Opteron 2.2GHz, 32GB RAM (8x4GB) 800MHz, 1.5TB (3x500GB) HDD, DVD-RW, Dual Embedded Broadcom NetXtreme II Gigabit Ethernet, RAID 5 ($3,031.08). We will also get a Buffalo LS-XH2.0TL 2TB External Storage ($314.99). With the estimated sales tax of $184.04, the final amount would be as specified above. If you could get us a purchase authorization by Friday, we could purchase the new equipment and install it over the weekend, which would avoid any network outage during workdays. The network would be fully functional and secure by Monday morning when everyone comes into work.

Bryan

NAVIGATION is
challenging: one
paragraph of 260 words.

Components of Expectations

- Explain overall expectation.
- Describe responsibilities.
- Provide deadlines.
- Discuss coordination.
- State goodwill.

Three components are central in setting expectations for those you manage: describing responsibilities, providing deadlines, and discussing coordination. Describing *responsibilities* means designating tasks and work outcomes to certain employees, providing *deadlines* means setting out the timeline by which the work should be accomplished satisfactorily, and discussing *coordination* involves providing guidelines for how employees should communicate and cooperate with one another. From time to time, you should also describe your own role and responsibilities to supervisees. When you do so, they see they are accountable to you and you are also accountable to them. This means you may need to occasionally own up to your own mistakes and accept responsibility when everything has not gone as expected.

Notice the differences between the less-effective and more-effective expectations messages in Figures 8.4 and 8.5, in which Bryan makes a new assignment and sets out

FIGURE 8.3

More-Effective Routine Request

---

smith & smith advertising

TO:	Andrea Johansen
FROM:	Bryan Atkins
CC:	Jenny Nguyen
DATE:	June 24, 2013
SUBJECT:	Request for Purchase Authorization for New Server

> SUBJECT LINE is short (7 words) but effective.

> REQUEST is stated clearly and up front.

Can you provide a purchase authorization for a new server and external drive? We should purchase this equipment as soon as possible to keep our information system as secure as possible. I recommend that we purchase the new server within two weeks.

The primary reason we need an additional server is that we will soon be vulnerable to data loss if we experience a system failure. Currently, our server runs on a 32-bit processor. In the near future, Microsoft will release an update to Windows 2008 that will end the life of this server. If we cannot run the most current version of Windows, we will soon fall behind in security and technology.

Jenny Nguyen from IT and I have determined that we can replace the soon-to-be-outdated server at minimal expense with a new server and an external drive. The proposed server will exceed the requirements of Windows Server 2008 R2 and allow for future expansion. This server will not require the purchase of an operating system (OS) or peripherals (keyboard, mouse, monitor, etc.). The Buffalo external storage will provide for a reliable backup solution for all the data housed on the server. We have priced the needed equipment as follows:

> RATIONALE is specific and clear.

Dell PowerEdge 2970, Quad Core AMD Opteron 2.2GHz, 32GB RAM (8x4GB) 800MHz, 1.5TB (3x500GB) HDD, DVD-RW, Dual Embedded Broadcom NetXtreme II Gigabit Ethernet, RAID 5	$3,031.08
Buffalo LS-XH2.0TL 2TB External Storage	$314.99
Estimated Sales Tax	$14.04
Estimated Total Cost	$3,530.11

Andrea, we would like to move forward as soon as possible with these purchases to make sure our system is secure. If you could get us a purchase authorization by Friday, we could purchase the new equipment and install it over the weekend, which would allow us to avoid any network outage during workdays. The network would be fully functional and secure by Monday morning when everyone comes into work.

> NAVIGATION is easy: Paragraphs are 40, 70, 89, and 67 words long.

---

the deadlines for Barry and John, two of his supervisees. The less-effective example violates the basic requirements of routine messages because it does not provide the key message clearly at the beginning. It is also difficult to read. In the more-effective message, Barry and John can grasp the key messages within seconds. They can process all of the information rapidly and understand the responsibilities, deadlines, and coordination associated with these new accounts.

FIGURE 8.4

Less-Effective Example of Setting Expectations

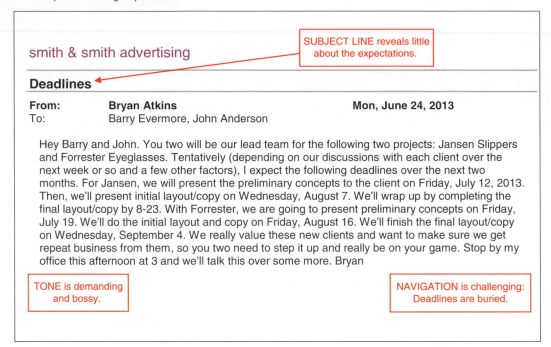

smith & smith advertising

SUBJECT LINE reveals little about the expectations.

Deadlines

| From: | Bryan Atkins | Mon, June 24, 2013 |
| To: | Barry Evermore, John Anderson | |

Hey Barry and John. You two will be our lead team for the following two projects: Jansen Slippers and Forrester Eyeglasses. Tentatively (depending on our discussions with each client over the next week or so and a few other factors), I expect the following deadlines over the next two months. For Jansen, we will present the preliminary concepts to the client on Friday, July 12, 2013. Then, we'll present initial layout/copy on Wednesday, August 7. We'll wrap up by completing the final layout/copy by 8-23. With Forrester, we are going to present preliminary concepts on Friday, July 19. We'll do the initial layout and copy on Friday, August 16. We'll finish the final layout/copy on Wednesday, September 4. We really value these new clients and want to make sure we get repeat business from them, so you two need to step it up and really be on your game. Stop by my office this afternoon at 3 and we'll talk this over some more. Bryan

TONE is demanding and bossy.

NAVIGATION is challenging: Deadlines are buried.

Providing Directions

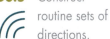

LO8.5 Construct routine sets of directions.

Components of Directions

- State goal.
- Give step-by-step directions.
- State goodwill.

Another common type of routine message provides directions for others. Messages that provide directions share many similarities with those that set expectations. The primary distinction is that directions typically include specific—often step-by-step—guidelines for accomplishing particular tasks.

Since describing step-by-step procedures is so specific, insufficient detail can frustrate your readers. For routine matters, you are generally safe reviewing your own work and making sure it is complete. For more technical and complicated procedures, make sure you have several people test the procedures to find where you can better clarify the steps involved.

In messages with procedures and directions, make the steps stand out clearly by enumerating each one. This helps your reader keep track of progress completing the tasks. Steps that are written in narrative form within a paragraph are typically difficult to follow.

Notice the differences between the less-effective and more-effective messages in Figures 8.6 and 8.7, where Bryan gives directions to John on how to make company travel arrangements. The less-effective example in Figure 8.6 has an unhelpful and careless tone, written almost entirely in passive voice. The message is abrupt and insufficiently detailed. Many readers will decode a meta message of "I don't have time for you." In the more-effective example in Figure 8.7, Bryan provides clear directions by pasting the human resources policies into the message and inserting his own comments as additional guidelines and tips. He also tells John where to go for more information. In reality, Bryan could have simply emailed "check the HR intranet portal." Yet, this more-effective message, written in just three to four minutes, is a strong sign of Bryan's willingness to help John. Many readers will decode a meta message of "I want to help you out as much as possible."

FIGURE 8.5

More-Effective Example of Setting Expectations

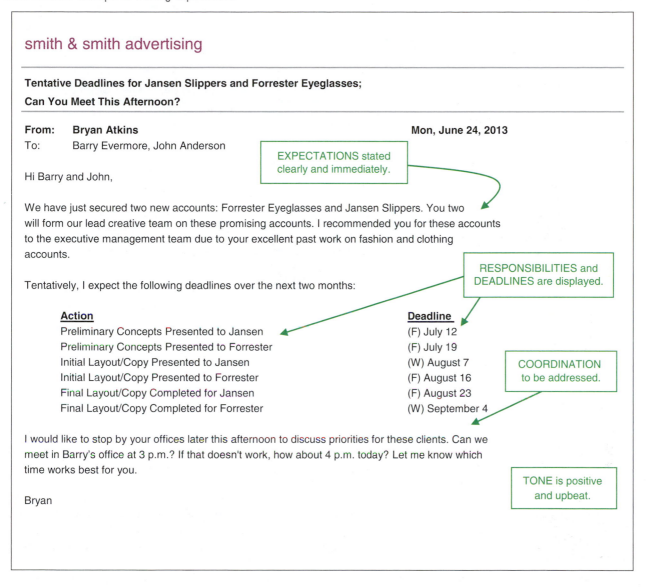

smith & smith advertising

Tentative Deadlines for Jansen Slippers and Forrester Eyeglasses;

Can You Meet This Afternoon?

| From: | **Bryan Atkins** | **Mon, June 24, 2013** |
| To: | Barry Evermore, John Anderson | |

Hi Barry and John,

EXPECTATIONS stated clearly and immediately.

We have just secured two new accounts: Forrester Eyeglasses and Jansen Slippers. You two will form our lead creative team on these promising accounts. I recommended you for these accounts to the executive management team due to your excellent past work on fashion and clothing accounts.

Tentatively, I expect the following deadlines over the next two months:

RESPONSIBILITIES and DEADLINES are displayed.

Action	Deadline
Preliminary Concepts Presented to Jansen	(F) July 12
Preliminary Concepts Presented to Forrester	(F) July 19
Initial Layout/Copy Presented to Jansen	(W) August 7
Initial Layout/Copy Presented to Forrester	(F) August 16
Final Layout/Copy Completed for Jansen	(F) August 23
Final Layout/Copy Completed for Forrester	(W) September 4

COORDINATION to be addressed.

I would like to stop by your offices later this afternoon to discuss priorities for these clients. Can we meet in Barry's office at 3 p.m.? If that doesn't work, how about 4 p.m. today? Let me know which time works best for you.

TONE is positive and upbeat.

Bryan

FIGURE 8.6

Less-Effective Directions

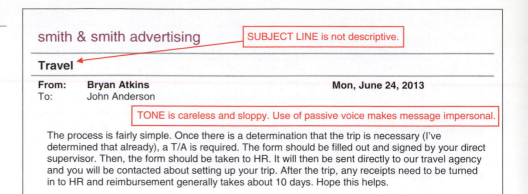

smith & smith advertising

Travel

| From: | Bryan Atkins | Mon, June 24, 2013 |
| To: | John Anderson | |

SUBJECT LINE is not descriptive.

TONE is careless and sloppy. Use of passive voice makes message impersonal.

The process is fairly simple. Once there is a determination that the trip is necessary (I've determined that already), a T/A is required. The form should be filled out and signed by your direct supervisor. Then, the form should be taken to HR. It will then be sent directly to our travel agency and you will be contacted about setting up your trip. After the trip, any receipts need to be turned in to HR and reimbursement generally takes about 10 days. Hope this helps.

FIGURE 8.7

More-Effective Directions

smith & smith advertising

DIRECTIONS are specific and clear.

Procedures for Setting Up Travel

| From: | **Bryan Atkins** | Mon, June 24, 2013 |
| To: | John Anderson | |

John,

For complete details, go to the *Travel* section of the **Human Resources intranet portal**. You will immediately find all policies and forms that you need.

Here are the basic steps pasted directly from the HR intranet portal with several *comments from me inserted in italics*.

1. Complete a "Travel Authorization" (T/A) form with approval signature from your immediate supervisor.

   (I'm the supervisor. You can get the latest T/A form off the HR intranet portal at the following link: T/A Form*.)*

2. Submit the T/A to Human Resources (HR). HR will forward it directly to our designated travel agency.

   (Our current designated travel agency is Dawson Travel.)

3. An agent from the travel agency will contact you directly and develop your trip itinerary with you. The travel agency will bill Smith & Smith directly for your airfare, accommodations, and car rentals.

   (You should do this right away. You may be able to choose an airline that you have frequent flier miles with if you can book far enough in advance. If you book within two weeks of the travel, you are required to use discount airlines.)

4. After completing your trip, turn in receipts for incidental expenses to HR. You will be reimbursed for these expenses and receive a daily stipend to cover meals.

   (Make sure to review the company policies so you know which incidental expenses are covered and how much your daily stipend will be.)

This should get you started. For questions about filling out the T/A, you'll get more help from HR. As soon as you get the T/A form filled in, just let me know and I'll sign it right away.

Bryan

TONE is professional and helpful.

Responding to Inquiries

The very nature of working with others involves asking and responding to questions. One of the most important strategies for responding to inquiries is to set off each question so your readers can quickly identify responses to particular questions. You generally can do this using bullets or numbered lists and/or special formatting (i.e., bold or italics). When choosing between bullets or numbered lists, consider whether the order of the items is important. If the order is important, use numbered lists. Otherwise, use bullets. Also, consider telling your readers where to get additional and more specific information by providing links to FAQ web pages or other relevant web pages.

Notice the difference between Bryan's less-effective and more-effective responses to an inquiry from a prospect in Figures 8.8 and 8.9. In the less-effective response in Figure 8.8, Bryan mixes responses in a single paragraph. (The original inquiry is located at the bottom of Figure 8.8; it is a poorly written inquiry with all the questions embedded in one paragraph.) In the more-effective response in Figure 8.9, Bryan gives each question its own section and highlights each in bold. By structuring the email this way, he helps the reader easily navigate the various answers. He also uses links to web pages with further information and attempts to schedule a face-to-face meeting where he can answer questions in a richer medium.

LO8.6 Compose routine responses to inquiries.

Components of Inquiry Responses

- Provide responses.
- State goodwill.

Creating Announcements

Business executives and managers routinely make announcements. Announcements are updates to policies and procedures, notices of events, and other correspondences that apply to a group of employees and/or customers. Announcements are one form of one-to-many communications.

Since announcements are generally broadcast to a large number of receivers (often as emails or corporate intranet posts), many employees and customers gloss over them. To prevent employees and customers from ignoring announcements, the subject line must be specific and must create interest. Furthermore, announcements, especially for events, should be designed to let readers gather all relevant information in 10 to 15 seconds. Thus, formatting is especially important.

In the less-effective announcement from Bryan about the upcoming social event (see Figure 8.10), he conveys little enthusiasm, runs all the pertinent information together, and provides incomplete information (i.e., *Which park? Can guests come?*). This message creates more questions than it answers. Bryan's more-effective announcement contains all the necessary ingredients of effective announcements (see Figure 8.11). The subject line explains what the event is and contains a call to action—an RSVP. The details of the event are set apart with bold labels, allowing the reader to gather the needed information in a matter of seconds. Readers will likely view this message as a positive, enthusiastic, and warm invitation.

LO8.7 Construct routine announcements.

Components of Announcements

- Gain attention.
- Give announcement.
- Provide details.
- Call to action.*
- State goodwill.

*For some announcements

Making Claims

Claims are requests for other companies to compensate for or correct the wrongs or mistakes they have made. As with other requests, you should immediately state what the *claim* is and what you expect the company to do for you. You also will provide a *rationale* for your claim in the body of the message and close with a call to *action*—a specific request.

As you write claims, keep in mind that your goal is to have your claim honored. Focus on facts first and emotions second, if at all. Lay out a logical, reasonable, and professional explanation for your claim. Emotional claims are far more likely to be rejected. Also, remember that you will often work with the same people again and again. So, be polite and focus on the long-term working relationship.

In Bryan's less-effective claim to the Prestigio Hotel about a billing error (see Figure 8.12), phrases such as "you have not honored" and "you overcharged" unnecessarily

LO8.8 Compose routine claims.

Components of Claims

- Make claim.
- Provide rationale.
- Call to action.
- State goodwill.

FIGURE 8.8

Less-Effective Response to an Inquiry

To...	Joel Yang [joel.yang@doityourselfsports.com]
Subject:	RE: Questions about Advertising

Arial   10   **B** *I* U

Hello Joel:

Thanks for getting in touch with us here at Smith & Smith. Answers to all of your questions can be found on our website (**Smith & Smith website**). Generally, you'll find that our rates are extremely competitive with other agencies. More important, we have a great record of return on investment and help you track this figure. Also, our agency has been at the forefront of all forms of online advertising and marketing for the past fifteen years. We have been instrumental in helping small companies rapidly grow their revenues and expand. See the following web page about our online advertising with examples of our work: **Smith & Smith online advertising and social media**. We can meet at a time and place convenient for you. This week I'm available from 2 to 4 on Tuesday, 9 to 11:30 on Wednesday, and in the morning or afternoon on Thursday. Please let me know a time that is best for you.

Bryan

> *Nonunified Response:*
> A single paragraph
> contains answers to all
> of the questions.

From: Joel Yang [joel.yang@doityourselfsports.com]
Sent: Mon, Jun 24, 2013 at 8:34 AM
To: Bryan Atkins [bryanatkins@smith+smith.com]
Subject: Questions about Advertising

Hi Bryan, I contacted Andrea Johansen about developing some ads. She recommended that I contact you directly. Basically, I'm interested in pricing for various advertising options. You've probably seen our used sports equipment stores around town. We've decided to change our business model and devote half of our retail space to new sports equipment. Anyway, we want to get the word out. We've always developed in-house advertising which I think has been amateurish. Of course, we don't have a big budget. So, we want quality advertising but we're concerned about pricing. How do your rates compare to other advertising agencies? Do you have any specialists in online advertising? What about with social media? When could we meet and talk about what you might provide us? Thanks a lot. Joel

FIGURE 8.9

More-Effective Response to an Inquiry

Hello Joel:

Thanks for getting in touch with us here at Smith & Smith. I suggest that we meet in person so we can learn more about your marketing and advertising needs. After we talk for 15 to 30 minutes, I could give you a good idea of what your options are and whether our agency is a good fit for you.

Our website (**Smith & Smith website**) has answers to each of your questions. I've responded briefly below with links to our website for more information:

How do your rates compare to other advertising agencies?

Our rates are extremely competitive with other agencies. More important, we have a great record of return on investment and help you track this figure. We also specialize in building brands, which is particularly important in your case since you are adjusting your business model to include new sports equipment. See the following web page with ten case studies of our clients and the returns they received on their advertising: **Smith & Smith case studies**.

Do you have any specialists in online advertising? What about in social media?

Yes. Our agency has been at the forefront of all forms of online advertising and marketing for the past 15 years. We have been instrumental in helping small companies rapidly grow their revenues and expand. See the following web page about our online advertising with examples of our work: **Smith & Smith online advertising and social media**.

When could we meet and talk about what you might provide us?

At a time and place convenient for you. I would be more than happy to visit your office. I am available during the following times this week:

Tuesday:	2 p.m. - 4 p.m.
Wednesday:	9 a.m. - 11:30 a.m.
Thursday:	9 a.m. - 11:30 a.m., 2 p.m. - 4 p.m.

Please let me know a time that is best for you. You can call directly anytime.

Bryan

Bryan Atkins
Account Executive
Smith & Smith Advertising
803-777-1848

SPECIFIC responses
to all questions.

NAVIGATION is easy with
questions as headings.

FIGURE 8.10

Less-Effective Announcement

smith & smith advertising   INFORMATION is incomplete.

Barbeque

From:	**Bryan Atkins**	Mon, June 24, 2013
To:	Smith & Smith Employees	

Hello everyone! We are having a barbeque cook-off at the park on August 17 at noon. This will be our first annual contest and we welcome you to try to win one of the great prizes with your own batch of barbeque. Please join us for lots of fun! You can RSVP me at batkins@smith+smith.com

Bryan Atkins

TONE lacks enough enthusiasm.

FIGURE 8.11

More-Effective Announcement

smith & smith advertising

Barbeque Cook-off on Saturday, Aug 17 – RSVP Requested

From:	**Bryan Atkins**	Mon, June 24, 2013
To:	Smith & Smith Employees	

Hello Fellow Employees!

INFORMATION is easy to process.

The social committee proudly announces the first annual barbeque cook-off at the park.

Please join us for an afternoon of fun, games, lots of yummy food, and a mystery band appearance.

Any employee can enter the barbeque cook-off contest. Just bring your own batch of barbeque if you are interested. Awards will be given, including 1st place: $500; 2nd place: $250; and 3rd place: $100. An esteemed panel of tasters (the social committee) will be the judges.

Location:	Lundstrom Park
Time:	Saturday, August 17, noon to 3 p.m.
Guests:	Bring up to three guests
What to Bring:	An appetite
Food:	Barbeque and catering from *Downtown Grille*

TONE is exciting and inviting.

Please RSVP with number of guests to Bryan Atkins atbatkins@smith+smith.com by June 26.

FIGURE 8.12

Less-Effective Claim

To...	Jeff Anderton [jeffanderton@theprestigiohotel.com]
Subject:	Please Correct Billing Mistakes on Hotel Stays Immediately

Hello Jeff:

I'm quite frustrated that we made an annual agreement with you at a rate of $124 per night for our employees that you have not honored. Within the past two months, two of our employees have stayed at the Prestigio for a total of 15 nights at a rate of $169. By my calculations, you overcharged us by $675. In addition, there should be a minor adjustment for taxes that we paid on a higher rate.

Please take care of this matter immediately by refunding us the overpaid amount. Thanks a lot.

TONE is accusatory and demanding.

Bryan

FIGURE 8.13

More-Effective Claim

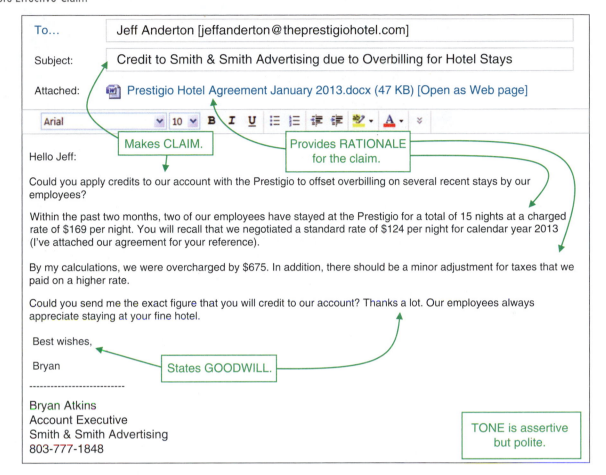

and perhaps unfairly question Jeff's intent. The message focuses first on frustration and second on the merits of the claim. Abrupt phrases such as "please take care of this matter immediately" can easily be misinterpreted as rude. Notice how the more-effective claim (see Figure 8.13) balances directness with politeness. Bryan justifies the claim with an objective description of the overbilling and provides an attachment with the agreement. He politely asks for an adjustment to the account while also complimenting Jeff on the excellent service the hotel provides. Note that in writing claims messages as well as any other kinds of messages, you may be able to save time by using voice recognition software (VRS), as discussed in the Technology Tips box on the next page.

Showing Appreciation

Employees at all levels of an organization desire to feel appreciated. Sadly, polls show that employees express thanks to one another less now than ever since polling on this issue began. Just 10 percent of employees say supervisors thank them daily. More than half (55 percent) of employees say they are thanked never, seldom, or only occasionally.[2]

A sincere expression of thanks also helps achieve business goals and strengthens work relationships. Joseph Ungoco of a popular public relations agency in New York is a staunch believer that thank-you notes help his agency maintain effective working relationships and strongly impact repeat business. He sends handwritten thank-you notes within 48 hours to partners and clients.[3]

LO8.9 Construct routine appreciation messages.

Components of Appreciation Messages

- Give thanks.
- Provide rationale.
- State goodwill.

TECHNOLOGY TIPS

VOICE RECOGNITION SOFTWARE

During the past decade, the accuracy and ease of using voice recognition software (VRS) have increased dramatically. You can use this software to rapidly put your thoughts in text format, allowing you to write routine and complex messages much more efficiently. You can use stand-alone VRS platforms (e.g., Dragon NaturallySpeaking, ViaVoice) or embed the software in your operating system (e.g., Microsoft Windows).

Keep in mind the following tips as you use voice recognition software for written business messages:

Take time to learn the software and increase its accuracy. You generally need some initial training sessions with the software so it recognizes your words accurately. You can train the software to recognize your voice with high accuracy within 15 to 30 minutes. Over time, you can add specialized terminology that you use frequently in your profession.

Use voice recognition software for planning and drafting your document. Most people are unable to write down thoughts as quickly as they can think of them. This is particularly the case during the brainstorming stage when you are grappling with many ideas. By using voice recognition software, you're more likely to get all those thoughts recorded as text.

Use VRS for routine messages. Since most routine messages are fairly straightforward and can be pieced together rapidly, you can often save time by using VRS. Even if you save just a few minutes per routine message, this may add up to several hours over the course of any given week due to the high volume of messages.

Review your messages carefully before sending. VRS is not perfect. It will inevitably make mistakes, so you need to carefully edit for accuracy. You should also check the message to make sure you have the right formality and tone for written communication. Many business professionals find that when using VRS, the act of speaking causes them to use less-formal language and phrases that require nonverbal cues.

Appreciation messages vary significantly in terms of formality. Thank-you notes for customers and clients or for special occasions demand more formality. Thank-you messages for colleagues and others you see each day should be less formal and should not feel over the top. In any case, several components are standard for appreciation messages. They should begin with an expression of *thanks*, provide a quick *rationale* for the thanks, and end with a statement of *goodwill*.

Appreciation messages should be genuine, simple, warm, and personal. To show your sincerity, focus exclusively on the recipient. Appreciation messages should not appear self-serving in any way; state any reference to yourself carefully to avoid drawing attention away from those you are thanking.

In the workplace, showing your appreciation will help build connections. Be careful, however, about excessive or exaggerated displays of gratitude. First, readers may view them as insincere. Second, they may cross boundaries of what is considered professional.

Notice the differences between Bryan's less-effective and more-effective appreciation messages to his team in Figures 8.14 and 8.15. In the less-effective example, the exaggerated and excessive phrases of gratitude (i.e., "a fabulous job," "feel fortunate," "you are all the best!") appear unprofessional or insincere. Also, the message contains far too much focus on Bryan and implies he now deserves thanks for his own actions (securing a new deal, providing lunch). In the more-effective example, Bryan focuses entirely on the group. He shows enthusiasm within professional boundaries.

FIGURE 8.14

Less-Effective Appreciation Message

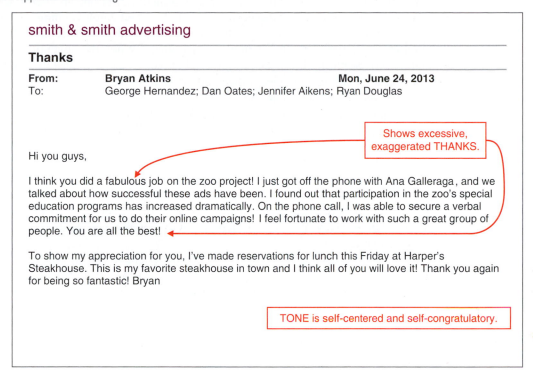

smith & smith advertising

Thanks

| From: | Bryan Atkins | Mon, June 24, 2013 |
| To: | George Hernandez; Dan Oates; Jennifer Aikens; Ryan Douglas | |

Hi you guys,

I think you did a fabulous job on the zoo project! I just got off the phone with Ana Galleraga, and we talked about how successful these ads have been. I found out that participation in the zoo's special education programs has increased dramatically. On the phone call, I was able to secure a verbal commitment for us to do their online campaigns! I feel fortunate to work with such a great group of people. You are all the best!

Shows excessive, exaggerated THANKS.

To show my appreciation for you, I've made reservations for lunch this Friday at Harper's Steakhouse. This is my favorite steakhouse in town and I think all of you will love it! Thank you again for being so fantastic! Bryan

TONE is self-centered and self-congratulatory.

FIGURE 8.15

More-Effective Appreciation Message

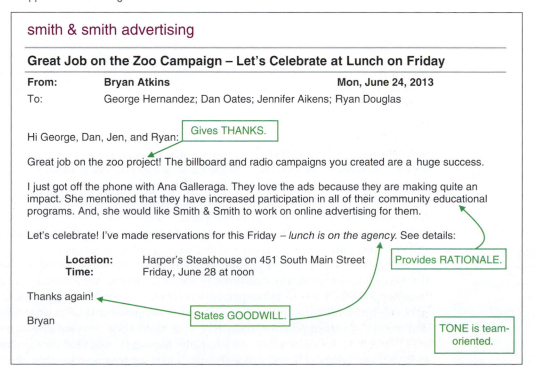

smith & smith advertising

Great Job on the Zoo Campaign – Let's Celebrate at Lunch on Friday

| From: | Bryan Atkins | Mon, June 24, 2013 |
| To: | George Hernandez; Dan Oates; Jennifer Aikens; Ryan Douglas | |

Hi George, Dan, Jen, and Ryan:

Gives THANKS.

Great job on the zoo project! The billboard and radio campaigns you created are a huge success.

I just got off the phone with Ana Galleraga. They love the ads because they are making quite an impact. She mentioned that they have increased participation in all of their community educational programs. And, she would like Smith & Smith to work on online advertising for them.

Let's celebrate! I've made reservations for this Friday – *lunch is on the agency.* See details:

Location:	Harper's Steakhouse on 451 South Main Street	*Provides RATIONALE.*
Time:	Friday, June 28 at noon	

Thanks again!

States GOODWILL.

Bryan

TONE is team-oriented.

Making Apologies

LO8.10　Compose apologies.

Even with the best of intentions, colleagues sometimes let one another down. Differences in communication style, personality clashes, and careless comments are sometimes factors in personal offenses. Business professionals who are high in emotional intelligence notice how their actions impact others. When they intentionally or unintentionally do harm, they seek to improve the workplace relationships right away. In some cases, making apologies is the appropriate response.

However, all apologies are not necessarily good apologies. As stated by management communication specialist Holly Weeks, "Offering the right apology, particularly in the corporate world, is not as simple as saying, 'I'm sorry.' Done right, an apology can enhance both reputations and relationships. Done wrong, an apology can compound the original mistake, sometimes to disastrous consequences."[4]

Effective apologies achieve several important results. First, they help repair working relationships so that you can refocus on solving problems together. Second, they can rebuild your reputation. When you've made offenses or mistakes that harm others, your credibility is weakened. Your reputation for competence, caring, and/or character may be questioned.[5]

Typically, an apology includes the following elements: *acknowledgment* of a mistake or an offense, an expression of *regret* for the harm caused, acceptance of *responsibility*, and a *commitment* that the offense will not be repeated. Effective apologies should be timely and sincere.

Apologies are ineffective when they are vague and cliché. For the apology to be effective, others must sense that the apologizer is sincere, genuine, and acting without an agenda. Effective apologies must focus on others, not you. During an apology, if the recipient decodes any behavior as defensive, it casts doubt on the apologizer's sincerity.[6]

Before apologizing, consider the business implications. If you are dealing with customers and clients, an apology may imply legal responsibility. For serious matters, you might seek the company's legal counsel. Internally, an apology may become a permanent record in a performance review or other files (in rare situations). So, you might consider the potential costs of an apology to your company and your career. Generally, however, apologies for routine mistakes and offenses pose little risk to either your company or your career. They are likely to restore and perhaps even enhance your company's and your personal credibility.

Notice Bryan's apology in Figure 8.16 for unfair statements he made at a meeting. The apology contains the basic elements: acknowledgment, regret, responsibility, and commitment. It is short, simple, sincere, and forward-looking. Colleagues who have known Bryan for years will likely accept the apology quickly and redirect their efforts to working together effectively.

Components of Apologies

- Make acknowledgment.
- Express regret.
- Take responsibility.
- Offer commitment.
- State goodwill.

Expressing Sympathy

LO8.11　Construct expressions of sympathy.

When your colleagues and other close professional contacts encounter personal losses—such as the sickness or even the passing away of loved ones—it is appropriate for you to extend your sincere sympathies. Although you may have maintained strictly professional relations with others, expressing condolences, concern, and support can help them cope with personal grief and pain.

The foremost requirement of any expression of sympathy is that it be sincere. These difficult moments are challenging and awkward. You may feel uncertain about what to say, which words to use. Your genuine concern will compensate for any deficiencies in the words you use. Typically, keep your expressions of sympathy brief. For deaths, state your support and concern to the person who has experienced the loss. Make the note personal by mentioning the deceased person by name and your positive impressions and memories. When possible, handwrite your expression of sympathy on a nice card (see Figure 8.17 for an example of a sympathy message). And read the Communication Q&A for one businessperson's thoughts on delivering routine messages of all kinds.

Components of Sympathy Messages

- Express sympathy.
- Offer support.
- State goodwill.

FIGURE 8.16

An Apology

---

smith & smith advertising

My Comments at Our Executive Management Meeting

| From: | Bryan Atkins | Mon, June 24, 2013 |
| To: | Executive Management Team | |

Dear colleagues,

This last Friday in our executive management meeting, I made several unfair comments.

> ACKNOWLEDGMENT of mistake.

I complained that several of you care more about our clients than you do about our employees. I also said that you ask our employees to work excessive hours on weekends and evenings because you are never willing to say "no" to our clients, even when they make unreasonable demands.

These statements were inaccurate and unfair. I have known each of you for many years, and I am certain that each of you cares deeply about our employees.

> Statement of REGRET.

Over the weekend, I thought about my comments a lot. I am frustrated that we—myself included—give in to unreasonable demands from a few of our clients. I think we end up putting too much stress on our employees as a result. I am sorry that I misdirected my frustration with the demands of our clients at each of you.

> Statement of RESPONSIBILITY.

I do hope that at our next executive management meeting, we can discuss how to negotiate with our clients when we view their demands as unreasonable. For my part, I will avoid any blaming. I would certainly like to hear your experiences, perspectives, and suggestions.

Bryan

> COMMITMENT to avoid such behavior in the future and approach frustrations constructively.

FIGURE 8.17

An Expression of Sympathy

COMMUNICATION Q&A

CONVERSATIONS WITH CURRENT BUSINESS PROFESSIONALS

Pete Cardon: How do most of your customers contact you? What kind of matters do they contact you about?

Aubrey Marshall: All of our major contact with our customers is through an online messaging system similar to email. Most customers are interested in routine things like price, quantity, availability, product consistency, product quality, shipping time, and basic quilting inquiries. Some just want to thank us for the products. Others tell us that the prices are too high, or question our shipping costs and so forth. I have found that customers expect to hear back right away. I make sure that customers get a complete response within one to two hours. My employees are trained to respond with detail-oriented messages. They also treat all people with courtesy, even if the customers have made unjustified requests or comments.

PC: How do you contact your suppliers?

AM: Most of our suppliers are based in Texas. We do 95 percent of our communication through email and the online ordering system. The other 5 percent of the time, we communicate by phone. This is usually if we have to talk about some differences of opinion or some other matter difficult to take care of by email.

PC: Do you expect to use social networking websites in the near future for communicating with customers and suppliers? Why?

AM: No, right now we only use social media for marketing. We have an online newsletter, a Twitter site, and a Facebook presence. We are trying to get ahead of our competition in the social media world. But we see this as marketing. When contacting customers and suppliers, the easiest medium is by email, but occasionally a phone call is required to help with any misunderstandings.

PC: For young professionals, what concluding advice would you give for creating effective daily communications?

AM: Always stay on top of your messages, whether they be through email or from a supplier's messaging system. Set aside time every day to respond. And never take shortcuts. Respond to every message carefully. You never know how much business you might lose if a customer feels that you have not provided a careful, in-depth response to questions and concerns. I also think that you need to train your employees to respond in a way that will drive repeat business. It's not as simple as you might think. You need to take time with your employees to talk about how best to respond to all types of daily messages.

Aubrey Marshall *started an online retail business in 2004 selling fabrics and notions to quilters. About 70 percent of her sales are in the United States. The remaining sales are primarily in Canada and Australia.*

Chapter Takeaway for *Routine Messages*

LO 8.1. Describe how delivering routine messages impacts credibility. (pp. 213–215)
Delivering effective routine messages improves your **reputation for personal credibility.**

It shows **competence** when you know how to manage and resolve routine business tasks.	It shows **caring** when you are responsive to others and show respect for their time.	It shows **character** when you live up to your promises and your company's commitments.

LO 8.2. Describe the process for developing routine business messages. (pp. 215–217)

Components of Routine Messages	
• State primary message (10 words or fewer).	• Restate request or key message in more specific terms.
• Provide details in paragraphs of 20 to 80 words.	• State goodwill.

LO 8.3. Construct routine business requests. (pp. 217–219)

Components of Requests		
• Make request.	• Call to action (for some).	See *examples of business requests* in Figures 8.2 and 8.3.
• Provide rationale.	• State goodwill.	

LO 8.4. Compose routine sets of expectations. (pp. 217–221)

Components of Expectations			
• Explain overall expectation.	• Provide deadlines.	• State goodwill.	See *examples of expectations messages* in Figures 8.4 and 8.5.
• Describe responsibilities.	• Discuss coordination.		

LO 8.5. Construct routine sets of directions. (pp. 220–222)

Components of Directions			
• State goal.	• Give step-by-step directions.	• State goodwill.	See *examples of directions* in Figures 8.6 and 8.7.

LO 8.6. Compose routine responses to inquiries. (pp. 223–225)

Components of Inquiry Responses		
• Provide responses.	• State goodwill.	See *examples of responses to inquiries* in Figures 8.8 and 8.9.

LO 8.7. Construct routine announcements. (pp. 223, 226)

Components of Announcements			
• Gain attention.	• Provide details.	• State goodwill.	See *examples of announcements* in Figures 8.10 and 8.11.
• Give announcement.	• Call to action (for some).		

LO 8.8. Compose routine claims. (pp. 223, 226–227)

Components of Claims		
• Make claim.	• Call to action.	See *examples of claims* in Figures 8.12 and 8.13.
• Provide rationale.	• State goodwill.	

LO 8.9. Construct routine appreciation messages. (pp. 227–229)

Components of Appreciation Messages			
• Give thanks.	• Provide rationale.	• State goodwill.	See *examples of appreciation messages* in Figures 8.14 and 8.15.

LO 8.10. Compose apologies. (pp. 230–231)

Components of Apologies			
• Make acknowledgment.	• Take responsibility.	• State goodwill.	See *an example of an apology* in Figure 8.16.
• Express regret.	• Offer commitment.		

LO 8.11. Construct routine expressions of sympathy. (pp. 230–231)

Components of Sympathy Messages			
• Express sympathy.	• Offer support.	• State goodwill.	See *an example of a sympathy message* in Figure 8.17.

Discussion Exercises

8.1 Chapter Review Questions (LO 8.1, LO 8.2)

A. Describe the AIM planning process for routine messages.

B. Explain the importance of reviewing for routine messages. What considerations should you make? What are your primary goals?

C. Identify the preferable message structures for various types of routine messages.

8.2 Communication Q&A Discussion Questions (LO 8.1, LO 8.2)

A. How does Aubrey Marshall approach routine communications?

B. What benefits and drawbacks does she see in electronic communication?

C. What piece of information or advice do you think is most useful?

Evaluation Exercises

8.3 Evaluating Routine Requests (LO 8.3)

A. Compare Bryan's less-effective and more-effective requests for a new server in Figures 8.2 and 8.3. Identify three ways in which Bryan improved the message.

B. How do you think the more-effective message will impact work outcomes?

C. How do you think the more-effective message will impact workplace relationships?

D. What two changes could you make to improve the more-effective example?

8.4 Evaluating Routine Expectations Messages (LO 8.4)

A. Compare Bryan's less-effective and more-effective messages regarding his expectations for Barry and John in their new assignment (see Figures 8.4 and 8.5). Identify three ways in which Bryan improved the message.

B. How do you think the more-effective message will impact work outcomes?

C. How do you think the more-effective message will impact workplace relationships?

D. What two changes could you make to improve the more-effective example?

8.5 Evaluating Routine Directions Messages (LO 8.5)

A. Compare Bryan's less-effective and more-effective messages giving directions for how to arrange company travel (see Figures 8.6 and 8.7). Identify the ways in which he improved the message.

B. How do you think the more-effective message will impact work outcomes?

C. How do you think the more-effective message will impact workplace relationships?

D. What two changes could you make to improve the more-effective example?

8.6 Evaluating Routine Inquiries (LO 8.6)

A. Compare Bryan's less-effective and more-effective responses to an inquiry from a client (see Figures 8.8 and 8.9). Identify three ways that he improved the message.

B. How do you think the more-effective message will impact work outcomes?

C. How do you think the more-effective message will impact workplace relationships?

D. What two changes could you make to improve the more-effective example?

8.7 Evaluating Routine Announcements (LO 8.7)

A. Compare Bryan's less-effective and more-effective announcements about the company social (see Figures 8.10 and 8.11). Identify three ways that he improved the message.

B. How do you think the more-effective message will impact work outcomes?

C. How do you think the more-effective message will impact workplace relationships?

D. What two changes could you make to improve the more-effective example?

8.8 Evaluating Routine Claims (LO 8.8)

A. Compare Bryan's less-effective and more-effective claims to the Prestigio Hotel about its rate (see Figures 8.12 and 8.13). Identify three ways that he improved the message.

B. How do you think the more-effective message will impact work outcomes?

C. How do you think the more-effective message will impact workplace relationships?

D. What two changes could you make to improve the more-effective example?

8.9 Evaluating Routine Appreciation Messages (LO 8.9)

A. Compare Bryan's less-effective and more-effective messages of appreciation to his staff (see Figures 8.14 and 8.15). Identify three ways that he improved the message.

B. How do you think the more-effective message will impact work outcomes?

C. How do you think the more-effective message will impact workplace relationships?

D. What two changes could you make to improve the more-effective example?

8.10 Evaluating Routine Apologies (LO 8.10)

A. Examine Bryan's apology in Figure 8.16. How do you think this apology will impact work outcomes?

B. How do you think this apology will impact workplace relationships?

C. What two changes could you make to improve the apology?

8.11 Evaluating Sympathy Messages (LO 8.11)

A. Examine Bryan's sympathy message in Figure 8.17. How do you think this sympathy message will impact work outcomes?

B. How do you think this sympathy message will impact workplace relationships?

C. What two changes could you make to improve the sympathy message?

8.12 Evaluating Your Approach to Writing (LO 8.1, LO 8.2)

Evaluate yourself with regard to each of the writing practices listed in the table below. Circle the appropriate number for each.

	1 – Rarely/Never	2 – Sometimes	3 – Usually	4 – Always
Before I write routine messages, I make sure I've gathered all of the relevant information.	1	2	3	4
Before I write routine messages, I spend a significant amount of time analyzing and piecing together the information.	1	2	3	4
Before I write routine messages, I learn as much as I reasonably can about the needs of the message receiver/s.	1	2	3	4
As I write routine messages, I think about how the message receiver/s will feel while reading the message.	1	2	3	4
As I write routine messages, I think about how the message receiver/s will respond.	1	2	3	4
As I write routine messages, I think about how quickly and easily the message receiver/s will be able to read the message.	1	2	3	4
Before sending a routine message, I place myself in the position of the message receiver/s and reread the message imagining how the message will be interpreted.	1	2	3	4
Before sending a routine message, I carefully double-check the entire message to make sure it is appropriate and accurate.	1	2	3	4
Before sending a routine message, I frequently ask people I trust to read the message or ask them how they would handle the communication.	1	2	3	4
Before sending a routine message, I use a spell-checker.	1	2	3	4

Add up your score and consider the following advice:

35–40: You are a *strategic, other-oriented* writer. You think about how to send a well-thought-out message that meets the needs of others. Continue with such awareness of the impact of your written messages.

30–34: You are a *careful, considerate* writer. You spend time thinking about the content of your message

and the needs of your message receiver/s. Consider taking more time in the planning process to think your message through even more carefully, and pay close attention to the needs and potential responses to your written messages by message receivers.

25–29: You are an *inconsistent but self-aware* writer. Sometimes you are careful about developing your message and considerate of the needs and reactions of others. Other times you are not. Always engage in excellent analysis when you craft your message and think carefully about your message receiver/s.

Under 25:   You *need to improve* your approach to writing. You likely send most messages without spending enough time to think through the problems and impacts on others. Often this approach is harmless.

Sometimes, however, you will not be influential in the way you want. Change your orientation to writing to spend most of your time preparing and reviewing.

After going through the self-assessment exercises, identify three specific goals you have for improving your approach to writing. Write four or five sentences about each goal.

Application Exercises

8.13 Request for a Letter of Recommendation (LO 8.1, LO 8.2, LO 8.3)

Find a specific job, internship, or graduate study listing that you would be interested in pursuing. Make sure it requires a letter of recommendation. Your task is to request a letter of recommendation from one of your instructors. Assume that you will write an email making the request.

 Answer the questions listed below to help you plan your request. Then write the request.

A. Why would your instructor want to write a letter of recommendation for you? What would increase your instructor's willingness and delight in writing a letter for you?

B. What tone will you try to project in your email?

C. What information about you would your instructor need to write an effective letter of recommendation?

D. How can you make it easier for your instructor to write a letter of recommendation?

E. How can you show courtesy to your instructor since she/he is using her/his own time to do a favor for you?

F. How will you order your message? What will be the subject line?

G. Write the email request for a letter of recommendation.

8.14 Writing a Memo with Group Goals and Expectations (LO 8.4)

Think about a group project you've worked on in school or at work. Ideally, you will choose a currently active group project. Assume the role of group leader (you can make up facts as necessary). Write a document that includes the following:

- Group member names.
- Group goals and ultimate outcomes.
- Group member roles.
- Timeline for completing various activities and coordinating with one another.

8.15 Writing Procedures for Getting into Graduate School (LO 8.5)

Go to the website of a graduate school you are interested in or to the graduate school website for your current university. Rewrite the directions for applying to a graduate program of interest to you. Make them clearer and simpler to read.

8.16 Responding to Inquiries (LO 8.6)

Assume you are an advisor for students in your program or major. A prospective student sends you the following message: "Hi, I'm interested in your major. Can you give me some information about it? What is the placement rate of your students in the workplace upon graduation? How much money do they usually get? What are the professors like? Do I have to have a minimum GPA to get in the program? Any information would be helpful. Thanks, Jack." Respond to this message with sufficient detail. Remember your goal is to make a favorable impression on this prospective student.

8.17 Making Announcements (LO 8.7)

Place yourself in the position of an advisor in your program. The upcoming semester will begin soon. Send an announcement to all current students with items they should be aware of for the upcoming semester. Include deadlines and make sure students will pay attention to the announcement.

8.18 Making Claims (LO 8.8)

Think about a product or service you have purchased in the past that did not work properly. Write a claim to the company about it. Explain why your claim is justified and suggest action. Focus on achieving an assertive but friendly tone.

8.19 Expressing Appreciation (LO 8.9)

Assume that you just received and accepted an offer for a job you've wanted. You believe one of your references may have been instrumental in helping you get the job. Write a note of appreciation.

8.20 Making Apologies (LO 8.10)

Assume you lost your temper when discussing a group project with one of your classmates. You left the meeting early because you were frustrated that your classmate insisted on doing everything his way. You still feel that he is dominating the project, but your behavior was inappropriate. Write an apology to your classmate in a way that repairs some of the damage between the two of you and allows the group to work more effectively together.

8.21 Expressing Sympathy (LO 8.11)

Assume your boss's mother has just passed away. Write a note that you could include in a card.

Endnotes

1. Dennis S. Reina and Michelle L. Reina, *Trust and Betrayal in the Workplace* (San Francisco: Berrett-Koehler Publishers, 2006): 19–20.

2. Joanna L. Krotz, "The Power of Saying Thank You," Microsoft Business, retrieved July 7, 2010, from www.microsoft.com/business/en-us/resources/marketing/customer-service-acquisition/the-power-of-saying-thank-you.aspx#Thepowerofsayingthankyou.

3. Ibid.

4. Holly Weeks, "The Art of the Apology," *Harvard Management Update* (May 19, 2003).

5. Barbara Kellerman, "When Should a Leader Apologize—and When Not?" *Harvard Business Review* (April 2006): 72–81; Weeks, "The Art of the Apology."

6. Ibid.

CHAPTER NINE

Persuasive Messages

Learning Objectives

After studying this chapter, you should be able to do the following:

LO9.1   Describe the relationship between credibility and persuasion.

LO9.2   Explain the AIM planning process for persuasive messages and the basic components of most persuasive messages.

LO9.3   Explain how the tone and style of persuasive messages impact their influence.

LO9.4   Create compelling internal persuasive messages.

LO9.5   Compose influential external persuasive messages.

LO9.6   Construct effective mass sales messages.

LO9.7   Evaluate persuasive messages for effectiveness and fairness.

In many business situations, you hope to persuade others. In internal business communications, you may want your boss, peers, or colleagues to consider or adopt your ideas when their perspectives differ from yours. In external business communications, you will want to persuade your clients, customers, and prospects to use your products and services. Persuasion involves influencing others to see the merits of your ideas and act on your requests, even when they initially resist. In this chapter, we explore strategies for persuading others through writing.

In some ways, all business messages contain an element of persuasion—that is, you are hoping to influence the way others think, feel, or behave. Many of the concepts in this chapter will enhance your ability to make any kind of request. However, the approaches in this chapter are most applicable to situations in which your audience will initially resist your requests.

Throughout this chapter, you will see examples of persuasive messages at Better Horizons Credit Union. The chapter case provides the background.

Chapter Case: Shifting Course at Better Horizons Credit Union

Who's Involved

Haniz Zogby, marketing specialist and loan officer
- Started working at Better Horizons nearly five years ago. She has worked 20 to 30 hours per week while attending college with a major in finance and a minor in event management.
- Started as a teller. Within a few years, she was promoted to positions of teller supervisor, loan officer, and marketing specialist.
- Currently working on marketing initiatives under the direction of Christine Russo.

Christine Russo, president and CEO
- Has worked at Better Horizons for approximately ten years.
- Currently interested in increasing the number of young members. With declining numbers of young members, she is concerned that the credit union does not have good long-term prospects.

Situation 1　Christine Wants to Build Support for New Banking Services That Meet the Needs of Younger Members

Christine recognized that people under the age of 30 were not joining the credit union. Christine wanted to write a message to board members about adopting marketing strategies and services that appeal to younger members. She planned to follow up by presenting her ideas in person at an upcoming meeting. The board is composed of longtime members who favor what they consider a "personal," "friendly," and "homey" credit union environment. They view moves to online marketing and services as breaking their brand of community and personal touch. The majority also oppose adding too many extra financial services, perceiving these services as "slick" and "too similar to banks."

Situation 2　Haniz Is in Charge of Recruiting Participants for a Local Charity Event

Christine asked Haniz to be in charge of recruiting credit union members to join this year's Hope Walkathon to support research on breast cancer. Better Horizons has assembled a walkathon team for this prominent community event each year for nearly a decade. Haniz is writing an email to send to all credit union members. The message will be modified slightly to appear as an announcement on the credit union website as well.

Situation 3   Haniz Needs to Create a Flyer Explaining the Benefits of Credit Union Membership Compared to Banks

Haniz is working on a flyer describing the benefits of membership at Better Horizons Credit Union. The flyer will be part of a packet of materials that is distributed to community members who participate in free financial planning and income tax assistance seminars offered by Better Horizons. Haniz is using the message to highlight the benefits of Better Horizons compared to local banks.

Situation 4   Haniz Is Helping to Develop a Sales Message for Auto Loans

Haniz and several other employees are working on sales messages for auto loans. In recent months, Better Horizon's senior management decided the credit union should become a "player" in the auto loans market. Few Better Horizons members take advantage of car loans, most assuming that dealer financing is cheaper and easier to get.

Task 1
How will Christine and Haniz write a message to board members that warms them up to ideas about new online services and marketing geared toward gaining younger members? (See the section on internal persuasive messages.)

Task 2
How will Haniz persuade credit union members to join the Hope Walkathon? (See the section on external persuasive messages.)

Task 3
How will Haniz develop a general-purpose flyer that shows the broad benefits of choosing Better Horizons Credit Union over banks? (See the "Constructing External Persuasive Messages" section.)

Task 4
How will Haniz develop sales messages for an auto loan campaign? (See the "Composing Mass Sales Messages" section.)

The Importance of Credibility in an Era of Mistrust and Skepticism

LO9.1 Describe the relationship between credibility and persuasion.

While credibility is critical to all business communications, its importance is heightened for persuasive messages. By definition, persuasion implies that you are communicating with someone who does not think or feel the same way as you do. So, your goal is to help your audience members identify with and find merit in your positions. If they question your credibility, they are unlikely to carefully consider your ideas, requests, or recommendations.

Persuasion is becoming more difficult as we live in a time of increasing mistrust. In Chapter 1, we discussed the declining levels of trust for nearly all professional groups, particularly business-related occupations. Michael Maslansky, one of the leading corporate communications experts, has labeled this the post-trust era (PTE):

> Just a few years ago, salespeople, corporate leaders, marketing departments, and communicators like me had it pretty easy. We looked at communication as a relatively

linear process. . . . But trust disappeared, things changed. . . . In a word, trust is out, skepticism is in.[1]

Over the past decade, Michael Maslansky and his colleagues have examined how language is used to persuade and motivate others. By interviewing hundreds of thousands of employees and customers in some 30 countries, they have found that the language of trust is more important than ever. Furthermore, they have noticed emerging trends in how language impacts trust. Strategies for persuasion that once worked are less effective in the PTE. Other strategies continue to work well. In this chapter, we sort through some of these basic principles of persuasive writing and identify those strategies that are most effective in the PTE.

Applying the AIM Planning Process to Persuasive Messages

LO9.2 Explain the AIM planning process for persuasive messages and the basic components of most persuasive messages.

Persuasion involves extensive planning: analyzing your *audience* to understand their needs, values, and how they are influenced; developing your *ideas* as you wrestle with the complicated business issues at hand; and creating a *message* structure that most effectively reduces resistance and gains buy-in. Many effective business communicators spend weeks and months learning about their target audiences, gathering information, and piecing together persuasive messages.

Understand Your Audience

To convince others to modify their own ideas and accept yours, you need to show that you care about them and that your ideas fit into their interests. This is the approach communication specialist Liz Simpson recommends:

> To succeed at the persuasion game, you have to be absolutely committed to understanding the other side's position as well as your own. Without that willingness to try on the other side's arguments, you simply cannot be persuasive. From that understanding will come the insights you need to move the other side over to your camp.[2]

This is true not only for ideas but also for products and services. Your best argument is always one that meets the needs and wants of your audience.

Understanding the needs and values of others is *not* simple. It requires a strong listening orientation. You will need to ask lots of questions to get beyond a surface understanding about the hopes, expectations, and hidden assumptions of your target audience. Once you know your target audience's needs and values, you are in a strong position to explain how your product, service, or idea benefits them.

In addition to understanding the needs and values of your target audience, you should consider the psychological principles that impact how people are influenced. Also, you should consider whether you are making a logical appeal or an emotional one in your persuasive messages.

Understand Methods of Influence
Dr. Robert Cialdini, a marketing psychologist, has spent his career studying how people are influenced in business and marketing environments. He has examined research in this area for four decades, plus he spent three years taking undercover jobs in car dealerships, telemarketing firms, fund-raising organizations, and other buyer-seller environments to learn the most influential ways of getting people to say yes. Based on his work, he has identified six principles of persuasion (aside from the price and quality of products and services). These principles include reciprocation, consistency, social proof, liking, authority, and scarcity.[3] Haniz's message to recruit credit union members for the Hope Walkathon offers an interesting example for applying these various principles (see Figure 9.7, p. 258, for her completed message).

Reciprocation is a principle of influence based on returning favors. As defined by Cialdini, "We should try to repay, in kind, what another person has provided us."[4] Cialdini cited an interesting study in which a professor sent Christmas cards to a random sample of strangers to see what would happen. Many of the card recipients reciprocated, sending cards to the professor without attempting to find out who he was. The study showed that even card receivers who did not know the card sender and who might not interact with the card sender in the future felt compelled to return the favor of sending a card. People tend to feel obligated to pay back others when they've received something of value.[5]

Haniz uses the principle of reciprocation in her message in several ways. For example, she focuses on a lengthy reciprocal relationship that the credit union has with the local breast cancer center, and the walkathon serves as the mechanism that draws the two organizations together. The credit union helps the center by generating walkathon donations, and the center helps the credit union and the larger community through more effective breast cancer treatment and education. Furthermore, the message implies a reciprocal relationship between the credit union and its members by offering various free items, such as a T-shirt, a water bottle, and a cancer guide, to members who are willing to participate in the walkathon.

Consistency is based on the idea that once people make an explicit commitment, they tend to follow through or honor that commitment. In other words, they want to stay consistent with their original commitment. Cialdini cited several studies to make this point. In one, psychologists found that horse racing fans become more confident that their horses would win after placing a bet. Once they made a final commitment, they were further convinced of the correctness of their choice.[6]

Haniz appeals to commitment and consistency in several ways. Foremost, she appeals to the credit union's long commitment to the fight against breast cancer. Some credit union members will want to continue to honor this long-standing collective commitment and will appreciate that their credit union is doing so. She also provides links in the message for people to immediately act on their interest in the walkathon. A link to register right now serves as an immediate commitment to participate.

Social proof is a principle of influence whereby people determine what is right, correct, or desirable by seeing what others do. Haniz employs several appeals to social proof in her letter. She describes the level of participation and contribution among members in last year's walkathon, implying that the popularity and financial impact of this event make it a good cause. Also, the walkathon itself is a type of social proof; the gathering of thousands of people wearing team T-shirts and marching in unison for a cause is powerful imagery.[7]

Liking is a principle of influence whereby people are more likely to be persuaded by people who they like.[8] Haniz appeals directly to this principle by describing Betty Williams, who is a breast cancer survivor, the benefactor of the breast center, a credit union member, and a participant in the walkathon. Betty Williams is presumably a person most people in the community know and like, a woman who many of the credit union members may know from running into her at the credit union or other community events, and a woman who is passionate about an important cause (a reason for liking). Haniz emphasizes in the message that walkathon participants will join this likable and respected community member at the walkathon.

Authority is a principle of influence whereby people follow authority figures. The number of celebrity endorsements in advertising is evidence of how authority can impact persuasion.[9] Although Haniz does not appeal to a national celebrity, she does appeal to a prominent local community member—again Betty Williams. With Betty's level of influence and personal experience combating cancer, she is likely seen as an authority. Furthermore, Haniz also appeals to members to support the Betty Williams Breast Center, a group of expert professionals who collectively are authorities on breast cancer.

Scarcity is a principle of influence whereby people think there is limited availability of something they want or need, so they must act quickly.[10] Haniz employs this principle in terms of time. She explains that the walkathon occurs only once each year (limited time period to participate) and that participants must sign up by a given deadline (limited time period to sign up).

You will apply these principles most often in external persuasive messages, and you should always apply them fairly. Cialdini describes them as "weapons of influence."[11] The very term *weapons* implies that they are powerful and can do harm. In the "Apply the FAIR Test" section near the end of the chapter, we further discuss the appropriate use of these principles.

Persuade through Emotion and Reason   Most people justify their business decisions based on the soundness of ideas, not feelings. Savvy business communicators, however, understand the importance of injecting emotion into their persuasive messages. While they appreciate the place of reason in business and consumer decisions, they understand that resistance to ideas, products, and services is often emotional. Conversely, they are aware that their target audiences often possess strong emotional attachment to competing ideas, products, and services. Thus, effective communicators find ways to appeal to the core emotional benefits of products, services, and ideas.[12]

Even in internal persuasive messages, emotional appeals are critical, as indicated by Craig Conway, president and CEO of PeopleSoft:

> Good communicators have an enormous advantage over poor communicators because so much of running a company is inspirational. . . . You just have to be able to persuade people that they are a part of something bigger. If you have a creative vision and you can communicate it in a compelling way to get people excited, you will recruit better people as a result. Then, it is easy to convince the world that you have a more dynamic company.[13]

Part of understanding your audience is identifying the needs and values that resonate emotionally for them.

Typically, internal persuasive messages focus mostly on logical appeals. External persuasive messages, with the exception of those that emphasize price, generally include strong emotional appeals. As you develop persuasive messages, think about how to get the right mix of logical and emotional appeals. Generally, you will supply both but emphasize one or the other. Keep in mind that even when you choose to make strong emotional appeals in written messages, you should generally avoid the tone of mass advertising, where exaggeration, sarcasm, and over-the-top appeals are acceptable and even effective. Later in the chapter, you will notice several messages created by Haniz and Christine—two based more strongly on logical appeals (Figures 9.5 and 9.8) and two on emotional appeals (Figures 9.7 and 9.9).

Develop Your Ideas

Idea development for persuasive messages is critical. Since your audience is resistant to the message, one of your key tasks is to establish credibility. Developing strong ideas in the interest of your audience helps you demonstrate your voice of competence. It involves gaining a deep understanding of the benefits and drawbacks of your ideas, products, and services. In addition, it involves gaining a thorough understanding of competing ideas, products, and services.

Thus, before attempting to persuade others, expert business communicators seek to understand products, services, and ideas in great depth so that they can speak from an authoritative and *competent* perspective. To address the issue of attracting younger credit union members, Christine and Haniz spend months learning about the strategies that other credit unions use. When Haniz works on a message that promotes her credit union over local banks, she carefully analyzes and compares the major products and services offered by her credit union and those of competing banks. When Haniz works on a message to persuade credit union members to join the Hope Walkathon, she learns all she can about participation in this event and how it helps in the fight against breast cancer.

Components of Persuasive Messages

- Gain attention.
- Raise a need.
- Deliver a solution.
- Provide a rationale.
- Show appreciation.
- Give counterpoints (optional).
- Call to action.

Set Up the Message Structure

Most business writing is **direct** and **explicit.** It is direct in that you begin with a main idea or argument and then provide the supporting reasons. It is explicit in that nothing is implied; statements contain full and unambiguous meaning. When you write directly and explicitly, you help your readers understand your message and you show respect for their time.

Compared to other business messages, persuasive messages are somewhat more **indirect** and **implicit.** They are sometimes indirect in that they provide the rationale for a request before making the specific request. They are sometimes implicit in that the request or some of the rationale for the request may be implied. In other words, sometimes the reader needs to read between the lines to grasp the entire meaning. Implicit statements politely ask people to do or think differently. Also, explicitly stating some types of benefits is considered poor form—for example, matters of financial or career gain in internal persuasive requests.[14]

Attention   The first task of most persuasive messages is to gain the attention of your readers. You can do this in a variety of ways, including asking a rhetorical question, providing a compelling or interesting fact, revealing a compelling statistic, issuing a challenge, or posting a testimonial.[15] For internal persuasive messages, the primary means of gaining attention is demonstrating a business need—a gap between what is and what could be.[16] You generally have more flexibility in external persuasive messages as you choose your attention-getters. See Table 9.1 for examples of attention-getters Haniz might use for some of her communication tasks.

Need, Solution, and Rationale   In the body of your message, your first task is to tie your product, service, or idea to the *needs* of your readers. The best way to reduce the resistance your reader may have is to show that your message meets your readers' needs. Once you've stated the need, you may describe your *solution,* which is a recommended product, service, or idea. Many readers will remain skeptical unless you provide convincing support. So, you will need to provide a strong *rationale,* meaning solid reasons why your product, service, or idea really benefits them. After all, you are more than likely attempting to influence skeptics.[17]

As you structure your message, consider how *direct* you should be. If your audience members are strongly and emotionally resistant to your solution, consider a more indirect approach so they warm up to your ideas before you suggest a solution. To make your message less direct, provide the rationale before the solution.

TABLE 9.1

Effective Attention-Getters

Type of Attention-Getter	Example
Rhetorical question	Did you know that average credit union members save $400 per year compared to bank customers?
Intriguing statistic	In the past five years, we've lost over 200 members—over 10 percent of our membership.
Compelling and unusual fact/s	You've probably heard car dealers boast about their near-zero percent interest rates—but there's a catch! By financing with car dealers, you give up your opportunity to receive manufacturer rebates and your power to negotiate on price.
Challenge	Please join our team in this year's Hope Walkathon in the fight against breast cancer.
Testimonial	"I never knew I could have so much negotiating power with a preapproved loan. By getting my car loan through Better Horizons, I negotiated a great deal with the car dealer. This is the way to buy cars!"

Appreciation   At some point in the body of the message, you should validate your readers by showing appreciation for their views and preferences. **Validation** implies that you recognize and appreciate others' needs, wants, ideas, and preferences as legitimate and reasonable. By validating your readers, you show respect for them and demonstrate a balanced perspective.[18]

Counterpoints   Traditionally, communicators overcame objections by providing counterpoints to any of the audience members' objections. In other words, they showed how their own ideas, products, or services were superior to the competing ideas, products, or services the audience favored.

Overcoming objections with counterpoints, however, is risky in the post-trust era. This approach may unnecessarily carry a *me-versus-you* tone and delegitimize the readers' concerns. Michael Maslansky, in his research about emerging trends in sales messages in the PTE, states that validation is "using words to let people know that their concerns are valid," and that it is the "polar opposite of overcoming objections."[19] He says the "new sales mantra [is to] agree with objections."[20] This perhaps ironic approach shows respect and balance because you validate the potential customer's feelings and ideas. When you validate your readers, they are more likely to accept the merits of your persuasive message.

Thus, consider carefully whether to include counterpoints to your readers' objections. When you know people well and believe that you will not create a *me-versus-you* adversarial stance, tactfully state how your ideas, products, and services outperform those of your readers.

Skilled business communicators understand that building support for their ideas takes time. Especially for persuasion within companies, you will generally use a mix of communication channels. Rarely will your ideas be accepted and enacted with one written message. However, one written message can make a powerful statement and open avenues of communication that lead to acceptance and adoption of your ideas.

Action   You conclude persuasive messages with a call to action, which asks your readers to take a specific step toward the purchase of a product or service or acceptance of an idea. However, a call to action should not be a hard sell; pressuring others is increasingly ineffective in the PTE.[21] In external persuasive messages, the call to action is typically a specific and explicit step. In internal persuasive messages, the call to action is sometimes explicit and sometimes implicit. It is more likely to be implicit for controversial change ideas and when corresponding with superiors who have ultimate decision-making authority.

> **Guidelines for Tone for Persuasive Messages**
>
> - Apply the personal touch.
> - Use action-oriented, lively language.
> - Write with confidence.
> - Offer choice.
> - Show positivity.

Getting the Tone and Style Right for Persuasive Messages

LO9.3 Explain how the tone and style of persuasive messages impact their influence.

The tone for persuasive messages should be confident and positive, yet at the same time avoid exaggeration or hype. This is tricky! You will no doubt need to make some trade-offs. The more confident and positive you make your message, the more you risk being perceived as pushy or exaggerated. As you reduce confidence and positivity, you risk your product, service, or idea being perceived as weak or unexciting. One benefit of asking colleagues to read your persuasive message before you send it is they can help you decide if you have achieved the right level of confidence and positivity without sacrificing believability.

The writing style of your message should be action-oriented and lively. But again, you risk being perceived as unbelievable or overly enthusiastic if you overdo the language. However, you risk being perceived as dull or unexceptional if you don't use engaging, lively language. Proofreading by yourself and with the help of colleagues will help you get the right writing style to set your message apart.

Apply the Personal Touch

Recently, a number of competing developers delivered presentations to a property owner, each hoping to persuade him to sell them 4,000 acres of much-sought-after property. The presentations were nearly identical, so the property owner was unsure how to choose the best developer. A few days later, the property owner received a handwritten thank-you note from one candidate. The property owner immediately awarded the deal to that developer because he had taken the time to write a message of appreciation.[22]

Often, your competitors are nearly identical to you. Your colleagues and customers will be more easily persuaded when you show interest in them personally, speak to them in personal terms, understand their specific needs, and demonstrate that you are seeking benefits for them. Personalizing your messages is not easy, though, as Michael Maslansky points out:

> For all of us, selling ideas or products or ourselves begins with a need to talk about something that we have and the audience should need, want, or agree with. The problem is that too often, we focus on the first part—what we want to sell, and too little on the second—why they want to buy . . . and yet, our audience demands increasingly that messages, products, and services speak directly to them.[23]

Creating messages that *speak directly* to customers and colleagues requires that you use language that helps your customers and colleagues feel the product, service, or idea is just for them.[24]

One of the primary strategies you can use to personalize persuasive messages is your selection of voice—either you-voice, we-voice, I-voice, or impersonal voice (as introduced in Chapter 2). Table 9.2 offers guidance on choosing the appropriate voice. Generally, you-voice is more effective in external persuasive messages to customers and clients because it emphasizes the benefits they receive from your products and services. From the customer's perspective, the you-voice shows them that they are the center of attention.

Writing in the you-voice to customers is more than just a stylistic choice. It forces you to consciously consider the readers' needs and wants. It forces you to personalize the message for them. By contrast, the we-voice in external messages can focus too much attention on your company and de-emphasize benefits to the customer. Notice the difference in overall tone in the two messages in Figures 9.4 and 9.5 (pp. 255–256). In the less-effective example, the you-voice is hardly used at all compared to the dominating we-voice. In the more-effective example, the you-voice takes center stage over the we-voice. The extensive use of you-voice in the more-effective message sends a strong meta message: *This message is about you.*

Another method of personalizing a message is to make your statements tangible. By definition, *tangible* means something can be touched; it is material or substantial. In a business communications context, making the statement **tangible** implies that the readers can discern something in terms that are meaningful to them. This allows the reader to sense the impact on a personal level.[25] You often can achieve a tangible feel by combining you-voice with specificity. Consider the examples in Table 9.3, from messages that Haniz is working on for the credit union.

As you reread your message, keep in mind the following advice from sales specialist Ralph Allora: "Read the letter aloud. If it doesn't sound like you're having a conversation with the client over the phone, then you're not using the right tone."[26] This in part is a test of whether you have personalized your message enough.

Use Action-Oriented and Lively Language

In persuasive messages, you have somewhat more license to write creatively. Focus on using action-oriented and lively words to achieve a sense of excitement, optimism, or

TABLE 9.2

Voice in Persuasive Messages

Voice	Appropriate Cases	Cautions	Examples
You-voice	Use in external persuasive messages to emphasize reader benefits.	Presumptuousness—assuming you know what is good for someone else	When you take out an auto loan, you get a variety of resources to help you in your car shopping, including a free copy of a Kelly Blue Book, access to free Carfax reports, Mechanical Breakdown Insurance (MBI), and Guaranteed Auto Protection (GAP).
			In this example, you-voice helps show direct benefits to the customers. Overuse across an entire message, however, may come across as presumptuous, overbearing, or exaggerated.
We-voice	Use in internal persuasive messages to emphasize shared work goals.	Presumptuousness—assuming you share common beliefs, ideas, or understanding with your colleagues	At Better Horizons, we've instilled a personal touch into every aspect of our business. We've reinforced this culture with face-to-face services. Our tellers welcome members by name. When members come into the credit union, they know we care about them as people, not just as customers. The warm, friendly, genuine, and personal approach we take to serving our members is why I'm so proud to work here.
			In this passage, we-voice instills a sense of shared values, priorities, and goals. We-voice can instill a strong sense of teamwork. When audience members have different perspectives, however, they may resent that you are stating agreement where it does not exist.
I-voice	Use in all persuasive messages sparingly.	Overuse implies self-centeredness	After examining the results of other credit unions, I am convinced that these tools can build emotional connections and loyalty with our members.
			In this example, I-voice is used to show a personal opinion and shows respect for audience members who are not yet fully persuaded. Frequent use of I-voice across an entire message, however, may come across as emphasizing your interests rather than those of the audience.
Impersonal voice	Use in persuasive messages to emphasize objectivity and neutrality.	Overuse may depersonalize the message	The basic difference between credit unions and banks is that credit union members own and control their credit unions whereas bank account holders have no stake or control in their financial institutions.
			In this example, impersonal voice helps show objectivity. An entire persuasive message in impersonal voice, however, may fail to connect on a personal level with the audience.

other positive emotions. Use strong nouns and verbs to add to the excitement of the message. Some sales messages sound dull because of overuse of and reliance on words such as *provide* and *offer*.[27] Across the entire message or thought, the action-oriented and lively language should emphasize a central theme. See Table 9.4 for examples from documents Haniz is working on for two of her projects.

TABLE 9.3

Making Tangible Statements

Less Effective	More Effective
Credit unions save members about $8 billion a year thanks to better interest rates and reduced fees.	On average, credit union members save $400 each year compared to bank customers thanks to lower loan rates and fees.
The benefit is not tangible. Customers are not sure what the benefit would be for them personally.	This benefit is tangible; the customers know how much they will save on an individual level.
In recent years, many credit unions have lost membership because younger individuals are not attracted to them.	In the past five years, we've lost over 200 members—over 10 percent of our membership. And we simply aren't attracting younger members.
This statement focuses on a general trend for credit unions but does not indicate an impact on a particular credit union.	This statement invokes a sense of what is happening right here at our credit union. Identifying the amount (as well as a percentage) helps the reader discern the impact.
We provide lower rates on car loans. Our car loan rates are between 1.5 and 1.75 percentage points less than at any of the banks in town.	**You pay lower rates on car loans.** You can get car loan rates at Better Horizons that are 1.5–1.75 percentage points less than at any other bank in town. Consider the savings: • On a 4-year $15,000 new car loan: You save about $680. • On a 4-year $5,000 used car loan: You save about $200.
This statement doesn't help the customers understand how much in dollars they would save on a car loan at Better Horizons.	This statement allows customers to easily think about how much savings they would receive by getting a car loan with Better Horizons.

TABLE 9.4

Using Action-Oriented and Lively Language

Less Effective	More Effective
The Betty Williams Breast Center has a nationally accredited program for treatment of breast cancer.	The Betty Williams Breast Center runs a nationally accredited program for treatment of breast cancer.
The weak verb *has* implies little action on the part of the Betty Williams Breast Center.	The action verb *runs* implies a full-fledged and active effort on the part of the Betty Williams Breast Center.
Better Horizons has always been known for its personal approach to our members. Our transactions have always occurred through face-to-face services. Our tellers are friendly to all members.	At Better Horizons, we've instilled a personal touch into every aspect of our business. We've reinforced this culture with face-to-face services. Our tellers welcome members by name. When members come into the credit union, they know we care about them as people, not just as customers.
Uses unexciting, weak verbs: *has been known, have occurred, are* (notice how passive verbs detract from a sense of action and engagement). The central theme of personalized service does not come through. For example, consider the contrast between *our tellers are friendly* versus *our tellers welcome members by name*.	Uses a positive, diverse set of action verbs: *instilled, reinforced, welcome, care*. Uses adjectives and nouns to further emphasize a central theme of personalized service: *personal touch, face-to-face services, name*.

TABLE 9.5

Writing with Confidence

Less Effective	More Effective
At our upcoming board meeting, I would like to discuss possible ways of appealing to younger members. We can talk about how various strategies might appeal to this group.	At our upcoming board meeting, I will present a vision of how we can build marketing strategies and product offerings to appeal to younger members. These strategies will not only attract younger members to our credit union but also increase our business across other age groups.
These statements are an attempt to achieve an other-orientation; they show sensitivity to involving others in the decision making. However, they show no confidence in the ideas or policies that the audience resists.	These statements imply confidence in the change message: These are ideas and policies that will make a difference. Furthermore, the writer can make them happen. The argument is logic-based but also contains an excitement about possibilities.
Please think about how Better Horizons can help you in your banking.	We encourage you to stop by Better Horizons and make direct comparisons with your current bank. You'll find that banking with Better Horizons saves you money, provides convenience when you travel, and offers services to meet nearly any banking need.
This nonspecific request sounds weak and unconfident. It gives the reader an excuse to easily dismiss the message.	This request lays down a challenge to make direct comparisons, confidently implying that Better Horizons can outperform competitors. It then directly states specific benefits to the potential member.

Write with Confidence

As you display more confidence in your idea, your product, or your service, you can more effectively influence your audience. Effective persuaders provide compelling and simple reasons for action. They should show confidence in these ideas, as illustrated in Table 9.5, again with examples from two of Haniz's projects. Emotionally, the writer's confidence allows the audience to gain confidence in the message. In internal persuasive messages, expressing confidence in key players, who can make the change occur, is crucial. These key players include upper-level executives who will actively endorse and authorize resources as well as those managers and employees who will put the ideas into motion.[28]

Offer Choice

Michael Maslansky and his research team have examined the reactions of tens of thousands of customers and clients to many types of written messages. In this section, we illustrate a few findings from the financial industry. For example, in Figure 9.1, you see four statements that were sent to respondents. In the hypothetical scenario that was presented to them, a company is attempting to do a good thing—give its employees an opportunity to put money in a retirement account.

The four statements state essentially the same thing but are phrased differently. Each is written fairly well and appeals to some individuals. The statement that appeals to the most people (40 percent) emphasizes choice rather than intent. It uses the you-voice rather than the we-voice, which is preferable for many messages written to consumers (this is most similar to a consumer situation). It contains three short sentences with 7, 2, and 27 words. The emphasis on choice (other-orientation), use of you-voice (other-orientation), and simple language combine to make this the most influential statement. By contrast, the other options each contain one long sentence (30, 36, and 27 words).

FIGURE 9.1

Most-Effective Statements to Persuade Skeptical Employees *(Creating Salary Deduction for 401(k) Scenario)*

Note: The survey involved a hypothetical situation where employers would automatically deduct 7 percent of an employee's salary and place it into a 401(k). This process would help employees save money for the future. The employees would have the option to opt-out.

Source: Adapted from *The Language of Trust: Selling Ideas in a World of Skeptics* by Michael Maslansky, Scott West, Gary DeMoss and David Saylor, Copyright © 2010 by Van Kampen Investor Services, Inc. Used by permission of Prentice Hall, a division of Penguin Group (USA) Inc.

Statement #1: This process is automatic, but not required. It's voluntary. If you don't want to be enrolled or you don't like any of the choices we made, you can always opt-down to a lower level or opt-out.

40%

Statement #2: We have established the investment rate and default option based on general retirement guidelines, but you may change your investment rate or stop participating in the plan at any time.

23%

Statement #3: We do not want to tell you what to do with the money, but we do want to help you understand your options and make the most of the money that you do save for retirement.

22%

Statement #4: We believe we have a responsibility to provide you with information and guidance about the most effective strategies for saving and investing to achieve your retirement goals.

15%

Percentage of Employees Who Preferred Statement

In the PTE, customers and clients consider choice an indicator of credibility. They view simple language (not implying lack of sophisticated knowledge) as a display of transparency and respect. In contrast, they view overly complex language as potentially deceptive.[29] Similarly, effective persuasive messages avoid statements that may be perceived as pressure tactics. Hard sells are increasingly ineffective in a PTE, especially in written format.[30] Compare Haniz's less-effective and more-effective persuasive statements in Table 9.6, all of which you will see again in her messages located later in the chapter.

In persuasive messages, always be careful about being perceived as presumptuous—unfairly assuming that you know or even share the thoughts, feelings, and intentions

TABLE 9.6

Emphasizing Choice

Less Effective	More Effective
You owe it to the women in your lives to make a difference.	You can help make a difference for women here in our community.
This appeal focuses on obligation and pressure. Most readers will not respond positively.	This appeal focuses on volunteerism and contribution to the community without telling the reader what to do.
The walkathon will be held on Saturday, October 6 at 9:00 a.m. at Central Park. Do your part to improve the lives of women in our community!	The walkathon will be held on Saturday, October 6 at 9:00 a.m. at Central Park. Please join Betty and the rest of the Better Horizons team for a day of fun, excitement, and hope!
This request is a guilt trip; it emphasizes the readers' duty.	This request recognizes the readers' choice to participate in a fun and exciting approach to a good cause.

of others. Many people are easily offended when you presume to know or even dictate how they will think, feel, or react to your messages.[31]

Show Positivity

Positivity in persuasive messages helps your audience focus on the benefits rather than the drawbacks of what you are trying to promote. Maslansky and his team's research helps demonstrate that subtle changes to more positive wording are generally more persuasive. For example, they asked consumers to identify which of three pairs of phrases were more persuasive in promotional material about investment options.

In the first pair of statements, 90 percent of consumers thought the statement *making sure you have enough money as long as you live* was more effective than the statement *managing longevity risk*. Overwhelmingly, the consumers thought the benefit (having long-term financial security) was more influential than the possible drawback (avoiding financial loss).

For the second pair of statements, 81 percent of consumers thought the statement *making sure you can afford to maintain your lifestyle* was more persuasive than the statement *managing inflation risk*. Similarly, the vast majority of consumers in the case thought that the benefit (maintaining your lifestyle) was more compelling than the drawback (possibly losing your current buying power).

For the third pair of statements, 63 percent of consumers thought the statement *making sure you can participate in the gains while reducing your downside risk* was more persuasive than *managing market risk*. In this case, consumers were more positively influenced by the statement about risk (a drawback) when it was preceded by a phrase about gains (the benefit).[32]

In addition to being positive, avoiding superlatives gives you the best chance of persuading your audience. Phrases such as *best product on the market, state-of-the-art technology,* or *best-in-class service* sound increasingly hollow. Maslansky's research with consumers shows that terms such as *comfortable retirement* rather than *dream retirement; protection* rather than *guarantee; financial security* rather than *financial freedom; effective* rather than *best of breed* are more persuasive.

Consumers perceive too-good-to-be-true statements as attempts to convince them of "the merits without making a rational argument. And they [too-good-to-be-true statements] fail because they suggest an inherent bias that ruins the integrity of the communicator."[33] Table 9.7 highlights the kinds of phrases that are increasingly ineffective with today's skeptical consumers. Table 9.8 contrasts messages from Haniz's projects that persuade with and without exaggeration.

TABLE 9.7

Statements to Avoid in the Post-Trust Era

Type	Examples That Don't Work
Trust me	"Trust me" or "We speak your language"
Unbelievable	"Your call is important to us" or "We care about our customers"
Too good to be true	"This is the right product for you" or "We give you guaranteed results"
Excuses	"What you need to understand is . . ." or "Our hands are tied"
Explanations	"This was taken out of context" or "I can explain"
Fear tactics	"Are you concerned about the security of your family?" or "Act now or you'll miss this opportunity"

Source: Adapted from *The Language of Trust: Selling Ideas in a World of Skeptics* by Michael Maslansky, Scott West, Gary DeMoss and David Saylor, Copyright © 2010 by Van Kampen Investor Services, Inc. Used by permission of Prentice Hall, a division of Penguin Group (USA) Inc.

TABLE 9.8

Avoiding Exaggeration and Superlatives

Less Effective	More Effective
You can trust us at Better Horizons to make your financial dreams come true.	As a nonprofit, member-controlled financial institution, Better Horizons can provide you with higher rates on savings accounts, better terms on loans, and lower fees.
This statement uses phrases that seem unbelievable *(you can trust us)* and exaggerated *(make your financial dreams come true)*. It is positive but not plausible.	This statement focuses on specific benefits and uses words that nearly all people view positively *(nonprofit, member-controlled, savings, better, lower fees)*. It is both positive and plausible.
Pay attention to these facts or risk losing money to banks.	Consider some of the following reasons to join Better Horizons and start saving today.
This statement focuses on fear and applies pressure. Most customers would consider the writer not credible.	This statement is inviting and nonthreatening. It uses pressure-free *(consider)* and positive *(join, start saving)* words.

Creating Internal Persuasive Messages

 **LO9.4** Create compelling internal persuasive messages.

Internal and external persuasive messages contain many common elements: they gain *attention*, raise a *need*, deliver a *solution*, provide a *rationale*, show *appreciation* for differences of opinion, give *counterpoints*, and call readers to *action*. Nevertheless, internal and external persuasive messages differ in some ways (see Table 9.9). Internal messages more often focus on promoting ideas, whereas external messages more often focus on promoting products and services. Also, internal persuasive messages tend to be slightly more direct and explicit, and they tend to be based on logical appeals.

TABLE 9.9

Components of Internal and External Persuasive Messages

	Internal Messages (Typically for Ideas)	External Messages (Typically for Products and Services)
Attention	Overview of a business problem	Catchy statement
Need	Description of a business problem	Description of unmet *needs* or *wants* of your customers
Solution	Description of *how* your idea or policy addresses the business problem	Description of *how* your product or service benefits customers
Rationale	Elaboration about *why* your idea or policy is the best option	Elaboration about *why* your product or service will benefit the customer
Appreciation	Appreciation for decision makers' perspectives and resistance to your ideas	Recognition of customers' resistance to your product or service
Counterpoints	Explanation of why your ideas are better than competing ideas (typically those of decision makers who comprise your target audience)	Explanation of why your product/service is better than competing products/services (typically those favored by the target audience)
Action	Recommendations for a course of action or further discussion about an idea or policy	Description of a specific step for the customer to take toward purchase of a product or service

FIGURE 9.2

Less-Effective Internal Persuasive Message

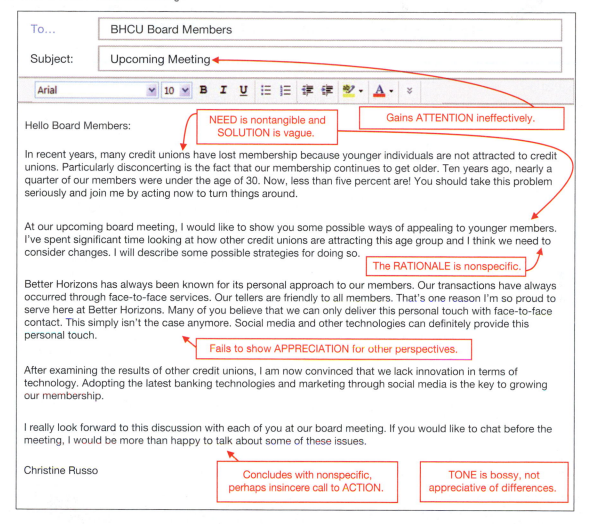

| To... | BHCU Board Members |
| Subject: | Upcoming Meeting |

Gains ATTENTION ineffectively.

Hello Board Members:

NEED is nontangible and SOLUTION is vague.

In recent years, many credit unions have lost membership because younger individuals are not attracted to credit unions. Particularly disconcerting is the fact that our membership continues to get older. Ten years ago, nearly a quarter of our members were under the age of 30. Now, less than five percent are! You should take this problem seriously and join me by acting now to turn things around.

At our upcoming board meeting, I would like to show you some possible ways of appealing to younger members. I've spent significant time looking at how other credit unions are attracting this age group and I think we need to consider changes. I will describe some possible strategies for doing so.

The RATIONALE is nonspecific.

Better Horizons has always been known for its personal approach to our members. Our transactions have always occurred through face-to-face services. Our tellers are friendly to all members. That's one reason I'm so proud to serve here at Better Horizons. Many of you believe that we can only deliver this personal touch with face-to-face contact. This simply isn't the case anymore. Social media and other technologies can definitely provide this personal touch.

Fails to show APPRECIATION for other perspectives.

After examining the results of other credit unions, I am now convinced that we lack innovation in terms of technology. Adopting the latest banking technologies and marketing through social media is the key to growing our membership.

I really look forward to this discussion with each of you at our board meeting. If you would like to chat before the meeting, I would be more than happy to talk about some of these issues.

Christine Russo

Concludes with nonspecific, perhaps insincere call to ACTION.

TONE is bossy, not appreciative of differences.

In contrast, external persuasive messages tend to be slightly more indirect and implicit, and they tend to be based on emotional appeals.

Christine, with the help of Haniz, constructed a letter to warm board members to the idea of adding new financial products and using more online and social networking tools to better reach younger members. Most board members are resistant to this message because they fear depersonalizing Better Horizons, which is known for its warm, community-oriented business model. In the less-effective message (see Figure 9.2), Christine is generally positive. However, she shows little confidence in the new ideas. The message generally contains short, dull, and nontangible comments.

In the more-effective message (see Figure 9.3), Christine personalizes the letter, addressing each board member individually, and begins with a tangible business problem. Then, she tactfully discusses her ideas and concludes with calls to action. The message contains conviction and vision without sounding too pushy. It uses a variety of implicit approaches to persuade board members that online services and social networking do not undermine personalized service. This message will open avenues for more constructive conversations when Christine meets with the board members in person.

In the more-effective message, Christine chooses to send the message in two forms. She sends it as a letter first (depicted in Figure 9.3) and as a follow-up email a few days

FIGURE 9.3

More-Effective Internal Persuasive Message

BETTER HORIZONS CREDIT UNION
Est. 1937

June 9, 2013

Matthew L. Poon, Ph.D.
19 Foxworthy Dr.
Pescaloosa, FL 91214

Gains ATTENTION effectively.

RE: Discussion at Our Upcoming Board Meeting about Gaining Younger Members

Provides compelling NEED and introduces SOLUTION.

Dear Dr. Poon:

In the past five years, we've lost over 200 members—over ten percent of our membership. This is largely because we are not attracting younger members. Ten years ago, nearly a quarter of our members were under the age of 30. Now, less than five percent are! Unless we can attract younger members, we risk a steady decline in membership over at least the next decade.

At our upcoming board meeting, I will present a vision of marketing strategies and product offerings to appeal to younger members. Not only will these strategies help attract younger members, they will also increase our business across other age groups. With several of our best employees, I've spent months examining how other credit unions attract members in this age group. I look forward to your feedback about implementing the following strategies to attract younger members:

Provides RATIONALE.

- Increasing our social networking presence on Facebook, Twitter, and blogs
- Promoting regular contests and events that cater to younger members (see for example a recent American Idol-like contest to create videos for credit unions at the following website: www.youngfreehq.com/contest/)
- Creating additional online account and lending services, including enhanced bill pay options
- Providing additional products geared to children of current members, including reloadable prepaid debit cards, teen checking and saving, mobile and online banking, and loan options for younger members (i.e., student loans, more car loan options)

At Better Horizons, we've instilled a personal touch into every aspect of our business. We've reinforced this culture with face-to-face services. Our tellers welcome members by name. When members come into the credit union, they know we care about them as people, not just as customers. The warm, friendly, genuine, and personal approach we take to serving our members is why I'm so proud to work here.

At first, I was concerned that online services and social networking might depersonalize the Better Horizons experience. I've often wondered over the past few months, *"Would these new services and technologies hurt our brand that is built on personal touch?"* After examining the results of other credit unions, I am convinced that these tools can build emotional connections and loyalty with our members. They can strengthen personal conversations with our members. And, they may be the key to growing our membership.

I really look forward to this discussion with each of you at our board meeting. If you would like to chat before the meeting, please call me anytime; I'd love to hear what you think.

You'll find an enclosed research report written by a leading credit union consultancy group that includes findings and recommendations about gaining younger members in credit unions. Can you take about 15 to 30 minutes to read through this report before the board meeting? The report has really influenced my ideas for moving the credit union forward. Thanks again for your support and ideas.

Best wishes,

Concludes with call to ACTION.

Christine Russo

Christine Russo
President and CEO
Better Horizons Credit Union

Shows APPRECIATION for other perspectives and subtly offers COUNTERPOINTS.

Enc.: Best Practices of Credit Unions Research Report

2737 Better Horizons Loop, Pescaloosa, FL 91214 • Phone: 803-784-7300 • Email: info@bhcu.org • Web: www.bhcu.org

later. In letter format, the message feels more personalized and shows the importance of the message. Likewise, it allows Christine to provide a printed-out enclosure as a courtesy.

Constructing External Persuasive Messages

Haniz writes two external persuasive messages. The first is a flyer for community members who are participating in free financial planning and tax assistance workshops sponsored and led by Better Horizons. The second is an email encouraging Better Horizons members to join the Hope Walkathon. The first message uses more logical appeals. It deals with reasons Better Horizons is a better option than local banks. The second message uses more emotional appeals. It focuses on pride in team and community, a sense of contribution to an important cause, and an exciting and hope-filled activity. It contains many facts but relies most heavily on garnering feelings of dedication and enthusiasm.

Notice the differences between the less-effective and more-effective examples in Figures 9.4 and 9.5. In the less-effective message (Figure 9.4), most components of persuasive messages are present except for a show of appreciation and a call to action.

LO9.5   Compose influential external persuasive messages.

FIGURE 9.4

Less-Effective External Persuasive Message Based on Logical Appeals

> This message does not highlight key ideas.

> This message is not personalized or tangible.

BETTER HORIZONS CREDIT UNION
Est. 1937

8 Reasons to Join Better Horizons Credit Union

Credit unions save members about $8 billion a year thanks to better interest rates and reduced fees. So, you can trust us to make your financial dreams come true. Pay attention to these facts or risk losing money to banks:

1. We are a member-based organization. That means our members can have a voice. They can serve on committees and even be elected to the Board of Directors.
2. We provide lower rates on car loans. We offer car loan rates at between 1.5 and 1.75 percentage points less than any of the banks in town.
3. We provide lower rates on unsecured loans. We offer unsecured loans at a full 2 percentage points lower than any bank.
4. We provide mortgages more conveniently and at lower costs to our members. For example, a 30-year mortgage is as low as 5.31 percent compared to rates of 5.35 to 5.42 percent at competitor banks in town. The average closing costs are $1,900 compared to between $2,800 and $3,000 at competitor banks.
5. We provide higher interest on checking and savings accounts. Currently, we offer between .3 and .5 percentage points more interest than any bank in town.
6. We charge less in fees. For example, overdraft fees at Better Horizons are $19 compared to $35 to $50 at other local banks.
7. We provide a free retirement and financial planning advisor. Better Horizons has always employed a full-time financial planning advisor to help members with any of their financial planning questions.
8. Credit unions are safer than banks. In the recent economic downturn, banks were five times more likely to fail than credit unions. Better Horizons has always been in excellent financial condition, even during economic downturns.

Please think about how Better Horizons can help you in your banking. Please stop by anytime and meet with Ms. Norah Stevens or another membership specialist to learn more. Or, fill out the online membership application. We look forward to seeing you!

2737 Better Horizons Loop, Pescaloosa, FL 91214 • Phone: 803-784-7300 • Email: info@bhcu.org • Web: www.bhcu.org

FIGURE 9.5

More-Effective External Persuasive Message Based on Logical Appeals

---

BETTER HORIZONS CREDIT UNION
Est. 1937

When You Join Better Horizons Credit Union, You're Not a Customer—You're an Owner

Eight Reasons to Join Better Horizons Credit Union | Gains ATTENTION. |

Did you know that average credit union members save $400 per year compared to bank customers? The basic difference between credit unions and banks is that credit union members own and control their credit unions whereas bank account holders have no stake or control in their financial institutions. As a nonprofit, member-controlled financial institution, Better Horizons can provide you with higher rates on savings accounts, better terms on loans, and lower fees. Consider some of the following reasons to join Better Horizons and start saving today:

1. **You come first.** You are not just a customer; you are an owner and member. That means you have a voice in how the credit union is run. You can serve on committees and even be elected to the Board of Directors.

2. **You pay lower rates on car loans.** You can get car loan rates that are between 1.5 and 1.75 percentage points less than at any of the banks in town. Consider the savings: | Provides a NEED and SOLUTION. |
   - On a 4-year $15,000 new car loan: You save about $680.
   - On a 4-year $5,000 used car loan: You save about $200.

3. **You pay lower rates on unsecured loans.** You can get unsecured loans for unforeseen expenses at much lower rates at credit unions than banks. On average, unsecured loans are a full 2 percentage points lower than any bank. Consider the savings:
   - On a 3-year $15,000 unsecured loan: You save about $640. | Provides RATIONALE. |
   - On a 3-year $5,000 unsecured loan: You save about $215.

4. **You can get mortgages more conveniently and at lower costs.**
   - You can get mortgages approved within one business day at Better Horizons.
   - On a 30-year mortgage, you can get a rate as low as 5.31 percent compared to rates of 5.35 to 5.42 percent at competitor banks in town. For a $200,000 mortgage, that amounts to a savings of between $1,800 and $4,900 over the course of the loan.
   - You can get closing costs that average $1,900 compared to between $2,800 and $3,000 at competitor banks.

5. **You earn higher interest on your checking and savings accounts.** Currently, you earn between .3 and .5 percentage points more interest than at any bank in town. That can add up fast. For an account with an average of $5,000, that will bring you an extra $15 to $25 per year.

6. **You pay less in fees.** If banking fees bother you, credit unions are the place for you. Overdraft fees, late payment fees on credit cards, and many other fees are lower at Better Horizons than at any local bank. For example, overdraft fees at Better Horizons are $19 compared to $35 to $50 at other local banks.

7. **You will have a free retirement and financial planning advisor.** Better Horizons has always employed a full-time financial planning advisor who can help you with your financial planning questions.

8. **Your savings are safest at credit unions.** In the recent economic downturn, banks were five times more likely to fail than credit unions. Better Horizons has always been in excellent financial condition, even during economic downturns. | Shows APPRECIATION for other perspectives. |

With all these benefits, why wouldn't everyone choose credit unions? That's a good question. Some people prefer banks because they often have branches and ATMs throughout the country, which is convenient for travel. Also, some people say that banks offer more services. And, many people don't know much about credit unions at all. We encourage you to stop by Better Horizons and make direct comparisons with your current bank. You'll find that banking with Better Horizons saves you money, provides convenience when you travel, and offers services to meet nearly any banking need.

Please stop by anytime and meet with Ms. Norah Stevens or another membership specialist to learn more. Or, fill out the online membership application. New members who complete an application before September 1 will receive $50 cash in their new checking account. | Concludes with call to ACTION. |

2737 Better Horizons Loop, Pescaloosa, FL 91214 • Phone: 803-784-7300 • Email: info@bhcu.org • Web: www.bhcu.org

However, it employs we-voice when the potential customer should be the entire focus of the message, and it does not provide tangible benefits.

By contrast, in the more-effective flyer (Figure 9.5), Haniz wrote a message that employs you-voice and describes tangible benefits to focus the entire message on the customer. The formatting makes each benefit stand out. The tangible statements help the customer quickly identify with the worth of the benefits; for example, saving $680 on a car loan (more-effective message) is a far clearer benefit than paying 1.5 to 1.75 percentage points less (as in the less-effective message).

The more-effective example also provides an influential appreciation statement (the less-effective example provides no appreciation statement) that anticipates the thoughts of skeptical consumers. In italics, it asks, *With all these benefits, why wouldn't everyone choose credit unions?* This validates the thinking of customers who might otherwise dismiss all these benefits as too good to be true. The paragraph explains why some people prefer banks and encourages customers to make direct comparisons themselves. Finally, the message concludes with a call to action—a cash reward to new members who join before September 1. Most effective sales messages provide incentives to motivate purchase of products or services.

Now notice the differences between the less-effective and more-effective external persuasive messages in Figures 9.6 and 9.7, both of which use emotional appeals to rally people to sign up for the Hope Walkathon. In the less-effective example (Figure 9.6), Haniz includes several statements that readers could perceive as guilt trips. It uses a series of extremely negative terms within the first few sentences (i.e., *deadliest, cancer deaths*) without providing hopeful words, an approach that could lead readers to think participating in the walkathon would make little difference. Furthermore, the

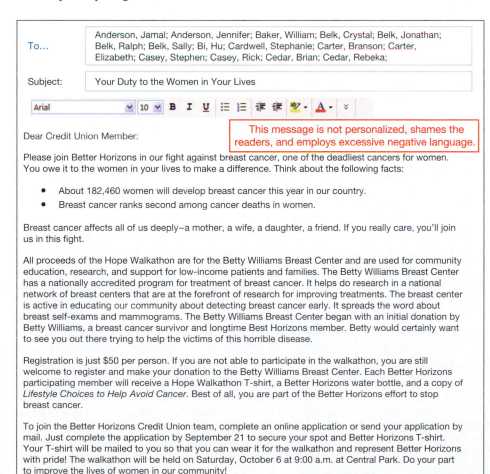

FIGURE 9.6

Less-Effective External Persuasive Message Based on Emotional Appeals

FIGURE 9.7

More-Effective External Persuasive Message Based on Emotional Appeal

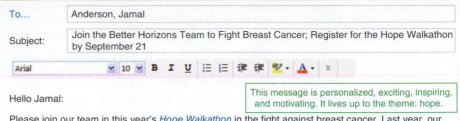

To... Anderson, Jamal

Subject: Join the Better Horizons Team to Fight Breast Cancer; Register for the Hope Walkathon by September 21

Arial 10 B I U

This message is personalized, exciting, inspiring, and motivating. It lives up to the theme: hope.

Hello Jamal:

Please join our team in this year's *Hope Walkathon* in the fight against breast cancer. Last year, our team of 415 members raised $23,000 for the Betty Williams Breast Center, located right here in our town.

Breast cancer affects our community deeply–but there is hope! Many advances in prevention and treatment are made possible by the proceeds from the Hope Walkathon. You can help make a difference for women here in our community.

Consider the following facts:

- About 50 women per year in our county are diagnosed with breast cancer.
- Seven of our credit union members were diagnosed with breast cancer last year (that we know of).
- About 1 in 8 women in our community will be diagnosed with breast cancer during their lifetime.
- Breast cancer is the second deadliest cancer in women.
- *The five-year survival rate for breast cancer is 95 percent when it is detected early.*

All proceeds of the walkathon go directly to the Betty Williams Breast Center and promote community education, research, and support for low-income patients and families. The Betty Williams Breast Center runs a nationally accredited program for treatment of breast cancer. It also contributes to a national network of breast centers that are at the forefront of research for improving treatments. The breast center is active in educating our community about detecting breast cancer early. It spreads the word about breast self-exams, mammograms, and other forms of prevention.

The Betty Williams Breast Center began with an initial donation by Betty Williams, a breast cancer survivor and longtime Best Horizons member. You can see her at the walkathon, where she will be participating for the 17th consecutive year!

Registration is just $50 per person. If you are not able to participate in the walkathon, you are still welcome to register and make your donation to the Betty Williams Breast Center. Each Better Horizons participating member will receive a Hope Walkathon T-shirt, a Better Horizons water bottle, and a copy of *Lifestyle Choices to Help Avoid Cancer*. Best of all, your money goes to a great cause.

To join the Better Horizons Credit Union team, complete an online application or send your application by mail. Please complete the application by September 21 to secure your spot and T-shirt. Your shirt will be mailed to you so that you can wear it for the walkathon.

The walkathon will be held on Saturday, October 6 at 9:00 a.m. at Central Park. Please join Betty and the rest of the Better Horizons team for a day of fun, excitement, and hope!

message is not personalized. Rather than focusing on the local and credit union communities, it exclusively examines the problem in a national context.

In the more-effective example (Figure 9.7), the message is far more personalized, upbeat, positive, and pressure-free. Instead of citing national statistics, it provides statistics about the local community and the credit union. It places more emphasis on Betty Williams, who is tied to the community and credit union. It describes the fun and excitement the reader will feel being part of a team. It does not avoid some of the negative terms (i.e., *deadliest, diagnosed*) associated with breast cancer; however, it uses far more positive and constructive words and phrases (i.e., *hope, prevention, treatment, survival, you can make a difference, 95 percent*) to create an overall hopeful and inspiring message. While both messages contain a call to action, the call to action in the more-effective example includes a direct link to sign up online. The more-effective example provides other links as well so readers can learn more about the walkathon and the Betty Williams Breast Center.

Advances in technology offer businesspeople many innovative options for delivering persuasive messages. The Technology Tips box on page 259 focuses on the use of video messages for internal messages, but video can also be a powerful tool for delivering external messages, persuasive and otherwise.

TECHNOLOGY TIPS

VIDEO SHARING IN THE WORKPLACE

Video sharing sites such as YouTube allow anyone to create and share video clips. The widespread popularity of YouTube reflects a deep desire by most people to be seen and heard. It also demonstrates the power that visual imagery can play in developing messages. Most companies have used YouTube, other social networking websites, and their own websites to distribute video marketing messages for many years. They have also realized the power of online videos for training and internal announcements.

Recently, however, companies have started giving employees the option of developing video podcasts. One of the first known such efforts was that of Microsoft, which in 2007 launched Academy Mobile, a YouTube-like website just for Microsoft employees and only for internal use. Employees can exercise their creativity to develop videos that increase camaraderie and share organizational knowledge. They can also gain strong name recognition within their companies.

Developing videos and podcasts in the workplace offers opportunities to persuade others and demonstrate thought leadership. When given the chance to share videos and podcasts in the workplace, keep these tips in mind:

Focus on the message. Plan your video message the same way as any other message: Analyze the needs of your colleagues (audience analysis), gather and analyze the most relevant information (idea development), and piece together the video message in a compelling and influential manner (message structuring).

Learn the software. Developing well-produced, professional videos takes more than a camera. Learn about video-editing software (such as Camtasia). Also, watch video podcasts created by popular colleagues (those colleagues who have a lot of followers).

Use the tools strategically. Develop video messages that benefit your company and your career. While entertainment value is important, your primary goal should be to educate your colleagues about a shared workplace challenge. Remember the online reputation that you seek. What skills and knowledge do you want to be known for? What personal traits do you hope to accentuate? How can you present yourself as a thought leader?

Composing Mass Sales Messages

LO9.6 Construct effective mass sales messages.

Even if you are not in a marketing position, you may participate in developing **mass sales messages**—messages sent to a large group of consumers and intended to market a particular product or service. Often in the form of mass emails, online ads, or sales letters, these messages generally have low success rates (ratio of number of purchases to number of message recipients). For example, a company sending out 7,000 sales letters may achieve only a 2 percent success rate (140 sales directly attributable to the mailings)—enough to make the effort profitable. Since mass emails and online ads are much less expensive than hard-copy sales letters (costs generally involve purchasing consumer email lists and online ads but no paper or postage), expected success rates may be much lower.

A secondary benefit of mass sales messages is that even when consumers do not respond with immediate purchases, these messages can raise a company's brand awareness. Consumers may keep the company in mind when making a purchase one, two, or more years in the future. On the other hand, many consumers resent mass sales messages. Excessive sales letters and spam emails may lower brand value in some cases.

While most of the principles from this chapter apply to sales messages, the structure of mass sales messages is adjusted to increase the success rate. Even modest improvements in the success rate—for example, from 2 percent to 3 percent—can make tens of thousands of dollars' difference in revenue. The model used most successfully for

Structure of Mass Sales Messages

- Gain attention.
- Generate interest.
- Build desire.
- Call to action.

mass sales messages is the AIDA approach: *attention*, *interest*, *desire*, and *action*. This approach begins and ends like other persuasive messages; it must first gain *attention* and it should end with a specific call to *action*.

Typically, the attention-getter needs to be livelier and even more provocative than with internal persuasive messages. After gaining attention, the next step is to build interest and curiosity. Then, the sales message should focus on building *desire*. That is, you want the potential customers thinking, "I want this product or service." You conclude with a specific call to action that the potential customer can take to begin the purchase process.

Most effective sales messages contain a **central sales theme.** Like other messages, sales messages are strongest when they contain a coherent, unified theme that consumers can recognize quickly. However, whereas your colleagues and clients who know you will grant you a window of 30 seconds or so to provide your main point, recipients of mass sales messages may give you only a few seconds. Thus, your sales message should stick to a single, recognizable theme that resonates within seconds.

One of the most common sales themes is price. Sales messages that focus on price tend to emphasize it immediately, generally in the attention-getter. Sales messages that emphasize other attributes typically de-emphasize price by making a brief mention of it near the end of the message. Some sales messages omit any references to price. This is a risky strategy for mass sales messages since most consumers expect at least some information about price right away.

In Figures 9.8 and 9.9, you can see two mass sales messages that Haniz and her colleagues created to promote the credit union's auto loans. In the first message

FIGURE 9.8

A Mass Sales Message with a Strong Logical Appeal

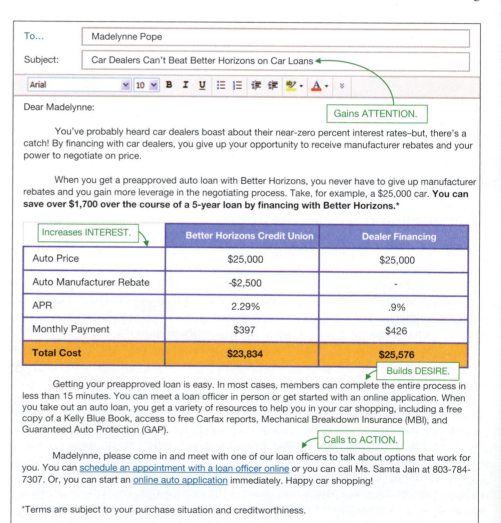

To...	Madelynne Pope
Subject:	Car Dealers Can't Beat Better Horizons on Car Loans

Dear Madelynne:

> Gains ATTENTION.

You've probably heard car dealers boast about their near-zero percent interest rates–but, there's a catch! By financing with car dealers, you give up your opportunity to receive manufacturer rebates and your power to negotiate on price.

When you get a preapproved auto loan with Better Horizons, you never have to give up manufacturer rebates and you gain more leverage in the negotiating process. Take, for example, a $25,000 car. **You can save over $1,700 over the course of a 5-year loan by financing with Better Horizons.***

> Increases INTEREST.

	Better Horizons Credit Union	**Dealer Financing**
Auto Price	$25,000	$25,000
Auto Manufacturer Rebate	-$2,500	-
APR	2.29%	.9%
Monthly Payment	$397	$426
Total Cost	**$23,834**	**$25,576**

> Builds DESIRE.

Getting your preapproved loan is easy. In most cases, members can complete the entire process in less than 15 minutes. You can meet a loan officer in person or get started with an online application. When you take out an auto loan, you get a variety of resources to help you in your car shopping, including a free copy of a Kelly Blue Book, access to free Carfax reports, Mechanical Breakdown Insurance (MBI), and Guaranteed Auto Protection (GAP).

> Calls to ACTION.

Madelynne, please come in and meet with one of our loan officers to talk about options that work for you. You can schedule an appointment with a loan officer online or you can call Ms. Samta Jain at 803-784-7307. Or, you can start an online auto application immediately. Happy car shopping!

*Terms are subject to your purchase situation and creditworthiness.

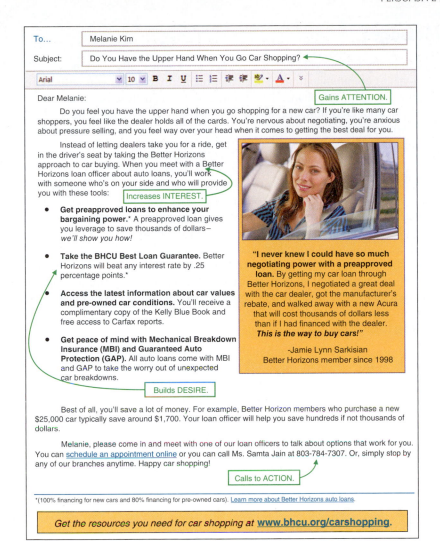

FIGURE 9.9

A Mass Sales Message with a Strong Emotional Appeal

(Figure 9.8), the central selling theme is price: Better Horizons Credit Union's auto loans cost less than dealer financing. So, the attention-getter focuses on this theme in the subject line and opening paragraph. The first paragraph arouses interest by pointing out the perhaps underappreciated fact that accepting low-rate dealer financing generally involves sacrificing rebates and negotiating power. The prominent and well-designed table likewise increases interest with its easy-to-process comparison between getting an auto loan versus dealer financing. The final paragraphs build desire by showing the ease and perks of getting an auto loan and providing information about how to apply right away. This sales message primarily makes a logical appeal.

In the next sales message (Figure 9.9), Haniz and her colleagues highlight a different sales theme with a primarily emotional appeal. In this message, they focus on going car shopping with confidence and strength, directly addressing an anxiety many car shoppers have of getting taken advantage of when making a car purchase. The emotional appeal involves several influence strategies, including social proof (with the testimonial of a satisfied member who has saved money by taking out an auto loan) and reciprocation (with the warm offer to get help from a loan officer and an invitation to "work as a team" against the car dealers). You typically have much more freedom of creative expression in mass sales messages than you do with other types of persuasive messages. Haniz uses this creative license with metaphorical language tied to playing cards ("upper hand," "dealer holds the cards") and driving ("take you for a ride," "get in the driver's seat").

Reviewing Persuasive Messages

LO9.7 Evaluate persuasive messages for effectiveness and fairness.

Always carefully review your persuasive messages, especially since nearly all of them are high-stakes communications. They can potentially provide you with more professional opportunities and enhanced credibility, or they can close off future opportunities and diminish your credibility. Likewise, because you are a representative of your organization, your persuasive messages may raise or decrease customer loyalty, revenues, and brand value.

Get Feedback and Reread

Persuasive messages are directed to others who *resist* your ideas, products, or services. Read your message carefully. Imagine yourself in your audience members' position and consider how they would respond. Make sure you ask trusted colleagues to read your messages. Ask them how they would respond and how they think you can better construct the message to get your intended results. You may be best served to seek out trusted colleagues who may be resistant in the same way as your audience. These colleagues may provide the most insight to you about crafting your message carefully.

Apply the FAIR Test

Persuasive messages can be intentionally designed to manipulate colleagues and customers. In a business communications context, **manipulation** involves attempting to influence others by some level of deception so you can achieve your own interests. You may face many strong temptations to manipulate others through persuasive messages—to elevate your career, get a commission on that extra sale, get that bonus for exceptional performance, or pad your ego for being right.

By applying the FAIR test, you can avoid sending persuasive messages that manipulate others. This is especially the case for sales messages because any misrepresentation of your product or service is unethical. Use Figure 9.10 as a guide as

FIGURE 9.10

Are Your Persuasive Messages FAIR?

Facts (How *factual* is your persuasive message?)
- Have you presented *all* the facts correctly?
- Have you presented information that allows colleagues, customers, and consumers to make informed decisions that are in their best interests?
- Have you carefully considered various interpretations of your data? Have you assessed the quality of your information?

Access (How *accessible* or *transparent* are your motives, reasoning, and information?)
- Are your motives clear or will others perceive that you have a hidden agenda? Have you made yourself accessible to others so that they can learn more about your viewpoints?
- Have you fully disclosed information that colleagues, customers, or consumers should expect to receive?
- Are you hiding any information that casts your recommendations in a better light? Are you hiding real reasons for making certain claims or recommendations?
- Have you given stakeholders the opportunity to provide input in the decision-making process?

Impacts (How does your communication *impact* stakeholders?)
- Have you carefully considered how your ideas, products, and services will impact colleagues, customers, and consumers?
- Have you made recommendations to colleagues, customers, and consumers that are in their best interests?

Respect (How *respectful* is your communication?)
- If you were the customer or the colleague, would you feel that the tone of the message was appropriate?
- Does the message offend or pressure? Does it show that your colleagues' and customers' needs are important?
- Would a neutral observer consider your communication respectful?

COMMUNICATION Q&A

CONVERSATIONS WITH CURRENT BUSINESS PROFESSIONALS

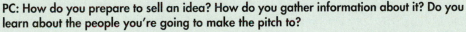

Pete Cardon: Can you describe a situation in which you had to persuade others about an idea that ended up having a big impact for your company?

Ron Fuller: When I worked at Microsoft, I had to persuade my general manager [GM] to not require my team to use a first-version product because it was simply not capable of supporting our needs. That was very difficult because GMs at Microsoft are expected to showcase new products in their own operations, so the pressure on my team was intense. After several weeks of testing, evaluation, and discussion, we found ourselves in a high-profile meeting where we were expected to declare our intentions to adopt the product. I was painfully torn between my clear obligation to do as instructed by management and what I felt was also an obligation to our large base of users within the company. Each member of my team, when called under the spotlight, agreed to adopt the new product while acknowledging the reservations. When it was my turn, I also agreed. However, I also spelled out as tactfully as I could the negative consequences for thousands of our pre-sales support engineers around the world. In light of this argument, the GM relented. Within one year, it became clear that this was the best outcome because the system my team created instead became one of the largest and most popular content distribution systems within the company.

PC: How do you prepare to sell an idea? How do you gather information about it? Do you learn about the people you're going to make the pitch to?

RF: Understanding the interests of the person you are trying to persuade is the most important part of formulating your pitch. The GM in my example was completely aware that adopting the new product would be problematic for thousands of field engineers and enormously costly for the company. But to him the cost was worth the benefit, at least from the perspective of his career. He wanted the news releases and analyst reports to highlight his use of the new product. The disaster that would follow would not command near the attention and would be seen, if seen at all, as an internal technical matter. It would not directly impact his performance review, his budget, nor his influence within the company. In the end, only a high-profile disclosure that he had been fully and publicly advised of the consequences in advance persuaded him to recalculate his interests.

PC: In your experience, what are some of the common mistakes employees make when trying to sell their ideas within a company?

RF: Failing to appeal to the interests of the right decision makers is probably the most common mistake. Often an employee will have a good idea, but if the people who make the decisions don't see it as being in their interest, the idea won't go very far. It's important to understand that the interest of the company and the interests of decision makers within management are not always the same thing. They usually should be, and often are, but not always.

Ron Fuller *is an information technology consultant. Following college he spent six years as a flight instructor, two years as a manager of the Olympic bobsled track, and a year as a stock trader. Then he found his passion: databases. He worked for six years at Microsoft and now works as an independent data management consultant, helping companies to better understand their businesses and their customers.*

you discuss with your colleagues whether your persuasive messages are fair. And by considering the experience of a business professional (see the Communication Q&A on this page), you can learn to be more thoughtful and skillful when crafting persuasive messages.

Chapter Takeaway for *Persuasive Messages*

LO 9.1. Describe the relationship between credibility and persuasion. (pp. 240–241)

Delivering effective persuasive messages improves your **reputation for personal credibility.**

It shows **competence** when you know everything about your product, service, or idea.	It shows **caring** when you explain how your product, service, or idea benefits others.	It shows **character** when you provide completely reliable and honest information.

LO 9.2. Explain the AIM planning process for persuasive messages and the basic components of most persuasive messages. (pp. 241–245)

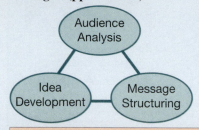

AIM Planning Process

Audience Analysis: Identify the needs of your audience and learn how it is influenced.

Idea Development: Gather extensive information about the products, services, and ideas that you are writing about.

Message Structuring: Gain attention, tie needs to benefits, provide rationale, show appreciation, and call your audience to action.

Components of Persuasive Messages

- Gain attention.
- Raise a need.
- Deliver a solution.
- Provide a rationale.
- Show appreciation.
- Give counterpoints (optional).
- Call to action.

Types of Attention-Getters

- Rhetorical question
- Intriguing statistic
- Compelling and unusual facts
- Challenge
- Testimonial

See *examples of attention-getters* in Table 9.1.

LO 9.3. Explain how the tone and style of persuasive messages impact their influence. (pp. 245–252)

Guidelines for Tone and Style for Persuasive Messages

- Apply the personal touch.
- Use action-oriented, lively language.
- Write with confidence.
- Offer choice.
- Show positivity.

See *examples of tone and style choices* in Tables 9.2 through 9.8.

LO 9.4. Create compelling internal persuasive messages. (pp. 252–255)

Components of Internal Persuasive Messages

- Gain attention: overview of a business problem
- Raise a need: description of a business problem
- Deliver a solution: description of *how* your idea or policy addresses the business problem
- Provide a rationale: elaboration about *why* your idea or policy is the best option
- Show appreciation: appreciation for decision makers' perspectives and resistance to your ideas
- Give counterpoints (optional): explanation of why your ideas are better than competing ideas (typically those of decision makers who comprise your target audience)
- Call to action: recommendations for a course of action or further discussion about an idea or policy

See *examples of internal persuasive messages* in Figures 9.2 and 9.3.

LO 9.5. Compose influential external persuasive messages. (pp. 255–259)

Components of External Persuasive Messages

- Gain attention: catchy statement
- Raise a need: description of unmet *needs* or *wants* of your customers
- Deliver a solution: description of *how* your product or service benefits customers
- Provide a rationale: elaboration about *why* your product or service will benefit the customer
- Show appreciation: recognition of customers' resistance to your product or service
- Give counterpoints (optional): explanation of why your product/service is better than competing products/services (typically those favored by the target audience)
- Call to action: description of a specific step for the customer to take toward purchase of a product or service

See *examples of external persuasive messages* in Figures 9.4 through 9.7.

LO 9.6. Construct effective mass sales messages. (pp. 259–261)

Structure of Mass Sales Messages			
• Gain attention.	• Generate interest.	• Build desire.	• Call to action.

See *examples of mass sales messages* in Figures 9.8 and 9.9.

LO 9.7. Evaluate persuasive messages for effectiveness and fairness. (pp. 262–263)

Reviewing Process

FAIR Test: Make sure your claims are factual and nondeceptive.

Proofreading: Carefully reread the message several times. Envision the response of your audience.

Feedback: Have trusted colleagues check for accuracy, honesty, and influence.

Key Terms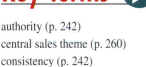

Discussion Exercises

9.1 Chapter Review Questions (LO 9.1, LO 9.2, LO 9.3)

A. Describe how credibility forms a basis for persuasion.

B. Explain how the tone and style of persuasive messages impact their persuasiveness. Specifically, address how personal touch, action-oriented language, confidence, choice, and positivity affect how message recipients respond.

C. Explain the AIM planning process for persuasive messages and the basic components of most persuasive messages.

9.2 Applying Key Terms (LO 9.1, LO 9.2, LO 9.3)

Explain each key term above and provide a concrete example of how it impacts persuasive messages.

9.3 Communication Q&A Discussion Questions (LO 9.1, LO 9.2, LO 9.3)

Read Ron Fuller's comments in the Communication Q&A section. Respond to the following questions:

A. When describing an idea that had a big impact on the company, Fuller mentioned that he was "painfully torn" between what he considered competing obligations. Explain what he did. What principles are illustrated here for engaging in fair and persuasive communications? How would you have approached a similar situation?

B. Fuller states that understanding the interests of others is the most important part of persuading them. The first example he provides of making a pitch, however, shows the complexity

of meeting the interest of others. The general manager he persuaded had competing interests. What were the competing interests? How should you handle situations where individuals have competing interests like this GM?

C. What are the key points Fuller makes about persuasion?

9.4 Should You Use Persuasion Sparingly? (LO 9.1, LO 9.3)

Some people suggest that all business communication is a form of persuasion—that is, you are attempting to motivate others to think and/or do as you suggest. Others suggest that you should use persuasion only in rare circumstances. For example, in the recent Dale Carnegie Training book called *The 5 Essential People Skills,* the authors write the following:

> It has been said that persuasion is like a savings account: The less you use it, the more you've got. Learn how to use your powers of persuasion well and at the appropriate moments. With time and practice, you'll be able to have positive influence on people's decisions in any number of areas.[34]

Write three or four paragraphs describing your perspectives on how often and when you should use persuasion in the workplace.

9.5 Character and Persuasion (LO 9.1, LO 9.7)

As Aristotle famously stated, "Character may almost be called the most effective means of persuasion." Do you think this is true in today's business world? Explain your viewpoints with three or four supporting points and examples.

Evaluation Exercises

9.6   Analyzing a Sales Message (LO 9.6)

Find an interesting sales message that you have received recently in the mail or through email. If you can't find one readily, go to the website of a company that sells products or services that interest you. Find a sales message of sufficient length to analyze. Analyze it in the following ways:

A. Which psychological tools of influence (consistency, reciprocation, social proof, authority, liking, scarcity) does it use? Provide examples.

B. What emotional appeals are used? What about logical appeals? Would you consider this sales message to be catering more to emotion or logic? Explain.

C. Do you consider this sales message warm and inviting?

D. Do you consider this sales message plausible?

E. Do you consider this sales message respectful?

F. Do you trust the sales message?

G. What are two changes you think could be made to improve its effectiveness?

9.7   Analyzing the Better Horizons Promotional Message (LO 9.5)

Analyze the Better Horizons flyer (Figure 9.6) in the following ways:

A. Which psychological tools of influence (consistency, reciprocation, social proof, authority, liking, scarcity) does it use? Provide examples.

B. What emotional appeals are used? What about logical appeals? Would you consider this messages as catering more to emotion or logic? Explain.

C. Do you consider this message warm and inviting?

D. Do you consider this sales message plausible?

E. Do you consider this sales message respectful?

F. Do you trust this message?

G. What are two changes you think could be made to improve its effectiveness?

9.8   Persuasion Self-Assessment (LO 9.1, LO 9.2, LO 9.3, LO 9.7)

Evaluate yourself with regard to each of the persuasive practices listed in the table below. Circle the appropriate number for each.

	1 – Rarely/Never	2 – Sometimes	3 – Usually	4 – Always
I can persuade others to see merit in my ideas even when they initially disagree.	1	2	3	4
Before trying to persuade others, I think about what their needs are.	1	2	3	4
Before trying to persuade others, I think about the best ways to influence them.	1	2	3	4
I feel comfortable expressing my viewpoints even when I know others disagree.	1	2	3	4
I can persuade others without offending them.	1	2	3	4
Even when others disagree with me, I offer my perspective without putting down their opinions.	1	2	3	4
I can write strong persuasive messages.	1	2	3	4
When I persuade others, I try to open up avenues for future discussion.	1	2	3	4
I realize that most people are not persuaded immediately. I communicate with others realizing that the process will likely involve many steps.	1	2	3	4
I show respect for others with whom I disagree.	1	2	3	4

Total your score and consider the following advice:

35–40:   You are an *effective persuader*. You likely influence others as intended in most cases. Continue honing your persuasive skills and ensure that you always act with the interests of others in mind.

30–34:   You are a *conscientious persuader*. You are aware of the needs of others, you are confident of presenting your perspectives, and you feel that you can show respect to others who think differently. Continue working on developing your persuasive abilities.

25–29:   You are an *average persuader*. You are persuasive in many cases, but you will be far more effective if you consistently apply principles of effective persuasion. Identify those areas where you most need to improve and you will see rapid improvement.

Under 25: You are a *less-effective persuader*. Think carefully about the areas in which you can most improve. You can dramatically change your influence on others by mastering just a few principles of persuasion.

Based on the self-assessment, identify three areas in which to improve your approach to persuasion. Write three goals and elaborate on each with a supporting paragraph.

Application Exercises

Case for Problems 9.9 through 9.11: Promoting New Services at Better Horizons Credit Union

Christine Russo works at Better Horizons and is developing several new services the credit union could offer. One idea is for credit union members to take a five-day cruise to the Bahamas. Two afternoons of the cruise will be devoted to financial planning workshops, including choices such as retirement planning, trusts and estates, insurance, charitable giving, taxes, and college savings. Also, a finance boot camp for teenagers will provide basic information about savings and checking accounts, loans, and budgeting.

In another initiative, Christine wants to set up a new rewards program for credit union members who use their Better Horizons debit or credit cards. Each purchase with the debit or credit card will contribute to their total reward points, which customers can redeem for brand-name merchandise, hotel accommodations, airline tickets, cruises, and other travel options (detailed in an online and paper merchandise and travel catalog). Members get one point for each dollar spent on their credit cards and one point for every two dollars spent on their debit cards. One advantage of the program is that points can be combined across accounts. So, family members or friends who are members of the credit union can transfer their points to one another's accounts and more quickly gain rewards. The program involves no fee, and members with the cards are automatically enrolled in the program.

9.9 Selling an Idea to the Better Horizons Board (LO 9.4)

Assume the role of Christine and write a letter to the board describing your ideas for the finance planning cruise and the new rewards program.

9.10 Promoting the Financial Planning Cruise to Better Horizons Credit Union Members (LO 9.5)

Write a sales message to Better Horizons members to promote the financial planning cruise. Feel free to add additional details (i.e., price and dates for the cruise).

9.11 Writing a Sales Letter for the New Better Horizons Special Rewards Card (LO 9.5, LO 9.6)

Write a sales message to Better Horizons members to promote the new rewards programs. Feel free to add additional details (i.e., types of rewards).

9.12 Creating a Message to Promote Joining a Student Club (LO 9.4, LO 9.5, LO 9.6)

A. Select a student club of interest to you. You may already be a member or you may know little about the club. In any case, write a message to encourage other students to join. Describe benefits that membership brings and specific steps for joining the club or learning more about it.

B. In a separate message, describe the students you are targeting; reasons for resistance among these students; how your message appeals to this group; and the mix of communication channels you'll use to distribute the message. Address the message to the president of the club.

9.13 Writing a Sales Letter for Your Computer Store (LO 9.6)

Assume you own a computer retail store located near your campus (give the store any name you want). You have sold fewer PCs in recent years due to the strong demand for Macs among university students. You will write a sales letter to reach all student housing units. Your goal is to encourage students to purchase PCs at your store. You can do online research to help you contrast PCs with Macs and identify pricing levels. In the sales letter, attempt to show students the advantages of PCs compared to Macs and get them to take specific steps to learn more about or even purchase a PC at your store.

9.14 Writing a Sales Letter for a Credit Union That Targets University Students (LO 9.6)

Write a sales letter that targets university students and promotes joining a local credit union. In addition to using materials from this chapter, go online and find comparisons of benefits between credit unions and banks. It's easy to find plenty of information in just 20 to 30 minutes.

9.15 Writing a Sales Letter for a Bank That Targets University Students (LO 9.6)

Write a sales letter that targets university students and promotes joining a local bank. Find information online about local credit unions and banks, select the financial institution that interests you the most, and then promote it with an effective sales letter.

9.16 Persuading University Students to Start a Retirement Account (LO 9.5, LO 9.6)

Write a message that targets university students and persuades them to start a retirement account. You'll find lots of information online about the benefits of starting a retirement account early. Spend a few hours learning about options before writing your letter.

Endnotes

1. Michael Maslansky, *The Language of Trust* (New York: Prentice Hall, 2010): 6.

2. Liz Simpson, "Get Around Resistance and Win Over the Other Side," *Harvard Management Communication Letter* (2003): 3.

3. Robert B. Cialdini, *Influence: The Psychology of Persuasion* (New York: HarperCollins, 2007).

4. Ibid: 17.

5. Ibid.

6. Ibid.

7. Ibid.

8. Ibid.

9. Ibid.

10. Ibid.

11. Ibid.

12. Ralph Allora, *Winning Sales Letters—From Prospect to Close* (New York: McGraw-Hill, 2009).

13. Meredith D. Ashby and Stephen A. Miles, *Leaders Talk Leadership: Top Executives Speak Their Minds* (New York: Oxford University Press, 2002): 160–161.

14. Matthew J. Mazzei, Christopher L. Shook, and David J. Ketchen, Jr., "Selling Strategic Issues: Crafting the Content of the Sales Pitch," *Business Horizons* 52: 539–543.

15. Beverly Ballaro, "Six Ways to Grab Your Audience Right from the Start," *Harvard Management Communication Letter* (2003): 3–5.

16. Mazzei et al., "Selling Strategic Issues: Crafting the Content of the Sales Pitch."

17. Tom Sant, *Persuasive Business Proposals: Writing to Win More Customers, Clients, and Contracts,* 2nd ed. (New York: AMACOM, 2004); Allora, *Winning Sales Letters—From Prospect to Close.*

18. Simpson, "Get Around Resistance and Win Over the Other Side."

19. Maslansky, *The Language of Trust*: 35.

20. Ibid: 37.

21. Allora, *Winning Sales Letters—From Prospect to Close*; Sant, *Persuasive Business Proposals: Writing to Win More Customers, Clients, and Contracts.*

22. Stephen M. R. Covey, *The Speed of Trust* (New York: Free Press, 2006).

23. Maslansky, *The Language of Trust*: 39.

24. Allora, *Winning Sales Letters—From Prospect to Close.*

25. Maslansky, *The Language of Trust.*

26. Allora, *Winning Sales Letters—From Prospect to Close.*

27. Ibid.

28. Mazzei et al., "Selling Strategic Issues: Crafting the Content of the Sales Pitch."

29. Maslansky, *The Language of Trust.*

30. Ibid.

31. Allora, *Winning Sales Letters—From Prospect to Close.*

32. Maslansky, *The Language of Trust*: 232–242.

33. Ibid: 116.

34. Dale Carnegie Training, *The 5 Essential People Skills: How to Assert Yourself, Listen to Others, and Resolve Conflicts* (New York: Simon & Schuster, 2009): 137.

CHAPTER TEN

Bad-News Messages

Learning Objectives

After studying this chapter, you should be able to do the following:

LO10.1 Describe how delivering bad news impacts your credibility.

LO10.2 Explain considerations for deciding which channels to use when delivering bad-news messages.

LO10.3 Summarize principles for effectively delivering bad-news messages.

LO10.4 Compose effective bad-news messages in person and in writing for various audiences, including colleagues, external partners, and customers.

LO10.5 Deliver and receive negative performance reviews constructively.

LO10.6 Review bad-news messages for effectiveness and fairness.

WHY DOES THIS MATTER?

Business inevitably involves giving bad or disappointing news to people. Perhaps you need to turn down a proposal, reject the business of a supplier, deny the claim of a customer, give a negative performance review to a subordinate, reject the idea of a colleague, explain that you do not like a product or service, notify your boss of mistakes you've made, or even tell employees that they will be laid off. Not all communications in business are pleasant. Because business is competitive by nature, turning others down is common.

Delivering really bad news is extremely stressful to most business professionals. In the Great Recession that began in 2008, 37 percent of human resource workers considered changing profession due to the frequency with which they were forced to deliver the news to employees that they were being laid off.[1] Management consultant Mark Blackham explained this uncomfortable predicament: "Bad news is bad news no matter how you spin it. It changes people's futures. This is one part of life that is not much fun, and you cannot make it better with words."[2]

In this chapter, we focus on several principles for delivering bad news in person and in writing. In the majority of workplace situations, you and your organization will continue to hold a working relationship with the recipients of bad news—whether they are colleagues, external partners, or customers. Therefore, your overarching goal is to create a path forward that is in the long-run interests of each person involved in the situation. Moreover, one of your goals is to help bad-news recipients maintain a positive image of your organization. Read the following short case, which will be the basis for five examples of delivering bad news shown throughout this chapter.

Chapter Case: Bad News at Marble Home Makeovers

Who's Involved

Juan Hernandez, business manager at Marble Home Makeovers (The business fabricates marble countertops, tiles, vanities, and bathtubs. It also installs and remodels home bathrooms and kitchens.)
- Overseeing fast growth as the company transitions from a small, regional company to a large, nationwide supplier

Cindy Cooper, loan officer at Wilson Citizen Bank
- Has acted as a small-business loan specialist for the prior four years

Jake Adelman, shift supervisor at Marble Home Makeovers
- Promoted to shift supervisor two years ago largely due to his ability to improve employee morale

Situation 1 (Tuesday afternoon) — Cindy Cooper Informs Juan That Marble Home Makeover's Credit Line Will Be Reduced Substantially

Cindy is in charge of small-business loans. Bank officials just decided that the bank was holding excessively risky credit lines with the majority of its small-business clients. Cindy was told to rein in dozens of these credit lines by reducing them by 50 to 75 percent. She called and met with several of these clients over the past week, many of whom stated they did not know how to meet the bank's sudden demands.

Next, Cindy needed to contact Juan and inform him that the bank would be cutting the credit line down from $100,000 to between $30,000 and $50,000. She knew this would be difficult news for Juan because Marble Home Makeovers faced some challenging cash constraints.

Situation 2
(Wednesday morning)

Juan Needs to Break the News to All Employees That Work Hours Will Be Reduced

Juan Hernandez sighed in frustration. He'd slept poorly last night because of anxiety. Today was going to be a long day. He had lots of bad news to pass around—to employees, suppliers, and customers. Juan had delivered bad news many times before, but it never got easy.

Juan gathered most of the employees for a 15-minute meeting. He broke the news that the company was temporarily suspending any overtime work and cutting back on shifts. Juan knew some of the workers lived from month to month and that these new changes would hurt them. The meeting, however, was cut short by a surprise safety inspection by an Occupational Safety and Health Administration (OSHA) officer. Thus, Juan needed to send out an email to clarify the news he had delivered in the meeting. He had not had a chance to answer all the questions, and some employees were not at work that day. He definitely wanted to get out more complete information right away.

Situation 3
(Wednesday afternoon)

Juan Needs to Tell a Supplier That He Has Selected a New Supplier

Juan's current supplier is a relatively small chemicals company run by Nick Jensen. Juan had relied exclusively on Nick's company for chemical supplies for the past three years. However, Juan had decided that a rival company was a better fit.

Situation 4
(Wednesday afternoon)

Juan Needs to Inform an Unhappy Customer That He Is Rejecting Her Claim

Juan needs to respond to an email complaint from a customer who complained that a marble countertop the company had installed in her home had a crack. She requested that Marble Home Makeovers replace the countertop or pay her $495 (the original price). The countertop had been manufactured and installed five years previously, well beyond the two-year warranty.

Situation 5
(Wednesday afternoon)

Juan Delivers Negative Feedback to an Employee

Juan conducts quarterly performance reviews for each of his shift supervisors. Today, he is meeting with Jake Adelman, who is one of the most popular employees in the company. Jake is outgoing, friendly, and inspiring to his workers. Juan has become close friends with Jake, and they regularly go out for lunch together.

One of Jake's primary responsibilities is to ensure that each outgoing shipment to construction wholesalers is complete and that all items are free of defects. In the past few months, however, several wholesalers have complained that Jake's shipments did not contain the correct items. In two cases, nearly every item in the shipments contained defects. Juan deemed Jake's quarterly performance as poor and knew he needed to confront Jake about these problems.

Task 1
How can Cindy inform Juan of changes to his credit line and also preserve business with Marble Home Makeovers? (See the section on delivering bad news in person to customers.)

Task 2
How can Juan write a message to employees informing them that they will have reduced work hours without excessively reducing employee morale and commitment? (See the section on delivering bad news in writing to colleagues.)

Task 3
How can Juan tell a longtime supplier that he has chosen a new supplier and still maintain goodwill? (See the section on delivering bad news in writing to external partners.)

Task 4
How can Juan reject this customer's claim but retain her loyalty? (See the section on delivering bad news in writing to customers.)

Task 5
How can Juan tell one of the most popular employees that he is not performing well? (See the section on delivering bad news in person for performance reviews.)

Maintaining Credibility When Delivering Bad News

LO10.1 Describe how delivering bad news impacts your credibility.

How you deliver bad news strongly impacts your credibility. Any perceived dishonesty or deception can damage your credibility.[3] Communication specialist Dave Zielinski described how failing to effectively deliver bad news during tough times can damage credibility over the long term:

> Employees, who have long memories, tend to remember how they were treated, not what marching orders they received, in times of corporate turmoil. When it comes to how they perceive the organization in the aftermath of such troubles, those who communicated openly, honestly and frequently will lay the foundation for future loyalty and overall organizational health.[4]

Zielinski's point is clear: Honesty and openness are key. Although people do not like to get bad news, they expect the truth.

Among the most trusted and successful sports agents and business advisors, David Falk is often recognized for his straightforward and honest approach to business. Basketball star Michael Jordan, who signed on with Falk as his agent, stated the following about him:

> There are moments in everyone's lives when you have to trust that your advisor will look you in the eye and tell you the truth, even when it's not what you want to hear. I always knew that David would tell me what he truly felt even when it wasn't popular or politically correct. As much as I always valued his skill for negotiation and his creativity in marketing, I especially admired his courage to express his convictions when it mattered most.[5]

Falk earned credibility because of his courage to deliver bad news: "Failing to tell the truth is not simply dishonest," he said, "it's ineffectual. . . . It took me a while but I came to recognize the beauty in being blunt. While I always tried to be respectful and mindful of the other person's feelings, I was also firm and to the point. . . . I believe being honest, even brutally so sometimes, creates the best atmosphere for long-term success."[6]

Falk's comments highlight the idea that trust and long-term success in business are built on honesty in bad-news situations. His experiences are not unique. Research shows that honesty and openness can lead to more trust in the bad-news bearer. The consulting firm Siegel+Gale conducted research about delivering bad news during the Great Recession. Through the research involving hundreds of customers of financial service companies, the consultants concluded the following:

> During this time of economic crisis, many organizations struggle to communicate unfavorable news—from lower earnings and shrinking market share, to cuts in service and increases in prices. While many assume that communicating bad news to customers shakes relationships and breeds mistrust, Siegel+Gale's latest . . . survey reveals that delivering bad

news the right way can actually strengthen customer relationships and lay the foundation for increased trust when conditions improve.[7]

Although one should never view the delivery of bad news opportunistically, those who deliver bad news appropriately enhance their credibility. It shows character on your part to tell people the truth, even when it's hard for all parties involved. In particular, bearing responsibility for your own role in causing the bad news shows your commitment to transparency and honesty, further bolstering character. It shows caring when you do all you can to lessen the impact of bad news on others and exhibit forward thinking that considers their needs. It shows competence when you have a track record of success in tough situations and demonstrate a good plan for overcoming the challenges you face.

Applying the AIM Planning Process for Bad-News Messages

Planning is critical to delivering bad news in a way that best serves all parties involved and leaves the door open for productive cooperation in the future. Yet, since bad news should be delivered in a timely manner, planning must be tackled as soon as possible. Many times, bad-news recipients are hurt less by the bad news than by how long it took to receive it. Your challenge, then, is to start planning efficiently as soon as you discover the unpleasant news.

Understand How the Bad News Will Affect Your Audience

Delivering bad news often creates stress, anxiety, and other strong emotions. You may feel eager to relieve yourself of these feelings. More than with other types of messages, you may need to work hard to focus your message on serving others. You can make the situation better for the recipients by understanding the nature of the bad news and its impacts on them, delivering the news in a timely manner, and choosing the right mix of communication channels.

Deliver the Bad News in a Timely Manner   The adage *no news is bad news* applies when colleagues, clients, or customers know you are in the process of making decisions that can impact them. In the absence of information, they often assume the worst. Sometimes, as people are wondering what the bad news may be, they may even pass their speculations on as part of the rumor mill. In these cases, you lose control of the message and can lose credibility if others think you have wrongfully withheld information. Never wait too long to deliver bad news.[8]

On the other hand, don't deliver bad news when you don't know the details, since this can cause unnecessary anxiety. For example, announcing that there *might* be budget cuts or layoffs or pay cuts without any specifics could cause more alarm than is warranted. You will be the judge of this.[9]

Choose the Right Mix of Channels   Generally, bad news is best delivered in person. This allows rich communication, where you can use verbal and nonverbal cues to show your concern and sensitivity. You get immediate feedback from those receiving bad news and can respond to their discomforts right away. In many unpleasant situations, you can immediately come up with options and solutions.

However, delivering bad news in writing also has advantages. By placing the bad news in writing, you can control the message more carefully and ensure that you state the bad news precisely and accurately. However, you do not have the ability to respond immediately if the message recipients misinterpret the bad news. Moreover, many people view bad news in written form as callous and impersonal. See Table 10.1 for a summary of advantages and disadvantages of delivering bad news in person and in writing.

Guidelines for Bad-News Messages

- Deliver the bad news in a timely manner.
- Choose the right mix of channels.
- Sympathize with the bad-news recipients and soften the blow.
- Provide a simple, clear rationale.
- Explain immediate impacts.
- Focus on solutions and long-term benefits.
- Show goodwill.

LO10.2 Explain considerations for deciding which channels to use when delivering bad-news messages.

TABLE 10.1

Advantages and Disadvantages of Bad News in Verbal and Written Forms

Verbal Delivery	Written Delivery
Advantages	*Advantages*
• Can use and observe nonverbal cues • Can more easily demonstrate intentions • Can more effectively clarify and explain the bad news • Can respond to concerns immediately	• Can craft message more carefully • Can document the message more easily • Can provide a message that serves as a reference (provide directions, suggestions, and options for future actions) • Can deliver message to more people more efficiently
Disadvantages	*Disadvantages*
• May hinder effective delivery, interpretation, and discussion of bad news due to strong emotions • Requires more time • Less able to document the bad news • Less able to provide directions that bad-news recipients can reference later	• Unable to demonstrate concern through nonverbal cues • Unable to immediately respond to concerns • Unable to work out mutual solutions • Less able to control long-term impacts on working relationships

As you consider which communication channels to use, analyze the nature of the bad news. In research from medical and social psychology literature, researchers have identified three aspects of the bad news that impact how you approach delivering it: severity, controllability, and likelihood. **Severity** is how serious or detrimental the bad news is. **Controllability** is the degree to which the bad-news message receiver can alter the outcome. **Likelihood** relates to the probability of the bad event occurring.[10]

As controllability decreases and likelihood and/or severity increase, richer channels of communication are most appropriate. For example, laying someone off should certainly be done in person. There is no controllability (the employee cannot undo being laid off), there is complete likelihood, and there is high severity (the employee will be unemployed and potentially without income and other benefits such as health insurance). When bad news becomes more controllable, less likely, and/or less severe, less-rich channels are more often justified. In Table 10.2, you can see appropriate responses in terms of richness for various combinations of severity and controllability.

Of course, your preferred communication channel is not always available. For example, if you work in a virtual team, you may not have the option of delivering bad news in person. Or if you hold a high-level leadership position, you simply cannot take time to speak to each person affected by your decisions. Where possible and appropriate, choose richer communication channels.

LO10.3 Summarize principles for effectively delivering bad-news messages.

Develop Your Ideas

Gathering the facts from a variety of sources is critical for bad-news messages. Often, you are dealing with emotionally charged issues, situations that are open to multiple interpretations, and/or situations where the potential consequences are severe. If you gather as much information as you can from a variety of sources, you're more likely to make objective judgments and propose fair solutions. Make sure you are aware of your own emotions and how they impact your thinking. You might ask yourself whether your reaction to the situation involves any defensiveness, rashness, or favoritism.

Structure Your Message

One choice you'll make when delivering bad news is whether to make your message more or less direct. For most bad-news messages, you'll ease into the bad news and allow the affected person to prepare for the potential shock. In less-direct messages,

Components of *Indirect* Bad-News Messages

• Ease in with a buffer.
• **Provide a rationale.**
• **Deliver the bad news.**
• Explain impacts.
• Focus on the future (as appropriate).
• Show goodwill.

Show concern.

TABLE 10.2

Types of Bad News and Richness of Communication Channels

Type of Bad News	Example	Written Only (Example: Email)	Verbal Not in Person (Example: Phone)	Verbal + Nonverbal Not in Person (Example: Video Call)	Verbal + Nonverbal in Person (Example: Meeting)	In Person + Written (Example: Meeting + Follow-up Memo)
Low Severity + High Controllability	Colleague's idea is rejected	*	*	*	*	*
Low Severity + Low Controllability	Customer claim is rejected (Figure 10.8)	*	*	*	*	*
Medium Severity + High Controllability	Vendor chooses another supplier (Figure 10.6)	*	✓	✓	✓	✓
Medium Severity + Low Controllability	Employees given fewer work hours (Figure 10.4)	✗	✗	✓	✓	✓
High Severity + High Controllability	Employee receives poor performance rating (Figure 10.10)	✗	✗	✗	✓	✓
High Severity + Low Controllability	Employee laid off	✗	✗	✗	✗	✓

✗ = rarely acceptable; * = depends on communication channel in use or preferred by bad-news recipient; ✓ = preferred.

you'll describe the rationale for the bad news first, whereas in more-direct messages, you'll give the bad news and then provide the rationale.

Sympathize with the Bad-News Recipient and Soften the Blow

When bad-news message recipients know you are concerned about them, they generally respond without antagonism and even appreciate your honesty. In person, most people make a judgment about your genuine concern for them based on many factors, including your past treatment of them and your nonverbal behavior. In writing, you are less able to use nonverbal behavior to show your sincere concern and appreciation.

For written messages, several techniques help the bad-news recipient prepare emotionally. First, using a neutral subject line often helps the reader recognize that the news will likely not be positive. However, since it is not direct (does not state the bad news), it allows the reader to momentarily adjust psychologically to accept the bad news.

Also, in some communications, you may use a one- or two-sentence buffer to start the bad-news message, which softens the blow. A **buffer** is a statement to establish common ground, show appreciation, state your sympathy, or otherwise express goodwill. Table 10.3 provides several examples, each of which is intended to draw connections between the message sender and message recipient and reduce the sudden emotional impact for the recipient.

When you show sympathy to your readers, you let them know you share their sorrow or trouble in some part. However, limit such expressions to one or two sentences, and make them sincere and professional. Avoid taking responsibility if you are not at fault. For example, the statement "We're sorry to hear about the crack in your countertop"

Components of *Direct* Bad-News Messages

- Ease in with a buffer.
- **Deliver the bad news.**
- **Provide a rationale.**
- Explain impacts.
- Focus on the future (as appropriate).
- Show goodwill.

Show concern.

TABLE 10.3

Buffers for Bad-News Messages

Type of Buffer	Example
Neutral statement	SUBJECT: Decision on Bid for Annual Contract with Marble Home Makeovers
Appreciation	Thank you for submitting your competitive bid to supply and deliver plastic resins for the upcoming year.
Sympathy	We're sorry to hear about the crack in your countertop.
Common ground	Reducing work hours creates unwanted financial challenges for our employees.
Compliment	Thank you for your excellent work, especially during this temporary period of cash flow challenges.

does not imply responsibility, whereas the statement "We're sorry that the countertop we installed has malfunctioned" may.

When delivering bad news, you may choose to use a form of buffer referred to as a **teaser message.** These messages, often written, signal to recipients that an upcoming conversation or other communication may involve unpleasant news. The teaser message prepares recipients emotionally yet does not reveal specific information. Neutral statements such as "I have some feedback to give you this afternoon" or "I'll share with you what our clients thought of your ideas" help employees prepare for news that may be partially negative.[11]

Deliver the Bad News
Throughout the delivery of bad news, find ways to express concern for recipients. By showing that you care, you may help them bear the news better and respond constructively. Generally, make the expression of concern brief, and stay attentive to the receiver's response. Be aware that excessive displays of concern may sound like a pity trip.

Get to the point fairly quickly—that is, express the bad news and explain the reasons for it clearly. Recipients of the bad news generally expect an explanation for why a decision was made. Stick to the facts so recipients will not try to fill in the blanks and come to the wrong conclusions. If you skirt around the bad news, your audience often views your efforts as evasive, thus weakening your credibility.[12]

In written bad-news messages, the neutral subject line and short buffer can soften the blow and show sympathy. However, make the buffer statement short, and, again, get to the bad news fairly quickly. You don't want readers to feel you are purposely downplaying or hiding the bad news by burying it within the message. You also don't want the readers to get their hopes up only to have them dashed later in the message. In these instances, bad-news recipients may even feel misled. If you find yourself writing an extremely indirect bad-news message, ask yourself whether you should instead meet in person or pick up the phone.

Provide a Clear Rationale and Specific Feedback
Recently, research about delivering bad news to customers in the financial industry has shown that when banks clearly explained the reasons for the bad-news decision, customers felt more trust toward the bank. In response to letters that offered little (i.e., "market conditions and maintaining profitability on your account") or no explanation, customers made comments such as the following: "This makes me feel like the bank wants to squeeze me for all they can. They're not interested in me as a loyal customer; I'm just a number to them." By contrast, customers who received full explanations in the letters were twice as likely to consider the organizations credible. They used statements such as the following: "They seemed honest and up-front. They were forthcoming and direct with their information, which is always good." Furthermore, the researchers showed

that clear, specific, and simple language built trust, whereas vague, general, and legal language created suspicion and anger.[13]

The most obvious and primary benefit of using simple and specific language is that recipients are more likely to interpret the information as honest and up-front. An additional reason to use simple and specific language is that bad-news recipients struggle to process information in bad-news situations. Since many recipients may experience strong emotions and begin thinking ahead about what the bad news means for them, they are less capable of processing complex information.

Explain Immediate Impacts

Once you've explained the bad news and the reasons for it, discuss the immediate impacts on recipients. In most situations, avoid moving directly to a discussion of what the bad news means for the company. Your focus should now be on the bad-news recipients, who will naturally be wondering, "What does this mean for me right now?"[14]

Resist the impulse to minimize the negative impact. By honestly describing the negative impacts, you address the foremost concern in the recipients' minds—themselves. If you skip this step, which many people prefer to do since it is not pleasant, you may lose the attention of the bad-news recipients for two reasons. First, they can't process other topics. They are fixated only on the potential impacts on themselves. Second, they may be annoyed if you move immediately to what you consider the silver lining, showing you are detached from their immediate needs.

Focus on Solutions and Long-Term Benefits

Most bad news is not permanent. In other words, it usually involves a temporary setback. So once you've described the immediate impacts on the recipients, move to a constructive, forward-looking approach. Where possible, describe realistic solutions, steps to overcoming the current problems, and/or the benefits that current sacrifices make possible. Ideally, you can describe solutions and benefits that the bad-news recipient can control.[15]

Focusing on solutions and long-term benefits should take a positive tone. However, be careful about the good news/bad news approach. The recipients of bad news may react negatively if they perceive that you are downplaying the impact of the bad news on them.[16]

Show Goodwill

Keeping the door open to working together constructively in the future should be one of your top priorities in nearly all cases. You may be demoting an employee from a current position today but promoting that same employee two or three years down the road. You may be denying the claim of a customer today but hoping for that customer's repeat business far into the future, and you're definitely trying to ensure that customer tells others that you are credible. You may say no to a supplier today but expect good terms on contracts from that same supplier in the future. It's not even uncommon for companies to ask laid-off employees to return to the company. In the process of delivering bad news, try not to burn bridges.

Getting the Tone, Style, and Design Right

When you discuss bad news with others, use your tone and nonverbal behaviors to show your interest and concern. Notice the recipient's nonverbal behavior as you deliver the news. Your ability to manage emotions—yours and others—during a bad-news discussion strongly influences your future working relationship. Research about providing feedback in performance reviews has shown that providing negative feedback with a positive tone actually makes employees feel more positive than when they receive positive feedback with a negative tone. In other words, the power of delivery often outweighs the content of your message in feedback situations.[17]

When you write your bad-news messages, carefully consider tone, style, and design. Aim for a *tone* of genuine concern in a professional manner. Also inject some positive direction to the message, but don't provide false hope or seem out of touch with the impacts on message recipients. Use a writing *style* that is simple, accurate, and jargon-free. Doing so helps people process information quickly and accurately. Since bad-news recipients may be experiencing strong emotions and allowing their thoughts to wander, they are less able to process information accurately. Therefore, use clear language that they will not misinterpret. Finally, maintain a simple *design.* If your message looks too slick, bad-news recipients may believe the message is designed more to impress than to meet their needs.

Delivering Bad News in Person to Clients

LO10.4 Compose effective bad-news messages in person and in writing for various audiences, including colleagues, external partners, and customers.

In any business, you develop close working relationships with clients over time. You become aware of their needs and hopes. In many cases, you've had to struggle to gain their business and you're constantly working to keep them satisfied with your products and services. Providing bad news to these clients is stressful, since you do not want to let them down, and you know that your success depends on their business.

In the first situation from the chapter case, Cindy Cooper needs to inform Juan Hernandez that the bank will reduce the credit line to his business by between 50 and 75 percent within a few months. Since Marble Home Makeovers is currently in a poor cash position, this new policy is serious and could be viewed as medium severity. Since the bank has some flexibility in establishing the new credit line terms (reduction of between 50 and 75 percent within 60 to 90 days), Juan may be able to negotiate the best possible terms. Therefore, he does have some control. In Cindy's less-effective approach (see Figure 10.1), she writes an email message, which is not as rich and personal as required based on the severity of this situation. In the more-effective delivery (see Figure 10.2), Cindy calls Juan, meets with him, and follows principles for delivering bad news effectively.

FIGURE 10.1

Less-Effective Delivery of Bad News to a Client

To...	Juan Hernandez
Subject:	Lower Credit Line Effective in 60 Days

| Arial | 10 | **B** *I* <u>U</u> |

Dear Mr. Hernandez:

Effective in 60 days from now, the outstanding credit line for Marble Home Makeovers will be reduced to $30,000. Your current outstanding balance of $94,345 far exceeds this new limit. We will move to collect if you are unable to meet these new requirements.

As you know, recent economic situations have resulted in changes in regulation standards as well as banks taking a closer look at the risk they bear. Accordingly, it has been deemed important to adjust our outstanding loans so that we bear an acceptable level of risk. In exhaustively examining our small-business loans and credit lines, it was determined that our credit lines should be lowered to achieve a more acceptable risk level. Due to the fact that we have deemed your credit line excessively risky, this adjustment is necessary.

Please call if you have any questions about the new credit line limits. I will be happy to help in any way.

Given the long-term working relationship between Cindy and Juan, this written message is impersonal. Furthermore, the message contains unnecessarily complex language.

Cindy Cooper

FIGURE 10.2

More-Effective Delivery of Bad News to a Client

Cindy was tired of telling her small-business clients the disappointing news that their credit lines would soon be severely reduced. She sighed and called the next person on her list: "Juan, the bank is making some adjustments to small-business credit lines. I'd like to meet in person as soon as possible to explain what this means for your business." Juan replied, "I can stop by this afternoon since I'm in town today." Having worked with Juan for over five years, she knew meeting the bank's demands would be challenging for his business.

> Phone call with a somewhat urgent but neutral tone serves as a BUFFER and allows Juan to prepare emotionally.

- [Later at the bank] -

Cindy: Juan, thanks for stopping by on such short notice. The bank is making some major changes to the terms of our small-business credit lines, and I wanted to let you know about these changes right away. Because of so many recent bank failures around the country, we requested an audit to help us evaluate our situation. The audit results showed that we hold far too much debt, and we're putting several policies into place to place the bank in a safer financial position. These policies will impact your business, so I wanted to explain the new terms and discuss how we can work together in meeting them.

> Provides RATIONALE for changes in credit line terms.

Juan: This sounds serious. What are the changes?

Cindy: For most small-business credit lines, including yours, we're reducing the credit line by between 50 and 75 percent. We expect to make the policy effective in between 60 and 90 days, and the bank will move to collect on outstanding credit above the new limits. Today, I'd like to discuss ways to lower your outstanding credit so that you'll remain on good terms once the new policy goes into place.

> Delivers the BAD NEWS.

Juan: Well, Cindy, this comes as quite a surprise. This will put tremendous strain on our business. Exactly how much do we need to pay back and in what time frame?

Cindy: In your case, you're currently using nearly $94,000 of your $100,000 credit line. We will cut the credit line to between $30,000 and $50,000 in 60 to 90 days. Based on our conversation today, including your ideas for reducing your outstanding balance, I'll make a determination this afternoon. What are your projections for cash flow over the next three to six months? What can you do to improve your cash situation rapidly?

> Explains IMMEDIATE IMPACTS.

Juan: We are facing some challenging cash constraints, but the long-term position looks strong. We've expanded during the past two years from a regional market to a national one. Our revenue has grown by 400 percent in just one year, and we've increased the number of employees from 15 to 50 in a year and a half. With all this growth, we've moved into a new building and invested heavily in new equipment and facility improvements.

We currently have five bids on several large projects. I expect us to get at least two of these. If we receive any of the five bids, we could immediately pay back the credit line.

Cindy: What if you do not receive any of the bids?

> Adopts a listening orientation.

Juan: In that case, our only option would be to lay off employees or reduce work hours. We do currently hold some excess inventory. We could temporarily reduce work hours and thus lower payroll expenses by relying on this inventory. . .

> Focuses on the FUTURE and shows GOODWILL.

[After continued discussion, Cindy decides to cut the credit line to $50,000 in 90 days since Juan has agreed to temporarily reduce payroll expenses. The employees will not be happy about this change.]

Delivering Bad News in Writing to Colleagues

One characteristic of high-performing organizations is that employees volunteer information with one another, even when it is bad news. In many organizations, however, employees are reluctant to share bad news. They do not want to disappoint others, and they do not want to be blamed. When many employees in an organization avoid sharing bad news, the result is the mum effect. The **mum effect** occurs when the chain of messages within an organization is filtered at each level to leave out or inaccurately state the bad news. The message that top executives often hear ends up being unrealistically rosy.

One tragic example of the mum effect is the 1986 space shuttle explosion. During the investigation, Nobel laureate Richard Feynman found that engineers had predicted the probability of a main engine failure at between 1 in 200 and 1 in 300. Top decision makers at the National Aeronautics and Space Administration (NASA), however, had been informed by reports that had progressively gotten more positive through several layers of bureaucracy, and they had thus believed the probability of main engine failure was closer to 1 in 100,000. While the shuttle disaster is an extreme example, businesses repeatedly underperform and even fail on projects due to the mum effect.[18]

When most employees deliver bad news and negative feedback to one another in open, honest, caring, and rich environments, organizations tend to exhibit higher morale. On the other hand, when most employees do not share bad news or do so impersonally, organizations tend to exhibit lower morale. In practice, many companies have cultures of delivering bad news impersonally. In a survey of 292 employees, only 37 percent stated that the primary means of delivering bad news in their companies was face-to-face meetings. The other primary means of bad-news delivery were emails (29 percent), letters and memos (12 percent), internal employee websites (8 percent), teleconferences or videoconferences (6 percent), and company newsletters (3.5 percent).[19]

McGraw Wentworth, a consulting firm, recently issued a report about delivering bad news during the Great Recession. The report explained, "Using an impersonal e-mail format to deliver bad news is very poor business form. Your employees will feel your organization has no respect for them. They will not forget the callous way they received bad news and when the economy turns around, they may be the first people looking for new opportunities."[20]

In all management positions, you will need to give bad news to your boss, your peers, or those you supervise from time to time. Your ability to deliver bad-news messages constructively will foster a transparent and open work culture. As appropriate, internal bad-news messages should show appreciation for the efforts of employees and look to the future.

In Juan's case, he is delivering news to the production workers that the company needs to reduce their hours for three months. He broke the news first in a rich environment—a meeting. Next, he is writing a follow-up to provide complete details and serve as a reference to employees. In the less-effective example (see Figure 10.3), Juan leaves out a buffer and focuses primarily on the needs of the company. This approach will anger many employees and reduce company loyalty. In the more-effective example (see Figure 10.4), Juan focuses on the employees—their needs and concerns. He does not sugarcoat the news. He clearly describes the reasons for reducing work hours. He also clearly explains the likely negative impacts (specific ranges of loss in income). Many employees will likely respect him for his openness and honesty. Juan concludes the message with forward-looking and positive thoughts about opportunities for the employees. This is appropriate as long as Juan can deliver on these promises.

FIGURE 10.3

Less-Effective Bad-News Message to Employees

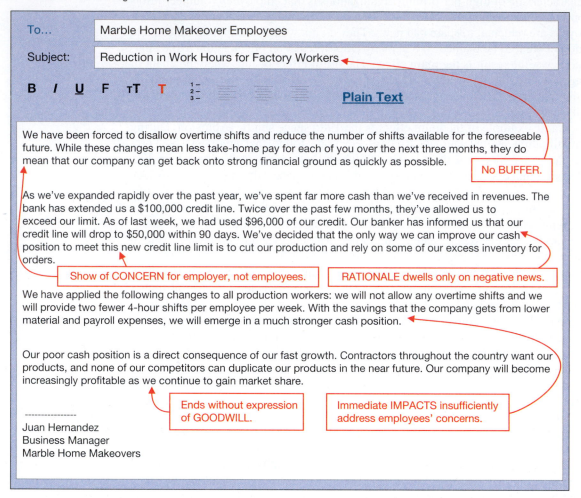

To...   Marble Home Makeover Employees

Subject: Reduction in Work Hours for Factory Workers

B *I* U F ᴛT T   1 – 2 – 3 –   **Plain Text**

We have been forced to disallow overtime shifts and reduce the number of shifts available for the foreseeable future. While these changes mean less take-home pay for each of you over the next three months, they do mean that our company can get back onto strong financial ground as quickly as possible.   `No BUFFER.`

As we've expanded rapidly over the past year, we've spent far more cash than we've received in revenues. The bank has extended us a $100,000 credit line. Twice over the past few months, they've allowed us to exceed our limit. As of last week, we had used $96,000 of our credit. Our banker has informed us that our credit line will drop to $50,000 within 90 days. We've decided that the only way we can improve our cash position to meet this new credit line limit is to cut our production and rely on some of our excess inventory for orders.

`Show of CONCERN for employer, not employees.`   `RATIONALE dwells only on negative news.`

We have applied the following changes to all production workers: we will not allow any overtime shifts and we will provide two fewer 4-hour shifts per employee per week. With the savings that the company gets from lower material and payroll expenses, we will emerge in a much stronger cash position.

Our poor cash position is a direct consequence of our fast growth. Contractors throughout the country want our products, and none of our competitors can duplicate our products in the near future. Our company will become increasingly profitable as we continue to gain market share.

`Ends without expression of GOODWILL.`   `Immediate IMPACTS insufficiently address employees' concerns.`

Juan Hernandez
Business Manager
Marble Home Makeovers

Delivering Bad News in Writing to External Partners

In most business positions, you will work extensively with external partners. External partners can include suppliers, consultants, or joint-venture partners. These are people you interact with often over extended periods. You will often have deep working relationships with them. Most often, you are better off breaking bad news to them in a rich communication channel—that is, in person or by phone. Writing makes sense, however, when you are providing a formal notice (i.e., rejecting a bid or proposal), when the bad news is not severe, or when your audience prefers corresponding in written form. When you break bad news in writing, you will generally follow up with a phone call or visit.

Juan has purchased extensively from Nick Jensen over the years, so rejecting his bid is not easy. In the less-effective example (see Figure 10.5), Juan does not provide useful feedback and does not indicate any interest in future work together. In other words, Juan has directed the message away from any business interest of Nick's. Nick may decode Juan's excessively personal display of concern (thanking him for

FIGURE 10.4

More-Effective Bad-News Message to Employees

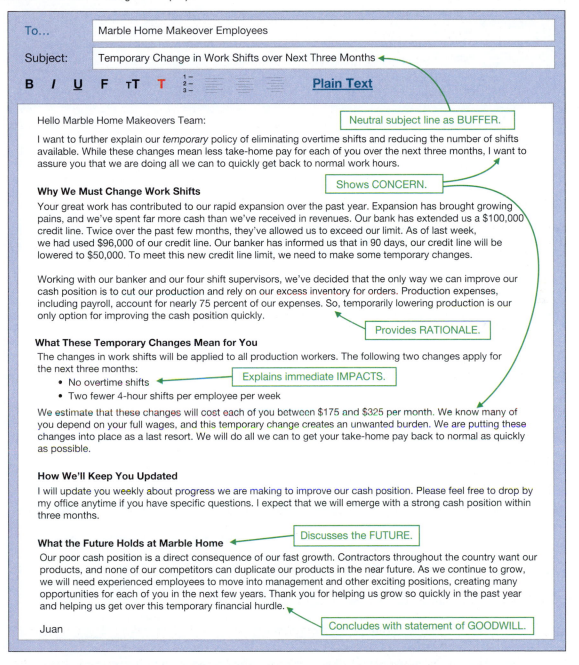

To... Marble Home Makeover Employees

Subject: Temporary Change in Work Shifts over Next Three Months ← Neutral subject line as BUFFER.

B *I* U F ᴛT T 1—2—3— Plain Text

Hello Marble Home Makeovers Team:

I want to further explain our *temporary* policy of eliminating overtime shifts and reducing the number of shifts available. While these changes mean less take-home pay for each of you over the next three months, I want to assure you that we are doing all we can to quickly get back to normal work hours.

Shows CONCERN.

Why We Must Change Work Shifts

Your great work has contributed to our rapid expansion over the past year. Expansion has brought growing pains, and we've spent far more cash than we've received in revenues. Our bank has extended us a $100,000 credit line. Twice over the past few months, they've allowed us to exceed our limit. As of last week, we had used $96,000 of our credit line. Our banker has informed us that in 90 days, our credit line will be lowered to $50,000. To meet this new credit line limit, we need to make some temporary changes.

Working with our banker and our four shift supervisors, we've decided that the only way we can improve our cash position is to cut our production and rely on our excess inventory for orders. Production expenses, including payroll, account for nearly 75 percent of our expenses. So, temporarily lowering production is our only option for improving the cash position quickly.

Provides RATIONALE.

What These Temporary Changes Mean for You

The changes in work shifts will be applied to all production workers. The following two changes apply for the next three months:

- No overtime shifts ← Explains immediate IMPACTS.
- Two fewer 4-hour shifts per employee per week

We estimate that these changes will cost each of you between $175 and $325 per month. We know many of you depend on your full wages, and this temporary change creates an unwanted burden. We are putting these changes into place as a last resort. We will do all we can to get your take-home pay back to normal as quickly as possible.

How We'll Keep You Updated

I will update you weekly about progress we are making to improve our cash position. Please feel free to drop by my office anytime if you have specific questions. I expect that we will emerge with a strong cash position within three months.

What the Future Holds at Marble Home ← Discusses the FUTURE.

Our poor cash position is a direct consequence of our fast growth. Contractors throughout the country want our products, and none of our competitors can duplicate our products in the near future. As we continue to grow, we will need experienced employees to move into management and other exciting positions, creating many opportunities for each of you in the next few years. Thank you for helping us grow so quickly in the past year and helping us get over this temporary financial hurdle.

Juan

Concludes with statement of GOODWILL.

being such a great friend and asking him out to lunch) as a less-than-straightforward way of saying no and an end to a working relationship. In the more-effective example (see Figure 10.6), Juan keeps it short, but he accomplishes the basic goals of a bad-news message. He expresses goodwill, explains why Marble Home chose another supplier, and leaves the door open to future business. Providing the rationale for this decision is helpful to Nick. It gives him an opportunity to improve the competitiveness of his company by focusing on these weaknesses. This professional

FIGURE 10.5

Less-Effective Bad-News Message to a Supplier

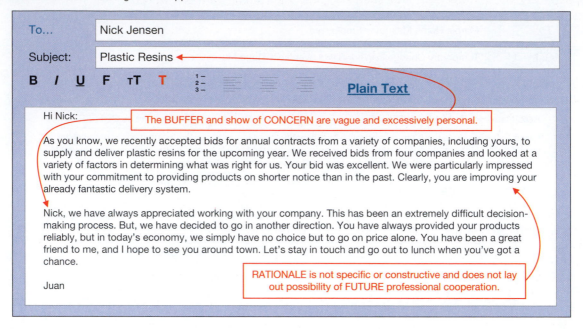

FIGURE 10.6

More-Effective Bad-News Message to a Supplier

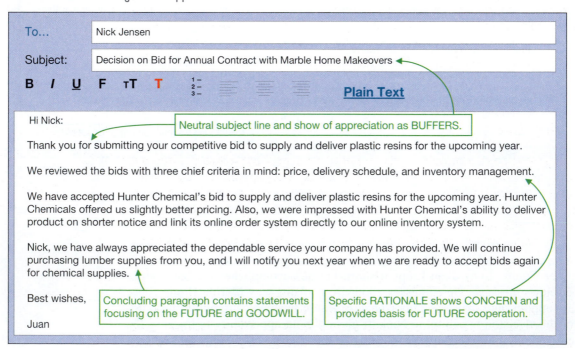

courtesy is not always appropriate or necessary. You'll be able to make this judgment based on the corporate culture where you work. Although Juan and Nick generally correspond by email, a follow-up phone call from Juan could strengthen their working relationship.

Delivering Bad News in Writing to Customers

In many positions, you will have direct contact with customers. You have probably already worked in jobs where you interacted extensively with customers and likely had to deliver bad news. You certainly have been an angry customer who has received bad news, so you can relate! Bad-news messages to customers contain the same essential components as other bad-news messages. However, when writing this kind of bad-news message, you want to emphasize the options available—solutions the customer has control over. In most bad-news situations, customers are interested only in solutions. They do not want long descriptions of why you can't meet their demands. Also, they do not want to be blamed for anything. Even when customers are at fault, use neutral language (avoid you-voice and use passive verbs) to point out mistakes.

Juan is in a situation with a customer who has made an unreasonable claim, so he is not going to replace the product or provide a refund. You will often encounter similar situations. In the less-effective example (see Figure 10.7), Juan unnecessarily blames the customer. Because he uses you-voice ("since you did not purchase the countertop with a warranty, you will not receive a refund"), the tone is accusatory and even confrontational. Furthermore, the message is not helpful enough. It offers some hastily written, vague advice. The customer will likely decode this response as uncaring.

In the more-effective message (see Figure 10.8), Juan provides both a buffer and expression of sympathy in the first sentence. Although Juan denies the claim, he provides thorough, detailed options for helping this customer. Most customers would be delighted with this level of responsiveness. This message expresses goodwill. In every part of the letter, the attention to detail and expressed hope to get the countertop fixed show goodwill.

In jobs where you interact often with customers, you are unlikely to have enough time to write an original bad-news message like Juan's to each customer. However, you probably face three or four broad types of complaints. By using templates with common explanations and solutions, you can quickly tailor a message to individual situations. For example, Juan could create a template that contained two options—one for customers who might fix the products themselves and the other for customers who might want a service visit. Then he could rapidly modify various details for the individual situation.

Delivering and Receiving Negative Performance Reviews

LO10.5 Deliver and receive negative performance reviews constructively.

Nearly all professionals engage in regular performance appraisals; sometimes they are appraising others, and sometimes they are themselves being appraised. Face-to-face reviews are often among the most stressful experiences for employees and sometimes for managers. These situations are particularly stressful when the manager must deliver negative performance reviews.[21] In this section, we will first consider the appraisal from the manager's point of view and then turn to the employee who is being appraised.

Delivering Negative Feedback

In most performance appraisals, you are evaluating excellent or good performers. In these cases, you should focus on an overall positive message. When evaluating poor performers, however, you should be clear about the need for improvement. You can

FIGURE 10.7

Less-Effective Bad-News Message to a Customer

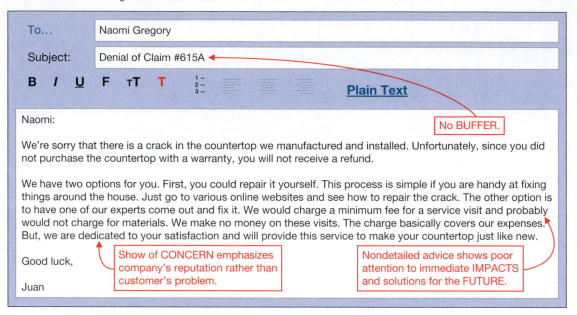

generally apply the principles we have discussed earlier in the chapter regarding delivering bad news. In addition, keep the following in mind:[22]

- *Adopt a team-centered orientation.* Even when you are evaluating a poor performer, maintain a mentality that you are working together as a team. Maintain a constructive, forward-looking tone.

- *Avoid sugarcoating the bad news.* Make sure the poor performer realizes she/he must improve (see the upcoming feedback section).

- *Explain the impacts of the individual's poor performance on organizational performance.* One major goal of performance appraisals is to help poor performers understand how they are hurting organizational performance.

- *Link to consequences.* Another major goal of performance appraisals is to help employees understand how poor performance impacts their employment opportunities at the organization as well as their ability to meet their career goals.

- *Probe for reasons performance is not higher.* Ask employees to discuss their perspectives on their poor performance. Often, you will identify root causes of poor performance that will help the employee improve rapidly. You may even uncover issues that impact the organization more broadly.

- *Emphasize problem solving rather than blaming.* As much as possible, adopt a positive, forward-looking tone. You are seeking solutions that help the poor performer improve. This is good for the poor performer's career, work relationships, and morale.

- *Be firm.* Many managers want to shrink from delivering negative feedback, especially when poor performers are defensive. Remain firm that the employee must improve.

You will undoubtedly need to deliver negative performance reviews from time to time. Your overall approach to these conversations and your choice of words are important in determining how useful the reviews are. Thus, use statements that offer clear and

FIGURE 10.8

More-Effective Bad-News Message to a Customer

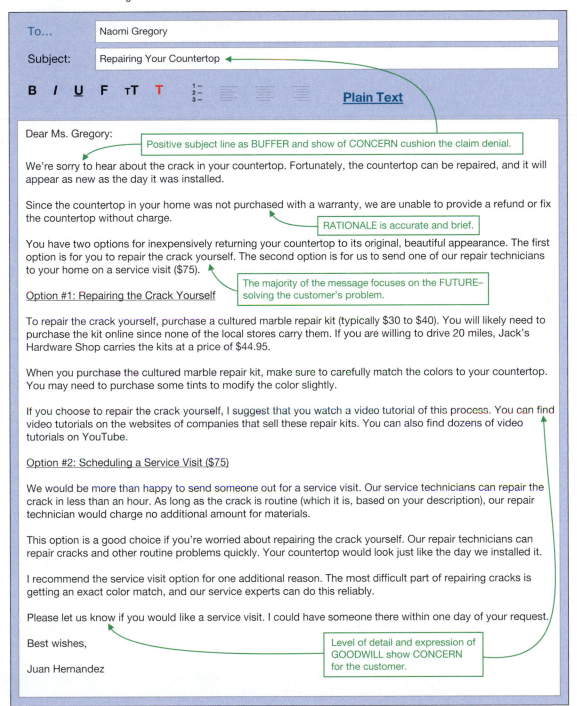

To... Naomi Gregory

Subject: Repairing Your Countertop

B *I* <u>U</u> F ᴛT **T** 1— 2— 3— **Plain Text**

Dear Ms. Gregory:

> Positive subject line as BUFFER and show of CONCERN cushion the claim denial.

We're sorry to hear about the crack in your countertop. Fortunately, the countertop can be repaired, and it will appear as new as the day it was installed.

Since the countertop in your home was not purchased with a warranty, we are unable to provide a refund or fix the countertop without charge.

> RATIONALE is accurate and brief.

You have two options for inexpensively returning your countertop to its original, beautiful appearance. The first option is for you to repair the crack yourself. The second option is for us to send one of our repair technicians to your home on a service visit ($75).

> The majority of the message focuses on the FUTURE–solving the customer's problem.

Option #1: Repairing the Crack Yourself

To repair the crack yourself, purchase a cultured marble repair kit (typically $30 to $40). You will likely need to purchase the kit online since none of the local stores carry them. If you are willing to drive 20 miles, Jack's Hardware Shop carries the kits at a price of $44.95.

When you purchase the cultured marble repair kit, make sure to carefully match the colors to your countertop. You may need to purchase some tints to modify the color slightly.

If you choose to repair the crack yourself, I suggest that you watch a video tutorial of this process. You can find video tutorials on the websites of companies that sell these repair kits. You can also find dozens of video tutorials on YouTube.

Option #2: Scheduling a Service Visit ($75)

We would be more than happy to send someone out for a service visit. Our service technicians can repair the crack in less than an hour. As long as the crack is routine (which it is, based on your description), our repair technician would charge no additional amount for materials.

This option is a good choice if you're worried about repairing the crack yourself. Our repair technicians can repair cracks and other routine problems quickly. Your countertop would look just like the day we installed it.

I recommend the service visit option for one additional reason. The most difficult part of repairing cracks is getting an exact color match, and our service experts can do this reliably.

Please let us know if you would like a service visit. I could have someone there within one day of your request.

Best wishes,

Juan Hernandez

> Level of detail and expression of GOODWILL show CONCERN for the customer.

targeted feedback, focus on actions and results rather than attitudes and intentions, and establish measurable and realistic expectations.

In the final situation from the opening case, Juan needs to give a negative performance evaluation to Jake, one of the shift supervisors. Juan does not want to harm his working relationship with Jake, and he's nervous about how Jake will react. In the next few pages, you'll find Juan's less-effective and more-effective approaches to

TABLE 10.4

Giving Clear and Targeted Feedback

Less Effective	More Effective
Juan: Jake, as usual, I'd like to thank you for how supportive you are of the employees. You really boost morale around here more than anyone else. . . . One thing I want to raise for the review is that on several of your shipments, our customers have complained. I think we should talk about how to avoid shipments that contain any items with defects. . . . Well, again, thank you for your efforts for the company and all your great work. See you later on for lunch.	*Juan:* Jake, for today's performance review, I want to focus on one issue: making sure all your shipments contain the correct items and that they are all defect-free . . . [spends most of time discussing how to improve in this area].
This sandwich approach to bad news (compliment–bad news–niceties) combined with Juan's roundabout language dilute the primary message that Jake needs to improve his performance. Juan may inadvertently send the signal that Jake's performance is not poor or that his mistakes are relatively insignificant.	This approach is clear and targeted. Jake will recognize the importance of improving in this area.

talking to Jake. You'll also find abbreviated versions of the performance appraisal in Figures 10.9 and 10.10.

Giving Clear and Targeted Feedback When providing feedback for poor performance, many managers want to soften the bad reviews so they employ the sandwich approach of good news–bad news–good news (compliment–negative feedback–niceties). However, the sandwich approach may inadvertently encourage poor performers. Instead, the review should emphasize the bad news so employees know how important it is for them to improve (see Table 10.4 for less-effective and more-effective examples of giving clear and targeted feedback).

Focusing on Actions and Results, Not Attitudes and Intentions Provide feedback only on that which is observable. You can accurately observe actions and results; however, you can never know the thoughts and feelings of others with certainty. Furthermore, if you focus on attitudes and intentions, you are far more likely to be perceived as judgmental and provoke defensiveness (see the less-effective and more-effective examples in Table 10.5).

Establish Measurable and Realistic Expectations Negative performance reviews without measurable and realistic goals may demoralize employees. Employees who receive negative reviews generally want a clear path to regaining positive ratings; they want to be on good terms with their supervisors, and they usually take pride in doing well. Make sure to discuss how they can improve performance in

TABLE 10.5

Focusing on Actions and Results, Not Attitudes and Intentions

Less Effective	More Effective
Juan: Jake, we've gotten a number of complaints from wholesalers that your shipments are not correct. I think this shows that you've been careless, and you're not really looking out for our customers. None of the other shift supervisors have had these problems—only you.	*Juan:* Jake, we have received four complaints about your shipments in the past month. In the most serious complaint, your shipment to Carnegie Homebuilders contained 14 sinks of the wrong size. The invoice you placed in the shipment did show the correct order, however. In addition, four of the sinks you shipped were cracked or chipped.
This critique focuses exclusively on characteristics of Jake— carelessness and inattentiveness.	This critique focuses on Jake's actions and the results of those actions. These comments are less likely to provoke defensiveness or a counterproductive response from Jake.

TABLE 10.6

Establishing Measurable Expectations

Less Effective	More Effective
Juan: Jake, we need to really focus on getting everything right from now on. I know you and your crew will do great and turn things around for our next performance review.	*Juan:* Jake, in our next quarterly performance review, we'll discuss how well you've done with your shipments. The standard will be to receive no complaints from customers for incorrect orders or for deficient products. Also, we'll discuss your progress on the goals you've outlined for managing your production crew. Thanks, Jake, for your ideas today, and I look forward to discussing your progress during the next few weeks and months.
This closing statement is vague. Jake does not know the standard by which Juan will evaluate him for the next performance review.	This closing statement is specific and measurable. Jake knows the standards by which Juan will evaluate him for the next performance review.

specific ways. You might even set up a development plan that includes action steps, timelines, specific goals, training, and resources needed. By setting clear expectations for improvement, you lay the groundwork for accountability later on (see Table 10.6 for less-effective and more-effective examples).

Increasingly, companies provide options for all or part of performance reviews to be conducted online. Typically, these online reviews allow you to give more frequent feedback to your employees. Read the Technology Tips section on page 292 for guidelines on delivering feedback with these systems.

Receiving Negative Feedback

In nearly all business positions, from entry-level to executive, you will have many opportunities to get feedback about your performance and potential. Seeking and receiving feedback, even when it's negative, will help you develop the skills you need to make an impact in the workplace and move into new positions. To accept negative feedback and respond to it well requires high emotional intelligence, since you may feel many emotions, including fear, anxiety, and perhaps even anger. To avoid counterproductive responses to negative emotions, learn to recognize and name these emotions. Then develop a reframing statement to respond more effectively. See Table 10.7 for ideas about reframing statements.[23]

TABLE 10.7

Reframing Your Thoughts to Initiate Feedback Conversations

Possible Negative Emotion	Counterproductive Response	Reframing Statement
Anger (*I'm mad at my boss because she doesn't pay attention to my work.*)	Acting out (complaining, showing irritability)	It's my responsibility to get feedback and guidance from my boss.
Anxiety (*I don't know what to expect.*)	Avoiding (*I'm too busy to get feedback.*)	Getting feedback can provide me with opportunities.
Defensiveness (*My boss doesn't know what he's talking about.*)	Not supporting the boss (*I'm not going to make him look good.*)	Being defensive prevents me from knowing what he thinks.
Fear of Reprisal (*I don't want to do this.*)	Denial (*I'm doing fine so I don't need feedback.*)	Getting an honest assessment of my work will help me.
Fear of Personal Rejection (*I'm worried she doesn't like me.*)	Withdrawal (being quieter than usual, feeling demotivated)	My performance on the job isn't related to whether she likes me.

FIGURE 10.9

Less-Effective Delivery of Bad News during a Performance Review

Juan: Jake, did you watch last night's game?
Jake: Yeah, that was awesome . . . [talk about sports for several minutes].

Juan: Well, let's get down to business. I'd like to thank you for how supportive you are of the employees. You really boost morale around here more so than anyone else . . . [continues talking about accomplishments and strengths for ten minutes].

Juan: One issue I want to raise for the review is that our customers have complained about several of your shipments. I think we should talk about how to avoid shipments that contain any items with defects.

Jake: I'll try to make sure that we don't have any mistakes on future orders. The other shift supervisors and I have talked about some ways of avoiding any future problems.

Juan: Jake, none of the other shift supervisors have had these problems—only you. I think this shows that you've been careless, and you're not really looking out for our customers.

Jake: Look, I'm sorry that there were some mistakes. But I'm not the one who packs the shipments. Those who are careless are the employees packing the shipments.

Juan: But, Jake, you're the one responsible for inspecting and approving the shipments, not the employees on your shift. Remember, every time our shipments have mistakes, it comes back on me. I have to take the fall for it with our owner. And I'm the one who has to hear the complaints from our customers.

Jake: OK, well, I'll make sure the employees on my shift are more careful.

Juan: We need to really focus on getting everything right from now on. I'm counting on you. Well, again, thank you for your efforts for the company and all your great work. See you later on for lunch.

The sandwich approach to delivering bad news dilutes the message and gives Jake a false sense that his performance is acceptable. Feedback and expectations are vague.

Juan encodes: I value you as an employee.

Jake decodes: Juan values my positive impact here.

Juan encodes: You have performed poorly with shipments. I want you to improve.

Jake decodes: Juan is making a blanket judgment by calling me *careless*. He is overlooking all the good work I do.

Jake encodes: You need to hold everyone responsible.

Juan decodes: Jake is making excuses and blaming others.

Juan encodes: You are the supervisor; you are responsible.

Jake decodes: Juan wants me to spend my time micromanaging my employees. And, he just cares about making himself look good.

Jake encodes: OK, I'll watch out for problems.

Juan decodes: Good, Jake's gotten the message he needs to improve.

Juan encodes: Now that you know my position, let's go to lunch.

Jake decodes: Great. Juan is generally happy with me and my performance.

FIGURE 10.10

More-Effective Delivery of Bad News during a Performance Review

Juan: Jake, for today's performance review, I want to focus most of our attention on one issue: making sure all your shipments contain the correct items and that they are all defect-free. We have received four complaints about your shipments in the past month. In the most serious complaint, your shipment to Carnegie Homebuilders contained 14 sinks of the wrong size. Four of those sinks were cracked or chipped. What do you think are some of the reasons for the incorrect shipments and the defective items?

Jake: I rely on my crew to produce defect-free items and pack the shipments. As a result, I don't actually see every shipment that goes out. Since I don't micromanage, I believe that my approach shows trust in the employees. Even though we have made a few mistakes, overall I think the working climate results in higher overall productivity.

Juan: I appreciate your focus on the employees, and I do think morale is high in your production crew. Ultimately, you bear responsibility for their performance, so I would like to discuss how to avoid costly shipment mistakes. The problems with the shipment to Carnegie Homebuilders cost us approximately $5,000 due to material and labor costs. I'm also concerned that they'll be less likely to choose us in the future. What are some ways you can manage your crew to avoid shipment mistakes in the future?

[Jake and Juan discuss approaches to managing the crew and improving quality for 30 minutes.]

Juan: Jake, for this quarter, I've given you an overall performance rating of 2, which indicates poor performance. This means that in the short term you're unlikely to receive a promotion or bonus. However, I'm confident in your ability and that of your crew to get all shipments correct . . . [Jake and Juan continue discussing the rating].

Juan: In our next quarterly performance review, we'll discuss how well you've done with your shipments. The standard will be to receive no complaints from customers for incorrect orders or deficient products. Also, we'll discuss your progress on the goals you've outlined for managing your production crew. Thanks, Jake, for your ideas today, and I look forward to discussing your progress during the next few weeks and months.

Jake realizes the severity of his poor performance. Juan's open, clear, specific, and problem-solving approach is not threatening and shows his commitment to supporting Jake's improvement efforts.

Juan encodes: I want to focus on your ability to get shipments correct.

Jake decodes: Juan is serious that I need to improve my shipments.

Jake encodes: My management style may cause some problems, but it also results in higher morale and productivity.

Juan decodes: Jake is not taking responsibility for the mistakes.

Juan encodes: Your management style has many benefits. It's still your responsibility to make sure shipments are correct. Incorrect shipments harm the company. Let's discuss ways to manage employees and avoid mistakes.

Jake decodes: Juan is looking out for the best interests of the organization.

Juan encodes: Your overall performance was poor for this quarter. I want you and your crew to succeed.

Jake decodes: I need to avoid any mistakes on shipments if I'm going to get promoted. Jake will support me if I show positive results.

Juan encodes: This is exactly how we will evaluate your performance.

Jake decodes: I know what Juan wants me to do.

TECHNOLOGY TIPS

PROVIDING PERFORMANCE FEEDBACK WITH APPRAISAL SOFTWARE

Most companies require performance reviews—some monthly, some quarterly, some annually—for all employees. Some innovative companies are now doing real-time performance reviews with social software. The social software allows supervisors and their employees to more regularly and interactively review employee performance. When you are in a supervisory position, you will be responsible for providing both positive and negative feedback to employees. Increasingly, you will provide this feedback with the use of appraisal software of some form.

As you provide feedback in online appraisal systems, keep in mind the following tips:

Provide regular and frequent feedback. One major benefit of appraisal software, particularly platforms that include social software, is that you can efficiently give your employees more feedback so they can increase performance. Establishing a regular pattern of feedback can increase your employees' motivation and performance.

Prepare your feedback carefully. Most appraisal software allows you to directly enter your comments into fields in a database. Once you enter the information, it is available to the employees and other managers. So, prepare your comments carefully. Consider drafting your comments in a word processing program first. If you're delivering negative feedback, you may first want to draft the feedback, wait a few hours or a few days, and then review your comments to ensure they are accurate and productive. Also, if you are giving negative feedback, first notify your employee in person. Use the moment to establish goals for improvement. Avoid blindsiding your employees by entering negative feedback in the performance database without first talking to them about it.

Keep your feedback objective and personal. Some employees feel that receiving feedback via appraisal software is too automated and impersonal. This is especially likely when the software is mostly composed of quantifiable and standard metrics that are used for all employees. These metrics do help provide consistency in feedback across the organization, but they lead some employees to "feel like a number." However your company's evaluation software is set up, find ways to provide more nuanced and open-ended feedback to recognize your employees' unique achievements. Make sure to include a shared, open-ended, goal-oriented, and positive discussion that keeps your employees motivated and productive.

Set up a face-to-face meeting as soon as possible if you detect hard feelings. Even in a social software environment that allows more interaction than do Web 1.0 communication tools, some employees may become discouraged with negative feedback or feel that feedback is not fair. Stay alert to such situations. When you notice this, set up a time to meet in person so that you can use a richer communication channel to reestablish rapport and reenergize your employees to focus on work goals.

Reviewing Bad-News Messages

LO10.6 Review bad-news messages for effectiveness and fairness.

The reviewing stage of bad-news messages is extremely important. Bad news involves unpleasant impacts on others, so you should carefully consider whether you are handling the situation appropriately. Also, since recipients can easily take bad news the wrong way and feel disappointed or angry, make sure to review your written and oral messages carefully so you can deliver the news respectfully.

Get Feedback and Reread

When writing bad-news messages, always reread them several times. Place yourself in the position of the recipients so you can try to imagine how they may feel and react. An extra 10 to 30 minutes of proofreading can lead to constructive work together in the future and avoid time lost resolving an unnecessarily escalated difference. Also, if the message does not need to be delivered immediately, consider writing it, waiting a few hours or days, and then rereading it. Often, you will find that your strong emotions, such as anxiety and nervousness, affected the tone of the original message. When you deliver a bad-news message in person, you have less control. Yet, you can still prepare

FIGURE 10.11

Are Your Bad-News Messages FAIR?

Facts (How *factual* is your communication?)

- Have I gathered all the relevant facts? Have I examined various accounts of the same events?
- Is my perspective of the facts influenced by defensiveness, favoritism, or some other bias?
- Is the rationale for this bad news based on sound facts and conclusions?

Access (How *accessible* or *transparent* are your motives, reasoning, and information?)

- Are my motives clear, or will others perceive that I have a hidden agenda?
- Is it clear how the decision was made?
- Am I giving enough information to bad-news recipients for them to respond well?
- Am I hiding any information that casts me in a better light or concealing the real reasons for the bad news?

Impacts (How does your communication *impact* stakeholders?)

- Have I considered all the ways in which this message will impact others in the near term and long term?
- What have I done to lessen the negative impacts on recipients?
- Am I doing what I can to provide opportunities—as appropriate—to the bad-news recipients?

Respect (How *respectful* is your communication?)

- Would recipients consider my communication respectful?
- Have I stated the message in a way that recognizes the inherent worth of others?

---

your intended message (mentally or in note form) and review it as you would a written bad-news message.

In some situations, consider asking trusted colleagues to review your message and give feedback. They may be able to give you a neutral and objective view of the situation. Generally, it is appropriate to talk to colleagues about bad-news messages that you plan to deliver to groups of customers or employees. However, it is not appropriate to ask others to read messages that include confidential matters. For example, negative feedback for an individual employee should typically be private.

Applying the FAIR Test

For all bad news, spend time reflecting on each component of the FAIR test before delivering the message. Since bad-news messages impact others in undesirable ways, take the time to make sure you have been as fair as possible. Read through some of the questions you might ask yourself in Figure 10.11. Also, consider the thoughts of James Sloan, the business professional featured in the Communication Q&A.

COMMUNICATION Q&A

CONVERSATIONS WITH CURRENT BUSINESS PROFESSIONALS

Pete Cardon: How often do you have to give bad news to others? What types of bad news?

James Sloan: Unfortunately, as the CFO, I often have to give bad news. The bad news I typically have to share is that certain business processes are not functioning as expected or are out of compliance with company policies or outside regulations. Occasionally, the news may include information related to an investigation of fraud or a violation with our company code of conduct. Furthermore, as a manager, I need to help my staff improve, and that includes being honest about poor performance or identifying areas of improvement.

PC: Can you describe a situation when you delivered bad news in person? How did you go about it?

JS: I think it is always best to deliver bad news in person. It allows for better interaction, a more thorough discussion, and information gleaned from body language. The receiver has less opportunity to read more into the underlying issue or to take things too personally, as we often tend to do.

Probably, the most difficult experiences I have had were related to terminating employees. On one occasion, I had to fly into Chicago and lay off several of my data-center managers and staff. Some had worked for the company for their entire careers. It was difficult and emotional. I made sure I was calm and honest but not overly emotional even though I could feel how devastating it was for some of them. I tried to be prepared to answer any question I thought they would ask, but there were a few I could not answer. So, I committed to get back to them. I tried to be positive and help them see beyond the moment. It did not always work, but I tried.

PC: Can you describe a situation when you delivered bad news in writing? How did you go about it?

JS: I had a manager who worked for me, based in Europe. He was a solid performer but did not like administrative tasks. This individual aspired to replace me, but the higher you move up within an organization, the more administrative your tasks tend to be. After several informal discussions related to certain administrative tasks, and after I allowed a period of time for change, I saw little improvement. I finally resorted to email that I intentionally sent on a Friday so he would have the entire weekend to digest what I had to say. The email addressed the topics we had discussed previously, with specific examples of dates when something was requested and when it was delivered or not. I made sure my facts were accurate and specific. I detailed the reasons for the tasks and further explained that while I fully supported him moving up in the organization, I could not honestly recommend him until he improved in this area. The email was honest and straightforward, and it upset him. However, over the weekend, he calmed down, and we had a good conversation on Monday. His performance improved; however, it is an area in which he will always struggle.

PC: What are some guidelines for choosing which communication channels to use?

JS: Dole is a worldwide organization that operates in 90 countries. Face-to-face communication is not always feasible, nor is speaking on the phone always convenient given all the time zones. My preferred order of communicating bad news is face-to-face, phone, and then email. However, I always follow up an email with a face-to-face meeting or a phone call.

PC: Why would you prefer email over a videoconference or webcast?

JS: Timeliness of communicating bad news is often critical. Setting up a videoconference often takes a lot of coordination and would result in a delay. Sometimes an email is the best way to initially communicate bad news. It is fast and provides the receiver an opportunity to read the information, digest it, and many times calm down enough to have a rational conversation about it. An email should always be followed up with a face-to-face meeting or a phone call. I feel a webcast is better for training or conducting online meetings than for communicating bad news.

PC: What happens in the workplace when people delay giving bad news?

JS: No one wants to be surprised with bad news. I find it best to communicate information as soon as I have it. Sometimes people hide the bad news, hoping it will go away, or they delay communicating it in the hopes it will get resolved. I have never seen any good that comes from delaying giving bad news.

PC: Can delivering bad news strengthen your work relationships or enhance your credibility? Do you have any examples?

JS: Absolutely! In order to have credibility, your colleagues need to know they can trust you. Part of acquiring trust is being honest. Honesty requires communicating the good and the bad equally. It is our human nature to want to be more positive and complimentary. We will give others a false sense of security and we will fail them by not helping them know areas where they can improve. We are doing a disservice to our colleagues by not helping them to be better.

PC: For young professionals, what concluding advice would you give for delivering bad news?

JS: Be positive, but be honest. Both qualities will take you far in any career. Whenever delivering bad news, make sure you are open about what the issue is and provide advice or guidance on how to improve the situation. Then, people will see that your goals are truly in their best interest and you are not simply one who points out faults just to bring others down. None of us is perfect, and if we are honest with ourselves and others, we can all improve together.

James Sloan *is vice president and chief financial officer of Dole Fresh Vegetables. He is a CPA and has had various financial roles over the course of his career. Before joining Dole, he worked at AT&T and Worthington Industries.*

Chapter Takeaway for *Bad-News Messages*

LO 10.1. Describe how delivering bad news impacts your credibility. (pp. 273–274)

Delivering effective bad-news messages improves your **reputation for personal credibility.**

It shows **competence** when you generate a forward-looking plan to overcome challenges.	It shows **caring** when you lessen the negative impacts on others and focus on their needs.	It shows **character** when you are completely transparent and honest.

LO 10.2. Explain considerations for deciding which channels to use when delivering bad-news messages. (pp. 274–275)

Guidelines for Choosing the Right Communication Channel for Bad-News Messages

• **Advantages of oral communication:** can use and observe nonverbal cues; can more easily demonstrate intentions; can more effectively clarify and explain the bad news; can respond to concerns immediately.	• **Advantages of written communication:** can craft message more carefully; can document the message more easily; can provide a message that serves as a reference (provide directions, suggestions, and options for future actions); can deliver message to more people more efficiently.	• When a bad-news message is more severe, more likely, and/ or less controllable, **choose richer communication channels when possible.**

LO 10.3. Summarize principles for effectively delivering bad-news messages. (pp. 275–279)

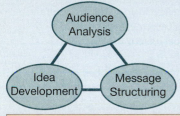

AIM Planning Process

Audience Analysis: Understand how the bad news will impact others and think carefully about how to best convey it.

Idea Development: Get your facts straight before delivering bad news and understand competing versions of events.

Message Structuring: Deliver the bad news in a productive manner. Ease into the bad news but avoid sugarcoating it.

Guidelines for Bad-News Messages

• Deliver the bad news in a timely manner.	• Sympathize with the bad-news recipients and soften the blow.	• Explain immediate impacts.
• Choose the right mix of channels.	• Provide a simple, clear rationale.	• Focus on solutions and long-term benefits.
		• Show goodwill.

LO 10.4. Compose effective bad-news messages in person and in writing for various audiences, including colleagues, external partners, and customers. (pp. 279–285)

Components of *Indirect* Bad-News Messages		Components of *Direct* Bad-News Messages	
Show CONCERN		Show CONCERN	
• Ease in with a buffer.	• Explain impacts.	• Ease in with a buffer.	• Explain impacts.
• **Provide a rationale.**	• Focus on the future (as appropriate).	• **Deliver the bad news.**	• Focus on the future (as appropriate).
• **Deliver the bad news.**	• Show goodwill.	• **Provide a rationale.**	• Show goodwill.

See *examples of bad-news messages* in Figures 10.1 through 10.8.

LO 10.5. Deliver and receive negative performance reviews constructively. (pp. 285–292)

Principles for Delivering Negative Performance Reviews		Style for Delivering Negative Performance Reviews
• Adopt a team-centered orientation.	• Link to consequences.	• Give clear and targeted feedback.
• Avoid sugarcoating the bad news.	• Probe for reasons performance is not higher.	• Focus on actions and results, not attitudes and intentions.
• Explain the impacts of the individual's poor performance on organizational performance.	• Emphasize problem solving rather than blaming.	• Establish measurable and realistic expectations.
	• Be firm.	

See *examples of delivering negative performance reviews* in Figures 10.9 and 10.10.

LO 10.6. Review bad-news messages for effectiveness and fairness. (pp. 292–293)

Reviewing Process

FAIR Test: Pay particular attention to the *impact* of the bad news on others and how to express it with *respect.*

Proofreading: Reread your message several times slowly, imagining how your message recipients will feel and respond.

Feedback: Ask several trusted colleagues who can empathize with the bad-news recipients to review your message.

Key Terms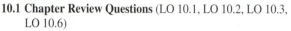

buffer (p. 276)

controllability (p. 275)

likelihood (p. 275)

mum effect (p. 281)

severity (p. 275)

teaser message (p. 277)

Discussion Exercises

10.1 Chapter Review Questions (LO 10.1, LO 10.2, LO 10.3, LO 10.6)

A. Describe reasons for hesitancy in delivering bad news and the impact of the mum effect.

B. Explain how delivering bad-news messages impacts credibility.

C. Describe the criteria for evaluating bad-news messages in terms of controllability, likelihood, and severity.

D. Explain considerations for deciding which channels to use when delivering bad-news messages.

E. Summarize principles for effectively delivering bad-news messages.

10.2 Key Terms (LO 10.1, LO 10.2, LO 10.3, LO 10.6)

Explain each key term and how it would impact a specific business communication situation.

10.3 Communication Q&A Discussion Questions (LO 10.1, LO 10.2, LO 10.3, LO 10.6)

Read James Sloan's thoughts about delivering bad news (pp. 293–294). Respond to the following questions.

A. According to Sloan, what are some principles for choosing an appropriate communication channel when delivering bad news?

B. How does he explain the relationship between delivering bad news and credibility?

C. He describes an experience when he had to deliver bad news in person. What approach did he take? Do you think this is an appropriate way to deliver bad news? Explain.

D. Sloan describes an experience when he had to deliver bad news in writing. What approach did he take? Do you think this is an appropriate way to deliver bad news? Explain.

E. What does he say about the timeliness of delivering bad news?

F. He mentions several times that one should be positive when delivering bad news. Explain how you think people can deliver bad news and be positive at the same time.

Evaluation Exercises ▶

10.4 Analyzing a Bad-News Message from Chrysler CEO Robert Nardelli to Employees (LO 10.3, LO 10.6)

In 2008, Bob Nardelli announced that Chrysler would lay off one-quarter of its white-collar managers. Read his email—Damon Lavrinc, "Bob Nardelli to Employees: We're Cutting 25% of Remaining White-Collar Jobs" (October 24, 2008) [Available at www.autoblog.com/2008/10/24/bob-nardelli-to-employees-we-want-a-25-cut-of-white-collar-job/]— and answer the following questions:

A. Is the bad news delivered immediately? Do you think it is delivered too directly? Too indirectly? Explain.

B. Is there a buffer? Is there an attempt to soften the blow? Explain.

C. How effective is the opening paragraph?

D. How effectively does the message explain immediate impacts?

E. Is the tone appropriate?

F. Conduct a FAIR test of the message.

G. Overall, what three changes would you suggest to make the bad-news message more effective?

10.5 Analyzing a Bad-News Message Delivered to You (LO 10.3, LO 10.6)

Describe a bad-news message you received in the workplace or at school. Evaluate the message in the following ways:

A. Was the bad news delivered in a timely manner? Do you think it was delivered too directly? Too indirectly? Explain.

B. Was there a buffer? Was there an attempt to soften the blow? Explain.

C. Were you told of or did you discuss immediate impacts?

D. Was the tone appropriate?

E. Was the delivery of bad news to you FAIR?

F. Overall, what three changes would have made the delivery of the bad news more effective?

10.6 Assess Your Ability to Deliver Bad News (LO 10.1, LO 10.2, LO 10.3, LO 10.6)

Evaluate yourself with regard to each of the practices listed in the table below. Circle the appropriate number for each.

	1 = Rarely/Never	2 = Sometimes	3 = Usually	4 = Always
When I need to pass on bad news, I avoid it as long as possible.	1	2	3	4
I have a hard time breaking bad news.	1	2	3	4
When I break the bad news, I understate how bad it really is.	1	2	3	4
When I pass on bad news, I use texts, emails, or other non-face-to-face messages to avoid conflict or uncomfortable situations.	1	2	3	4
I try to meet people in person or make a phone call, even when it's inconvenient, rather than using email or texts to pass on bad news.	1	2	3	4

Add up your score and consider the following advice:

16–20: You are *conflict avoidant.* You usually avoid delivering bad news because you feel uncomfortable doing so. When you break bad news, you understate it. You generally have good intentions, but sometimes you make matters worse by not confronting uncomfortable situations. Try thinking about the benefits to you and the bad-news recipients when delivering bad news right away.

12–15: You are *somewhat conflict avoidant.* You often avoid unpleasant conversations and communications. Sometimes, you prefer to leave issues unresolved rather than risk the uncomfortable interactions to address these issues.

10–11: You *sometimes confront bad news in a timely manner.* In many situations, you confront uncomfortable situations right away, yet you shy away from doing so in other cases.

Under 10: You *usually confront bad news in a timely manner.* You confront bad news and difficult situations immediately and with sensitivity.

Write three goals you have for constructively delivering bad news in the workplace.

10.7 Assess Your Prior Experiences Delivering Bad News (LO 10.1, LO 10.2, LO 10.3)

Briefly describe your own experiences delivering bad news in the following ways:

A. Delivering it too late and negatively affecting the bad-news recipient more than you intended.

B. Delivering it right away and creating the best possible outcomes for all involved.

C. Delivering it using a communication channel that wasn't appropriate.

D. Delivering it using a communication channel that was appropriate.

E. Not telling the whole truth.

Based on these experiences, write three principles for delivering bad news that you will live by in the workplace. Elaborate on each with one paragraph.

Application Exercises

Case for Problems 10.8 through 10.10: Bad News at Jensen Chemicals and Hardware Depot

Nick Jensen shook his head in frustration as he read Juan Hernandez's email notifying him that his company had lost the bid to supply chemicals to Marble Home Makeovers for the upcoming year. He'd had a hunch that his uncle's store, Jensen Chemicals and Hardware Depot, would not get the bid. However, it was still disappointing, and he was worried that unless the store changed its business model, it would be out of business within five years. The store had lost nearly 30 percent of its business in supplying chemicals in the past two years. It simply couldn't compete with larger regional companies.

Nick knew he needed to talk to his uncle, Mike Jensen, the owner. Mike owned five businesses but no longer got involved much in managing them. He spent about half of his time on

vacations. Nick thought he should email Uncle Mike and tell him what he considered ominous signs for his company. He might recommend that they sell this portion of the business to a larger chemical manufacturer and supplier, and get out of chemicals altogether. They would probably take a loss to do so, but selling now could also help them cut their losses. Nick knew his uncle loved having a stake in chemicals. He was also embarrassed that while Mike had entrusted him with a management position, the chemical portion of the business was performing so poorly. The good news, however, was that business-to-business hardware sales were in great shape.

Nick dreaded several other pieces of bad news he needed to deliver right away. Over a decade ago, during their most profitable years, management at Jensen Chemicals and Hardware Depot had implemented many benefits. One program allowed employees to be reimbursed for their tuition for up to two classes per semester if they received grades of a B or higher. Currently, 20 employees consistently took advantage of the program. Nick needed to inform all employees that the program would be discontinued immediately, as it cost the company too much. Employees currently enrolled could be reimbursed for courses during the present semester. Employees who had fewer than four courses left to receive an undergraduate degree would continue receiving reimbursement until they graduated. This included just three employees.

Finally, Nick needed to inform customers that the Jensen Chemicals and Hardware Depot Elite Customers program would be discontinued after the current rewards cycle. Under the program, customers who spent over $1,000 in a calendar year automatically qualified for a 10 percent discount on all purchases in the following year. The program had been quite popular, and Nick knew that many customers would be upset. However, he had done the math and felt it was a money loser for the company. To soften the disappointment to customers, in letters to all previous Elite Customers, he was including a 20 percent discount coupon on any single purchase. In addition, customers could still reach Elite Customer status for this year and qualify for discounts next year.

10.8 Writing a Bad-News Message about Jensen Chemicals and Hardware Depot (LO 10.4)

Assume the role of Nick and write an email to your uncle explaining why you think the company needs to get out of chemicals. You think the chemicals division could be sold for around half a million dollars. You currently have about $740,000 in debt related to the chemicals division. You would need to lay off ten employees, all of whom have been loyal to the company for many years. However, you think it's necessary because the chemical division lost nearly $200,000 last year, and you expect things to get worse.

10.9 Writing a Bad-News Message about Elimination of Tuition-Reimbursement Program (LO 10.4)

Assume the role of Nick and write a bad-news announcement to all employees explaining the elimination of the tuition-reimbursement program. Explain that the company has lost money in three of the four prior years and that you need to take actions to make the company profitable again.

10.10 Writing a Bad-News Message about Elimination of Elite Customer Program (LO 10.4)

Assume the role of Nick and write a bad-news announcement to all former Elite Customers explaining the elimination of the program.

10.11 Rewriting a Corporate Bad-News Message (LO 10.4)

In 2008, Bob Nardelli delivered news that Chrysler would lay off one-fourth of its white-collar managers. Read his email—Damon Lavrinc, "Bob Nardelli to Employees: We're Cutting 25% of Remaining White-Collar Jobs" (October 24, 2008) [Available at www.autoblog.com/2008/10/24/bob-nardelli-to-employees-we-want-a-25-cut-of-white-collar-job/]—and then rewrite it to make it more effective.

Endnotes

1.   Ed Frauenheim, "Over HR: Is It Time to Get Out?" *Workforce Management* (January 22, 2009): 22.

2.   "Comment on Breaking Bad News," *New Zealand Management* 55, no. 9 (2008): 16.

3.   McGraw Wentworth, "Tips on Delivering Bad News," *The ViewsLetter* 12, no. 2 (2009): 1–4.

4.   Dave Zielinski, "Crisis Presenting: How to Deliver Bad News," *Presentations* (February 1, 2001).

5.   David Falk, *The Bald Truth* (New York: Gallery Books, 2009): xiii.

6.   Ibid: 73, 79, 91.

7.   Siegel+Gale, *Turning Bad News into Good Vibes* (New York: Siegel+Gale, 2009): 1.

8.   Lauren Dixon, "Good Practices for Delivering Bad News," retrieved July 20, 2010 from http://webatsimon.com/good-practices-for-delivering-bad-news/ (April 13, 2010); "Comment on Breaking Bad News."

9.   McGraw Wentworth, "Tips on Delivering Bad News."

10.   Kate Sweeny and James A. Shepperd, "Being the Best Bearer of Bad Tidings," *Review of General Psychology* 11, no. 3 (2007): 235–257.

11.   "Does It Matter How Your Boss Delivers Bad News to Employees?" retrieved July 25, 2010, from http://www.a2ethics.org/node/246.

12.   Dixon, "Good Practices for Delivering Bad News."

13.   Siegel+Gale, *Turning Bad News into Good Vibes*: 4.

14.   Dixon, "Good Practices for Delivering Bad News."

15.   Michael Maslansky, *The Language of Trust* (New York: Prentice Hall, 2010).

16.   McGraw Wentworth, "Tips on Delivering Bad News"; Sherry Law, "How to Soften Blow When You Have to Give Bad News," *Denver Business Journal* (August 18, 2006).

17.   Daniel Goleman, Richard Boyatzis, and Annie McKee, "Realizing the Power of Emotional Intelligence: Primal Leadership," *Harvard Business Review* (December 2001): 42–51.

18.   ChongWoo Park, Ghiyoung Im, and Mark Keil, "Overcoming the Mum Effect in IT Project Reporting: Impacts of Fault Responsibility and Time Urgency," *Journal of the Association for Information Systems* 9, no. 7 (2008): Article 17; A. Tesser and S. Rosen, "The Reluctance to Transmit Bad News," *Advances in Experimental Social Psychology* 8 (1975): 193–232.

19. PRWeb, "Only One-Third of Companies Give Employees Bad News Face-to-Face—IABC Study," retrieved July 20, 2010, from www.jobbankusa.com/news/business_human_resources/companies_give_employees_bad_news.html (January 20, 2006).

20. McGraw Wentworth, "Tips on Delivering Bad News."

21. Rebecca Knight, "Delivering an Effective Performance Review," *Harvard Business Review blog* (November 3, 2011).

22. Ibid; Kathleen Jordan, *Performance Appraisal: The Basics* (Boston: Harvard Business Press, 2009); Brian Cole Miller, *Keeping Employees Accountable for Results* (New York: American Management Association, 2006).

23. Adapted from table in Jay M. Jackman and Myra H. Strober, "Fear of Feedback," *Harvard Business Review* (April 2003): 101–107.

CHAPTER ELEVEN

Crisis Communications and Public Relations Messages

Learning Objectives

After studying this chapter, you should be able to do the following:

LO11.1 Explain how crisis communications and public relations messages impact organizational reputation.

LO11.2 Describe the nature of crisis management in today's organizations.

LO11.3 Apply the AIM planning process to crisis communications.

LO11.4 Construct effective and responsible crisis messages.

LO11.5 Explain how to handle external complaints and negative rumors.

LO11.6 Review crisis communications for fairness and effectiveness.

LO11.7 Describe the role of public relations messages in today's organizations.

LO11.8 Apply the AIM planning process to public relations messages.

LO11.9 Construct effective and responsible public relations messages.

LO11.10 Review public relations messages for fairness and effectiveness.

WHY DOES THIS MATTER?

We have frequently discussed the role of personal credibility in fostering successful communication. Your colleagues, clients, customers, and other contacts respond to you far more positively when they perceive you as credible. Similarly, a company's credibility is closely linked to many areas of business performance, including total sales and revenue, repeat business, word-of-mouth marketing, and customer satisfaction—to name just a few.

Personal credibility and organizational credibility are correlated. When you gain or lose a reputation for credibility with your professional contacts, you enhance or detract from your company's credibility. Likewise, when your company gains or loses credibility, you also lose personal credibility.

In this chapter, we'll explore the importance of crisis communications and public relations (PR) messages with the view that credibility is a foundation for both. One major goal of crisis communications is to protect and repair an organization's credibility during crises, while one of the major goals of public relations messages is to enhance a company's credibility. Throughout the chapter, we'll also refer to a company's *reputation* as a measure of its credibility.

Traditionally, crisis communications and public relations messages were delegated exclusively to public relations professionals and upper-level executives. However, in the Social Age, when employees are increasingly visible and available to stakeholders, most business professionals contribute to an organization's crisis communications and public relations messages. Furthermore, many organizations have found that young professionals are particularly adept with these communications. For example, when Ernst & Young developed a Facebook recruiting page, its younger employees proved to be the most effective at interfacing with potential hires and encouraging them to apply. Similarly, many younger professionals serve as first responders to negative messages in blogs, discussion forums, corporate websites, and other online locations.[1] Of course, upper-level executives and crisis management teams continue to prepare and deliver most high-stakes crisis communications.

Your ability to effectively craft and deliver crisis and public relations messages can pay great dividends over the course of your career. Social Age companies are increasingly aware of the importance of maintaining and enhancing organizational reputation. A standard expectation for promotion to mid- and upper-level business positions is adeptness in these areas. Companies entrust these positions to business professionals who understand how to safeguard a company's reputation.

Furthermore, since you will represent your department or team within your organization, your ability to enhance its reputation will often lead to better opportunities and more resources for your group. In turn, you can gain a reputation as a leader who raises the profile of your work teams and units. Thus, the principles for developing effective crisis communications and PR messages are critical in many aspects of your daily work. Read the following short case, which is the basis for many of the examples provided throughout this chapter.

LO11.1 Explain how crisis communications and public relations messages impact organizational reputation.

Chapter Case: Building, Maintaining, and Repairing Credibility at Better Horizons Credit Union

Who's Involved

Christine Russo, president and CEO
- During her tenure as president, one of her primary goals has been to build Better Horizon's brand value.

Haniz Zogby, marketing specialist and loan officer
- Haniz works on a variety of PR messages under the direction of Christine. She has also played a role in crafting various crisis communications and PR messages.

Crisis Situations

As the president and CEO of the Better Horizons Credit Union (BHCU), Christine Russo spends much of her time attempting to enhance the reputation of the organization. In her five-year tenure as president, two priorities have been preparing for crises and engaging in public relations.

Last year, BHCU faced two unexpected crises: (1) a hurricane and (2) a breach of security to the Better Horizons member database. The hurricane made two of BHCU's branches inoperable due to rain and wind damage. Some credit union members lost homes. Most members were without power for at least three days and could not return to their homes during that period. In the other crisis, BHCU's data center was hacked, potentially compromising the private information of all credit union members.

Public Relations Situations

Traditionally, BHCU has placed most of its PR messages in a quarterly newsletter. Now, Christine and Haniz are developing weekly PR content for their website as well as for various social media. Christine and Haniz intend to add PR messages and stories about the following in the next few weeks: BHCU's commitment to financial literacy, a local high school student who has saved money for college, retirement planning seminars, and experiences of the Better Horizons team at a local walkathon. They also want to draw more traffic to the BHCU Facebook page by creating a writing contest.

Crisis Tasks
How did Christine and BHCU employees manage communications during the hurricane crisis?
How did they communicate with credit union members during the hacking crisis to protect members and minimize damage to the credit union's reputation? (See the "Creating Crisis Messages" section.)

PR Tasks
How will Christine and Haniz develop influential PR messages? (See the "Creating PR Messages" section.)

Crisis Communication Messages

LO11.2 Describe the nature of crisis management in today's organizations.

All companies should be prepared to handle crises—unforeseen disruptions to business operations that involve threats to public safety, major financial loss, and reputation loss. Companies face many types of crises, including natural disasters, product failures, technological failures, work-site accidents, management misconduct or criminal behavior, and various forms of negative press coverage.[2] The costs of crises can be enormous. For example, in 2000 and 2001, Ford suffered regular, negative press about

FIGURE 11.1

The Stages of Crisis Management

Pre-Crisis Preparation
- Create a crisis management plan.
- Assign and train a crisis management team.
- Regularly conduct exercises to test the crisis management plan.
- Develop sample responses to various types of crises.

Crisis Responses
- Act to help victims and ensure public safety; provide stress and trauma counseling.
- Monitor the situation carefully and stay updated with the facts.
- Provide quick, accurate, and consistent communications through all available communication channels; tailor messages to each stakeholder group.

Post-Crisis Actions
- Keep stakeholders informed about recovery and corrective efforts.
- Update the crisis management plan based on lessons learned.
- Engage in public relations to repair the organization's reputation.

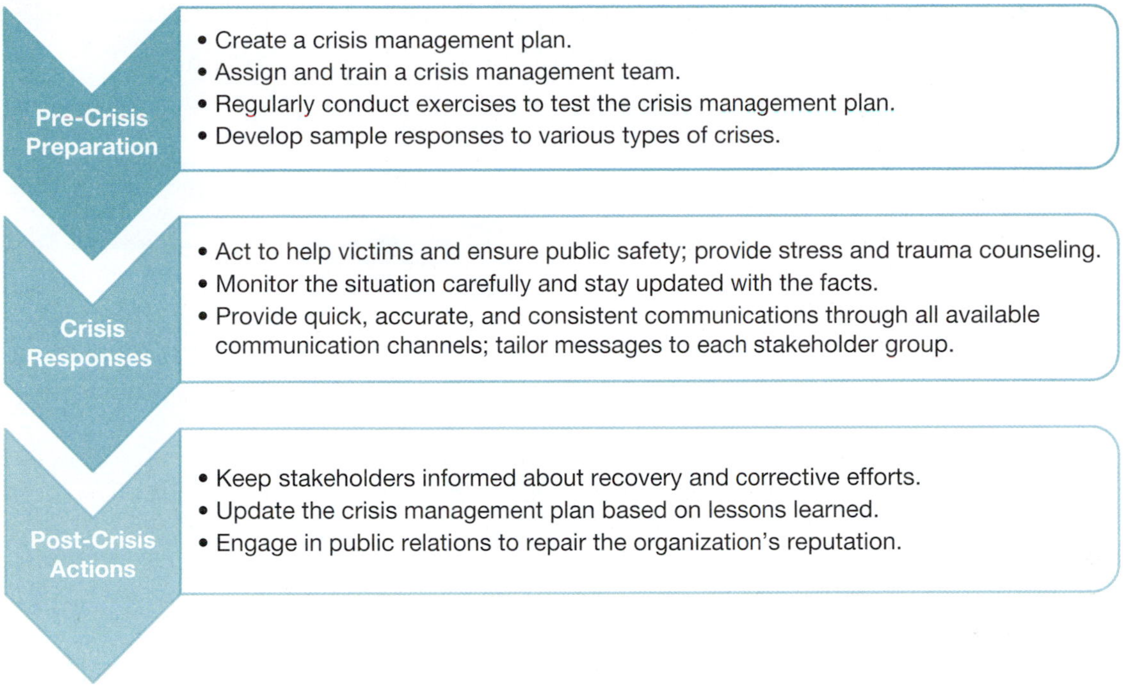

unusually high numbers of deadly rollover crashes in Ford Explorers. Ford attributed the problems solely to the Bridgestone/Firestone tires. Bridgestone/Firestone blamed the design of the Ford Explorer. One economic-impact study showed that the crisis—largely played out in public—cost Ford $10 billion in lost sales, stock losses, plant closings, recalls, and other factors.[3]

Although companies cannot foresee crises precisely, they should operate under the assumption that crises will occur—that is, it's not a matter of if, but when. To minimize and correct damage to victims and avoid excessive reputation loss, companies should excel at all stages of crisis management: pre-crisis planning, crisis responses, and post-crisis actions (as depicted in Figure 11.1).[4]

Before a crisis occurs, companies should create and regularly update response plans. These plans should designate crisis management teams and identify the roles of key players. Moreover, crisis response teams should conduct annual exercises to test the company's ability to respond. As Dean Tougas, a crisis communication planner at Boeing, explained, "There can't be a learning curve. . . . Everyone involved in the response to a crisis has to be able to become immediately productive in handling it. That's why it's critical to run training programs and build infrastructure."[5]

Another key component of preparation is developing a crisis communications plan. The plan should address how the company will inform each group of stakeholders about crisis events (see Figure 11.2). A company's crisis communications—even during high-stress events—should be quick, accurate, and consistent. Unless a company prepares for crises with plans and regular exercises, it is unlikely to achieve this standard.[6]

The response stage involves rapidly confronting the crisis. The primary responsibility of the company is to help victims and remove any danger to stakeholders. With a well-developed plan in place, which includes designation of crisis management teams and roles, a company can often rapidly and effectively meet the needs of victims and other stakeholders. An important but secondary responsibility during the response stage is to preserve an organization's reputation. During the crisis response stage, the

FIGURE 11.2

Stakeholder Groups

company should attempt to reach all stakeholders through appropriate communication channels. The examples of crisis communications in the next few sections involve written communications during the crisis response stage. The principles, however, apply to oral communications as well.

In the post-crisis stage, the business has returned to normal operations and the crisis situation has been resolved or stabilized. During this stage, the company should implement a consistent stream of public relations messages (discussed in the second half of the chapter) to repair its reputation. In some cases, this effort may last many years. For example, in response to the 2010 oil spill in the Gulf of Mexico, BP has made many efforts to compensate for the damage it caused and regularly develops PR messages to repair its reputation. It continues to prominently feature these efforts on its corporate website.

LO11.3 Apply the AIM planning process to crisis communications.

Applying the AIM Planning Process for Crisis Communication

The planning process for crisis communications must be thorough but compressed. Providing victims and other stakeholders with timely and accurate information to avoid further loss is next to impossible without a designated communication plan as part of a larger, regularly updated crisis response plan. With such a plan in place, a crisis communications team can act swiftly to help its stakeholders avoid further losses and help the company restore its credibility.

Audience Analysis for Crisis Communications   Crisis messages should be designed with particular stakeholders in mind. Typically, crisis communication teams determine those stakeholders who are most affected and make contact with them as soon as possible. Often crisis communication teams focus on external stakeholders and fail to provide employees with enough information. Yet, for 80 to 85 percent of crisis situations, employees are the first or second most-important stakeholders.[7]

Crisis communication teams should focus not only on what information to provide but also on how they can show empathy. The success of many crisis messages hinges on the recipients' emotional reactions to them. In many cases, customers, employees, and other stakeholders are willing to forgive companies if they provide timely and accurate information and make good-faith, caring efforts to improve the situation.[8]

TABLE 11.1

Types of Crises and Levels of Company Responsibility

Victim Crises (Minimal Responsibility)	Accident Crises (Low Responsibility)	Preventable Crises (Complete Responsibility)
• Natural disasters • Rumors about organization • Workplace violence committed by former or current employee • Product tampering by individual outside the organization	• Stakeholder claims that organization is not operating appropriately • Industrial accidents due to technology and equipment failures • Product failure due to technology and equipment failures	• Industrial accidents due to employee errors • Harm to consumers from product failures due to employee errors • Management actions that are unlawful and/or place stakeholders at risk

Many of these judgments about whether the response is in *good faith* or *sincere* or *caring* are made quickly. Thus, the crisis communication team should develop and deliver crisis communications under the assumption that they must gain trust and emotional commitment from various stakeholders rapidly.

Idea Development for Crisis Communications
Although companies should provide crisis information as soon as possible, they must provide accurate information. The crisis communications team must rapidly assemble the facts, put meaning to the information they collect, and take positions about the best ways for stakeholders to protect themselves. In this tense and sometimes chaotic stage immediately following a crisis, the communications team often works with incomplete and suspect information. Thus, team members must make judgments about the relevancy, accuracy, and legitimacy of the information they do have.[9]

One primary task during the idea development stage is to define the nature of the crisis because this will help the team formulate appropriate messages. Crises can be broadly classified into three types: victim crises, accident crises, and preventable crises (see Table 11.1).[10] In a **victim crisis,** stakeholders generally do not hold companies responsible. For example, an earthquake may affect the operations of a company and the safety of its employees, yet stakeholders will not believe the company is at fault. In an **accident crisis,** stakeholders hold companies responsible but understand that what happened was not intentional and was difficult to foresee. For example, a workplace accident due to equipment failure would typically be considered unintentional, but stakeholders would still assign some responsibility to the company. In a **preventable crisis,** stakeholders believe the company is to blame and is completely responsible for the damages and losses to stakeholders. Typically, if company employees are found to be at fault for the crisis, stakeholders assign complete responsibility to the company.

The crisis management team should also identify whether the crisis involves *intensifying factors* to help decide how to develop appropriate crisis communications. When the company has a negative reputation or a history of prior problems relating to the crisis, then the danger to the company's reputation is intensified.

Message Structure for Crisis Communications
The primary purpose of crisis communications is to help victims and other stakeholders. A secondary purpose is to avoid or repair reputation loss. You can use various types of statements as depicted in Table 11.2 and described in this section to develop appropriate crisis messages. Based on the type of crisis and whether there are intensifying factors, you can map out the necessary components of effective crisis communications (see Table 11.3).[11]

- *Express concern.* As noted, stakeholders make judgments about the company's empathy and caring within 30 seconds.[12] By showing concern immediately, you establish credibility. This allows you to more effectively provide for stakeholders'

Components of Crisis Communications

- Express concern.
- Explain corrective actions.
- Provide instructions.
- Give an excuse/justification (for certain types of crises).
- Provide compensation/apology (for certain types of crises).

TABLE 11.2

Types of Responses in Crisis Communication

Type of Statement	Explanation
Concern	Express concern to all affected by the crisis.
Corrective actions	Describe specific steps the organization is taking to correct the problem and minimize damage.
Instructions	Tell stakeholders what to do to protect themselves and stay informed and updated.
Attack the accuser	Where relevant, attack the credibility of the accusing individuals or groups.
Denial	Deny that there is a crisis or that the organization has any responsibility.
Excuse	Minimize the organization's responsibility by denying intent to harm or pointing out inability to control events.
Justification	Minimize the perceived damage of the crisis.
Reminder	Enumerate past good works of the organization.
Ingratiation	Praise stakeholders for their actions in dealing with the crisis.
Compensation	Offer money or gifts to victims.
Apology	Take full responsibility for the crisis and ask for forgiveness.

TABLE 11.3

Types of Crises and Appropriate Responses

Type of Crisis	Concern	Corrective Actions	Instructions	Excuse and/or Justification*	Compensation and/or Apology
Victim crises	x	x	x		
Victim crises*	x	x	x	x	
Accident crises	x	x	x	x	
Accident crises*	x	x	x	x	x
Preventable crises	x	x	x	x	x

*With intensifying factors

Note: Crisis communicators may always consider the use of *reminders* and *ingratiation*. They should consider *denial* and *attack the accuser* for unjustified rumors and attacks against the company.

needs. It also protects your company; expressions of sympathy reduce the number of claims against an organization.[13] So, ensure that you have the right spokesperson and have that person express concern immediately. The spokesperson should be someone who expresses sympathy well, understands the situation well, and knows how to offer an appropriate level of confidence in the company and its efforts to resolve the crisis.

- *Explain corrective actions.* Some stakeholders are harmed—physically, psychologically, and/or financially—by crises. During the crisis, many stakeholders experience anxiety about potential losses to their physical or financial safety. Thus, one of stakeholders' most immediate concerns is what the company is doing to stop, minimize, and/or compensate for their damages. After you have expressed concern, talk about what the company is doing to resolve the crisis. Often in the initial stages, crisis communication teams have little or conflicting information. During these confusing moments, avoid making statements about the causes of the crisis or what your company's exact response will be. Instead, describe the process the company is using to investigate the situation, and express the company's commitment to formulating a response as soon as it can.[14]

- *Provide instructions.* Not only do stakeholders want to know what the company is doing for them in a crisis, but they also want to know what they should do to avoid any further physical or financial harm. So, provide specific instructions on how stakeholders can protect themselves and get assistance dealing with damage. Use as many communication channels as possible. Since this information changes rapidly during a crisis, consider prominent places on your website for updating information. Blogs are especially useful during crises. Companies that have used blogs in this way have been able to reduce complaints and improve their reputation (see Figure 11.5, which shows a blog for Better Horizons with regular updates following a crisis).[15]

- *Give an excuse or provide justification.* When stakeholders will hold the company responsible for the crisis (accident and preventable crises), the crisis communication team should consider providing excuses or giving justification. If the company supplies reasons it's not at fault or could not have foreseen or controlled the events, stakeholders may assign less responsibility. However, these strategies are not without risk. Some stakeholders may hold the company even more responsible if they do not believe the excuses or justifications or if they find them illegitimate.

- *Issue an apology and explain compensation.* In preventable crises, the company is at fault. The crisis communication team should explain how the company will compensate victims, and it should issue an apology. In recent years, stakeholders have increasingly expected apologies from business leaders. When leaders apologize, it becomes a public record of companies' efforts to repair the damage they have caused. As communication specialist Barbara Kellerman explains, "A successful apology can turn enmity into personal and organizational triumph—while an apology that is too little, too late, or too transparently tactical can bring on individual and institutional ruin."[16]

Creating Crisis Messages

Once crisis communication teams have planned their messages, they must act under significant time pressures to compose them. They must also act quickly to modify them for various media: letters, emails, web pages, blogs, texts, radio and television broadcasts, and so on. Members of crisis communication teams should work closely to ensure that they develop consistent messages.

In Figures 11.3 through 11.7, you can see more-effective and less-effective crisis messages developed at Better Horizons. In each case, Christine Russo, the CEO, took the lead in crafting the messages. She involved other top managers and employees in the process. In the first communication, Christine deals with the impacts of a hurricane on the credit union's operations (see Figures 11.3 and 11.4). This crisis is a victim crisis since credit union members will not hold the credit union responsible. Nonetheless, the credit union is severely impacted by damage to its buildings and equipment, and the homes of credit union members have been damaged as well. Christine writes a letter to be distributed by mail and manually at credit union locations. It clearly shows concern, explains actions that Better Horizons is taking to help, and provides directions for affected credit union members. She also modifies this message for a website post and sends it by email and text message as well (see Figure 11.5).

LO11.4 Construct effective and responsible crisis messages.

FIGURE 11.3

Less-Effective Communication for a Victim Crisis

BETTER HORIZONS CREDIT UNION
Est. 1937

September 8, 2012

Dear Credit Union Member:

> Focuses primarily on the actions of the credit union with little show of CONCERN for victims.

I would like to explain the Better Horizons response to the recent hurricane. Following the hurricane, I directed my team to move swiftly to restore banking services, provide and coordinate emergency relief, and donate to the Red Cross and other emergency relief efforts. I want you to know that Better Horizons will quickly resume all services as usual.

Since our area has been declared a national disaster area, you may be eligible for federal aid. Federal aid is controlled by the National Credit Union Administration (NCUA). You may contact NCUA directly. For BHCU members in affected areas, I have authorized BHCU to help those members severely affected by the hurricane in a number of ways, such as possibly restricting loan payments and terms and guaranteeing lines of credit. We will also waive ATM surcharges and fees if you can demonstrate you were forced to make these transactions as a result of evacuations. To show our support for your generosity, we will also allow free domestic wires to affected areas and charitable organizations based on a preapproved list of organizations. I'm also pleased to announce that we will assist you by cashing FEMA disaster assistance checks and government benefit checks.

> Explains CORRECTIVE ACTIONS without sufficient detail.

To show our commitment to the community, I have also authorized various BHCU employees to coordinate basic relief supplies, provide access to computers, and other efforts. In good times and bad times, you can see that Better Horizons is there for you.

Please call our toll-free BHCU hurricane hotline (1-888-700-BHCU) for more information.

Best wishes,

Christine Russo

Christine Russo
President and CEO
Better Horizons Credit Union

> Provides INSTRUCTIONS for getting up-to-date information and contacting credit union representatives only by phone.

2737 Better Horizons Loop, Pescaloosa, FL 91214 • Phone: 803-784-7300 • Email: info@bhcu.org • Web: www.bhcu.org

---

In the second communication, Christine deals with a security breach to the credit union's member database (see Figures 11.6 and 11.7). This is an accident crisis. Although the attack is from an unknown outsider, many credit union members will hold the credit union responsible for not protecting their sensitive information adequately. Christine finds out about the crisis in the early evening and works all night with a team of trusted employees to develop an immediate response. By the morning, she sends out an email to alert all credit union members to the potential danger that their information has been stolen. She expresses concern, provides a list of corrective actions, and gives detailed directions about how members can protect themselves.

Christine also gives a short excuse and justification. She explains that major banks have also experienced hacking events recently and that bank customers have not been adversely affected. So, Christine implicitly points out that these failures in data protection occur to major financial institutions with more resources for security (which excuses Better Horizon's inability to prevent the attack) and that banking customers were not harmed (justifies members in feeling less threatened). This excuse and justification may lessen the reputation loss for Better Horizons.

FIGURE 11.4

More-Effective Communication for a Victim Crisis

BETTER HORIZONS CREDIT UNION
Est. 1937

September 8, 2012

Dear Credit Union Member:

> Shows CONCERN.

One week ago, the most damaging hurricane in our history severely impacted credit union members. By our estimation, nearly 150 members lost their homes, approximately 900 members suffered major damage to their homes, and almost half of our members lost power for nearly three days. Fortunately, we are not aware of any loss of life or life-threatening injuries.

In the wake of the hurricane, BHCU employees moved swiftly to restore banking services, provide and coordinate emergency relief, and donate to the Red Cross and other emergency relief efforts. If you have been impacted by the hurricane, we pledge to help you get back on your feet.

Since our area has been declared a national disaster area, **you may be eligible for federal aid**. Federal aid is controlled by the National Credit Union Administration (NCUA). You may contact NCUA directly: 1-888-584-6847or www.ncua.gov.

For BHCU members in affected areas, BHCU will take the following actions to help **alleviate hurricane-related banking hardships**:

- *Restructure loan payment terms* and extend due dates up to 90 days
- *Guarantee lines of credit* through the National Credit Union Share Insurance Fund
- *Waive any ATM surcharges and fees* due to evacuations
- *Allow free domestic wires* to affected areas and charitable organizations
- *Cash FEMA disaster assistance checks* and government benefit checks

> Explains CORRECTIVE ACTIONS.

BHCU is also facilitating **other relief efforts** and providing information about the following:

- *Basic relief supplies*. A Red Cross relief center is located in the parking lot of the Forest Grove branch. You can get water, meals, and other essential supplies.
- *Access to computers*. BHCU has set up a computer center (50 computer terminals) at our Forest Grove branch. You may use the computers for no charge between 7 a.m. and 9 p.m. daily.
- *How your union membership may help you*. If you are a union member, AFL-CIO may be negotiating immediate help, such as continuing pay, health and welfare plans, and instant access to pension funds. We have an AFL-CIO representative at our Forest Grove branch to answer any questions.

To learn how BHCU can help ease your financial hardships, please set up a time to meet with a BHCU representative as soon as possible. You can set up a meeting time by calling the toll-free BHCU hurricane hotline (1-888-700-BHCU) or by scheduling a time online at the BHCU website (www.bhcu.org). The website also contains up-to-the-minute information about BHCU efforts to help you overcome your financial hardships.

Best wishes,

Christine Russo

Christine Russo
President and CEO
Better Horizons Credit Union

> Provides INSTRUCTIONS.

2737 Better Horizons Loop, Pescaloosa, FL 91214 • Phone: 803-784-7300 • Email: info@bhcu.org • Web: www.bhcu.org

FIGURE 11.5

Crisis Updates on a
Corporate Blog

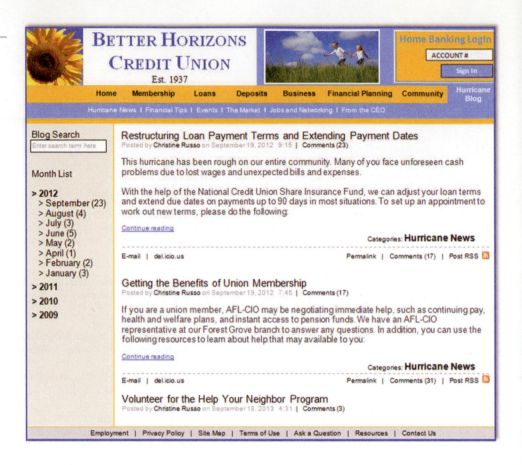

LO11.5   Explain how to
handle external
complaints and
negative rumors.

Responding to External Complaints and Handling Negative Rumors in the Social Age

One of the foremost challenges to organizations in the emerging Social Age is managing negative rumors. Bloggers and reporters with negative views of an organization, activists who oppose an organization, disgruntled employees, dissatisfied customers, and many others can use social media to gain a large platform and voice their grievances. These opinions may be difficult to rebut. Furthermore, dissatisfied stakeholders can use various social media—social networks, wikis, blogs—to rapidly harm a company's reputation.[17]

For example, in July 2011, Netflix abruptly raised monthly subscription fees from $9.99 to $15.98 for subscribers of streaming and DVD delivery services. Hundreds of thousands of irate customers posted angry comments on Netflix's Facebook page and website, and their own Facebook pages, Twitter messages, and other social media. The intense social media reactions led to extensive mainstream press coverage. Within two months, the stock value fell by more than 60 percent.[18] (See Figures 11.17, 11.18, and 11.19 in the exercises at the end of the chapter for messages sent by Netflix during this crisis.)

In addition to crises that companies themselves create, as in the Netflix example, crises created by unfounded rumors can also substantially harm corporate reputation. Often, these rumors emerge from individuals with basically no resources other than social media platforms: blogs, tweets, text messages, Facebook groups, YouTube videos, and online petitions. After the BP oil platform disaster, an individual set up a fake BP public relations Twitter account with negative and even disparaging comments about BP. The fake BP Twitter account gained more followers than the real BP Twitter account. This shows the power that single stakeholders with few or no financial resources can have in the Social Age.

Crises resulting from direct attacks on a company's reputation often require the company to forcefully deny and/or attack the accusers. However, even when the rumors are false, strong denials and counterattacks bear risks. In these delicate situations, the premise should be that perceptions are more important than reality. When your company is under attack, consider the following principles:[19]

- *Gather the facts.* Negative rumors often contain some elements of truth. To respond effectively and fairly, you should quickly assemble all the facts.

- *Avoid heavy-handedness (show of force).* In July 2009 the Horizon Realty Group sued a former tenant who had sent the following tweet to a few dozen followers: "Who said sleeping in a moldy apartment was bad for you? Horizon really thinks it's okay." The lawsuit, claiming damages of $50,000, quickly became a national headline story because the company appeared to be reacting with disproportionate force. The apartment group lost the suit, and its excessive show of force created a highly public loss of corporate reputation.

- *Respond quickly.* In the social media world, companies cannot take a week to respond to a tweet. Respond to unfounded rumors rapidly.

- *Use the appropriate channels.* Companies should choose channels to match their audiences. If the company is responding to a video on YouTube, it should use YouTube to respond. One recent example occurred when Domino's U.S. president created an apology video on YouTube in response to a YouTube video that employees had created to show disgusting and unsanitary things they did to pizzas before delivering them. This response quickly shifted the story from what Domino's employees had done wrong to what the Domino's CEO had done right and unconventionally.

- *Rely on external advocates.* Since stakeholders often distrust companies during periods of negative rumors, companies should seek trusted external organizations and individuals to come to their defense. For example, in January 2010, Royal Caribbean was attacked severely in the press and in social media when it docked a luxury cruise liner just 60 miles from where an earthquake had leveled Port-au-Prince, Haiti. Hours later, the CEO blogged about Royal Caribbean's role in providing jobs to Haiti and the use of its ships to deliver humanitarian aid. However, it wasn't until external advocates—the United Nations, the World Trade Organization, Sustainable Travel International, and the Kenan Institute for Ethics—came to its defense that stakeholders again trusted Royal Caribbean.

- *Respond with credentials.* When a company is attacked unfairly through social media, it should rebut the charges with credentials. For example, when Target was unfairly attacked for not supporting equal rights, it immediately responded with its concrete record of achievements, including having been recognized in the "Top 50 Companies for Diversity" (awarded by DiversityInc), "Top 10 Companies with the Highest Percentage of Women Directors" (awarded by Corporate Women Directors International), and "World's Most Ethical Companies" (awarded by the Ethisphere Institute).

A company that recently applied all these strategies in response to negative rumors is Timberland, which has a long history of applying an eco-friendly approach to producing and selling outdoor clothes, boots, and shoes. Yet, in 2009, Timberland unexpectedly found itself the target of Greenpeace, an organization devoted to stopping environmental destruction. A Greenpeace report and series of press releases attacked Timberland for contributing to deforestation in Amazon rain forests.

Initially, Timberland CEO Jeff Swartz and his management team were infuriated. They viewed the attacks as unfair and unsubstantiated. They also felt wronged, since Timberland had for years placed the issue of deforestation as one of its top environmental priorities. For example, Timberland had planted one million trees in China. Swartz's first impulse was to attack the accuracy of Greenpeace's report. However, he

FIGURE 11.6

Less-Effective Communication for an Accident Crisis

To...	Peter Gutke
Subject:	Loss of Personal Information

Arial   10   **B** *I* <u>U</u>

Dear Mr. Gutke:

Does not express CONCERN in opening sentences.

Last night (July 16) at approximately 7 p.m., we discovered that an unauthorized individual (or group) hacked into our data system and accessed account information.

We are still investigating this incident. We believe that the hacker was able to access some of your personal information and could attempt to use your information in unauthorized and illegal manners.

We have acted immediately to try to protect you. We have temporarily suspended online banking services, hired an external security firm to conduct a thorough investigation of this incident, and started a process to increase our data security and infrastructure. We apologize for the temporary suspension. As soon as online banking services resume, we will notify you. With the exception of online banking services, you may use all other banking services as usual.

You may be at risk for identity theft. We are not certain that the hacker retrieved your data, but we cannot yet rule out that possibility. Upon learning of the intrusion, Better Horizons immediately purchased a $500,000 insurance policy for each credit union member to cover the following in the case of identity theft: legal costs, identity-restoration costs, and lost wages.

Explains CORRECTIVE ACTIONS in dense, difficult-to-read passages.

We urge you to take the following steps to protect your good name and avoid any potential financial loss: Avoid any potential scams—by email, telephone, or mail—where you are asked for sensitive and confidential information. Better Horizons will never contact you and ask for your confidential information (such as a social security number). Monitor your account statements and check your credit reports for any fraudulent activity. Also, act proactively and take control of this situation. Remember that you are entitled to one free credit report annually from each of the major credit bureaus. You can order your free credit report at www.annualcreditreport.com. Also, Better Horizons will provide free credit reporting service for the upcoming year as requested. You can—free of charge—request that credit bureaus place a fraud alert on your file. This will require creditors to take extra steps to verify your identity and reduce the likelihood that another person could get credit in your name. You can click on any of the following links to make this request to any of the major credit bureaus: Experian, Equifax, and TransUnion. You may want to learn more about how to avoid identity theft at the U.S. Federal Trade Commission's website: www.consumer.gov/idtheft. This website provides additional information and resources to protect your identity.

Please be aware that we are doing everything possible to avoid this situation occurring again. But, the sophistication of many hackers increases daily. Even some major banks with millions of dollars to invest in security systems and personnel have experienced similar hacking events in recent months. In these events, the information of approximately 45 million banking customers was hacked.

Please contact us with any specific questions or concerns. You may call our dedicated phone line (803-784-7399), email us, (identitysecurity@bhcu.org), or visit the web page where we have posted up-to-date information about actions taken by BHCU to remedy this situation (www.bhcu.org/security).

Sincerely,

Christine Russo, President and CEO

The JUSTIFICATION/EXCUSE bears a helpless, nonconfident tone.

Provides INSTRUCTIONS with details buried in long paragraphs. Without hyperlinks and phone numbers, the burden of taking these steps is more frustrating and painstaking for credit union members.

FIGURE 11.7

More-Effective Communication for an Accident Crisis

To...	Peter Gutke
Subject:	Loss of Personal Information

`Arial` ⌄ `10` ⌄ **B** *I* <u>U</u> ≔ ≔ ⇥ ⇥ ✏ ⌄ **A** ⌄ ⌄

Dear Mr. Gutke:

Last night (July 16) at approximately 7 p.m., we discovered that an unauthorized individual (or group) hacked into our data system and accessed account information. We are deeply concerned about protecting your identity, and we are working around the clock to ensure you are not impacted negatively by this situation.

> Shows CONCERN.

We are still investigating this incident. We believe that the hacker was able to access the following information from your account profile: credit union account numbers (but not passwords), credit card numbers (but not security codes), credit card expiration dates, email address, phone number, address, and birth date.

In response to the hacking, we have taken the following actions:

> Explains CORRECTIVE ACTIONS.

1. Temporarily suspended online banking services
2. Hired an external security firm to conduct a thorough investigation of this incident
3. Started a process to increase our data security and infrastructure

We expect to reinstate online banking services in the next 24 to 72 hours. We apologize for the temporary suspension. This is a precautionary measure as we continue our investigation. As soon as online banking services resume, we will notify you. With the exception of online banking services, you may use all other banking services as usual.

You may be at risk for identity theft. We are not certain that the hacker retrieved your data, but we cannot yet rule out that possibility. Upon learning of the intrusion, Better Horizons immediately purchased a $500,000 insurance policy for each credit union member to cover the following in the case of identity theft: legal costs, identity-restoration costs, and lost wages.

We urge you to take the following steps to protect your good name and avoid any potential financial loss:

- Avoid any potential scams—by email, telephone, or mail—where you are asked for sensitive and confidential information. Better Horizons will never contact you and ask for your confidential information (such as a social security number).
- Monitor your account statements and check your credit reports for any fraudulent activity.

> Provides INSTRUCTIONS.

You may consider the following information to help you stay vigilant in protecting yourself:

- You are entitled to one free credit report annually from each of the major credit bureaus. You can order your free credit report at www.annualcreditreport.com. Also, Better Horizons will provide free credit reporting service for the upcoming year as requested.
- You can—free of charge—request that credit bureaus place a fraud alert on your file. This will require creditors to take extra steps to verify your identity and reduce the likelihood that another person could get credit in your name. You can click on any of the following links to make this request to any of the major credit bureaus: Experian, Equifax, and TransUnion.
- You may want to learn more about how to avoid identity theft at the U.S. Federal Trade Commission's website: www.consumer.gov/idtheft. This website provides additional information and resources to protect your identity.

Mr. Gutke, we deeply regret that your personal information may have been stolen. We will do all in our power to help you protect your identity. We are acting immediately to fortify our data security and stop such hacking attacks in the future. Several major banks have experienced similar hacking events in recent months. In these events, the information of approximately 45 million banking customers was hacked. To date, none of this information has been used for identity theft efforts.

Please contact us with any specific questions or concerns. You may call our dedicated phone line (803-784-7399), email us (identitysecurity@bhcu.org), or visit the web page where we have posted up-to-date information about actions taken by BHCU to remedy this situation (www.bhcu.org/security).

Sincerely,

> Gives brief JUSTIFICATION/EXCUSE.

Christine Russo, President and CEO

and his public relations team quickly concluded that they wanted to engage rather than antagonize these activists. The reality was that Timberland sourced about 7 percent of its leather from cows in Brazil. In some cases, cattle farmers had clear-cut rain forests for pasturing. The company had to step back and admit, though its environmental efforts had been excellent, it was not sure if the leather purchased from Brazil came from suppliers who illegally cut down forests for pasture.

Within the few weeks following the Greenpeace press release, more than 65,000 activists sent emails threatening to boycott Timberland and created a media firestorm. In most cases, the activists copied or paraphrased talking points from Greenpeace press releases.[20] As Swartz explained, "I figured if that many people were taking the time to send an e-mail, there must be at least half a million not sending e-mails who were also pissed off. That's a big number. Our brand's reputation was at stake."[21]

Read through Table 11.4, which displays some of the communications of Timberland, Greenpeace, and environmental activists over a five-month period. You will notice that Timberland gradually developed its message, increasingly adopted the right tone, focused on the needs of activists, and diffused a surge of anger against the company into an appreciation for the company's efforts to combat deforestation.[22]

TABLE 11.4

Timberland's Response to Accusations from 65,000 Online Activists[23]

Date	Messages	Note
June 1, 2009	**Greenpeace issues the report "Slaughtering the Amazon"** and encourages environmental activists to contact companies at fault: "While the US-based companies behind reputable global brands like Adidas, Nike, Reebok, and Timberland appear to believe that Amazon sources are excluded from their products, our investigations expose for the first time how their blind consumption of raw materials fuels deforestation and climate change. . . . Take action now: Ask Nike, Adidas, Timberland, Reebok, Clark's and Geox to refuse to use leather that is destroying the Amazon."	Without advance notice to Timberland, Greenpeace begins a full-scale campaign against them.
June 1, 2009	**Activists immediately flood Timberland with angry emails** such as the following: "Dear Mr. Swartz, I am concerned that, given your company's dependence on leather to make shoes sold around the world, you may be supporting forest destruction, slave labor, the expulsion of indigenous groups within the Amazon Rainforest, and global climate change. . . . As a consumer, I want to be confident that when I buy your shoes I have not contributed to Amazon destruction and climate change. . . . I look forward to hearing what steps you will take to help solve this problem."	Beginning on June 1, nearly 65,000 activists wrote complaints to Timberland similar to this.
June 3, 2009	**Greenpeace continues to ask activists to contact Timberland.** One such request appeared in a blog post called "Timberland Needs to Hear From You" on the Greenpeace website: "Now is the time to save the Amazon and our climate, and every step will count. Ask Timberland to step up already. . . . We're disappointed with Timberland, but they can still do the right thing—especially if they hear from you. If you receive an email from Timberland, please respond with a question: Can you prove that my Timberlands are not destroying the Amazon? And please cc: Kking@Timberland.com so that you know they are getting your feedback."	Greenpeace continued its aggressive campaign against Timberland.

TABLE 11.4

(*Continued*)

Date	Messages	Note
June 1–4, 2009	**During the first four days of the campaign, Timberland replied to every email complaint with a lengthy, somewhat defensive email:** "Thank you for your inquiry. . . . We take our environmental and community impact very seriously and work hard to do our part to preserve the planet by planting trees, reducing our contribution to global warming, developing environmentally-conscious products and encouraging civic action. . . . We do source some leather from Brazil, but we have been assured that the material is not sourced from deforested areas. . . . We share your concerns about deforestation. . . . Timberland's tree planting initiative has resulted in more than one million trees planted across the globe since 2001. . . . We plan to plant another million trees by the end of 2011."	Timberland showed respect for and agreement with the activists' views. Timberland *avoided heavy-handedness* and *used the appropriate channels* by responding by email in the correct language (determined by the location of IP addresses).
June 5, 2009	**Starting on the fifth day, Timberland decided on a less-is-more approach:** "Thank you for your inquiry. . . . Timberland is committed to minimizing the environmental impact of our business operations. We're interested in engaging with Greenpeace and others in our industry about this situation."	Timberland continued to respond to all email complaints within hours. Managers admitted to themselves they needed more information about sourcing and committed to *gathering all the facts.*
July 24, 2009	**After striking an agreement with Greenpeace, Timberland crafted a new message on July 24:** "For more than 20 years, Timberland's approach to supplier relationships has been one of active, mutual engagement. . . . Our principles apply in the Amazon, and so we are working closely with our supplier in Brazil to ensure they have an action plan in place that addresses their commitment to an immediate moratorium on deforestation in the Amazon Biome, and of course refraining from sourcing products from indigenous or protected lands or entities that engage in slave labor."	Timberland announced its commitment to devote more resources to stopping deforestation in the Amazon.
July 29, 2009	**Greenpeace announced Timberland's leadership efforts in avoiding deforestation** in the Amazon in a Greenpeace website story called "Timberland Steps It Up a Notch, Commits to Amazon Protections": "Working with Greenpeace, Timberland released a policy that will require its leather suppliers to commit to a moratorium on purchasing any cattle raised in newly deforested areas within the Amazon Rainforest. . . . 'Timberland has raised the bar for environmentally and socially responsible leather sourcing policies in the Amazon. They have taken an important step by not only committing to avoid leather from cattle raised in newly deforested areas, but by working with existing suppliers like Bertin, to move the Brazilian cattle sector toward supporting a moratorium on any new cattle expansion into the Amazon Rainforest,' said Lindsey Allen, Greenpeace forests campaigner."	Ultimately, Timberland worked and partnered with Greenpeace to promote a shared cause: ensuring suppliers did not engage in deforestation. This partnership allowed Timberland to *rely on external advocates* as it repaired its reputation.
October 30, 2009	**On October 30 Timberland sent a lengthy email update signed by CEO Jeff Swartz to everyone who'd contacted the company on this issue:** "Three months later, real progress to report. . . . Last month [our supplier] publicly announced their official Amazon cattle moratorium . . . and is working aggressively to meet traceability targets to ensure the origin of all the cattle they source is acceptable and not contributing to Amazon deforestation. . . . For its part, Greenpeace has done an outstanding job gathering data, creating a complete and compelling case for the issue, and mobilizing its tens of thousands of supporters. . . . Their effort has driven change into the system. We applaud their activism."	After Timberland took a more active role in stopping deforestation in the Amazon, it followed up with each of the 65,000 activists who had lodged complaints to explain actions taken and express shared purpose.

FIGURE 11.8

Are Your Crisis Communications FAIR?

Facts (How *factual* is your communication?)

- Have you presented *all* the facts correctly?
- Have you presented information that allows stakeholders to make informed decisions that are in their best interests?
- Have you carefully considered various interpretations of your data? Have you assessed the quality of your information?

Access (How *accessible* or *transparent* are your motives, reasoning, and information?)

- Have you fully disclosed information that stakeholders need?
- Are you hiding information that casts you in a better light or real reasons for making certain claims or recommendations? Have you put your interests ahead of the interests of the victims?
- Have you given victims the opportunity to provide input in the decision-making process?
- Have you used all available communication channels to reach victims?

Impacts (How does your communication *impact* stakeholders?)

- Have you thought about how your communication will help or even hurt others? How could you learn more about these impacts?
- Have you made recommendations to stakeholders that are in their best interests?

Respect (How *respectful* is your communication?)

- Would those you are communicating with consider your communication respectful?
- Would a neutral observer consider your communication respectful?

 LO11.6 Review crisis communications for fairness and effectiveness.

Reviewing Crisis Messages

Whenever you plan and create crisis communications, you are participating in a consequential effort. You are directly representing your company to your many stakeholders. In many cases, your communications may help them avoid further loss. Certainly, the reputation of your company is in your hands, so it's particularly important to take care with the following.

Proofreading and Getting Feedback for Crisis Messages   During the crisis response stage, you will likely be pressed for time. In these tense moments, rereading your written crisis communications is essential. Pay special attention to accuracy. In some crises, your stakeholders' physical and financial security are at stake. Also, if possible, consider having your legal counsel read your messages before you distribute them.

Applying the FAIR Test to Crisis Communications   As with other communications, ask yourself and discuss with others whether your crisis messages are fair. Ask questions such as those listed in Figure 11.8 to ensure you are communicating in the interests of others.

Public Relations Messages

 LO11.7 Describe the role of public relations messages in today's organizations.

We begin this section by discussing the role of public relations in today's organizations. Then, since PR messages are viewed with more skepticism and distrust than most other business messages, we briefly examine strategies for achieving credibility despite that skepticism. Next, we focus on developing effective PR messages.

The Role of Public Relations Today

The public relations (PR) function occupies an increasingly important role in companies and other organizations for several reasons. In the emerging Social Age, companies are less able to generate predictable media exposure due to the shrinking options in mass advertising (especially in television), the increasingly fragmented media landscape (people turning to many sources and media for information), and the growing importance of online consumer reviews and activist blogs.[24] Since so many consumers rely on social media for information, the public relations field is among the business areas most rapidly adopting Social Age practices. Still, the success of these PR messages is far more difficult to control and measure than just a decade ago.

Traditionally, PR was viewed as media relations, and the primary vehicle for PR messages was press releases. Over the past several decades, during the Information Age, the scope of PR broadened and became a key component of the marketing mix.[25] PR has been defined as "the management function that establishes and maintains mutually beneficial relationships between an organization and the various publics on whom its success depends."[26] In other words, PR is fundamentally about *building relationships* with employees, customers, communities, the media, and other stakeholders.

A primary goal of building these relationships is to improve corporate reputation or credibility. Elliot Schreiber, one of the foremost authorities on public relations, recently defined **corporate reputation** on the Institute for Public Relations website:

> From the perspective of the organization, reputation is an intangible asset that allows the company to better manage the expectations and needs of its various stakeholders, creating differentiation and barriers vis-à-vis its competitors. From the perspective of stakeholders, reputation is the intellectual, emotional and behavioral response as to whether or not the communications and actions of an organization resonate with their needs and interests.[27]

This definition reveals several key aspects of reputation. First, it is an asset; it has value. Studies suggest that reputation directly contributes to between 3 and 7.5 percent of annual revenues. For some companies, reputation can increase revenue even more. Second, having a positive reputation is not enough. A company's reputation must differentiate it from its competitors. Third, a primary goal of public relations is managing the expectations of stakeholders. And most important, through public relations, a company develops a reputation that delivers value to stakeholders based on their own needs and interests.[28]

Gaining Credibility through PR in the Post-Trust Era and the Social Age

Ironically, while the goal of PR involves reputation management, the field of PR has among the worst reputations. In Figure 11.9, you will see the results of a recent survey about the perceived credibility of various professionals.[29] Public relations executives were viewed as the least credible, with just 14 percent of adults believing that information coming from PR executives was credible.

This skeptical view of PR professionals and messages is not new. For decades, many customers, employees, and other stakeholders have viewed PR messages as spin.[30] However, the problem of developing credible PR messages is even more challenging in the post-trust era and the Social Age. People trust traditional media sources less than ever before. Furthermore, most people think that discerning the truth is more difficult

Principles for PR Communications

- Establish and maintain credible relationships with stakeholders.
- Build PR activities around a brand or strategic launch.
- Complete full cycles in PR campaigns.
- Communicate the *good* your company does.
- Adapt your PR messages to Information Age and Social Age communication channels.

A person like yourself — 52%
Doctor/health care specialist — 52%
Nonprofit organization representative — 47%
Academic — 44%
Financial industry specialist — 43%
Regular employee of a company — 35%
CEO/leader of your company — 32%
CEO of a company — 26%
Public relations executive — 14%

0%   20%   40%   60%

FIGURE 11.9

If You Heard Information from Each of These Sources, How CREDIBLE Would the Information Be?

Source: Edelman Trust Barometer 2007 as presented in Andy Beal and Judy Strauss, *Radically Transparent: Monitoring and Managing Reputations Online*, John Wiley & Sons, Inc., 2008. Reprinted with permission of John Wiley & Sons, Inc.

FIGURE 11.10

Less-Effective Invitation to a Blogger

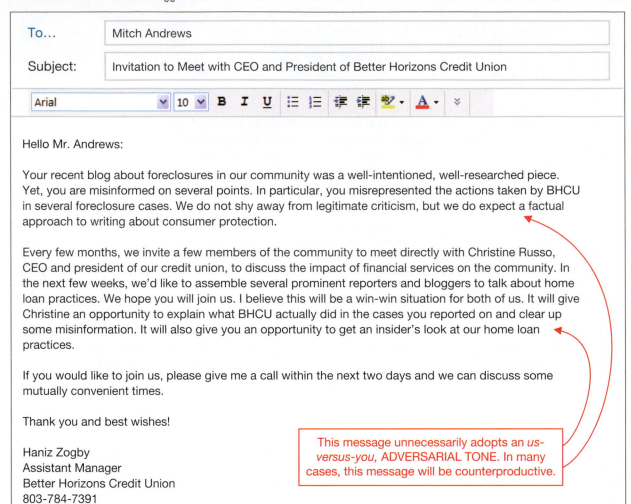

| To... | Mitch Andrews |
| Subject: | Invitation to Meet with CEO and President of Better Horizons Credit Union |

Hello Mr. Andrews:

Your recent blog about foreclosures in our community was a well-intentioned, well-researched piece. Yet, you are misinformed on several points. In particular, you misrepresented the actions taken by BHCU in several foreclosure cases. We do not shy away from legitimate criticism, but we do expect a factual approach to writing about consumer protection.

Every few months, we invite a few members of the community to meet directly with Christine Russo, CEO and president of our credit union, to discuss the impact of financial services on the community. In the next few weeks, we'd like to assemble several prominent reporters and bloggers to talk about home loan practices. We hope you will join us. I believe this will be a win-win situation for both of us. It will give Christine an opportunity to explain what BHCU actually did in the cases you reported on and clear up some misinformation. It will also give you an opportunity to get an insider's look at our home loan practices.

If you would like to join us, please give me a call within the next two days and we can discuss some mutually convenient times.

Thank you and best wishes!

Haniz Zogby
Assistant Manager
Better Horizons Credit Union
803-784-7391

This message unnecessarily adopts an *us-versus-you,* ADVERSARIAL TONE. In many cases, this message will be counterproductive.

than ever due to a fragmented media landscape and uncertainty about the information provided on Social Age tools such as websites and blogs.[31]

Since PR messages are *usually* treated with skepticism, establishing credibility and showing sincere goodwill should be primary goals in your public relations efforts. Consider the following pieces of advice.

Develop Credible Relationships   Public relations can be viewed as an unending process of building and nurturing relationships with stakeholders. The range of PR relationship-building activities is broad: It includes lobbying, sponsoring community events, holding press conferences, setting up public speeches, organizing company tours for the public and the media, providing public service announcements, and penning op-ed articles, to name a few.

A company builds credibility in its relationships to the degree that it achieves three types of responsibility: economic responsibility (similar to competence), ethical responsibility (similar to character), and social responsibility (similar to caring).[32] **Economic responsibility** means producing products and services that meet the needs of customers and clients; **ethical responsibility** means that corporate activities comply with high ethical and legal standards; and **social responsibility** means that companies *give back*, serve, and meet the social interests of their communities.

FIGURE 11.11

More-Effective Invitation to a Blogger

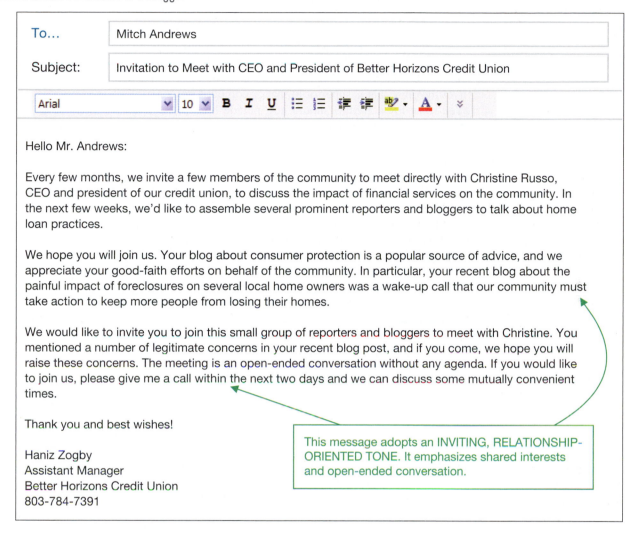

To...   Mitch Andrews

Subject: Invitation to Meet with CEO and President of Better Horizons Credit Union

Arial   10   B I U

Hello Mr. Andrews:

Every few months, we invite a few members of the community to meet directly with Christine Russo, CEO and president of our credit union, to discuss the impact of financial services on the community. In the next few weeks, we'd like to assemble several prominent reporters and bloggers to talk about home loan practices.

We hope you will join us. Your blog about consumer protection is a popular source of advice, and we appreciate your good-faith efforts on behalf of the community. In particular, your recent blog about the painful impact of foreclosures on several local home owners was a wake-up call that our community must take action to keep more people from losing their homes.

We would like to invite you to join this small group of reporters and bloggers to meet with Christine. You mentioned a number of legitimate concerns in your recent blog post, and if you come, we hope you will raise these concerns. The meeting is an open-ended conversation without any agenda. If you would like to join us, please give me a call within the next two days and we can discuss some mutually convenient times.

Thank you and best wishes!

Haniz Zogby
Assistant Manager
Better Horizons Credit Union
803-784-7391

This message adopts an INVITING, RELATIONSHIP-ORIENTED TONE. It emphasizes shared interests and open-ended conversation.

In the post-trust era (PTE), credible relationships are critical for creating effective PR messages. When stakeholders view the company as credible, they trust its PR messages; when they view the company as not credible, they distrust those messages. When stakeholders have unformed opinions of a company, the typical PTE response is to treat PR messages skeptically. In situations where stakeholders view a company neutrally or as not credible, one of the best PR approaches is to find outside parties who will talk positively about the company or endorse it. By establishing relationships with prominent, visible, and credible opinion makers who are willing to make endorsements, companies may gain positive public exposure.

In the emerging Social Age, developing credible relationships with important opinion makers is critical. One approach is to learn about bloggers who write about your industry or business. Then, consider developing relationships with them, inviting them on-site, being transparent, and giving them raw information. If they get to know you and you provide them with firsthand information about your company, they are less likely to write potentially damaging blog posts that are skewed by less-credible external information.[33] Figures 11.10 and 11.11 present invitations from Haniz to a blogger who has written about the industry unfavorably. In the less-effective example (Figure 11.10), Haniz's invitation adopts an us-versus-you tone. It emphasizes that she is right and he is wrong, thus closing off conversation and relationship-building. By contrast, in the more-effective example (Figure 11.11), Haniz demonstrates a listening-centric orientation by extending an invitation for real dialogue.

Build a Brand or Strategic Promotion

One primary goal as you build relationships with stakeholders should be to differentiate your company's brand, products, and services from those of competitors. In other words, the goal is not just to gain positive public exposure. Rather, it is to carve out a distinctive corporate reputation for delivering value that is superior to that of competitors.

Yet, most PR activities should not include hard sells. They are intended to build and reinforce a brand in a no-pressure manner that avoids the feel of mass advertising. Potential customers should never perceive PR activities as strictly self-serving.

Among the most visible PR activities for companies are charitable ones. Companies that contribute to their stakeholder communities also gain brand value. For example, Cisco, a major computer networking company, created the Cisco Networking Academy. This program contributes networking equipment to high schools and develops training programs for teachers and students. This type of giving directly impacts thousands of students and provides opportunities for career success. It also fills a shortage of qualified network administrators—up to a million, according to some estimates. This philanthropic effort is strategic because it increases demand for networking equipment and also reinforces Cisco's brand as the networking leader. Thus, corporate giving sets in motion a virtuous cycle that provides value for companies and their stakeholders.[34]

Better Horizons Credit Union also provides various community outreach programs, including free financial planning courses, a financial literacy fair, and volunteers for the Junior Achievement program in public schools. These activities succeed to the degree that stakeholders recognize Better Horizons as a financial institution that takes a personalized approach to financial planning, which is the brand Better Horizons seeks.

Complete the Campaign Cycle

A strategic approach to public relations involves campaigns—a series of methodical activities over a certain time period to meet defined PR objectives (see Figure 11.12). At the heart of PR campaigns is listening and research. Listening to stakeholders and applying a research approach at each stage in a campaign cycle ensures that PR activities create the most value for a company and

FIGURE 11.12

The PR Campaign Cycle

its stakeholders. The ongoing conversations via social media—especially Facebook, Twitter, YouTube, and activist blogs—create an environment in which companies continuously listen and research what stakeholders are saying and hearing about their companies. Part of the listening and research approach involves staying well informed of current events and markets that impact corporate reputation.[35]

The first step in most PR campaigns is to establish objectives. These objectives may include increasing word of mouth, increasing media attention to products and services, or increasing positive views of the company's brand, products, and services. Traditionally, the two most common measures of PR success were media mentions and word of mouth.[36] Now, companies are developing more sophisticated measures of PR success and evaluating not only positive press but also impact on competitive advantage. Once the objectives are established, the next steps involve identifying key stakeholders, developing key messages, identifying strategies and related tactics, and setting budgets and timelines. Finally, all effective campaigns involve evaluation.[37]

Communicate the Good the Company Does for Stakeholders

Companies should regularly and honestly publicize stories and articles about the good deeds they do. Informing stakeholders about the economic and social value the company provides enhances its reputation.[38] Companies should also make their high ethical standards visible to all stakeholders—identifying themselves as ethical corporate citizens. Similarly, companies should communicate their core values. Otherwise, some stakeholders will assume that the company operates only in a self-serving manner.[39]

Transition from Information Age PR to Social Age PR
The transition to truly networked communication will take decades. Some business functions have been quicker to adopt social media. Public relations is among the business functions that has done so the most rapidly.

In Social Age PR, business professionals can circumvent the traditional media and use communication channels that more quickly reach stakeholders. In this social media environment, PR professionals will increasingly give stakeholders the opportunity to talk back.[40] However, using social media for PR has several disadvantages: Most people think social media messages are less reliable than messages in traditional media outlets and print. Also, controlling the message is more difficult because of the fragmented, two-way nature of the social media environment. Some consumer analysts even suggest that social media allow customers and other stakeholders to vent more rage than in other forums.[41]

Most medium and large organizations have created social media teams that handle public relations. These teams (1) develop formal social media policies; (2) monitor internal and external communities; (3) engage online communities with fan pages, corporate blogs, online innovation forums, and meetings with prominent bloggers; and (4) act as first responders by acknowledging mistakes and warding off crises when negative, brand-threatening social media activity occurs.[42]

In addition to Social Age PR strategies, companies will continue to employ many Information Age PR strategies for the foreseeable future. In Figure 11.13, you can see some Better Horizon PR messages. You will notice that many of them are provided on static web pages, which is an Information Age approach. Other tools involve social media, such as video sharing, blogs, microblogs (often referred to as *tweets*), social networking websites, and texting.

As you develop PR messages, choose the communication channels that best enable you to reach your stakeholders; some respond more to messages via Web 1.0 tools, whereas others prefer PR communications through Web 2.0 tools. Keep in mind that using a particular communication channel (print, web page, social media) is not a strategy. Rather, developing a PR message with a target audience in mind is a strategy.

While your PR strategy will stay the same, you will modify your PR messages to reflect the norms and values generally associated with Information Age versus Social

FIGURE 11.13

PR Messages in the Emerging Social Age

Website with Regular PR Stories

Social Networking Site with Engaging Content

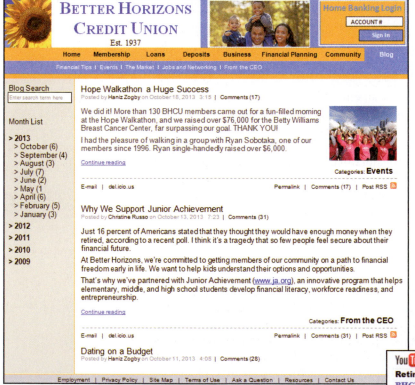

Corporate Blogs with Regular, Personalized Content

Texting to Facilitate Immediate Two-Way Communication

@hanizzobgy
Haniz Zogby

Congratulations to the Better Horizons walkathon team for raising $76,000 for the Betty Williams Cancer Center! Thank you!!!!

Microblogs (Tweets)

Online Videos on YouTube Channel

TABLE 11.5

Tools for PR Messages: Information Age Audiences and Social Age Audiences

Information Age	Social Age
Tone • Formal and professional • Authoritative and expert-based • Planned and professional	*Tone* • Less formal and social • Authentic and transparent • Spontaneous, conversational, and personalized
Tools Online media kits and newsrooms (press releases and responses to press inquiries) E-newsletters and e-blasts Online media databases Internet wire distribution services (PR Newswire, Business Wire) Video news releases/Video on demand	*Tools* Corporate blogs and microblogs Corporate social networking pages Online forums (online and in person) with key stakeholders Meetings with influential bloggers and online activists

Age communication tools. As shown in Table 11.5, the tone of Information Age communication tools, such as e-newsletters and online newsrooms, is generally more formal, professional, authoritative, and well crafted. By contrast, the tone of Social Age communication tools is typically less formal (but rarely informal), more authentic, and more spontaneous.[43]

Applying the AIM Planning Process for Public Relations Messages

LO11.8 Apply the AIM planning process to public relations messages.

Traditionally, companies issued press releases in a news story format to describe product launches, sponsored events, financial results, charitable donations, awards, and other *newsworthy* stories. These PR messages were labeled press releases because they were issued to editors and reporters of newspapers, magazines, and other media outlets. Editors and reporters then crafted their own stories from the material in the press releases. Similarly, companies often sought public exposure through the media by writing op-ed pieces or letters to the editor.

Although companies now use many communication channels and often bypass the traditional media to distribute PR messages, the legacy of press releases and op-eds continues. Most companies have a section of their websites, often labeled *pressroom* or *newsroom,* for PR stories and opinion pieces that follow the press release or op-ed style.

Audience Analysis for Public Relations Messages Nearly all public relations messages are targeted and adapted to particular stakeholder groups (see Figure 11.2, page 304). If you tailor your messages for each group, you increase the likelihood that group members will perceive your distinctive brand. The nine broad stakeholder categories were once quite tidy. In the Social Age, however, stakeholder groups straddle geographic and institutional boundaries, so you may need to think carefully about how to conceptualize your audiences.[44]

As you develop PR messages, answer questions such as the following about each stakeholder group:

● How much do they know about your company? How positively or negatively do they view it?

● What is their view of your brand value? Are they satisfied with your performance in the following areas: economic responsibility, social responsibility, and ethical responsibility?

● From what sources do they get information about you and your competitors? Through which communication channels can you best reach them?

TABLE 11.6

TABLE 11.6

Matching Influence Techniques to Public Relations Efforts

Influence Technique	Example
Reciprocation	Better Horizons offers free financial planning workshops. Although these workshops are provided without obligation, many participants gain a favorable view of Better Horizons and choose to reciprocate by becoming members.
Commitment	In the financial planning workshops, participants make commitments to adopt various financial planning strategies and goals. They often use Better Horizons and other financial institutions' services and planning tools to stay consistent with these commitments.
Social proof	The Better Horizons website provides stories and images of community members engaging in a good cause by participating in the Hope Walkathon. These stories and images combine to show what the community values and what it considers *right*.
Liking	Better Horizons invites various journalists and bloggers to meet the CEO in person for lunch. These interactions allow key media figures to gain personal relationships with Better Horizons executives. Ideally, as journalists and bloggers get to know them on an up-close-and-personal level, they will like them and, as a result, avoid ascribing negative intentions to them.
Authority	Better Horizons sponsors an annual financial literacy fair that features the prominent radio host of a personal finances show. By doing so, Better Horizons establishes an appeal to an authority figure.
Scarcity	By holding the financial literacy fair just once per year, Better Horizons allows just a short window of opportunity for people to participate, which increases interest. Furthermore, the fair features a nationally acclaimed keynote speaker who may not ever be back in town.

To make your PR efforts most effective, find ways to influence stakeholders so that they view your company's distinctive brand favorably and so that they are more likely to support your company through positive word of mouth and purchases. Robert Cialdini's influence techniques (described in Chapter 9) are useful in shaping stakeholders' views through PR messages.[45] See Table 11.6 for various strategies Better Horizons uses in PR efforts and messages to influence stakeholders.

Idea Development for PR Messages Since a primary goal of PR is to create distinctive brand value for a company, any individual message should be considered a piece in this larger effort. So, the first step is to clarify your company's brand and, through discussion, gain a shared sense of the brand message. Without this agreement among colleagues, a company may produce nonunified, perhaps even confusing, messages.

Many PR messages center on drawing positive attention to products and services, especially those that are newly launched, recently improved, or recently awarded or otherwise recognized. Developing your ideas for PR messages involves understanding these products and services completely and accurately. Furthermore, it involves identifying which products and services the company intends to highlight. Thus, it requires discussions of the company's strategy for promoting various products and services. Once you have done all this, you are ready to act much like a news reporter. You gather accurate and reliable information that tells a compelling story of what the company has done.

Message Structure for PR Messages In the press release style, which still accounts for most written PR messages, the main components include a headline, dateline, the story, a boilerplate, and contact information.

The *headline* immediately captures the attention of stakeholders. Next, the *dateline* allows readers to identify when the story occurred. Then, the *PR story*—whether it's announcing a product launch, an act of charity, an event, or many other types of notable corporate activities—is written in third person in what is often referred to as *inverted pyramid style.*

The *story* should answer the basic questions of *who, what, when, where,* and *why* quickly within the first paragraph—the widest part of the inverted pyramid. The story then provides supporting details—the second tier of the inverted pyramid. At the end of the PR story, a *boilerplate* or *positioning statement* briefly explains background about the company: the nature of its business, its products and services, its customers, and its *unique selling position,* meaning what distinguishes it from competitors.[46] Typically, minor PR messages are just 100 to 300 words, and major announcements are generally 500 to 800 words.[47]

Another common approach to PR messages is the op-ed style. Traditionally, a corporate leader would write an opinion piece in first person about a challenge or issue shared by the company and the public. As with press releases, the scope of the op-ed approach for PR has grown. Just a decade ago, op-eds were written for newspapers and other periodicals on an irregular basis. Now, however, the op-ed style is common on corporate blogs, where business leaders can regularly share their opinions and experiences.

Components of PR Messages
Press release style: • Headline • Dateline • PR story • Boilerplate • Contact information • Call to action

Creating PR Messages

Once you have planned your message, you are ready to write it with a focus on achieving excellence in tone, style, and design. Because most stakeholders will make rapid judgments and be skeptical of your motives and interests, you want a friendly tone. Also, use words, phrases, and sentences that help you achieve transparency and objectivity. Stakeholders realize that the message contains your version of reality, and they may perceive your version as skewed toward your own interests rather than theirs. If you can convince your audience members that you are writing objectively and in their interests, you will encounter far less resistance.

LO11.9 Construct effective and responsible public relations messages.

Your primary aim regarding style is to make your message easy to process. As you would for a newspaper article, you will write in short paragraphs and sentences so that skimmers can quickly gather pertinent information.

Most PR messages are now distributed electronically via multimedia platforms, such as websites and even email. PR messages in print form are often packaged in nicely designed annual reports, social responsibility reports, and so on. These messages frequently involve extensive use of photographs, video, and graphic design features. For your most important PR messages, consider using professionals to incorporate good aesthetic design.

In Figures 11.14 and 11.15, you can see two sets of PR messages from Better Horizons. The first is an announcement about the Better Horizons Annual Financial Literacy Fair and is developed in press release style. The message is developed to attract community members to the event and to promote Better Horizons' brand and values. The message is warm, inviting, and front-loaded. The second message is in op-ed style. Christine, Better Horizons president, uses a we-voice (see Chapter 5) to describe the company's commitment to the Junior Achievement program. This reinforces Better Horizons' commitment to financial literacy in the community, affirms its commitment to its partner (Junior Achievement), and promotes its brand and values. Since this op-ed style piece is written on a blog, it also allows interaction with stakeholders, who can post their own comments. For more about using corporate blogs, read the Technology Tips box on page 328.

FIGURE 11.14

A Public Relations Message in the Press Release Style on a Web Page

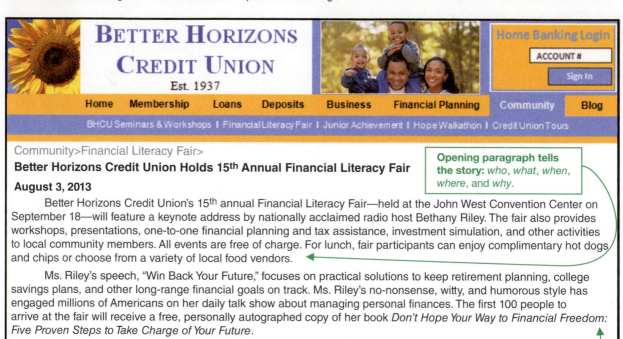

LO11.10 Review public relations messages for fairness and effectiveness.

Reviewing Public Relations Messages

PR messages are often extremely consequential, and your company's reputation is on the line. Therefore, make sure to carefully review what you've written. You may have weeks and months to review some messages. For others, however, you may face pressing time constraints. In either case, proofread carefully, get at least some feedback, and apply the FAIR test.

Proofreading and Getting Feedback for PR Messages

If you are writing PR messages for a midsized or large organization, you will likely work with a team. At the very least, you will work with a marketing director or blog editor. Working with editors and PR teams allows you to receive plenty of feedback. For online PR messages, you also get feedback from readers. They may leave comments,

FIGURE 11.15

A Public Relations Message in Op-Ed Style on a Blog

BETTER HORIZONS
CREDIT UNION
Est. 1937

Home Banking Login
ACCOUNT #
Sign In

Home | Membership | Loans | Deposits | Business | Financial Planning | Community | Blog

Financial Tips | Events | The Market | Jobs and Networking | From the CEO

Blog Search

Enter search term here

Month List

> **2013**
> October (6)
> September (4)
> August (3)
> July (7)
> June (2)
> May (1
> April (6)
> February (5)
> January (3)
> **2012**
> **2011**
> **2010**
> **2009**

Why We Support Junior Achievement

Posted by **Christine Russo** on October 13, 2013 7:23 | Comments (31)

Just 16 percent of Americans stated that they thought they would have enough money when they retired, according to a recent poll. I think it's a tragedy that so few people feel secure about their financial future.

At Better Horizons, we're committed to getting members of our community on a path to financial freedom early in life. We want to help kids understand their options and opportunities.

That's why we've partnered with Junior Achievement (www.ja.org), an innovative program that helps elementary, middle, and high school students develop financial literacy, workforce readiness, and entrepreneurship.

We believe Junior Achievement programs work because they rely on community volunteers with real-world business experience to guest-teach courses. The courses are structured to give students hands-on, practical, and real business experiences.

In the past ten years, BHCU employees have volunteered nearly 2,000 hours as guest teachers. Our water-cooler conversations here at work often center on our wonderful experiences working with the young people of our community.

We are optimistic about the financial future of these students because they are learning and committing to the fundamentals of financial planning. A few months ago on this blog, we highlighted the experiences of Jasmine Jenkins, a local high school student who was deeply impacted by her Junior Achievement course in 7th grade (www.bhcu.org/blog/jasminejenkins). She started a college savings plan and amassed nearly $14,000. Next week, she will start her first semester at PVU, becoming the first member of her family to go to college! If you ask Jasmine, she'll be the first to tell you that Junior Achievement made this dream possible for her.

Please join me in supporting Junior Achievement in any way you can – volunteering, contributing, or simply recommending it to your local schools.

COMMENTS
❝❝ Showing 31 comments

Luis   3 hours ago

I could not possibly agree more. Our young people need to start planning early, especially in these uncertain times. JA was a critical part of inspiring me to start my own small business. Christine, count me in as someone who will volunteer.

jenharding   1 day ago

I've taught two JA courses in the past. I've noticed two things. First, the students are hungering for chances to really get involved in projects that feel real. In each of the classes I taught, we created actual companies. Second, most of the students lack quite basic attitudes and skills necessary to compete in the business world. The JA programs help these kids gain these attitudes and skills quickly.

Christine touched on the key take-away. We've got to get our kids started sooner in developing financial know-how. Preparing for careers and understanding financial planning is more complicated now than it was in past decades.

TECHNOLOGY TIPS

CORPORATE BLOGS

Nearly all companies now use corporate blogs as part of their online public relations efforts. These blogs are also useful during crises, allowing companies to provide constant updates from a central location. Consider the following approaches:

Spend time learning about blogs. If you and those assigned to developing a blog are novices, invest time learning about best practices in blog writing. Look at your competitors' blogs and those of companies within your industry. You'll find plenty of information to help you map out a strategy.

Humanize your blogs. This is a place on your website where you give your readers a glimpse into the human, personal side of your business. Talk about the lighter sides of business and expose your personality—all in a way that strengthens your brand.

Facilitate and encourage conversations. Use your blogs to start online conversations. Let your readers come inside and feel like they are part of the community. This is a great opportunity to listen to your customers and other stakeholders to find out what they want and expect from you. Respond to comments so that readers feel heard. Avoid, however, deleting comments, even when they are negative.

Provide regular, fresh content. Your readers will only follow your blog if you update it frequently and provide original content. Aim for fun, authentic, and useful posts. Consider how-to posts that focus on lifestyle interests and hobbies.

Revolve your blog entries around a consistent theme. If you don't have a unifying theme, readers cannot make sense of the blog or understand why they should return to it regularly. Ideally, you will develop themes that build your brand value.

Introduce your bloggers and establish their credibility. Several employees will likely write your corporate blog. You can enhance these bloggers' credibility by providing short profiles: their pictures, personal backgrounds, and areas of expertise.

Connect your blog to other social media. To increase the impact and gain followers, allow readers to subscribe to your blog via an RSS feed and connect via other social media such as Facebook, Twitter, and YouTube.

Source: Reprinted courtesy of Southwest Airlines.

allowing you to evaluate how helpful or valuable they find your online messages. Also, with web analytics, you can get a sense of how many and what type of visitors read your messages. Thus, PR messages have built-in means of being proofread and getting feedback.

You can make this team approach to developing PR messages more effective if you respond well to the comments of others within your own team as well as those stakeholders who comment online. Avoid responding to negative feedback defensively. Use these comments to guide your future PR efforts.

Applying the FAIR Test to Public Relations Messages

As with other communications, ask yourself and discuss with others whether your PR message is fair to others. Ask questions such as those listed in Figure 11.16 to ensure you are communicating in the interests of others.

FIGURE 11.16

Are Your Public Relations Communications FAIR?

Facts (How *factual* is your communication?)

- Have you presented *all* the facts correctly?
- Have you presented information that allows stakeholders to make informed decisions that are in their best interests?
- Have you carefully considered various interpretations of your data? Have you assessed the quality of your information?
- When interpreting your information, have you looked at it from the perspectives of stakeholders?

Access (How *accessible* or *transparent* are your motives, reasoning, and information?)

- Are your motives clear, or will others perceive that you have a hidden agenda?
- Have you fully disclosed information that stakeholders need?
- Are you hiding any information to cast yourself in a better light or any real reasons for making certain claims or recommendations?
- Have you given stakeholders the opportunity to provide input in the decision-making process?

Impacts (How does your communication *impact* stakeholders?)

- Have you considered how your communication impacts all stakeholders?
- Have you thought about how your communication will help or even hurt others? How could you learn more about these impacts?
- Have you made recommendations to stakeholders that are in their best interests?

Respect (How *respectful* is your communication?)

- Would those you are communicating with consider your communication respectful?
- Would a neutral observer consider your communication respectful?

Always avoid spinning the truth. Nearly all public relations professionals can tell dozens of stories about the damage done to corporate reputations when messages failed to provide complete or accurate information *(facts),* covered up information *(access),* overlooked potential fallout on stakeholders *(impacts),* and failed to consider stakeholders *(respect).* Any dishonesty can come back to haunt you.[48]

As you evaluate how to tell PR stories, be honest and stay grounded in reality. While the goal of PR campaigns is to improve the corporate reputation in ways that give distinct advantages compared to competitors, seasoned PR professionals caution against raising the expectations of stakeholders too much. In the short run, you may boost your corporate image. In the long run, however, if your claims were overblown, stakeholders will likely realize that their high expectations were not met and recognize that you overpromised.

For example, the former head of PR at AT&T, Dick Martin, admits that he and his team excessively promoted a merger between AT&T and Time Warner because they viewed the deal from an overly optimistic perspective. Later, Martin said, "So when things began to go amiss for the company, we had a more difficult time controlling the damage than if we had been more modest in laying out our plans."[49] He believes the lesson of this public relations nightmare is simple: "Don't fall in love with your own story."[50]

Many legal and ethical considerations affect the public relations field. Be aware of PR-related regulations within your industry and company. In particular, be aware of regulations that exist for copyrights and trademarks and the communication activities of publicly traded companies. As you consider how to compose and distribute PR messages ethically, seek the guidance of organizations such as the Public Relations Society of America and the International Association of Business Communicators (IABC), which have developed guidelines.[51] In addition, consider the thoughts of PR professional Steven Craig in the Communication Q&A on page 330.

COMMUNICATION Q&A

CONVERSATIONS WITH CURRENT BUSINESS PROFESSIONALS

Pete Cardon: How can you use PR messages to build relationships with stakeholders?

Steven Craig: One key is building strong relationships with local communities and media. In the past few years, I've worked on a lot of campaigns for a copper mine. The mine is one of the largest economic contributors to the local community. It's also one of the largest polluters. So, the mine is a mixed blessing to the area. In a very real sense, the mine's existence depends on the favorable views of local community members.

PR professionals at the mine are constantly developing messages that center on its role as an economic engine and its progress in its environmental responsibility. They use focus groups to stay informed about the perspectives of community members. That way they can tailor the PR messages to what people are thinking right now. If they find that people are concerned about pollutants, they can develop PR messages about recent changes, such as relying more on natural gas than coal to reduce emissions or increased use of alternative energy sources.

Not only is the content of the PR messages important, so is the timing. The mine depends on getting regulations and permits for its operations. Gaining these regulations and permits would be next to impossible without local support. Many of the PR campaigns are timed to increase positive press prior to applying for various permits.

PC: How do PR messages contribute to an organization's brand value?

SC: Consumers make many of their decisions solely based on brand value. Brand value is built in many ways, including through PR messages. Typically, if your brand value is strong, people notice your advertisements. If your brand value is weak, your ads get lost among the hundreds of other advertising messages out there.

The mine I mentioned earlier has built goodwill over generations. Everyone in the local area at least knows someone—a friend or relative—who has worked there. The mine tries to capture this feeling of community and economic legacy as part of its brand value.

PC: What are some of the most common mistakes you've seen in PR messages?

SC: You really need to stay with the same broad message. I've seen many cases where advertising and public relations firms or clients get anxious to change their look and change their message. But the public doesn't respond to constantly shifting brands. It's like all of a sudden if your friend changes his personality, it confuses you and makes you wonder if you really know this person. PR and ad campaigns are just the same. You need to develop a good message, establish your brand, and stay the course with consistent messages. This is especially the case for companies without large advertising budgets.

Steven Craig *has worked on dozens of public relations campaigns during his 20 years in the advertising industry. He started his career working for public relations and advertising firms such as Penna Powers and DSW. He currently owns his own advertising firm.*

Chapter Takeaway for *Crisis Communications and PR Messages*

LO 11.1. Explain how crisis communications and public relations messages impact organizational reputation. (pp. 301–302) Delivering effective crisis communications and PR messages improves **your company's credibility.**

For crisis communications, you show **competence** when you implement a crisis communications plan to rapidly assist victims and stakeholders. For PR messages, you show **economic responsibility** when you produce excellent products and services.

For crisis communications, you show **caring** when you demonstrate your genuine concern to help victims and stakeholders. For PR messages, you show **social responsibility** when you give back to your stakeholder communities.

For crisis communications, you show **character** when you ensure the company lives up to its legal and ethical responsibilities. For PR messages, you show **ethical responsibility** when you abide by high ethical values and legal standards.

LO 11.2. Describe the nature of crisis management in today's organizations. (pp. 302–304)

Pre-Crisis Preparation
- Create a crisis management plan.
- Assign and train a crisis management team.
- Regularly conduct exercises to test the crisis management plan.
- Develop sample responses to various types of crises.

Crisis Responses
- Act to help victims and ensure public safety; provide stress and trauma counseling.
- Monitor the situation carefully and stay updated with the facts.
- Provide quick, accurate, and consistent communications through all available communication channels; tailor messages to each stakeholder group.

Post-Crisis Actions
- Keep stakeholders informed about recovery and corrective efforts.
- Update the crisis management plan based on lessons learned.
- Engage in public relations to repair the organization's reputation.

LO 11.3. Apply the AIM planning process to crisis communications. (pp. 304–307)

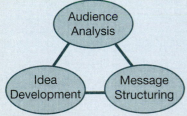

AIM Planning Process

Audience Analysis: Focus first on victims and most-impacted stakeholders. Use all communication channels to get messages out.

Idea Development: Gather various versions of the events, identify impacts and solutions, and analyze the nature of the crisis.

Message Structuring: Express concern, explain corrective actions, and provide instructions.

Type of Crisis	Concern	Corrective Actions	Instructions	Excuse and/or Justification	Compensation and/or Apology
Victim crises	X	X	X		
Victim crises*	X	X	X	X	
Accident crises	X	X	X	X	
Accident crises*	X	X	X	X	X
Preventable crises	X	X	X	X	X

*With intensifying factors

LO 11.4. Construct effective and responsible crisis messages. (pp. 307–313)

Components of Crisis Communications

- Express concern.
- Explain corrective actions.
- Provide instructions.
- Give an excuse/justification (for certain types of crises).
- Provide compensation/apology (for certain types of crises).

See *examples of crisis communications* in Figures 11.3 through 11.7.

LO 11.5. Explain how to handle external complaints and negative rumors. (pp. 310–315)

Principles for Responding to External Complaints and Rumors		
• Gather the facts.	• Respond quickly.	• Rely on external advocates.
• Avoid heavy-handedness (show of force).	• Use the appropriate channels.	• Respond with credentials.

See *examples of handling negative rumors* in Table 11.4.

LO 11.6. Review crisis communications for fairness and effectiveness. (p. 316)

Reviewing Process

FAIR Test: Always be honest with your *facts*, provide *access* to your decision making, and consider *impacts* on stakeholders.

Proofreading: For crisis messages, ensure complete accuracy.

Feedback: Access all avenues for feedback: colleagues, legal counsel, stakeholders.

LO 11.7. Describe the role of public relations messages in today's organizations. (pp. 316–323)

Principles for PR Communications
• Establish and maintain credible relationships with stakeholders.
• Build PR activities around a brand or strategic launch.
• Complete full cycles in PR campaigns.
• Communicate the *good* your company does.
• Adapt your PR messages to Information Age and Social Age communication channels.

LO 11.8. Apply the AIM planning process to public relations messages. (pp. 323–325)

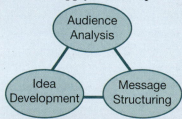

AIM Planning Process

Audience Analysis: Identify the unique needs and values of stakeholder groups and employ principles of influence.

Idea Development: Analyze how the PR message can fit into a unified PR effort that promotes distinctive brand value.

Message Structuring: Organize the PR message in press release style: headline, dateline, story, boilerplate, and contact info.

LO 11.9. Construct effective and responsible public relations messages. (pp. 325–327)

Components of PR Messages	
Press Release Style	
• Headline	• Boilerplate
• Dateline	• Contact information
• PR story	• Call to action

See *examples of PR messages* in Figures 11.10, 11.11, 11.13, 11.14, and 11.15.

LO 11.10. Review public relations messages for fairness and effectiveness. (pp. 326–329)

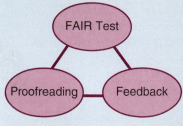

Reviewing Process

FAIR Test: Always be honest with your *facts*, provide *access* to your decision making, and consider *impacts* on stakeholders.

Proofreading: Check for contribution to brand value.

Feedback: Access all avenues for feedback: colleagues, legal counsel, stakeholders.

Key Terms

accident crisis (p. 305)

corporate reputation (p. 317)

economic responsibility (p. 318)

ethical responsibility (p. 318)

preventable crisis (p. 305)

social responsibility (p. 318)

victim crisis (p. 305)

Discussion Exercises

For additional cases and exercises related to crisis communications and public relations messages, see the online resources.

11.1 Applying Key Terms (LO 11.1, LO 11.2, LO 11.7)

Explain each of the key terms and provide a concrete example of how it impacts crisis communications and/or PR messages.

11.2 Crisis Communications Discussion Questions (LO 11.2, LO 11.3, LO 11.4, LO 11.5, LO 11.6)

Describe the role of crisis communications in today's organizations. Respond to the following questions in one or two well-thought-out paragraphs per question:

A. How can a company plan for crises, which by nature are often unpredictable?

B. What strategies should companies use to combat unfounded online rumors?

C. How should companies respond to victim crises, accident crises, and preventable crises?

D. How should a company choose which stakeholders take priority during a crisis?

11.3 Public Relations Discussion Questions (LO 11.7, LO 11.8, LO 11.9, LO 11.10)

Explain the role that public relations plays in today's organizations. Respond to the following questions in one or two well-thought-out paragraphs per question:

A. What are the goals of public relations efforts?

B. What are the defining characteristics of corporate reputations?

C. How is public relations changing in the post-trust era and emerging Social Age? How is it remaining the same?

D. Why do stakeholders so often view public relations messages skeptically?

E. What are the three aspects of credible PR efforts? Explain.

F. Explain what the PR campaign cycle is. Describe the importance of each stage: (a) listen/research; (b) set objectives; (c) identify stakeholders; (d) develop key messages; (e) establish strategy and tactics; (f) create timeline and budget; and (g) evaluate.

11.4 Best Practices in Crisis Communications (LO 11.2, LO 11.3, LO 11.4, LO 11.5, LO 11.6)

Choose an area of interest within crisis communications. You might consider the type of crisis (victim crisis, accident crisis,

preventable crisis) and/or the medium of communication (i.e., blogging, press conferences). Describe best practices for your selected topic in four or five paragraphs. You may use resources from a variety of public relations professional groups that provide a wealth of free information on their websites. Also, at these websites, you may find a specific topic of interest to you. Consider using the following as resources:

- Institute for Crisis Management (http://crisisexperts.blogspot.com/)
- Public Relations Society of America (www.prsa.org)

11.5 Best Practices in Public Relations (LO 11.7, LO 11.8, LO 11.9, LO 11.10)

Choose an area of interest within public relations. For example, you might choose from topics such as events and tours, meetings with stakeholders, PR campaigns, corporate social responsibility efforts, corporate blogs, or many others. Describe best practices in this area in four or five paragraphs. You may use resources from a variety of public relations professional groups that provide a wealth of free information on their websites. Also, at these websites, you may find a specific topic of interest to you. Consider using the following as resources:

- Arthur W. Page Society (www.awpagesociety.com)
- Public Relations Society of America (www.prsa.org)
- Center for Corporate Citizenship (www.bcccc.net)
- Institute for Public Relations (www.instituteforpr.org)
- Ragan (www.ragan.com)

11.6 Communication Q&A Discussion Questions (LO 11.1, LO 11.7, LO 11.8, LO 11.9)

Read the comments of Steven Craig in the Communication Q&A section and respond to the following questions:

A. What key points does Craig make about PR messages?

B. He mentions that one of his clients works extensively with focus groups. In your opinion, what, if any, ethical issues are raised by tailoring PR messages to what stakeholders think?

C. He states that it's extremely important to stay on message over time with PR. Explain his viewpoint and add your own thoughts about this notion.

D. He also raises the issue of timing. Based on his thoughts and your own, explain several principles for effectively timing PR messages.

11.7 Ethics in Crisis Communications and Public Relations
(LO 11.3, LO 11.6, LO 11.8, LO 11.10)

Look at the Code of Ethics for the Public Relations Society of America (you can find it at www.prsa.org/AboutPRSA/Ethics/CodeEnglish/). The PRSA advocates six professional values: advocacy, honesty, expertise, independence, loyalty, and fairness. Choose two of these and do the following:

A. Elaborate on your two chosen values. Provide details about their meaning and how you can ensure that your crisis communications and PR messages comply with these two values.

B. Explain the primary challenges to living up to your two chosen professional values.

C. Choose a company of interest to you. What specific steps can this company take to live up to your two chosen professional values?

Evaluation Exercises

11.8 Evaluate Crisis Communications (LO 11.3, LO 11.5, LO 11.6)

Find a crisis message from a company of your choice. If you have a difficult time finding one, consider the following recent corporate crises and find a related crisis message:

- Go Daddy's response when its CEO killed an elephant in Zimbabwe, causing many customers to cancel accounts (2011).
- Netflix's response to social media outcries after it raised monthly prices by 60 percent (2011).
- Japanese carmakers' (Toyota, Honda, Nissan) response to earthquake and tsunami (2011).
- BP's response to the Deepwater Horizon oil spill (2010).
- Mattel's comments on the recalls of over 11 million toys due to safety concerns (2007).

Answer the following questions related to the crisis message you have chosen:

A. Review the components of crisis messages—concern, corrective actions, instructions, attack against the accuser, denial, excuse, justification, reminder, ingratiation compensation, and apology (see Table 11.2 for descriptions of each).

B. Which components are included? Which are missing that should have been included? Explain.

C. How well did the crisis communication meet the needs of victims and other stakeholders?

D. Do you believe the communication was completely fair? Explain.

E. What are three aspects of the crisis message that could have been improved? Explain.

11.9 Analyze a Corporate Apology from Toyota CEO Akio Toyoda (LO 11.3, LO 11.6)

In early 2010, Toyota was forced to recall millions of its vehicles due to reports of gas pedal malfunctions. Dozens of drivers reported that their cars suddenly and unavoidably accelerated. Several incidents resulted in deaths. Toyota CEO Akio Toyoda appeared before the U.S. Congress to extend his apologies and discuss how the company would take responsibility. Read the summary and full text of Toyoda's apology at www.nytimes.com/2010/02/25/business/global/25toyota.html and www.cbsnews.com/8301-503544_162-6235105-503544.html.

Analyze the apology in the following ways:

A. In what ways is the apology direct? Indirect?

B. How does the apology express goodwill?

C. Does the apology include any positive comments? Give examples. Are these appropriate?

D. Does the apology include enough detail?

E. Does the apology include enough information about how Toyota will take responsibility?

F. Do you think the apology has aspects that are uniquely Japanese? Explain.

G. What three things would you have done differently or adjusted in the apology?

11.10 Evaluate a Press Release for a Company of Choice (LO 11.8, LO 11.10)

Choose a press release from a company of interest. Generally, you can access recent press releases by visiting a company's online pressroom (generally labeled *pressroom, newsroom,* or *media*). Answer the following questions about your selected press release:

A. Which stakeholder groups is this message written for? How well does it meet their needs?

B. What are the key messages? How well do they tie into the company's brand value or strategic promotion of certain products or services?

C. How well does the release tell a compelling PR story?

D. Does it contain a boilerplate? What does the boilerplate emphasize about the company?

E. Overall, how effective do you think this press release is? What two suggestions do you have for improving it?

11.11 Evaluate a Corporate Blog for Public Relations Content (LO 11.8, LO 11.10)

Find a corporate blog of interest to you. Read five entries and respond to the following questions:

A. What are the five topics of the blog entries? How do these entries tie into a theme?

B. Does the theme support the company's brand value or strategic promotion of certain products or services? Explain.

C. Which stakeholder groups is this blog written for? How well does it meet their needs?

D. What types of stakeholders would regularly follow this blog? Why?

E. What three suggestions do you have for improving the public relations value of this corporate blog?

11.12 Evaluate a Social Responsibility Report (LO 11.8, LO 11.10)

Read a corporate social responsibility report. You can generally find such reports in the pressroom section or investors' section of the website. Respond to the following questions:

A. What major initiatives, activities, and charitable giving does your selected company engage in to meet its social responsibility to stakeholders?

B. How would you define the company's brand? Do these social responsibility activities tie into the company's brand?

C. How well do the social responsibility activities improve or enhance corporate reputation?

D. What two suggestions do you have for better or further tying the social responsibility activities to the company's brand value?

E. What three suggestions do you have for improving the social responsibility report?

Case for Exercises 11.13 through 11.15 and 11.22 through 11.24: Netflix and Related Communications

In July 2011, Netflix abruptly separated its DVD-delivery and streaming services, increasing monthly subscription fees from $9.99 to $15.98 for subscribers who wanted to continue both services. Hundreds of thousands of irate customers posted angry comments on Netflix's Facebook page and website, and their personal Facebook accounts, Twitter messages, and other social media. The intense outcry led to extensive mainstream press coverage. Customers were angered by the drastic price increases and also the abrupt and confusing messages about them.

After two months of complaints via social media and traditional press, a public relations misstep had turned into a full-blown crisis. Netflix CEO Reed Hastings offered an apology on the Netflix website to try to contain the crisis (see Figure 11.19). In the message, he added that Netflix would create a new business called Qwikster to carry its DVD-delivery business. Within a month, Netflix abandoned the idea and retained the Netflix name for DVD-delivery and streaming services.

The short-term damage was severe. During the third quarter of 2011, Netflix lost approximately 1 million subscribers. Netflix shares fell from around $299 in July 2011 to $130 in September 2011. Yet, Netflix earnings rose 63 percent during the same quarter. Some analysts suggest that Netflix made a good, even necessary, business decision.[52] Nearly all public relations and crisis communication experts, however, agree that Netflix handled the communications poorly, unnecessarily alienated many customers, and damaged its corporate reputation (see Figures 11.17 and 11.18 for original announcements of the price increase).[53]

FIGURE 11.17

Original Email Message Sent to Netflix Customers[54]

Dear Ryan,

We are separating unlimited DVDs by mail and unlimited streaming into two separate plans to better reflect the costs of each. Now our members have a choice: a streaming only plan, a DVD only plan, or both.

Your current $9.99 a month membership for unlimited streaming and unlimited DVDs will be split into 2 distinct plans:

Plan 1: Unlimited Streaming (no DVDs) for $7.99 a month
Plan 2: Unlimited DVDs, 1 out at-a-time (no streaming) for $7.99 a month

Your price for getting both of these plans will be $15.98 a month ($7.99 + $7.99). You don't need to do anything to continue your memberships for both unlimited streaming and unlimited DVDs.

These prices will start for charges on or after September 1, 2011.

You can easily change or cancel your unlimited streaming plan, unlimited DVD plan, or both, by going to the Plan Change page in Your Account.

We realize you have many choices for home entertainment, and we thank you for your business. As always, if you have questions, please feel free to call us at 1-888-357-1516.

–The Netflix Team

Source: Reprinted with permission of Netflix.

FIGURE 11.18

Longer Version of Announcement on Netflix Corporate Blog[55]

Jessie Becker, here to share two significant changes at Netflix with you.

First, we are launching new DVD only plans. These plans offer our lowest prices ever for unlimited DVDs – only $7.99 a month for our 1 DVD out at-a-time plan and $11.99 a month for our 2 DVDs out at-a-time plan. By offering our lowest prices ever, we hope to provide great value to our current and future DVDs by mail members. New members can sign up for these plans by going to DVD.netflix.com.

Second, we are separating unlimited DVDs by mail and unlimited streaming into separate plans to better reflect the costs of each and to give our members a choice: a streaming only plan, a DVD only plan or the option to subscribe to both. With this change, we will no longer offer a plan that includes both unlimited streaming and DVDs by mail.

So for instance, our current $9.99 a month membership for unlimited streaming and unlimited DVDs will be split into 2 distinct plans:

Plan 1: Unlimited Streaming (no DVDs) for $7.99 a month
Plan 2: Unlimited DVDs, 1 out at-a-time (no streaming), for $7.99 a month.

The price for getting both of these plans will be $15.98 a month ($7.99 + $7.99). For new members, these changes are effective immediately; for existing members, the new pricing will start for charges on or after September 1, 2011.

Why the changes?

Last November when we launched our $7.99 unlimited streaming plan, DVDs by mail was treated as a $2 add on to our unlimited streaming plan. At the time, we didn't anticipate offering DVD only plans. Since then we have realized that there is still a very large continuing demand for DVDs both from our existing members as well as non-members. Given the long life we think DVDs by mail will have, treating DVDs as a $2 add on to our unlimited streaming plan neither makes great financial sense nor satisfies people who just want DVDs. Creating an unlimited DVDs by mail plan (no streaming) at our lowest price ever, $7.99, does make sense and will ensure a long life for our DVDs by mail offering. Reflecting our confidence that DVDs by mail is a long-term business for us, we are also establishing a separate and distinct management team solely focused on DVDs by mail, led by Andy Rendich, our Chief Service and Operations Officer and an 11 year veteran of Netflix.

Now we offer a choice: Unlimited Streaming for $7.99 a month, Unlimited DVDs for $7.99 a month, or both for $15.98 a month ($7.99 + $7.99). We think $7.99 is a terrific value for our unlimited streaming plan and $7.99 a terrific value for our unlimited DVD plan. We hope one, or both, of these plans makes sense for our members and their entertainment needs.

As always, our members can easily choose to change or cancel their unlimited streaming plan, unlimited DVD plan, or both by visiting Your Account.

Source: Reprinted with permission of Netflix.

FIGURE 11.19

CEO's Apology from Netflix Website[56]

I messed up. I owe everyone an explanation.

It is clear from the feedback over the past two months that many members felt we lacked respect and humility in the way we announced the separation of DVD and streaming, and the price changes. That was certainly not our intent, and I offer my sincere apology. I'll try to explain how this happened.

For the past five years, my greatest fear at Netflix has been that we wouldn't make the leap from success in DVDs to success in streaming. Most companies that are great at something – like AOL dialup or Borders bookstores – do not become great at new things people want (streaming for us) because they are afraid to hurt their initial business. Eventually these companies realize their error of not focusing enough on the new thing, and then the company fights desperately and hopelessly to recover. Companies rarely die from moving too fast, and they frequently die from moving too slowly.

When Netflix is evolving rapidly, however, I need to be extra-communicative. This is the key thing I got wrong.

In hindsight, I slid into arrogance based upon past success. We have done very well for a long time by steadily improving our service, without doing much CEO communication. Inside Netflix I say, "Actions speak louder than words," and we should just keep improving our service.

FIGURE 11.19

(*Continued*)

But now I see that given the huge changes we have been recently making, I should have personally given a full justification to our members of why we are separating DVD and streaming, and charging for both. It wouldn't have changed the price increase, but it would have been the right thing to do.

So here is what we are doing and why:

Many members love our DVD service, as I do, because nearly every movie ever made is published on DVD, plus lots of TV series. We want to advertise the breadth of our incredible DVD offering so that as many people as possible know it still exists, and it is a great option for those who want the huge and comprehensive selection on DVD. DVD by mail may not last forever, but we want it to last as long as possible.

I also love our streaming service because it is integrated into my TV, and I can watch anytime I want. The benefits of our streaming service are really quite different from the benefits of DVD by mail. We feel we need to focus on rapid improvement as streaming technology and the market evolve, without having to maintain compatibility with our DVD by mail service.

So we realized that streaming and DVD by mail are becoming two quite different businesses, with very different cost structures, different benefits that need to be marketed differently, and we need to let each grow and operate independently. It's hard for me to write this after over 10 years of mailing DVDs with pride, but we think it is necessary and best: In a few weeks, we will rename our DVD by mail service to "Qwikster."

We chose the name Qwikster because it refers to quick delivery. We will keep the name "Netflix" for streaming.

Qwikster will be the same website and DVD service that everyone is used to. It is just a new name, and DVD members will go to qwikster.com to access their DVD queues and choose movies. One improvement we will make at launch is to add a video games upgrade option, similar to our upgrade option for Blu-ray, for those who want to rent Wii, PS3 and Xbox 360 games. Members have been asking for video games for many years, and now that DVD by mail has its own team, we are finally getting it done. Other improvements will follow. Another advantage of separate websites is simplicity for our members. Each website will be focused on just one thing (DVDs or streaming) and will be even easier to use. A negative of the renaming and separation is that the Qwikster.com and Netflix.com websites will not be integrated. So if you subscribe to both services, and if you need to change your credit card or email address, you would need to do it in two places. Similarly, if you rate or review a movie on Qwikster, it doesn't show up on Netflix, and vice-versa.

There are no pricing changes (we're done with that!). Members who subscribe to both services will have two entries on their credit card statements, one for Qwikster and one for Netflix. The total will be the same as the current charges.

Andy Rendich, who has been working on our DVD service for 12 years, and leading it for the last 4 years, will be the CEO of Qwikster. Andy and I made a short welcome video. (You'll probably say we should avoid going into movie making after watching it.) We will let you know in a few weeks when the Qwikster.com website is up and ready. It is merely a renamed version of the Netflix DVD website, but with the addition of video games. You won't have to do anything special if you subscribe to our DVD by mail service.

For me the Netflix red envelope has always been a source of joy. The new envelope is still that distinctive red, but now it will have a Qwikster logo. I know that logo will grow on me over time, but still, it is hard. I imagine it will be the same for many of you. We'll also return to marketing our DVD by mail service, with its amazing selection, now with the Qwikster brand.

Some members will likely feel that we shouldn't split the businesses, and that we shouldn't rename our DVD by mail service. Our view is with this split of the businesses, we will be better at streaming, and we will be better at DVD by mail. It is possible we are moving too fast — it is hard to say. But going forward, Qwikster will continue to run the best DVD by mail service ever, throughout the United States. Netflix will offer the best streaming service for TV shows and movies, hopefully on a global basis. The additional streaming content we have coming in the next few months is substantial, and we are always working to improve our service further.

I want to acknowledge and thank our many members that stuck with us, and to apologize again to those members, both current and former, who felt we treated them thoughtlessly.

Both the Qwikster and Netflix teams will work hard to regain your trust. We know it will not be overnight. Actions speak louder than words. But words help people to understand actions.

Respectfully yours, Reed Hastings, Co-Founder and CEO, Netflix

Source: Reprinted with permission of Netflix.

11.13 Evaluate a Bad-News Email Message in Terms of PR Principles (LO 11.3, LO 11.5, LO 11.6)

Based on the Netflix announcement contained in Figure 11.17, respond to the following questions:

A. How effectively does this email follow principles for bad-news messages? (You may need to glance at Chapter 10 to refresh your memory.)

B. How could the message be rewritten to reinforce the following PR principles: establish and maintain credible relationships with stakeholders; build PR activities around a brand or strategic launch; adapt your message to Social Age communication channels?

C. What are your three primary recommendations for improving this message? Be specific and elaborate on your ideas.

11.14 Evaluate a Bad-News Blog Post in Terms of PR Principles (LO 11.3, LO 11.5, LO 11.6)

Based on the Netflix announcement contained in Figure 11.18, respond to the following questions:

A. How effectively does this blog post follow principles for bad-news messages? (You may need to glance at Chapter 10 to refresh your memory.)

B. How could the message be rewritten to reinforce the following PR principles: establish and maintain credible relationships with stakeholders; build PR activities around a brand or strategic launch; adapt your message to Social Age communication channels?

C. What are your three primary recommendations for improving this message? Be specific and elaborate on your ideas.

11.15 Evaluate a Crisis Apology (LO 11.3, LO 11.5, LO 11.6)

Based on Netflix CEO Reed Hastings's apology (see Figure 11.19), respond to the following questions:

A. How would you classify this crisis: a victim crisis, an accident crisis, or a preventable crisis? In what other ways would you describe this crisis?

B. What components of a crisis communication does this message contain—concern, corrective actions, instructions, excuse, justification, compensation, apology, reminders, ingratiation, denial, attack the accuser?

C. Evaluate each component you've identified. How effective is each? Be specific.

D. Overall, what three major recommendations would you make?

11.16 Evaluate Timberland's Approach to Stopping Negative Rumors (LO 11.3, LO 11.5, LO 11.6)

Based on Table 11.4, answer the following questions about Timberland's management of negative rumors.

A. How did Timberland avoid heavy-handedness? Give at least two specific examples.

B. Do you think Timberland responded quickly enough? Explain your views.

C. The table shows some email responses from Timberland. What other communication channels could Timberland have used? What is the value of using these other channels?

D. In what way did Timberland use external advocates? What are three other options the company had for using external advocates?

E. What are two options Timberland could have used for responding with credentials?

F. Choose one of the email messages from Timberland and give three suggestions for improving it.

Application Exercises

11.17 Plan a Crisis Message (LO 11.3)

Identify a company of interest. Assume that the CEO or other key executive is arrested on a domestic violence charge. The executive admits an altercation but denies the seriousness of the charges. Respond to the following questions:

A. What stakeholders will you craft a message for? What communication channels will you use? Who will be in charge of crafting the communications?

B. What type of information will you provide for each stakeholder group? What will you do to keep stakeholders updated?

C. How will you structure your messages? What are the key components you will provide in your crisis communications? Elaborate about what you mean and be specific for each of the components you describe.

11.18 Plan Public Relations Messages (LO 11.8)

Identify a company of interest and do the following:

A. Explain the company's brand value and how PR messages can help it build its brand.

B. Using Figure 11.2 as a guide, categorize and describe this company's major stakeholders. You will likely need to reclassify or split some of the categories. For example, you might consider further segmenting the customer group.

C. Describe PR efforts the company does or could do that match the six forms of psychological influence as illustrated in Table 11.6.

D. Outline three PR messages the company could create. For each, explain the key messages, major content, communication channel, and targeted stakeholders

11.19 Rewrite a Crisis Message (LO 11.4)

In 2008, Bob Nardelli delivered news that Chrysler would lay off one-quarter of its white-collar managers. Read his email—at www.autoblog.com/2008/10/24/bob-nardelli-to-employees-we-want-a-25-cut-of-white-collar-job/—and then rewrite it to make it more effective.

11.20 Rewrite a Press Release (LO 11.9)

Find an interesting press release from a company of choice. Assume you will modify it for a different communication channel and a different target stakeholder. For example, if you found a press release written for the media, you could rewrite it as a blog entry for customers. Rewrite the press release accordingly.

11.21 Rewrite a Blog Entry (LO 11.9)

Find a corporate blog entry of interest to you. Rewrite the blog entry as a press release. Assume that you are writing it for the media or for potential investors.

11.22 Plan and Rewrite the Netflix Bad-News Email Announcement (LO 11.8, LO 11.9)

Based on the Netflix announcement contained in Figure 11.17, do the following:

A. Write a detailed AIM planning document and devote at least five paragraphs to analyzing your audience, developing your ideas, and structuring your message.

B. Rewrite the bad-news email.

11.23 Plan and Rewrite the Netflix Bad-News Blog Announcement (LO 11.8, LO 11.9)

Based on the Netflix announcement contained in Figure 11.18, do the following:

A. Write a detailed AIM planning document and devote at least five paragraphs to analyzing your audience, developing your ideas, and structuring your message.

B. Rewrite the bad-news announcement.

11.24 Plan and Rewrite the Netflix Apology (LO 11.3, LO 11.4)

Based on Netflix CEO Reed Hastings's apology (see Figure 11.19), do the following:

A. Write a detailed AIM planning document and devote at least five paragraphs to analyzing your audience, developing your ideas, and structuring your message.

B. Rewrite the crisis apology.

Endnotes

1. Gerald C. Kane, Robert G. Fichman, John Gallaugher, and John Glaser, "Community Relations 2.0," *Harvard Business Review* (November 2009): 45–50.

2. W. Timothy Coombs and S. J. Holladay, "Helping Crisis Managers Protect Reputational Assets: Initial Tests of the Situational Crisis Communication Theory," *Management Communication Quarterly* 16: 165–186; W. Timothy Coombs, "Impact of Past Crises on Current Crisis Communications: Insights from Situational Crisis Communication Theory," *Journal of Business Communication* 41: 265–289; W. Timothy Coombs, "Crisis Management and Communications," *Institute for Public Relations* (October 30, 2007), available at www.instituteforpr.org/topics/crisis-management-and-communications/.

3. Linda M. Hagan, "For Reputation's Sake: Managing Crisis Communication," in Elizabeth L. Toth, *The Future of Excellence in Public Relations and Communication Management* (Mahwah, NJ: Lawrence Erlbaum Associates, 2007): 413–440; Dan Ackman, "Tire Trouble: The Ford-Firestone Blowout," *Forbes* online (June 20, 2001), available at http://www.forbes.com/2001/06/20/tireindex.html.

4. Coombs and Holladay, "Helping Crisis Managers Protect Reputational Assets"; Coombs, "Impact of Past Crises on Current Crisis Communications"; Coombs, "Crisis Management and Communications."

5. Richard Bierck, "What Will You Say When Disaster Strikes?" *Harvard Management Communication Letter* (May 2002): 1.

6. Coombs and Holladay, "Helping Crisis Managers Protect Reputational Assets"; Coombs, "Impact of Past Crises on Current Crisis Communications"; Coombs, "Crisis Management and Communications."

7. Bierck, "What Will You Say When Disaster Strikes?": 1–4.

8. Ibid.

9. Joanne E. Hale, Ronald E. Dulek, and David P. Hale, "Crisis Response Communication Challenges: Building Theory from Qualitative Data," *Journal of Business Communication* 42, no. 2 (2005): 112–134.

10. Coombs and Holladay, "Helping Crisis Managers Protect Reputational Assets"; Coombs, "Impact of Past Crises on Current Crisis Communications"; Coombs, "Crisis Management and Communications."

11. Ibid.

12. Georgia Credit Union Affiliates, "How to Communicate When a Crisis Occurs," retrieved August 29, 2011, from http://www.gacreditunions.org/advocacy/public_influence/crisis/how_to_communicate.php.

13. Coombs and Holladay, "Helping Crisis Managers Protect Reputational Assets"; Coombs, "Impact of Past Crises on Current Crisis Communications"; Coombs, "Crisis Management and Communications."

14. Alice M. Tybout, "Let the Response Fit the Scandal," *Harvard Business Review* (December 2009): 82–88.

15. Yan Jin and Brooke Fisher Liu, "The Blog-Mediated Crisis Communication Model: Recommendations for Responding to Influential External Blogs," *Journal of Public Relations Research* 22 no. 4 (2010): 429–455.

16. Barbara Kellerman, "When Should a Leader Apologize—and When Not?" *Harvard Business Review* (April 2006): 74.

17. Kane et al., "Community Relations 2.0."

18. Hayley Tsukayama, "Netflix Faces Backlash over Price Changes," *Washington Post* online (July 13, 2011), available at http://www .washingtonpost.com/blogs/faster-forward/post/netflix-faces-backlash -over-price-changes/2011/07/13/gIQAs8QHCI_blog.html.

19. Leslie Gaines-Ross, "Reputation Warfare," *Harvard Business Review* (December 2010): 70–76.

20. Jeff Swartz, "Timberland's CEO on Standing Up to 65,000 Angry Activists," *Harvard Business Review* (September 2010): 39–43.

21. Ibid: 40.

22. Ibid: 39–43.

23. Passages in the "Messages" column are verbatim from the following sources: Swartz, "Timberland's CEO on Standing Up to 65,000 Angry Activists": 43; "Top Name Brands Implicated in Amazon Destruction," retrieved February 20, 2012, from www.greenpeace.org/ usa/en/news-and-blogs/news/slaughtering-the-amazon/; "Timberland Needs to Hear from You," (June 3, 2009) retrieved February 20, 2012, from www.greenpeace.org/usa/en/news-and-blogs/campaign -blog/timberland-needs-to-hear-from-you/blog/25613/; "Timberland Steps It Up a Notch, Commits to Amazon Protections: New Policy Sets Deadline for Bertin to Support Moratorium on Cattle Expansion into the Amazon," (July 29, 2009) retrieved February 20, 2012, from www.greenpeace.org/usa/en/news-and-blogs/news/ timberland-steps-it-up-072909/.

24. David Robinson, "Public Relations Comes of Age," *Business Horizons* 49 (2006): 247–256.

25. Phil Hall, *The New PR: An Insider's Guide to the Changing Face of Public Relations* (North Potomac, MD: Larstan Publishing, 2007).

26. Lucy Harr and Dick Radtke, *PR for CUs* (Madison, WI: Credit Union Executives Society, 2004): 1.

27. Elliot S. Schreiber, "Reputation," *Institute for Public Relations* website (December 2, 2008), www.instituteforpr.org/topics/reputation/.

28. Ibid.

29. Edelman Trust Barometer 2007 as presented in Andy Beal and Judy Straus, *Radically Transparent: Monitoring and Managing Reputations Online* (Indianapolis, IN: Wiley Publishing, 2008).

30. Hall, *The New PR: An Insider's Guide to the Changing Face of Public Relations;* Kirk Hallahan, "Seven Models of Framing: Implications for Public Relations," *Journal of Public Relations Research* 11, no. 3 (1999): 205–242.

31. Donald K. Wright and Michelle D. Hinson, "How Blogs and Social Media are Changing Public Relations and the Way It Is Practiced," *Public Relations Journal* 2, no. 2 (2008): 1–21; Hall, *The New PR: An Insider's Guide to the Changing Face of Public Relations;* Kane, et al., "Community Relations 2.0"; Deirdre Breakenridge, *PR 2.0: New Media, New Tools, New Audiences* (Upper Saddle River, NJ: Pearson Education, 2008).

32. Schreiber, "Reputation."

33. Bill Margaritas and David B. Rockland, "Leading Brands and the Modern Social Media Landscape," *Ketchum Webinar* (November 18, 2010).

34. Michael E. Porter and Mark R. Kramer, "The Competitive Advantage of Corporate Philanthropy," *Harvard Business Review* (December 2002): 56–68.

35. Breakenridge, *PR 2.0: New Media, New Tools, New Audiences.*

36. Robinson, "Public Relations Comes of Age."

37. Kane et al., "Community Relations 2.0."

38. Pekka Aula and Saku Mantere, *Strategic Reputation Management: Toward a Company of Good* (New York: Routledge, 2008).

39. Rosanna M. Fiske, "The Business of Communicating Values," *Harvard Business Review* blog (July 26, 2011), retrieved August 3, 2011, from http://blogs.hbr.org/cs/2011/07/the_business_of_ communicating.html.

40. Breakenridge, *PR 2.0: New Media, New Tools, New Audiences.*

41. Chris Taylor, "How Social Media Are Amplifying Customer Outrage," retrieved July 29, 2011, from www.cnn.com/2011/TECH/social .media/07/22/social.media.outrage.taylor/.

42. Kane et al., "Community Relations 2.0."

43. Breakenridge, *PR 2.0: New Media, New Tools, New Audiences;* Hall, *The New PR: An Insider's Guide to the Changing Face of Public Relations;* Patty Deutsche, *Elements of a PR Plan* (San Francisco: e-agency, 2011).

44. Kane et al., "Community Relations 2.0": 45.

45. Andy Green, *Effective Personal Communication Skills for Public Relations* (Philadelphia: Kogan Page, 2006).

46. Ibid.

47. Deutsche, *Elements of a PR Plan.*

48. Baruch Fischhoff, "Getting Straight Talk Right," *Harvard Business Review* (May 2006): 24–25.

49. Dick Martin, "Gilded and Gelded: Hard-Won Lessons from the PR Wars," *Harvard Business Review* (October 2003): 47.

50. Ibid: 44.

51. Larry F. Lamb and Kathy Brittain McKee, *Applied Public Relations: Cases in Stakeholder Management* (Mahwah, NJ: Lawrence Erlbaum Associates, 2005).

52. Darren Murph, "Reed Hastings' Netflix Spinoff Isn't About DVD Success, It's About Hedging the Stream," retrieved February 25, 2011, from www.engadget.com/2011/09/19/ editorial-reed-hastings-netflix-spinoff-isnt-about-dvd-succes/.

53. Ryan M. Healy, "How Netflix Could Have Made Bad News Better," retrieved from http://www.ryanhealy.com/ netflix-bad-news-better/.

54. Ibid.

55. Jessie Becker, "Netflix Introduces New Plans and Announces Price Changes," retrieved from http://blog.netflix.com/2011/07/netflix -introduces-new-plans-and.html.

56. Reed Hastings, "An Explanation and Some Reflections," retrieved from http://blog.netflix.com/2011/09/explanation-and-some -reflections.html.

Reports and Presentations

PART FIVE

CHAPTER TWELVE

Research and Planning for Business Reports

After studying this chapter, you should be able to do the following:

LO12.1   Explain how planning and conducting business research for reports impacts your credibility.

LO12.2   Create research objectives that are specific and achievable.

LO12.3   Explain principles of effective design for survey questions and choices.

LO12.4   Develop charts and tables to concisely display data and accentuate key messages.

LO12.5   Evaluate the usefulness of data sources for business research.

LO12.6   Conduct secondary research to address a business problem.

LO12.7   Evaluate research data, charts, and tables for fairness and effectiveness.

WHY DOES THIS MATTER?

Hear Pete Cardon explain why this matters.

bit.ly.com/CardonWhy12

In your career, you'll be responsible for reading and preparing an amazing variety of business reports. Common types include business plans, project reports, status or progress reports, financial plans, marketing plans, strategic plans, and technical reports. Reports can range from a single page to thousands of pages. One characteristic is common to all types: the purpose is to provide sound information, analysis, and advice to decision makers.

Compared to most daily business correspondence, reports are considered more reliable, authoritative, thorough, and final. As decision-making tools, they are typically commissioned by and written for middle-level or upper-level managers or external stakeholders (i.e., loan officers, stockholders). Because of their role in decision making, most reports take much more time to create than daily business correspondence. Furthermore, many reports are written collaboratively since they contain complex information that requires the talents and resources of many professionals.

Many reports rely on business research. A person who can conduct business research will have many opportunities for success and advancement. Research is the process of searching for knowledge. In business, you may want to know how consumers think and feel; understand employees' attitudes about a new policy; forecast sales based on past performance and carefully selected assumptions; use internal data to identify consumer behavioral patterns; or examine data to address a variety of business problems.

Conducting and reporting research can enhance your credibility in a variety of ways. You demonstrate an often rare competency in the workplace when you can zero in on core business problems and collect and analyze data that relates to these problems. You show caring by involving key decision makers in the process and conducting research that meets their needs. Also, your character is significantly enhanced when decision makers recognize that they can count on you to deliver results in an objective and unbiased fashion.

In this chapter, we consider several approaches to planning and conducting research for reports. Overall, the purpose is to gather and analyze data that will drive excellent decision making and high organizational performance. First, we focus on setting research objectives, a process that ensures you identify the most relevant data for your business goals. Then, we examine the processes of primary and secondary research to ensure that you will gather reliable data. We also discuss how to effectively present numerical and other information in charts, graphs, and tables so that your complex data is easy to understand and supports your key messages. Read the following case, which serves as the basis for examples provided in Chapters 12 and 13.

LO12.1 Explain how planning and conducting business research for reports impacts your credibility.

Chapter Case: Analyzing Customer Satisfaction at the Prestigio Hotel

Who's Involved

Jeff Anderton, marketing assistant
- Has worked at the Prestigio for three months
- Roles include marketing of meetings and conventions to professional groups and tracking customer satisfaction
- Graduated a year ago with a marketing major and statistics minor

Andrea Garcia, general manager
- Has worked as general manager for one year
- Started at the Prestigio nearly nine years ago in a position similar to Jeff's marketing assistant position
- Expects thorough data and analysis before making decisions

The Situation

The Prestigio is a four-star hotel that gains much of its business from conventions and meetings. In recent years, it has lost revenue in nearly all areas. In particular, for each of the past two years, the Prestigio has lost between 5 and 10 percent in revenues for conferences. Thus, Andrea wonders if they need to reevaluate their strategy on meetings. She is concerned about the drop in business and wants good research to understand how to move forward.

Andrea recently asked Jeff to work on three marketing research projects. She expects him to complete them in roughly three months.

For the first project, she wants Jeff to analyze guest satisfaction at the Prestigio compared to its three chief competitors: the Grand Swan, Great Falls, and Wyatt. She wants Jeff to use an online hotel rating system to conduct the analysis. Andrea also wants to know if satisfaction ratings have improved in relation to two recent initiatives: increasing the guest-to-staff ratio and increasing the amount of customer-service training. Jeff determines that he can best gather the data with primary research, through a survey he will develop.

For the second project, Andrea wants Jeff to conduct a survey about guest satisfaction among conference attendees. She is particularly interested in guests for three-day conferences. One issue she wants to address is their purchase of and satisfaction with Internet service in their guest rooms. As with the first task, Jeff decides that the best way to address Andrea's research objectives is to develop a survey.

For the third project, Andrea wants Jeff to gather information about eco-friendly or green meetings. Traditionally, the Prestigio has not focused on green meetings. However, in the past year, Andrea has noticed that meeting planners and other guests frequently inquire about green meetings. She wants to know if the Prestigio should invest more resources in such options. Jeff will use a combination of primary and secondary research to address the research objectives for this project.

Task 1
Gather and analyze guest satisfaction ratings for the Prestigio and its competitors.

Task 2
Conduct a survey of recent conference attendees to evaluate conference satisfaction.

Task 3
Gather information about best practices in green meetings.

Analyzing Your Audience for Business Reports

The planning stage for many types of business reports—especially those based on research—often takes months, even years. Like other communications, you can apply the AIM planning process to develop your message based on good ideas that meet the needs of decision makers.

The first step in developing research-based business reports is identifying what decision makers want to accomplish. In many cases, they will commission the reports and have clear goals in mind. In other cases, they do not have clear goals. In all cases, you should spend time with your target audience of decision makers to carefully consider their primary business goals, research objectives, and expectations.[1]

During the research and report writing process, consider updating decision makers and involving them in the process. This increases the likelihood that you will develop a report that is useful to them.

Developing Your Ideas with Primary Research

With a clear understanding of what decision makers want from reports, you are ready to begin research. For important business decisions, gathering data can take weeks, months, and even years. Since many reports are intended to aid high-stakes decision making, getting the right information, analyzing it correctly, and making related recommendations needs to be done carefully and completely.

Business research can be broadly categorized as primary and secondary. **Primary research** refers to the analysis of data that you, people from your organization, or others under your direction (i.e., consultants) have collected. **Secondary research** refers to the analysis of data collected by others with no direction from you or members of your organization.

Primary research is generally most reliable and useful for your business reports because you can focus it to meet your specific research objectives and get feedback directly related to your organization and its needs. However, conducting primary research is often time-consuming, intrusive, and expensive. In some cases, primary research might suffer from a bias toward preexisting opinions and beliefs. For example, a marketing director who is convinced that a new product will be successful when it hits market may misinterpret consumer research to fit his/her preexisting opinions. Common types of primary research include analysis of internal data, survey research, focus groups, interviews, and case studies.

In this chapter, we focus on one of the most common types of primary research: surveys. Survey research is increasingly common because of the ease with which online surveys can be administered (see Technology Tips on page 361). Generally, survey research involves administering written questionnaires. Most survey questions are **closed questions:** They restrict respondents to certain answers (rating scales, multiple choice, etc.). Some survey questions are **open-ended questions,** allowing respondents to answer in any way they choose. Closed questions can be more easily quantified and analyzed. However, open-ended questions allow you to understand an issue in more depth.

Developing Research Objectives

Once you have identified what your audience of decision makers needs, you will carefully define your research problems. Defining research problems involves stating your research objectives in specific, targeted, and achievable statements. Notice in Table 12.1 how Jeff develops research objectives for two of his research projects.

Creating Surveys

With online survey technology readily available and easy to use, you will likely have many opportunities to use it in the workplace. Surveys are particularly useful because you can quickly get the responses of dozens if not hundreds of colleagues, current or potential customers, or members of other groups of interest. Online surveys are a nice

LO12.2 Create research objectives that are specific and achievable.

LO12.3 Explain principles of effective design for survey questions and choices.

TABLE 12.1

Creating Research Objectives

Less Effective	More Effective
Determine how satisfied our conference guests are.	Determine guest satisfaction among conference attendees for key conference amenities and services.
This objective is not specific enough. The statement does not lead to a focused approach to research.	This objective is specific. The statement leads to a focused approach to research.
Understand green meetings.	Identify key trends impacting the market demand for green meetings held at hotels.
This objective is not specific. It is too broad and lacks context.	This objective is specific. It focuses on a context that is relevant to the Prestigio.

tool because you can automatically dump all the data you collect into a spreadsheet. Of course, online surveys are not always convenient or possible, so you will sometimes use traditional paper-and-pencil questionnaires.

Ideally, you will have opportunities to learn about effective survey design, data collection, and analysis in some of your university courses. If you don't have this opportunity, many excellent books can help you develop your survey research skills. However, to develop your survey skills, you will need more than how-to knowledge. You also need to practice several times; there's no substitute for conducting several surveys and using the data to solve business problems in the workplace.

Generally, surveys should be short. Rarely can you get accurate data from surveys that take longer than five minutes to complete. Most consumer research questionnaires contain fewer than five or six questions. If the survey takes too long, respondents may become impatient and provide less-than-accurate responses or skip questions. The exception is when you pay respondents to take a survey. The obvious drawback is the high cost.

Another key to getting reliable data is designing the survey questions effectively. Survey questions should be (a) simple to answer, (b) non-leading, (c) exhaustive and unambiguous, and (d) limited to a single idea.

Survey Questions Should Be Simple to Answer
As you design most surveys, envision respondents who are eager to complete the items quickly and who will spend minimal time thinking about any given item. Survey questions should contain short questions and response options. Thus, respondents should be able to read the entire question in 10 to 20 seconds and select a response that matches their true opinions and feelings within just a few seconds. In Table 12.2, you will notice how Jeff is developing survey questions for his research about guest satisfaction.

Survey Questions Should Be Non-Leading
Be sure the questions in your survey are **non-leading.** A leading question is one that suggests an answer. Often, the leading question is designed to gain a preferred response from the survey

TABLE 12.2

Creating Simple Survey Questions

Less Effective	**More Effective**
On a scale from 1, not satisfied, to 4, extremely satisfied, how satisfied were you in the following areas related to your conference experience (if you have no opinion or did not use the following services, simply mark N/A)?	**How satisfied were you with the following aspects of your conference experience?**

Less Effective

	1	2	3	4	N/A
Conference Meals	○	○	○	○	○
Internet Pricing	○	○	○	○	○
Internet Speed in Rooms	○	○	○	○	○

More Effective

	1– Not Satisfied	2– Somewhat Satisfied	3– Satisfied	4– Extremely Satisfied	N/A-Not Applicable
Conference Meals	○	○	○	○	○
Internet Pricing	○	○	○	○	○
Internet Speed in Rooms	○	○	○	○	○

The question is 39 words long. Many respondents will be confused about how to answer the questions without labels for the numerical values.	The question contains just 12 words. Formatting and labels allow respondents to quickly and precisely process the information.

TABLE 12.2

(*Continued*)

Less Effective	More Effective
Rank-order each of the following guest services and amenities in providing value to you during your conference stay. (Rank-order each item. Place a 1 next to your favorite item, a 2 next to your second-favorite item, and so on. Do not place a number next to an amenity or service that you did not use during your stay.) _____ Spa _____ Fitness center _____ Outdoor swimming pool _____ Prestigio golf course _____ Prestigio comedy club _____ One of the Prestigio restaurants	Which of the following GUEST SERVICES AND AMENITIES did you use during your conference stay? **Check ALL that apply.** ☐ Spa ☐ Prestigio golf course ☐ Fitness center ☐ Prestigio comedy club ☐ Outdoor swimming pool ☐ One of the Prestigio restaurants
This question is complicated to answer. Many respondents will not spend time to carefully rank each item. Other responses may be inaccurate or unreliable.	This question is easy to answer. Respondents are given just one choice and can make this judgment within a few seconds.

designer's perspective. Sometimes, leading questions are phrased to imply how a respondent should answer. For example, the following leading question would likely lead many respondents to provide insincere answers: *As a citizen in the country with the most per capita carbon emissions in the world, how interested are you in learning about green meeting options?* Leading questions often do not allow respondents to provide their genuine thoughts or impressions. So, leading questions in surveys can produce unreliable and unusable information (see Table 12.3).

Survey Choices Should Be Exhaustive and Unambiguous   Survey choices should be complete. Being **exhaustive** means that all possibilities are available, and being **unambiguous** means that only one choice is appropriate (see Table 12.4).

Survey Questions Should Contain One Idea   Survey questions that contain more than one idea are difficult for respondents to answer (see Table 12.5).

TABLE 12.3

Creating Non-Leading Survey Questions

Less Effective	More Effective
To show my support for the green meeting movement, I would recommend the Prestigio as a good site for a business conference. 1. Strongly disagree 2. Disagree 3. Neutral 4. Agree 5. Strongly agree	I would recommend the Prestigio as a good site for a business conference. 1. Strongly disagree 2. Disagree 3. Neutral 4. Agree 5. Strongly agree
This survey question is leading. It suggests to respondents a correct or right answer. It would not provide reliable or useful results.	This survey question is non-leading. It does not suggest or manipulate a response. It would likely provide useful data.

TABLE 12.4

Creating Exhaustive and Unambiguous Survey Choices

Less Effective	More Effective
Age: A. Under 30 B. 31 to 40 C. 41 to 50 D. 50 to 64	Age: A. 30 and under B. 31 to 40 C. 41 to 50 D. 51 to 65 E. Over 65
These choices are neither exhaustive nor unambiguous. They are not exhaustive because respondents who are 65 and over would not have a choice to select. They are not unambiguous because two of the choices overlap (C and D); in other words, a person who is 50 could select either option.	These choices are both exhaustive and unambiguous. Any respondent of any age would find just one correct response.

TABLE 12.5

Creating Survey Questions with a Single Idea

Less Effective	More Effective
How much do you know about green meetings and possible savings on these meetings? A. Nothing at all B. A little C. Some D. A lot	How much do you know about green meeting options for your business? A. Nothing at all B. A little C. Some D. A lot
This question contains two ideas: (1) what the respondent knows about green meetings; and (2) what the respondent knows about possible savings on green meetings. This is confusing to the respondent and impossible for the researcher to interpret.	This question contains one idea. As a result, the question is easy for the respondent to answer and easy for the researcher to analyze.

Furthermore, they are impossible to correctly analyze. Notice Jeff's completed survey in Figure 12.1.

Analyzing Your Data

Once you've conducted your surveys, your next step is to analyze the data. This job may feel exhilarating. Or it may feel overwhelming and even daunting. Even small sets of data from relatively few survey questions can be analyzed and configured in nearly limitless ways. As you develop your primary research skills, consider the following advice:

1. *Learn as much as you can about forecasting and other forms of statistical and quantitative analysis.* Unless you apply good principles of analysis, you can easily get flawed results. Furthermore, unless you are careful, you can without any intention of doing so allow your preconceived ideas and biases to affect how you interpret the data.

2. *Learn as much as you can about spreadsheet, database, and statistical software.* You likely will have a course in spreadsheet software (i.e., Excel). Make the most

FIGURE 12.1

Example of Simple, Easy-to-Complete Online Survey

Feedback on Your Conference Stay at *The Prestigio*	Exit this Survey

Thanks for your participation in this survey. When you complete this survey by clicking the "Done" button, you will be given a printable coupon worth $10 at any Target store.

1. Gender:

◯ Male
◯ Female

2. Age:

◯ Under 30 ◯ 51 to 65
◯ 31 to 40 ◯ Over 65
◯ 41 to 50

3. Income Level:

◯ Under $30,000 ◯ $50,000–$75,000
◯ $30,000–$40,000 ◯ $75,000–$100,000
◯ $40,000–$50,000 ◯ Over $100,000

4. How many days of Internet service did you purchase during your conference visit?

◯ 0 ◯ 2
◯ 1 ◯ 3

5. How satisfied were you with the following aspects of your conference experience?

	1– Not Satisfied	2– Somewhat Satisfied	3– Satisfied	4– Extremely Satisfied	N/A– Not Applicable
Conference Meals	◯	◯	◯	◯	◯
Internet Pricing	◯	◯	◯	◯	◯
Internet Speed in Rooms	◯	◯	◯	◯	◯
Business Center	◯	◯	◯	◯	◯
Staff & Service	◯	◯	◯	◯	◯
Meeting Rooms	◯	◯	◯	◯	◯

6. Please respond to the following statements based on your experiences during your recent conference at the Prestigio.

	1– Strongly Disagree	2– Disagree	3– Neutral	4– Agree	5– Strongly Agree
Overall, I was satisfied with the conference experience.	◯	◯	◯	◯	◯
I would like to attend another business conference held at the Prestigio.	◯	◯	◯	◯	◯
I would recommend the Prestigio as a good site for a business conference.	◯	◯	◯	◯	◯

Which of the following GUEST SERVICES AND AMENITIES did you use during your conference stay? Check ALL that apply.

☐ Spa ☐ Outdoor swimming pool ☐ Prestigio comedy club
☐ Fitness center ☐ Prestigio golf course ☐ One of the Prestigio restaurants

[Done]

of this training and continue experimenting with it to feel comfortable analyzing data. Also, develop a basic understanding of databases. All companies store tremendous amounts of information in databases. If you understand basic database design, you will know what types of information you can extract to answer your research questions. Finally, statistical software (i.e., SPSS, SAS, SYSTAT) can help you conduct analyses far more rapidly and efficiently than can spreadsheet software.

3. *Rely on others in your analysis.* You will likely work with colleagues who have quantitative analysis skills in certain disciplines and for certain types of business problems, and you can turn to them for technical help. Also, you can turn to others for analytical help, because when you analyze data in a group, you are less likely to inadvertently misinterpret the data.

4. *Stay focused on your business problem and look for the big picture.* Often, company databases or survey data contain so much information that you can easily be overwhelmed by the many ways to use it. As you discipline yourself to focus on your key research problems, you are less likely to get bogged down looking at tangential issues.

Communicating with Charts and Tables

Nearly all business activities and goals are measured and quantified: profit and loss, operating expenses, marketing expenditures, employee turnover, performance evaluations, market share, budgets, customer behavior, quality, and so on. Simply put, business executives and managers communicate with numbers. Some management experts even describe the ability to communicate numbers as a core managerial competency. Thus, in this section, we'll focus on using charts and tables to communicate numerical information.

After conducting survey research or other forms of business research, you typically have many statistics and figures that you could include in reports to decision makers. However, presenting this information effectively is challenging. In fact, most managers are poor at communicating numerical information. Also, while business managers tend to like numbers, few listeners and readers can absorb a lot of them at one sitting. As one communication expert mentioned to managers, "The chances are good that you love numbers a lot more than most of your audience members do. . . . Overloading your audience members with data is a sure way to guarantee they'll forget almost everything you say."[2] Although most managers communicate with numbers with the intention of persuading and inspiring, they most often end up confusing or boring their audience.

The most fundamental mistake that executives and managers make when communicating with numbers is failing to focus on the main message, which tends to be nonnumerical. Phrases such as, "I'm going to spend a few minutes going through the numbers," or "Let me give you some background by running through the numbers" can cause your audience to tune out.[3] As you will learn in more detail in the next sections, your presentation's takeaway message should be your first and primary consideration when communicating with charts and tables. As you read through the next few pages, notice how Jeff designs charts and tables for his research at the Prestigio Hotel. In particular, pay attention to how these charts and tables are useful for Andrea, who is the general manager and primary decision maker.

LO12.4 Develop charts and tables to concisely display data and accentuate key messages.

Designing Effective Charts   Charts can effectively convey complex numerical information in a simple, appealing format. A well-designed chart can express a strong message and leave a lasting visual impression on viewers and readers. Since many viewers and readers immediately gravitate to them, charts have the potential to draw readers into a document or presentation almost instantaneously.

Overall, the message of the chart is central. As Dona Wong, graphics director of *The Wall Street Journal* from 2001 to 2010, explained, "It is the content that makes graphics interesting. When a chart is presented properly, information just flows to the viewer in the clearest and most efficient way. There are no extra layers of colors, no enhancements to distract us from the clarity of the information."[4] As with other business messages, planning is the key component of developing charts.

Effective business communicators carefully select the few data relationships that most support their business messages. Top graphic designer Nigel Holmes, who is credited with coining the term *explanation graphics,* notes that charts must do more than describe or inform. They should explain important business ideas or relationships that support the key messages of a communication. Furthermore, charts should not require much mental effort for the reader. As Holmes points out, "Charts that don't explain themselves are worse than no charts."[5]

Throughout this chapter you'll find charts and tables that illustrate the strategic use of data to address the concerns of Andrea from the chapter case. While dozens of chart options are available, this section focuses on the three types used primarily within the workplace: line charts, pie charts, and bar charts. Several other chart and figure types are illustrated with less detail. Mastering the design principles of these most common and relevant charts will enable you to create other, less-common types if you choose to do so.

Generally, **line charts** are useful for depicting events and trends over time. For example, stock prices over time would make the most sense when presented in the form of a line chart. **Pie charts** are useful for illustrating the pieces within a whole. Market share would be best illustrated with a pie chart. **Bar charts** are useful to compare amounts or quantities. The bar chart, with its many forms, is the most versatile of these charts since it can be used to compare many types of data.

Creating Effective Charts

As you create charts, focus on the following criteria: (a) title descriptiveness, (b) focal points, (c) information sufficiency, (d) ease of processing, and, most important, (e) takeaway message. In the following pages, you will find a discussion of each of these criteria. Also, you will find less-effective and more-effective examples for each major type of chart. Each of the examples is supplemented with explanations about these five criteria.

Title Descriptiveness   Most readers look first at the chart's title to grasp its message. Thus, the title should explain the primary point of the chart. However, it must be short enough for the reader to process quickly (generally less than ten words). In some cases you may add a subtitle if the short title is not sufficient.

Consider Figure 12.2, which illustrates identical information with a less-effective and more-effective line chart. In the less-effective chart on the left, the chart title is a short and relatively unhelpful phrase, "Staff & Service Ratings." By contrast, the chart title in the more-effective chart on the right uses a title and a subtitle. The main title, "Improvement in Staff & Service Ratings," uses the first word to immediately point out the main theme of the chart. The subtitle, in just seven words, accentuates the idea that the improvement was intentional or goal-based ("Raising Our Performance") and that the improvement far exceeded that of primary competitors.

Focal Points   A chart should draw the reader's attention to the most-critical relationships and ideas. Much like unified paragraphs (Chapter 3), in which all sentences focus on one main idea, each of the chart's focal points should support one main idea. The focal points can be visually generated in many interesting ways—for example, font choices (**bold**, *italics*), color, size, and callout boxes.

In the more-effective line chart in Figure 12.2, a variety of focal points highlight the improvement in staff and service ratings at the Prestigio. The callout box centered in the chart directs the reader to the point in time when the Prestigio launched its staff and service initiative, allowing the reader to trace the improvement in ratings since that time. The Prestigio data series is emphasized with a darker, thicker line that is placed on top of the other data series (for the other hotels).

Information Sufficiency Just how much information should you include in your charts? Charts should contain enough information for the reader to quickly and reasonably understand the ideas that are being displayed. Clear labels and legends should demonstrate what is being measured and in what units. In some cases, readers will expect to know data values at each point within the chart.

Although the ineffective line chart in Figure 12.2 does contain a legend showing which lines correspond to which hotels, the meaning of the *y*-axis is not as clear. A reader may assume that the data comes from a survey, since *ratings* is in the title, but be unsure what the range or direction of the scale is. By contrast, the more-effective line chart in Figure 12.2 contains a note indicating the range of the scale. Many charts place this information in a label along the *y*-axis.

Ease of Processing Another basic purpose of a chart is to convey complicated information as quickly as possible. If your readers can't process the information rapidly, they will lose interest. To some degree, this requires a balancing act with information sufficiency. The more information you provide, the more difficult it may be for some readers to process the chart quickly. By selecting only the necessary information and placing labels and data at appropriate places, you enable your reader to process the information quickly and efficiently. Ideally, your reader should grasp the key ideas within 10 to 15 seconds.

The less-effective line chart in Figure 12.2 reveals several processing problems. The most serious is that the legend forces the reader to glance back and forth between the lines and the legend to correctly link the data series. Another problem is that the Prestigio data series, which should be the center of attention, is placed underneath the other lines, with no special formatting features to make it stand out. The more-effective chart is far easier to process. Data labels appear directly next to each line so that the reader does not have to glance back and forth between the legend and the plot area. Furthermore, the Prestigio line is bolder and thicker, and it is placed in front of the other lines to draw the intended attention.

Takeaway Message An effective chart leaves a lasting impression about your key point. Will your readers remember your intended main message in two hours? If not, your chart had little impact. The takeaway is the essence of your chart—how the information, title, focal points, and other formatting combine to convey a lasting message. Overall, the ineffective line chart in Figure 12.2 leaves little lasting impression. The reader who studies the chart carefully might see that the Prestigio's staff and service ratings improved more than did those of competitors, but the reader has to get through a compilation of colored lines with little or no contextual reference. Furthermore, the chart offers no explanation for why this change in ratings may have occurred. By contrast, a reader can rapidly process the more-effective line chart in Figure 12.2. The title, focal points, and simple design lead to one strong takeaway message: The Prestigio launched a staff and service initiative that has successfully improved customer satisfaction compared with its major competitors. Figures 12.3, 12.4, and 12.5 present other types of charts with less-effective and more-effective variations. Figures 12.6 and 12.7 present a variety of other useful formats for charts.

General Rules of Chart Formatting

Although formatting a chart is secondary to creating a powerful takeaway message, it is by no means unimportant. Since visuals have an impact even before the reader begins reading, ineffective formatting can give the reader an impression of sloppy or imprecise work.

FIGURE 12.2

Less-Effective and More-Effective Line Charts

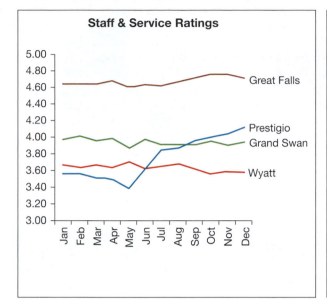

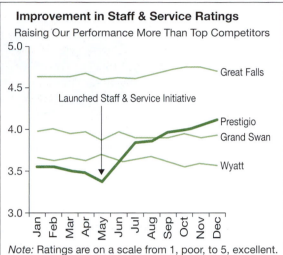

Note: Ratings are on a scale from 1, poor, to 5, excellent. All ratings were retrieved from the Wahoo travel website and are averaged for each month across the year.

	Key Design and Formatting Problems in Less-Effective Chart	**Adjustments in More-Effective Chart**
Title descriptiveness	Nondescriptive, bland title. It does not tie into any primary message.	Title and subtitle focus on intentional improvement.
Focal points	Lacks focal points. All parts of the chart are treated equally—thus, there is no emphasis or indication of what should be the key points of comparison.	The callout box focuses attention on the staff and service initiative as the cause of rising customer satisfaction. A darker, thicker line with a bold label draws attention to the Prestigio data series.
Information sufficiency	Inadequate information about the rating scale. What do the numbers represent? What is the year for which data was gathered?	The note provides information about the rating scale.
Ease of processing	Legend placed on the right side. This forces the reader to move back and forth between the legend and the data series in the plot area. Further, the colors do not aid in the information presentation.	Instead of a legend, data labels are placed directly at the end of each data series (line) to make identification of each hotel's performance easier. Additionally, the color scheme is kept to a minimum, thereby prominently displaying the dramatic rise in ratings.
Takeaway message	Staff and service ratings have improved for the Prestigio over the past year. However, the message requires too much effort for the viewer and could easily be missed or forgotten quickly.	All elements of the chart capture the message that the Prestigio staff and service initiative has successfully improved customer satisfaction compared to competitors.

FIGURE 12.3

Less-Effective and More-Effective Pie Charts

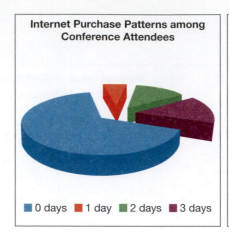

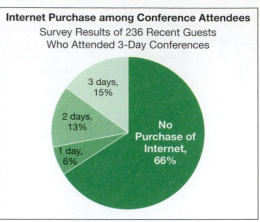

	Key Design and Formatting Problems in Less-Effective Chart	Adjustments in More-Effective Chart
Title	Descriptive but unexciting title.	Descriptive title focuses attention on the fact that these are 3-day conference attendees.
Focal points	The main focal point is the large pie slice. The colors used give a very dense and dark feeling to the visual.	The primary focal point is the slice highlighting those not purchasing any Internet service. It is labeled more effectively ("No Purchase of Internet" versus "0 days" in the less-effective chart) and is written in bold text on a darker-colored background to draw attention to this key point.
Information sufficiency	Absence of data label on each slice makes this chart difficult to interpret.	Data labels are provided in percentages.
Ease of processing	Legend is placed on the bottom. This forces the reader to move back and forth between the legend and the pie slices in the plot area. Also, the breakaway, 3-D shape of the object skews the data. The pie slices are not arranged for fastest processing.	Data series names and data labels are placed together in the pie slices to foster easy processing. The largest pie slice is located at 12 o'clock for quick recognition (most people read pie charts beginning at 12 and continue to read in a clockwise direction).
Takeaway message	Most conference attendees do not purchase Internet services. However, getting the message requires a great deal of effort and could easily be missed or forgotten quickly.	All aspects of the chart collectively demonstrate that conference attendees are unlikely to purchase Internet services.

FIGURE 12.4

Less-Effective and More-Effective Bar Charts

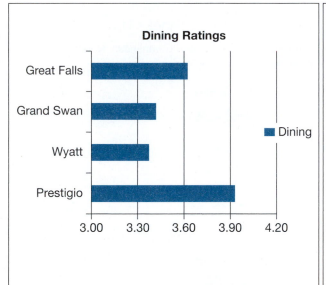

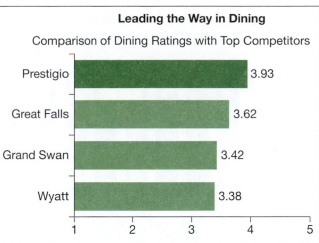

	Key Design and Formatting Problems in Less-Effective Chart	**Adjustments in More-Effective Chart**
Title descriptiveness	Nondescriptive, bland title.	Title immediately recognizes the Prestigio's leading position in dining ratings.
Focal points	Lacks focal points. All bars are treated equally.	Darker color of the Prestigio bar draws attention to it.
Information sufficiency	Inadequate information about the rating scale.	A note about the rating scale and inclusion of data labels provides sufficient information.
Ease of processing	The legend is unnecessary and distracting. The items are not ordered effectively (the order is neither alphabetical nor quantitative) to help draw rapid comparisons. The large gap size compared to bar width reduces quick processing. The axis increments are in rarely used units (generally, units in multiples of 2, 5, and 10 are more natural).	The chart is arranged in descending order by average ratings to make comparisons easier. Bar width in comparison to gap width is most conducive to rapid processing.
Takeaway message	The takeaway message is that the Prestigio has higher dining ratings. However, the message is weak and could easily be glossed over or forgotten.	The Prestigio occupies the proud position of leading its competitors in dining ratings. This is a strong, optimistic, and memorable message.

FIGURE 12.5

Ineffective Clustered-Column Chart and More-Effective Panel of Charts

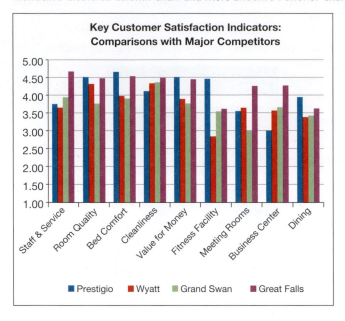

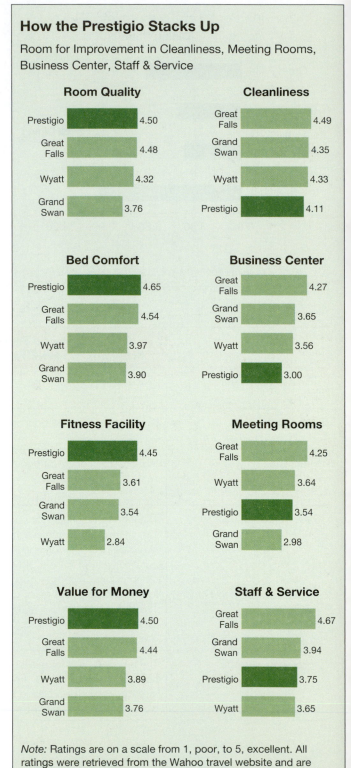

	Ineffective Clustered-Column Chart	**Effective Alternative: Panel of Charts**
Title	Descriptive but bland.	Curiosity building ("How the Prestigio Stacks Up"); a call to action ("Room for Improvement in . . .").
Focal points	None. Too cluttered.	Prestigio rankings and position for each rating area.
Information sufficiency	No data labels.	Data labels provided for each rating area.
Ease of processing	Nearly impossible. Too much information. Not sorted.	Simple and easy processing for each rating area. Charts are organized by relative performance (excellent performance on left side, needs improvement performance on right side).
Takeaway message	No key point related to the ratings.	The Prestigio is elite in various areas compared to its competitors, but is behind in other key areas.

FIGURE 12.6

Other Common Charts for Statistical Data

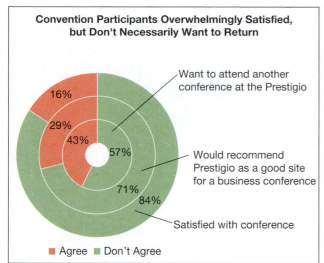

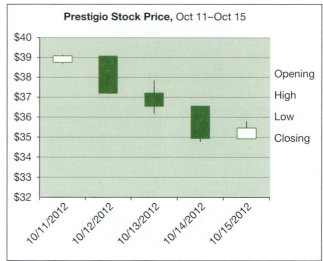

Doughnut charts allow you to represent wholes. Unlike pie charts, you can present more than one data series.

High-low charts allow you to show values that fluctuate. These charts are often used for stock prices.

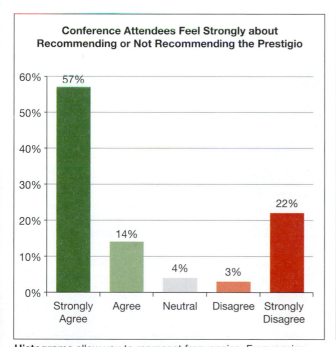

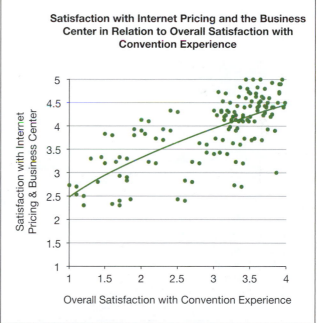

Histograms allow you to represent frequencies. Frequencies often reveal data relationships not easily visible by looking at averages.

Scatter plot or **X-Y charts** allow you to include pairs of data on an x-y plot. Many scatter plots contain trend lines to reveal data relationships.

FIGURE 12.7

Common Charts for Organizational Structures, Projects, and Processes

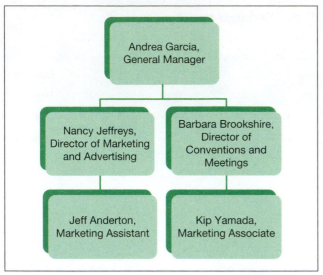

Org charts allow you to show who various personnel report to.

Gantt charts allow you to show progress on aspects of projects. These charts are frequently used as part of project management.

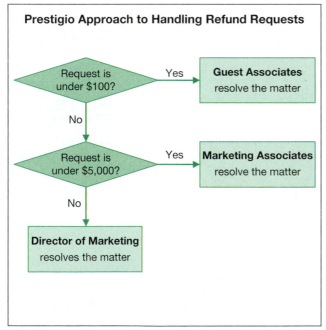

Flowcharts allow you to depict a series of steps in a process or procedure to help others make decisions.

Chevron lists or charts allow you to show a set of sequential steps and provide subpoints for each step.

Generally, the formatting should be as simple as possible and should accentuate the key data relationships. If a formatting feature detracts from the key points, remove or improve it. Table 12.6 provides general formatting guidelines for charts.

Designing Effective Tables

Generally, charts are the most effective way of quickly demonstrating a key point or relationship. However, charts are limited in the amount of information they can provide.

TABLE 12.6

Formatting Guidelines for Specific Chart Types

Chart Type	Formatting Guidelines
All charts	• Ensure that all data is appropriately labeled. • Avoid using too many bright colors; they can be distracting. • Use darker colors to represent your most important data series. • Avoid unusual fonts or too many special effects. • Avoid 3-D charts. • Ensure that all text is horizontal. • Avoid white type on dark backgrounds in most cases.
Line	• Scale should be about two-thirds of the range included in the chart. • Series names should be placed on or attached directly to lines. • Only four or fewer data series (lines) should be included.
Pie	• Largest slice should begin at 12 o'clock and go clockwise; second-largest slice should begin at 12 o'clock and go counterclockwise. • Exploding slices should be used sparingly. • Pie slices should complete a whole (add up to 100% of a data series).
Bar	• Bars should be about twice the width of the space in between bars. • Baseline should always be zero. • Bars should be arranged in ascending or descending order in most cases. • Legend should only be used if the chart has two or more data series.

Tables, by contrast, allow you to provide more data with additional precision. Because of this, charts are generally better for highlighting a key idea, and tables are generally better for comprehensiveness and precision.

Evaluating the Effectiveness of Tables   Like charts, tables are typically more effective with simple formatting. In addition, the way a table presents data can affect the clarity of its message. Consider, for example, the tables in Figure 12.8, which are based on identical data. Place yourself in the position of the reader and assume you have the following question: "Does higher income level correspond with higher likelihood of purchasing Internet services?" It is difficult to answer this question quickly by looking at the less-effective table. By contrast, glancing at the more-effective table rapidly reveals that purchasing no Internet service (0 days) strongly correlates with the lowest income bracket (under $30,000/year).

The less-effective table is cluttered due to excessive grid lines, poor labels, and non-indented items. By contrast, the more-effective table limits the number of grid lines. Furthermore, each grid line serves a distinct purpose. The initial grid lines separate the column labels from the survey data. Subsequent grid lines separate each category of data, including those for all respondents, gender, and income level. Indents of items within each category further accentuate the distinctions between categories.

The second table also is more effective because numerical adjustments have been made. The first table contains *counts* of respondents who responded in certain ways. Counts make it difficult for readers to make effective comparisons quickly. Yet, many readers are also interested in knowing how many people participated in a survey. By converting the counts into percentages, the more-effective table enables readers to process the information more easily. Placing the counts in parentheses makes the data comprehensive.

General Rules of Table Formatting   Overall, more-effective formatting and numerical conversion make a significant impact on the usefulness of a table. The general guidelines in Table 12.7 will help you create more effective tables.

FIGURE 12.8

A Less-Effective and More-Effective Table

Less-Effective Table

Survey Results

During the three days of the conference you attended at the Prestigio, how many days did you purchase Internet service?				
Days of Internet Service	0	1	2	3
All Respondents	154	15	31	36
Gender				
Male	82	8	15	22
Female	72	7	16	14
Income				
Under $30,000	15	0	1	2
$30,000–$40,000	41	4	3	7
$40,000–$50,000	48	3	11	12
$50,000–$75,000	33	6	7	8
$75,000–$100,000	12	2	4	4
Over $100,000	5	0	5	3

More-Effective Table

Internet Service Purchases among Conference Guests

	Days of Internet Service Purchased (Number of Respondents in Parentheses)				
	0 Days	**1 Day**	**2 Days**	**3 Days**	**Total (#)**
All Respondents	65.5% (154)	6.4% (15)	13.2% (31)	15.3% (36)	236
Gender					
Male	64.6% (82)	6.3% (8)	11.8% (15)	17.3% (22)	127
Female	66.1% (72)	6.4% (7)	14.7% (16)	12.8% (14)	109
Income					
Under $30,000	83.3% (15)	0.0% (0)	5.6% (1)	11.1% (2)	18
$30,000–$40,000	74.5% (41)	7.3% (4)	5.5% (3)	12.7% (7)	55
$40,000–$50,000	64.9% (48)	4.1% (3)	14.9% (11)	16.2% (12)	74
$50,000–$75,000	61.1% (33)	11.1% (6)	13.0% (7)	14.8% (8)	54
$75,000–$100,000	54.5% (12)	9.1% (2)	18.2% (4)	18.2% (4)	22
Over $100,000	38.5% (5)	0.0% (0)	38.5% (5)	23.1% (3)	13

TABLE 12.7

Formatting Guidelines for Tables

Issue	Formatting Guidelines
Order	• Order your entries appropriately (alphabetical or numerical order of categories, or ascending/descending order of values of comparison).
Indentation	• Indent or otherwise set apart items within a category.
Data series	• Present comparative data series vertically.
Column/Row labels	• Label columns and rows effectively.
Grid lines	• Use grid lines for every three to five rows at natural breaks (new categories); readers can easily scan rows under this simple design technique. • Avoid grid lines on all borders; this tends to clutter the table. • Avoid alternating background colors on rows in most cases; this is also distracting and unnecessary.

TECHNOLOGY TIPS

USING ONLINE SURVEY SOFTWARE

Conducting surveys has become increasingly easy with various software, such as SurveyMonkey, Qualtrics, and various add-ins for meeting and social software. The software, in many cases, helps you rapidly create survey questions. It often contains a pool of existing questions you can even select from.

In an online format, you can send the survey link to anyone in your contact list, including colleagues and customers. In other words, such software gives you greater access to survey respondents than was possible as recently as a few years ago. Furthermore, many companies specialize in helping you gain access to millions of potential respondents (called an *online panel*). When you conduct marketing or consumer research, these companies can help you get a large sample size for nearly any demographic of interest.

Source: Reprinted with permission of Survey Monkey, www.surveymonkey.com.

Another benefit of using online surveys is that the data is immediately dumped into a database or spreadsheet in a form you can quickly analyze. Some online survey software even provides immediate reports that include summary and crosstab statistics (although you'll often want to manipulate the data yourself to dig deeper and get answers to particular questions).

As you use online survey software, keep in mind the following tips:

Apply the same careful and thorough standards you would to any form of business research. The ease of creating online surveys often leads business professionals to use them carelessly, not putting enough time into designing the survey questions.

Avoid overusing online surveys. Again, because of the ease of administering online surveys, employees in many organizations are bombarded with surveys. As a result, employees often suffer respondent fatigue and respond to surveys less carefully. The results of the survey are only as good as the careful input of your respondents.

Developing Your Ideas with Secondary Research

In most cases, primary research is ideal. You can carefully tailor it to your specific business problems. Primary research, however, takes a lot of time and money. Even with sufficient resources, your organization may lack access to certain types of data. Generally, a far less-expensive approach is secondary research. One advantage of nearly all secondary research is that someone else already spent the time to conduct and write it up.

Evaluating Data Quality

As you collect secondary research, carefully evaluate it in terms of data quality. Concern yourself with the following issues:

- **Reliability** relates to how dependable the data is—how current and representative.
- **Relevance** of the data relates to how well it applies to your specific business problem.
- **Adaptability** relates to how well the research can be altered or revised to meet your specific business problem.

LO12.5 Evaluate the usefulness of data sources for business research.

TABLE 12.8

Strengths and Limitations of Data Quality for Primary and Secondary Research Sources

	Reliability	**Relevance**	**Adaptability**	**Expert-Based**	**Bias**
Primary Research	High	High	High	Medium – High	Goals and preexisting notions of the researcher
White Papers	Low – High	Medium – High	Low	Medium – High	Organizational mission and objectives
Industry Publications	Medium – High	Medium – High	Low	Medium – High	Mission of the publication/editing team
Business Periodicals	Medium – High	Low – Medium	Low	Low – High	Mission of the publication/editing team
Scholarly Journals	High	Low	Low	High	Theoretical significance
External Blogs, Wikis, and Other Websites	Low – High	Medium – High	Low	Low – High	Writers' career objectives
Business Books	Medium – High	Low – High	Low	Medium – High	The latest, greatest idea mentality; easy fixes

- **Expertise** relates to the skill and background of the researchers to address your business problem.
- **Biases** are tendencies to see issues from particular perspectives. The possibility of biases does not necessarily imply that secondary research is unreliable; however, when using such research, view the data cautiously and keep in mind the ultimate objectives of the researchers.

Some secondary research reports cost thousands of dollars to purchase, whereas others are free. You have a variety of options to choose from with secondary research, including white papers, industry publications, business periodicals, scholarly journals, external blogs, and business books. Each of these types of secondary data has benefits and drawbacks (see Table 12.8). Thus, you will inevitably face trade-offs as you select secondary data.

White papers are reports or guides that generally describe research about solving a particular issue—perhaps one similar to the one you are encountering. They are issued by governments and organizations. White papers are readily available on many corporate and other organizational websites. However, they are often biased, since white papers are often produced by industry groups with an agenda or companies with specific marketing goals related to the white paper. Thus, when you rely on white papers, you should learn about the agendas of the sponsoring organizations.

Industry publications are written to cater to the specific interests of members in particular industries. These can include periodicals and reports. Industry reports often are highly reliable, relevant, and expert-based. However, industry reports are generally expensive, ranging from several hundred dollars to thousands of dollars. Generally, the more reliable the industry reports are, the more expensive they are. Fortunately, many business libraries carry a variety of expensive industry reports and publications that are free for you to use as long as you are enrolled at your university.

Business periodicals (magazines, newspapers) provide stories, information, and advice about contemporary business issues. They are often written by well-respected business journalists and experts. However, most articles in magazines and periodicals will have limited value in applying to your specific business problems and your organization. Furthermore, these articles often rely on anecdotal evidence rather than carefully controlled experiments and survey research. Periodicals that are industry publications are often far more relevant than general business magazines and articles.

Scholarly journals contain business research that is extremely reliable. The information comes from carefully controlled scientific research processes and has been reviewed by experts in the field. However, scholarly business articles rarely provide useful information for business problems that you will focus on in the workplace. Rather, scholarly articles focus on more theoretical and abstract issues. Furthermore, they are generally written with a level of statistical analysis and/or theoretical background that is difficult to understand.

External blogs and other online resources provide a plethora of information. Since most blogs are not formally edited or reviewed, the range in reliability is enormous. As you progress in your career, you will find those blogs that are reliable and relevant to the types of business problems you face. If you rely on blogs, make sure you carefully determine the expertise of the blog writer/s.

Business and management books range greatly in terms of their overall usefulness. Fortunately, you can usually better assess the usefulness of business and management books than other secondary sources because of the many online reviews available and the ability to preview sections of the books (online and in person at bookstores or libraries). Online reviews can help you gauge how useful various books can be for your particular business problems.

Conducting Library Research

LO12.6 Conduct secondary research to address a business problem.

Most university libraries have rich stores of information on business. Aside from a significant collection of books across a wide range of disciplines and topics, your library likely contains a wealth of digital resources. You likely also have access to thousands of company and industry reports (each of which cost hundreds and thousands of dollars to consumers); articles from hundreds of business periodicals, including *The Wall Street Journal, Forbes, Bloomberg Businessweek,* and many others; industry-specific periodicals and reports; scholarly journals; and many, many more avenues for research.

Most university libraries subscribe to dozens of online databases. Popular and useful ones with business research and articles include EBSCO Business Source Complete, ProQuest, IBISWorld, Hoover's, Global Financial Database, Conference Board, eMarketer, Mint Global, NetAdvantage by Standard & Poor's, Thomson One, and others. In Figure 12.9, you'll see a few examples of these databases and how they present information for your research. In the EBSCO Host window, you'll notice the many search options available. In the ProQuest window, you can see links to specialized reports, on such topics as trends and forecasts, market research, or SWOT analyses. In the IBISWorld window, you can see the categories of information in a particular industry report. Working from this screen, Jeff can access reliable information about key success factors, cost structure benchmarks, technology, and many other topics about hotels in the United States.

Navigating the many resources in these databases and identifying the ones that will be most useful to you take time. You might consider spending several weeks browsing these various databases simply to become familiar with what's available. You should also seek a business librarian to help you identify those databases that best match your interests and needs.

Each of the databases contains search features, and several basic strategies will help you make the most of them. When you manually search, you can use Boolean operators *(and, or)* to widen your search. For example, when Jeff wants to find more information about "green meetings," his initial search of this phrase yields 33 results. By looking for both words separately (using *and*), his search yields over 2,000 results.

FIGURE 12.9

Finding Valuable Information with Library Resources

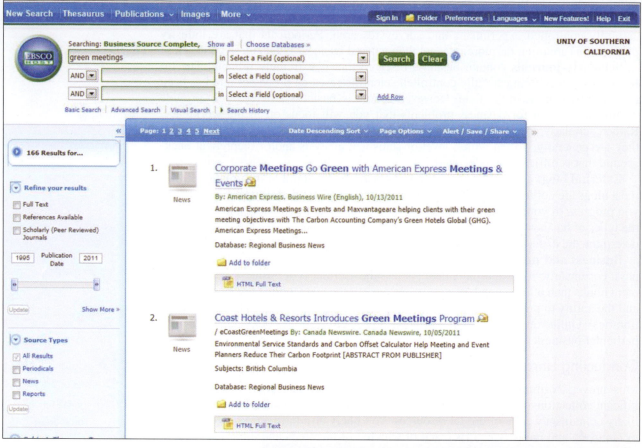

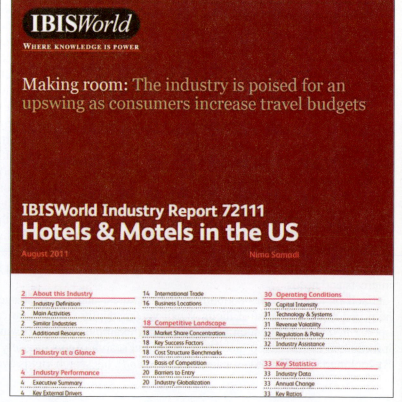

TABLE 12.9

Strategies for Using Search Terms Effectively

Strategy	Example	Number of Hits in ProQuest
Use Boolean operators	Green Meetings Green *and* Meetings Green *or* Meetings	33 2,016 33,313
Use alternative keywords	Eco-Friendly *and* Conventions Eco-Friendly *and* Meetings Green *and* Conventions	20 56 489
Use closely related ideas	Green *and* Hotels Eco-Friendly *and* Hotels Eco-Friendly *and* Convention Centers	66 71 13

FIGURE 12.10

Using Suggested Terms in Online Business Databases

By looking for either phrase (using *or*), he finds over 33,000 results (see Table 12.9). Also, consider using alternative keywords and closely related ideas. Finding the right sources requires persistence. You might spend hours looking for useful information and then rapidly find dozens of relevant and useful sources.

Once you enter your terms, most online business databases provide a list of suggested topics based on commonly indexed terms. These can be very helpful. Notice, for example, Figure 12.10. You will see the many combinations of indexed terms that result from a manual search for eco-friendly hotels in ProQuest. By clicking on these various suggested searches, you can rapidly find which combinations of search terms yield the best results.

Documenting Your Research

As you collect secondary research, keeping track of the information sources is critical. Decision makers expect excellent documentation of your information because this helps them evaluate the credibility of your report. Since they often make high-stakes decisions based on reports, they expect to know *exactly* what the basis is for facts, conclusions, and recommendations you present.

When you keep track of your sources during the research stage, you can efficiently and accurately document your report. Many novice report writers waste time during the drafting stage trying to retrace their steps and find the sources for certain pieces of information. Worse, they may make errors in documentation by providing an incorrect source, casting doubt on the credibility of the report.

To avoid these problems, experienced writers have a system for recording all sources during the research stage. Not all report writers use the same system; some use word processing software, while others use spreadsheets or databases. The key is to create a system that allows you to accurately and efficiently record sources for your information. In Figure 12.11, you can see how Jeff combines taking notes with keeping track

FIGURE 12.11

System for Recording Secondary-Research Sources during Note Taking

Torrence, S. (2010, November). Change the world one meeting at a time: APEX/ASTM sustainability standards nearly set. *Corporate Meetings & Incentives, 29*(11), 18–21.

- According to MeetGreen, a 3-day conference with 300 attendees creates waste equivalent to 33 small vehicles; water resources that would fill half of an Olympic-sized swimming pool; greenhouse gases to fill 25 million basketballs.
- Convention Industry Council Accepted Practices Exchange (APEX) is collaborating to work on APEX/ASTM Sustainable Meetings Standards. These evolving standards can be found at the following website: Meetingsnet.com/green/apex-astm-sustainability-standards
- 9 areas of APEX/ASTM standards: (a) accommodation; (b) audiovisual and production; (c) communications and marketing; (d) destinations; (e) exhibits; (f) food and beverage; (g) meeting venues; (h) on-site offices; (i) transportation.
- The EPA initiated green meetings standards with the formation of Green Meeting Industry Council
- Government planners often required to comply with standards

Richard K. Miller & Associates (2010). *2010 Travel & Tourism Market Research Handbook* (Loganville, GA: Author).

- Green Meeting Industry Council envisions a green meeting industry with zero net environmental impact by 2020
- MeetingNews 2010 survey of meeting planners:
  - 93 percent report they at least occasionally use green meetings
  - Most common green meeting practices are the following: reduce paper by using digital alternatives (79%); on-site recycling programs (61%); host cities that requires less travel (48%)
  - 10 percent measure carbon footprint
  - 40 percent say there are not enough green meeting venues
  - 46 percent believe green meetings are too expensive
- Websites that measure carbon footprint of events: carboncounter.org; carbonfootprint.com; carbonfund.org; myfootprint.org; zerofootprint.net

Lowe, M. C., (2010, October). The greening of hotels: A look at what major chains are doing to support eco-friendly meetings. *Meetings & Conventions, 45*(10), 45–56.

- *Kimpton:* In 2005 became first brand to package green meetings. Gained clients such as Microsoft and Aveda. Uses EarthCare Meetings nine-point standard. Standards include the following: 100 percent recycled paper; all meeting correspondence is electronic; catering ingredients sourced locally; eco-friendly cleaning products; organic tea at coffee stations; motion-controlled lighting in all meeting spaces; unused food donated. They have found that green meetings do not cost more – in fact cost less.
- *Fairmont Hotels & Resorts:* Eco-Meet program was initiated in 2007. It focuses on four main areas.
  - Eco-accommodation: Information to guests about how to be more environmentally conscious during stay; all rooms with recycling bins; energy-efficient lighting; water-conservative plumbing
  - Eco-service: dishes/cutlery instead of disposable plates/plastic untensils; recycling bins; reusable items such as silk flowers and linen napkins
  - Eco-cuisine: local, seasonal, organically grown foods from with 100 miles; 50 percent reduction in animal proteins (use vegetable proteins instead)
  - Eco-programming: electronic registration, check-in, paper reduction efforts. Carbon offsets, energy certificates (planting trees, lower-carbon technologies)
- Fairmont's results per person: three fewer plastic water bottles, two fewer aluminum cans, three fewer paper plates, two fewer sets of disposable cutlery.
- *Hilton:* LightStay: analyzes 200 operational practices. Helps planners estimate environmental impact. Gives planners options.
- *Hyatt:* Meet and Be Green Initiative: 3 percent rebate for following 10-point green guidelines. Requires hotel and attendees to consciously lower impacts.
- *Marriott:* has offered green meetings since 2008. 3,600 employees are certified Marriott Green Planners.

of his sources. This approach helps him organize his information and allows him to rapidly provide documentation once he begins drafting his report.

Using Online Information for Business Research

For most business research, the information you can access through business databases and other sources at your library is generally the most reliable. However, you will also likely use Internet searches outside your library system to find relevant information on your topic. As you do so, keep in mind the following strategies:

- *Always evaluate data quality.* The range in quality on the web is immense. Make sure you're not using sources that are uninformed or inaccurate.

- *Do more than just "Google it."* You can employ many strategies for online research, including the following:

  - *Go to reputable business and industry websites and conduct searches.* For example, Jeff may go directly to general periodical or business news sites such as *Bloomberg Businessweek* or CNBC.com to do searches. Or he may go to industry sites. When he goes to the Convention Industry Council website, he finds a variety of sources that are not available at his library and that are more current than the information in business databases (see Figure 12.12).

  - *Find online discussions and forums about your selected topic.* You can learn what current professionals are saying about a topic by visiting online discussions and forums. For example, on LinkedIn, you can view the conversations of thousands of professionals on any given topic. Notice in Figure 12.13 the many options that Jeff has to choose from. Each of these groups holds dozens of ongoing conversations about current practices in the industry.

  - *Search beyond text-based information.* Increasingly, you can access a wealth of information in video and audio format. For example, when Jeff is seeking information about green meetings, a few simple searches yield thousands of online

FIGURE 12.12

Using Industry Websites for Research

Source: Reprinted with permission of Convention Industry Council, www.conventionindustry.org.

FIGURE 12.13

Using Online Groups and
Discussion Forums for
Research

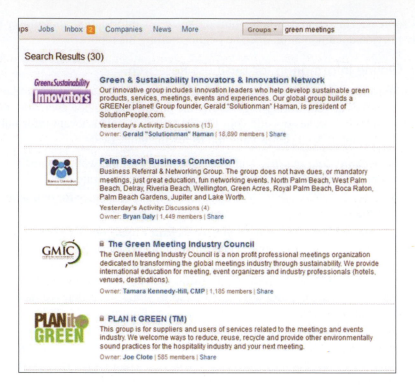

videos on YouTube (see Figure 12.14). By viewing a few of these videos, he
identifies many green meeting practices that hotels are using. He also gets information from speeches and presentations that he could not find elsewhere.

- *Be persistent.* In the age of the Internet, many of us are accustomed to quick answers. Getting solid business information, however, rarely involves quick answers.
Try as many approaches as you can to find the data you need.

FIGURE 12.14

Using Online Videos for
Research

Applying the FAIR Test to Your Research Data and Charts

LO12.7 Evaluate research data, charts, and tables for fairness and effectiveness.

As you conduct research for your reports, frequently evaluate whether you are being fair. For example, whether you are doing primary or secondary research, make sure you are examining all the available facts and interpreting them from various perspectives. A common problem is that business professionals may enter into research with preexisting assumptions or even conclusions. In primary research, such assumptions may lead you to ask the wrong questions or interpret the data incorrectly. In secondary research, they may lead you to gather only information that matches your assumptions and conclusions. For example, if Jeff already assumes that developing and marketing green meetings makes business sense for the Prestigio, he may inadvertently gravitate to information that supports his position and avoid information that does not, thus misleading his readers.

Another way you may unintentionally mislead a reader is with numerical data. However, you can take a few steps to ensure that you represent data fairly and avoid losing credibility. First, whenever you are unsure of a data relationship, discuss it with your colleagues. Collectively, you will often arrive at a fair way to represent the information. Also, ask yourself if you have provided enough information for your readers and audience members to make informed and accurate judgments.

Some business professionals show only the data that supports their points. In other words, they cherry-pick the data in their favor. This practice is deceptive. Furthermore, some business professionals distort information, even though it is technically correct. Charts, for example, can be manipulated to exaggerate or misinform. Notice Table 12.10, which contains two versions of the same chart.

As you collect, analyze, and present data to others, ensure that you provide all the relevant *facts,* even if they don't fit into convenient conclusions. Grant *access* to your data. Your full disclosure of data to colleagues, clients, and others in your business dealings will pay long-term dividends in terms of credibility. Many businesses emphasize transparency on an institutional level. As an individual, when you make compelling numerical arguments through charts, tables, and other formats while also

TABLE 12.10

Creating Fair Charts

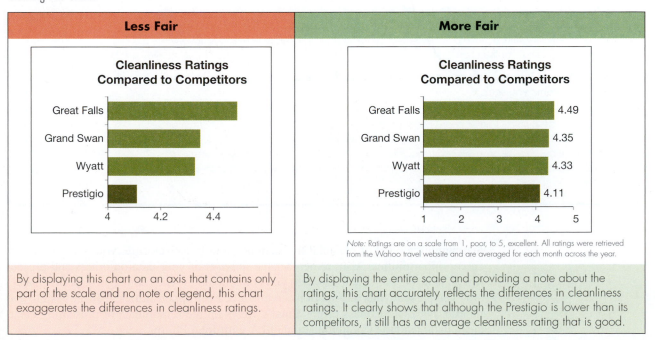

By displaying this chart on an axis that contains only part of the scale and no note or legend, this chart exaggerates the differences in cleanliness ratings.

By displaying the entire scale and providing a note about the ratings, this chart accurately reflects the differences in cleanliness ratings. It clearly shows that although the Prestigio is lower than its competitors, it still has an average cleanliness rating that is good.

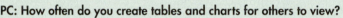

COMMUNICATION Q&A

CONVERSATIONS WITH CURRENT BUSINESS PROFESSIONALS

Pete Cardon: In the business world, why is it important to create tables and charts for numerical data?

John Phillip: Business leaders are inundated with data, some relevant and some irrelevant. I have seen meetings derailed because the executives can't immediately see the significance of a PowerPoint slide. When used effectively, tables, graphs, and charts focus the audience on the key point and make the information easier for the audience to retain. Focusing attention on the key business drivers leads to more fruitful discussions and action. In my work, my primary duties include developing financial targets for the five-year strategic plan and the annual operating plan, creating current-quarter and full-year outlooks, and reporting results in monthly operating reviews. For each of these activities, I'm responsible for preparing presentations to deliver to senior executives. I have found that these presentations need to maintain consistent themes or story lines.

John Phillip *has worked as a finance manager and financial analyst for the past 12 years in a Fortune 100 company.*

PC: How often do you create tables and charts for others to view?

JP: Every day—in a variety of forms, ranging from tables included within the body of an email to formal executive presentations.

PC: How do you choose when to use tables and charts?

JP: All communications need to be appropriately tailored to the audience. Tables are effective when I want the audience to know the numbers; I often use tables in less-formal communications, especially with my level of the organization and below. Charts are a great way to visually show comparative data and trends. Every formal presentation that I create contains charts because they easily focus on the key data.

PC: How are the charts you create today different from those you created just after completing your business program?

JP: The biggest improvement I have made is that I now clearly identify the information I want to communicate *before* I create the chart. The chart is just a tool in achieving the communication objective. The type of chart I use depends on what I want the audience to take away. Other improvements are subtle: I experiment with the scale, color, font size, and legend placement. These seemingly little things make a large difference in the ability of the audience to quickly be drawn to the emphasis of the chart.

PC: How often do you see colleagues create poor or ineffective charts? What are the most common problems you see?

JP: It is very easy to go overboard when presenting data, and I have seen quite a few ineffective charts. To be truthful, I have been responsible for one or two of them. The most common error is a chart that does not support the story line. This creates confusion in the audience. Another common error is an overly complicated chart. I tend to stick with simple charts, i.e., pie charts, bar charts, and line charts. More complicated charts often take too long to explain or confuse the message.

maintaining a level of personal transparency and full disclosure, you will gain many career opportunities. Also, remember the *impacts* of your data on others and present it with *respect*. For example, when you collect data on your colleagues' performance, how you present your information can impact career opportunities, team cohesion, and morale. For one business professional's views on the importance of presenting clear, clean data, read the Communication Q&A with John Phillip.

Chapter Takeaway for *Research and Planning for Business Reports*

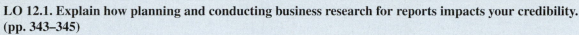

LO 12.1. Explain how planning and conducting business research for reports impacts your credibility. (pp. 343–345)

Planning and conducting research for business reports demonstrates **your personal credibility.**

It shows **competence** when you can collect, analyze, and present business research.	It shows **caring** when you collect business research that fills an unmet need for others.	It shows **character** when you collect, analyze, and report your research data fairly.

LO 12.2. Create research objectives that are specific and achievable. (p. 345)

See *examples of research objectives* in Table 12.1.

LO 12.3. Explain principles of effective design for survey questions and choices. (pp. 345–350)

Principles for Survey Question Design	
• Simple to answer	• Exhaustive and unambiguous
• Non-leading	• Single idea

See *examples of survey question design* in Tables 12.2 through 12.5. See a complete online survey in Figure 12.1.

LO 12.4. Develop charts and tables to concisely display data and accentuate key messages. (pp. 350–361)

Criteria for Evaluating Charts	
• Title descriptiveness	• Ease of processing
• Focal points	• Takeaway message
• Information sufficiency	

See *examples of charts and tables* in Figures 12.6 through 12.7.

LO 12.5. Evaluate the usefulness of data sources for business research. (pp. 361–363)

Criteria for Evaluating Data Quality	
• Reliability	• Expertise
• Relevance	• Biases
• Adaptability	

LO 12.6. Conduct secondary research to address a business problem. (pp. 363–368)

Principles for Secondary Research
• Use business databases such as EBSCO, IBISWorld, and Hoover's.
• Document your research.
• Conduct online research carefully, strategically, and creatively.

See *an example of documenting research during the note-taking stage* in Figure 12.11.

LO 12.7. Evaluate research data, charts, and tables for fairness and effectiveness. (pp. 369–370)

Facts: Present all relevant facts, even when they don't fit nicely into convenient conclusions. Avoid exaggeration or any other distortion of the facts.

Access: Grant access to your data to decision makers and others affected by your report. Focus on transparency and disclosure.

Impacts: Consider how the data in your report will impact stakeholders.

Respect: Ensure that your presentation of the data demonstrates respect for stakeholders.

Key Terms

adaptability (p. 361)

bar charts (p. 351)

biases (p. 362)

business and management books (p. 363)

business periodicals (p. 363)

chevron lists (p. 358)

closed questions (p. 345)

doughnut charts (p. 357)

exhaustive (p. 347)

expertise (p. 362)

external blogs (p. 363)

flowcharts (p. 358)

Gantt charts (p. 358)

high-low charts (p. 357)

histograms (p. 357)

industry publications (p. 362)

line charts (p. 351)

non-leading (p. 346)

open-ended questions (p. 345)

org charts (p. 358)

pie charts (p. 351)

primary research (p. 345)

relevance (p. 361)

reliability (p. 361)

scatter plots (p. 357)

scholarly journals (p. 363)

secondary research (p. 345)

unambiguous (p. 347)

white papers (p. 362)

Discussion Exercises

12.1 Chapter Review Questions (LO 12.1, LO 12.2, LO 12.3, LO 12.4, LO 12.5)

A. Explain the features that distinguish reports from other types of business correspondence.

B. Describe ways in which you can enhance your credibility by creating reports.

C. Discuss the advantages and drawbacks of both primary and secondary business research.

D. Describe strategies for understanding the needs of your audience for reports.

E. Explain why developing clear research objectives is so crucial to business research.

F. Describe principles for effective survey questions.

G. Summarize the primary reasons for using charts and tables.

H. Explain at least three general design principles for charts.

I. Describe unique design and formatting principles that apply to line charts, pie charts, and bar charts.

J. Explain the criteria for judging the quality of research data.

12.2 Communication Q&A Discussion Questions (LO 12.4, LO 12.7)

In the Communication Q&A section, when asked about choosing when to use tables and charts, John Phillip stated, "All communications need to be appropriately tailored to the audience. Tables are effective when I want the audience to know the numbers. I often use tables in less-formal communications, especially with my level of the organization and below. Charts are a great way to visually show comparative data and trends."

A. Based on this statement as well as your own experience, list and elaborate on three or four general guidelines for choosing between tables and charts.

B. Consider John Phillip's answers, and in two or three paragraphs, explain why simpler is better when it comes to charts. Also, explain the strategy behind developing effective charts.

C. Mark Twain is famously quoted as saying, "Figures often beguile me, particularly when I have the arranging of them myself; in which case the remark attributed to Disraeli would often apply with justice and force: 'There are three kinds of lies: lies, damned lies, and statistics'" (from Twain's autobiography). Do you believe this is the case with charts? Explain in three to five paragraphs specific approaches you can use to ensure that your charts are considered credible.

12.3 Combining Quantitative and Communication Skills (LO 12.1, LO 12.4, LO 12.5, LO 12.6)

Lloyd C. Blankfein, chairman and CEO of Goldman Sachs, was asked, "What would you like business schools to teach more of, or less of?" He responded:

> Look, I think it's very important to teach people to have a healthy respect for facts and information. And you know, to paraphrase Keynes, "to change minds when facts change." That's why I think certain careers—and maybe not intuitive careers—do very well. There's a lot of lawyers floating around Wall Street. There's a lot of engineers. A lot of people who deal in facts and have an appreciation for facts. A quantitative thing is very helpful. I was a social studies major, but you need to be numerate. If you have those good quantitative skills, it's very, very helpful.[6]

Based on Blankfein's comments and your own opinions, respond to the following questions:

A. Why are quantitative skills so highly valued in various business disciplines?

B. How important do you think quantitative skills will be to your career? In what ways?

C. What are your strongest areas in terms of quantitative skills? Weakest areas?

D. What are your strongest areas in terms of spreadsheet software? Weakest areas?

E. What are five goals you have for improving your quantitative skills?

Evaluation Exercises

12.4 Evaluating Charts and Tables in Annual Reports
(LO 12.4)

Choose an annual report from a company that interests you. Select several tables and graphs from the report. Evaluate each in terms of design. Describe at least three effective and less-effective aspects

for each chart and graph. Also, make one recommendation for improving them.

12.5 Evaluating Charts about Exports (LO 12.4)

Examine each of the following charts (Figures 12.15A, B, and C) and respond to the questions below:[7]

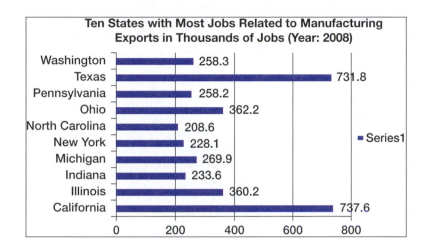

FIGURE 12.15A

Ineffective Bar Chart

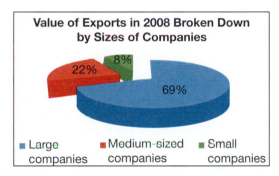

FIGURE 12.15B

Ineffective Pie Chart

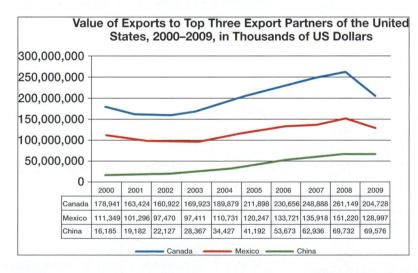

FIGURE 12.15C

Ineffective Line Chart

For each of the above charts, describe their weaknesses in terms of the following: (a) title descriptiveness, (b) focal points, (c) information sufficiency, (d) ease of processing, and (e) takeaway message.

Application Exercises

12.6 Developing Research Objectives (LO 12.2)

Choose three topics of interest that you could research. Write three specific research objectives that could provide a clear direction for you to collect primary data or gather secondary research.

12.7 Conducting Survey Research (LO 12.3)

Individually or in groups, select a business problem that you can learn more about by conducting survey research. You will create an online survey for all of your classmates to take, so design your project around the assumption that you are finding out what university-aged students think or feel about the topic. Design the survey so that it can be completed in three to five minutes. Do the following:

A. Create the survey with between 5 and 15 survey questions.
B. Administer the survey.
C. Identify the major findings and conclusions.
D. State related recommendations.
E. Create two tables that summarize findings from the survey.
F. Create two charts that display key messages related to the data.
G. Write a report that includes your objectives, methodology, findings, conclusions, and recommendations.

12.8 Learning about Online Business Databases at Your Library (LO 12.6)

Identify five online business databases available through your library. For each, explain what the key advantages are and provide one limitation. When you have written about each database, write a concluding statement that identifies which databases are most useful for your business interests.

12.9 Evaluating Data Quality (LO 12.5)

Find five data sources related to a topic that interests you. Analyze reliability, relevance, adaptability, expertise, and biases.

12.10 Creating Charts from the Apple Annual Report[8] (LO 12.4)

Assume you are working for Apple and are summarizing key financial and sales data for presentation to an external audience, such as potential investors or media reporters. You would like to create charts to quickly summarize your performance and allow others to compare your performance across operating segments and product lines.

Use the two tables below to create the following charts. Remember to follow effective design principles.

A. Create a line chart to show net sales growth from 2005 to 2009.
B. Create a line chart to show Mac unit sales in the four major operating segments (Americas, Europe, Japan, and Retail) from 2007 to 2009.
C. Create a bar chart to show net sales for the top five product groups in 2009.
D. Create a pie chart to show net sales for all product groups in 2009.
E. Create a pie chart to show unit sales by product groups in 2009.
F. Identify two key relationships or comparisons from the table. Create charts that best illustrate these relationships or comparisons.
G. As directed by your instructor, exchange your charts with a partner from your class. Evaluate one another's chart designs in terms of title descriptiveness, focal points, information sufficiency, ease of processing, and takeaway message.

Table of Selected Financial Data for Apple, 2005–2009

	2009	2008	2007	2006	2005
Net sales	$42,905	$37,491	$24,578	$19,315	$13,931
Net income	$8,235	$6,119	$3,495	$1,989	$1,328
Earnings per common share:					
Basic	$9.22	$6.94	$4.04	$2.36	$1.64
Diluted	$9.08	$6.78	$3.93	$2.27	$1.55
Cash dividends per common share	$—	$—	$—	$—	$—
Earnings per common share:					
Basic	$893,016	$881,592	$864,595	$844,058	$808,439
Diluted	$907,005	$902,139	$889,292	$877,526	$856,878
Cash, cash equivalents, and marketable securities	$33,992	$24,490	$15,386	$10,110	$8,261
Total assets	$47,501	$36,171	$24,878	$17,205	$11,516
Long-term debt	$—	$—	$—	$—	$—
Total liabilities	$15,861	$13,874	$10,347	$7,221	$4,088
Shareholders' equity	$—	$—	$—	$—	$—

Notes: Currency figures in millions of dollars; share amounts in thousands; dividends are actual figures.

Table of Net Sales for Apple, 2007–2009

	2009	Change	2008	Change	2007
Net Sales by Operating Segment:					
Americas net sales	$18,887	15%	$16,447	38%	$11,907
Europe net sales	11,810	28%	9,233	69%	5,469
Japan net sales	2,279	32%	1,728	59%	1,084
Retail net sales	6,656	−9%	7,292	67%	4,362
Other Segments net sales (a)	3,273	17%	2,791	59%	1,756
Total net sales	$42,905	14%	$37,491	53%	$24,578
Mac Unit Sales by Operating Segment:					
Americas Mac unit sales	4,120	4%	3,980	32%	3,019
Europe Mac unit sales	2,840	13%	2,519	39%	1,816
Japan Mac unit sales	395	2%	389	29%	302
Retail Mac unit sales	2,115	4%	2,034	47%	1,386
Other Segments Mac unit sales (a)	926	17%	793	50%	528
Total Mac unit sales	10,396	7%	9,715	38%	7,051
Net Sales by Product:					
Desktops (b)	$4,324	−23%	$5,622	40%	$4,023
Portables (c)	9,535	9%	8,732	38%	6,313
Total Mac net sales	13,859	−3%	14,354	39%	10,336
iPod	8,091	−12%	9,153	10%	8,305
Other music-related products and services (d)	4,036	21%	3,340	34%	2,496
iPhone and related products and services (e)	13,033	93%	6,742	NM	630
Peripherals and other hardware (f)	1,475	−13%	1,694	30%	1,303
Software, service, and other sales (g)	2,411	9%	2,208	46%	1,508
Total net sales	$42,905	14%	$37,491	53%	$24,578
Unit Sales by Product:					
Desktops (b)	3,182	−14%	3,712	37%	2,714
Portables (c)	7,214	20%	6,003	38%	4,337
Total Mac unit sales	10,396	7%	9,715	38%	7,051
Net sales per Mac unit sold (h)	$1,333	−10%	$1,478	1%	$1,466
iPod unit sales	54,132	−1%	54,828	6%	51,630
Net sales per iPod unit sold (i)	$149	−11%	$167	4%	$161
iPhone units sold	20,731	78%	11,627	NM	1,389

Notes: Currency figures in millions of dollars; unit figures in thousands; per unit figures are actual amounts; NM = Not Meaningful.
(a) Other Segments include Asia Pacific and FileMaker.
(b) Includes iMac, Mac mini, Mac Pro, and Xserve product lines.
(c) Includes MacBook, MacBook Air, and MacBook Pro product lines.
(d) Consists of iTunes Store sales, iPod services, and Apple-branded and third-party iPod accessories.
(e) Derived from handset sales, carrier agreements, and Apple-branded and third-party iPhone accessories.
(f) Includes sales of displays, wireless connectivity and networking solutions, and other hardware accessories.
(g) Includes sales of Apple-branded operating system and application software, third-party software, AppleCare, and Internet services.
(h) Derived by dividing total Mac net sales by total Mac unit sales.
(i) Derived by dividing total iPod net sales by total iPod unit sales.

12.11 Revising Charts about Exporting (LO 12.4)

A. Revise the ineffective bar chart from Exercise 12.5.

B. Revise the ineffective pie chart from Exercise 12.5.

C. Revise the ineffective line chart from Exercise 12.5.

D. With your instructor's direction, consider evaluating your charts against those of your peers in the class. Decide which charts are most effective and share them with the class.

12.12 Evaluate Various Types of Secondary Research Data (LO 12.5)

Based on a topic of interest, find at least one of each of the following types of sources: white paper, industry publication, business periodical, scholarly journal, external blog, and business book. Evaluate each of the sources in the following areas: reliability, relevance, adaptability, expertise, and bias.

12.13 Planning Research at the Prestigio (LO 12.2, LO 12.3, LO 12.5, LO 12.6)

A. Assume the role of Jeff Anderton and conduct research about green meetings. Specifically, your assignment is to identify best practices for green meetings from the perspective of vendors, compare marketing approaches, and evaluate the strategic and financial importance of offering green meetings. Do the following: Write three specific research objectives.

B. Explain strategies for collecting research for each objective.

C. Write three research questions that you could ask conference attendees that would help you understand what consumers think about green meetings.

D. Identify three online sources about green meetings. Evaluate each in terms of the following: reliability, relevance, adaptability, expertise, and biases.

Endnotes

1. David Kintler and Bob Adams, *Independent Consulting: A Comprehensive Guide to Building Your Own Consulting Business* (Avon, MA: Streetwise, 1998).

2. Roly Grimshaw, "Communication by Numbers," *Harvard Management Communication Letter* 8, no. 3 (2005): 3–4.

3. Ibid; Dona M. Wong, *The Wall Street Journal Guide to Information Graphics: The Dos and Don'ts of Presenting Data, Facts, and Figures* (New York: W. W. Norton & Company, 2010).

4. Wong, *The Wall Street Journal Guide to Information Graphics*, p. 13; Stephen Few, *Show Me the Numbers: Designing Tables and Graphs to Enlighten* (Oakland, CA: Analytics Press, 2004).

5. Kirsten D. Sandberg, "Easy on the Eyes: A Design Legend Tells How to Turn Complex 'Real World' Information into Clear Visual Messages," *Harvard Management Communication Letter* 5, no. 8 (2002): 3–5.

6. New York Times Corner Office Blog, "Teamwork," retrieved June 15, 2010, from http://projects.nytimes.com/corner-office/ Teamwork.

7. Based on data retrieved June 15, 2010, from http://www.trade.gov/mas/ian/Jobs/Reports/2008/jobs_by_state_totals.html.

8. Steven P. Jobs and Peter Oppenheimer, *2009 Annual Report Filing for Apple* (Form 10-K/A filed to the United States Securities and Exchange Commission, January 25, 2010), retrieved June 15, 2010, from http://www.apple.com/investor/.

CHAPTER THIRTEEN

Completing Business Reports

Learning Objectives

After studying this chapter, you should be able to do the following:

LO13.1 Explain how completed reports affect your credibility.

LO13.2 Demonstrate excellent thinking by applying a precision-oriented style to reports.

LO13.3 Design your reports to aid in decision making.

LO13.4 Project objectivity in reports.

LO13.5 Review reports for effectiveness and fairness.

WHY DOES THIS MATTER?

Hear Pete Cardon explain why this matters.

bit.ly.com/CardonWhy13

Your primary goal as you draft business reports is to improve decision making. More so than routine business correspondence, reports should be built on thorough, precise, and reliable information and analysis, and should offer advice to help decision makers—typically middle-level and upper-level managers—make informed choices. As a report writer, your personal credibility is tied to how well you provide facts, conclusions, and positions that help decision making (competence), involve decision makers and address their needs (caring), and report information honestly and transparently (character).

Chapter 12 discussed collecting primary and secondary research for business reports and displaying the data in meaningful charts and tables. In this chapter, we focus on putting it all together. As you do with other written documents, when writing reports, you'll focus on achieving the right style, design, and tone. We focus first on style, emphasizing the importance of absolute precision. Next, we discuss design, which you can use to ensure that decision makers rapidly pull out the most important pieces of information. Finally, we focus on achieving an objective tone.

This chapter contains two sample reports: one based on primary research and one based on secondary research. There are far too many types of reports to display in this chapter. You can see examples of a business proposal and a business plan in Appendix C. Also, you can see additional examples of reports (such as a status report) in the online resources at www.mhhe.com/cardon.

The examples throughout this chapter are based on the continued case of the Prestigio Hotel. Read the chapter case to get reacquainted with the situation.

LO13.1 Explain how completed reports affect your credibility.

Chapter Case: Reporting about Customer Satisfaction at Prestigio Hotels

Who's Involved

Jeff Anderton, marketing assistant
- Has worked at the Prestigio for three months
- Roles include marketing the meeting facilities to business/professional groups and tracking customer satisfaction
- Graduated a year ago with a marketing major and statistics minor

Andrea Garcia, general manager
- Has worked as general manager for one year
- Started at the Prestigio nearly nine years ago in a position similar to Jeff's marketing assistant position
- Expects well-analyzed, organized, polished reports

The Situation

Andrea has asked Jeff to write two reports from information he has collected and analyzed. Andrea has placed a high priority on these reports. The first report she wants completed is about the future of green meetings. She views this as an area of strategic concern. Jeff has collected secondary research and interviewed several hotel managers who have successfully marketed green meetings. Now, he needs to think about how to put all the information together.

The second report is based on survey data of conference attendees. Jeff will distribute this report to all marketing team members. The Prestigio marketing team has been conducting a similar survey for the past five years and uses this annual guest satisfaction report to benchmark performance over time. The team will begin working on a new strategic plan in the upcoming months and needs as much reliable information as possible.

Task 1	**Task 2**
Jeff will compose a report about the current market for green meetings and recommend courses of action for the Prestigio.	Jeff will work with one of his colleagues to write a report about the results of a survey he administered to conference attendees at the Prestigio.

Demonstrate Excellent Thinking by Applying a Precision-Oriented Style

LO13.2 Demonstrate excellent thinking by applying a precision-oriented style to reports.

The most basic and critical component of any report is precision in thinking as reflected in style—meaning that it offers accurate, well-documented facts; good reasoning for conclusions; and a solid basis for recommendations (see Figure 13.1). The foundation for these facts, conclusions, and recommendations must be a well-stated business problem or challenge. In short, a report that facilitates effective decision making must demonstrate excellence in thinking.

In Jeff's case, he spends several months working from start to finish on his two research projects. After clearly articulating the business problem, he collects all the necessary information, carefully checks the reliability of each of his sources, examines the facts from many angles as he develops conclusions and recommendations, and asks various colleagues about their perspectives. His critical thinking skills allow him to apply a precision-oriented style to his reports.

Start with a Clear Statement of the Business Problem or Challenge

Placing a clear statement of the central business problem or challenge at the beginning helps establish the purpose and value of the report. Without such a statement, reports lack direction and may be perceived as unimportant.

Problem statements are most effective when they provide the unique context of the problem for the organization and reflect an appropriate sense of urgency. Typically, such statements should be one to three paragraphs long. Notice how Jeff establishes the direction of his green meetings report in Table 13.1.

FIGURE 13.1

Excellence in Thinking for Reports

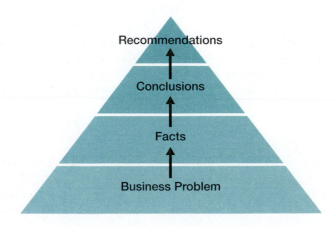

TABLE 13.1

Problem Statement or Business Challenge

Less Effective	More Effective
Since 2008, our revenues from conventions and meetings have declined by roughly 23 percent. One reason that we may have not rebounded is that we still do not provide options for clients who want green meetings.	Since 2008, our revenues from conventions and meetings have declined by roughly 23 percent. Since meetings constitute nearly 60 percent of our total revenues and form the basis for our reputation as a high-class provider of events, we may need to seek new ways of rebuilding our conventions and meetings business. Like many hotels and organizations dependent on business travel, the Prestigio Hotel has lost revenue due to the Great Recession that began in late 2007. However, unlike some others in the meetings and conventions industry, we have not rebounded. Meeting Professionals International (2011) reports that by 2010, hotels and other organizations that hosted meetings had already recovered from the recession. From 2010 to 2011 in the meetings industry, there was an 8 percent increase in the number of meetings held, and revenues per meeting increased by 5 percent from $188,000 to $197,000. One reason we may not have rebounded is that we still do not provide options for clients who want green meetings. Our director of conventions and meetings, Barbara Brookshire, has noticed that many meeting planners inquire about such options. She is certain that we have lost business because we do not provide green meetings, and she expects that meeting planners will increasingly request these options.
This brief statement does suggest one reason revenues may have dropped. However, it lacks contextual details that provide the urgency to solve this problem.	This problem statement provides sufficient context to communicate the severity of the situation. Not only has the Prestigio lost revenue in meetings, but also meetings constitute the most important element of its business, and the recession cannot be used as an explanation for the continued fall in revenue. Furthermore, anecdotal evidence suggests a reason for the lost revenue.
Since 2008, we have evaluated guest satisfaction and future intentions among conference attendees with an annual survey. This report provides the results of this year's survey as well as year-to-year comparisons for the past five years.	Guest satisfaction has always been the foundation for repeat business. With so many online reviews of hotels readily available to meeting planners, the importance of achieving high guest satisfaction ratings is more important now than ever. Since 2008, we have used an annual survey to evaluate guest satisfaction, assess future intentions of conference attendees, and determine how we can improve guest satisfaction. This report provides the results of this year's survey as well as year-to-year comparisons for the past five years.
This statement fails to explain the basic purpose and value behind conducting the surveys.	By adding a few additional thoughts in just two sentences, this problem statement establishes the importance of using the surveys to improve guest satisfaction and, consequently, repeat business. Furthermore, it explains the increased urgency of this effort.

Use Fact-Based Language

Precision in reports relies on facts. You can raise the credibility of your report by (a) supplying the facts with precision; (b) providing supporting details for your conclusions; (c) carefully dealing with predictions and cause-effect statements (see Table 13.2); and (d) responsibly citing your research sources (see the next section about documenting secondary research).

Document Secondary Research and Avoid Plagiarism

By nature, decision makers adopt a methodical and skeptical approach to making investments, changing strategies, and making other substantial changes. They expect quality information to make these decisions. By documenting your sources, you allow decision makers to judge the quality of your data. Decision makers are also looking for

TABLE 13.2

Using Fact-Based Language

Less Effective	More Effective
Nearly all of our respondents reported satisfaction with their conference experiences.	Overall, the vast majority (84%) of our respondents reported satisfaction with their conference experiences.
This fact is imprecise and open to interpretation.	By providing the exact percentage in parentheses, this fact is precise.
One of the strongest indicators that meeting planners expect green meetings options is that they increasingly inquire about such meetings in RFPs.	One of the strongest indicators that meeting planners expect green meetings options is that they increasingly inquire about such meetings in RFPs. A recent survey showed that *71 percent of meeting planners already do or plan to inquire about green initiatives on RFPs for meeting venues* (Shapiro, 2009).
Without a supporting fact, this conclusion may be viewed as unsubstantiated or merely the writer's opinion.	This conclusion is immediately substantiated with a supporting statistic (fact). Because the author provides a citation, decision makers can view the original research if they want to.
The return on investment for providing green meeting options is guaranteed to be at least 300 percent and potentially as high as 500 percent. Investing in green meetings would certainly be a wise choice moving forward.	Based on our conversations with three individuals who have introduced green meeting options at hotels comparable to ours, we concluded that the return on investment for developing a basic infrastructure for green meetings is strong—as high as 500 percent. Each hotel has invested $150,000 to $250,000 annually to build green meeting infrastructures. Although precisely determining how much return is due to new green meeting options is difficult, each of these individuals attributes between $500,000 and $1.3 million in additional revenue due to providing green meeting options (J. Hardaway, personal communication, October 14, 2012; K. Cafferty, personal communication, October 15, 2012; M. Dipprey, personal communication, October 14, 2012).
This statement guarantees that the investment will bring a return. Many decision makers would view the statement as naïve.	This set of statements demonstrates a cautious but confident analysis that the investment may reap substantial returns. It treats statements about prediction and cause and effect carefully, and it includes source information.

signals that you have been methodical in collecting, analyzing, and reporting findings. By documenting your sources, you display your thorough, detail-oriented approach.

Typically, you should provide a reference list at the end of the report that contains all your sources. Also, throughout your document, you should provide citations to indicate the information you have drawn from other sources. You can use a variety of *documentation* systems, including APA and MLA styles. You can see examples of these two styles in Table 13.3. You should, however, use an official style guide to document with precision. Style guides contain hundreds of rules for various types of sources. Additionally, many websites contain the most current documentation guidelines, including the APA style website (www.apastyle.org) and the Purdue Online Writing Lab (http://owl.english.purdue.edu/owl/). Also, if you will spend a lot of time writing reports that need documentation, you might explore some of the available software to help in this process (see the Technology Tips section on page 392).

Although you will generally base your reports on secondary research, you must still demonstrate your originality in thought. That is, your goal is to combine information from your various sources in novel and insightful ways and thereby generate your own conclusions and recommendations.

To develop original reports, make sure that you avoid all forms of **plagiarism.** According to the Merriam-Webster dictionary, to plagiarize is to "steal and pass off (the ideas of another) as one's own" and "to commit literary theft."[1] Thus, plagiarism is serious; it is literally stealing the ideas of others.

TABLE 13.3

References in APA and MLA Documentation Styles

	APA	MLA
Book	Zavada, N., & Spatrisano, A. J. (2007). *Simple steps to green meetings and events: The professional's guide to saving money and the earth.* (Portland, OR: Meeting Strategies Worldwide).	Zavada, Nancy, and Amy Spatrisano. *Simple Steps to Green Meetings and Events: The Professional's Guide to Saving Money and the Earth.* Portland: Meeting Strategies Worldwide, 2007.
Report from an Organization (white paper)	MeetGreen. (2010). *Oracle Open World sustainable event report.* (Portland, OR: Author).	MeetGreen. *Oracle Open World Sustainable Event Report.* Portland: Author, 2010.
Scholarly or Scientific Journal	Kim, Y., & Han, H. (2010). Intention to pay conventional-hotel prices at a green hotel – a modification of the theory of planned behavior. *Journal of Sustainable Tourism, 18*(8), 997–1014.	Kim, Yunhi, and Heesup Han. "Intention to Pay Conventional-Hotel Prices at a Green Hotel – A Modification of the Theory of Planned Behavior." *Journal of Sustainable Tourism* 18.8 (2007): 997–1014. Print.
Magazine/Periodical	Lowe, M. C. (2010, October). The greening of hotels: A look at what major chains are doing to support eco-friendly meetings. *Meetings & Conventions, 45*(10), 45–56.	Lowe, Michael C. "The Greening of Hotels: A Look at What Major Chains Are Doing to Support Eco-Friendly Meetings." *Meetings & Conventions* Oct. 2010: 45–56. Print.
Newspaper	White, M. C. (2010, August 16). For hotels, eco-friendly ideas await a friendlier economy. *The New York Times*, p. B5.	White, Martha C. "For Hotels, Eco-Friendly Ideas Await a Friendlier Economy," *The New York Times* 16 Aug. 2010: B5. Print.
Web Page	Environmental Protection Agency. (2010, May 12). Greening your meetings and conferences: A guide for federal purchasers. Retrieved from www.epa.gov/epp/pubs/meet/greenmeetings.htm	Environmental Protection Agency. "Greening Your Meetings and Conferences: A Guide for Federal Purchasers." *epa.gov.*, 12 May 2010, Author. Web. 24 Oct. 2012.
Article from Online Periodical	Campbell, S. (2008, January). Shades of green. *Elite Meetings.* Retrieved from www.elitemeetings.com/docs/shades-of-green.php	Campbell, Susan. "Shades of Green." *Elite Meetings*, Elite Meetings International, Jan. 2008. Web. Oct. 2012.
Personal Interviews	(J. Hardaway, personal communication, October 14, 2012)* *not included in reference list; used as in-text citation only.	Hardaway, Jack. Personal Interview. 14 Oct. 2012.
In-Text Citations	(Kim & Han, 2010)	(Kim and Han)

To avoid plagiarism on a sentence and paragraph level, document all references to the ideas of others, including (1) direct quotations, (2) paraphrases, and (3) other instances in which you borrow or reference the ideas of others. **Direct quotations** are verbatim restatements from another source. Use direct quotations only when the quotation contains a particularly compelling combination of words, flows effectively with your paper, and emphasizes the credibility of the original speaker or writer. In most situations, you should paraphrase rather than use direct quotations. **Paraphrasing** involves using your own words to express the meaning of the original speaker or writer. When you paraphrase, you significantly alter the original words and sentence structure, but you still need to give credit to the original speaker or writer for the idea. Notice Table 13.4 for examples of using direct quotations and paraphrasing in ways that avoid plagiarism.[2]

TABLE 13.4

Citing Secondary Sources of Information and Avoiding Plagiarism

Original Statement from Source	In July 2008, as the process became more involved, the committee began working with ASTM International, a voluntary standards-development organization. Through each stage, members of the ASTM community have read and voted on the evolving document, including people unfamiliar with the meetings industry. Spatrisano was hoping to submit the standards for the final balloting process at the end of September. "There have been some philosophical disagreements," notes Spatrisano, "such as how you determine what 'recycled' means, as in whether a recycled item contains preconsumed products or just postconsumed. That's one of the issues we are tied up in." Source: Braley, S. J. F. (2010, October). Guidelines for green meetings: M&C previews the forthcoming APEX Initiative. *Meetings & Conventions*, *45*(10), 57.

Situation	Plagiarized Statement	Non-Plagiarized Statement
Direct quotations	Spatrisano explained that there have been some philosophical disagreements such as how you determine what "recycled" means (Braley, 2010).	As Spatrisano explained, "There have been some philosophical disagreements . . . such as how you determine what 'recycled' means" (Braley, 2010, p. 57).
	Although this statement contains an in-text citation, it is plagiarized because it does not use quotation marks to indicate verbatim statements from Spatrisano.	*This statement correctly identifies the direct quotation with quotation marks and includes a source and page number.*
	In July 2008, as the process became more involved, the committee began working with ASTM International, a voluntary standards-development organization.	"In July 2008, as the process became more involved, the committee began working with ASTM International, a voluntary standards-development organization" (Braley, 2010, p. 57).
	This statement is extremely deceptive; it presents verbatim text from another source without any documentation.	*This statement is technically not plagiarized. It uses quotation marks and indicates the source and page number of the original source. However, direct quotes should be used selectively, and this statement is unlikely to flow more smoothly than a simple paraphrase.*
Paraphrasing	The ASTM/APEX process became more involved in July 2008, when ASTM International (a voluntary organization that develops standards) became involved. ASTM community members studied and voted on an evolving document at various stages. The final balloting will end around September after Spatrisano submits the standards (Braley, 2010).	The Convention Industry Council has partnered with ASTM International to develop industry standards for green meetings. These evolving standards will go up for vote in September (Braley, 2010).
	This statement is plagiarized because it retains essentially the same set of ideas with nearly identical phrases and sentence structures. Such minor alterations are not considered paraphrasing.	*This statement reflects the meaning of the original source but is reworded sufficiently. It correctly identifies the source of the information. It is effective to the degree it flows with the ideas before and after the paraphrasing.*
Other forms of borrowing the ideas of others	The process of developing industrywide standards is complicated. For example, even coming to agreement about the definition of a seemingly basic term such as *recycled* is a matter of contention. Currently, members are divided as to whether recycled items refer to those with *preconsumed* or *postconsumed* products (Braley, 2010).	The process of developing industrywide standards is complicated. For example, Amy Spatrisano, principal of MeetGreen, has indicated that even coming to agreement about the definition of a seemingly basic term such as *recycled* is a matter of contention. Currently, members are divided as to whether recycled items refer to those with *preconsumed* or *postconsumed* products (Braley, 2010).

TABLE 13.4

(Continued)

Situation	Plagiarized Statement	Non-Plagiarized Statement
	This statement partially identifies the source of this information. However, it can provide more complete accounting of where the information came from by identifying who originally stated these ideas.	*By including a reference to the person who originally provided these ideas, this article provides more complete information about the original source of ideas.*

The best way to avoid plagiarism on a documentwide level is to demonstrate originality of thought—supplying your own ideas, conclusions, and recommendations that you support by weaving together information from a variety of sources. If the majority of ideas in your report are based on just one or two sources, your report is essentially plagiarized.

Base Recommendations on Facts and Conclusions in the Report

One of the foremost goals of many reports is to give good advice, but business professionals often fail to sufficiently connect their recommendations to their facts and conclusions. If decision makers are to take your report seriously and feel comfortable acting on it, they must be able to see clear connections between the facts and conclusions you present and the related recommendations, as depicted in Figure 13.2.

Provide Specific and Actionable Recommendations

In addition to being based on facts and conclusions in the report, recommendations must be specific and actionable. Many business professionals run out of steam by the end of the report or are reluctant to take a firm position, so they provide vague and sometimes superficial recommendations. Make sure you provide recommendations that are sufficiently detailed and realistic for decision makers (see Table 13.5). You can

FIGURE 13.2

Basing Recommendations on Facts and Conclusions

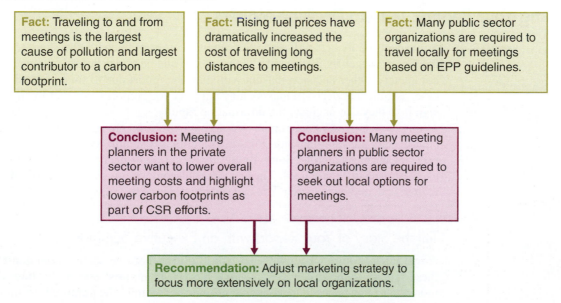

TABLE 13.5

Making Recommendations Specific and Actionable

Less Effective	More Effective
Gain certification as a green meetings provider.	*Gain recognition and certification from organizations creating green meeting standards.* Gaining certification will immediately place us in a select group of venues. The process of gaining certification will help us develop further knowledge about providing green meetings. Moreover, this effort allows us to meet evolving industry standards and promote ourselves with these third-party endorsements. We seek to do the following in the upcoming year: A. Achieve Level 1 compliance for each of the nine standards in the APEX/ASTM green meeting standards. B. Gain Green Seal certification as a green meetings provider. C. Gain recognition as a green hotel on websites such as Travelocity. D. Join the Green Meeting Industry Council.
This recommendation is somewhat specific but not actionable. It does not provide any clear steps to take.	This recommendation contains a rationale as well as specific steps that decision makers would view as actionable.
Focus on energy-efficient transportation for our guests.	*Get a fleet of hybrid or alternative fuel vans.* Many meeting planners on RFPs request that hotels provide energy-efficient transportation options. Doing so can significantly lower the overall carbon footprint of the conference and serves as a high-profile illustration of our commitment to eco-friendly meetings. Our initial estimates suggest that we could replace our four-van fleet for roughly $100,000 (after trade-in or sale of our existing fleet).
This recommendation is vague. It can refer to many types of actions and indicates a superficial, nonthorough effort to provide advice.	This recommendation is specific and provides elaboration about a detail all decision makers are interested in: cost.

elaborate on your recommendations with a section on your rationale, the implications of your recommendations, and clear steps to take toward implementation.

Designing Your Reports to Help Decision Makers

LO13.3 Design your reports to aid in decision making.

Some decision makers will read your reports from start to end. Others will try to glean the key messages by first reading the summary and headings before reading the report completely. Other decision makers will skim the report due to time pressures. In any case, assume that decision makers may not read your report from start to end, and design it so they can navigate the information rapidly.

One way to make your report easy to navigate is to provide a structure that decision makers are familiar with. Figure 13.3 contains sample structures from common types of business reports. Some formal reports contain many additional components, as illustrated in Figure 13.4. These additional components can be classified as front matter, text, and back matter. You can see examples of full, formal reports in the online learning materials.

Tell the Story of Your Report with an Executive Summary

As you glance through Figure 13.3, you'll notice that one section common to all of these reports is the *executive summary*. Nearly all reports, especially those that are more than a few pages long, contain one at the beginning. The purpose is to summarize

FIGURE 13.3

Common Structures for Business Reports[3]

Components of a Survey Report

Executive Summary
Introduction and
    Background
Methodology
Findings
Conclusions
Recommendations
References
Appendices

Components of a Trend Report

Executive Summary
Introduction
Background
Trend Analysis
Recommendations
References
Appendices

Components of a Business Proposal

Cover Page
Executive Summary
Current Situation
Specific Objectives
Deliverables Overview
Timeline
Results Enhancers
Pricing

Components of a Business Plan

Cover Page
Executive Summary
Business Description
    and Vision/General
    Company Description
Business Objectives
Description of the
    Market/Market
    Analysis
Description of the
    Products and Services
Organization and
    Management
Marketing and Sales
    Strategy
Financial Management
Appendices

Components of a Strategic Plan

Cover Page
Executive Summary
SWOT Analysis
Vision, Mission, Values
Strategic Objectives
Action Items
Implementation
Process
Evaluation

Components of a Progress Report

Executive Summary
Introduction
Background
Accomplishments
Problems
Future Plans/Timeline
Conclusion
References
Appendixes

Components of an Annual Report

Cover
Narrative Statements
    (letter to stockholders
    from the CEO—
    functions as executive
    summary, company
    overview, mission
    statement, history)
Financial Statements
    (income statement,
    balance sheet, cash
    flow, auditor's report)
References
Appendixes

Components of a SWOT Analysis

Executive Summary
Strengths
Weaknesses
Opportunities
Threats
Recommendations
References
Appendixes

Components of a Marketing Plan

Executive Summary
Market Research
Product
Competition
Mission Statement
Marketing Strategies
Pricing
Positioning/Branding
Budget
Marketing Goals/
    Objectives

FIGURE 13.4

Components of a Formal Report[4]

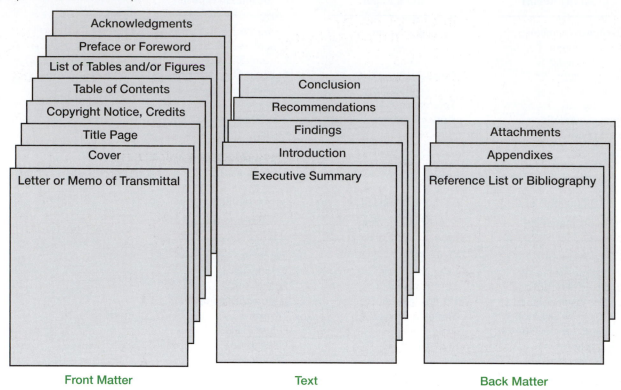

Front Matter   Text   Back Matter

the most important contents, including key findings, conclusions, and recommendations, so that busy executives and other decision makers can quickly understand and act on the report.[5] A good executive summary "demonstrates that you can clearly focus on your goals and state, in no-nonsense fashion, who you are, what you want, and where you are going."[6] Generally, an executive summary should be about one page long for every 10 to 20 pages in the report. You can see two examples of executive summaries on pages 394 and 402 as well as two examples in Appendix C with a business proposal and a business plan.

Provide the Story Line with Descriptive Headings and Other Content Markers

Nearly all reports contain *headings* to help readers quickly navigate. Particularly with reports, decision makers often skim from section to section to find information. At a minimum, you will include first-level headings. For reports over five pages, you will likely use second-level headings and perhaps even third-level headings (see Table 13.6). In addition to accurately showing what is contained in each section, headings should also demonstrate the basic logic of a report. Notice in the left-hand column in Table 13.6 how Jeff uses headings to develop the basic story line of the report: problem ⇨ opportunities and risks ⇨ best practices ⇨ potential rewards ⇨ advice/recommendations.

Although your reports must generally follow a fairly standard order with regard to contents, you do have some flexibility in how you label your headings. Where possible, opt for descriptive titles and headings that help your readers quickly recognize

TABLE 13.6

Providing Clear Headings That Support a Story Line

Heading Structure (should stay consistent throughout document)	**Title (14-pt bold)** **Level-1 Heading (11-pt bold)** *Level-2 Heading (11-pt italicized)*
Title is descriptive	**Should the Prestigio Hotel Develop and Market Green Meetings?**
Story of the report	**Executive Summary**
Business problem or challenge	**Introduction to Green Meetings**
Opportunities and risks	**Market Demand for Green Meetings** *Many Public Sector Organizations Are Required to Hold Green Meetings* *Many Private Sector Organizations Seek Green Meetings as Part of CSR Efforts* *Many Organizations Are Pursuing More Local Options for Meetings* **Risks of Marketing Green Meetings**
Best practices	**Best Practices and Standards for Green Meetings** *Current Best Practices for Green Meetings* *Emerging Standards for Green Meetings*
Potential rewards	**Return on Investment for Green Meetings**
Advice	**Recommendations**

TABLE 13.7

Creating Headings to Help Decision Makers Navigate the Document

Less Effective	More Effective
A Report of the Current Market Situation for Green Meetings with Related Recommendations	Should the Prestigio Hotel Develop and Market Green Meetings?
This title is difficult to process with a variety of noun clusters.	This title is more intriguing and signals to the decision maker the central direction of the report.
Best Practices	Best Practices and Standards for Green Meetings
This brief heading in isolation tells little about the contents of the section.	The addition of just a few words clarifies what will be included in this section.

the value and contents of any given section. Notice in Table 13.7 how minor changes can make headings more efficient and engaging.

Use Preview Statements to Frame Your Messages and Accentuate Takeaway Messages

Reports are often lengthy and dense, so preview statements can help decision makers follow the direction of your text. Also, preview statements frame the message, allowing readers to create a mental map of your key takeaway messages (see Table 13.8).

TABLE 13.8

Providing Clear Preview Statements

Less Effective	More Effective
In our research, we found several trends that we discuss in the upcoming pages.	In our research, we found the following trends regarding green meetings: (a) many public sector organizations are required to hold green meetings; (b) many private sector organizations seek green meetings as part of corporate social responsibility (CSR) efforts; and (c) many organizations are pursuing local options for meetings.
This short, abrupt statement leaves readers with no direction about the trends. If the readers do not read further, they will not have any indication of the key takeaway messages.	This preview statement—in just a few sentences—creates the mental map for decision makers as they read further and groups the takeaway messages all in one place.

TABLE 13.9

Using Charts to Support the Story Line of the Report

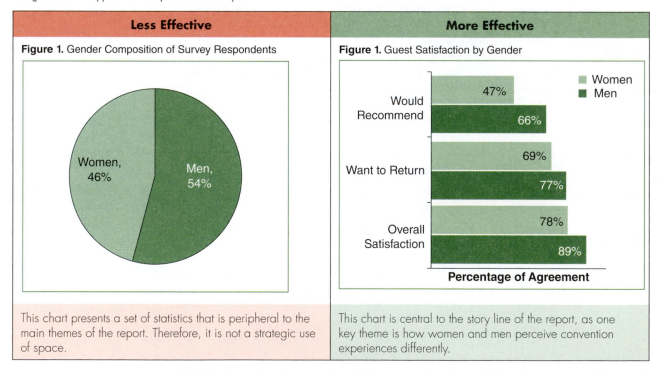

Less Effective	More Effective
Figure 1. Gender Composition of Survey Respondents	**Figure 1.** Guest Satisfaction by Gender
This chart presents a set of statistics that is peripheral to the main themes of the report. Therefore, it is not a strategic use of space.	This chart is central to the story line of the report, as one key theme is how women and men perceive convention experiences differently.

Insert Charts and Tables to Draw Attention to Your Key Points

Reports based on research data frequently include *tables* and *figures* (including charts) to supplement the text. You will apply principles for tables and charts that you learned in Chapter 12. Keep in mind that the purpose of tables and charts is first and foremost to fit into the story line you have established for your report. Also, tables and charts should simplify or clarify complicated numerical information that may bog down your reader in text (see Table 13.9).

TABLE 13.10

Applying Bulleting

Less Effective	More Effective
Within the past few years, surveys show that the *majority* of meeting planners strongly consider green meeting options. For example, the following survey results are typical: In a 2009 survey, 51 percent of meeting planners reported increasing efforts to run green meetings (Drammeh, 2009); in a 2010 survey, 93 percent of meeting planners stated that they would at least occasionally use green meetings (Richard K. Miller & Associates, 2010); and in a 2011 survey, 51 percent said green meetings were more highly prioritized than before (Green Meetings Portland, 2011).	Within the past few years, surveys show that the *majority* of meeting planners strongly consider green meeting options. For example, the following survey results are typical: • In a 2009 survey, 51 percent of meeting planners reported increasing efforts to run green meetings (Drammeh, 2009). • In a 2010 survey, 93 percent of meeting planners stated that they would at least occasionally use green meetings (Richard K. Miller & Associates, 2010). • In a 2011 survey, 51 percent said green meetings were more highly prioritized than before (Green Meetings Portland, 2011).
This passage is too dense to read and process quickly.	By using bullets, readers can much more quickly digest the information.

Apply Bulleting and Enumerated Lists to Make Passages Easier to Process

Since reports often contain dense information, using bulleting and enumerated lists can help readers rapidly process and group information (see Table 13.10). On the other hand, when too much of the report is in bullet points, it can create a choppy, staccato-like effect.

Create a Cover Page, a Table of Contents, and Appendixes

Reports of more than ten pages often include a *cover page*. Regardless of length, formal reports—especially those submitted to external decision makers (i.e., loan officers, venture capitalists, stockholders)—always include a cover page. At a minimum, the cover page should include a title, names of those who wrote and/or are submitting the report, and a date. For formal reports, companies often rely on internal or external graphic designers, public relations professionals, and other document design specialists to create a visually appealing document. The cover page is generally the most emphasized aspect of this document design.

Likewise, a *table of contents* is expected for nearly any report over ten pages long. The table of contents contains all first-level headings and sometimes all second-level headings. Providing a well-designed table of contents immediately creates an impression that you are organized.[7] You can see an example of a business plan with a table of contents in Appendix C.

Reports also frequently include *appendixes* to provide reference materials. For example, common information in appendixes include financial statements, marketing materials, detailed data tables, brochures, references, résumés, and biographies.

Achieving Objectivity and Positivity through Tone

Achieving a positive, *can-do* tone in your communications is appropriate in nearly all business situations. In many business reports, projecting positivity is also important. However, more so than positivity, you should project objectivity—the sense that you are providing information, analysis, and advice that is sound, reliable, and unbiased. In other words, project objectivity first and positivity second. Furthermore, ensure that

LO13.4 Project objectivity in reports.

TECHNOLOGY TIPS

USING SOFTWARE TO PROVIDE STRUCTURE AND DOCUMENTATION

Most word processing software packages—notably Microsoft Word—contain features to help you provide structure and documentation to your reports.

Using Word, you can accomplish some of the following tasks in your reports:

- Create a table of contents that can be automatically updated as you make revisions.

- Create your own styles that apply to headings (Title, Heading 1, Heading 2).

- Use captions for tables and figures that automatically update numbers as you work on the document.

- Use cross-referencing so that if you change the order of referenced objects, any references to objects in the text are updated with the new object reference number.

- Use co-authoring tools.

You can also use Word to help you document the information contained in your reports. Typically, you'll use the following sequence:

Create a source. You'll use a simple wizard that walks you through the information you need to provide. Word automatically generates the reference in APA or MLA style and places it in the reference list.

Create an in-text citation. Within your report where you want to insert a citation, simply use the Insert Citation feature, select the reference, and click OK: Word automatically inserts a properly formatted in-text citation.

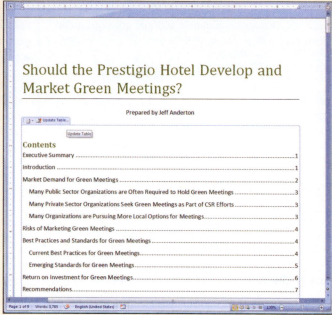

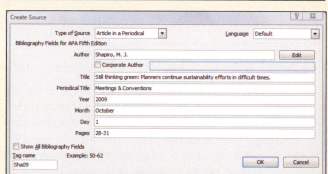

TABLE 13.11

Striking an Objective Tone While Also Projecting Positivity

Less Effective	More Effective
Generally, the research indicates that market demand for green meetings is growing, with the majority of meeting planners showing interest. The following features define the increasing demand: (a) many public sector organizations are required to hold green meetings; (b) many private sector organizations seek green meetings as part of CSR efforts; and (c) many organizations are pursuing more local options for meetings. Currently, demand far outstrips supply. This provides us with a golden opportunity to gain market share before other meeting venues develop green meeting options. Hotels of comparable size to the Prestigio have reported phenomenal return on investment for next to nothing as far as developing and marketing green meetings. Even though we can't predict the future market with certainty, the exponential growth of this market shows its forward trajectory, and we should make sure we're not the latecomers for this trend. As a result, the Prestigio should make short-term investments to provide some green meeting options, and also position us to invest heavily to meet future long-term demand. We should immediately take the following actions to break into the green meetings market before it's too late: 1. Hire a green meetings specialist. 2. Get a fleet of hybrid or alternative fuel vans. 3. Gain recognition and certification as a green meetings venue from reputable third-party organizations. 4. Adjust marketing strategy to focus more extensively on local organizations. 5. Reevaluate prospects in the public sector. 6. Feature our green meeting options prominently in marketing materials.	Generally, the research indicates that market demand for green meetings is growing, with the majority of meeting planners showing interest. The following features define the increasing demand: (a) many public sector organizations are required to hold green meetings; (b) many private sector organizations seek green meetings as part of CSR efforts; and (c) many organizations are pursuing more local options for meetings. Right now is a good time to develop green meetings because demand far outstrips supply. Hotels of comparable size to the Prestigio have reported strong return on investment for minimal investments in developing and marketing green meetings. However, the future demand is neither clear nor certain. As a result, the Prestigio should make relatively small, short-term investments to provide some green meeting options. This will position us to invest more heavily as we learn more about the long-term demand. In particular, we recommend the following actions during the next year: 1. Hire a green meetings specialist. 2. Get a fleet of hybrid or alternative fuel vans. 3. Gain recognition and certification as a green meetings venue from reputable third-party organizations. 4. Adjust marketing strategy to focus more extensively on local organizations. 5. Reevaluate prospects in the public sector. 6. Feature our green meeting options prominently in marketing materials.
The tone of this passage projects excessive enthusiasm and perhaps a rush to action. Some of the adjectives are exaggerated, perhaps displaying an imprecise, unprofessional approach to the report.	The tone of this passage projects objectivity. The adjectives are businesslike and measured. A tempered *can-do* attitude emerges without sacrificing the sense that the research is methodical, thorough, and unrushed.

your enthusiasm and strong positive emotion do not appear to cloud your judgment. In Table 13.11, notice the comparisons between two alternative approaches to writing an executive summary. As you read through these passages, consider how to strike the right balance between objectivity and positivity.

Assessing Key Features of a Completed Report

In the upcoming pages, you can see two examples of business reports. The first (Figure 13.5) is based on secondary research. It can be classified as a *business trend* or *business issue* report. The second (Figure 13.6) is based on survey results, which is primary research. Although you will find that reports vary greatly in purpose and length, as you glance through these examples, consider the key features to strive for in all your reports: value to decision makers, precision, documentation, easy navigation, and objectivity.

FIGURE 13.5

Business Report with Secondary Research

Should the Prestigio Hotel Develop and Market Green Meetings?

Prepared by Jeff Anderton
October 2012

Executive Summary

The executive summary tells the story of the report so the busy reader can get the gist of the content.

In the past few years, potential clients have increasingly requested green meeting options. As a result, Prestigio managers have increasingly wondered whether providing such options could increase revenues in our conventions and meetings business. This report addresses whether the Prestigio should develop and market green meeting options. It contains analysis in the following areas: (a) market demand for green meetings; (b) risks of marketing green meetings; (c) best practices and standards for green meetings; (d) return on investment for green meetings; and (e) recommendations.

Generally, the research indicates that market demand for green meetings is growing, with the majority of meeting planners showing interest. The following features define the increasing demand: (a) many public sector organizations are required to hold green meetings; (b) many private sector organizations seek green meetings as part of CSR efforts; and (c) many organizations are pursuing more local options for meetings. Right now is a good time to develop green meetings because demand far outstrips supply.

Hotels of comparable size to the Prestigio have reported strong return on investment for minimal investments in developing and marketing green meetings. However, the future demand is neither clear nor certain. As a result, the Prestigio should make relatively small, short-term investments to provide some green meeting options. This will position us to invest more heavily as we learn more about the long-term demand. In particular, we recommend the following actions during the next year:

The executive summary concludes with recommendations.

1. Hire a green meetings specialist.
2. Get a fleet of hybrid or alternative fuel vans.
3. Gain recognition and certification as a green meetings venue from reputable third-party organizations.
4. Adjust marketing strategy to focus more extensively on local organizations.
5. Reevaluate prospects in the public sector.
6. Feature our green meeting options prominently in marketing materials.

Introduction begins with statement of and brief background to the problem.

Introduction to Green Meetings

Since 2008, our revenues from conventions and meetings have declined by roughly 23 percent. Since meetings constitute nearly 60 percent of our total revenues and form the basis for our reputation as a high-class provider of events, we may need to seek new ways of rebuilding our conventions and meetings business.

The Great Recession that began in late 2007 led to lost revenue for all hotels and organizations dependent on business travel. However, unlike others in the conventions and meetings industry, Prestigio has not rebounded in

FIGURE 13.5

(Continued)

the past few years. Meeting Professionals International (2011) reports that by 2010, hotels and other organizations that hosted meetings had already recovered from the recession. From 2010 to 2011 in the meetings industry, there was an 8 percent increase in the number of meetings held, and revenues per meeting increased by 5 percent from $188,000 to $197,000.

One reason we may have not rebounded is that we still do not provide options for clients who want green meetings. Our director of conventions and meetings, Barbara Brookshire, has noticed that many meeting planners inquire about green meeting options. She is certain that we have lost business because we do not provide such meetings, and she expects that meeting planners will increasingly request these options.

Introduction concludes with a review of report contents.

The purpose of this report is to examine the following aspects of green meetings: (a) current and projected market demand; (b) risks of developing and marketing green meetings; (c) best practices and emerging standards related to green meetings; and (d) potential return on investment. We conclude the report with recommendations about the degree to which the Prestigio Hotel should develop and market green meetings.

Market Demand for Green Meetings

Headings clearly state section content.

Increasingly, meeting planners expect green meetings options. Just five to six years ago, surveys of meeting planners showed that a *minority* showed strong interest in green meetings, with roughly 18 to 43 percent in various surveys deeming them important (Drammeh, 2009; Gecker, 2008). Around 2009, the market demand quickly accelerated. Within the past few years, surveys show that the *majority* of meeting planners strongly consider green meeting options. For example, the following survey results are typical over the past few years:

- In a 2009 survey, 51 percent of meeting planners reported increasing efforts to run green meetings (Drammeh, 2009).
- In a 2010 survey, 93 percent of meeting planners stated that they would at least occasionally use green meetings (Richard K. Miller & Associates, 2010).
- In a 2011 survey, 51 percent said green meetings were more highly prioritized than before (Green Meetings Portland, 2011).

One of the strongest indicators that meeting planners expect green meetings options is whether they inquire about them in RFPs. A recent survey showed that *71 percent of meeting planners do or plan to inquire about green initiatives on RFPs for meeting venues* (Shapiro, 2009).

In-text citations allow readers to know exactly where the information came from.

Venues that currently offer green meeting options are in a strong competitive position. Several industry analysts have reported that the demand for green meetings is far greater than the supply (Campbell, 2008; Environmental Protection Agency, 2010). In one survey, 40 percent of meeting planners said there are not enough green meeting venues (Richard K. Miller & Associates, 2010).

While surveys of meeting planners and forecasts by industry analysts point to a continuing and increasing demand, not much information is available about the market size for green meetings. In our research, we found that the following trends will increasingly impact market size: (a) many public sector organizations are required to hold green meetings; (b) many private sector organizations seek green meetings as part of corporate social responsibility (CSR) efforts; and (c) many organizations are pursuing local options for meetings.

FIGURE 13.5

(Continued)

Many Public Sector Organizations Are Required to Hold Green Meetings

Government agencies are leading the way in demanding green meetings (Torrence, 2010). Many government groups are increasingly required to abide by *Environmentally Preferable Purchasing* (EPP). The following EPP standards are the overarching principles that apply to green meetings:

- Include environmental factors as well as traditional considerations of price and performance as part of the normal purchasing process.
- Emphasize pollution prevention early in the purchasing process.
- Examine multiple environmental attributes throughout a product's or service's life cycle.
- Compare relative environmental impacts when selecting products and services.
- Collect and base purchasing decisions on accurate and meaningful information about environmental performance. (Environmental Protection Agency, 2010)

The application of these EPP principles demonstrates that the major sources of waste and pollution for meetings are the following: marketing of events and registration; travel to the event; hotel stays; food services; exhibition halls; and local transportation. As a result, government meeting planners increasingly emphasize green meetings with the following components: location that minimizes travel; eco-friendly meeting facilities and processes; local transportation; eco-friendly catering; and eco-friendly promotion, marketing, and registration practices (Environmental Protection Agency, 2010).

Many Private Sector Organizations Seek Green Meetings as Part of CSR Efforts

> These level-2 headings allow rapid comprehension of key supporting points.

One of the primary motivations for planning green meetings is to fulfill corporate CSR initiatives. Nearly all Fortune 500 organizations have developed CSR plans that include green initiatives, and, increasingly, small- and medium-sized organizations emphasize green initiatives as part of CSR plans. Many stakeholders expect that being a good corporate citizen must include these green initiatives (Gecker, 2009). Meeting planners, then, often seek out green meetings to satisfy CSR plans. In fact, 42 percent of meeting planners say that they plan green meetings with CSR in mind (Meeting Professionals International, 2011).

With the prominent role of green initiatives as part of CSR efforts, green meetings will likely become a major focus because meetings are among the least green activities for many organizations. According to MeetGreen, a three-day conference with 300 attendees creates waste equivalent to the mass of 33 small vehicles; water resources that would fill half of an Olympic-sized swimming pool; and greenhouse gases to fill 25 million basketballs (Torrence, 2010). Furthermore, one well-known meeting standards organization, the Green Meeting Industry Council, envisions a green meeting industry with zero net environmental impact by 2020 (Richard K. Miller & Associates, 2010).

Many Organizations Are Pursuing Local Options for Meetings

The major cause of pollution for meetings is travel to and from these events. As a result, many organizations that are seeking to minimize carbon footprints are holding meetings that are more local. Because of increased demand for green meetings combined with the impact of higher fuel costs, 32 percent of meeting planners say they are planning more local events and 29 percent say they will hold more virtual meetings (Edelstein, 2011a). This trend may mean that event venues need to increasingly market locally.

FIGURE 13.5

(Continued)

Risks of Marketing Green Meetings

Although the demand for green meetings is growing, developing and marketing green meetings is not without risks. While it is true that meeting planners increasingly ask about green meetings in RFPs, there is little evidence to show the impact of such options on the ultimate selection of a meeting venue. In particular, clients resist green meetings for the following reasons (Campbell, 2008):

- *Many meeting planners incorrectly believe green meetings are more expensive.* In reality, most green meetings cost less than non-green meetings. Yet, many meeting planners and other decision makers perceive that green meetings cost more (Gecker, 2009; Lowe, 2010; MeetGreen, 2010). In one survey, 46 percent of meeting planners agreed that green meetings are too expensive (Richard K. Miller & Associates, 2010).
- *Some executives and senior managers are not interested in green meetings.* Although meeting planners organize and coordinate most of the communication between their organizations and meeting venues, they are rarely the final decision makers. Sometimes meeting planners express interest in green meetings only to lack support from decision makers in their organizations (Campbell, 2008).
- *Many potential clients view green meetings as lower-quality experiences.* Many meeting planners worry that although green meetings are eco-friendly and may even save money, they provide a lower-quality experience (Campbell, 2008). This is largely a misperception. In one recent study of conventions held in three common meeting destinations (Orlando, Florida; Birmingham, Alabama; Columbus, Ohio), the researchers found that green meeting practices were correlated with higher satisfaction among convention attendees (Lee, Brieter, & Choi, 2011).
- *Some meeting planners are unaware of green meeting options.* Because of the limited supply of venues that offer legitimate green meeting options, some meeting planners assume that they will not find a venue up to their expectations (Campbell, 2008).

Many of the risks of marketing green meetings are based on misperceptions. Thus, any successful development and marketing of green meetings must focus on educating the client base about the actual costs and actual quality of green meetings (Campbell, 2008).

Best Practices and Standards for Green Meetings

Although meeting planners increasingly seek green meeting options, they often hold varied views of exactly what constitutes a green meeting. During the past five years, the options developed and marketed by major hotel chains have established current best practices. Furthermore, in the past few years, various third-party organizations have begun developing concrete standards for green meetings.

Current Best Practices for Green Meetings

Most major hotel chains now offer green meeting options that can serve as effective models for smaller hotel groups such as the Prestigio. Fairmont's *Eco-Meet* program, initiated in 2007, is often considered among the industry innovators. Other major hotel chains—including Hilton, Hyatt, and Marriott—have followed Fairmont's lead and established comparable programs. The *Eco-Meet* program focuses on four main areas (Lowe, 2010):

- *Eco-accommodation:* provide information to guests about how to be more environmentally conscious during their stays; place recycling bins in all rooms; use energy-efficient lighting and water-conservative plumbing.

– Page 4 –

Headings support common story lines and rationales in business decision making, including terms such as benefits, risks, *and* best practices.

FIGURE 13.5

(Continued)

- *Eco-service:* use dishes/cutlery instead of disposable plates/plastic utensils; provide recycling bins; use reusable items such as silk flowers and linen napkins for restaurant and catering services.

- *Eco-cuisine:* source local, seasonal, and organically grown foods from with 100 miles; attain a 50 percent reduction in animal proteins (use vegetable proteins instead).

- *Eco-programming:* use electronic registration and check-in; engage in paper reduction efforts; purchase carbon offsets and energy certificates.

Some insight about which green meeting options are most often implemented can be gained from recent studies. One study of meeting planners showed that the three most common practices to achieve green meetings were the following: reducing paper by using digital alternatives (79%); providing on-site recycling programs (61%); and selecting host cities that require less travel (48%) (Richard K. Miller & Associates, 2010).

Emerging Standards for Green Meetings

Even with many major hotel chains developing and marketing green meetings, however, the concept of exactly what constitutes green meetings is not clearly defined, and there is no industrywide agreement (Lee, Brieter, & Choi, 2011). Because of the growing demand, the Convention Industry Council and ASTM International are developing the APEX/ASTM Environmentally Sustainable Meeting Standards.* These standards are the most comprehensive and most respected set of green meeting standards in the industry.

The APEX/ASTM standards will address nine areas: (a) accommodation; (b) audiovisual and production; (c) communications and marketing; (d) destinations; (e) exhibits; (f) food and beverage; (g) meeting venues; (h) on-site offices; and (i) transportation (Convention Industry Council, n.d.; Torrence, 2010). These nine standards involve four levels of compliance from minimal to zero-waste meetings (level one to level four). Currently, there are about 30 pages of standards. Some meeting planners view the standards as most applicable to large conventions (Braley, 2010). Soon, meeting venues may gain certification for compliance with APEX/ASTM standards (Convention Industry Council, n.d.).

Another set of standards that are particularly relevant for public sector meetings was developed by the Environmental Protection Agency (EPA). The EPA requires government agencies to include the following questions in RFPs for meetings ("Be Green," 2009):

1. Do you have a recycling program? If so, please describe.
2. Do you have a linen/towel reuse option that is communicated to guests?
3. Do guests have easy access to public transportation or shuttle services at your facility?
4. Are lights and air conditioning turned off when rooms are not in use? If so, how do you ensure this?
5. Do you provide bulk dispensers or reusable containers for beverages, food, and condiments?
6. Do you provide reusable serving utensils, napkins, and tablecloths when food and beverages are served?
7. Do you have an energy-efficiency program? Please describe.
8. Do you have a water-conservation program? Please describe.

---

*The Convention Industry Council is a leading advocate for the meetings, conventions, and exhibitions industry. It is composed of 103,500 individuals and 19,500 organizations involved in the meetings industry. It produces the Accepted Practices Exchange (APEX), which is a set of industrywide standards for the meetings, conventions, and exhibitions industry. ASTM International is an organization that establishes international voluntary consensus standards. It is represented by members from 135 countries and develops standards based on the guiding principles of the World Trade Organization.

Footnotes used for additional information.

FIGURE 13.5

(Continued)

9. Does your facility provide guests with paperless check-in and checkout?

10. Does your facility use recycled or recyclable products? Please describe.

11. Do you source food from local growers or take into account the growing practices of farmers that provide the food? Please describe.

12. Do you use bio-based or biodegradable products, including bio-based "cafeteriaware"? Please describe.

13. Do you provide training to your employees on these green initiatives? Please describe. What other environmental initiatives have you undertaken, including any environment-related certifications you possess, EPA voluntary partnerships in which you participate, support of a green suppliers network, or other initiatives?

Aside from the APEX/ASTM and EPA standards, other certification and compliance programs exist. For example, another third-party certification program is the Green Seal certification (Lee, Brieter, & Choi, 2011). Various websites, such as Travelocity and Yahoo, designate hotels as green hotels. In some cases, even travel companies and agencies have created measures of green compliance. For example, American Express Meetings and Events recently created a metric that measures carbon, water, and waste for each meeting venue (Edelstein, 2011b). In addition to venue certification, some hotel chains provide in-house certification for green planners. For example, Marriott has certified 3,600 employees as Marriott Green Planners (Lowe, 2010).

Return on Investment for Green Meetings

Although surveys of meeting planners show growing interest in green meetings, little data exists about the return on investment for developing and marketing green meetings. Furthermore, little is known about how often green meeting options are a deciding factor for meeting planners. Rather, much of the research and advice about green meetings focuses more on social responsibility than profitability.

We talked to three individuals during the past month who have initiated green meetings in their hotels as a marketing strategy: Jack Hardaway, Director of Meetings at Lionwood Hotels; Melanie Dipprey, General Manager of Silver Lake Hotel and Resort; and Kirsley Cafferty, Director of Sales at the Easton Inn. Each of these individuals is extensively involved in marketing meetings at their hotels, all of which are similar in size to our hotel. Each has initiated green meetings during the past 18 to 24 months.

Based on our conversations with them, we concluded that the return on investment for developing a basic infrastructure for green meetings is strong – as high as 500 percent. Each hotel has invested approximately $150,000 to $250,000 annually to build their green meetings infrastructures. Although precisely determining how much return is due to new green meeting options is difficult, each hotel attributes between $500,000 and $1.3 million in additional revenue due to providing green meeting options (J. Hardaway, personal communication, October 14, 2012; K. Cafferty, personal communication, October 15, 2012; M. Dipprey, personal communication, October 14, 2012).

These hotels have taken the following actions, which require little investment, to develop and market their green meetings: (a) hired or trained full-time green meetings specialists; (b) sought out public sector organizations; (c) gained Green Seal certification; and (d) created a web page about green meeting options (J. Hardaway, personal communication, October 14, 2012; K. Cafferty, personal communication, October 15, 2012; M. Dipprey, personal communication, October 14, 2012). In addition, Lionwood Hotels has started ensuring that at least half of all catered food is sourced from within 50 miles of their hotels. They believe their focus on local, organic foods has been the deciding factor in two groups selecting their hotel for conventions (J. Hardaway, personal communication, October 14, 2012).

Report relies on firsthand interviews in addition to secondary research. The firsthand information addresses difficult-to-find secondary information.

– Page 6 –

FIGURE 13.5

(Continued)

Recommendations

With the majority of meeting planners to some extent prioritizing green meetings, most large hotel chains moving toward heavily promoting such options, and a unique opportunity to gain market share given the current undersupply of hotels providing these options, we should move immediately to develop and market green meetings. However, because the future demand for green meetings and related services is not well understood (even among the major hotel chains), we recommend a short-term strategy. An initial one-year strategy requires little initial investment but positions us to move forward aggressively in years to come as we gain a clearer understanding of the market demands. Specifically, we recommend the following actions in the next year:

1. *Hire a green meetings specialist*. An experienced green meeting planner or marketer could help us develop green meeting options and provide the needed expertise to develop longer-term plans.

2. *Get a fleet of hybrid or alternative fuel vans*. Many meeting planners on RFPs request that hotels provide energy-efficient transportation options. Providing local transportation with energy-efficient vans can significantly lower the overall carbon footprint of conferences held at our hotel and serve as a high-profile illustration of our commitment to eco-friendly meetings. Our initial estimates suggest that we could replace our four-van fleet for roughly $100,000 (after trade-in or sale of our existing fleet).

3. *Gain recognition and certification as a green meetings venue from reputable third-party organizations*. Gaining certification will immediately place us in a select group of venues. Moreover, the process of gaining certification will help us develop knowledge about providing green meetings. This effort also allows us to meet evolving industry standards and promote ourselves with these third-party endorsements. Specifically, we can accomplish the following actions in the upcoming year:

    a. Achieve Level 1 compliance for each of the nine standards in the APEX/ASTM green meeting standards.
    b. Gain Green Seal certification as a green meetings provider.
    c. Gain recognition as a green hotel on websites such as Travelocity.
    d. Join the Green Meeting Industry Council.

4. *Adjust our marketing strategy to focus more extensively on local organizations*. Most organizations are realizing that travel to and from the host city of an event is the least eco-friendly aspect of meetings. As a result, we suggest increasing our marketing efforts to organizations located within 500 miles to build more local clientele for our services.

5. *Reevaluate prospects in the public sector*. Government agencies are among the most progressive organizations that are seeking green meeting options. As we position ourselves as a green meetings provider, we should market aggressively to public sector organizations.

6. *Feature our green meeting options prominently in marketing materials*. We should feature our new options prominently on our website and develop contract language that favors green meetings. On the website, we should address frequently asked questions and address frequent misperceptions about green meetings.

Enumerated list contains recommendations. They are set apart in italics and followed by a short rationale to allow decision makers to understand the ideas clearly.

Recommendations are specific and achievable. They are based on needs and opportunities described in the body of the paper.

FIGURE 13.5

(*Continued*)

References

"Be Green: 14 Questions for Your Hotel." (2009, July 1). Retrieved from
www.meetingsnet.com/green/venue/0701-epa-hotel-questions/

Braley, S. J. F. (2010, October). Guidelines for green meetings: M&C previews the forthcoming APEX Initiative.
Meetings & Conventions, 45(10), 57–60.

Campbell, S. (2008, January). Shades of green. *Elite Meetings* [online]. Retrieved from
www.elitemeetings.com/docs/shades-of-green.php

Convention Industry Council. (n.d.). APEX/ASTM environmentally sustainable meeting standards. Retrieved from
www.conventionindustry.org/StandardsPractices/APEXASTM.aspx

Cumming, P., & Pelham, F. (2010). *Making events more sustainable: A guide to BS 8901*. (London: BSI Group).

Drammeh, J. (2009, February 15). Green meetings good for business. Connect Meetings Intelligence [online].
Retrieved from www.connectyourmeetings.com/2009/02/15/green-meetings-good-for-business/

Edelstein, L. G. (2011a, May). Slammed by fuel costs: Planners say oil prices are directly affecting meetings.
Meetings and Conventions, 46(5), 20–21.

Edelstein, L. G. (2011b, October 18). *American Express releases green meetings measurement tool*. Retrieved
from www.meetings-conventions.com/articles/american-express-releases-green-meetings-measurement-
tool/c44242.aspx

Environmental Protection Agency. (2010, May 12). *Greening your meetings and conferences: A guide for
federal purchasers*. Retrieved from www.epa.gov/epp/pubs/meet/greenmeetings.htm

Gecker, R. (2009, July). Lean and green: How companies that are cutting budgets still manage to make their
meetings sustainable. *Corporate Meetings & Incentives, 28*(7), 16–20.

Kim, Y., & Han, H. (2010). Intention to pay conventional-hotel prices at a green hotel – a modification of the
theory of planned behavior. *Journal of Sustainable Tourism, 18*(8), 997–1014.

Meeting Professionals International (2011). *FutureWatch 2011*. (Dallas, TX: RR Donnelley & Sons Company).

Lee, J., Breiter, D., & Choi, Y. (2011). Quality of a green destination as perceived by convention attendees:
The relationships between greening and competitiveness. *Proceedings of the 16th Graduate Students
Research Conference in Hospitality and Tourism.*

Lowe, M. C., (2010, October). The greening of hotels: A look at what major chains are doing to support
eco-friendly meetings. *Meetings & Conventions, 45*(10), 45–56.

MeetGreen. (2010). *Oracle Open World sustainable event report*. (Portland, OR: Author).

Pizam, A. (2009). Green hotels: A fad, ploy or fact of life? *International Journal of Hospitality Management, 28*(1), 1–5.

Richard K. Miller & Associates (2010). *2010 Travel & Tourism Market Research Handbook* (Loganville, GA: Author).

Shapiro, M. J. (2009, October 1). Still thinking green: Planners continue sustainability efforts in difficult times.
Meetings & Conventions, 44(10), 28–31.

Spatrisano, A., & Wilson, N. J. (2007). *Simple steps to green meetings and events: The professional's guide to
saving money and the earth*. (Portland, OR: Meeting Strategies Worldwide).

Torrence, S. (2010, November). Change the world one meeting at a time: APEX/ASTM sustainability standards
nearly set. *Corporate Meetings & Incentives, 29*(11), 18–21.

Travel Portland and Oregon Convention Center. (2011, October 23). Green meetings. Retrieved from
www.greenmeetings.travelportland.com/

Reference list (in
APA style)
allows decision
makers and
other readers to
follow up on
information and
make judgments
about data quality.
It also inspires
confidence in the
writer as organized
and detail-oriented.

FIGURE 13.6

Business Report with Primary Research

Guest Satisfaction among Conference Attendees
2012 Report
The Prestigio

Prepared by Barbara Brookshire and Jeff Anderton
January 2013

Executive Summary

Survey Details: To determine guest-satisfaction levels, we surveyed 264 convention attendees who participated in three- or four-day conventions between January and October 2012.

Key Findings:
- Satisfaction ratings for key guest services and amenities: conference meals, 76 percent; meeting rooms, 75 percent; staff and service, 69 percent.
- Key indicators of repeat business: overall guest satisfaction, 84 percent; willingness to recommend the Prestigio, 57 percent.
- Overall satisfaction ratings by gender and income: women, 78 percent; men, 89 percent; higher-income, 66 percent, lower-income, 88 percent.
- Overall satisfaction in the past five years: 2008, 87 percent; 2009, 81 percent; 2010, 79 percent; 2011, 79 percent; 2012, 84 percent.

Key Conclusions:
- We fell short of our 85 percent satisfaction targets in the following areas: conference meals, meeting rooms, and staff and service.
- We received high ratings for our restaurants, which are the most popular guest service and amenity. Preferences for other guest services and amenities are highly variable based on gender and income.
- We fell short of our goals for overall satisfaction and willingness to recommend the Prestigio.
- We found that women and higher-income guests tend to be less satisfied, less willing to return, and less willing to recommend the Prestigio. Women and higher-income guests are also less satisfied with conference meals and staff and service.
- We have made significant improvement over the past year in nearly all satisfaction ratings following four years of declines.

Recommendations:
- Examine how we can raise satisfaction among women and higher-income conference attendees.
- Adapt our marketing of meetings to the group composition of prospects.
- Continue our customer service initiatives to improve staff and service ratings.
- Reexamine our catering services to improve conference meals.

This executive summary is in structured format (compared to the narrative format of the executive summary in Figure 13.5). The headings allow decision makers and other readers to easily distinguish between survey details, findings, conclusions, and recommendations.

1

FIGURE 13.6

(Continued)

Introduction

Guest satisfaction has always been the foundation for repeat business. With so many online reviews of hotels readily available to meeting planners, the importance of achieving high guest satisfaction ratings is more important now than ever. Since 2008, we have evaluated guest satisfaction and future intentions among conference attendees with an annual survey to help us determine how we can improve guest satisfaction. This report provides the results of this year's survey as well as year-to-year comparisons for the past five years.

Survey Purpose and Administration

This year, we asked the following broad research questions:

- How satisfied are conference attendees with conference services and amenities?

- What hotel amenities do conference attendees use during their conference stays?

- How likely are our conference attendees to contribute to future business?

Most of the survey questions have remained identical since we started these annual surveys. Some unique questions are inserted into the survey each year to address particular areas of strategic concern. Survey questions are provided in the Appendix of Survey Questions.

The survey was administered online. The survey link was sent to 534 guests who had participated in three- or four-day conferences between January 2012 and October 2012. Altogether, 236 respondents completed the survey, garnering a participation rate of roughly 44 percent.

Findings and Conclusions from This Year's Survey

Findings and conclusions can be grouped into three broad areas: (1) satisfaction with conference services and amenities; (2) use of Prestigio guest services and amenities during conference stays; and (3) overall satisfaction and future intentions among conference attendees.

Satisfaction with Conference Services and Amenities

Between two-thirds (64%) and three-fourths (76%) of respondents expressed satisfaction with various conference services and amenities (see Table 1). Based on these findings, we made the following conclusions:

- *We fell short of our goals in the following areas: conference meals, meeting rooms, and staff and service*. In January 2012, we set goals to reach at least 85 percent satisfaction for these three key areas. Barbara Brookshire, our Director of Conventions and Meetings, has indicated that 85 percent satisfaction in these areas would place us in the elite category compared to our competitors. We fell between 9 and 16 percent short of these goals.

- *Our guests are most satisfied with conference meals and meeting rooms*. While our goal remains to reach 85 percent satisfaction for our conference services and amenities, we generally view 75 percent satisfaction as good performance. Therefore, we consider satisfaction with conference

> Level-1 and Level-2 headings help readers make sense of the report information.

2

FIGURE 13.6

(Continued)

meals and meeting rooms acceptable. However, we may not have the unique competitive advantage in this area that we did five years ago.

- *Many of our guests are unhappy with Internet pricing and the business center.* Roughly one in three respondents was not satisfied with these services.

Table 1. Satisfaction with Conference Services and Amenities

	Conference Meals	Meeting Rooms	Staff and Service	Internet Pricing	Business Center
All Respondents	76% (179)	75% (178)	69% (163)	66% (155)	64% (152)
Gender					
Male	85% (108)	76% (97)	72% (91)	73% (93)	56% (71)
Female	65% (71)	74% (81)	66% (72)	57% (62)	74% (81)
Income					
Under $40,000	89% (65)	77% (56)	78% (57)	38% (28)	64% (47)
$40,000–$75,000	73% (94)	76% (97)	68% (87)	76% (97)	66% (84)
Over $75,000	57% (20)	71% (25)	54% (19)	86% (30)	60% (21)

Note: Altogether, 236 respondents took the survey. Percentages and number of respondents (in parentheses) refer to those who responded *satisfied* or *extremely satisfied* on the survey.

Use of Prestigio Guest Services and Amenities during Conference Stays

By far, the most used guest services and amenities by conference attendees are the Prestigio restaurants, with over half (53%) of our respondents stating they ate there during their conference stays. Roughly 30 to 40 percent of respondents reported using the comedy club (39%), the fitness center (35%), or the swimming pool (31%). Relatively few of our conferences guests reported using the spa or golf course (see Table 2). Based on these findings, we made the following conclusions:

- *The restaurants are most convenient for use during conference stays.* Other internal surveys show that our non-conference guests tend to frequent the fitness center, the swimming pool, and the golf course more so than our restaurants. We believe that conference attendees most

> Tables allow decision makers to examine the data themselves and make their own judgments.

Table 2. Use of Prestigio Guest Services and Amenities during Conference Stay

	Prestigio Restaurants	Comedy Club	Fitness Center	Swimming Pool	Spa	Golf Course
All Respondents	53% (126)	39% (92)	35% (82)	31% (73)	19% (45)	8% (18)
Gender						
Male	46% (59)	53% (67)	38% (48)	29% (37)	2% (3)	11% (14)
Female	61% (67)	23% (25)	31% (34)	33% (36)	39% (42)	4% (4)
Income						
Under $40,000	33% (24)	22% (16)	18% (13)	33% (24)	1% (1)	3% (2)
$40,000–$75,000	62% (79)	50% (64)	39% (50)	30% (39)	17% (22)	7% (9)
Over $75,000	66% (23)	34% (12)	43% (15)	29% (10)	63% (22)	20% (7)

Note: Altogether, 236 respondents took the survey. Percentages and number of respondents (in parentheses) refer to those who responded *satisfied* or *extremely satisfied* on the survey.

3

FIGURE 13.6

(Continued)

likely use the restaurants more than other services and amenities because of their busy conference schedules.

- *Use of guest services and amenities is highly variable based on gender and income.* We discuss this further in the *Differences by Gender and Income* section.

Overall Satisfaction and Future Intentions among Conference Attendees

Overall, the vast majority (84%) of our respondents reported satisfaction with their conference experiences. Nearly three out of four (73%) respondents stated that they would want to attend another conference at the Prestigio, and nearly six in ten respondents (57%) said they would recommend the Prestigio as a good site for a business conference (see Table 3). Based on these findings, we made the following conclusions:

- *We fell short of our goals for overall satisfaction and willingness to recommend the Prestigio.* In January 2012, we set goals for overall satisfaction at 90 percent and willingness to recommend the Prestigio at 65 percent. We fell short by 6 to 8 percentage points. We have found that these two survey questions are good indicators of repeat and referred business.

- *Overall satisfaction, desire to return to the Prestigio, and willingness to recommend the Prestigio are highly variable on gender and income.* We discuss this further in the *Differences by Gender and Income* section.

Table 3. Overall Satisfaction and Future Intentions among Conference Attendees

	Overall Satisfaction	Want to Return	Would Recommend
All Respondents	84% (198)	73% (173)	57% (135)
Gender			
Male	89% (113)	77% (98)	66% (84)
Female	78% (85)	69% (75)	47% (51)
Income			
Under $40,000	88% (64)	81% (59)	67% (49)
$40,000 –$75,000	87% (111)	74% (95)	57% (73)
Over $75,000	66% (23)	54% (19)	37% (13)

Note: Altogether, 236 respondents took the survey. Percentages and number of respondents (in parentheses) refer to those who responded *satisfied* or *extremely satisfied* on the survey. The full wording for survey items was as follows: Overall, I was satisfied with the conference experience; I would like to attend another business conference held at the Prestigio; I would recommend the Prestigio as a good site for a business conference.

Table notes give additional information to decision makers to evaluate the data quality and relevance.

Differences by Gender and Income

For the first time, we analyzed this year's guest satisfaction survey by taking into account gender and income. We found major differences and arrived at the following conclusions:

- *Women and higher-income guests tend to be less satisfied, less willing to return, and less willing to recommend* (see Figure 1). A review of findings in Table 3 reveals that women and higher-income guests are far less likely to express satisfaction on those items that we consider barometers of future and repeat

4

FIGURE 13.6

(Continued)

business. On the issue of willingness to recommend, roughly half (47%) of women reported that they are willing to recommend, whereas roughly two-thirds (67%) of men said they would recommend the Prestigio. The difference is even larger by income level. Just one-third (37%) of high-income respondents said that they would recommend the Prestigio, whereas roughly two-thirds (67%) of lower-income respondents said that they would do so.

- *Women and higher-income guests are less satisfied with conference meals and staff and service,* as revealed in Table 1. In past years, we have identified these as key factors leading to overall satisfaction. The gaps are especially wide for conference meals. Whereas the vast majority (85%) of men were satisfied with conference meals, just two-thirds (65%) of women were satisfied. The gap is wider when considering income level. Whereas nearly all (89%) lower-income respondents were satisfied with conference meals, just over half (57%) of higher-income respondents felt this way.

- *Women conference attendees tend to disproportionately choose Prestigio restaurants and the spa. Men conference attendees disproportionately choose the comedy club and the golf course.* Women attendees' top two choices of guest services and amenities are Prestigio restaurants (61%) and the spa (39%), whereas men attendees' top two choices are the comedy club (53%) and the Prestigio restaurants (46%). Men are roughly three times as likely to use the golf course (11% to 4%).

- *Higher-income guests tend to disproportionately choose the spa and the golf course; middle-income guests tend to disproportionately choose the comedy club; and lower-income guests tend to utilize all hotel services and amenities less with the exception of the swimming pool.* Higher-income guests are three to four times more likely to use the spa and golf course compared to middle-income guests. Lower-income guests rarely if ever use the spa and golf course.

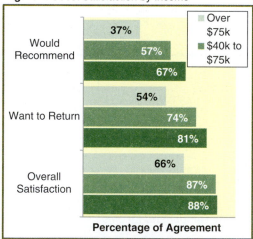

Figure 1. Guest Satisfaction by Gender

Figure 2. Guest Satisfaction by Income

> Charts reveal the key findings.

These conclusions regarding the experiences of women and higher-income guests are quite concerning. We deal mostly with meeting planners who are women, and our women respondents likely reflect the expectations of these meeting planners. Furthermore, we pride ourselves in providing high-class conference experiences—those that we assume would cater to the tastes of higher-income guests.

5

FIGURE 13.6

(*Continued*)

Comparison of Guest Satisfaction Rates over the Past Five Years

Comparisons of survey results over the past five years reveal several basic trends (see Table 4 for complete results):

- *Overall satisfaction and willingness to recommend have increased over the past year*. From 2008 to 2011, overall satisfaction and willingness to recommend fell 10 and 13 percentage points, respectively. However, in the past year (2011 to 2012), overall satisfaction and willingness to recommend improved 5 and 8 percentage points, respectively (see Figure 3).

- *Satisfaction with conference meals and staff and service has increased over the past year*. From 2008 to 2011, satisfaction with conference meals and staff and service decreased 19 and 3 percentage points respectively. However, in the past year (2011 to 2012), satisfaction with conference meals and staff and service increased 8 and 7 percentage points, respectively.

- *Most indicators of satisfaction have returned to levels from five years ago*. In general, nearly all indicators of satisfaction showed steady deterioration from 2008 to 2011 with the past year showing improvement back to near-2000 levels of satisfaction.

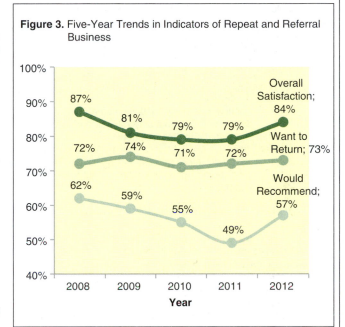

Figure 3. Five-Year Trends in Indicators of Repeat and Referral Business

The report provides perspective by comparing current satisfaction rates with those of past years.

Table 4. Year-to-Year Comparisons of Key Satisfaction Indicators, 2008–2012

	2008	2009	2010	2011	2012
Indicators of Repeat and Referral Business					
Overall Satisfaction	87%	81%	79%	79%	84%
Want to Return	72%	74%	71%	72%	73%
Would Recommend	62%	59%	55%	49%	57%
Conference					
Conference Meals	87%	76%	74%	68%	76%
Meeting Rooms	77%	71%	74%	76%	75%
Staff & Service	65%	64%	61%	62%	69%
Internet Pricing	-	-	-	-	66%
Business Center	-	-	-	-	64%

6

FIGURE 13.6

(*Continued*)

Recommendations

1. *Examine ways to raise satisfaction among women and higher-income conference attendees*. We view women and higher-income guests as particularly important to our success. Most meeting planners we work with are women and likely reflect the perspectives of our female guests more so than our male guests. Furthermore, since we pride ourselves on providing high-end conference services, we should examine why our higher-income guests are less satisfied. To better understand how we can raise guest satisfaction among women and higher-income conference attendees, we should take the following actions:

    a. Set up focus groups with women and higher-income guests to gain a more in-depth understanding of their concerns and suggestions for improvement.

    b. Informally talk to some of our women and higher-income guests during conferences and catalog these guests' feedback in a lessons-learned database.

    > *These recommendations demonstrate thoughtful examination of the survey findings. Decision makers will take these seriously.*

2. *Adapt our marketing of meetings to the group composition of prospects*. We now have a much better understanding of how the gender and income level of our guests impact which amenities and services they use. We should adapt our marketing materials to appeal more strongly to certain groups. For example, each year we host meetings for the Northern Hunters Association, with over 90 percent male membership, and the Farmers Healthcare Group, comprised mostly of female nurses.

3. *Continue our customer service initiatives to improve staff and service ratings*. Our recent initiatives to improve personalized guest service appear to have been successful. Given our emphasis on guest service as a foundation for all of our improvements, we should ensure we maintain a high staff-to-guest ratio, provide incentives for exceptional guest service, and continue our intensive two-month mentoring and training program for new guest attendants.

4. *Reexamine our catering services to improve conference meals*. Five years ago, our guests were overwhelmingly satisfied with conference meals. In fact, many guests recommended repeat business in large part due to the excellent meals. To cut costs, we have changed catering services over the past five years, and the result has been far lower guest satisfaction with meals. To strengthen or regain our reputation for high-end conference experiences, we should identify ways to return to 2008-level guest satisfaction for conference meals.

7

FIGURE 13.6

(Continued)

Appendix of Survey Questions

1. Gender:

2. Age:

3. Income Level:
   a. Under $30,000
   b. $30,000–$40,000
   c. $40,000–$50,000
   d. $50,000–$75,000
   e. $75,000–$100,000
   f. Over $100,000

4. How many days of Internet service did you purchase during your conference visit?
   *a. 0   b. 1   c. 2   d. 3

5. How satisfied were you with the following aspects of your conference experience? (on the following scale: 1, not satisfied; 2, somewhat satisfied; 3, satisfied; 4, extremely satisfied).

   a. Conference meals
   b. Internet pricing*
   c. Internet speed in rooms*
   d. Business center
   e. Staff and service
   f. Meeting rooms

6. Please respond to the following statements based on your experiences during your recent conference at the Prestigio (on the following scale: 1, strong disagree; 2, disagree; 3, neutral; 4, agree; 5, strongly agree).

   a. Overall, I was satisfied with the conference experience.
   b. I would like to attend another business conference held at the Prestigio.
   c. I would recommend the Prestigio as a good site for a business conference.

7. Which of the following guest services and amenities did you use during your conference stay? Check all that apply.*
   ❏ a. Spa
   ❏ b. Fitness center
   ❏ c. Outdoor swimming pool
   ❏ d. Prestigio golf course
   ❏ e. Prestigio comedy club
   ❏ f. One of the Prestigio restaurants

*Survey items added to this year's survey.

> *Decision makers perceive primary and secondary research as more credible when the related procedures, sources, and other information are provided. However, much of this information takes up a lot of space. As a result, appendixes and other back-report sections are used to provide complete information for inquisitive readers.*

8

Reviewing Your Reports for Fairness and Effectiveness

LO13.5 Review reports for effectiveness and fairness.

As with other written documents, you will always review your reports to ensure that you have been fair to yourself and your readers. Also, you want to make sure the report is as effective as possible.

Since research-based reports are generally commissioned for high-stakes decisions, you have likely worked collaboratively with others. If you've developed the report by yourself, you should still try to get other perspectives before you officially submit it. When possible, discuss the report with the ultimate decision makers so that you can best tailor the final product to their needs.

As you review the report by yourself and with others, run through it numerous times, each time considering a different perspective. For example, review the entire document several times for accuracy and precision in logic. Review it at least once,

COMMUNICATION Q&A

CONVERSATIONS WITH CURRENT BUSINESS PROFESSIONALS

Pete Cardon: What are some keys to writing effective reports?

Rich Harrill: Reports should be comprehensive in their presentation of data and information, but should also have a strong, succinct executive summary for busy industry and community leaders. The report should be well organized with a table of contents. Tables, graphs, and charts need to be used only where relevant to illustrate an example. The same rule goes for appendixes. I always provide a brief PowerPoint presentation to go with the document. It is often this presentation that is circulated among interested parties rather than the report itself. Project reports should be attractive. I now prefer "perfect" bound documents to messy, spiral binding. A writing and editing mentor once told me that you should write so that the reader can understand every word. He offered very simple but very effective advice in a world that sometimes uses esoteric words and concepts as a replacement for simple and direct communication.

PC: How do you facilitate effective team writing on reports?

RH: I believe it is best to let individual team members write in their own voice and style. In some cases I might provide a very loose style sheet to guide certain requirements. However, I generally suggest structural or content changes to the authors. When the manuscript comes back after this first pass, an experienced editor and I will edit thoroughly and try to integrate the different styles. It is a good editor's job to weave the submissions together in a way that results in a coherent document with consistent style and tone.

PC: Has report writing changed during your career?

RH: Yes, and quite drastically. Increasing competition among individuals and firms has upped the ante on report writing. Years ago, a report that was technically great was held to minimal aesthetic standards. Today, a report must have both style and substance. The data or information must be great, the document must look appealing, and it must be accessible to many different clients and constituents—from laypersons or reporters to politicians and bureaucrats. No matter how good the methodology or analysis used to produce the report, it will go unnoticed if it is not interesting, compelling, and even "sexy." This trend is now the rule rather than the exception in the age of viral marketing and social media.

PC: For young professionals, what concluding advice would you give about creating business proposals and reports?

RH: Cultivate your own sense of style and substance. Be technically proficient but also confident and appealing. The report should be an extension of your own brand—classy and attractive to people that work with you and would like to work with you. Shoot for timeless qualities in composition. Develop an ear for pauses and breaths, the same way you develop good conversational skills that make you popular with friends and colleagues. Good technical report writing is not much different; the researcher is disseminating information in a way that defies fad and will be relevant to readers many years from now.

Rich Harrill *is director of the Alfred P. Sloan Foundation Travel and Tourism Industry Center and the International Tourism Research Institute at the University of South Carolina. He has written dozens of reports for government and private sector clients.*

imagining yourself in the position of decision makers to improve it based on what you perceive as their needs. Also, review it at least once for typos or mechanical errors. Make sure you review the report over several sittings and several days if possible, since you are unlikely to catch all of the changes you would ideally make in just one sitting. And for the perspective of an experienced business professional on writing reports, see the Communication Q&A with Rich Harrill.

Chapter Takeaway for *Completing Business Reports*

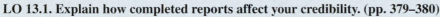

LO 13.1. Explain how completed reports affect your credibility. (pp. 379–380)
Completing business reports demonstrates **your personal credibility.**

It shows **competence** when you provide facts, conclusions, and positions that help decision making.	It shows **caring** when you involve decision makers and address their needs.	It shows **character** when you report all information honestly and provide access to your rationale.

LO 13.2. Demonstrate excellent thinking by applying a precision-oriented style to reports. (pp. 380–386)

Recommendations

Conclusions

Facts

Business Problem

Style: Apply precision-oriented language and display excellence in thinking.

See *examples of a clear problem statement* (Table 13.1), *fact-based language* (Table 13.2), *citations to avoid plagiarism* (Table 13.4), *recommendations based on facts and conclusions* (Figure 13.2), and *specific and actionable recommendations* (Table 13.5).

LO 13.3. Design your reports to aid in decision making. (pp. 386–391)

Design: Provide easy navigation so that decision makers can quickly identify key points and themes.

See *examples of common headings/sections in reports* (Figure 13.3), *common components of formal reports* (Figure 13.4), *use of headings as a storyline device* (Table 13.6), *wording for headings* (Table 13.7), *use of preview statements* (Table 13.8), *effective charts* (Table 13.9), and *bulleting and enumerated lists* (Table 13.10).

LO 13.4. Project objectivity in reports. (pp. 391–409)

Tone: Emphasize objectivity and project a tempered can-do attitude.

See *examples of objective tone* (Table 13.11).

LO 13.5. Review reports for effectiveness and fairness. (pp. 409–410)

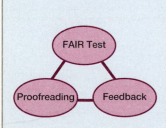

FAIR Test

Proofreading   Feedback

Reviewing Process
FAIR Test: Make sure facts, conclusions, and positions are as objective as possible. Make any of your biases apparent.
Proofreading: Check for precision and excellence in thinking. Ensure that your report is complete but easy to navigate.
Feedback: Involve as many trusted colleagues and partners as possible. Ideally, involve decision makers.

Key Terms

direct quotations (p. 383)   paraphrasing (p. 383)   plagiarism (p. 382)

Discussion Exercises

13.1 Chapter Review Questions (LO 13.1, LO 13.2, LO 13.3, LO 13.4)

For each of the following items, respond with one or two paragraphs.

A. Explain the significance of stating the business problem or challenge at the beginning of a report.

B. Discuss the various ways in which reports should be precise.

C. Describe the value of good documentation in your research reports.

D. Explain what it means for recommendations to be specific and actionable.

E. Discuss how charts should be used in reports.

F. Describe how you can strike a tone of objectivity in a report and also project positivity.

G. Explain various approaches for reviewing reports.

13.2 Communication Q&A Discussion Questions (LO 13.1, LO 13.2, LO 13.3)

Read the Communication Q&A section with comments from Rich Harrill. Respond to the following questions:

A. What does Harrill offer as keys to writing effective reports?

B. According to Harrill, how should you lead a team writing effort?

C. How has report writing changed in recent years, according to Harrill? What does this mean for your approach to report writing?

D. Harrill repeatedly mentions getting advice and feedback from others. In some cases, he relies on hired editors. In other cases, he gets informal feedback. Why is it so important to get feedback for your report writing? What steps can you take in your report writing to get more feedback from others? How should you select others you will approach for advice?

13.3 Complete SBA Training for Business Plans (LO 13.1, LO 13.2, LO 13.3)

Go to the Small Business Administration website (www.sba.gov) and complete the online training for "Starting a Business" (www.sba.gov/training/index.html), which takes about 30 minutes. In three to five paragraphs, describe the key points of developing a business plan that apply to writing effective reports.

Evaluation Exercises

13.4 Evaluating a Business Report (LO 13.1, LO 13.2, LO 13.3, LO 13.4)

Choose a business report to evaluate. Answer the following questions related to it:

A. How effectively does the report tell a story?

B. How effectively are headings used?

C. How effectively are charts, figures, and/or other graphics used?

D. How effectively are research results presented?

E. Overall, how reliable and useful is this report? Explain.

F. What three aspects of the report would you like to model in your report writing?

G. What three aspects of the report do you think should be improved?

You can find numerous reports online; often these are white papers. Ideally, search for a topic of interest. For example, if you are interested in the future of shopping malls, you could conduct an Internet search with a search phrase such as *future of shopping malls "white paper,"* and you will likely find dozens of options to choose from. Spend 10 to 15 minutes to find a report that is interesting to you.

Application Exercises

13.5 Writing a Survey Report and Marketing Plan for an Ice Cream Shop (LO 13.1, LO 13.2, LO 13.3)

Assume you are planning to open an ice cream shop on campus. There are currently no ice cream shops within three miles of your campus. You are deciding between leasing space in the student center or opening a stand-alone shop on the outskirts of campus. You recently surveyed just over 400 university students to identify their preferences. The following table contains the results.

Gender						
	Female		**Male**		**Total**	
	#	**%**	**#**	**%**	**#**	**%**
How often do you go to an ice cream parlor in a given month?						
0 times	26	14%	40	19%	66	16%
1 time	73	38	112	53	185	46
2 to 4 times	83	43	57	27	140	35
5 or more times	9	5	4	2	13	3
Would you prefer a drive-through versus sit-down?						
Drive-through	51	27	95	45	146	36
Sit-down	140	73	118	55	258	64
Which do you prefer?						
Ice cream	77	40	170	80	247	61
Frozen yogurt	102	53	43	20	145	36
Sherbet	12	6	0	0	12	3
How do you like your ice cream prepared?						
Sundae	57	30	38	18	95	24
Cone	47	25	40	19	87	22
Cup	64	34	67	31	131	32
Milkshake	23	12	68	32	91	23
What's your favorite condiment?						
Candy	35	18	93	44	128	32
Cookies	31	16	49	23	80	20
Flavored syrup	57	30	52	24	109	27
Nuts	45	24	19	9	64	16
Fruit	23	12	0	0	23	6
Have you bought store novelties in the past (i.e., shirts, hats, etc.)?						
Yes	111	58	178	84	289	72
No	80	42	35	16	115	28
How many scoops do you typically prefer?						
1	112	59	42	20	154	38
2	71	37	140	66	211	52
3	8	4	31	15	39	10
How much are you willing to pay for a one-scoop ice cream cone?						
$1.00–$1.50	67	35	45	21	112	28
$1.51–$2.00	105	55	64	30	169	42

(Continued)

	Gender					
	Female		Male		Total	
	#	%	#	%	#	%
$2.01–$2.50	13	7	62	29	75	19
$2.51 or more	6	3	42	20	48	12
How much are you willing to pay for a two-scoop ice cream cone?						
$1.51–$2.25	73	38	43	20	116	29
$2.26–$3.00	76	40	40	19	116	29
$3.01–$3.50	31	16	84	39	115	28
$3.51 or more	11	6	46	22	57	14
Would you prefer an all-you-can-eat ice cream shop?						
Yes	25	13	158	74	183	45
No	166	87	55	26	221	55

Write a marketing report that includes your survey objectives, methodology, findings, and conclusions. Also, provide your related marketing recommendations.

13.6 Writing a Proposal for a Student Club (LO 13.1, LO 13.2, LO 13.3)

Assume your university has recently developed a grant program for student clubs. The goal of the program is to award between $5,000 and $10,000 per club for activities that promote academic research and/or travel to industry conferences.

Choose a student club of interest and write a proposal that describes the purpose of your club and a specific project that the grant money would support. Provide a rationale for how you will use the money, a timeline for completing your project (or travel), and a description of deliverables. (Look at the proposal in Appendix C as a guide.)

13.7 Writing a Survey Report about Mobile Phone Use in the Workplace (LO 13.1, LO 13.2, LO 13.3)

Ashley Foxe works for Process Leadership, a large consulting group that advises companies in North America, Europe, and Asia. It typically works on one- to six-month projects with companies that are trying to develop more open and collaborative work environments. The Process slogan is *leading with culture*, implying that entire companies need to share work values to maximize their productivity.

Ashley's role with Process Leadership is to write research reports or white papers that are available free of charge. These research reports are distributed on the Process Leadership home page and are intended to reinforce the Process brand of improving corporate culture. Process generally disseminates press releases about the research. Often, the research is picked up in newspaper, business magazines, and other professional publications. Each time the research is mentioned, it serves as free marketing and advertising for Process Leadership.

Ashley recently conducted a survey project about mobile phone use in the workplace. She conducted a nationwide survey of full-time business professionals with annual salaries over $30,000. She compiled the following data tables from the survey.

TABLE A

Demographics of Survey Respondents

Gender	Count	Percentage
Male	186	53.1%
Female	164	46.9
Age Group		
21–30	35	10.0
31–40	95	27.1
41–50	87	24.9
51–65	133	38.0
Income		
$30,000 to $39,999	41	11.7
$40,000 to $49,999	46	13.1
$50,000 to $59,000	53	15.1
$60,000 to $69,999	31	8.9
$70,000 to $79,999	40	11.4
$80,000 to $89,999	33	9.4
$90,000 to $99,999	29	8.3
$100,000 to $149,999	50	14.3
$150,000 or more	27	7.7
Total	350	100

TABLE B

Appropriateness of Mobile Phone Use in Meetings by Gender

	Male		Female		Total	
	Rarely	**Never**	**Rarely**	**Never**	**Rarely**	**Never**
Bringing phone to meeting	34.5	11.4	33.7	24.0	34.0	21.7
Checking time with phone	26.9	30.6	27.4	30.5	27.1	30.6
Checking incoming calls	26.3	25.8	31.1	21.3	28.6	27.4
Checking text messages	30.1	41.4	30.5	50.6	30.3	45.7
Answering a call	35.5	41.3	25.6	64.0	30.9	56.3
Excusing self to answer call	36.0	18.8	30.5	23.8	33.4	21.1
Writing and sending texts	26.9	54.3	22.0	65.2	24.6	51.3
Browsing the Internet	28.5	43.5	26.8	53.0	27.7	48.0

TABLE C

Appropriateness of Mobile Phone Use in Meetings by Age Group

	21–30		31–40		41–50		51–65	
	Rarely	**Never**	**Rarely**	**Never**	**Rarely**	**Never**	**Rarely**	**Never**
Bringing phone to meeting	20.0	8.6	28.4	12.6	35.6	28.7	40.6	27.1
Checking time with phone	37.1	2.9	22.1	26.3	28.7	34.5	27.1	38.3
Checking incoming calls	25.7	5.7	24.2	24.2	27.6	32.2	33.1	32.3
Checking text messages	28.6	20.0	30.5	37.9	32.2	50.6	21.3	54.9
Answering a call	22.9	42.9	36.8	42.1	34.5	51.4	26.3	67.7
Excusing self to answer call	31.4	11.4	23.2	16.8	313.1	25.3	37.6	24.1
Writing and sending texts	22.9	34.3	30.5	45.3	28.7	51.4	18.0	75.9
Browsing the Internet	28.6	20.0	32.6	32.6	24.1	57.5	26.3	60.2

TABLE D

Attitudes toward Texting and Making Calls with Mobile Phones

	Males	**Females**	**21–30**	**31–40**	**41–50**	**51–65**	**Total**
Overall, using mobile phones for *TEXTING* in the workplace . . .							
Reduces miscommunication.	37.6	34.8	54.3	42.1	33.3	21.3	36.3
Makes communication more efficient.	41.4	45.7	71.4	55.8	41.3	34.6	47.7
Improves relations with colleagues.	32.3	21.3	60.0	37.9	28.7	11.4	30.9
Improves relations with clients.	36.6	26.8	54.3	34.7	31.0	24.8	32.0
Makes work easier.	43.5	40.2	65.7	56.8	35.6	21.3	42.0
Overall, using mobile phones for *CALLS* in the workplace . . .							
Reduces miscommunication.	64.0	53.7	77.1	74.7	55.2	45.9	51.3
Makes communication more efficient.	70.4	65.2	88.6	81.1	66.7	54.1	68.0
Improves relations with colleagues.	51.3	51.3	88.6	70.5	60.9	42.1	51.3
Improves relations with clients.	66.1	61.6	88.6	82.1	60.9	46.6	64.0
Makes work easier.	65.6	64.0	88.6	75.8	63.2	51.9	64.9

Take the role of Ashley and write a white paper on mobile phone use in the workplace. You can include any other information you find useful. Include sections for data collection, survey findings and conclusions, and recommendations. Make sure to include at least a few charts or figures that illustrate compelling points. Remember your corporate slogan as you develop the report.

13.8 Write a Business Plan for a Franchise (LO 13.1, LO 13.2, LO 13.3)

Choose a franchise that interests you. Write a business plan for the franchise in your location (or location of your choice) that includes the following:

- Executive summary
- Introduction
- Management
- Marketing
- Financial projections
- Financial needs

Be creative with your management and marketing ideas. You may not be familiar with creating financial projections, but do your best and simplify this step if necessary. The point of this assignment is to practice writing the plan. Work with your instructor to decide what is acceptable.

You can find possible franchises for this project by searching online for franchising opportunities. Most franchisors supply plenty of information about requirements to open a franchise.

You may want to consult several online articles about writing business plans. You can find many good resources. For example, consider the following article: Jeff Elgin, "Writing the Franchise Business Plan," *Entrepreneur* online (September 5, 2005). Available at www.entrepreneur.com/franchises/buyingafranchise/franchisecolumnistjeffelgin/article79626.html.

13.9 Conducting Survey Research (LO 13.1, LO 13.2, LO 13.3)

Individually or in groups, select a business problem you can learn more about by conducting survey research. You will create an online survey for all of your classmates to take, so design your project around the assumption that you are finding out what university-aged students think or feel about the topic. Design the survey so that respondents can complete it in three to five minutes. Once you have conducted the survey, write a report that includes your objectives, methodology, findings, conclusions, and recommendations.

13.10 Write a Report about a Business Trend (LO 13.1, LO 13.2, LO 13.3)

Using research from your university library, write report in APA or MLA documentation style that accomplishes the following:

A. States a business problem or challenge (you might imagine yourself in a position within a company of interest).

B. Describes and substantiates a trend that impacts business.

C. Provides recommendations for how your company can respond to the trend to become more competitive.

Endnotes

1. "Plagiarize," retrieved March 1, 2012, from *Merriam-Webster Online Dictionary* at http://www.merriam-webster.com/dictionary/plagiarize.

2. "What Is Citation?" retrieved March 1, 2012, from *Plagiarism.org* website at http://www.plagiarism.org/plag_article_what_is_citation.html; "Plagiarism FAQs," retrieved March 1, 2012, from *Plagiarism.org* website at http://www.plagiarism.org/plag_article_what_is_citation.html; "What Is Plagiarism?" retrieved March 1, 2012, from *Plagiarism.org* website at http://www.plagiarism.org/plag_article_what_is_citation.html.

3. David Kintler and Bob Adams, *Independent Consulting: A Comprehensive Guide to Building Your Own Consulting Business* (Avon, MA: Streetwise, 1998); Brian R. Ford, Jay M. Bornstein, and Patrick T. Pruitt, *The Ernst & Young Business Plan Guide* (Hoboken, NJ:

John Wiley & Sons, 2007); Small Business Administration, "Write a Business Plan," retrieved September 15, 2010, from Small Business Administration website at www.sba.gov/smallbusinessplanner/plan/writeabusinessplan/index.html.

4. Roberta Moore, Patricia Seraydarian, and Rosemary Fruehling, *Pearson Business Reference and Writer's Handbook* (Upper Saddle River, NJ: Pearson Education, 2010).

5. Joy Roach, Daniel Tracy, and Kay Durden, "Integrating Business Core Knowledge through Upper Division Report Composition," *Business Communication Quarterly* 70, no. 4 (2007): 431–449.

6. Joseph Covello and Brian Hazelgren, *Your First Business Plan,* 5th ed. (Naperville, IL: Sourcebooks, 2005): 12.

7. Ibid.

CHAPTER FOURTEEN

Planning Presentations

Learning Objectives

After studying this chapter, you should be able to do the following:

LO14.1 Describe how planning your presentations leads to credibility.

LO14.2 Analyze presentation audiences in terms of message benefits, learning styles, and communicator styles.

LO14.3 Organize and gather content for a preview, view, and review.

LO14.4 Develop effective slide presentations.

LO14.5 Use the story line approach to presentations.

LO14.6 Evaluate your presentations for fairness and effectiveness.

WHY DOES THIS MATTER?

Presentations have many purposes, including promoting a new business or idea, reporting on the status of projects or product performance, helping management and employees stay informed about business policies, or selling a product or service. Presentations give you opportunities to connect deeply with your audiences and convey and control your messages carefully.

Presentations place a spotlight on you and allow you to maintain and even build your credibility. When you clearly know what you're talking about, audiences judge you as competent. When you show that you are interested in the needs of your audience, they judge you as caring. When you offer your views honestly and transparently, audiences judge you as having character.

Although speaking is a normal part of every day for you, making business presentations is not necessarily automatic or natural. As speech expert Thomas Leech explained, "Developing proficiency in oral communications doesn't occur automatically. The ability to speak may have come much as did walking and breathing, but speaking well to groups is another matter."[1] As you read this chapter, identify the areas that will help you most in developing your presentation skills. This chapter focuses on planning your content. The next one focuses on delivering that content effectively.

Read the chapter case about Shannon Browne and her plans to revamp a sales presentation. In particular, note what she views as her unique challenges. Throughout the chapter, you'll see how she attempts to overcome these challenges while crafting her presentation.

Hear Pete Cardon explain why this matters.

bit.ly.com/CardonWhy14

LO14.1 Describe how planning your presentations leads to credibility.

Chapter Case: Planning Presentations at Sinosourcing Experts

Who's Involved

Shannon Browne
- Has worked as a sales rep at Sinosourcing Experts for five months
- Recently graduated with a major in supply chain management and a minor in Chinese

The Situation

Shannon recently accepted a sales rep position at Sinosourcing Experts, which combines her interests in global supply chains and the Chinese culture. Sinosourcing Experts helps small businesses outsource their manufacturing to China. It markets its services in North America and maintains offices in Los Angeles, Shanghai, and Hong Kong. At the Chinese offices, Sinosourcing has nearly 30 employees, including sourcing experts, engineers, and import/export specialists. These employees are the go-betweens in setting up and ensuring quality manufacturing in China for small North American companies.

Shannon's job is to gain new clients in North America. She spends most of her time giving presentations to small-business owners about how they can move some of their manufacturing to China and save on manufacturing costs. One approach the company uses to gain new clients is to set up small seminars about manufacturing in China. Between 15 and 20 participants attend each seminar at sites around the country. The seminars last three hours and culminate with Shannon's 45-minute presentation. Typically, she gets one or two new clients at each presentation.

Shannon wants to revamp her presentation to increase her success. In particular, she wants to overcome several basic misconceptions and stereotypes that many seminar participants hold about manufacturing in China, most of which are negative. While many of these seminar participants believe that production costs are lower, they assume that quality suffers and time to market for new products takes too long. Some participants have the impression that moving production to China would involve supporting labor abuses in sweatshop-type factories that violate standard safety practices. Others assume that Chinese management is unsophisticated and ideological (Communist).

Task 1
Prepare the basic content of the presentation to explain the benefits of outsourcing manufacturing while also addressing concerns.

Task 2
Develop slides to supplement the presentation and reinforce the key messages.

Planning the Content of Your Presentation

As you design your presentations and speeches, the AIM planning process will help you, just as it does in the writing process. You'll analyze your *audience* to make sure you're addressing their needs and speaking to them in the way that is most appealing and easy to learn. You'll develop your *ideas* by identifying the key facts and conclusions related to your topic. You'll also construct your *message* to focus on the key takeaway concepts and to provide supporting points throughout. In this chapter, we do not focus on developing your ideas, since this process is largely similar to that for writing. We instead discuss analyzing your audience and structuring your message, since these processes have some unique features for presentations. Then, we discuss designing electronic slides, since these are commonly included in many professional presentations.

LO14.2 Analyze presentation audiences in terms of message benefits, learning styles, and communicator styles.

Analyze Your Audience

Understanding the needs of your audience is one of your first tasks as you develop your presentations. Of course, this is complicated by a variety of factors. Your audiences for presentations may differ in size and makeup, and in some cases, you won't know who they will be. As you do your homework about the audience, answer the following questions to the degree possible:

How Will Audience Members Benefit from the Product, Service, or Ideas I Am Proposing?
This is the single most important question you can use to guide you as you design your presentation. In particular, focus on benefits that fulfill an unmet need.[2]

In Shannon's case, she focuses primarily on how small businesses can reduce production costs by outsourcing some or all of their manufacturing in China. This is an unmet need for many small businesses because they often compete with larger businesses that have the resources and know-how to move productions overseas. Most small businesses, by contrast, lack the resources and know-how to do this successfully.

What Do the Audience Members Already Know about My Product, Service, or Ideas?
Find out whatever you can about your audience members' knowledge level. If people know little about your product, you will need to

spend a proportionately higher amount of your presentation time to inform them. Also, try to find out where they have gotten their information or how they have developed their perceptions about the topic. Knowing this allows you to more effectively deal with misinformation.

In Shannon's case, she has found that seminar participants understand little about manufacturing in China. Much of what they know is based on news headlines or short 30-second news stories. Many of their judgments about the Chinese business and political environment come from short sound bites during highly charged political debates. Because many participants have such superficial understanding of manufacturing in China, her company allots three hours for the seminar, hoping to provide a deep understanding. Her culminating 45-minute presentation specifically addresses outsourcing for small businesses.

What Are My Audience Members' Chief Concerns?   Considering this question is particularly important for presentations. Whereas you can take time to gather your thoughts when responding in writing to someone's concerns, in presentations and other face-to-face communications you must respond immediately.

Shannon recognizes that most small-business owners have superficial knowledge about manufacturing in China. They've often heard about the great cost savings but little else. Many people have stereotypes of sweatshops and unfair labor practices. Similarly, they may think that products made in China are of lower quality. Many seminar participants also hold a negative view of what they perceive as a Communist approach to business. In Shannon's presentations, she wants to make sure to not only inform but also overcome incorrect stereotypes.

Who Are the Key Decision Makers?   Your presentation is generally intended to draw support from your whole audience. Typically, however, some people in your audience have more impact on your ability to achieve your work objectives than do others. These key decision makers are the ones you want to influence the most.

For internal presentations, think about those individuals who have the most influence and authority to act on your ideas. For presentations to clients, customers, and prospects, think about which individuals are the decision makers for their organizations or who you perceive as the most likely prospects for future business. Focus most of your attention on them.[3]

Shannon generally finds out about people who have signed up for her presentations before they arrive. She checks their company websites to learn about their businesses and gets a general sense for how well Sinosourcing Experts can meet the needs of their businesses. She typically identifies 5 or 6 out of the 15 to 20 people who attend her seminars who she considers the top prospects. Of course, she maintains flexibility since she doesn't have complete information.

What Will Appeal to Your Audience?   You can influence your audience by employing a combination of emotional and analytical appeals. Oral communications, especially speeches and presentations, are well suited to strong emotional appeal, as they create bonds between the speaker and the audience and emotional connections with products, services, and ideas. At the same time, your speeches and presentations will include a set of ideas that you want your audience to appreciate analytically. Plan to make both emotional and analytical connections with your audience.

As you're thinking about emotional and analytical appeals, consider the communicator styles of your audience (see Chapter 2). *Sensers* will appreciate your ability to stay on point and discuss immediate goals. Emotionally and analytically, they are attracted to action-oriented and results-oriented language and logic.

Feelers will appreciate your ability to discuss business relationships—such as benefits to work teams and colleagues and loyalty to customers and clients. Emotionally, feelers will connect to you with your use of "we" language and other relationship-centered

---

Principles of Audience Analysis

Identify the following:
- Audience benefits
- Existing knowledge
- Concerns
- Decision makers
- Appeals
- Communicator style
- Learning style

terms. Analytically, feelers will connect with your holistic approach to business benefits. They are attracted to business logic that includes more than just bottom-line measures of performance.

Thinkers will appreciate your ability to provide all of the facts and avoid rushing to judgment about conclusions. Thinkers generally pride themselves on a dispassionate (nonemotional) approach to decision making and may be turned off by what they consider blatant and irrelevant appeals to emotion. However, this in no way implies that emotional appeal is unimportant to thinkers. Thinkers are often emotionally connected to precise language; well-designed and conceptualized charts, models, and other figures; and the ability to handle tough questions.

Intuitors will appreciate your ability to present visionary ideas. Emotionally, they connect to out-of-the-box thinking and emphasis on strategic initiatives. They want to feel a part of something larger than themselves. Analytically, they respond to discussing concepts first and facts last.

Over time, Shannon has found that seminar participants inevitably represent a mix of all the communicator styles. However, she has noticed that her groups of small-business owners contain a high percentage of thinkers and intuitors. The thinkers often have engineering backgrounds and have branched off from a larger company to focus on a manufacturing niche of interest to them. The intuitors are often those who crave freedom, don't want a boss, and have a vision of creating revolutionary products. Shannon adjusts her presentation to these types of communicators and their backgrounds.

What Is the Learning Style of Your Audience?
As with communicator styles, audience members have different learning styles. **Visual learners,** who make up about 40 percent of the population, learn best from illustrations and simple diagrams that show relationships and key ideas. They also enjoy gestures and metaphors. Ironically, text-based PowerPoint slides do not appeal to them much. On the other hand, PowerPoint slides rich in images and figures do help visual learners respond to your message. **Auditory learners,** who also comprise roughly 40 percent of the population, like loud, clear voices and believe emotion is best conveyed through voice. **Kinesthetic learners,** who make up about 20 percent of the population, need to participate to focus their attention on your message and learn best. They need group activities, hands-on activities, or breaks at least every 20 minutes.[4]

Shannon ensures that she has content and activities that appeal to each of these types of learners. She presents slides with images and diagrams to appeal to visual learners, speaks with conviction and enthusiasm to appeal to auditory learners, and provides a handout for participants to fill out to appeal to kinesthetic learners.

Develop Your Message

As with written reports, successful presentations rely on well-developed takeaway messages, supporting information, and structure. You'll get lots of advice during your career about how to deliver a successful presentation. Much of this advice is good because delivery is important. However, developing your content is still the most critical factor in presentation success, so prepare your content before you spend too much time on your delivery.[5]

Identify a Few Takeaway Messages
Your first task is to identify the two or three key messages you want to convey. Once you've developed these key messages, everything in the presentation should lead back to them.[6] Particularly for presenting to busy executives, summarize your key takeaway messages at the outset and reemphasize them several times.[7]

Overall, your presentation will be most effective if you focus on how your key messages relate to the common interests of your audience. At the same time, be cautious about trying to please everyone. Some presenters broaden their messages in an attempt

Components of Presentations

- Preview (10–15 percent of time)
  - Attention-getter
  - Positioning statement
  - Overview: Takeaway messages
- View (85–90 percent of time)
  - Takeaway message #1
  - Takeaway message #2
  - Takeaway message #3
- Review (5 percent of time)
  - Recap
  - Call to action

to appeal to everyone in the audience. This approach is risky, however, since broadening the message so much may dilute its impact and power.[8]

In Shannon's case, her takeaway messages are relatively simple: Your small business can reduce manufacturing costs, improve quality control, and reduce time to market by manufacturing in China. Shannon makes sure that nearly everything in her presentation leads back to these key messages.

Structure Your Presentation with a Clear Preview, View, and Review[9]
Most audience members expect your presentation to include a **preview,** view, and review (analogous to the introduction, body, and conclusion in written documents). Typically, your preview occupies roughly 10 to 15 percent of your presentation time, your view takes up the vast majority (85 to 90 percent) of your time, and the review takes up the least time (5 percent).

LO14.3 Organize and gather content for a preview, view, and review.

Provide a Compelling Preview

The beginnings of your presentations and speeches are critical. Audience members who do not know you well often form quick impressions about you and your message. Even people who know you fairly well generally decide quickly if your message is important to them. Dana LaMon, who lost his sight at the age of four but went on to achieve a highly successful career as a judge and professional speaker, suggests that audiences make up their minds in the first minute or two of the presentation:

> As an administrative law judge for 26 years, I have heard and written decisions in about 6,400 cases. My unscientific estimate is that in about 95 percent of them, I knew what I would decide before the hearing was over. After 19 years in Toastmasters and 16 years as a professional speaker, I have learned that the audience, too, will make quick decisions. They will judge a speaker and his or her speech well before the presentation is done. That is why I have come to believe that the most important part of my speech is the opening.[10]

In other words, during that first few minutes, audience members have their answers to the following questions: Am I going to listen? Am I going to benefit from what is said? Will it be valuable enough to take with me? Am I going to act on what I hear?

The *preview* should generally include an attention-getter, a positioning statement, and an overview. The preview should accomplish the following: create interest, show benefits, demonstrate value, and encourage action (all related to the four questions in the prior paragraph).

Choose an Effective Attention-Getter
In research among executives, the factors most likely to attract their attention were the following: The message was personalized, it evoked an emotional response, it came from a trustworthy source, and it was concise. In particular, personalized and emotion-evoking attention-getters led executives to pay close attention to presentations more than twice as often.[11]

Stephen Denning, one of the world's foremost authorities on leadership communication, spent decades working for the World Bank. While leading World Bank initiatives and meeting leaders throughout the world, he learned that influence in presentations depends heavily on first garnering attention. He explained:

> Successful leaders communicate very differently from the traditional, abstract approach to communication. In all kinds of settings, they communicate by following a hidden pattern: first, they get attention. Then they stimulate desire, and only then do they reinforce with reasons.[12]

The primary goals of attention-getters are to get your audience members emotionally invested in your presentation and engaged in thinking about your ideas. Table 14.1 focuses on seven types of attention-getters that Shannon could use in her presentation: rhetorical questions, vivid examples, dramatic demonstrations, testimonials or quotations, intriguing statistics, unexpected exercises, and challenges. This is not a

TABLE 14.1

Types of Effective Attention-Getters

Attention-Getter	Example
Rhetorical question	How many of you have heard for years about the great opportunities to source from and manufacture in China? How many of you have thought it's too complicated for a business your size to even consider this? In these tough times, when larger competitors have tremendous advantages in product costs, many small-business owners are asking these questions. "China" comes to mind, but you avoid exploring the possibility further because you assume it just won't work for your small business. Today I'm going to explain how you can do it.
	This attention-getter immediately evokes thinking about personal experiences for audience members. It focuses on an unmet need (getting costs down), and it is positive. It is also concise: it takes roughly 35 seconds to deliver (89 words).
Vivid example	One of our more recent clients was a small computer cable manufacturer. To give you a sense of the possibilities of producing in China, I want to quickly paint a picture of the options this small business had to choose from in China.
	In the city of Dongguan, about one hour from Hong Kong, there's a roughly 20-square-mile area with more than 50 computer cable manufacturers. Also in this area, there are roughly 100 suppliers of computer cable parts. Suppliers and manufacturers in many cases even share offices to create a seamless production process. It's amazing to be on the ground and see the tens of thousands of managers, engineers, and workers in such a small geographic area who are zeroed in on a particular product niche. I've not seen this type of concentration of efforts in any other place in the world. You have dozens of manufacturing alternatives within a few minutes' drive of one another.
	By contrast, here in the United States, this small company was 500 miles distant from its competitors and 1,000 miles from its suppliers. It's no wonder that producing in China can save money on manufacturing costs, and with such proximity to competitors and suppliers, you can get your products to market far faster.
	This example captures the attention of the audience with its vivid, story-based description of the manufacturing options available to a recent client. Many audience members will envision the manufacturing environment in their minds and wonder what comparable options await them in China. This example would take roughly 90 to 95 seconds to deliver (214 words). To keep the audience engaged, Shannon should communicate passion and enthusiasm.
Dramatic demonstration	(Holding two computer cables that appear identical) These two computer cables probably look the same to each of you. In fact, one of our recent clients made both of them. This one (holding out the first cable) was manufactured here in the States. It cost about $4 to make. After manufacturing, both cables were inspected and electronically tested. On average, cables like this fail the test 3 percent of the time. This other cable (holding out the second cable) was produced in southern China. It cost about $1.50 to make. Under the same inspection standards, less than 1 percent of these cables that were made in China failed quality tests.
	This attention-getter gives the audience a tangible sense of a reduction in production costs and improvement in quality control. This demonstration is delivered in approximately 40 to 45 seconds (93 words).
Testimonial or quotation	Marble Home Makeovers, a small manufacturer of fabricated marble, is a small business that just moved much of its manufacturing to China. Its business manager, Juan Hernandez, recently told me that they increased sales by $3 million last year due to the ability to offer better pricing. In a few moments, I will show you a video of his experience.
	This short statement focuses on the testimonial of a client. It emphasizes a dramatic rise in sales, which appeals to small-business owners emotionally and rationally. It would take just 25 seconds to deliver (60 words). Ideally, a compelling video testimonial will be provided as well.
Intriguing statistic	Probably many of you have heard the talk of saving 30, 40, even 60 percent on manufacturing costs in China. Probably fewer of you have heard that time to market for products manufactured in China can be one to three months faster than if you manufactured them in the United States.

TABLE 14.1

(Continued)

Attention-Getter	Example
	This attention-getter focuses on an exciting statistic for small-business owners (potential savings on production costs of up to 60 percent) and an unexpected one (time to market falling by one to three months). Not only does this meet their needs, it gets audience members thinking about how it's possible to manufacture at such a distance but get products to market sooner. This concise statement takes roughly 20 seconds to deliver (51 words).
Unexpected exercise	As we get started, I'd like each of you to get a partner and tell them your three most important goals for manufacturing. Let's take about two or three minutes and then I'd like you to report on what your partner told you.
	Most people attending a seminar or workshop do not expect to be involved early on. By quickly getting participants talking, you may also get them to open up and relax. In this exercise, they will explicitly talk about their own goals, which will remain on the forefront of their minds as Shannon gets into the presentation. Another benefit for Shannon is she can now adapt her presentation to the needs of the audience more effectively. This is a great approach for kinesthetic learners.
Challenge	Today I'm going to describe the experiences of several small-business owners who have successfully moved all or part of their production to China. In some cases, these small businesses have doubled or even tripled their net income within a few years. As I explain their experiences, think about your small business. Think about the similarities these small businesses have with yours and what this means for your business moving into China. At the same time, think about the unique obstacles your business has.
	This direct challenge to audience members to conceptualize and envision how the content of the presentation applies to their own businesses will help many of them become more engaged and active during the presentation. This is a concise opening at just 30 to 35 seconds (84 words).

comprehensive list; however, these strategies are among the most effective.[13] Think about how you might use each option in a presentation.

People enjoy humor in presentations. Generally, however, avoid opening with jokes. Few people do well when they open with jokes. Communication specialist Nick Morgan explains:

> You need to start with something clever enough to catch everyone's attention, but you're at your most nervous, and thus it's hard to shine like you want to. So how to get started? The traditional advice—still followed by many business speakers—is to begin with a joke. . . . For everyone except the professional comedian, this is bad counsel indeed. You're at your worst in terms of nerves. Don't compound the problem by setting for yourself one of the most difficult public speaking chores of all right off the bat: Delivering a punch line with brilliant comic timing. It's extremely difficult to do under the best of circumstances—even for seasoned professionals.[14]

Even if you're one of the rare breed of people who can consistently pull them off, opening jokes may have unintended consequences. Audience members may remember your jokes more than your key messages, so if you choose a humorous opening, tie it to your key messages.

Starting with an overwhelming set of facts and numbers or telling the story of your company may not be particularly effective either. If you choose to give background on your company, do so concisely, and make sure you connect the story of your company to the needs of your audience.[15]

Creating a Positioning Statement A **positioning statement** frames your message in appealing terms to your audience members and demonstrates clear and valuable benefits to them. The positioning statement should be as concise as possible—ideally one to two sentences. With the attention-getter, you engage and capture interest. With the positioning statement, you demonstrate that your presentation is worth paying close attention to for its entirety.

In Shannon's case, she selects the following positioning statement: "Today I'm going to discuss how small businesses like yours can easily move some or all of your manufacturing to China to lower production costs and achieve other manufacturing goals. In fact, I'm going to explain how you could have a manufacturing presence in China in as little as one month." This positioning statement is strong. It speaks directly to the needs of small manufacturers who are seeking lower costs. It also employs positive, upbeat, and client-focused language.

Providing an Overview Statement   The final part of the preview is the overview. Ideally, you can state your overview in one to three sentences in simple, conversational language. Immediately after Shannon makes her positioning statement, she provides an overview: "I'm going to focus on three primary benefits of sourcing and manufacturing in China: The first and most compelling reason is that you can reduce production costs by 40 to 60 percent; the second reason is that you can maintain and even increase the quality of your products; and the final reason is that you can cut time to market for your products by one to three months." This overview segments the presentation in terms of three key benefits or takeaway messages. These benefits are easy to remember and they are couched in the you-voice to help audience members think about the benefits to their own businesses.

Justify Your Views

The majority of your presentation will be devoted to expressing and supporting your **views**—your two, three, or four key messages. Recognize that many of your audience members are skeptical. After all, you will likely be asking them to commit to your products, services, or ideas at the expense of their time, money, or other resources. In other words, you are generally asking people to take some type of professional and/ or personal risk. Make sure you can back up your main positions with strong support material, including specific cases or examples, stories and illustrations, analogies, statistics and facts, quotations, or your own professional experiences.[16]

Use support materials in moderation, however. You can easily overwhelm your audience. Furthermore, most audience members prefer certain types of supporting material during presentations. For example, personalized case studies are more likely to influence audience members than statistics. At the same time, avoid any weak evidence, since that will undermine your case, and be prepared with additional support material if audience members request it.[17] Furthermore, gain a sense of your audience members' preferences. For example, thinkers are typically more influenced by quantitative information whereas feelers are typically more influenced by personal experiences.

Executive communication coach Roly Grimshaw observes that the most serious mistake business managers make is to present the evidence (numbers, statistics, facts) first, or only the evidence, and leave out their primary conclusions or central positions.[18] A more successful approach is the **PREP method,** which involves stating your *position,* providing the *reasons,* giving an *example* or providing evidence, and then restating your *position.*[19] Table 14.2 provides an instance of the PREP method from Shannon's presentation. As you read through this example, think about what Shannon gains from starting and ending with her position.

Conclude with an Effective Review

The **review** comprises a small percentage of your presentation time. However, make sure to have a strong finish—this is the place where you are hoping to gain buy-in on specific actions. First, you will recap your message in just a few sentences. Then, you'll provide a call to action, where you'll ask the audience members to make specific

Components of PREP Method

- Position
- Reasons
- Example
- Position

TABLE 14.2

The PREP Method

	Sample Statements
Step 1: **Position**	It's challenging for most small businesses to set up manufacturing in China.
Step 2: **Reasons**	It's challenging because of the major barriers of entry: finding and developing relationships with Chinese suppliers and manufacturers, having engineers on the ground to ensure quality production, bearing the costs of facilitating communication, and learning to deal with another business culture.
Step 3: **Example**	Let me give you a quick example of clients who we've worked with to successfully set up manufacturing in the past year. Their initial efforts to manufacture in China were costly and disappointing.
	Ten years ago and prior to our involvement, a marble fabrication company tried to set up manufacturing on their own. They sent a team of three managers to China on a two-week trip to meet potential manufacturers. They spent nearly $20,000 on the first trip and did little but eat meals with several manufacturers.
	A year, three more trips, and another $75,000 in travel expenses later, they were still confused about who to partner with. They had met a dizzying array of Chinese business managers and government officials.
	They finally settled on one manufacturer to produce a newly designed marble countertop. The first small batch turned out great. Then, they ordered a large batch of countertops worth nearly $300,000. When the shipment arrived, the quality was so poor they could not sell any of them. The Chinese manufacturer refused to reimburse them or remanufacture the order. The company tried to seek legal recourse with no success.
	Since they had no one on the ground in China to identify a reliable manufacturer in the first place, monitor quality once production started, nor resolve contract disputes, they ended up losing nearly half a million dollars. They also had unhappy customers at home who did not have products on time.
Step 4: **Position**	So, without access to relationships with Chinese manufacturers and suppliers and an on-the-ground presence to monitor operations, small businesses can find it very challenging and costly to set up production in China.

commitments. For example, Shannon often ends with the following call to action: "Thank you for attending this seminar. I want to quickly mention how you can get a more specific understanding of the savings you can achieve by producing in China. In your packets, I've enclosed a free estimate form. If you can provide some fairly basic information about one of your products, we could have cost estimates and shipping details back to you within a week. The estimate is free. There is no obligation at all to receive an estimate." This call to action is nonthreatening and is the natural next step for seminar participants to become clients.

Design Appealing Slides

Businesspeople frequently use PowerPoint or other electronic slide presentations as visual aids for their presentations (see the Technology Tips feature on page 434 for alternatives to PowerPoint). The reason for doing so is compelling. Good visuals can increase communication effectiveness and persuasiveness by about 50 percent.[20] After all, about 75 percent of what people learn comes visually; 12 percent through hearing; and 12 percent through smell, taste, and touch.[21]

However, poorly designed or poorly selected visuals can actually detract from presentation effectiveness.[22] While the use of electronic slides is often effective and nearly ubiquitous for business presentations, take caution. People in the workplace sometimes mock poor electronic slide presentations as *suffering death by PowerPoint*. Consider some of the comments in Figure 14.1 from business leaders.[23]

While well-designed electronic slide presentations can dramatically increase audience learning, poorly designed ones can draw intense negative reactions, as evidenced

LO14.4 Develop effective slide presentations.

FIGURE 14.1

Avoiding Death by PowerPoint

I actively despise how people use PowerPoint as a crutch. I think PowerPoint can be a way to cover up sloppy thinking, which makes it hard to differentiate between good ideas and bad ideas. I would much rather have somebody write something longhand, send it in ahead of the meeting and then assume everybody's read it, and then you start talking, and let them defend it. The question from the beginning of the meeting to the end of the meeting is, "Have we added value: yes or no?" And I would say that if the meeting is mostly the presentation of a deck of PowerPoint slides, you conveyed information, but you didn't actually add value.

-Cristóbal Conde, CEO of SunGard

I prefer that people not go through a slide deck. If you're working in an area, and you are running a business, you ought to be able to stand up there and tell me about your business without referring to a big slide deck. When you are speaking, people should focus on you and focus on the message. They can't walk away remembering a whole bunch of different things, so you have to have three or four really key messages that you take them through, and you remind them of what's important.

-James J. Schiro, director at Pepsico

Death by PowerPoint occurs because of the bullet trap. Speakers and presenters often reduce their presentations to series of bullets and thoughts in outline form. As a result, they often bore their audiences and lose connection with their audiences.

-Ellen Finkelstein, communication specialist

by the quotations in Figure 14.1. Make sure your electronic slide presentations aid rather than detract from your presentation objectives. Consider the following advice as you design your slides:

You Are the Focus of Your Presentation   From the beginning of the design process, resist the urge to make your slides the primary focal point; they are just an aid. Ideally, audience members will focus their eyes on you for the majority of the presentation. Consider the comments of Judith Humphrey, a prominent executive trainer:

> Great leaders understand that they are the best visual. They instinctively know that their message will come through best if the audience looks at them and listens to them—with no distractions. Audiences that divide their attention will only be able to partially commit to you. PowerPoint slides are usually a dumbed-down version of the narrative script you are delivering. Visuals rely on bullet points; you speak in full sentences, with illustrations and stories. Slides are dispassionate; your voice and gestures provide passion and emphasis. So in deflecting the audience's attention away from you to the bullet points, you're reducing the quality of your material and its impact on the audience.[24]

Create a Storyboard with Your PowerPoint Slide Titles   Make sure that your presentations *tell a story* to your audience. To check whether your slides provide a flowing narrative rather than a disjointed set of ideas, line up your slide titles (see Table 14.3). Ask yourself whether the slide titles move naturally through the narrative of your presentation.[25]

Shannon chooses to set up most of her titles as questions, which is a strategy that elicits thought and engagement. Collectively, these questions address hallmark issues of stories, such as *who? where? why? when?* and *how?* The order of these slides also includes the elements of a classic narrative of persuasion: attention, need and solution, rationale, counterpoints, and call to action (see Chapter 9).

Setting out the titles in this storyboard approach helps you see which slides you really need. A common misperception of electronic slide presentations is that more is better. In fact, using fewer slides can help you tell the story more effectively. As one recruiter in a recent *Wall Street Journal* study stated, "Students seem to think a better

TABLE 14.3

Setting Up Slide Titles to Help You Make a Smooth, Logical Presentation

Slide #	Title	Story Line
1	Manufacturing in China: How Your Small Business Can Do It	Positive overarching theme in the title slide: You can do this.
2	Why China?	*Attention:* shows benefits of manufacturing in China
3	What Are the Challenges?	*Need:* shows challenges to small businesses in outsourcing manufacturing
4	What Does *Sinosourcing* Do for Small Companies Like Yours?	*Solution:* shows the benefits that Sinosourcing provides through its services
5	Who Works for *Sinosourcing*?	*Rationale/Counterpoints:* describes who provides these services and why they are qualified; addresses concerns that Chinese managers are not sophisticated
6	How Does *Sinosourcing* Identify Suppliers and Manufacturers?	*Rationale/Counterpoints:* describes process for finding excellent suppliers and manufacturers; addresses concerns about manufacturing quality, labor practices, and safety standards
7	What's the *Sinosourcing* Process?	*Rationale/Counterpoints:* describes the process for Sinosourcing working with clients; addresses concerns that the process takes too long
8	We Want to Partner with You	*Call to Action:* sets up invitation to get free cost estimate

grade is assigned based on the number of slides in a presentation. In real life, you have 10 minutes to present to management. If you can't get the whole story in that time on two or three slides, you're dead in your career."[26]

In Shannon's presentation (see Figure 14.2), she uses a total of eight slides—one slide for every five to six minutes of her 45-minute presentation. As a rule, avoid showing more than one slide for every minute to two minutes of a presentation.

Design Your Slides for Ease of Processing In relation to speeches and presentations, you have likely heard of the KISS method: *Keep it simple, stupid.* Creating simple presentations is a good strategy. However, a more overarching and effective strategy is to focus on ease of processing. Your goal is to take your often complex data, relationships, and ideas and illustrate and depict them in easy-to-learn ways. Consider the following approaches to facilitate ease of processing:[27]

- *Limit the amount of information on any given slide.* Readers should be able to grasp the content within 10 to 15 seconds. For text, rarely should you use more than ten words per line and more than five to six lines.
- *Use font sizes that all audience members can read easily.* For titles, use at least 24-point fonts; for body text, use at least 18-point fonts.
- *Focus on and highlight key information.* Use bold, italics, and other formatting features to make key phrases or key components in figures stand out.
- *Use plenty of white space.* White space is effective for borders and between items and text on slides; it provides an uncluttered appearance.
- *Use high-contrast backgrounds and colors.* Make sure backgrounds do not obscure text. For dark text, use light backgrounds. For light text, use dark backgrounds.

FIGURE 14.2

Less-Effective and More-Effective Slides for *Sinosourcing* Presentation

Manufacturing in China : How Your Small
Business Can Do It

Shannon Browne
Sales Representative

Key message
does not
stand out
clearly; most
prominent
text is the
sales rep's
name.

Clip art on
title slide
does not
convey
professional
image.

More-Effective Opening Slide

Manufacturing in China:
How Your Small Business Can Do It

Shannon Browne, Sales Representative

Sinosourcing Experts, LLC
Meeting Your Sourcing Needs in China

Key message
for the
presentation
stands out
effectively.

More
professional
with official
company logo.

Less-Effective Slide #2

Why China?

- Save on costs up to 60%
- Keep the same quality for your products
- Even reduce the time it takes to put new products on the market
- Case Study: Marble Home Makeovers

No key words
or formatting
lead to less
impactful
slide.

Some
components
are nothing
more than
cues for the
presenter
("Case Study:
Marble Home
Makeovers").

More-Effective Slide #2

Why China?

Cost: You can reduce manufacturing costs by **40-60%**

Quality: You can maintain or improve quality control

Efficiency: You can reduce time to market by 1 to 3 months

Marble Home Makeovers

Sinosourcing Experts, LLC
Meeting Your Sourcing Needs in China

Formatting and
key words help
reinforce
primary
messages
rapidly.

Video case/
testimonial is
strong support.

FIGURE 14.2

(*Continued*)

More-Effective Slide #3

What Are the Challenges?

Top Five Concerns of Small Businesses Outsourcing in China

1. Choosing the right suppliers/manufacturers — 89%
2. Understanding government bureaucracy — 83%
3. Communicating effectively — 74%
4. Maintaining an on-the-ground presence — 73%
5. Resolving contractual/legal disputes — 65%

Percentage of Small Business Owners

Source: Sinosourcing Survey of 157 small businesses from the USA and Australia.

Sinosourcing Experts, LLC
Meeting Your Sourcing Needs in China

This chart is easier to process on a screen because it contains condensed information without sacrificing accuracy.

More-Effective Slide #4

What Does *Sinosourcing* Do for Small Companies Like Yours?

- Connects you with reliable suppliers/ manufacturers
- Helps you get permits and licenses
- Facilitates immediate communication with partners
- Monitors every phase of production
- Ensures that contract terms are met

Sinosourcing Experts, LLC
Meeting Your Sourcing Needs in China

This slide is more effective because it shortens the phrases for each bullet point and contains more white space.

Less-Effective Slide #3

What Are the Challenges?

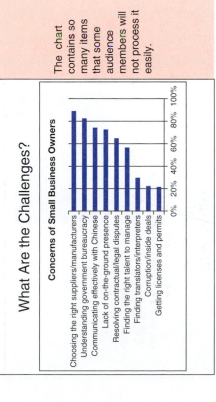

Concerns of Small Business Owners

Choosing the right suppliers/manufacturers
Understanding government bureaucracy
Communicating effectively with Chinese
Lack of on-the-ground presence
Resolving contractual/legal disputes
Finding the right talent to manage
Finding translators/interpreters
Corruption/inside deals
Getting licenses and permits

0% 20% 40% 60% 80% 100%

The chart contains so many items that some audience members will not process it easily.

Less-Effective Slide #4

What Does *Sinosourcing* Do for Small Companies Like Yours?

- Connects your company with reliable Chinese suppliers and manufacturers
- Monitors every phase of production at the factory (from design to shipment)
- Facilitates immediate communication with suppliers and manufacturers
- Ensures that contract terms are met
- Dramatically reduces your production costs

This slide contains far too much text. Audience members will be unable to grasp key concepts quickly.

FIGURE 14.2

(*Continued*)

More-Effective Slide #5

Who Works for Sinosourcing?

Our Experts:
12 Sourcing Experts/Quality Inspectors
10 Engineers and Designers
4 Import/Export Specialists
3 Legal/Contract Specialists
5 Field Reps in the USA

Education and Background:
All employees have master's degrees
All employees are bilingual
All employees have extensive manufacturing experience

Offices:
Shanghai, Hong Kong, Los Angeles

Sinosourcing Experts, LLC
Meeting Your Sourcing Needs in China

Pictures of Chinese managers that display professionalism and expertise quickly dispel stereotypes that some seminar participants have of Chinese managers.

More-Effective Slide #6

How Does *Sinosourcing* Identify Suppliers and Manufacturers?

Strict Safety/ Human Rights Standards:
SA800 and CPSIA compliant
Regular visits with factory managers and workers

Strict Quality/ Sustainability Standards:
ISO 14001 compliant
Regular factory audits

Sinosourcing Experts, LLC
Meeting Your Sourcing Needs in China

Pictures of clean, modern factory floors help overcome perceptions of decrepit, poor-quality manufacturing.

Less-Effective Slide #5

Who Works for Sinosourcing?

Our Experts:
12 Sourcing Experts/Quality Inspectors
10 Engineers and Designers
4 Import/Export Specialists
3 Legal/Contract Specialists
5 Field Reps in the USA

Education and Background:
All employees have master's degrees
All employees are bilingual
All employees have extensive manufacturing experience

Offices:
Shanghai, Hong Kong, Los Angeles

This slide contains convincing information but does not contain any visual features to resonate with audiences emotionally.

Less-Effective Slide #6

How Does *Sinosourcing* Identify Suppliers and Manufacturers?

- We abide by strict safety and human rights standards
  o SA800 and CPSIA compliant
  o Regular visits with factory managers and workers
- We abide by strict quality and sustainability standards
  o ISO 14001 compliant
  o Regular factory audits

The image in this photo does not relate to quality or safety standards.

FIGURE 14.2

(*Continued*)

More-Effective Slide #7

What's the *Sinosourcing* Process?

Step 1
You provide product information.
- specifications
- drawings/designs
- material requirements

Step 2
Identification of 3 to 5 manufacturers with price quotes.
⏱ 2– 5 wks

Step 3
Sample order.
⏱ 1– 5 wks

Step 4
Production begins.*
- target price
- timelines
- quantities
⏱ 1– 4 wks for first batch
*batch or continuous

Step 5
Shipment to you.
2–3 wks

Average time for entire process until delivery of first batch: **11 weeks.**

Sinosourcing Experts, LLC
Meeting Your Sourcing Needs in China

This diagram helps seminar participants rapidly conceptualize the process of setting up production in China.

More-Effective Slide #8

We Want to Partner with You

Please contact us to consider your options:
Phone: 803-760-5983
Email: info@sinosourcingexperts.com
Web: www.sinosourcingexperts.com

Sinosourcing Experts, LLC
Meeting Your Sourcing Needs in China

The final slide is a warm, inviting picture that helps engender trust in the Chinese employees at Sinosourcing Experts.

Less-Effective Slide #7

What's the Process?

1. You provide specifications, drawings/designs, material requirements, target price, and timelines/quantities

2. We ensure that the product information you supplied is complete and then identify 3 to 5 potential manufacturers. This takes roughly 2–4 weeks. We obtain 3 to 5 price quotes. This takes just 2–5 days.

3. We facilitate a sample order in which you quickly receive samples to assess your satisfaction with the manufacturer. This typically takes 1–5 weeks for routine items.

4. Mass production (batch or continuous production) begins upon your approval.

5. Shipment of products. Sinosourcing completes all specifications and documentations with your approval.

Most audience members won't be able to quickly gather all of the details when this slide is projected on a screen.

Less-Effective Slide #8

We Want to Partner with You

Please contact us to consider your options:
Phone: 803-760-5983
Email: info@sinosourcingexperts.com
Web: www.sinosourcingexperts.com

The image expresses warmth but does not reinforce key messages nor overcome negative stereotypes that some audience members hold.

TECHNOLOGY TIPS

ALTERNATIVES TO POWERPOINT

In many work environments, PowerPoint slides have become the standard visual aid for presentations and meetings. Even if you're great at using them, you might consider other types of visual aids and props to add impact, creativity, or simply variety to your presentations.

Try other electronic slide and presentation software. Consider trying Prezi, Google Docs, SlideRocket, 280 Slides, or other software packages to see what you're most comfortable with. Many presenters find that presentation software such as Prezi does not box them into bullet-point-based, linear presentations and provides more flexibility.

Use smart boards, whiteboards, or chalkboards. The act of writing as you go with keyboards, markers, or chalk may allow you to engage your audience more effectively because you are presenting in the moment, avoiding the structure or order of electronic slides, and getting input from your audience as you go. Furthermore, you may find that drawing objects freehand allows you to depict ideas more accurately and forcefully than you can with the drawing tools in PowerPoint. Still, make sure you avoid spending too much time facing away from the audience.

Experiment with new presentation technologies. Hundreds of new and emerging presentation technologies are *social*. In other words, they allow you to get information and feedback from your audience and incorporate it into your presentation. By experimenting with these technologies, you'll learn to tap into the incoming messages while also controlling your message or the conversation.

- *Use compelling images in moderation.* One of the basic reasons to use electronic slide presentations in the first place is to display images. You can use these images to convey powerful messages efficiently and with emotional power, especially for the visual learners in your audience. But make sure you are selective. Too many pictures, poor-quality pictures, or off-message pictures may detract from your message.

- *Develop simple charts and diagrams.* Charts and diagrams can be particularly helpful for simplifying complex data relationships. Make sure to use charts and figures that the audience can process in a matter of seconds. Otherwise, they have to spend an excessive amount of time trying to understand the chart or diagram and they're not paying attention to you. In some cases, they may give up and become annoyed.

- *Get professional design help when possible.* For high-stakes presentations, consider getting help from public relations or design specialists. If you are part of a large organization, you can often get this help internally. In many cases, well-designed templates may already exist. For smaller organizations, you may need to hire outside help.

For advice from an expert, read the Communication Q&A with James Robertson on page 438.

Applying the Story Line Approach to Your Presentations

LO14.5 Use the story line approach to presentations.

Earlier in this chapter, you learned about the PREP method of providing rich examples to support your positions. You also learned that you should create electronic slides with a story line approach. This section explains how you can apply a story line approach to your entire presentation and enhance your ability to connect with and influence others.

The story line approach is useful for various types of presentations because it allows your listeners to engage on a deeper level emotionally and intellectually. Emotionally, they often feel a bond with you as a speaker. Furthermore, they tend to internalize stories, even developing their own parallel stories that evoke commitment, determination, sympathy, and other emotions. However, stories are far more than emotional tools. Research shows that people remember stories more easily than they do abstract information, and they are more likely to act on what they hear via stories.[28]

When James E. Rogers, president and CEO of Duke Energy, was asked, "What would you like business schools to teach more of, or less of?" he had this to say:

> What I would really teach is how to write, and how to speak and make presentations. I've overused this term in this conversation, but *it's the ability to pull the salient facts together and tell a story, so that people feel it, sense it, they're convinced by it, and want to do something because of it.*
>
> My first full-time job, I worked at night as a newspaper reporter, going to school during the day. So, I really started out covering police news, and then federal courts and political news. And I really kind of developed a sense of the importance of trying to find the essence of the story and trying to arrange the facts in some chronology to make sense out of it. In a sense, as a CEO, part of my job is not only to help develop direction but to teach the storytelling. Those early years as a reporter gave me a sense of that in terms of how to tell the story, how to communicate.[29]

Rogers is not the only business professional who emphasizes storytelling. Jathan Janove, who did extensive HR training about sexual harassment in the early to mid-1990s, described his transition to storytelling for presentations. Penalties to employers and employees had increased substantially, and his job was to explain new laws governing appropriate behavior. As he lectured employees, he found that they often resented the perceived intrusiveness of the new laws and the fear tactics of describing harsh penalties. And they found the lectures boring. Here is what Janove did:

> It didn't take a great leap to realize that this training wasn't working, so I adopted a new approach, jettisoning scare-you-straight legal points. I substituted stories illustrating types of behaviors employees should avoid and how they unwittingly get themselves in trouble. Something amazing happened: Suddenly, the rooms were full of bright eyes. Discovering that telling stories is an excellent way to train employees about workplace law, I began collecting parables.[30]

Janove further explained that once he adopted a story-based approach to business training, he became far more influential. Audiences listened more attentively, learned more, and changed their behaviors.

You can use stories in many kinds of business presentations. For example, Sally Herigstad, a CPA and consultant to *MSN Money,* spoke about using this strategy for delivering financial presentations:

> Financial presentations tell a story. You're not just showing a collection of profit-and-loss statements and balance sheets—you're telling a story that your audience needs to hear. It may be a story of a new company with promising growth. Or maybe it's a story about meeting market challenges. Whatever your story is, stick to it: Toss everything that doesn't help you tell it in a compelling, easy-to-follow way. Tell your story with simplicity and clarity.[31]

Typically, stories for business connect facts with people and their business goals. Ideally, they are true, factual, and based on real events. In some cases, they may be hypothetical, but listeners still must find them realistic and relevant.[32] Generally, stories for business include the following components:[33]

- *Plot:* a business situation that involves challenges or tensions to overcome and a clear beginning and end.
- *Setting:* the time, place, characters, and context of the business situation.

FIGURE 14.3

Telling Stories to Connect with and Influence Audience Members

For this job, I love the opportunity to travel around the country and meet so many small-business owners. One thing I've learned from these meetings is that small-business owners care about their employees and that they are loyal to them. They know their employees on an entirely different level than executives at large companies do.

Most small-business owners who are contemplating outsourcing manufacturing really suffer at the thought of laying off any of their employees. They can appreciate the business benefits – the cost savings, the potentially faster time to market, even the possibility of higher quality. Yet, they have a hard time swallowing the fact that they may have to shut down some or all of their manufacturing operations and put their valued employees out of jobs, especially in tough times like this. I suspect many of you have considered this painful possibility as well.

Throughout our conversation, I've mentioned the example of Marble Home Makeovers. The business manager there, Juan Hernandez, knew that they had to sell product for less if they were going to stay competitive. He worried they might even go out of business. I've already mentioned how successful they were in terms of turning around their business by moving some of their manufacturing to China. However, I haven't mentioned the impacts on the employees.

Of course, Juan agonized over the thought of laying off up to 30 of his factory workers. Many of these employees were neighbors and close friends. Over half the factory workers had been with the company for over five years.

Ultimately, Juan made a plan that he felt made business sense but also was as fair as possible to employees. He retained ten of the employees to manufacture customized products for local customers, he moved five employees to office or service positions, and he had to lay off 15 employees. Although he was not required to do so, he gave two months of pay as severance to these laid-off employees.

Within a year, the business grew so quickly that Juan hired nearly ten local community members into marketing and office positions, including two of the employees he had to lay off. He projects that if the company continues to do so well, within two to three years, they will have more local employees than they did prior to outsourcing some of the manufacturing positions to China.

Juan's experience is common. Outsourcing does require some painful decisions. Yet, it does keep your business more competitive, and you may hire more local employees in the long run.

Plot: This plot is about how small-business owners can responsibly outsource manufacturing to China.

Setting: The setting focuses on Juan Hernandez at Marble Home Makeovers, an example Shannon has used elsewhere in her presentation. He makes a painful decision to lay off some workers and outsource some work to China to keep the business competitive.

Resolution: By outsourcing, the business grows, and Juan is able to hire more local employees.

Moral or lesson: In the long run, outsourcing keeps businesses competitive and may allow hiring more local employees.

At 426 words, this story would take roughly 2½ to 3 minutes.

- *Resolution:* a solution to the challenges or tensions.
- *Moral or lesson:* a point to the story.

In Figure 14.3 you'll find a story Shannon uses for her presentation about outsourcing to China. It contains a plot, a setting, a resolution, and a moral. It speaks directly to a concern nearly all small-business owners have—laying off workers. This story is part of a larger story line that Shannon carries across her entire presentation.

Keep in mind that stories should be short. Even when audience members are engaged, their patience is limited. They expect to get the point quickly. Typically, stories should last 30 seconds to one minute. In some cases, a story can last two to three minutes. Use your judgment and pay attention to your audiences. To help you identify how long a story is, time it while you rehearse. Or write it out and estimate how much time it will take to tell. Most people are comfortable with speaking at about 150 to 160 words per minute (this is the pace of most audio books). So, a 75-word story takes roughly 30 seconds, and a 150-word story takes about one minute.

It takes time to gather true stories for your presentations, so be alert for good ones. Remember, the purpose is always to make a point, not to entertain. If the stories have entertainment value, that's an added bonus.

Reviewing Your Presentations for Fairness and Effectiveness

LO14.6 Evaluate your presentations for fairness and effectiveness.

Review your presentations in the same way you review your written communications. In the first place, double-check every aspect of your supplementary materials as well as the technology you will use to ensure that it is perfect and working. Typos on electronic slides can be a glaring display of carelessness. Also, seek feedback from colleagues and clients before and after your presentations. Ask them how they would change the presentation to better meet their needs.

As with all of your communications, ask yourself how fair your business presentations are. Is the content based on *facts?* Have you granted others *access* to your real motives and reasoning? Have you been forthright about *impacts* on audience members and other stakeholders? Have you ensured that you show *respect* for audience members (see Figure 14.4)?

In Shannon's case, she evaluates her presentation in each regard. In particular, she has provided claims about savings in manufacturing costs, improving quality control, and decreasing time to market for products. Shannon is comfortable with these claims.

FIGURE 14.4

Are Your Presentations FAIR?

Facts (How *factual* is your presentation?)
- Have you presented *all* the facts correctly?
- Have you presented information that allows colleagues, customers, and consumers to make informed decisions that are in their best interests?
- Have you carefully considered various interpretations of your data? Have you assessed the quality of your information?

Access (How *accessible* or *transparent* are your motives, reasoning, and information?)
- Are your motives clear, or will others think you have a hidden agenda? Have you made yourself accessible to others so that they can learn more about your viewpoints?
- Have you fully disclosed information that colleagues, customers, or consumers should expect to receive?
- Are you hiding any information to cast your recommendations in a better light or real reasons for making certain claims or recommendations?

Impacts (How does your communication *impact* stakeholders?)
- Have you carefully considered how your ideas, products, and services will impact colleagues, customers, and consumers?
- Have you made recommendations to colleagues, customers, and consumers that are in their best interests?

Respect (How *respectful* is your presentation?)
- Does the message offend or pressure in any way? Does it show that your colleagues' and customers' needs are important?
- Would a neutral observer consider your communication respectful?

COMMUNICATION Q&A

CONVERSATIONS WITH CURRENT BUSINESS PROFESSIONALS

Pete Cardon: What types of presentations do you give?

James Robertson: In the course of a year I typically give two or three "keynote" presentations at conferences or conventions and many internal presentations on strategy, business plans, or technology directions to people above and below me in the organization. Many of my presentations come in the form of general communication and update meetings to staff teams or working groups where I need to deliver a consistent and accurate message on a topic as their leader.

PC: How do you prepare for the presentations?

JR: The key to a successful presentation is knowing your audience and practicing your message. Regardless of how big or small the group, make sure you spend plenty of time preparing. I dedicate many hours of practice to making sure that the 20 or 30 minutes I'll have in front of them comes off without a hitch. The audience is always the wild card, but anticipating their response is important.

PC: In what ways do you see PowerPoint used effectively in the workplace?

JR: Presentations resonate with me more when they convey a simple message. There is an old saying "a picture says a thousand words." I recently delivered a presentation where I did not have a single word on any of the slides, but the pictures on those slides conveyed the message. Humans are very visual and experiential, and they retain visuals in memory more easily than they do words. While not all presentations are purely visual, the best ones I've ever seen, or have given, involved more use of graphics and pictures and less use of words and text.

PC: In what ways do you see PowerPoint used ineffectively in the workplace?

JR: I hate presentations where the slides consist only of words or numbers or very complicated charts I can't read at a distance or really understand. That's the ultimate turnoff and will put your audience to sleep in a hurry.

See more of Mr. Robertson's comments about presentations at the end of the next chapter.

James Robertson *is vice president of Global Data Networks and Information Technology Security at Turner Broadcasting. He has worked at Turner Broadcasting for 15 years and runs a global operations team of over 200 IT professionals.*

The company has tracked the success of its clients for many years and identifies these claims as valid and accurate. She provides *access* to her motives: She wants to get new clients for Sinosourcing. She is also clear about *impacts*—even those that harm others—of outsourcing. For example, she tells seminar participants that outsourcing requires them to lay off employees in their communities (see Figure 14.3). Finally, Shannon is respectful in every way. For example, many of the seminar participants raise concerns based on misperceptions about manufacturing in China. She listens to them respectfully and corrects their misperceptions without sounding judgmental. For additional thoughts on delivering presentations from an experienced professional, read the Communication Q&A with James Robertson.

Chapter Takeaway for *Planning Presentations*

LO 14.1. Describe how planning your presentations leads to credibility. (pp. 419–420)

Planning presentation content demonstrates **your personal credibility.**

It shows **competence** when you demonstrate that you know what you're talking about.	It shows **caring** when you provide content that meets the needs of others.	It shows **character** when you provide honest and transparent content.

LO 14.2. Analyze presentation audiences in terms of message benefits, learning styles, and communicator styles. (pp. 420–423)

Principles of Audience Analysis	Learner Types
Identify the following: • Audience benefits • Decision makers • Communicator style • Existing knowledge • Appeals • Learning style • Concerns	• Visual • Auditory • Kinesthetic

LO 14.3. Organize and gather content for a preview, view, and review. (pp. 423–427)

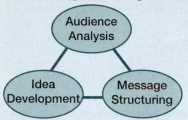

AIM Planning Process

Audience Analysis: Identify how the message benefits the audience and make it easy to process.

Idea Development: Identify your presentation goals, key messages, and supporting details.

Message Structuring: Give a preview of your message, justify your views, and end with a review.

Components of Presentations: Preview, View, Review

Types of Attention-Getters: Rhetorical Question, Vivid Example, Dramatic Demonstration, Testimonial or Quotation, Intriguing Statistic, Unexpected Exercise, Challenge

See *examples of attention-getters* in Table 14.1.

PREP Method: Position, Reasons, Example, Position

See *an example of a PREP statement* in Table 14.2.

LO 14.4. Develop effective slide presentations. (pp. 427–434)

Principles for Developing Slides	
• Create a storyboard with your PowerPoint slide titles.	• Use plenty of white space.
• Design your slides for ease of processing.	• Use high-contrast backgrounds and colors.
• Limit the amount of information on any given slide.	• Use compelling images, charts, and figures.
• Use font sizes that all audience members can read easily.	• Get professional design help when possible.
• Focus on and highlight key information.	

See *less-effective and more-effective examples of slides* in Figure 14.2.

LO 14.5. Use the story line approach to presentations. (pp. 434–437)

Components of Effective Stories for Business	See *an example of a story for business* in Figure 14.3.
Plot, Setting, Resolution of challenge, Moral	

LO 14.6. Evaluate your presentations for fairness and effectiveness. (pp. 437–438)

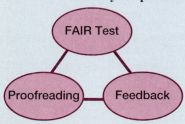

Reviewing Process

FAIR Test: Focus on presenting factual information and being clear about impacts on others.

Proofreading: Make sure your electronic slides, handouts, and other supplementary materials are perfect.

Feedback: Ask colleagues and clients what they would like you to change about your presentation.

Key Terms

Discussion Exercises

14.1 Chapter Review Questions (LO 14.1, LO 14.2, LO 14.3, LO 14.4, LO 14.5, LO 14.6)

For each of the following items, respond with one or two paragraphs.

A. Explain why presenters must be aware of audience members' chief concerns.

B. Discuss the importance of knowing which people in an audience are decision makers.

C. Describe how presentations can be adapted to people of different communicator and learning styles.

D. Discuss the value of identifying just a few takeaway messages.

E. Explain the role of the preview, view, and review in presentations.

F. Describe common types of attention-getters. Explain the two types that you generally consider most effective.

G. Identify common types of support materials for presentations.

H. Explain principles of effective electronic slide use for presentations.

I. Describe the story line approach to presentations.

14.2 Communication Q&A Discussion Questions (LO 14.2, LO 14.4, LO 14.5)

Read the Communication Q&A section with comments from James Robertson. Respond to the following questions:

A. What does Robertson say about preparing for presentations?

B. What tips does he give for connecting with the audience?

C. What does he say about effective and ineffective electronic slide presentations?

D. Why does he prefer visual slides over text- or number-heavy slides?

14.3 Using Stories for Presentations (LO 14.5)

Read the following quotation from Stephen Denning:

These days, command-and-control approaches are unlikely to generate positive responses in employees, let alone the marketplace. The era when top managers could simply give orders and expect their will to be done has long gone. As a result, leaders have turned to storytelling to overcome barriers to communication. Since time immemorial, human beings have used stories to spread religions, win support for political agendas or launch wars. And as we look around the business world, stories are everywhere. Managers think in stories, they remember in stories, they plan in stories, they express hopes and fears and dreams in stories, and they make decisions in stories. Storytelling is already part of our world.

Moreover, storytelling is not a rare skill possessed by a few people born with the gift of gab. All human beings start spontaneously telling stories at age 2 and go on doing it for the rest of their lives. They tell stories effortlessly in social settings. Leadership storytelling involves taking a capacity that people already have and applying it for constructive purposes. Anyone can master the discipline.[34]

Based on Denning's comments and your own experiences, respond to each of the following items:

A. Why are stories an effective communication tool compared to command-and-control approaches?

B. What are some steps people can take to become effective storytellers?

C. What are some of the risks of storytelling?

14.4 Overcoming "Death by PowerPoint" (LO 14.4)

James E. Rogers of Duke Energy was asked, "What would you like business schools to teach more of, or less of?"

I believe there is such a thing as death by PowerPoint. Because I believe, and this is the storyteller in me and maybe the former newspaper reporter, that I'd much rather have someone write a two-page summary of what they're thinking. When you're forced to sit and write it, not only are you getting the subject, verb, predicates right, but you're tying the sentences together and ideas together. PowerPoints are just bullets, bullets, bullets, and when you actually have to write something, you start to develop a more cohesive logic. I think words really make a difference—what you say, how you say it. A lot of energy needs to go into how you present the idea. And I'm not talking about spin. I'm really talking about making the idea come alive through a story.[35]

Based on these comments, respond to each of the following items:

A. What are some specific ways in which you think PowerPoint lowers the level of effective business thinking?

B. What are some specific ways that you can alter the design of electronic slide presentations to bring out good business thinking?

C. What do you think is the difference between spin and story in a business presentation?

14.5 Avoiding Bad PowerPoint Presentations (LO 14.4)

Read the various comments by business leaders in Figure 14.1. Respond to the following questions with one or two paragraphs each:

A. What are the key points that these leaders make about PowerPoints?

B. For each key theme or key point you've identified, make counterpoints. Explain another perspective on the issue and/or explain how to use PowerPoint slides without encountering this problem.

Evaluation Exercises

14.6 Evaluating an Electronic Slide Presentation (LO 14.4)

Find an electronic slide presentation you are interested in on the SlideShare website (www.slideshare.net). In three to five paragraphs, describe the following:

A. The electronic slide presentation.

B. Use of white space.

C. Use of charts, diagrams, and other figures.

D. Use of pictures and other images.

E. Use of text.

F. Three recommendations to improve the electronic slide presentation.

14.7 Self-Assessment: Your Approach to Planning Presentations (LO 14.2, LO 14.3, LO 14.4)

Evaluate yourself with regard to each of the practices listed in the table below. Circle the appropriate number for each.

Statement	1 – Rarely/Never	2 – Sometimes	3 – Usually	4 – Always
I carefully select two or three key messages that I want to get across for my presentations.	1	2	3	4
I design my presentations so that nearly every aspect leads back to one of my main points.	1	2	3	4
I repeat my main points at least several times during a presentation.	1	2	3	4
I provide an overview at the beginning of my presentations that includes my key messages.	1	2	3	4
I think carefully about how my key messages meet the needs of my audiences.	1	2	3	4
I think carefully about how to adapt my key messages to the preferred communicator styles of my audience members.	1	2	3	4
I think carefully about how to adapt my key messages to the preferred learning styles of my audience members.	1	2	3	4
I provide enough support materials to make my key messages convincing.	1	2	3	4
I speak with confidence about my key messages.	1	2	3	4
I conclude with a call to action that is built upon my key messages.	1	2	3	4

Add up your score and consider the following advice:

35–40: You are a *strategic, other-oriented presenter*. You think about how to prepare and deliver a presentation that meets the needs of others. Continue with such awareness of the impact of your written messages.

30–34: You are a *careful, considerate presenter*. You spend some time thinking about the content of your message and the needs of your audience members. Take time to think your message through even more carefully and pay close attention to the needs and potential responses to your written messages by audience members.

25–29: You are an *average* presenter. Sometimes you are careful about developing your message and considerate of the needs and reactions of others. Other times you are not. Get in the habit of taking time to carefully craft your message.

Under 25: You *need to improve* your approach to presenting. You likely don't spend enough time thinking through the key messages and their impacts on others. You will be far more influential if you spend more time preparing your messages and delivering them with your audience members in mind.

Once you complete the assessment, write three paragraphs about the three specific ways in which you can improve your ability to prepare and deliver your key messages in presentations.

14.8 Evaluating Learning and Communicator Styles (LO 14.2)

Based on the descriptions of communicator styles (sensers, feelers, thinkers, intuitors) and learning styles (visual, auditory, kinesthetic) described in the "Analyze Your Audience" section of this chapter, do the following:

A. Describe your learning and communicator styles (you may consider yourself a combination of various styles).

B. Discuss how your learning and communicator styles may impact how you prefer to receive presentations.

C. Discuss how your learning and communicator styles may impact how you plan and deliver presentations.

D. Explain a few ways you can adapt your presentation style to learning and communicator styles other than your own.

14.9 Interviewing a Business Professional about Planning for Presentations (LO 14.1, LO 14.2, LO 14.3, LO 14.4)

Interview a business professional about best practices in planning business presentations. Write four to five paragraphs about the interview and address the following issues:

A. Planning themes and key points.

B. Adapting the presentation to the needs and preferences of the audience.

C. Using attention-getters or other strategies to engage the audience in the opening moments.

D. Preparing examples and support for key ideas.

E. Developing electronic slides and handouts.

F. Using technology.

14.10 Conducting a FAIR Test of a Recent Presentation (LO 14.6)

Think about a presentation you made recently. Assess how you did in terms of the following:

A. Did you present the facts correctly?

B. Did you present all the relevant facts?

C. Did you present any information that would be considered misleading?

D. Did you make your motives clear, or will others perceive that you have a hidden agenda?

E. Did you hide any of the real reasons for making certain claims or recommendations?

F. Did you seek the opinions and ideas of those impacted by your communication?

G. Did you think about how your communication will help or even hurt others?

H. Would others consider your presentation respectful?

Application Exercises

14.11 Planning Attention-Getters (LO 14.3)

Using Table 14.1 as a guide, do the following:

A. Identify a topic for a presentation.

B. Write how you could use each type of attention-getter: rhetorical question, vivid example, dramatic demonstration, testimonial or quotation, intriguing statistics, unexpected exercise, and challenge.

C. Explain the three approaches you believe would be most effective.

14.12 Creating Positioning and Preview Statements (LO 14.3)

A. Identify a topic for a presentation.

B. Write a positioning statement.

C. Write a preview statement.

14.13 Employing the PREP Method to Take Positions (LO 14.3)

Identify a key position that you intend to make during your presentation. Using Table 14.2 as a guide, write out how you could use the PREP (Position—Reasons—Example—Position) method to effectively convey this position to your audience.

14.14 Creating a Storyboard for Your Presentation (LO 14.4)

Identify a topic of interest. Create a storyboard (similar to the one displayed in Table 14.3) to outline the titles, content, and related story line of your PowerPoint slides.

14.15 Creating Electronic Slides (LO 14.4)

Create an electronic slide presentation for your topic of interest. Ensure that it conveys your key messages effectively.

14.16 Creating Electronic Slides from Reports (LO 14.4)

Many times in the workplace, you will create a written report and provide an oral presentation as well. Select a written report and develop a set of electronic slides that could be used to present it. If you have not developed your own report, consider the following options:

- A report or other written message in the textbook. For example, you could consider the following: Green Meetings in Chapter 13 or Guest Satisfaction Ratings among Conference Attendees in Chapter 13.

- An annual report from a company of interest.

- A white paper from a company of interest.

Endnotes

1. Thomas Leech, *How to Prepare, Stage, and Deliver Winning Presentations,* 3rd ed. (New York: American Management Association, 2004): 9–10.

2. Lin Grensing-Pophal, "Presentations That Sell without Offending," *Society for Human Resource Management* website (July 1, 2004).

3. Harry Mills, *Power Points! How to Design and Deliver Presentations That Sizzle and Sell* (New York: AMACOM, 2007).

4. Nick Morgan, "Reach Audience Members Where They Learn," *Harvard Management Communication Letter* (May 2002): 9.

5. Mills, *Power Points! How to Design and Deliver Presentations That Sizzle and Sell.*

6. Leech, *How to Prepare, Stage, and Deliver Winning Presentations.*

7. Ibid.

8. Mills, *Power Points! How to Design and Deliver Presentations That Sizzle and Sell.*

9. This section is adapted from the work of Mills, *Power Points! How to Design and Deliver Presentations That Sizzle and Sell.*

10. Dana LaMon, "Making the Moment Meaningful," *Toastmaster* online (November 2007), available at www.toastmasters.org/ToastmastersMagazine/ToastmasterArchive/2007/November/MomentMeaningful.aspx.

11. Stephen Denning, *The Secret Language of Leadership: How Leaders Inspire Action through Narrative* (San Francisco: John Wiley & Sons, 2007).

12. Ibid.

13. Ibid.

14. Nick Morgan, "Opening Options: How to Grab Your Audience's Attention: Six Great Ways to Begin a Presentation," *Harvard Management Communication Letter* (June 2003): 3–4.

15. Denning, *The Secret Language of Leadership: How Leaders Inspire Action through Narrative.*

16. Leech, *How to Prepare, Stage, and Deliver Winning Presentations.*

17. Mills, *Power Points! How to Design and Deliver Presentations That Sizzle and Sell.*

18. Roly Grimshaw, "Communication by Numbers," *Harvard Management Communication Letter* 8 no. 3 (2005): 3–4.

19. Nick Morgan, "How to Put Together a Great Speech When You're Under the Gun," *Harvard Management Communication Letter* (September 2003): 3–4.

20. Leech, *How to Prepare, Stage, and Deliver Winning Presentations*; Mills, *Power Points! How to Design and Deliver Presentations That Sizzle and Sell.*

21. Mills, *Power Points! How to Design and Deliver Presentations That Sizzle and Sell.*

22. Leech, *How to Prepare, Stage, and Deliver Winning Presentations.*

23. New York Times Corner Office Blog, "Communication," retrieved June 15, 2010, from http://projects.nytimes.com/corner-office/Communication; New York Times Corner Office Blog, "Simplicity,"

retrieved June 15, 2010, from http://projects.nytimes.com/corner-office/Simplicity; Stephen M. Kosslyn, *Clear and to the Point: 8 Psychological Principles for Compelling PowerPoint Presentations* (Oxford: Oxford University Press, 2007): 1; Ellen Finkelstein, "Sidestep the PowerPoint Trap," *Toastmaster* online (May 2009), available at www.toastmasters.org/ToastmastersMagazine/ToastmasterArchive/2009/May/SidestepPowerPoint.aspx.

24. Judith Humphrey, "You Are the Best Visual," *Harvard Management Communication Letter* (October 2011): 10–11.

25. Grimshaw, "Communication by Numbers."

26. Ronald Alsop, "Poor Writing Skills Top M.B.A. Recruiter Gripes," *The Wall Street Journal,* January 17, 2006.

27. Kosslyn, *Clear and to the Point: 8 Psychological Principles for Compelling PowerPoint Presentations;* Leech, *How to Prepare, Stage, and Deliver Winning Presentations;* Sally Herigstad, "Giving Effective Financial Presentations with PowerPoint," *Toastmaster* online (July 2008), available at www.toastmasters.org/ToastmastersMagazine/ToastmasterArchive/2008/July/PresentationswithPowerPoint.aspx; Mills, *Power Points! How to Design and Deliver Presentations That Sizzle and Sell.*

28. John Seely Brown, Stephen Denning, Katalina Groh, and Laurence Prusak, *Storytelling in Organizations: Why Storytelling Is Transforming 21st Century Organizations and Management* (Burlington, MA: Elsevier Butterworth-Heinemann, 2005); Roger C. Schank, *Tell Me a Story: A New Look at Real and Artificial Memory* (New York: Charles Scribner's Sons, 1990); Walter Swap, Dorothy Leonard, Mimi Shields, and Lisa Abrams, "Using Mentoring and Storytelling to Transfer Knowledge in the Workplace," *Journal of Management Information Systems* 18, no. 1 (2001): 95–114; Michael W. McLaughlin, "Getting Clout from Speaking Engagements," *Society for Human Resource Management* website (May 5, 2010); Judith Tingley, "Walking a Fine Line: How Much Personal Information Should Speakers Share?" *Toastmaster* online (March 2009), available at www.toastmasters.org/ToastmastersMagazine/ToastmasterArchive/2009/March/Walking-a-Fine-Line.aspx; Jathan Janove, "A Story Is Worth a Thousand Lectures," *HR Magazine* 54, no. 7 (July 1, 2009) [online version]; Mills, *Power Points! How to Design and Deliver Presentations That Sizzle and Sell.*

29. New York Times Corner Office Blog, "Communication."

30. Janove, "A Story Is Worth a Thousand Lectures."

31. Herigstad, "Giving Effective Financial Presentations with PowerPoint."

32. David Armstrong, *Managing by Storying Around* (New York: Doubleday, 1992).

33. Adapted from Robert F. Dennehy, "The Executive as Storyteller," *Management Review* 88, no. 3 (1999): 40–43; Roger C. Schank, *Tell Me a Story: A New Look at Real and Artificial Memory* (New York: Charles Scribner's Sons, 1990).

34. Stephen Denning, "Stories in the Workplace," *Society for Human Resource Management* website (October 1, 2008).

35. New York Times Corner Office Blog, "Communication."

CHAPTER FIFTEEN

Delivering Presentations

Learning Objectives

After studying this chapter, you should be able to do the following:

LO15.1   Describe how presentation delivery impacts your credibility.

LO15.2   Deliver presentations with authenticity, confidence, and influence.

LO15.3   Apply the SOFTEN model of nonverbal communication for presentations.

LO15.4   Use slides and handouts to supplement your presentation effectively.

LO15.5   Interact effectively with your audience.

Chapter Case: Attracting New Clients at Sinosourcing Experts

Who's Involved

Shannon Browne
- Has worked as a sales rep at Sinosourcing Experts for five months
- Recently graduated with a major in supply chain management and a minor in Chinese

The Situation

Shannon has prepared a new presentation about how Sinosourcing Experts can help small manufacturers outsource some of their manufacturing in China. Now she is ready to try it on several groups of small-business owners and managers. She's nervous, though, and uncertain about the outcome.

Task 1
Connect with audiences, gaining their trust and confidence.

Task 2
Deliver a persuasive and memorable explanation of the benefits of working with Sinosourcing.

Establish Presence

Presenting gives you an excellent opportunity to connect deeply with your colleagues, your clients, and your other contacts. It allows you to express your views in a rich, two-way environment. As you do with your written communication, you will aim to strike the right style and tone in your presentations. Moreover, you will strive to establish a "presence," something great speakers and presenters are often described as doing. Having presence means commanding attention, garnering respect for your ideas, engaging your listeners, and even inspiring your audiences to action. In this section, we focus on strategies you can use to enhance your presence as you deliver your presentations.

Establish Credibility

For internal presentations, you often present to people who know you well and who have already formed opinions about your credibility; they have a sense of your competence, caring, and character. However, internal presentations still provide you the opportunity

LO15.1 Describe how presentation delivery impacts your credibility.

to change others' views of you. Without appearing self-serving, find ways to increase your perceived credibility. Use the presentation to show your thorough understanding of a business issue. Frame your ideas in ways that show clear benefits to your company, its employees, and its stakeholders. In every way, display honesty and openness.

For external presentations, you are often dealing with people who have superficial impressions of your credibility. You have opportunities before, during, and after your presentation to bolster your credibility. Before the presentation, you can make information about your background available or have someone introduce you with a brief statement.

During the presentation, you establish your competence by showing that you know the content well. You show your caring by connecting emotionally with audience members and adapting to their needs. You show your character by being open and honest. After your presentation, following up as appropriate with audience members shows your caring and character as well. Some audience members may raise issues for you to look into or ask for additional information. Comply with these requests promptly and you will establish a reputation for responsiveness.

LO15.2 Deliver presentations with authenticity, confidence, and influence.

Maintain Authenticity

Standing in front of an audience feels anything but natural for many business professionals. Yet, nearly all audience members are making judgments about you and your message based on their perceptions of your authenticity. One of your primary goals as you develop your presentation skills is to find ways to present your real self to your audiences. Barbara De Angelis, a well-known communication specialist and speaker, explained the importance of maintaining authenticity:

> I often work with speakers who can't understand why they aren't more successful, or why they become so anxious in front of others. Often, they make the mistake of trying to imitate other speakers who they believe are more powerful or more skilled, or they mechanically follow learned formulas for successful public speaking. However, by doing this, they are unintentionally disconnecting from one of their greatest assets—and one of the secret ingredients for being successful: their authenticity. . . . People can sense when we are trying too hard, or faking confidence, or projecting an image that doesn't feel natural. When people see us appearing inauthentic, it makes them uneasy. And we actually appear awkward or nervous.[1]

As you read this chapter about presentation delivery, focus on making a few changes at a time. Attempting to alter too many of your presentation techniques at once may detract from your ability to speak naturally and genuinely. Add new presentation techniques to your repertoire constantly, but also make sure to draw on your natural strengths.

Know Your Material and Rehearse

By running through your presentations several times, you allow yourself to become more comfortable with the content, work out weakly connected areas, and identify parts that you want to emphasize through tone and nonverbal communication. Also, rehearsing allows you to time your presentation so you know if you need to add or remove content.

Far too many speakers and presenters avoid rehearsing. The presentation itself is often the first run-through. Executive speech coach Nick Morgan observed the following about this approach:

> The sad truth is that when you wing it, the performance is rarely as good in the audience's memory as it is in the speaker's. The reason is that your heightened adrenaline literally makes you feel better—more energy, more enthusiasm, more acuity—and so you rate your own performance better. What the audience all too often sees, on the other hand, is disorganization, fumbled examples, and the vagueness that comes from not knowing your material thoroughly.[2]

Rehearsing may involve running through the presentation in your mind or out loud. Ideally, you do it out loud. Consider videotaping your presentation so that you can get a sense of the overall impact of your ideas, the flow of your content, and the delivery of your presentation.

Many speakers and presenters use notes. Notes are not necessarily considered a weakness; however, use them sparingly or, ideally, not at all. Rehearsing will help you determine if you want or need notes. If you use them, rehearsing helps you choose which notes you need and allows you to become comfortable handling your notes in a nondistracting way.

Overcome Fear and Speak with Confidence

Nearly everyone gets nervous and even fearful of presenting in public, especially in unpredictable and high-stakes circumstances. Many polls show that adults fear public speaking more than death. Responding to these various polls, Jerry Seinfeld once joked, "At a funeral, the average person would rather be in the casket than giving the eulogy."[3] Other polls show that public speaking is among the most serious phobias among adults, with the fear of snakes the only phobia surpassing it (see Figure 15.1).[4]

Experiencing some nervousness as you speak and present is normal. Even experienced speakers get stage fright from time to time. Unexpected circumstances, for example, may cause unusual nervousness—unfamiliar or intimidating audience members, technology failure, pressure to perform with a skeptical audience, noticing the speech is being recorded, and many other reasons.[5]

Feeling some nerves is not necessarily bad. It shows you care about making an effective presentation. And feeling some nerves can heighten your ability to deliver forcefully and passionately. Nervousness is dysfunctional only when it impairs your ability to deliver your content. In most presentations, certain parts are the most critical—for example, a call to action (see Chapter 14)—and at the same time, they have the least-certain outcome. Sometimes, out of nervousness, presenters do not follow through completely at these moments. If nervousness means you

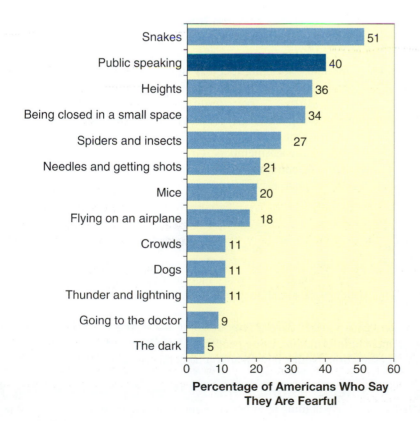

FIGURE 15.1

Top Fears of American Adults

Source: Geoffrey Brewer, "Snakes Top List of Americans' Fears: Public Speaking, Heights and Being Closed in Small Spaces also Create Fear in Many Americans" (March 19, 2001), retrieved from Gallup Polls online, http://www.gallup.com/poll/1891/snakes-top-list-americans-fears.aspx. Copyright © 2001 Gallup, Inc. All rights reserved. The content is used with permission; however, Gallup retains all rights of republication.

shortchange yourself at those critical moments, use techniques to help you manage your nervousness.[6]

Consider some of the following recommendations:[7]

Engage in Relaxation Techniques

Consider some of the following options:

- Stretching.
- Meditating.
- Going hiking or exercising (a day or so before your presentation).
- Listening to music.
- Going to a movie.

- Watching a sunset.
- Thinking about the things in your life you are grateful for, such as your cherished relationships.
- Letting your mind go blank.
- Counting backward from 100.

Become Aware of Your Breathing

Taking several deep breaths is a great technique to quickly alleviate anxiety. Also, consistently taking full breaths leads to improved tone and timber of your voice as well as better, more confident posture.

Practice Visualization

Envision yourself speaking with confidence and ease. Imagine making nonverbal connections with your audience. Think about how you will respond to audience questions. In your mind, play out your presentation and see yourself succeeding.

Focus on Friendly Faces Initially to Gain Composure and Confidence

Inevitably, the presence of some audience members will make you more nervous than others. It may be a critical boss, a skeptical client, a person you disagree with often, or someone who intimidates you for other reasons. In the opening moments of your presentation, when you are most apt to suffer from nervousness, look at those in the audience with whom you are most friendly. This will help calm you during those ever-important first moments.

Watch Your Food and Beverage Intake

Pay attention to foods and beverages that impact your nervousness. Some people avoid or minimize caffeine intake on speech days to avoid jitters. Others avoid dairy products, since they can coat the mouth and throat and make speaking feel less smooth. Notice how various foods and beverages affect your body and adjust accordingly.

Get Comfortable with Audience Members before Starting Your Presentation

One of the best ways of relaxing immediately before your presentation is to speak with audience members. Greet them at the door, walk around the room, engage in small talk, and find other ways to break the ice and help you and your audience members warm up to each other.

Focus on People

If you make your speech about people, your audience members are more likely to trust your commitment to them and others: People like to hear about people. Also, a strong people-focus will allow you to liven up dry facts and statistics. Try the following methods of making your speech about people.[8]

Make People the Subject of Your Sentences

Especially when you present numerical information, using people as the subjects of your sentences humanizes your presentation. Notice how Shannon does this in Table 15.1.

Introduce Colleagues and Refer to Them by Name during Your Presentation

By naming members in your organization or other relevant people,

TABLE 15.1

Making People the Subject of Your Sentences

Less Effective	More Effective
Our internal research shows that we have achieved an 82 percent client satisfaction rate in terms of perceived quality improvement since moving operations to China.	Our quality inspectors consistently survey our clients to make sure we're getting the right fit for them. The vast majority of our clients—82 percent—say that quality has improved since moving production to China.
This statement is compelling but dry and impersonal to some audience members.	This statement is compelling because of the people involved: the quality inspectors who conduct the surveys and the clients who are happy with quality improvements.

TABLE 15.2

Introducing Colleagues by Name

Less Effective	More Effective
Our engineers have extensive experience in the Chinese manufacturing environment.	Our engineers collectively have over 80 years of experience in the Chinese manufacturing environment. For example, our lead engineer, Jack Chang, completed his master's degree in engineering at the University of Kentucky and has spent the past 15 years in outsourced manufacturing in China. Jack knows exactly how to identify manufacturers and suppliers to meet your standards.
This statement is good but could be improved by elaborating on who these engineers are.	This statement is stronger with its focus on Jack Chang and his experience. It helps some listeners relate to and even develop a feeling of trust for the company's engineers.

TABLE 15.3

Using Names of Audience Members

Less Effective	More Effective
It's common for small-business owners to think about manufacturing in China for years without taking any real action.	Just a few minutes ago, I was speaking to Jim here in the front row. He mentioned that he's thought about the possibilities in China for over a decade. Five years ago, he went on a local Chamber of Commerce trip to China but ended up thinking his company simply didn't have the time or money to explore this option any further. Jim's experience is common. Many small-business owners have wondered about manufacturing in China but never thought it was possible for them.
This statement is good but is not personalized. It is essentially a "faceless" comment and thus may be less persuasive.	This statement makes the point in a personalized, relatable manner. It shows the presenter is connected to the experiences of the audience.

you help your audience members feel they are getting to know these important individuals (see Table 15.2).

Use Names of Audience Members as Appropriate When you know the names of those in your audience, consider using their names from time to time to personalize your presentation (see Table 15.3).

Stay Flexible

Presentations rarely go as planned. Knowing your content perfectly will help you adapt to unexpected circumstances. Maintaining a flexible approach will help you think on your feet for unanticipated events. Consider the following ways of staying flexible.

Arrive Early Arriving early lets you notice if you have any surprises in terms of equipment, room layout, or people in attendance. If so, you may be able to make adjustments before the presentation begins. When presenting in a place you've never been before, arrive at least an hour or two early.

Focus on the Needs of Your Audience Some presentations can get off course when audience members raise questions or make comments. If you are preoccupied with your own agenda only, you can become flustered or disorganized if someone poses a question. Be ready to adapt to the immediate needs of your audience so you can quickly modify your presentation based on their requests. If you spend time anticipating possible questions, you will generally be prepared to answer them at any point in your presentation and segue back into the flow.

When You Lose Your Place, Don't Panic All presenters inevitably lose their train of thought from time to time. When this happens, you can try a few strategies. One is simply to pause until you regain your composure and your line of thinking. Within a few seconds, you will often get back on target. What seems like an eternity to you will be but a short pause to audience members. Many audience members will not even notice you lost your place. Another strategy is to repeat the last statement you made (five or six words). Doing so will help you regain your thought process.

Never Tell Your Audience Things Haven't Gone as Expected Many presenters instinctively tell the audience about problems that have disrupted the presentation (i.e., technology failures, misplaced handouts). Resist the urge to mention these mishaps. To many audience members, this sounds like excuse-making and detracts from your key messages and/or your credibility. Most audience members will never know that anything out of the ordinary happened if you simply proceed with slightly modified plans.

Always Have a Plan B If you have electronic slides to display, be prepared for a situation where the projector does not work and you need to speak without them. If you recognize factual problems in your handouts at the last moment, be prepared to present without them. Know ahead of time how you'll present under these situations.

Know What Your Key Messages Are You can often leave out parts of your presentations as necessary with little change in impact as long as you know your three or four key messages and accentuate them throughout your presentation.

Use the Room to Your Advantage

You will inevitably present in rooms of various sizes and layouts. Generally, you connect with your audiences best if you position yourself close to them and establish eye contact with them. Consider the following advice.

Position Yourself Where People Can See You Easily Walk around the room before your presentation to check the vantage points that various audience members will have. After you do this, you can generally determine where you can stand to get the most eye contact with your audience. Also, think about how you can be closest to them. If your audience members have taken all the back seats and left the front seats empty, move closer to them to reduce the spatial barrier. Or, politely ask your audience members to move forward to the front of the room.

Move Around But Avoid Distracting the Audience During presentations of more than five to ten minutes, you can keep the audience more engaged by moving around the room. This draws the focus to you and allows you to gain spatial proximity with most of your audience members at some point during your presentation. However, some movements can be distracting. For example, excessive pacing may show that you're nervous. Or, since you will likely be standing and your audience members will likely be seated, getting too close may make them feel that you are hovering over them.

Use Podiums and Tables Strategically Many rooms are set up with podiums or tables, where presenters can place notes and other materials. Standing behind a podium or table can help you project authority and add to the formality of the presentation. If you do use a podium to achieve these goals, make sure you stand upright. Avoid leaning on or gripping the podium, which indicates nervousness. Also, consider whether a podium, table, or other object placed between you and your audience creates a barrier to connection. If you stand in front of the podium or table, you can get closer to your audience physically. As a result, you may achieve a more friendly, accessible, and casual tone.

Communicate Nonverbally

Your audience members consciously and subconsciously make a variety of judgments about your credibility and your message based on your nonverbal behavior. Gary Genard, president of Public Speaking International, had this to say about nonverbal communication:

> How comfortable a speaker is in his own skin, how he stands and moves, how he looks at others in the room, his tone of voice, even the clothes he wears—together, these variables constitute a constant flow of data running underneath whatever the speaker is saying . . . leaders know how to move boldly and decisively. There is nothing tentative about their movements and gestures—instead, they literally command the space through which they move.[9]

Consider the **SOFTEN model of nonverbal communication** in your presentations: smile, open stance, forward lean, tone, eye contact, and nod. By focusing on these nonverbal behaviors, you can display confidence and strength while also showing warmth and concern.[10]

Smile Use your facial expressions to connect with your audience members and show your enthusiasm for your topic. Audience members are more likely to warm up to you when you put forth positive, can-do emotion.

Open Stance Most people consider an open stance as more warm and inviting. Excessively putting your hands on your hips, folding your arms, crossing your legs, and gripping a podium or other objects closes you off from some people and implies less warmth. Keeping your arms to your sides or gesturing with palms up is more inviting to the audience.

Forward Lean Facing your audience directly with a slight forward lean and upright posture shows confidence and interest. By contrast, leaning back, slouching, and lowering one's shoulders imply timidity and lack of confidence.

Tone Use your voice to express enthusiasm or other intended emotion. To make sure everyone in the room can hear the confidence of your message, project your voice adequately. Also, speak at a reasonable pace. Rushing your presentations is often a sign

LO15.3 Apply the SOFTEN model of nonverbal communication for presentations.

of nervousness. First impressions of self-confidence and empathy often come from a slower rate of speaking with fewer gestures.[11] On the other hand, many audience members tune out when you speak too slowly and may even think you are unprepared.

Evaluating your own voice is difficult, since the voice you hear is not what your listeners hear.[12] Consider recording your voice so you can evaluate your tone and pace. Also, ask people you trust to evaluate the tone, pace, and emotion conveyed by your voice during presentations.

Eye Contact   Maintaining eye contact with your audience is among the most important forms of nonverbal communication. It creates an immediate sense of connection when you meet audience members eye to eye. The very act of keeping eye contact forces you to think about your listeners. It helps you evaluate and adjust your presentation as you observe your audience members' reactions. Perhaps most important, eye contact facilitates trust. Many people partially judge the truthfulness of a message from eye contact.[13]

Nod   Use gestures that show affirmation and acceptance of your audience members. For example, nodding indicates that you agree or recognize the value of what others say. Gesture with your hands, arms, body, and head to achieve positive connections with your audience. Attempt to read your audience and get a sense for how much energy they have. Research shows that morning speakers should have medium energy and match most audiences' lower energy levels with a conversational tone. Afternoon and evening speakers can increase their expressiveness and energy.[14]

Remember to be natural. While you can improve your nonverbal communication to better connect with your audience, it takes time. Try out new forms of nonverbal communication incrementally. And be aware that people often misread body language. The more you pay attention to your audience's reactions, the more you will be able to identify how people respond to your nonverbal communication.[15]

Dress for Success

Business professionals are frequently advised to *dress for success,* especially for important events such as speeches and presentations. How you dress can make a big impact on how others perceive you. In a recent survey, 41 percent of employers stated that employees who dressed professionally were more likely to be promoted. This figure rises to 55 percent in certain industries, such as financial services.[16]

Most attire can be placed on a continuum from formal to casual. Common categories along this continuum are formal business, business casual, and casual. **Formal business dress,** at one end of the continuum, is intended to project executive presence and seriousness. It is distinguished by business suits, typically dark and conservative, accompanied by collared, button-down dress shirts. For men, neckties are essential.

Business casual dress is one step down in formality along the continuum. It is intended to project a more comfortable, relaxed feel while still maintaining a high standard of professionalism. Business casual dress is interpreted broadly and varies significantly by location and company. As a result, business casual can be divided into *high-level business casual* and *low-level business casual.* In Figure 15.2, you can see three levels of attire: formal business, high-level business casual, and low-level business casual. Business casual dress is probably the most common form of dress in the workplace today, with 43 percent of adults in a recent survey identifying that as their typical workplace attire.[17]

Casual dress is the least formal option. It is rare in a business-related setting.[18] While some companies have implemented casual Fridays, nearly half of executives and managers feel that employees dress too casually on these days.[19] If your company allows casual Fridays, make sure your attire continues to project a professional image.

FIGURE 15.2

Formality of Workplace Attire

Formal Business

Men
Tailored business suits
Dress shirts
Neckties
Leather shoes

Women
Tailored business suit with pants or skirt
Dress shirts
Hosiery or socks
Leather shoes

Business Casual (high-level)

Men
Suit coats, sports coats, or blazers
Button-down collar shirts
Neckties optional
Leather shoes

Women
Pantsuits and tailored separates
Closed-toe or closed-heel shoes

Business Casual (low-level)

Men
Button-down collar shirts or polo-type shirts
Khakis or chinos
Leather belts and shoes
Conservative footwear

*Women**
Dress shirt
Dress pants or skirt
Conservative footwear

*Standards for women vary more than for men.

Your attire, and the level of formality you choose, projects a range of messages (see Figure 15.3). Generally, formal business attire projects authority and competence, high-level business casual is associated with productivity and trustworthiness, and low-level business casual is associated with creativity and friendliness.[20]

For business presentations, you should generally dress up slightly more formally than your audience. Also, consider the messages you intend to send. Younger professionals may not yet have established traits such as authority and competence, whereas they are often assumed to be friendly. So, younger professionals can gain significantly by dressing more formally.

FIGURE 15.3

Messages Sent by Formality
of Workplace Attire

Source: Peter W. Cardon and
Ephraim A. Okoro, "Professional
Characteristics Communicated by
Formal versus Casual Workplace
Attire," *Business Communication
Quarterly* 72 no. 3 (2009):
355–360.

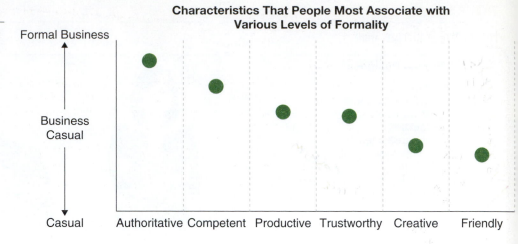

Characteristics That People Most Associate with
Various Levels of Formality

Use Visual Aids and Handouts

LO15.4 Use slides and
handouts to
supplement your
presentation
effectively.

You can powerfully supplement your presentations with visual aids and handouts. In fact, many audiences expect both. In this section, we discuss how to use these items to increase your presentation effectiveness.

Use Visuals without Losing Focus on You

In Chapter 14, we discussed the design of electronic slides. Another option for presentations is the screencast video, described in the Technology Tips feature on page 455. Regardless of the technology you use, your goal is to keep yourself as the main focus of the presentation. Even with well-designed slides or videos, however, keeping the focus on you during the presentation can be challenging. Keep in mind the following tips as you present:

Avoid Turning Out the Lights in Most Cases Many presenters turn out the lights so that the audience can more easily view the slides. This makes the slides, rather than you, the focal point for the duration of the presentation. Some audience members may also get drowsy in low light. In some rooms, you can dim the lights next to the screen, but if you do, make sure that you are in full light to your audience.

Don't Start Your Slides Right Away The opening moments of your presentation are too valuable to devote to slides. Use at least the opening one to two minutes to make a personal connection with your audience. Then begin your slides.

Speak to Your Audience, Not the Screen The single most important strategy is to face your audience. Presenters often spend too much time looking at their slides with their back or side to the audience.

Interpret, Don't Read Your Slides When you simply read your slides, you reduce yourself to nothing but a narrator. Since audience members can read your slides more quickly than you can recite what they say, the slides become the primary source of information. When you explain and elaborate on the content in your slides, you draw your audience's attention to you as the primary source of information.

Preview the Slides before Showing Them To keep the focus on you and more effectively control the timing of your message, introduce your slides before

CREATING SCREENCAST VIDEOS

Business professionals—especially executives, human resource professionals, and sales and marketing professionals—increasingly use screencast videos to reach audiences remotely. Many software packages, such as Camtasia, Adobe Captivate, and Jing, allow you to develop presentation videos that record the activity on your computer screen and combine it with video, audio, and other files. As you develop these screencast videos, keep in mind the following tips:

Plan your production and make several trial runs. A screencast video requires you to take the roles of producer, director, and actor all in one. You can choose elements to display on your screen, such as PowerPoint slides, spreadsheets, word processing documents, or other types of files. Simultaneously, you can narrate as you display the content and can even provide video of yourself. After recording, you have many tools available to edit your production.

Create short, concise videos. Most screencast videos are short. For example, most how-to videos

created by companies and posted on YouTube or their own websites last one to five minutes.

Use the right resources. You can use free screencast software and inexpensive video cameras and microphones to make screencasts; however, it's generally worth the investment to purchase state-of-the-art screencast software and the right cameras and microphones, especially if you intend to create professional-grade screencasts.

you show them. When you move to a slide without any introduction, the audience automatically focuses on the slide more than on you.

Use a Remote Control to Advance Slides When Possible
Using a remote control to move from slide to slide allows you to move around as you talk and more effectively engage with your audience. It also allows you to maintain more eye contact, since using a keyboard requires glancing down.

Avoid Standing in Front of the Slide Projection
Make sure to stand to the side of the slide projection area. Standing in front of the projection causes two problems. It makes the slide more difficult to view. But, perhaps worse, it distorts your appearance.

Use Blank Slides Strategically
If you plan to speak for lengthy periods without referencing your slides, consider displaying a blank slide so that the screen does not become a distraction.

Use Handouts Effectively

Handouts generally make sense for detailed, numerical, and other information that is difficult to project adequately onto a screen. Also, you may want audience members to complete certain handouts during or after the presentation. For example, Shannon provides a handout on which seminar participants describe a manufacturing project they want to outsource.

However, handouts can distract your audience and take attention away from you. One primary advantage of presentations is that you have high control over what message your audience members hear, especially compared to written communications. As soon as you distribute handouts, you may lose this control, since some audience members will immediately begin looking through the handouts and lose their focus on you.

If you can, wait until the end of your presentation to distribute handouts. This allows you to maintain more control over the message. If you need to use handouts during the presentation, consider how you might distribute them without losing control, especially during the opening one to two minutes of your presentation. Recall that audience members form many of their deepest impressions during this initial part of your presentation. Many presenters have lost the opportunity to connect effectively during their openings because of rustling handouts.

Interact with Your Audience

LO15.5 Interact effectively with your audience.

Good speakers involve the audience as much as possible without getting off message and taking too much time. A few ways to interact with your audience include fielding questions during the presentation as well as mingling and following up with audience members afterward.

Field Questions

Many of your presentations will involve a question-and-answer (Q&A) portion. You may ask for questions at the conclusion of your presentation or invite questions throughout. When you take questions, you show you are interested in your listeners' real concerns and needs. You also have an opportunity to clarify points you may have misstated or omitted. Of course, fielding questions involves a number of risks: Your audience members may ask you difficult ones and may even get you off topic. The solution is to reinforce your key messages while also addressing the needs of your questioners. Practice the following strategies to make the Q&A go as smoothly and effectively as possible:[21]

Pause before Answering   This gives you time to reflect and quickly develop the best response. It also gives the impression that you are thoughtful. In some cases, you may feel under pressure during questioning. Pausing helps you stay calm and collected.

Be Honest   During questioning, many presenters are so committed to supporting their own positions that they respond with exaggeration or with excessive confidence. This is a mistake. Admit when you do not know the answer. Explain that you would like to get an answer to the question and seek an opportunity to continue the conversation later on. Notice in Table 15.4 how Shannon responds when she doesn't have a firm answer to a question.

Show Appreciation   Fielding questions allows you to develop an emotional bond with the questioner. You can do so by sincerely showing thanks, recognizing the importance of the question, and otherwise validating the questioner, as Shannon does in the more-effective example in Table 15.5.

TABLE 15.4

Responding Honestly to a Question

Less Effective	More Effective
Q. *Recently, the Chinese yuan has been strengthening against the dollar. Won't that mean smaller savings for your clients in the future?*	
A. The exchange rates move around from time to time. I don't follow this much, but I do know that sometimes it's actually in your favor. You really don't have to worry about this much because the changes are relatively small and pretty much even out over time.	**A.** I'm not exactly sure how much the exchange rates have impacted savings for our clients in recent months. I know that we expect the Chinese yuan to continue strengthening, and this will definitely impact how much you can save. I can get a good answer to you within a few days. I'll talk to one of our finance specialists and several of our clients. If you'll be available, I can give you a call then.
Shannon's response glosses over the fact that she is not informed enough to give an accurate answer. Although she attempts to put a positive spin on the issue, she may appear to dismiss some listeners' genuine concerns.	Shannon states that she is uncertain. However, she demonstrates a willingness to get the answer from reliable sources and promises to provide that information within a few days. Overall, she gains credibility with her upfront, helpful response.

TABLE 15.5

Showing Appreciation

Less Effective	More Effective
Q. *Do we work completely through sales reps here in the U.S., or do we get to talk directly with your contract specialists and engineers in China? Do we get to talk directly with the manufacturers you work with?*	
A. We try to arrange for you to talk with anyone involved with your contract by . . .	**A.** That's a good question. Most business owners are quite concerned about communicating directly with those who are responsible for manufacturing their products. We facilitate this direct and timely communication by . . .
This is a good, rational response but could be improved with additional validation of the questioner.	By briefly validating the importance of the question, Shannon demonstrates that she relates directly with this concern and that Sinosourcing is committed to facilitating this communication. The response is strong on both the rational and the emotional levels.

Be Concise   Short responses are effective for several reasons. First, the question may be of interest to just one or a few of your audience members. Second, the longer your response, the more likely you are to stray from your key messages or excessively repeat them. As a rule of thumb, keep most responses to between 20 and 45 seconds. Pay close attention to your audience members during Q&A to see if they are remaining interested and engaged. Notice Table 15.6 to compare Shannon's less- and more-concise responses.

Reframe the Question to Match Your Agenda   You should have fairly clear objectives for your presentation. When your listeners ask questions that could derail your agenda, find ways to tactfully reframe the conversation in favor of your objectives, as Shannon does in the examples in Table 15.7.

Mingle and Follow Up

When you complete your presentation, your work is not complete. In most cases, this is a good opportunity to work the room, further connecting with your audience. You can get additional feedback and discuss future endeavors with your listeners.

TABLE 15.6

Being Concise

Less Effective	More Effective
Q. *Can you give me another example of a small business that's saved more than 50 percent on manufacturing?*	
A. Sure. I could give you dozens of examples. Let me tell you about one of our client companies that manufactures souvenir items . . . (continues on for three to four minutes largely repeating the same key points).	**A.** On our website, we present case studies. You can read about 15 of our client companies and find detailed information about their performance in terms of savings, time to market, and quality control. With so many cases, you can easily find a company that manufactures a product similar to yours and get a good point of reference for your set of challenges.
By providing such a lengthy answer, Shannon may inadvertently lose audience members who have already gotten her key points.	In this brief response (20 to 30 seconds), Shannon provides new information (a section on the website with case studies) and touches on but does not belabor key takeaway points. This response has broad appeal, since it offers audience members a resource where they may locate companies facing challenges similar to their own.

TABLE 15.7

Reframing a Question to Match Your Agenda

Less Effective	More Effective
Q. *I'm quite skeptical that our company could save as much as you're suggesting. Can you really guarantee that we'll save at least 40 percent on manufacturing?*	
A. Well, actually, we can't guarantee how much you'll save. But, I can tell you that the average savings for our clients is between 40 and 60 percent.	**A.** The average savings for our clients is between 40 and 60 percent. Sometimes it's slightly less, and sometimes it's slightly more. The great part about our system is we get bids from reliable suppliers, and then *you* can determine what the savings will be. We guarantee enforcement of any contract you enter. In other words, you can receive bids without cost or commitment and estimate your own savings. If the savings are attractive by your estimation, then you can choose to move forward.
This question challenges the basic premise that Sinosourcing can help a company manage risk in decision making. It may raise doubts throughout the audience. While the response is true, it fails to reframe the question to explain how Sinosourcing *can* help companies manage risk.	This response reframes the conversation by emphasizing how Sinosourcing helps clients manage risk and take control in the decision-making process.

Similarly, in the days following the event, you can reach out to your audience members. Follow up on any promises you made about providing additional information. If possible, send a quick email note to thank people for attending. Set in motion steps that turn a onetime presentation into an ongoing professional relationship.

Be a Supportive Audience Member

You will likely be an audience member more often than you are a presenter. Take this role seriously. Do all you can to support the presenter. Show interest by maintaining eye contact and sitting up straight. Avoid behaviors that may distract the presenter, such as glancing at your mobile phone or yawning. Make comments and ask questions

COMMUNICATION Q&A

CONVERSATIONS WITH CURRENT BUSINESS PROFESSIONALS

Pete Cardon: Do presentations generally go as expected?

James Robertson: You can have many things working against you when presenting. Everything from the audiovisual equipment not behaving to the slide deck not working as expected, and then there's the dynamics of the audience. Many technical problems can be corrected by spending a few minutes beforehand making sure everything works, but always be aware of the presenting "gremlins," and always have a plan if something does trip you up. The key to overcoming these problems is to know the subject, know the audience, and practice the presentation so that even if the technology fails, you still deliver on message.

The hardest thing to plan for is the human factor: *How will the audience react to your message? Will they agree or disagree with your point of view?* and *Will they speak up or keep quiet during Q&A?* Be prepared by thinking about some of the questions you'd ask if you were looking at the information presented. Anticipating and planning the answers will help you get all the way to closure.

PC: What are some of the keys to connecting with your audience?

JR: I've found that you need to set the stage with a scenario or situation that's applicable to the subject you're discussing. Linking this topic back to your message provides a powerful opening and grabs the audience attention from the start. This can be as simple as opening with something you've read in a magazine or a newspaper or something you've seen on TV or a life experience you've had. The key is to make sure you bridge between the experience you're opening with and the topic you're presenting on.

During the presentation, always talk to the audience and not to the slides. Practice makes perfect.

At the end of the presentation, leave them with a closing that reinforces the message. Again, it can be an experience or just a good summary of what you discussed, but with a punch that they remember. I try and leave my audience with no more than three points they can take away with them, but those three points should encapsulate the essence of the message.

PC: For young professionals, what concluding advice would you give about developing skills to give great presentations?

JR: Much of real success in business is being able to "tell your story" well. Whether presenting a project to gain financial funding or rolling out goals to staff, it's critical that you are confident and persuasive. People will follow a leader they believe in, so it's important to cultivate your credibility. Being able to connect to any audience is a critical skill, so look for any opportunity to present and hone your presentation skills. It will become one of your most important skill sets.

James Robertson *is vice president of Global Data Networks and Information Technology Security at Turner Broadcasting. He has worked at Turner Broadcasting for 15 years and runs a global operations team of over 200 IT professionals.*

that help the presenter stay on message. Publicly express appreciation for the merits of the presentation. Privately offer advice for making the presentation more useful.

Being a supportive audience member has many advantages. In most cases, you share professional interests with the presenter. As a result, the success of the presentation is a team effort. Furthermore, your reputation for being a supportive audience member may be reciprocated when you take the role of presenter. For further insights on delivering presentations, read the Communication Q&A with James Robertson.

Chapter Takeaway for *Delivering Presentations*

LO 15.1. Describe how presentation delivery impacts your credibility. (pp. 445–446)

Delivering presentations demonstrates **your personal credibility.**

It shows **competence** when you know and provide valuable content.	It shows **caring** when you are responsive to the expectations of your audience.	It shows **character** when you display complete openness and honesty.

LO 15.2. Deliver presentations with authenticity, confidence, and influence. (pp. 446–451)

Principles for Establishing Presence

• Establish credibility.	• Focus on people.	• Use the room to your advantage.
• Maintain authenticity.	• Start and finish strong.	• Communicate nonverbally.
• Know your material.	• Stay flexible.	• Dress for success.
• Speak with confidence.		

Principles for Focusing on People

• Make people the subject of your sentences.	• Use names of audience members.
• Introduce colleagues by name.	

See *examples of focusing on people* in Tables 15.1, 15.2, and 15.3.

Principles for Staying Flexible

• Arrive early.	• When you lose your place, don't panic.	• Always have a plan B.
• Focus on the needs of the audience.	• Never tell your audience things haven't gone as expected.	• Know what your key messages are.

LO 15.3. Apply the SOFTEN model of nonverbal communication for presentations. (pp. 451–454)

Principles of the SOFTEN Model

• *S*mile	• *F*orward lean	• *E*ye contact
• *O*pen stance	• *T*one	• *N*od

LO 15.4. Use slides and handouts to supplement your presentation effectively. (pp. 454–456)

Principles for Using Slides

• Avoid turning out the lights in most cases.	• Interpret, don't read your slides.	• Avoid standing in front of the slide projection.
• Don't start the slides right away.	• Preview the slides before showing them.	• Use blank slides strategically.
• Speak to your audience, not the screen.	• Use remotes to advance slides.	

LO 15.5. Interact effectively with your audience. (pp. 456–459)

Principles for Fielding Questions

• Pause before answering.	• Show appreciation.	• Reframe the question to match your agenda.
• Be honest.	• Be concise.	

See *examples of fielding questions* in Tables 15.4, 15.5, 15.6, and 15.7.

Key Terms

business casual dress (p. 452)

casual dress (p. 452)

formal business dress (p. 452)

SOFTEN model of nonverbal
communication (p. 451)

Discussion Exercises

15.1 Chapter Review Questions (LO 15.1, LO 15.2, LO 15.3, LO 15.4, LO 15.5)

For each of the following items, respond with one or two paragraphs.

A. Discuss how you can establish and build credibility before, during, and after your presentations.

B. Describe the importance of authenticity for presentations. Discuss how you can plan and rehearse for presentations and also maintain authenticity.

C. Discuss some strategies for overcoming nervousness and fear before and during presentations. Describe the three strategies you believe are most effective for you.

D. Describe strategies for making people the focus of your presentations.

E. Explain the SOFTEN model of nonverbal communication.

F. Describe strategies for using slides and handouts without distracting the audience from what you have to say.

G. Describe strategies for effectively fielding questions during or after your presentation.

15.2 Communication Q&A Discussion Questions (LO 15.1, LO 15.2, LO 15.4, LO 15.5)

Read the comments from James Robertson. Respond to the following questions:

A. What is Robertson's advice for when things go awry with technology?

B. What tips does he give for connecting with your audience?

C. What does he say is the hardest thing to prepare for and why?

D. What does he explain about how to start and end a presentation?

Evaluation Exercises

15.3 Evaluating an Effective Presentation (LO 15.2, LO 15.3, LO 15.4)

Think about a recent presentation you attended that you found effective. In three to five paragraphs, describe why it was effective. Include the following aspects in your analysis, referring to Chapter 14 if necessary for a refresher on preview-view-review:

A. Description of the presentation.

B. Key points.

C. Preview.

D. View.

E. Review.

F. Electronic slides or other visual aids.

G. Nonverbal behavior.

15.4 Evaluating a Corporate Presentation (LO 15.2, LO 15.3, LO 15.4)

Go online and find a business presentation that interests you. You can generally find presentations easily on company websites (usually in the Media, Newsroom, or Investors sections), YouTube, or business websites (e.g., CNBC). Evaluate the presentation and include the following in your analysis, referring to Chapter 14 if necessary for a refresher on preview-view-review:

A. Description of the presentation.

B. Key points.

C. Preview.

D. View.

E. Review.

F. Electronic slides or other visual aids.

G. Nonverbal behavior.

15.5 Assessing One of Your Recent Presentations (LO 15.1, LO 15.2, LO 15.3, LO 15.4, LO 15.5)

Think about a presentation you delivered recently. In three to five paragraphs, address the following issues, referring to Chapter 14 if necessary for a refresher on preview-view-review:

A. Description of the presentation.

B. Key points.

C. Preview.

D. View.

E. Review.

F. Electronic slides or other visual aids.

G. Nonverbal behavior.

H. Three improvements you would make if you did the presentation again.

15.6 Video Recording Your Presentation (LO 15.1, LO 15.2, LO 15.3, LO 15.4, LO 15.5)

Record one of your presentations and then do the following:

A. Immediately following your presentation, draft your basic impressions of your performance.

B. Watch the video recording three times as follows:

- On the first viewing, observe the overall impact of your presentation.
- On the second viewing, turn the volume off and observe your nonverbal behaviors.
- On the third viewing, close your eyes and listen. Pay attention to the speed, volume, pitch, variety, and enthusiasm in your voice.

After completing steps A and B above, answer the following questions about your presentation:

A. How effective was your opening?

B. How effective was your nonverbal communication (e.g., voice quality, eye contact with audience)?

C. How effective was the content of your presentation (e.g., relevance to audience, logical order, impact)?

D. How persuasive was your presentation?

E. How well did you connect with your audience?

F. Overall, name two major strengths and two major weaknesses of your oral presentation.

G. If you were going to deliver this same presentation again, what three adjustments would you make?

H. What are the two presentation skills you believe you most need to improve? Explain.

Application Exercises

For exercises 15.7 through 15.10, prepare five- to ten-minute presentations. Make sure you first identify your key messages and analyze your audience based on information in the textbook. Create a clear and compelling preview, view, and review (see Chapter 14). If directed by your instructor, create electronic slide presentations.

15.7 Presentation to the Board about Changing Direction at Better Horizons Credit Union (LO 15.1, LO 15.2, LO 15.3, LO 15.4, LO 15.5)

Assume the role of Christine Russo (see Chapter 9). Based on the information in Chapter 9, create a presentation to the board about building marketing strategies and product offerings for younger members. You could base a large part of the presentation on Figure 9.4.

15.8 Presentation to College Students about Joining Better Horizons Credit Union (LO 15.1, LO 15.2, LO 15.3, LO 15.4, LO 15.5)

Assume the role of Haniz Zogby (see Chapter 9). Based on the information in Chapter 9, create a presentation to university students

to persuade them to join Better Horizons Credit Union. You could base part of the presentation on Figure 9.6.

15.9 Presentation Asking for Participation in the Hope Walkathon (LO 15.1, LO 15.2, LO 15.3, LO 15.4, LO 15.5)

Assume the role of Haniz Zogby (see Chapter 9). Based on the information in Chapter 9, create a presentation to encourage credit union members to participate in the Hope Walkathon. You could base part of the presentation on Figure 9.8.

15.10 Presentation about Changes at Marble Home Makeovers (LO 15.1, LO 15.2, LO 15.3, LO 15.4, LO 15.5)

Assume the role of Juan Hernandez (see Chapter 10). Based on the information in Chapter 10, create a presentation to employees about temporary changes in work shifts. You could base the presentation on Figure 10.4.

Endnotes

1. Barbara De Angelis, "Communicating with Authenticity," *Toastmaster* online (June 2007), available at www.toastmasters.org/ToastmastersMagazine/ToastmasterArchive/2007/June/Authenticity.aspx.

2. Found in Nick Morgan, "How to Put Together a Great Speech When You're Under the Gun," *Harvard Management Communication Letter* (September 2003): 3. He was citing Phillip Khan-Pami, *Blank Page to First Draft in 15 Minutes: The Most Effective Shortcut to Preparing a Speech or Presentation* (Miami, FL: How To Books, 2002).

3. http://www.time.com/time/magazine/article/0,9171,994670-1,00.html.

4. Geoffrey Brewer, "Snakes Top List of Americans' Fears: Public Speaking, Heights and Being Closed in Small Spaces Also Create Fear in Many Americans," (March 19, 2001), retrieved August 22, 2010,

from *Gallup* online: http://www.gallup.com/poll/1891/Snakes-Top-List-Americans-Fears.aspx.

5. Karen L. Twichell, "Stage Fright—Why Now?" *Toastmaster* online (January 2010), available at www.toastmasters.org/ToastmastersMagazine/ToastmasterArchive/2010/January/Stage-Fright.aspx.

6. Thomas Leech, *How to Prepare, Stage, and Deliver Winning Presentations,* 3rd ed. (New York: American Management Association, 2004).

7. Twichell, "Stage Fright—Why Now?"; Judi Bailey, "Beauty and the Beast: Changing Your Fear from Fiend to Friend," *Toastmaster* online (December 2007), available at www.toastmasters.org/ToastmastersMagazine/ToastmasterArchive/2007/December/BeautyandtheBeast.aspx; Gabrielle B. Dahms, "Good Posture = Good

Breathing," *Toastmaster* online (June 2008), available at www
.toastmasters.org/ToastmastersMagazine/ToastmasterArchive/2008/
June/Departments/HowToPDF.aspx; Harry Mills, *Power Points! How
to Design and Deliver Presentations That Sizzle and Sell* (New York:
AMACOM, 2007).

8.   Kevin Johnson and Tennille-Lynn Millo, "Put Your Audience in
Your Speech," *Toastmaster* online (August 2007), available at www
.toastmasters.org/ToastmastersMagazine/ToastmasterArchive/2007/
August/Audience.aspx.

9.   Gary Genard, "Leveraging the Power of Nonverbal Communication,"
Harvard Business Management Communication Letter (2004): 3–4.

10.   Mills, *Power Points! How to Design and Deliver Presentations
That Sizzle and Sell.*

11.   Dave Zielinski, "Body Language Myths," *Toastmaster*
online (September 2007), available at www.toastmasters.org/
ToastmastersMagazine/ToastmasterArchive/2007/September/Myths.aspx.

12.   Nancy Sebastion Meyer, "That's Not My Voice—Is It?" *Toast-
master* online (February 2009), available at www.toastmasters.org/
ToastmastersMagazine/ToastmasterArchive/2009/February/
Departments/Manner-of-Speaking.aspx.

13.   Mike Landrum, "Speaking Eye to Eye: A Meeting of the Eyes
Denotes a Meeting of the Minds," *Toastmaster* online (December
2009), available at www.toastmasters.org/ToastmastersMagazine/
ToastmasterArchive/2009/December/Articles/Speaking-Eye-to-Eye.aspx.

14.   Zielinski, "Body Language Myths."

15.   Ibid.

16.   R. Haefner, "How to Dress for Success for Work," retrieved
January 27, 2009, from www.cnn.com/2008/LIVING/worklife/07/30/
cb.dress.for.success/index.html (July 30, 2008).

17.   Joseph Carroll, "Business Casual Most Common Work Attire,"
Gallup Poll (October 4, 2007).

18.   Thomas Kiddie, "Recent Trends in Business Casual Attire and
Their Effects on Student Job Seekers," *Business Communication Quar-
terly* (September 2009): 350–354; Beverly Langford, *The Etiquette
Edge: The Unspoken Rules for Business Success* (New York: American
Management Association, 2005).

19.   Accountemps, "Survey Shows Relaxed Attire May Be Too Relaxed at Many Firms," May 25, 2000, http://www.accountemps.com/
PressRoom?id=151 (accessed January 10, 2010).

20.   Based on studies from the following sources: Peter W. Cardon
and Ephraim A. Okoro, "Professional Characteristics Communicated
by Formal versus Casual Workplace Attire," *Business Communication
Quarterly* 72, no. 3 (2009): 355–360; J. V. Peluchette and K. Karl,
"The Impact of Workplace Attire on Employee Self-Perceptions,"
Human Resource Development Quarterly 18, no. 3 (2007): 345–360;
J. V. Peluchette and K. Karl, "Dressing to Impress: Beliefs and Attitudes
regarding Workplace Attire," *Journal of Business and Psychology* 21,
no. 1 (2006): 45–63.

21.   Granville N. Toogood, *The New Articulate Executive: Look, Act,
and Sound Like a Leader* (New York: McGraw-Hill, 2010).

CHAPTER SIXTEEN

Employment Communications

Learning Objectives

After studying this chapter, you should be able to do the following:

LO16.1   Identify your key selling points for the job application process.

LO16.2   Evaluate the primary needs of employers for positions of interest.

LO16.3   Set up the message structure for résumés and cover letters.

LO16.4   Highlight your qualifications with effective tone, style, and design.

LO16.5   Create chronological and functional résumés to highlight your key selling points.

LO16.6   Develop a list of references that will improve your employment prospects.

LO16.7   Compose effective cover letters that highlight your key selling points.

LO16.8   Review your job application documents for effectiveness and fairness.

LO16.9   Develop strategies for responding to common job interview questions.

LO16.10   Explain etiquette for following up after job interviews.

LO16.11   Explain etiquette for leaving an organization with grace and foresight.

Searching for jobs can be exhilarating. It involves hopes for new beginnings and possibilities! Many job applicants also find the process stressful, intimidating, and scary. In recent years due to the recession, one reality is that the number of applicants exceeds the number of positions. However, with determination, patience, and planning, you can land a job that will help you move forward in your career. In this chapter, you will focus on developing a job application package that allows you to identify and highlight your key selling points in a way that meets the needs of employers. Quickly read the following case that is the basis for examples you will see throughout the chapter.

Chapter Case: Haniz Applies for Jobs

Who's Involved

Haniz Zogby
Marketing specialist and loan officer at Better Horizons Credit Union
Florida State University, Class of 2013
Major: Finance; *Minor:* Event Management

The Situation

Haniz Zogby will graduate soon. She has worked for Better Horizons Credit Union for five years and feels a high level of job security. At Better Horizons, she has been given many opportunities to assist and, in some cases, direct promotional campaigns. However, she typically spends less than half of her time involved in marketing. Haniz wants a job where she has more responsibility, spends more of her time on innovative marketing campaigns, and makes more money.

Task 1
Haniz wants to write a résumé that effectively portrays her selling points.

Task 2
Haniz wants to write cover letters that introduce her to employers and explain her value to them.

Task 3
Haniz wants to interview effectively and show she's ready for the job.

Applying the AIM Planning Process to Résumés and Cover Letters

Preparing for the job application process is similar to preparing for other forms of business communication: It involves analyzing your audience (meeting the needs of your employers), developing your ideas (identifying your key selling points), and setting up the message structure. Your end products—cover letters and résumés—are persuasive messages that show how you meet the needs of your prospective employers.

Identify Your Key Selling Points

To create résumés and cover letters that serve your long-term career interests, your first step should be to carefully evaluate your career ambitions and qualifications. In this process, you clarify your professional goals for the short term (one to two years) and long term (five to ten years), identify the skills you have developed at school and work, and sort out the attributes that define who you are as a professional. As with other business communications, you attempt to identify your most important and strongest features so you can develop a concise and compelling message about the value you will bring to your prospective employers.

To help you identify your interests, abilities, and attributes, you might consider completing a self-inventory (see Figure 16.1 with an example of Haniz's self-inventory). Start by writing your career goals. Even if you don't yet have clear ones in mind, do your best to imagine the type of work you would like to be doing in five and ten years. Allow yourself enough time to do some soul-searching and research about careers as you develop your goals.

Identifying your career goals helps you accomplish several things in the job search process. First, it helps you frame your résumé and cover letter to project your career hopes. Second, it helps you evaluate how well your abilities and attributes prepare you for your desired career. This process allows you to address those areas where you most need improvement. Finally, it shows employers that you are serious, as well-defined career goals imply seriousness in your approach to work.

Once you have written down your career goals, identify your abilities and attributes.[1] **Abilities** are skills and knowledge that can be applied to accomplishing work tasks. **Attributes** are personal traits or characteristics. In the job application process, employers are often looking for more than your abilities. They're trying to figure out the kind of person you are. These judgments often come in the form of adjectives, such as *reliable, analytical,* or *people-oriented.* These attributes are difficult to measure precisely, but they indicate how well you'll fit into the company culture, how much effort and commitment you'll put into your work, and how you'll impact the work of others.

FIGURE 16.1

Self-Inventory of Career Interests and Job-Related Abilities and Attributes

Haniz Zogby
April 1, 2013

My Career Goals
1. To act in a leadership role to develop and market financial services for credit unions
2. In five to ten years, to hold an influential marketing position within a credit union group

My Strongest Professional Abilities
1. Developing strong professional relationships with clients and vendors
2. Attracting new members to credit unions through referrals, seminars, mailings, and online social networking
3. Organizing members to participate in credit-union-sponsored financial workshops and community events

My Strongest Professional Attributes
1. Trusted and reliable on important campaigns
2. Innovative and creative in approach to marketing and promotions
3. Passionate about the credit union industry

Areas Where I Need to Improve
1. Conducting customer surveys, statistical analysis, and survey reporting
2. Earning a reputation for excellence outside of my local community

TABLE 16.1

Abilities and Attributes That Establish Credibility in the Job Application Process

	Abilities (Skills and/or Knowledge)	Attributes (Enduring Approaches to Work)		
Competence (Task)	Function-specific (e.g., marketing, finance) Company/Industry Technology Analysis/Research	Achievement-oriented Ambitious Analytical Assertive Creative Can-do attitude Curious	Decisive Detail-oriented Entrepreneurial Independent Inquisitive Passionate	Problem solver Resourceful Results-oriented Seeks challenges Takes initiative Visionary
Caring (Relationships)	Communication/Interpersonal Teamwork Emotional intelligence Leadership Intercultural	Customer-oriented Diplomatic Empathetic Flexible Generous	Inspiring Loyal Motivational People-oriented Persuasive	Responsive Sensitive Supportive Team-oriented Tolerant
Character (Values)	Familiarity with corporate culture and values Dedication to the success of the company Knowledge of business ethics	Accountable Committed Constant Dedicated Dependable	Fair Hardworking Honest Open-minded Optimistic	Reliable Responsible Straightforward Trustworthy Unbiased

Employers consider your mix of attributes as they try to determine if you have the right *chemistry*—an intangible that human resource professionals say they weigh heavily in the decision to hire. Fifteen percent of HR professionals say it accounts for 75 percent or more of the decision. Nearly four in ten (39 percent) say it accounts for about 50 percent of the decision.[2]

One useful way of analyzing your *abilities* and *attributes* is in terms of credibility. To do so, consider the features of competence (ability to accomplish work tasks), caring (ability to maintain effective workplace relationships), and character (ability to uphold corporate norms and standards). Competence focuses on the technical skills to achieve work tasks. In Table 16.1, you can see examples of abilities and attributes associated with competence, caring, and character.

Understand the Needs of Your Potential Employers

When hiring you, employers are making a huge investment. They will only make this investment when you demonstrate that you meet *their* needs. You can learn how well you fit the needs of employers by conducting a thorough job search and carefully analyzing those positions that are most compatible with your abilities and attributes.

LO16.2 Evaluate the primary needs of employers for positions of interest.

Completing a Thorough Job Search Process
Looking for jobs takes a lot of time. It's not uncommon for the process—from finding a position announcement to application to offer—to take three to six months (or even longer in some industries). Your thorough search for the best potential positions at the initial stages can save you a lot of time and increase the likelihood you'll get a position that is in your long-term interests.

Use all the resources available to learn about your options and ensure that you apply for the jobs that are good fits for you. You likely have a career center located in your college or university. Spend some time talking to experts there and make a plan for exhaustively searching for jobs that match your interests and qualifications. Where possible, contact and get involved with professional organizations and visit organizational

TABLE 16.2

Most Common Sources of Professional Networking

Skills	Percentage
1. Friends/relatives	**67**
2. Colleagues	**56**
3. Supervisors or managers	26
4. Conferences, trade shows, conventions	26
5. Clients	25
6. Business meetings	24
7. Professional societies/trade associations	22
8. Job search and career websites	19
9. Professional social networking websites (e.g., LinkedIn)	19
10. Social networking websites (e.g., Facebook)	16
11. Mentors and coaches	12
12. Job fairs	8
13. Alumni associations	6
14. Professors	5

Note: Percentage of employees that use these forms of professional networking for employment.
Source: From Society for Human Resource Management, "SHRM Poll: Networking Professionally: Employee Perspective,"
January 2009. Reprinted with permission via Copyright Clearance Center.

websites to learn about options. Go to job fairs on and off campus to see what opportunities are open and to practice networking in a competitive environment.

Certainly you're aware of the many job websites to search for positions (e.g., monster .com, careerbuilder.com). Your college or university may even recommend particular websites. Use all the available online options, but also make sure you are networking in the traditional sense as well—talking to friends, relatives, and colleagues. Even in the Social Age, the most common forms of networking for employment opportunities remain people you know well (see Table 16.2).[3]

Analyze the Needs of Potential Employers   One of the best ways to understand an employer's needs is to carefully read and analyze the job position announcement. Then, group the requests in the announcement in terms of abilities and attributes (for an example, see Figure 16.2, where Haniz did this for a job announcement). Once you've done this, you're in a good position to decide whether you match these criteria and, if so, to frame your résumé and cover letter to highlight these abilities and attributes.

In addition to analyzing the job position announcements, consider other strategies to gain insight about what the company is seeking. Some job announcements include contact information for a company representative. You might call this person, express your interest, and find out more. By doing this, you connect with an influential company representative and gain insight not provided in the job announcement.

Also, learn all you can about the company. Spend time researching its strategic goals. Find out about its unique challenges, and think about how you might fit into the company's plans to face these challenges.

FIGURE 16.2

Analyzing a Job Posting for Key Needs

Job Summary	**Credit Union Field Marketing Specialist**
Location 84341 **Job Type** Full Time **Reference Code** 831481809	**Organization:** Anchor Federal Credit Union Network **Education Required:** College Degree **Experience Required:** 1–3 Years **Position Description:** Works with managers throughout the Anchor Federal Credit Union network to develop local marketing events to promote Credit Union membership. Coordinates all activities for each event, including supply distribution, prizes, and duration of campaign, budget, marketing support, and staffing. Responsible for tracking results and providing recommendations for future events. Also is responsible for collecting and maintaining data related to market conditions of each proposed site. Performs various other marketing and support functions when not traveling including general promotional development, membership surveys, collateral production and tracking, retiree package mailings, and other projects as assigned by the VP of Marketing. **Position Requirements:** Develops individual marketing activities to support branch growth and/or agency events. Travels to various locations throughout the country to organize events. Analyzes market conditions to ensure that the marketing activity is in line with the demographics of that particular region. Provides annual profile of demographics for each region. Oversees budget for each activity. Is responsible for reporting variances on a monthly basis. Works with outside vendors to solicit participation in marketing activities. Actively promotes the participation of both staff and monetary contributions from these outside sources. Works with VP and AVPs of branches to set priorities and establish goals for each event. Tracks results of each event and analyzes the success/shortfall of each. Distributes reports for review. Tracks marketing collateral inventory for branches and DMs. Ensures timely distribution and proper inventory controls. Develops mailings for account generation and retention. Develops ongoing mail programs to DMs and BCO managers for relationship development throughout the agency side of the business. Makes routine phone calls to HR managers, DMs, and BCO managers to establish event schedules, coordinate Financial Finesse seminars, and maintain relationships throughout the organization. Performs other duties as assigned. **Position Attributes:** *Candidate must be able to travel 25–30% domestically. *A minimum of 2 years of field marketing and sales experience. *Candidate must have presentation skills and experience.

Abilities wanted

Marketing: local marketing events, market analysis, marketing reports (written and oral), sales letters and other mailings to generate membership, seminars.
Relationship management: work with branch managers to organize local events and set marketing strategies; staffing for events; maintain intra-organizational relationships and relationships with outside vendors.
Communication: distribute event schedules, disseminate marketing reports, encourage participation, make sales presentations.

Attributes wanted

Ambitious: must be able to take initiative on organizing many events and meet deadlines.
Creative: must develop attractive and compelling marketing events and campaigns.
Organized: must be able to manage many simultaneous projects, events, and relationships.

LO16.3 Set up the message structure for résumés and cover letters.

Set Up the Message Structure for Résumés and Cover Letters

Your résumé should tell a story of the value you can provide to a company. Like other persuasive messages, it is stronger if you have a central sales theme. By choosing two or three abilities and attributes to highlight, you can craft a compelling document that shows how you meet the needs of employers.

A mistake that many job applicants make is trying to display everything they do well. This approach often ends up sending a scattered message and diluting a central sales theme about your key abilities and attributes.

Generally, employers prefer single-page résumés, although it is increasingly acceptable to create two-page résumés.[4] As a university student, however, aim for a single page. If you find yourself using more than one page, you are likely weakening the message about your key selling points. Condensing all your experience may be painful, but keep in mind that executives are more than three times as likely to complain about résumés that contain too much information than they are about résumés that contain too little.[5] Typically, résumés contain the following major sections: name block, career summary or objective, education, and experience.

Name Block   Most résumés begin with your name and contact information. This section allows recruiters to easily find your contact information (i.e., address, phone, email). This section should not contain any distracting information, such as an unprofessional email address.

Career Summary or Objective (Optional)   The second component expresses your career goals or your interest in a specific position or line of work. It is typically no more than one sentence long. Increasingly, objective statements are considered optional. Some hiring managers believe they are becoming obsolete.

In place of objective statements, many job seekers now provide short profiles. These profiles, often called *career summary* or *summary of qualifications,* present your qualifications in 100 words or less. Career summaries are inherently focused on the needs of others (employers), whereas objective statements tend to focus on the needs of self (the job seeker). You can see an example of a summary of qualifications in Figure 16.6 on page 480.

Education   This section summarizes your experiences in higher education and professional training. Most university students place the education section before the work experience section, since it generally highlights studies in a discipline directly related to the jobs they are seeking.

Consider providing some information that distinguishes or explains the uniqueness and value of your education. For example, a short list of related coursework helps employers understand the content of your program. You might also include class projects, practicum, service learning projects, or other educational experiences that highlight your key abilities and attributes.

Include your GPA if it is high (3.5 or higher) or required. Also, if you have achieved any academic credentials or awards, mention them. For example, being on the dean's list or graduating summa cum laude are well-recognized honors. If you received scholarships or other academic awards that employers may not recognize, include a short note that explains why the awards are significant.

Generally, do not include information about your high school education. Employers are not interested. However, during your high school years, you may have been involved in work or other relevant activities that emphasize your key abilities and attributes. This type of information may be appropriate for the work experience or "additional information" sections of your résumé.

Work Experience   In this section, also called *employment history or experience,* list your accomplishments and responsibilities from prior jobs in chronological order beginning with your current or most recent one.

Some students wonder if they should include unpaid internships in this section. Typically, you should, since they are relevant and legitimate professional experiences. In fact, the abilities and attributes students gain from internships are often more relevant and transferable to sought-after positions than those from their previous paid positions.

If you have little or no work experience, you shouldn't panic. You can highlight your abilities and attributes by listing achievements and experiences in school and community activities. In the online resources, you can find several sample résumés of individuals who do not have much work experience. Of course, you should make a priority of establishing a job history right away to bolster your credibility in the eyes of potential employers.

Additional Information   Education and work experience often account for the majority of your résumé content. You can provide a variety of other information, however, to accentuate your key abilities and attributes. In fact, some of the additional information may be critical to showing who you are as a person—your attributes. You have a great deal of flexibility with other information you display. You might consider including some of the following sections:

- Technology Skills
- Professional Associations
- School Clubs
- Honors and Awards
- Certifications and Licensure
- Community Activities
- Volunteer Work
- Training
- Language Abilities

As you think about additional information to provide, the standard is simple: *Does providing this information carry on a narrative of your key abilities and attributes?* Keep in mind that many employers are particularly looking for job candidates with strong technology and interpersonal skills.[6] You can highlight these skills when you showcase your community and volunteer work, professional and student affiliations, and computer skills. Do not include such personal information as marital status, age, religion, or sexual orientation, as none of this is relevant.

Getting the Tone, Style, and Design Right for Résumés and Cover Letters

Once you've analyzed your key abilities and attributes and gathered information to place in your résumé, you're ready to present the information in a compelling manner. The tone, style, and design must be perfect. Employers often skim your résumé on the first pass. Unless you can present your main credentials within 15 to 30 seconds, you may be eliminated from the job pool. Even if potential employers reward your well-designed résumé with a second look, they are unlikely to spend a lot of time. In one survey of hiring managers, 24 percent said they spent less than two minutes reviewing a résumé, 32 percent spent three to five minutes, 23 percent spent six to ten minutes, and just 16 percent spent more than ten minutes.[7]

This section is about developing your résumé so that you can make the most of the small window you have with potential employers. What can you do to show your distinctive combination of abilities and attributes? What can you do to make your experience stand out? What can you do to persuade prospective employers that you will be a good investment for them? In short, how can you make sure that potential employers rapidly understand your story: the unique abilities and attributes that will deliver value to them?

Emphasize Accomplishments with Action Verbs

As you describe your accomplishments and experiences, begin your statements with action verbs (see Table 16.3 for a list). By doing so, you highlight your abilities and attributes in a way that emphasizes action and results.

LO16.4 Highlight your qualifications with effective tone, style, and design.

Principles of Effective Résumés

- Emphasize accomplishments with action verbs.
- Quantify accomplishments where possible.
- Position your most important contributions first.
- Group and label information to increase ease of reading.
- Remove irrelevant details.
- Avoid buzzwords and jargon.
- Be exact and avoid any errors.
- Group and label information to improve ease of reading.
- Format to distinguish pieces of information.
- Select a simple yet visually appealing layout.

TABLE 16.3

Action Verbs for Résumés

**Management/
Supervision**
Assigned
Evaluated
Executed
Facilitated
Hired
Managed
Mentored
Monitored
Motivated
Organized
Oversaw
Planned
Scheduled
Screened
Selected
Strengthened
Supervised
Trained

Leadership
Authorized
Decided
Delegated
Directed
Enabled
Encouraged
Enlisted
Executed
Formed
Guided
Implemented
Influenced
Initiated
Instituted
Led
Set goals

Marketing/Sales
Accumulated
Advertised
Attained
Boosted
Broadened

Contracted
Demonstrated
Developed
Exceeded
Excelled
Gained
Generated
Improved
Increased
Launched
Marketed
Proposed
Raised
Secured
Sold

Finance/Accounting
Allotted
Appraised
Assessed
Audited
Averted
Balanced
Budgeted
Controlled
Corrected
Cut
Earned
Estimated
Evaluated
Forecasted
Interpreted
Prepared
Preserved
Projected
Reconciled
Reduced

**Teamwork/
Communication**
Coached
Collaborated
Coordinated
Described
Encouraged

Explained
Informed
Mediated
Negotiated
Persuaded
Presented
Promoted
Publicized
Reported
Specified
Summarized
Supported
Teamed with

Analysis/Research
Analyzed
Compiled
Conducted
Detected
Diagnosed
Explored
Gathered
Identified
Inspected
Interpreted
Operated
Performed
Proved
Quantified
Researched
Reviewed
Solved
Studied
Surveyed
Tested

Administration
Administered
Arranged
Edited
Installed
Maintained
Processed
Purchased
Recorded

Reorganized
Reviewed
Screened
Streamlined
Systematized
Updated

Customer Service
Assisted
Clarified
Confronted
Delivered
Greeted
Handled
Maximized
Met
Minimized
Performed
Provided
Resolved
Responded
Served
Settled
Treated
Worked with

Innovation/Creativity
Built
Completed
Conceptualized
Created
Defined
Designed
Developed
Devised
Formulated
Innovated
Invented
Modernized
Ranked
Received
Recognized
Revolutionized

Select your action words strategically. Without exaggerating, choose verbs that make your key abilities and attributes jump off the page. For example, if you want to show that you are a leader, a series of statements beginning with action verbs such as *guided, initiated,* and *led* paint a more vivid picture than the statement *I am a good leader.*

By the same token, avoid verbs that undersell your abilities and attributes. Many university students use weak verbs when describing their significant customer service and administrative experiences. Phrases such as *answered calls, entered information in the computer,* and *waited tables* do not emphasize transferable abilities and attributes.

TABLE 16.4

Using Action Words to Emphasize Accomplishments

Less Effective	More Effective
Responsible for marketing efforts for younger members.	Developed and ran marketing campaigns targeting young professionals and university students that resulted in approximately 55 new members in the past year.
Without an action word, this statement sounds unnecessarily weak and passive.	By starting with strong action words, this statement illustrates a sense of goal setting and achievement.
Answered phones.	Greeted clients and scheduled appointments in person and by phone.
Although this statement starts with an action word, it emphasizes a menial, nonskilled effort.	This action word immediately draws attention to Haniz's focus on her customer orientation and value for a business.
Kept track of tanning products.	Took inventory of all items sold in the store.
This statement emphasizes a duty without any reference to the business importance of the task.	This statement illustrates a sense of purpose in accomplishing an important business task.

Rather, they focus on menial duties and do not focus on professional outcomes. Read through some of the less-effective and more-effective statements in Table 16.4 and notice how action verbs can bolster your credibility.

Quantify Accomplishments Where Possible

Your potential employers want to know how valuable your contributions have been in your prior jobs. So, where possible, describe key contributions and how they impacted the bottom line. Often, even when you can't say for certain how much you impacted financial results, you can provide numbers that show the significance of your work. Notice the contrasts between less-effective and more-effective examples in Table 16.5 and how quantification strengthens the more-effective statements.

Position Your Most Important Contributions First

The order in which you place your accomplishments and other supporting details shows how you prioritize them. The supporting details you place first or second under

TABLE 16.5

Quantifying Accomplishments

Less Effective	More Effective
Supervised other tellers in the teller department.	Supervised six tellers—responsible for the overall direction, coordination, and evaluation of unit.
Without a quantity, potential employers might assume a rather inconsequential set of supervision duties.	With a number of tellers noted, potential employers see that the applicant has supervised a team.
In charge of effort to support local breast cancer awareness event.	Organized a group of 83 members to participate in a local breast cancer walkathon.
Without quantification and an action word to begin this statement, this phrase emphasizes responsibilities rather than accomplishments.	By quantifying the performance (recruiting 83 members), this accomplishment stands out as exceptional.

TABLE 16.6

Positioning Most Important Contributions First

Less Effective	More Effective
• Greeted clients and scheduled appointments in person and by phone • Assisted with purchasing of medical supplies and processing of client orders • Managed financial bookkeeping for the company using QuickBooks	• Managed financial bookkeeping for the company using QuickBooks • Assisted with purchasing of medical supplies and processing of client orders • Greeted clients and scheduled appointments in person and by phone
This list emphasizes customer skills and de-emphasizes financial bookkeeping skills. If the goal is to display financial abilities, then the list is not effective.	This list emphasizes financial abilities with less emphasis on purchasing and customer service.

each heading in your résumé form the deepest impressions about your abilities and attributes. Furthermore, because most potential employers skim, they may only see the first one or two supporting details for each heading. So, strategically arrange this information to highlight your best features (see Table 16.6).

Remove Irrelevant Details

Writing résumés and cover letters requires the discipline to tell a story of how your key abilities and attributes will provide value to an employer. You should generally avoid details about your personal life, especially those that some people may find objectionable or unprofessional (e.g., politics or religion). Other information—although technically OK on a résumé—should be provided only if it helps develop your narrative. Generally, avoid listing personal interests and hobbies unless this information takes up little space and accentuates your key abilities and attributes (see Table 16.7).

Avoid Clichés, Buzzwords, and Jargon

As you craft your job application, show enthusiasm for potential positions without resorting to clichés. Many clichés, such as *dream job* or *track record of success,* fail to highlight your abilities and attributes for a few reasons. First, they do not communicate

TABLE 16.7

Removing Unnecessary Details

Less Effective	More Effective
Community Activities and Accomplishments Volunteer, VITA, Columbia, SC (giving up my Saturdays in support of a good cause) Church Choir (my church choir contains professional-level talent and tours internationally) Member of the National Association of Federal Credit Unions Volunteer Gymnastics Coach, Columbia, SC Varsity Basketball Overall MVP (2005–2006), Team Captain (2005–2006)	**PROFESSIONAL ASSOCIATIONS AND COMMUNITY ACTIVITIES** **Member,** National Association of Federal Credit Unions, Arlington, VA, 2010 to present **Volunteer Tax Consultant,** Volunteer Tax Assistance Program (VITA), Columbia, SC, 2008 to present **Volunteer Coach,** Elite Gymnastics Summer Camp, Columbia, SC, 2003 to 2007 (summers)
This list contains several unnecessary pieces of information. The references to the church choir and high school sports are interesting; however, in limited space, they do little to highlight Haniz's key abilities and attributes.	This condensed list better frames the activities in a professional light and in terms of Haniz's key abilities and attributes. She retains one sports item (gymnastics coach) to show her leadership abilities and commitment to the community.

TABLE 16.8

Avoiding Clichés

Less Effective	More Effective
The Credit Union Marketing Specialist position you posted is my dream job.	My successes in attracting new credit union members would translate well into the requirements of your Credit Union Marketing Specialist position. I am eager to speak with you by phone or in person to learn more about the position and explain how I can contribute.
This statement is inherently me-centered and naïve.	This statement projects credibility and shows an interest in dialogue about the position.

your specific accomplishments. Second, many potential employers perceive these statements as showing unrealistic or naïve expectations about a job or inflated beliefs about abilities (see Table 16.8).

Be Exact and Avoid Errors

Potential employers examine your résumé with intense scrutiny. On the first pass, many discard it immediately if it contains typos or other careless errors. In one recent survey, roughly three out of four financial executives (76 percent) said they would eliminate job applicants with just one or two typos on their résumés (see Figure 16.3).[8] In other words, the standard is high, and few potential employers are forgiving. For an example of poor proofreading, see Table 16.9.

Throughout the job application process, potential employers will apply exacting attention to all of the information in your documents and interviews. Any inconsistency or questionable information may damage or disqualify your chances. Often, potential employers judge your character when they see seemingly contradictory information. So be accurate and precise in setting out dates of employment, job responsibilities and accomplishments, educational background, and all other aspects of the résumé and cover letter.

Group and Label Information to Improve Ease of Reading

When you have long lists of items, consider grouping the information to help recruiters quickly grasp your abilities (see Table 16.10). If you don't group lists of four or more items, recruiters will often skip or gloss over them. Furthermore, by grouping items on your résumé, you show your understanding of related skill sets.

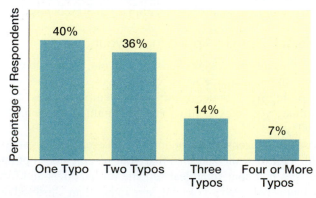

Responses from Senior Financial Executives

FIGURE 16.3

How Many Typos in a Résumé Does It Take for You to Decide Not to Consider a Job Candidate for a Position in Your Company?

Source: Accountemps, "Have a Keen Eye for Derail," July 14, 2009, http://www.accountemps .com/PressRoom?id=2491 (accessed November 20, 2010). Reprinted with permission of Robert Half International.

TABLE 16.9

Proofreading for Typos and Misspellings

Less Effective	More Effective
Increased the moral of the unit and gained incite into managing frontline employees.	Increased the morale of the unit and gained insight into managing frontline employees.
These spelling errors (moral, incite) would not be detected with spell-check software.	The spelling is correct in this case.

TABLE 16.10

Grouping and Labeling to Highlight the Employment Narrative

Less Effective	More Effective
Computer Skills: MS Word, MS Excel, MS Access, MS PowerPoint, Prezi, MS Publisher, MS Project, QuickBase, MS Outlook, QuickBooks, Powerscan Loan Display, WebEx	*Project Management/Scheduling:* QuickBase, MS Project, MS Outlook *Finance/Accounting:* QuickBooks, Powerscan Loan Display *Spreadsheets and Databases:* MS Excel, MS Access *Presentations/Publishing:* WebEx, MS PowerPoint, Prezi, MS Publisher, MS Word
Since the list contains 12 items, recruiters are unlikely to read through it. Furthermore, they are unlikely to distinguish the various types of software skills.	Once the list is grouped, recruiters can quickly (within three or four seconds) recognize the types of software skills involved.
Major coursework: ECON 2013, 2023; ACG 2021, 2071, 3171, 3331; FIN 3244, 4424, 4324, 4329, 4453; MAN 3240, 4720.	*Primary coursework:* bank administration, investments, marketing of financial services, event management.
This list of major courses provides little meaningful information and does not feed into an employment narrative.	Because these courses are grouped into three or four areas that feed into an employment narrative, potential employers understand the gist of the academic program rapidly and see its place in Haniz's set of abilities and attributes.

Format to Distinguish Pieces of Information

As you format your résumé, focus on ease of processing and consistency. Imagine recruiters who are reviewing dozens if not hundreds of résumés in a day. They are likely skimming on the first pass to see if your résumé deserves more attention. So make sure they can gather the most pertinent information quickly. By formatting your document effectively with bold, italics, spacing, and other features, you can help recruiters understand your primary abilities and attributes within 20 to 30 seconds (see Table 16.11).

Select a Simple Yet Visually Appealing Layout

The last step in the résumé process is choosing a layout. Many job candidates instinctively worry about the appearance in the early stages of résumé writing, especially when they are working from model documents or templates. Resist this natural urge and focus on planning your message first and fine-tuning its tone and style. Then, select an appealing layout.

You can choose from dozens of layout options and even design your own. Generally, seek layouts with a lot of white space so that your résumé does not appear cluttered. Also, choose designs that contain a clear scheme for headings and formatting. Make sure that the content is balanced across the page rather than clustered on one side.

TABLE 16.11

Formatting to Distinguish Key Pieces of Information

Less Effective	More Effective
Work Experience Better Horizons Credit Union, Pescaloosa, FL Marketing Specialist/Loan Officer Jan 2011 to present	**WORK EXPERIENCE** BETTER HORIZONS CREDIT UNION, Pescaloosa, FL **Marketing Specialist/Loan Officer Jan 2011 to present**
With formatting the same for company, position, and dates, this information is difficult to pick out quickly. This problem is amplified over an entire document.	With unique formatting applied to section headings (centered, capitalized, bolded), company (capitalized, left aligned), position (bolded, left aligned), and dates (bolded, right aligned), employers can pick out key pieces of information rapidly and within seconds gain a good sense of employment and education histories.

Creating Chronological and Functional Résumés

One of your first choices as you assemble your résumé is the format. The two major options are **chronological résumés,** which present the information grouped by work and education over time, and **functional résumés,** which present the information in terms of key skills. The most common and generally preferred format, especially for young professionals, is the chronological résumé. One recent survey showed that 75 percent of hiring managers preferred them, whereas 17 percent preferred functional résumés, and 8 percent had no preference.[9]

Functional résumés draw special attention to your key skills. They are most often used by professionals with extensive (more than 15 years) experience and individuals with little or no work experience. Experienced professionals use them as a way to streamline a lengthy list of jobs, many of which involved similar accomplishments and experiences. Inexperienced individuals often use them to emphasize key skills developed through a combination of school, community, volunteer, and other types of activities while de-emphasizing a lack of work experience.

Consider creating both a chronological and a functional résumé to determine which format is more effective at selling your key abilities and attributes. The process of creating both types may even give you insight about how to present your selling points. So, even if you don't think you'll use a functional résumé, writing one will likely give you ideas to improve and refine your chronological résumé (or vice versa). Notice the ineffective chronological résumé in Figure 16.4 and the effective chronological and functional examples in Figures 16.5 and 16.6.

You will also need to develop an online résumé, a professional profile, and perhaps even an online portfolio. Creating an online presence for your job search often provides you with more flexibility because you can use keywords, hyperlinks, and examples of your finest work. Figure 16.7 features Haniz's approach to developing an online presence with a LinkedIn page, an online résumé on a personal webpage, and an online profile on the monster.com website.

For some positions, you may be asked to provide text or scannable résumés (examples of these are provided in the online resources for the textbook). Generally, these formats allow employers to upload data into a database and search a set of résumés electronically. A few strategies can increase the effectiveness of these types of résumés. For example, when you convert your standard résumé into a scannable one, adjust the content to gain success with the robot. Typically, you can do this by using nouns instead of verbs for job duties and accomplishments, and packing keywords early in your résumé.[10]

Generally, employers prefer to receive résumés in standard format through electronic channels. In a recent survey of employers, 71 percent stated a preference for standard

LO16.5 Create chronological and functional résumés to highlight your key selling points.

Components of Chronological Résumés

- Name block
- Summary of qualifications *or* Career objective (optional)
- Education
- Work experience
- Additional information

Components of Functional Résumés

- Name block
- Summary of qualifications *or* Career summary
- Skills
- Additional information

FIGURE 16.4

An Ineffective Chronological Résumé

Haniz Zogby
164 Founders Ridge Court, Havana, FL 32333
Phone: 850-784-7391; email: hanizzogby@gmail.com

<u>Education</u>
Florida State University, Tallahassee, Florida, Graduation: May 2013, BS in Finance, Minor in
Event Management GPA: 3.714 (Magna Cum Laude)
Major coursework: ECON 2013, 2023; ACG 2021, 2071, 3171, 3331; FIN 3244, 4424, 4324, 4329,
4453; MAN 3240, 4720 3.924 GPA at Woodbridge High School (7th in Class), Palmetto Scholarship

<u>Work Experience</u>
Better Horizons Credit Union, Irmo, SC
Marketing Specialist/Loan Officer, Oct 2011 to present
   • Extend business and personal loans to credit union members
   • Assist with promotional programs
   • Responsible for marketing efforts for younger members
   • In charge of effort to support local breast cancer awareness event
Teller Supervisor, Oct 2010 to Oct 2011
   • Responsible for all cash reserves at the credit union
   • Helped with referral and sales programs
   • Balanced monthly general ledgers
   • Supervised other tellers in the teller department
   • In charge of the entire unit and its activities
Teller, July 2008-Oct 2010
   • Managed banking transactions for members in a helpful and efficient manner
   • Recognized as the top referral getter among the tellers
Palmetto Home Medical, Columbia, SC
Receptionist/Billing Assistant, May 2005 - May 2008 (summers)
   • Answered phones
   • Data entry into the computer
Ultra Tan, Blythewood, SC
Salon Attendant, September 2007 to May 2008
   • Cleaned the salon
   • Answered questions that customers had
   • Kept track of tanning products
<u>Computer Skills</u>
MS Word, MS Excel, MS Access, MS PowerPoint, Prezi, MS Publisher, MS Project, QuickBase,
MS Outlook, QuickBooks, Powerscan Loan Display, WebEx

<u>Community Activities and Accomplishments</u>
Volunteer, VITA, Columbia, SC (giving up my Saturdays in support of a good cause)
Church Choir
Member of the National Association of Federal Credit Unions
Volunteer Gymnastics Coach, Columbia, SC
Varsity Basketball Overall MVP (2005-2006), Team Captain (2005-2006)

<u>Study Abroad</u>
Cass Business School, Dubai, United Arab Emirates
   • Took business classes in a multicultural environment
   • Observed one of the most dynamic business environments in the world
   • Took Arabic language courses

The excessively plain appearance of this résumé does not create a positive initial impression.

Recruiters will have a challenging time identifying key attributes and abilities.

Text appears cluttered because it is mostly on the left-hand side of the page without space in between.

The lack of **bold,** *italics,* or other formatting features makes it difficult to rapidly identify key pieces of information.

The focus on responsibilities as opposed to accomplishments fails to sufficiently highlight abilities.

Weak verbs do not emphasize high-order thinking and transferable skills for business.

Sections with additional information do not effectively highlight key attributes and abilities.

FIGURE 16.5

An Effective Chronological Résumé

Haniz Zogby	164 Founders Ridge Court, Havana, FL 32333 • 850-784-7391 • hanizzogby@gmail.com *LinkedIn*: linkedin.com/in/hanizzogby • *Online Portfolio*: sites.google.com/site/hanizzogby

EDUCATION

FLORIDA STATE UNIVERSITY, Tallahassee, Florida
Bachelors of Science in Finance, Minor in Event Management   **Graduation: May 2013**
- *Primary coursework*: bank administration, investments, marketing of financial services, event management
- *Study abroad*: one semester at Cass Business School in Dubai focusing on international finance and marketing
- *GPA*: 3.7; *Awards*: Magna Cum Laude

WORK EXPERIENCE

BETTER HORIZONS CREDIT UNION, Pescaloosa, FL
Marketing Specialist/Loan Officer   **Jan 2011 to present**
- Developed and ran marketing campaigns targeting young professionals and university students that resulted in approximately 55 new members in the past year
- Established a reward points program that was adopted by nearly 30 percent of members
- Organized a group of 83 members to participate in a local breast cancer walkathon
- Extend business and personal loans to credit union members

Teller Supervisor   **Dec 2009 to Jan 2011**
- Implemented and tracked referral and sales programs in the teller department
- Balanced monthly general ledgers, including branch and teller over/short
- Managed all cash reserves at the credit union
- Supervised six tellers; responsible for the overall direction, coordination, and evaluation of unit

Teller   **July 2008 to Dec 2009**
- Handled banking transactions for members in a helpful and efficient manner
- Obtained the most referrals in the teller unit during the entire year (2009)

PALMETTO HOME MEDICAL, Columbia, SC
Receptionist/Billing Assistant   **May 2005 to July 2008 (summers)**
- Managed financial bookkeeping for the company using QuickBooks
- Assisted with purchasing of medical supplies and processing of client orders
- Greeted clients and scheduled appointments in person and by phone

ULTRA TAN, Blythewood, SC
Salon Attendant   **Sept 2007 to May 2008**
- Sold tanning packages and tanning lotions
- Took inventory of all items sold in the store
- Resolved customer concerns related to products, billing, and scheduling

COMPUTER SKILLS

Project Management/Scheduling: QuickBase, MS Project, MS Outlook
Presentations/Publishing/Word Processing: WebEx, MS PowerPoint, Prezi, MS Publisher, MS Word
Finance/Accounting: QuickBooks, Powerscan Loan Display; *Spreadsheets and Databases*: MS Excel, MS Access

PROFESSIONAL ASSOCIATIONS AND COMMUNITY ACTIVITIES

Member, National Association of Federal Credit Unions, Arlington, VA, 2010 to present
Volunteer Tax Consultant, Volunteer Tax Assistance Program (VITA), Pescaloosa, FL, 2008 to present
Volunteer Coach, Elite Gymnastics Summer Camp, Columbia, SC, 2003 to 2007 (summers)

This simple but nicely formatted résumé allows recruiters to rapidly identify key abilities and attributes.

Distinctive and consistent formatting for headings (Centered **BOLD CAPS**), organizations (CAPS), position (**Bold**), and dates (right-aligned **bold**) make information easy to identify.

Specific accomplishments enhance credibility of claims.

Strong action verbs emphasize transferable management and marketing abilities.

Grouping helps rapidly display key computer skills.

Selective display of associations and community activities highlights key abilities and attributes.

FIGURE 16.6

An Effective Functional Résumé

Haniz Zogby

164 Founders Ridge Court, Havana, FL 32333 • 850-784-7391 • hanizzogby@gmail.com
LinkedIn: www.linkedin.com/hanizzogby • *Online Résumé:* https://sites.google.com/site/hanizzogby

Qualifications Summary
Ambitious credit union professional with record of successful marketing through local events, seminars, mailings, online social networking, and referrals. Knowledgeable of best practices in marketing for credit unions and innovative financial services for credit unions. Committed to leading marketing efforts to increase credit union membership and empower those who use local credit unions.

Skills

Marketing for
Credit Unions
• Developed and ran marketing campaigns targeting young professionals and university students that resulted in approximately 55 new members in the past year
• Established a reward points program that nearly 30 percent of members adopted
• Implemented and tracked referral and sales programs in the teller department

Event
Management
• Organized a group of 83 members to participate in a local breast cancer walkathon
• Set up regular seminars about retirement plans, investing, and business loans for credit union members
• Minored in Event Management and completed team projects for a charity fund-raiser (organized a music concert), a sports event (set up a kids' night), and a wedding

Leadership
• Participated in all major decisions for Better Horizons Credit Union during the past year as assistant manager
• Supervised six tellers; responsible for the overall direction, coordination, and evaluation of entire teller unit
• Involved in leadership roles at work, school, and community for the past ten years

Technology
• Excel at using software to facilitate project management and scheduling (QuickBase, MS Project, MS Outlook)
• Comfortable with a variety of online and face-to-face presentation software platforms (WebEx, MS PowerPoint, Prezi)
• Advanced-level use of a variety of finance, accounting, spreadsheet, and database software (QuickBooks, Powerscan Loan Display, MS Excel, MS Access)
• Expert at word processing and publishing software (MS Publisher, MS Word)

Employment History

07/2008–present	BETTER HORIZONS CREDIT UNION, Pescaloosa, FL *Marketing Specialist/Loan Officer* (01/2011–praesent), *Teller Supervisor* (12/2009–01/2011), *Teller* (07/2008–12/2009)
05/2005–07/2008 (summers)	PALMETTO HOME MEDICAL, Columbia, SC, *Receptionist/Billing Assistant*
09/2007–05/2008	ULTRA TAN, Blythewood, SC, *Salon Attendant*

Education

Bachelors of Science in Finance, Minor in Event Management, FLORIDA STATE UNIVERSITY, Tuscaloosa, FL, Graduation: 05/2013.

Study Abroad, one semester of business classes at CASS BUSINESS SCHOOL, Dubai, UAE

Community Involvement

Volunteer Tax Consultant, VOLUNTEER TAX ASSISTANCE PROGRAM (VITA), Columbia, SC, 2008–present.

Volunteer Coach, ELITE GYMNASTICS SUMMER CAMP, Columbia, SC, 2003–2007 (summers).

This cleanly formatted résumé sends signals of professionalism and orderliness.

The qualifications summary contains a concise statement that highlights key abilities and attributes.

By grouping skills, Haniz demonstrates what she has to offer in a matter of seconds.

A brief employment history section helps recruiters judge the depth and consistency of her experience.

The education and community involvement sections contain only a few strategically selected items that focus on her key messages.

FIGURE 16.7

Online Profiles on Social Networking and Job Websites

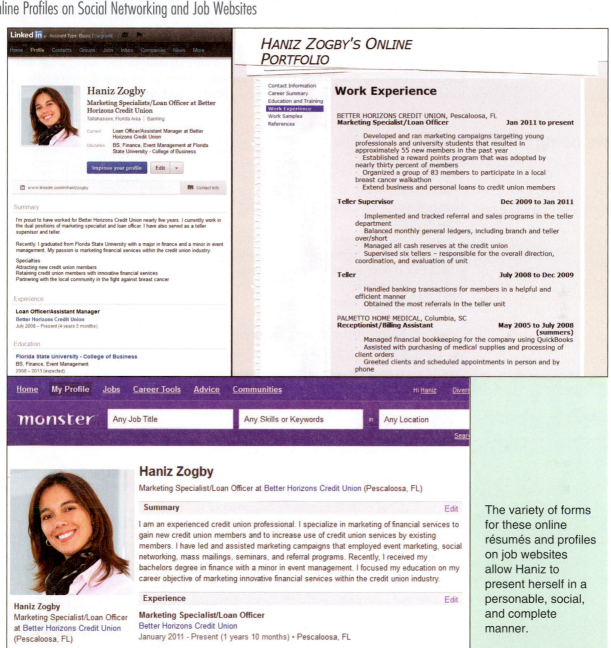

The variety of forms for these online résumés and profiles on job websites allow Haniz to present herself in a personable, social, and complete manner.

résumés, 21 percent for standard résumés in text format, 3 percent for scannable résumés, and 5 percent expressed no preference. In terms of delivery, 46 percent preferred receiving the résumé as an attachment to an email, 38 percent preferred receiving it via the company website, 7 percent preferred receiving paper copies by mail, and 9 percent had other preferences. Some preferred résumés pasted within the email rather than sent as attachments due to security concerns. Most employers who use application websites expect résumés to be uploaded in their entirety, whereas some employers have set up their websites so applicants can submit particular sections of résumés.[11]

Developing a Reference List

LO16.6 Develop a list of references that will improve your employment prospects.

You will need to provide a list of personal references as part of most job applications. Some job applicants put off this task until the last minute, often underestimating its significance. In fact, your references may be among the most important factors in gaining a new position.

One recent study showed that for professional positions, 62 percent of employers call three or more references from applicants' lists of references, 18 percent call two references, 3 percent call just one reference, 8 percent call more than three references, and just 9 percent do not contact any references.[12] As you construct your list of references, consider these tips:

Develop Relationships with Potential References over Time

Well before you need to apply for a position, compile a list of people who can provide credible accounts of your qualifications. Consider people who work in fields and industries that interest you. Also consider professors with whom you have established a relationship over several semesters, ideally in classes directly related to your sought-after positions.[13]

Contact Your References Ahead of Time

Before you place any names on your list, reach out to those individuals and, as a courtesy, ask permission to use their names. A short email may be enough to accomplish this request, but consider meeting in person or calling to explain the positions you are applying for and recent experiences you've had. These short conversations allow your references to speak about you with enthusiasm and up-to-date information. Also, these conversations give you a chance to seek advice about how to handle the job application process. Generally, also send these individuals your most updated résumé so they are aware of the information that potential employers have.

Some of your references will be former supervisors. Forward-thinking job applicants stay in touch with past supervisors from time to time to keep them updated with their career developments. Even small but sincere gestures such as sending yearly holiday cards can lead to favorable comments when these former supervisors speak with your potential employers.[14]

Think about whether you should include your current supervisor as a reference. In some cases, she or he will understand and even encourage your efforts to seek new positions and will serve as an excellent reference. In other cases, however, your supervisors may be unhappy that you want to leave your current position. For example, if your supervisor thinks your job search indicates a lack of dedication to your current job, you may find your professional opportunities diminishing. If you're uncomfortable telling your supervisor that you're searching for a new position, you likely should not provide him/her as a reference.

Thank Your References

Your references will undoubtedly wonder how your job search fares. Stay in touch with them about progress you've made. When your job search is over, thank them for

FIGURE 16.8

References List

Haniz Zogby | 164 Founders Ridge Court, Havana, FL 32333 • 850-784-7391 • hanizzogby@gmail.com
LinkedIn: linkedin.com/in/hanizzogby • *Online Résumé*: sites.google.com/site/hanizzogby

REFERENCE LIST

Christine Russo
CEO and President
BETTER HORIZONS CREDIT UNION
Address: 1488 Altura Dr.
Pescaloosa, FL 32315
Phone: 850-971-0234
Email: russo@betterhorizons.com
Relationship: Ms. Russo has been my supervisor for the past five years. She is intimately familiar with my work in the following positions: marketing specialist, loan officer, teller supervisor, and teller.

Jim Harrill, CPA
Owner
HARRILL TAX ASSOCIATES
Address: 3419 Main Street
Havana, FL 32333
Phone: 850-972-3188
Email: jamesharrilljr@harrilltax.com
Relationship: Mr. Harrill trained me and supervised my work as a volunteer tax consultant for the VITA program. He is familiar with my work ethic and commitment to the community.

Jamie McPherson, Ph.D.
Associate Professor of Finance
FLORIDA STATE UNIVERSITY
Address: 719-C Thurmond Tower
Tallahassee, FL 32302
Phone: 850-777-1848
Email: mcpherson@fls.edu
Relationship: Dr. McPherson taught two of my courses and served as an advisor for my honors thesis about emerging financial services in credit unions.

Jack Gerardi
Owner and President
PALMETTO HOME MEDICAL
Address: 18 Foxborough Lane
Columbia, SC 29201
Phone: 803-798-1312
Email: jgerardi@palmettohomemed.com
Relationship: Mr. Gerardi supervised my work as a receptionist and billing assistant for 3-1/2 summers.

Consistent formatting allows recruiters to quickly gather key information.

Formatting that matches the résumé formatting shows attention to detail and a touch of class.

A brief statement about relationships with references demonstrates professionalism and helps recruiters make judgments about the value of each one.

---

their participation in the process. These shows of goodwill may come in handy over the years as you ask these same individuals for assistance in future job searches.

Complete a Consistently Formatted, Well-Detailed Reference List

When you construct the list of references, check the job announcement to see how many references are required. If it does not provide a number, list three to five individuals. Make sure you provide current contact information. In addition, consider providing a brief (one or two sentences) description of your professional or school relationship to each reference. Finally, format the list of references to be compatible with your résumé (see Figure 16.8).

Constructing Cover Letters

Cover letters describe your interest in and qualifications for a position. Whereas you may have one, two, or at most three versions of your résumé for various positions, you must uniquely tailor each cover letter to a particular position. No two cover letters should be the same.

LO16.7 Compose effective cover letters that highlight your key selling points.

The role of cover letters has changed in recent years. Some hiring managers no longer read them. One recent survey showed that just over half (56 percent) of employers request them.[15] Yet, even with this slightly declining interest, you should write perfect cover letters because a majority of hiring managers still read them, and when they do, cover letters likely send your first impression.

Your primary goal for cover letters is to sell your key abilities and attributes in a way that matches the needs of the employer for a particular position. As you do with sales letters, you build excitement and optimism that you can excel in the posted position. Unlike mass sales letters, however, cover letters deliver the message that you are writing to one particular employer, and only that employer.

Keep in mind the following advice:[16]

Components of Cover Letters

• Interest in position.
• Match with position.
• Call to action.

The Cover Letter Often Forms the First Impression

Since many potential employers read your cover letter (or a condensed version of it as an email) first, it forms the first impression of you. Therefore, it must be perfect. As an error-free message, the cover letter can immediately place you in the upper echelons. A New York tutoring company, Inspirica, recently sought out writing tutors. In 93 percent of the 220 cover letters, HR specialists found writing errors.[17]

Clearly Identify the Position You Are Applying For

Your potential employer is likely reviewing applications for many—sometimes hundreds or thousands—of positions at the same time. Many employers use electronic application systems to clearly identify the positions that applicants are seeking. In any case, clearly and prominently identify the position you are applying for in your cover letter. The subject line is often a good location for this information.

Be Focused and Concise

In recent years, potential employers have come to expect shorter, more concise cover letters. This is in part due to larger application pools for each position. Thus, you should generally aim for three to five targeted paragraphs.

In such limited space, focus on your main selling points—your key abilities and attributes—and how these selling points match the needs of your employer. By taking this focused approach, you create a prism from which the employer will interpret your résumé, thus strengthening the story you are telling of your qualifications.

Show a Confident and Enthusiastic Tone without Exaggerating or Displaying Arrogance

One of the most challenging aspects of the cover letter is getting the tone right. Employers are looking for employees who can contribute, so you should mention how your unique abilities can help the company. Yet, hiring managers may view excessive self-praise as arrogance.

Also, you should show your interest in the position and the company, as hiring managers will be trying to gauge your enthusiasm and commitment levels. At the same time, you will want to avoid flowery language, which hiring managers may find off-putting and not businesslike.

Tailor Your Cover Letter to the Job Posting and Needs of the Employer

By carefully reading the job announcement, you can prioritize your selling points so they are tailored to the position of interest. This approach not only accentuates your ability to do the job, it also shows that you have researched the position and are responsive to the needs of the company. The Internet provides many avenues for job seekers to learn about companies. Read the Technology Tips feature on page 488 to learn about one approach.

FIGURE 16.9

An Ineffective Solicited Cover Letter

164 Founders Ridge Court, Havana, FL 32333
850-784-7391
hanizzogby@gmail.com

May 15, 2013

Human Resources Department
Anchor Federal Credit Union Network
158 Anchor Loop
Raleigh, NC 27601

Hello Hiring Committee:

Please consider my application for the Credit Union Marketing Specialist position. I think you will find that I possess the skills that you are looking for.

My mother always has said, "The sky's the limit." I have always admired her sense of optimism. One reason I admire the credit union model is because of my mom. My mother was a teller for nearly 20 years, and I followed in her footsteps. She always felt that she was doing good for the community by working in a credit union, and I have gained this deep sense of commitment to the community through credit unions as well. In my current workplace, I have been promoted more quickly than any other employees. You will find that I am ambitious, organized, and I am passionate about marketing credit unions. My passion has driven me to success at Better Horizons Credit Union and will propel me to success at Anchor Federal Credit Unions if you give me a chance.

I want to illustrate to you the kind of abilities I can bring to Anchor Federal Credit Union Network by describing a recent marketing campaign that I ran. About one year ago, our CEO, Christine Russo, determined that we needed to gain younger members. She has relied on me often to help come up with ideas for important marketing campaigns, and she turned to me in this instance as well. After thoroughly examining best practices throughout the industry, we came up with a set of financial services and advertising ideas that resulted in approximately 55 new members. Our branch manager recognized this campaign as the most effective marketing effort during her 15 years at the credit union. I'm proud of this kind of effort and I can deliver this level of result at Anchor Federal Credit Union if you give me the chance.

The job you posted is my dream job. It combines my love of credit unions with my skills and interests in event management. You will notice on my résumé that not only do I have training in event management, but I also have experience using events as marketing tools for Better Horizons Credit Union. I thrive in these environments where I need to bring people together for fun and exciting events. Thank you for your attention to this letter. I hope that we can meet to further our discussions.

Sincerely,

Haniz Zogby

This letter contains too much text and long paragraphs. The body has 405 words and two long paragraphs of 138 and 143 words. Many busy recruiters will not read it carefully.

Because of excessive personal information and emotion, this cover letter lacks a professional and serious tone.

The use of clichés, such as "the sky's the limit" and "dream job," shows naiveté.

The closing does mention future contact but is vague.

Adapting for Unsolicited Letters

Most people gain their positions through formal job announcements—that is, jobs *solicited* by companies. When applying for these jobs, you will write a **solicited cover letter,** since it is for an open position that a company advertises (see Figures 16.9 and 16.10 for examples of ineffective and effective solicited cover letters). In some cases, however, you may seek employment with a company that does not even have an open position. In these cases, you will submit an **unsolicited cover letter,** since the company has not requested job applications.

When writing unsolicited cover letters, you make several modifications. You must first find out as much as possible about the employer so that you can explain how you fit the employer's needs. Also, you should open immediately with a proposition about how you can add value, and summarize your key abilities and attributes quickly, often

FIGURE 16.10

An Effective Solicited Cover Letter

---

164 Founders Ridge Court, Havana, FL 32333
850-784-7391
hanizzogby@gmail.com

May 15, 2013

Mr. Jacob Garcia, Director of Human Resources
Anchor Federal Credit Union Network
158 Anchor Loop
Raleigh, NC 27601

RE: Credit Union Marketing Specialist Position (Job Posting #831481809)

Dear Mr. Garcia:

My successes in attracting new credit union members would translate well into meeting the requirements of your Credit Union Marketing Specialist position. I am eager to speak with you by phone or in person to learn more about the position and explain how I can contribute.

During nearly five years at Better Horizons Credit Union, I have excelled at many of the responsibilities you are seeking, including marketing to increase membership, tracking the success of marketing activities, coordinating marketing events and efforts, and delivering presentations to partners and potential clients. I have helped gain new credit union members by developing marketing campaigns with many of the techniques you are seeking, including event marketing, mailings, referral programs, seminars, and online social networking.

One of my most successful marketing campaigns occurred last year when I was given the responsibility of increasing membership among young professionals and university students. I developed mailings, an online social networking campaign, and seminars that resulted in approximately 55 new members. Our branch manager, Ms. Christine Russo, recognized this campaign as the most effective marketing effort during her 15 years at the credit union.

During my time working at Better Horizons Credit Union, I have been rapidly promoted and given critical marketing responsibilities due to my leadership, initiative, creativity, and performance. I can make these same contributions to the Anchor Credit Union Network.

Please call me at your convenience to arrange an interview. You can reach me at my mobile phone (850-784-7391) between 9 a.m. and 6 p.m. daily.

Sincerely,

Haniz Zogby

This cover letter is brief but focused, stating key abilities and attributes in a professional and confident manner. The body contains 257 words. The longest paragraph is 75 words. Recruiters are far more likely to read this letter.

The letter demonstrates awareness of the needs of the employer and how her skills match those needs.

This letter conveys a professional and confident tone.

The closing statement is assertive and specific in requesting contact. Yet, it is not overbearing or pushy.

---

in bulleted form (see Figure 16.11 for an example of an unsolicited cover letter in email form).[18]

Reviewing Your Résumés and Cover Letters

LO16.8 Review your job application documents for effectiveness and fairness.

Your job application must be perfect. Recruiters rarely have any tolerance for inaccuracies in a résumé. Furthermore, they won't hire you unless you present your selling points effectively.

On the most basic level, you should make sure every element of your job application correctly portrays your abilities and attributes, so you must avoid any urge to

FIGURE 16.11

An Unsolicited Referral Cover Letter

To: Lucy Sharapova <l.sharapova@easterncu.org>

Subject: Expansion Plans for the Eastern Credit Union Network

📎 Zogby_Haniz_Resume.docx (48.00

B *I* <u>U</u> F ᴛT T ₁₂₃ ≣ ≣ ≣   **<<Plain Text**

Dear Ms. Sharapova:

After reading about your credit union network's expansion plans in the *Credit Union Leadership Journal*, I am eager to join your marketing team. My skills in attracting new credit union members through event marketing, mailings, referral programs, seminars, and online social networking could help you achieve your ambitious growth plans.

I am an experienced credit union professional with extensive marketing experience and financial background. My marketing successes include the following:

- Attracting 55 new members within one year in a marketing campaign targeting young professionals and university students
- Developing a reward points program that was adopted by nearly 30 percent of our members
- Establishing referral and sales programs in our teller department that significantly increased membership and member use of financial services

You can learn more about my qualifications by reading my attached résumé. Also, please see my online résumé and LinkedIn profile. My online résumé contains actual samples from marketing campaigns I have led. It contains mailings, content from the Better Horizons website, and video of two marketing seminars that I organized and presented.

I am seeking an entry-level marketing position in a credit union network with potential for advancement based on performance. As far as location, I am flexible and willing to relocate anywhere. I am seeking an opening salary range of $50,000 to $60,000.

Please give me a call at your convenience to arrange an interview. You can reach me on my mobile phone (850-784-7391) between 9 a.m. and 6 p.m. daily. Also, I plan to give you a call within the next two weeks to learn more about potential job openings and explore the possibility of a job interview.

Best regards,

Haniz Zogby

Mobile Phone: 850-784-7391
Email: hanizzogby@gmail.com
Online Résumé: linkedin.com/in/hanizzogby
LinkedIn Profile: sites.google.com/site/hanizzogby

The message is concise. The body has just 276 words. Further, the short paragraphs and bulleted items allow the recruiter to get the gist within 15 to 30 seconds.

The subject line focuses on the needs and ambitions of the employer.

Links to her online résumé and LinkedIn profile allow the recruiter to learn more if she is interested.

The tone is confident and assertive without being demanding.

As an unsolicited request for a job interview, this message is more up-front about issues such as salary and promotional opportunities.

exaggerate. You should also review your documents over and over to ensure they emphasize your selling points in a compelling manner. Consider getting the opinion of many people about your résumé. You might start with some individuals in the career center and a few of your professors.

Also, try to get the opinions of some people in positions that match your career interests. Since business professionals interpret résumés quite differently, you may get some conflicting advice. This is normal. Even all hiring managers won't agree about what makes the best résumé. However, by getting many opinions, you'll be able to make decisions about strategies that enhance your likelihood of success in the job search process.

TECHNOLOGY TIPS

GETTING AN INSIDER'S VIEW OF POTENTIAL EMPLOYERS

Most job seekers use Internet job postings and advertisements to find and apply for jobs. Most also have used LinkedIn and other professional networking websites to find opportunities. However, few job seekers get an inside look at the companies that interest them.

A variety of websites can help you get insiders' perspectives about companies. One example of this type of website is Glassdoor.com, where you can find reviews about any company of interest from its current and former employees. You can learn how satisfied employees are with the company, what the company culture is like, what advancement opportunities there are, and even salary ranges for various positions.

By getting as much inside information about a company as possible, you

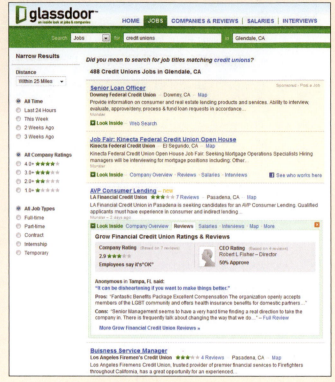

Source: Courtesy of Glassdoor.

can determine if the company culture and job opportunities match your expectations before you ever apply. Furthermore, this inside information can help you prepare for the job application and interview process. It may even help you in the salary negotiations once you have a job offer.

Acing the Job Interview

Your cover letter, résumé, list of references, and other pieces in your job application package set the stage for the most consequential part of the process—the interview. When you have secured an interview, you have made the initial cut and are likely deemed a good candidate. You are now competing against the best candidates for the position.

Many job applicants spend little time preparing for the interview, essentially winging it. At this crucial stage—where hiring managers are making their decisions—preparation often sets apart those who receive offers and those who do not. In this section, we focus on a few parts of the job interview: dressing appropriately, using appropriate etiquette, responding to interview questions, and following up.

Dress for the Interview and Pay Attention to Etiquette

One of the first signals of professionalism you give at a job interview relates to your clothing choices (notice, for example, the items related to dress in Figure 16.12).[19] As much as possible, gain a sense ahead of time about the dress standards at the company

FIGURE 16.12

Most Serious Problems in the Job Application/Interview Process

Nationwide Survey of Hiring Managers

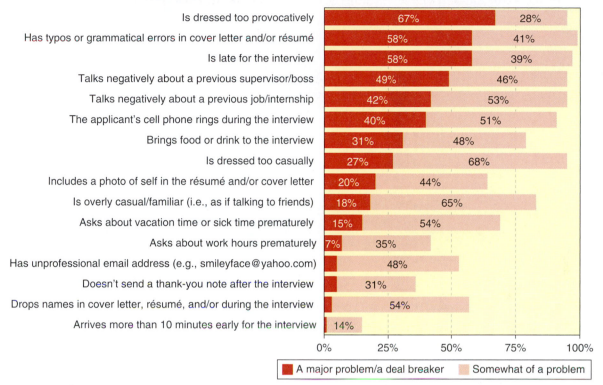

	A major problem/a deal breaker	Somewhat of a problem
Is dressed too provocatively	67%	28%
Has typos or grammatical errors in cover letter and/or résumé	58%	41%
Is late for the interview	58%	39%
Talks negatively about a previous supervisor/boss	49%	46%
Talks negatively about a previous job/internship	42%	53%
The applicant's cell phone rings during the interview	40%	51%
Brings food or drink to the interview	31%	48%
Is dressed too casually	27%	68%
Includes a photo of self in the résumé and/or cover letter	20%	44%
Is overly casual/familiar (i.e., as if talking to friends)	18%	65%
Asks about vacation time or sick time prematurely	15%	54%
Asks about work hours prematurely	7%	35%
Has unprofessional email address (e.g., smileyface@yahoo.com)		48%
Doesn't send a thank-you note after the interview		31%
Drops names in cover letter, résumé, and/or during the interview		54%
Arrives more than 10 minutes early for the interview	14%	

Source: From Society for Human Resource Management, "SHRM Poll: Interviewing Do's and Don'ts for Job Seekers," September 15, 2009. Reprinted with permission via Copyright Clearance Center.

where you are interviewing. Generally, you should dress up, even when the company has a fairly casual environment. Typically, err on the side of conservative dress—that is, wear well-pressed, clean, and nicely fitted clothes. Avoid over-accessorizing with too much jewelry, flashy glasses, or other items. Consider a dress rehearsal at home to feel at ease in your chosen outfit.[20]

During your visit to the company—before, during, and after the formal interview—pay attention to appropriate etiquette. Most hiring managers expect you to maintain a certain level of formality. Greet those you meet with handshakes and enthusiasm.

Respond Effectively to Interview Questions

The moment of truth for hiring managers generally occurs during the job interview. Many make fairly quick judgments about your abilities and attributes. In a recent survey of 498 human resource professionals, one-third (33 percent) made not-to-hire decisions within 5 minutes, and another third (30 percent) made that decision within 15 minutes.[21] Your window may be brief to make the case that you are a good fit for the company. To prepare for the questions you may be asked, consider the following tips:

Respond to Questions Strategically, Confidently, and Concisely

As you crafted your cover letter and résumé, you identified those professional abilities and attributes that meet the needs of your employer. These are your selling points, and you should find ways throughout the interview to emphasize them. You are strategic to the degree that you find ways to bring up these selling points.

LO16.9 Develop strategies for responding to common job interview questions.

TABLE 16.12

Common Job Interview Questions for Entry-Level Business Positions

Type of Interview Question	Examples
Introduction questions	• Tell me about yourself. • How was your flight here? Did you find this office easily? • How was your flight here? How do you like living in _____?
Education and training	• Why did you choose your school? • Why did you choose your major? • What was your favorite part of your program? Least favorite?
Knowledge of company and industry	• What do you know about our company? • What do you think are some of our main business challenges? How can you help? • What trends do you see in this industry?
Work experience	• How did you get your last job? • Why did you leave your last job? Have you ever been fired? • What did you like least about your last job?
Approaches to work, goals, and successes	• Why did you apply for this job? • What are you looking for in a job? • How will you be successful in this position? • What were some tough decisions you had to make at your last job? • What are your biggest accomplishments? • Tell me about a project you worked on in your most recent job. How did you contribute to its success? • What do you wish you had accomplished but were unable to? • Can you tell me about a difficult situation you encountered at work? How did you respond? How did you get your team to work effectively? • Can you tell me about a situation where you had to work under pressure and deal with deadlines?
Personal attributes	• What are your strengths? Weaknesses? • What would your current boss say are your greatest strengths and weaknesses? • Are you creative? Hardworking? Ambitious? • What have you learned from your past jobs?
Interpersonal, team, management, and leadership skills	• What types of people do you like to work with? • What types of people do you think are most difficult to work with? • What is your leadership/management style? • Do you have top management potential? • How well do you work in teams? • What is your communication style when working with others? • Have you had to make an unpopular decision or announcement? How did you do it?

Also, show confidence. While you should avoid bragging, you need to emphasize your abilities and attributes. Some job applicants are uncomfortable doing this. Claim credit for work you have accomplished. Say "I" instead of "we" during the job interview more often than you would otherwise as you talk about accomplishments at work. Yet, at the same time, maintain a balance between taking credit for your individual accomplishments and demonstrating your team orientation.[22]

Finally, give concise answers. Most responses should be between 30 seconds and two minutes. Briefer answers are generally too abrupt, and longer answers are often unfocused. Also, longer answers disrupt the conversational nature of the job interview.

In Table 16.12, you'll find many common types of interview questions. Be prepared to respond to any of them strategically, confidently, and concisely. In Table 16.13,

TABLE 16.13

Responses to Common Job Interview Questions

Less Effective	More Effective
Q. *Tell me about yourself.*	**Q.** *Tell me about yourself.*
A. Well, I'm a recent graduate with a degree in finance. I also minored in event management. I have worked for a credit union for the past five years. I started out as a teller and moved up from there. Prior to working at the credit union, I worked at a medical supplies company and a tanning salon. Outside of that, I've been heavily involved in sports my whole life. And, that brings me right up until now, ready to move into a new position.	**A.** About five years ago, I took a position as a teller at a credit union. I found that I really loved the credit union approach to providing financial services. Within months, I realized that this was a career direction for me. I was fairly quickly promoted into other positions—first as a teller supervisor and then as loan officer and marketing specialist. While working at the credit union, I also went to Florida State University, where I majored in finance and minored in event management. I focused all of my studies on my deep interest in marketing financial services for credit unions. One reason I'm so intrigued by the position is that it combines several of my key interests.
This response is factual but does not directly lead into a coherent, inspiring account of Haniz's selling points.	This statement captures Haniz's background, naturally describes several of her selling points, and ties her selling points to the needs of the position. At 115 words, this statement would take roughly 45 seconds to one minute to state.
Q. *It looks like you just graduated. Tell me about your university experience.*	**Q.** *It looks like you just graduated. Tell me about your university experience.*
A. I had a great time in school. I had great professors all the way through my program in finance. I made great friends. One of the most exciting parts of my schooling was studying in Dubai for a semester, which really opened my eyes to the world. The only part I didn't like about school was the pressures of working full-time for most of my four years and also studying on the side. But, I think I grew a lot from the experience.	**A.** Going to Florida State University was a great experience and helped me improve my skills in marketing financial services. Early on in my finance program, I took a variety of classes about banking and investments that helped me think about financial services we could offer at Better Horizons. Also, I used a lot of what I learned in my event management minor to think about events we could run at the credit union. I think my favorite semester was when I went abroad to Dubai. I was fascinated to see that the businesses in that country are using so many creative and innovative approaches to event marketing. I've tried to use some of those techniques I saw in Dubai at Better Horizons.
This response provides a general overview of Haniz's experience but fails to provide a sense that she was pursuing a set of goals. The response does not contain selling points.	This response ties Haniz's university experiences into her professional goals and accomplishments. It highlights her key selling points and shows her goal-directed approach to work.
Q. *Why do you want to leave your current job?*	**Q.** *Why do you want to leave your current job?*
A. My job at Better Horizons Credit Union has given me many opportunities, but I am often frustrated with the conservative approach that our Board has taken to developing new services. My immediate supervisor usually agrees with my ideas, but she understands that the Board will not approve our most ambitious ideas. So, she falls in line. Better Horizons has been a great learning experience, but I'm simply ready to move on to a more ambitious work environment.	**A.** Leaving Better Horizons Credit Union will not be easy for me. I've enjoyed working closely with so many of my colleagues, and getting to know the community has been wonderful. Last year, when I helped run our campaign that brought in so many younger members, I realized that I wanted to be part of a larger credit union network in a position where I could spend more of my time developing marketing events and facilitating coordination between branches. I think this is where my strengths lie, and as far as I can tell, a good match for your position.
By stating her displeasure with the Board and the less than ambitious work culture, Haniz makes a risky statement. Some hiring managers will worry that Haniz does not work well with others.	By focusing on the satisfying aspects of the position she intends to leave, Haniz is more likely to give the impression that she is a committed, team-oriented employee. She segues her response into the needs of the current position.

(Continued)

TABLE 16.13

(*Continued*)

Less Effective	More Effective
Q. *How well do you work in teams?*	**Q.** *How well do you work in teams?*
A. I take a win-win mentality into all team projects. I really believe that one plus one can make three if you work together as a team. I think if you ask anyone who I've worked with, they'll tell you that I facilitate a productive work environment where we're feeding off one another's ideas and where the end result is a creative and effective solution.	**A.** I enjoy working in teams to meet marketing objectives. Last year's marketing campaign that resulted in 55 new members was the result of a five-member team at Better Horizons. I was asked to head up the team and focused on events and social media, while the other team members worked on their specialty areas, such as market research, print advertising, and radio spots. Even though we each had our specialties, we had to work together extensively to make sure we created a unified marketing message. We also pushed one another to come up with better ideas. I don't think we could have achieved such a successful campaign without one another.
This clichéd, vague response does little to convey Haniz's real ability to work in teams.	This response shows Haniz's ability to work in teams through a concrete example. It inspires confidence that Haniz is a team player and genuinely understands the economic value of working in teams.
Q. *Do you have management experience? What is your approach to managing others?*	**Q.** *Do you have management experience? What is your approach to managing others?*
A. Yes. As a teller supervisor, I supervised a unit of six tellers. I was responsible for coordinating, scheduling, and the overall performance of the group. I think the most important part of managing is being open. The tellers always knew where I was coming from and vice versa.	**A.** Yes. At Better Horizons, I've managed the teller department and led a variety of marketing campaigns that required bringing together the ideas and resources of credit union employees and members. I have been most successful when I've followed several principles. First, I think it's important to set a vision and articulate the big goals. Second, I think it's critical to get everyone's ideas about how to achieve the goals. Finally, I think you have to find ways to gain buy-in and create incentives for others to engage in the goals. Here's how I did this with our mailing campaign to attract more members . . .
This response is too short. While the response is positive, it fails to lead into Haniz's selling points of developing marketing campaigns.	This response answers the question and also transitions to Haniz's selling points.
Q. *What are your weaknesses?*	**Q.** *What are your weaknesses?*
A. I can't really think of any weaknesses off the top of my head. Well, I guess one thing is that I never settle for anything less than excellence. Some people who accept mediocrity sometimes say I'm a control freak, but I get the job done. So, in one way you could view this as a weakness, but from the business viewpoint, it's a net plus.	**A.** One of the things I noticed in the job posting is that you are looking for someone with the ability to conduct member surveys. I wish I could say that I had experience doing surveys in my current job. I think it is critical to include surveys as part of market analysis. I took several courses about conducting surveys and statistical analysis, yet I haven't applied this knowledge to real business problems. I look forward to developing my abilities in this regard and would welcome any training or mentoring.
This question is common in job interviews. Many job candidates view it as a trick question and evade it or state a weakness that could really be viewed as a strength. This response does not show that Haniz is self-aware enough to improve quickly on the job.	This response shows that Haniz is self-aware. It also reveals her ambitious, goal-setting nature and recognition of what she needs to do to provide value for her potential employer.

you'll see some sample responses from Haniz. As you read these questions, think about how the hiring manager is likely responding.

Be Perceptive about What Hiring Managers Are Evaluating
Hiring managers ask most questions with specific goals in mind. They are trying to evaluate how well your abilities and attributes match the needs of the position and fit into the corporate culture. Thus, they will ask a variety of questions about your education, work experience, and knowledge of their company. In most questions, you can fairly easily discern what they are trying to find out about you.

Other interview questions, however, may be more difficult to "read." With such questions, think about what kinds of judgments the interviewer might make. For example, when hiring managers ask you to introduce yourself, they want to know how you see yourself; it gives them a glimpse into your sense of your life and career direction, your priorities, and your work values. When they ask you what your weaknesses are, they are generally less concerned about what you can't do now but rather what you can do later. They are trying to see how self-aware you are and if you are likely to improve over time. Even questions in small talk—such as how your flight was, how your hotel room is, or how your football team is doing—are asked by hiring managers to make judgments about your emotional intelligence.

Tell Success Stories
Throughout this book, we've discussed the importance of stories. During job interviews, telling stories about your successes can create a positive connection between you and your potential employers. By telling success stories, you provide specific and concrete examples as evidence of your abilities and attributes. Also, these stories often offer a glimpse into who you are as a person.[23]

One approach to telling success stories is the **STAR method** (Situation – Tasks – Actions – Results). Table 16.14 shows how Haniz uses the STAR method to briefly but convincingly respond to the question *How well do you work with deadlines?* Read through this example and compare its specificity to an abstract, nonspecific response,

TABLE 16.14

The STAR Approach to Responding to Interview Questions

	Example Statements
	Q. *How well do you work with deadlines?* **A.** I'm quite used to meeting deadlines, and actually, I've done some of my best work when I had to hit a deadline. One example occurred recently in organizing a group of credit union employees and members to participate in a local walkathon to support breast cancer.
SITUATION where you created a positive outcome	For over a decade, our credit union has been a prominent supporter of the event, but our participation has decreased almost every year. Last year, our group was comprised of just 15 people, most of whom were employees. Altogether, we only raised around $600.
TASKS you were assigned as part of a process	Two weeks before the deadline for signing up, our president approached me and asked me if I could head up a promotional effort to get a larger group from the credit union. She suggested that I aim for at least 30 people and focus on getting more of our members on the walkathon team, especially newer members.
ACTIONS you took that led to outcome	Within a few days, another marketing specialist and I had set up some incentives for members to participate, such as a free T-shirt and a water bottle. We developed promotional messages that we sent out by email and via our Facebook page and our website. I think what made the most difference is that we asked tellers to distribute flyers each time a member came in for a transaction.
RESULTS that occurred	Ultimately, we recruited 83 walkers and raised nearly $10,000 for our local breast cancer center. We also were able to get a variety of new members to join our walkathon team and connect on a deeper level with our credit union community.

TABLE 16.15

Questions by Job Candidates in First Interviews

Less Effective	More Effective
• What kind of salary are you offering for this position? • How often can I work from home? • Is there a strong benefits package?	• Can you tell me about the company culture? • If there were any one thing you could change about the company culture, what would it be? • What are you looking for in the person who takes this position? • How do you evaluate employees' performance? • What are the next steps in the process? • Who would I report to in this position? What management style does this person have? • Do you have any concerns about my ability to succeed in this position?

such as "I work well under pressure and deadlines. In fact, I thrive under these conditions and often produce my best results."

As you tell success stories, make sure that they respond directly to interview questions and reveal your best selling points. Also, make sure your stories stay relatively brief. Generally, responses that are longer than one to two minutes are too long. You might consider writing out five or six success stories you could use in a job interview.

Avoid Criticizing Your Former Organizations, Supervisors, and Colleagues   If you glance back at Figure 16.12, you will notice that among the worst offenses in job interviews is speaking negatively of your current or past employers. If you express negativity, hiring managers may wonder how well you get along with others and what attitude you bring to work. When you are asked questions such as *Why do you want to leave your current job* or *What is your least favorite part of your job,* be prepared with an honest response that is constructive, forward-looking, and complimentary if possible.

Ask Questions   Generally, your interviewer will ask you what questions you have. Come prepared with some. When interviewees do not ask questions, hiring managers often view them as uninterested or inexperienced. In Table 16.15, you will notice several questions that are not effective and others that are generally effective.[24]

Typically, if you ask about salary, compensation, and other perks on the first interview, you may inadvertently send the meta message "this is all about me." One survey showed that less than one-third of hiring managers thought it was OK for interviewees to bring up salary on the first interview.[25] Of course, these are considered appropriate topics on second or third interviews when a potential employer is showing strong interest in you.

LO16.10 Explain etiquette for following up after job interviews.

Follow Up after the Job Interview

Sending a note of appreciation following an interview is a good strategy. In a poll of 150 senior executives, 88 percent stated that sending a thank-you note could increase chances of employment. When asked how many job applicants actually did send thank-you notes, executives estimated that just 51 percent of candidates do so.[26]

Within a few hours to one day after your interview, send a thank-you note. Your primary goal should be to express goodwill and confirm your interest in the position (see Figure 16.13). The note should be brief and genuine. Some job applicants wonder whether they should send a thank-you email or a thank-you card. In a recent survey, 50 percent of HR professionals said that sending a thank-you email is the best way of expressing thanks. Nearly one-third (28 percent) said it's best to send a thank-you

FIGURE 16.13

Thank-You Note Following an Interview

Short, professional thank-you note shows professionalism, appreciation, and interest.

Attached résumé, LinkedIn profile address, and informative online résumé provide recruiters with additional information if they choose to look at it.

note by regular mail. Also, some HR professionals (17 percent) recommend sending a thank-you email right away *and* sending a thank-you note by regular mail.[27] Clearly, the only "right" answer is that you should send one.

Unless the interviewers tell you that you should wait until they contact you, feel free to follow up with their progress in making a selection. Many job applicants feel hesitant to follow up, assuming that they may annoy or nag hiring managers. Generally, however, your polite follow-ups show that you want the position and that you are persistent. As shown in Figure 16.14, most hiring managers expect you to follow up, with nearly half (43 percent) stating you should check back at least once per week.

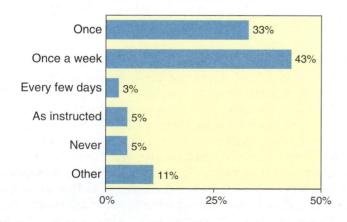

FIGURE 16.14

How Often Should You Check Back after Being Interviewed?

Nationwide Survey of Human Resource Professionals

Source: From Society for Human Resource Management, "SHRM Poll: Interviewing Do's and Don'ts for Job Seekers," September 15, 2009. Reprinted with permission via Copyright Clearance Center.

Leaving an Organization

LO16.11 Explain etiquette for leaving an organization with grace and foresight.

When you accept a new position, you can extend several courtesies to your current employer and ensure that you leave on good terms so that your supervisors can provide a positive recommendation in the future if you need it. In the first place, you should inform your supervisor that you are leaving immediately, preferably in person. Show graciousness and appreciation for the professional opportunities you have been given. Be careful about bragging or boasting about your new position, which will imply to some of your colleagues that you do not appreciate the sacrifices that many of your supervisors and colleagues likely made for you.[28] In addition to telling your supervisor in person that you are leaving, you may be required to write a formal resignation. Write a brief, warm, and appreciative letter (see Figure 16.15).

FIGURE 16.15

Resignation Letter

BETTER HORIZONS CREDIT UNION
Est. 1937

May 14, 2013

Christine Russo, President and CEO
Better Horizons Loop, Pescaloosa, FL 91214

RE: Notice of Resignation

Dear Christine:

I am writing to inform you of my resignation from Better Horizons Credit Union effective May 31, 2013.

Leaving BHCU is an extremely difficult decision. Please accept my deep gratitude for the many professional opportunities you have provided me.

Most of all, I will miss the people of BHCU. When we say the "Better Horizons family," we are not exaggerating.

Best wishes to you and the credit union for continued growth and success!

Sincerely,

Haniz Zogby

Haniz Zogby
Better Horizons Credit Union

This concise letter provides all needed components: a resignation date and an expression of goodwill.

Expression of goodwill and gratitude is professional, warm, and sincere.

COMMUNICATION Q&A

CONVERSATIONS WITH CURRENT BUSINESS PROFESSIONALS

Peter Cardon: What do you think are some ways students can make themselves stand out in the job application process?

Nancy Vaccaro: The application process is your opportunity to promote your unique attributes and emphasize what sets you apart from other applicants. Think about how best to communicate what relevant skills you can bring to an organization. Employers are looking for applicants who are motivated for success, so be sure to highlight work that you've done in and out of the classroom setting such as internships, volunteer jobs, or class projects. While it may sound basic, you should always be thorough, neat, and pay attention to detail on the application. Avoid using overarching, generic comments such as "open to any position." As you start your job search, take a focused approach and target your application to a specific job or position.

Nancy Vaccaro *is an HR manager at NBCUniversal. She has held HR management positions for over 15 years at The Walt Disney Company, Mattel, and Easton-Bell Sports.*

PC: What do you think are some keys to developing an effective résumé? What are some of the most common mistakes you see?

NV: Employers typically spend just a few seconds reviewing a résumé. This means you have a very small window of opportunity to catch and hold the attention of a recruiter and, ultimately, a hiring manager. Be mindful of typos and grammatical errors. Provide as much detail as possible without being too wordy. Generally, one to two pages for your résumé is acceptable. Always provide current contact information, and stay clear of listing an email address that runs the risk of reading and sounding inappropriate or unprofessional. Make your résumé visually appealing by steering clear of fonts that clutter the page. Take a thoughtful approach and speak not only to what you've accomplished, but how you did it. As a hiring manager, I look for candidates who are motivated, forward-thinkers, and not just "doers."

As you tailor your résumé, use keywords and terminology that are directly related to the job for which you're applying. It's not uncommon for organizations to use talent management or recruiting tools that parse résumés and search for keywords electronically. But do this with care! If you're unable to demonstrate the correlation between the keywords and your own work experience and skill set, employers will know very quickly that you are not a fit for their needs or their organizations. With all this said, it's just as important to add some personality to your résumé and make it interesting so it doesn't read too much like a job description. Consider your résumé as a marketing tool or an advertisement of your skills, accomplishments, and achievements. What sets YOU apart from all other candidates? Highlight your unique tangible and intangible qualities and transferable skills. How would you apply them? How can they add value to an organization? You're branding yourself as the type of employee that employers want on their team and in their organization.

PC: What do you think are some keys to an effective job interview? What are some of the most common mistakes you see?

NV: Prepare for the interview in advance by researching and familiarizing yourself with the company and the job description. I've often interviewed candidates who weren't able to tell me what they knew about the company and couldn't articulate their understanding of the job. In the eyes of prospective employers, this is a sign that you don't care and you aren't taking your job search seriously. You should come prepared with a list of questions to ask at the end of the interview as well as questions you anticipate will be asked of you. Don't be surprised if you're asked to provide real examples of items that you've listed as accomplishments on your résumé. Stay engaged, pay attention in the interview, and take notes, as some of your prepared questions will inevitably be answered in the course of the interview, and others will arise. Lastly, always demonstrate your level of professionalism and interest in the job by sending a thank you note or email to all those you've interviewed with.

PC: What is the most important piece of advice for business students in gaining an entry-level business position?

NV: Network! Network! Network! Build your network through social media tools like LinkedIn, Facebook, and Twitter. Understand your career goals, stay positive, and have confidence in your abilities! Good luck!

Chapter Takeaway for *Employment Communications*

LO 16.1. Identify your key selling points for the job application process. (pp. 466–467)

Effective résumés, cover letters, and interviews enhance **your personal credibility.**

It shows **competence** when you demonstrate skills and/or knowledge to complete work tasks.	It shows **caring** when you demonstrate the ability to manage effective workplace relationships.	It shows **character** when you demonstrate that you uphold high professional norms and standards.

See *skills and attributes that reflect competence, caring, and character* in Table 16.1.

See *an example of a self-inventory* in Figure 16.1.

LO 16.2. Evaluate the primary needs of employers for positions of interest. (pp. 467–469)

See *an example of analyzing a job posting for key needs* in Figure 16.2.

LO 16.3. Set up the message structure for résumés and cover letters. (pp. 470–471)

Components of Chronological Résumés	**Components of Functional Résumés**
• Name block	• Name block
• Summary of qualifcations *or* Career objective (optional)	• Summary of qualifications *or* Career summary
• Education	• Skills
• Work experience	• Additional information
• Additional information	

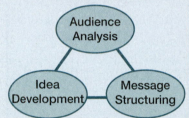

AIM Planning Process
Audience Analysis: Identify the abilities and attributes that add value to employers.
Idea Development: Identify your career interests and job-related abilities and attributes.
Message Structuring: Match your abilities and attributes to the needs of employers.

LO 16.4. Highlight your qualifications with effective tone, style, and design. (pp. 471–477)

Principles of Effective Résumés	
• Emphasize accomplishments with action verbs.	• Avoid buzzwords and jargon.
• Quantify accomplishments where possible.	• Be exact and avoid any errors.
• Position your most important contributions first.	• Group and label information to improve ease of reading.
• Group and label information to increase ease of reading.	• Format to distinguish pieces of information.
• Remove irrelevant details.	• Select a simple yet visually appealing layout.

See *examples of action words* in Tables 16.3 and 16.4; *quantifying accomplishments* in Table 16.5; *positioning contributions* in Table 16.6; *removing unnecessary details* in Table 16.7; *avoiding clichés* in Table 16.8; *proofreading for typos and misspellings* in Table 16.9; *grouping and labeling* in Table 16.10; and *formatting to distinguish key pieces of information* in Table 16.11.

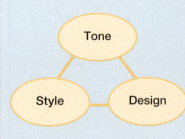

Tone, Style, and Design
Tone: Tell the story of your abilities and attributes with tempered enthusiasm and confidence. Avoid a me-first mentality.
Style: Display an action orientation and ensure a consistency of facts throughout your employment application.
Design: Make sure that employers can pick out key pieces of information to understand your story quickly.

LO 16.5. Create chronological and functional résumés to highlight your key selling points. (pp. 477–482)

See *examples of ineffective and effective chronological résumés* in Figures 16.4 and 16.5.

See *an example of a functional résumé* in Figure 16.6.

See *examples of online profiles on social networking and job websites* in Figure 16.7.

LO 16.6. Develop a list of references that will improve your employment prospects. (pp. 482–483)

See *an example of a reference list* in Figure 16.8.

LO 16.7. Compose effective cover letters that highlight your key selling points. (pp. 483–487)

Components of Cover Letters
● Interest in position
● Match with position
● Call to action

See *examples of ineffective and effective solicited cover letters* in Figures 16.9 and 16.10.

See *an example of an unsolicited referral cover letter* in Figure 16.11.

LO 16.8. Review your job application documents for effectiveness and fairness. (pp. 486–489)

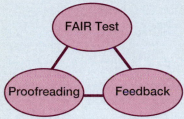

Reviewing Process
FAIR Test: Make sure every element of your job application package is factual and accurate.
Proofreading: Review your documents many times to avoid any errors or inconsistencies.
Feedback: Get feedback from fix or six trusted individuals about the effectiveness of your documents.

LO 16.9. Develop strategies for responding to common job interview questions. (pp. 489–494)

See *common interview questions* in Table 16.12.

See *ineffective and effective responses to interview questions* in Table 16.13.

Components of STAR Stories	
● Situation	● Actions
● Tasks	● Results

See *an example of a STAR story* in Table 16.14.

See *examples of ineffective and effective questions by job candidates* in Table 16.15.

LO 16.10. Explain etiquette for following up after job interviews. (pp. 494–495)

See *an example of a thank-you note following an interview* in Figure 16.13.

LO 16.11. Explain etiquette for leaving an organization with grace and foresight. (p. 496)

See *an example of a resignation letter* in Figure 16.15.

Key Terms

abilities (p. 466)

attributes (p. 466)

chronological résumé (p. 477)

functional résumé (p. 477)

solicited cover letter (p. 485)

STAR method (p. 493)

unsolicited cover letter (p. 485)

Discussion Exercises

16.1 Chapter Review Questions (LO 16.1 to LO 16.11)

A. How can identifying your job interests, abilities, and attributes help you develop an effective résumé?

B. In what ways can you categorize your key abilities and attributes to project credibility?

C. What are some ways of identifying the key abilities and attributes employers are seeking for unfilled positions?

D. What are the benefits and drawbacks of chronological and functional résumés?

E. What strategies can you use to project competence and confidence but not arrogance in your job application messages?

F. What is the underlying purpose of grouping and labeling data on your résumé?

G. What strategies can you use to develop a reliable reference list for your job searches?

H. What are the key factors in appropriate etiquette for your job interview?

I. Explain how the STAR approach to answering interview questions can help you display your key abilities and attributes.

J. What are some principles to abide by when leaving a position?

16.2 Using All Communication Channels in the Job Search Process (LO 16.2)

Recently, Terry J. Lundgren, CEO and president of Macy's, was asked, "[Do you have] any job-seeking advice for college grads?" Here's what he had to say:

Use whatever contact you have to try to get your résumé read. That's the most important thing—just to get it in front of people. Because we're all flooded with, of course, thousands and thousands of résumés in a company of our size, and getting your résumé read is not an automatic. And so do what you can do to get it in front of the people who matter who will read it. It's not the CEO typically, by the way; it's the HR person or the head of recruiting or head of training or whatever. Third, don't stop there. Don't just do it online, because it's easy to do it online. Do it online and then put it in an envelope and send it to the top company that you're interested in pursuing. And then follow up with a phone call, and talk to the assistant and say: "I just want to make sure that my résumé's getting read. I'm very interested in your company, and it's really important to me. And I just want to know—can you give me advice?—is there anything that I can do to get my résumé in front of your boss?" Whatever you have to say, just to show the most important thing—that you're hungry. And to convince them, maybe you use a little of your acting skills. And I'll probably relate it to

college dating—you know, use a little, "I'm really interested in you"— to say: "This is the company I want to work for. Yours is the company that I want to work for." And then once you get, hopefully, more than one opportunity, you're back in charge to say, "Where do I want to go and where do I want to work."[29]

Based on Lundgren's comments and your own perspectives, respond to the following questions:

A. Explain what Lundgren means by showing "you're hungry" for a position. Describe ways in which you can show hunger in a positive way.

B. What does he suggest about the effectiveness of relying exclusively on electronic means to submit job applications? What combination of communication channels do you consider optimal for gaining a job of interest?

C. He suggests that you should view the process like dating. In what ways does this analogy make sense to you? Explain.

16.3 Identifying What Employers Are Seeking (LO 16.2)

Recently, Anne Berkowitch, co-founder and chief executive of SelectMinds, discussed how her approach to hiring new employees has evolved:

I started out recruiting for skills that I knew I didn't have and I didn't understand intuitively. I was putting way too much emphasis on skills and background and what I could see on paper. I wasn't trusting myself to evaluate whether these were the right people. I'd say I went through a spate where I made the wrong hires. Then I said, "I have to do this differently, and I'm just going to trust my instinct about the right kind of person to bring onto this team." I had to hire people who had skills and experience I needed, but who they were as a person played a much bigger role in what I looked for. The people I want to hire share a number of characteristics. They're smart. They're problem solvers. They're good at what they do. They are honest with themselves, which to me is extremely important. If you're not honest with yourself, then too much of your energy goes toward managing what you're saying to everybody else, rather than what you should be doing. They are curious and they want to do things outside their comfort zone. They're passionate—it doesn't matter about what. It could be about theater. It could be about your kids. The other quality is they're people who want to be part of a group to build something. They're not looking for title. They're really motivated by coming on board. At this point, I feel like I could talk to somebody for five minutes and have a good sense of whether they have those qualities, and I'll be right 85 percent of the time.[30]

A. Explain what you think Berkowitch means when she says she started prioritizing hiring employees for "who they were as a person" more so than by their skills and experience?

B. What attributes does she look for in particular when hiring new employees? Are these attributes that you can demonstrate on paper? Explain.

C. She says she can judge whether a person fits her company within five minutes. Do you believe that hiring managers can do this reliably? Assuming that you have only five minutes to demonstrate your value to a hiring manager, what would you want to stand out about yourself?

16.4 Showing Passion for a Company (LO 16.2)

Maigread Eichten, CEO and president at The FRS Company, recently described the importance of knowing about and having passion for a company:

> I interview a ton of people and I get really frustrated with interviews, to be honest, because I find that people come in a lot of times and they don't even know that much about the company, which I find just really odd. I went to business school, and I decided I wanted a PepsiCo internship. They were only taking one intern, so my shot at getting this Pepsi internship was slim to none, because I had no experience. But I decided I wanted this internship and what I did was—I think about this all the time when I interview people, sort of, why don't they do this to me?— I researched all the people coming to campus to interview. I knew everything about them. I knew everything about Pepsi-Cola and the PepsiCo company. I knew everybody in the UCLA recruiting office and I wrote the story of myself as a brand and I came up with a whole talk about why Pepsi should hire me, and the assets I could bring. I had called up the two or three people who had been Pepsi interns from other campuses, and I found out every single thing that they had done as interns. So I had done all that work before I took this interview. I was one of the four people they took back to New York for an interview, and I got this internship. I was probably also incredibly annoying, but I certainly was super qualified. And what I would say to my kids is, to get the job you need two things. You need the functional skills, but then you also have to be super prepared, and you have to have incredible passion. You have to make that person want to hire you. They have to have a reason to hire you. There's no excuse why you can't have that. I'm just really surprised by some of the people I interview. A few people, when I say "FRS," they say, "I haven't tried the product." If they say that, the interview is over.[31]

A. Eichten explains that job candidates should have "incredible passion." What do you think are some ways you can appropriately show passion for a company during the job search process?

B. She stated that she was likely viewed as "annoying" during the hiring process because of her persistence. How much should a job candidate follow up? How much should a job candidate contact a potential employer?

Evaluation Exercises

16.5 Interviewing with a Hiring Manager about Job Application Best Practices (LO 16.1, LO 16.2)

Contact a hiring manager (consider any person you know who is involved in the hiring process) and arrange a time to interview that person for 30 minutes to one hour. Ask the hiring manager about the following related to hiring new employees:

A. Most common mistakes on résumés and cover letters.

B. Aspects in résumés and cover letters that make successful job candidates stand out.

C. Keys to successful interviews.

D. Common mistakes at job interviews.

E. Appropriate ways to follow up after interviews.

After the interview, write a two-page report detailing best practices for successfully navigating the job application process and getting a job. Tailor your report to undergraduate students who are seeking entry-level professional positions.

16.6 Getting Feedback on Your Résumé and Cover Letter (LO 16.3, LO 16.4, LO 16.5, LO 16.7, LO 16.8)

To determine how well you are promoting your selling points (your two or three key abilities and two or three key attributes), do the following in this order:

A. Write down your key selling points.

B. Create your résumé and cover letter to highlight these key selling points.

C. Without providing what you believe are your key selling points, ask a trusted classmate/colleague/professor to review your résumé and cover letter. Specifically, ask your peer to answer the following questions:

1) Based on these documents, what do you think my key selling points are? Ask your peer to mention abilities or skills and attributes or traits.

2) Do my key selling points stand out clearly? Do you think my résumé and cover letter provide a consistent message about my selling points?

3) What suggestions do you have for me to improve these documents?

After getting responses from your peer, answer the following questions:

A. What did your peer say were your key selling points? What did your peer say about how well your selling points stood out?

B. How closely aligned were your peer's observations with what you intended to be your key selling points?

C. Based on your peer's observations, what modifications should you make to your résumé and cover letter to better highlight your selling points?

16.7 Getting Feedback on Your Résumé from a Professional in Your Desired Discipline/Industry (LO 16.3, LO 16.4, LO 16.5, LO 16.8)

Find a professional in the discipline and/or industry that interests you. Ask this person to review your résumé and give you feedback about the following: (a) strength of your résumé in gaining the position you seek; (b) advice for improving the résumé; (c) areas of your résumé that may appear less credible or perhaps even exaggerated; and (d) advice for increasing career opportunities. Turn in the following:

A. Revised résumé.

B. Document detailing what you learned from the business professional and what changes you made to your résumé as a result.

16.8 Getting Feedback on Your Résumé from Classmates (LO 16.3, LO 16.4, LO 16.5, LO 16.8)

Form a group of three to four classmates. Read one another's résumés, spending three to five minutes per résumé. As you read, focus on how well the person communicates key abilities and attributes. Debrief by explaining the following:

A. Key abilities and attributes communicated by the résumé.

B. Two or three areas in which the résumé could be improved.

C. Any areas in the résumé that seem less substantiated than others.

Individually, write two to three paragraphs about the comments and advice you received from the other members in your group.

Application Exercises

16.9 Evaluate Your Key Selling Points (LO 16.1)

Using Table 16.1 and Figure 16.1 as guides, do the following:

A. State your career goals.

B. Describe the three or four abilities and three or four attributes that you want to stand out most prominently in your job application package. Why do you want these skills and attributes to stand out?

C. Name the two or three abilities and attributes you most want to develop.

16.10 Analyze a Job Announcement of Interest to You (LO 16.2)

Find a job announcement for a position of interest to you. Using Figure 16.2 as a guide, do the following:

A. Group and categorize the key abilities and attributes that are being sought.

B. Describe your fit with these abilities and attributes.

C. Explain how you can compensate for abilities or attributes that you have not yet fully developed.

16.11 Using Action Words (LO 16.4)

Using Tables 16.3, 16.4, and 16.5 as guides, do the following:

A. Choose ten of the action words and create statements that you could use on your résumé with your accomplishments.

B. Make five statements of accomplishments that you could place on your résumé that include quantification (e.g., increased sales by 12 percent).

16.12 Creating a Résumé (LO 16.3, LO 16.4, LO 16.5)

Create a perfectly polished résumé.

16.13 Creating Functional and Chronological Résumés (LO 16.3, LO 16.4, LO 16.5)

Create two versions of your résumé—a chronological and a functional résumé. In addition to these two documents, create a separate

document that describes the advantages and disadvantages of using each type.

16.14 Creating a Reference List (LO 16.6)

Create a reference list with five individuals whom you could trust to provide good professional endorsements of your abilities. Provide all contact information and a brief statement about how each person knows you.

16.15 Creating a Cover Letter (LO 16.7)

Choose a job announcement that interests you. Write a cover letter that is addressed to the contact person/organization in this announcement.

16.16 Telling Stories with the STAR Method (LO 16.9)

Write down how you would answer one of the following interview questions using the STAR method: (a) Can you tell me about a challenge you overcame at work? (b) Can you give me an example of how you showed leadership at work? or (c) Can you tell me about one of your recent successes at work? You can substitute school experiences for work experiences if you'd like.

16.17 Writing a Thank-You Note (LO 16.10)

Choose a job position that interests you. Assume you have just completed the job interview. Write a thank-you message that you think appropriately expresses gratitude and improves your chances in the hiring process.

16.18 Writing a Resignation Letter (LO 16.11)

Assume that you will be resigning from a job (you can use a current/past position). Write a message that states when you will leave, shows your appreciation, and ensures goodwill with the employer in the future.

Endnotes

1. KSA (Knowledge, Skills, Abilities) approach for federal jobs.

2. Society for Human Resource Management, "SHRM Poll: Interviewing Do's and Don'ts for Job Seekers," (September 15, 2009), retrieved from *Society for Human Resource Management* website http://www.shrm.org/Research/SurveyFindings/Articles/Pages/InterviewingDosandDonts.aspx.

3. Society for Human Resource Management, "Networking Professionally: Employee Perspective" (January 12, 2009), retrieved from *Society of Human Resource Management* website http://www.shrm.org/Research/SurveyFindings/Articles/Documents/OEnetworking.pdf.

4.   Accountemps, "Survey Shows Longer Resumes Now More Acceptable," March 20, 2007, http://www.accountemps.com/PressRoom?id=1840 (accessed January 10, 2010).

5.   Accountemps, "The Devil Is in the 'Resume' Details: Typos or Grammatical Errors Most Common Resume Mistake, Survey Shows," March 31, 2005, http://accountemps.rhi.mediaroom.com/index.php?s=189&item=250 (accessed January 10, 2010).

6.   Accountemps, "Most Wanted: 'People' People: Survey Shows Interpersonal Skills Can Trump Technical Knowledge in Job Search," October 29, 2009, http://accountemps.rhi.mediaroom.com/index.php?s=189&item=863 (accessed January 10, 2010).

7.   Accountemps, "More Than Half of Executives Surveyed Spend Five Minutes or Less Screening a Resume," January 17, 2001, http://accountemps.rhi.mediaroom.com/index.php?s=189&item=328 (accessed January 10, 2010).

8.   Accountemps, "Have a Keen Eye for Derail," July 14, 2009, http://www.accountemps.com/PressRoom?id=2491 (accessed November 20, 2010).

9.   Accountemps, "Form over Function: Three-Quarters of Executives Surveyed Prefer Chronological Resumes from Job Seekers," http://www.accountemps.com/PressRoom?id=2527 (accessed January 10, 2010).

10.   Nicole Amare and Alan Manning, "Writing for the Robot: How Employer Search Tools Have Influenced Résumé Rhetoric and Ethics," *Business Communication Quarterly* 72, no. 1 (2009): 35–60.

11.   Nancy Schullery, Linda M. Ickes, and Stephen E. Schullery, "Employer Preferences for Résumés and Cover Letters," *Business Communication Quarterly* 72, no. 2 (2009): 163–176.

12.   Accountemps, "Put In a Good Word for Me," August 13, 2003, http://www.accountemps.com/PressRoom?id=367 (accessed January 10, 2010).

13.   Kim Isaacs, "Get Your References Together for Your Job Search," retrieved October 6, 2011, from http://career-advice.monster.com/job-search/getting-started/prepare-your-references/article.aspx.

14.   Therese Droste, "Help Your References Help You," retrieved October 6, 2011, from http://career-advice.monster.com/job-search/getting-started/Help-Your-References-Help-You/article.aspx.

15.   Schullery et al., "Employer Preferences for Résumés and Cover Letters."

16.   Kim Isaacs, "Cover Letters to Recruiters," Monster.com Advice blog, retrieved January 20, 2011, from http://career-advice.monster.com/resumes-cover-letters/cover-letter-tips/cover-letters-to-recruiters/article.aspx.

17.   JoAnn S. Lublin, "The Keys to Unlocking Your Most Successful Career," *The Wall Street Journal Career Journal* [online] (July 6, 2010).

18.   Kim Isaacs, "Cold Cover Letters," Monster.com Advice blog, retrieved January 20, 2011, from http://career-advice.monster.com/resumes-cover-letters/Cover-Letter-Tips/Cold-Cover-Letters/article.aspx.

19.   Society for Human Resource Management, "SHRM Poll: Interviewing Do's and Don'ts for Job Seekers."

20.   Kathy Gurchiek, "Dress to Impress, Not Stress, the Hiring Manager," *Society for Human Resource Management HR News* [online] (November 1, 2010).

21.   Society for Human Resource Management, "SHRM Poll: Interviewing Do's and Don'ts for Job Seekers."

22.   Eve Tahmincioglu, "Avoid 'the Seven Deadly Sins of Interviewing'" (August, 29, 2010), MSNBC Careers blog, retrieved January 10, 2011, from www.msnbc.msn.com/id/38882416/ns/business-careers.

23.   Harrison Barnes, "Use Personal Stories to Connect with an Employer and Get a Job," Harrison Barnes blog, retrieved January 10, 2011, from www.aharrisonbarnes.com/use-stories-to-get-a-job-and-connect-with-an-employer/.

24.   Tory Johnson, "Land That Job: What Interviewers Really Want You to Ask Them" (April 19, 2010), retrieved October 7, 2011, from http://abcnews.go.com/GMA/JobClub/questions-job-interview/story?id=10409243.

25.   Accountemps, "Most Executives OK with Applicants Asking about Compensation by Second Interview" (March 18, 2009), http://accountemps.rhi.mediaroom.com/index.php?s=189&item=165 (accessed January 10, 2010).

26.   Accountemps, "Thanks, But No Thanks: Survey Shows Thank-You Notes Influence Hiring Decisions, but Only Half of Candidates Send Them" (August 9, 2007), http://accountemps.rhi.mediaroom.com/index.php?s=189&item=203 (accessed January 10, 2010).

27.   Society for Human Resource Management, "SHRM Poll: Interviewing Do's and Don'ts for Job Seekers."

28.   Beverly Langford, *The Etiquette Edge: The Unspoken Rules for Business Success* (New York: American Management Association, 2005).

29.   *New York Times* Corner Office Blog, "Career Advice," retrieved June 15, 2010, from http://projects.nytimes.com/corner-office/Communication.

30.   Adam Bryant, "Learn to Lead from the Back of the Boat," *New York Times* Corner Office Blog (September 4, 2010), retrieved September 6, 2010, from http://www.nytimes.com/2010/09/05/business/05corner.html?ref=business.

31.   *New York Times* Corner Office Blog, "Career Advice."

Punctuation, Number Usage, and Grammar

This appendix includes rules that cover many common writing issues. For a complete review of language mechanics guidelines, consult a comprehensive guidebook such as the *Gregg Reference Manual*. Also, use the online resources, including exercises and assessments.

Overview of Terms Used in This Appendix

Nouns are words or phrases that refer to persons, places, objects, qualities, or activities.

Subjects are nouns that are the primary topics of a sentence. The subject determines the verb form used in the sentence (see rule G2, page 517).

Verbs are words or phrases that express action or existence.

Predicates are verb phrases that in combination with a subject make a complete sentence.

Adjectives are words or phrases that modify nouns.

Adverbs are words or phrases that modify adjectives, verbs, or adverbs.

Prepositions are words that show the relationships between nouns (e.g., *at*, *in*, *by*, *from*, *with*).

Coordinating conjunctions connect words, phrases, or clauses; examples include *and*, *but*, *or*, and *nor*.

Clauses contain a subject and a predicate. **Independent clauses** express a complete thought and can stand alone, whereas **dependent clauses** cannot stand alone.

Participles are words that share characteristics of verbs and adjectives. *Present participles* end in *ing*; *past participles* end in *ed*; and *perfect participles* are a combination of a form of the verb "to have" and a past participle.

Punctuation and Formatting

Commas

Commas have two functions: (1) to set off nonessential expressions that break the flow of a sentence and (2) to separate items in a sentence so that their relationships to one another are clear. *Nonessential* expressions, if removed, do not alter the meaning of the sentence or make the sentence incomplete. Table A.1 lists ten key rules related to commas, with examples. Each rule in this section is identified by a letter (C, for comma) and a number.

TABLE A.1

Comma Rules

Rules	Examples
C1. Use commas to distinguish essential from nonessential information (essential expressions do not require commas; nonessential expressions do require commas).	✔ Sergey Brin and Larry Page, <u>who were attending Stanford at the time</u>, developed the initial technology for Google searches. **Explanation:** The *who* clause is nonessential because a specific person is mentioned; the information does not narrow down who the people are. ✔ Graduate students <u>who were attending Stanford University at the time</u> developed the initial technology for Google searches. **Explanation:** The *who* clause is essential because it further specifies, or narrows down, who the students are – students *at Stanford*. ✔ Google's initial public offering <u>occurred in 2004, the same year that</u> Google developed a multiyear alliance with AOL Europe. **Explanation:** A comma is required after the year 2004 since the following expression does not further specify which year and is thus nonessential. ✔ Google's initial public offering <u>occurred in the same year that</u> Google developed a multiyear alliance with AOL Europe. **Explanation:** A comma is not required because the *that* clause further specifies which year and is thus an essential expression.
C2. Use commas to set off interrupting expressions.	✔ Larry, <u>rather than Sergey</u>, was listed as the inventor on the patent for Google's original search mechanism. **Explanation:** The underlined expression interrupts the flow of the sentence from subject to verb. ✔ Eric Schmidt, <u>the CEO at Google since 2001</u>, was previously Chairman of the Board and CEO at Novell. **Explanation:** The underlined expression is an appositive and interrupts the flow of the sentence from subject to verb. ✔ Google's largest market, <u>which accounts for 47 percent of revenues</u>, is the United States. **Explanation:** The underlined expression provides further but nonessential information and interrupts the flow of the sentence from subject to verb. ✔ Google offers a variety of applications, <u>such as Google Docs and Google Calendar</u>. **Explanation:** The underlined expression is additional and nonessential information. ✔ Google, <u>in my opinion</u>, is the best technology company to work for. **Explanation:** Independent thoughts interrupt the flow of the sentence and require commas. ✔ Google Chrome, <u>if you're looking for an open-source web browser</u>, may be a fit for you. **Explanation:** Dependent clauses in the middle of the sentence must be set off by commas. ✔ Double-digit annual sales growth at Google during the past three years, <u>in spite of the recession and increased competition</u>, demonstrates the strong demand for Google products and services. **Explanation:** This nonessential prepositional phrase in the middle of the sentence interrupts the flow of the sentence. **Note:** Many clauses that require commas in the beginning or middle of a sentence do not require one when they are at the end of the sentence. ✔ Google Chrome may be a fit for you <u>if you're looking for an open-source web browser</u>. **Explanation:** This dependent clause at the end of the sentence does not interrupt the flow of the sentence, so no comma is needed. ✔ Double-digit annual sales growth at Google during the past three years demonstrates the strong demand for Google products and services <u>in spite of the recession and increased competition</u>. **Explanation:** This prepositional phrase at the end of the sentence does not interrupt the flow of the sentence, so no comma is needed.

TABLE A.1

(Continued)

Rules	Examples
C3. Use a comma following a transitional expression.	✔ <u>Also</u>, Google's social networking website has gained little acceptance in the United States. **Explanation:** Transitional expressions such as *also* help readers relate sentences to one another. Transitional expressions are followed by commas. ✔ <u>As a result</u>, Google purchased a new mobile display ad provider to increase its revenues in mobile advertising. **Explanation:** Transitional expressions such as *as a result* help readers relate sentences to one another. Transitional expressions are followed by commas.
C4. Use a comma between two independent clauses separated by *and*, *but*, *or*, or *nor*.	✔ Sergey Brin is currently the President of Technology<u>, and</u> Larry Page is currently the President of Products. **Explanation:** Two independent clauses are separated by a comma and coordinating conjunction. **Exception:** When an introductory expression applies to both independent clauses, a comma is not placed between the independent clauses. ✔ Since Google's organizational restructuring in 2001, Sergey Brin has served as the President of Technology <u>and</u> Larry Page has served as the President of Products. **Explanation:** A comma is not placed between the independent clauses because the introductory expression applies to both of them. **Exception:** Short compound sentences often do not require a comma (generally less than 12 to 13 words). Sergey is in charge of technology <u>and</u> Larry is in charge of products. **Explanation:** This sentence is short (13 words) and is understood easily without a comma separating the two independent clauses.
C5. Use commas in a series with three or more items.	✔ Google's client services include <u>Google Toolbar, Google Chrome, and Google Pack</u>. **Explanation:** Each of these three items in a series is separated from one another by a comma. ✔ Google has developed an innovative culture by <u>setting up an informal work environment, providing the top incentives in the industry, and encouraging employees to spend 20 percent of their time on their own projects</u>. **Explanation:** Each of the three items in the series is separated from one another by a comma. ✔ Google spends far above industry averages in the following areas: <u>marketing, training, and research and development</u>. **Explanation:** Each item in the series is separated by commas. Notice that *research and development* is a single item.
C6. Use a comma between two independent adjectives preceding a noun.	✔ Google has long been recognized as an <u>innovative, unconventional</u> company. **Explanation:** *Innovative* and *unconventional* each independently modifies *company*. **Note:** There are two quick ways to identify independent adjectives. First, if you can place the word *and* between the two adjectives without changing the meaning, then they are independent (innovative and unconventional). Second, if you can reverse the order of the adjectives without changing the meaning, then they are independent (unconventional, innovative).

TABLE A.1

(Continued)

Rules	Examples
C7. Use a comma after introductory expressions.	✔ <u>After Google had installed solar panels at Googleplex</u>, it continued its environmental efforts by placing herds of goats around the campus so that mowing the lawns was not necessary. **Explanation:** Commas are always placed after introductory dependent clauses.
	✔ <u>By installing thousands of solar panels at Googleplex</u>, Google showed its commitment to environmental causes. **Explanation:** Commas are always placed after introductory participial phrases.
	✔ <u>To show its commitment to environmental causes</u>, Google has installed thousands of solar panels at Googleplex. **Explanation:** Commas are always placed after introductory infinitive phrases.
	✔ <u>Under the new set of corporate policies</u>, Google will only lease LEED-certified buildings. **Explanation:** Commas are placed after long (five or more words) introductory prepositional phrases.
	Common Exceptions*
	Short introductory adverbs that explain *when* (e.g., next week), *how often* (e.g., frequently), *where* (e.g., at the office), or *why* (e.g., for this reason) do not require commas afterward.
	✔ <u>A few years ago</u> Google became part of the public debate over network neutrality. **Explanation:** An introductory adverb that expresses *when* does not require a comma.
	✔ <u>Often</u> the company issues public statements regarding its stand on this issue. **Explanation:** An introductory adverb that expresses *how often* does not require a comma.
	✔ <u>At Google</u> the leadership team believes that users should have complete control over the content they view. **Explanation:** An introductory adverb that expresses *where* does not require a comma.
	✔ <u>For this reason</u> Google supports network neutrality. **Explanation:** An introductory adverb that expresses *why* does not require a comma.
	Short (less than five words) introductory prepositional phrases that do not contain a verb, a transitional phrase, or an independent comment do not require commas.
	✔ <u>In the interview</u> Google's CEO emphasized the company's commitment to network neutrality. **Explanation:** A comma is not required because the introductory prepositional phrase is short (three words) and does not contain a verb, a transitional phrase, or an independent thought.
	✔ <u>In the interview with Google's CEO</u>, he emphasized the company's commitment to network neutrality. **Explanation:** A comma is required because the introductory prepositional phrase is long (five or more words).
	✔ <u>In the statement</u> he explained that broadband carriers should not be allowed to control content. **Explanation:** A comma is not required because the introductory prepositional phrase is short (three words) and does not contain a verb, a transitional phrase, or an independent thought.
	✔ <u>In making this statement</u>, he demonstrated Google's position that broadband carriers should not be allowed to control content. **Explanation:** A comma is required. Though the introductory prepositional phrase is short (four words), it contains a verb.
	*A lot of variation exists in how writers apply these exceptions. Many writers use commas after all introductory expressions to avoid analyzing each situation.

TABLE A.1

(*Continued*)

Rules	Examples
C8. Use commas in dates.	✔ Tuesday, May 10 **Explanation:** A comma separates a day and a date. ✔ May 10, 2011 **Explanation:** A comma separates a date and a year. ✔ May 2011 **Explanation:** A comma does not separate a month and a year. ✔ Between May 10, 2011, and May 13, 2011, there were 13 billion Google searches. **Explanation:** A comma follows a date-year combination in the middle of a sentence.
C9. Use commas as needed for clarity.	✘ At the Googleplex campus building engineers have identified several approaches to reducing carbon emissions. **Explanation:** Although technically correct (*At the Googleplex campus* is a short introductory adverb), many readers will wonder what the subject of the sentence is. Is it *building engineers* or just *engineers*? ✔ At the Googleplex campus, building engineers have identified several approaches to reducing carbon emissions. **Explanation:** The comma between campus and building clearly shows that *building* modifies *engineers*. ✘ In 2010 37 of Google's top employees left and took positions at Facebook. **Explanation:** Although technically correct (*In 2010* is a short introductory adverb), readers may misunderstand or become momentarily confused with two sets of numbers placed next to one another. ✔ In 2010, 37 of Google's top employees left and took positions at Facebook. **Explanation:** A comma between the two numbers clarifies that they do not belong together. **Alternatively:** In 2010 thirty-seven of Google's top employees left and took positions at Facebook. **Explanation:** Spelling out one of the numbers clarifies that the two numbers do not belong together.
C10. Common misuses of commas.	✘ Google, provides a number of inexpensive enterprise products. **Explanation:** Commas do not separate subjects from verbs. ✘ Google provides, a number of inexpensive enterprise products. **Explanation:** Commas do not separate verbs from objects. ✘ Google provides a number of free, services. **Explanation:** Commas do not separate adjectives from nouns. ✘ The CEO, of Google has prioritized the launch of enterprise products to compete directly with Microsoft. **Explanation:** Commas do not separate related prepositional phrases. ✘ Sergey Brin is currently the President of Technology, and is a member of the board of directors. **Explanation:** Commas do not separate two predicates with a single subject. ✘ Sergey Brin is currently the President of Technology, Larry Page is currently the President of Products. **Explanation:** Commas do not separate two independent clauses not connected with a coordinating conjunction (this is called a *comma splice*). ✘ Google's stock price rose rapidly, after it went public. **Explanation:** Commas do not separate a dependent clause at the end of a sentence. ✘ To acquire On2 Technologies, was a key move in improving Google's video compression capabilities. **Explanation:** Commas do not separate infinitives that serve as subjects from verbs. ✘ Acquiring On2Technologies, was a key move in improving Google's video compression capabilities. **Explanation:** Commas do not separate gerunds that serve as subjects from their related verbs. ✘ Google's nearly, limitless email service is free. **Explanation:** Commas do not separate adverbs from adjectives.

Semicolon Rules

Rules	Examples
S1. Use a semicolon between two closely related independent clauses omitting *and*, *but*, *or*, or *nor*.	✔ Google's business model focuses on providing applications free of charge to users and receiving revenue through <u>advertising; Microsoft's</u> business model focuses on selling applications to users without the clutter of advertising. **Explanation:** The semicolon separates two closely related independent clauses to emphasize their relatedness.
	Alternatively: Google's business model focuses on providing applications free of charge to users and receiving revenue through <u>advertising. Microsoft's</u> business model focuses on selling applications to users without the clutter of advertising. **Explanation:** A period separates two independent clauses.
	✘ Google's business model focuses on providing applications free of charge to users and receiving revenue through <u>advertising, Microsoft's</u> business model focuses on selling applications to users without the clutter of advertising. **Explanation:** A comma does not separate two independent clauses (unless connected by a coordinating conjunction). Using a comma in this way is called a comma splice.
S2. Use a semicolon between two independent clauses separated by transitional expressions.	✔ Google's business model focuses on providing applications free of charge to users and receiving revenue through <u>advertising; on the other hand,</u> Microsoft's business model focuses on selling applications to users without the clutter of advertising. **Explanation:** Semicolons separate two independent clauses separated by a transitional expression.
	✔ Google offers more than 30 major products and services; however, Google derives 90 percent of its revenues through Google Web Search. **Explanation:** Semicolons separate two independent clauses separated by a transitional expression.
S3. Use semicolons between items in a series that contains internal commas.	✔ Google's major offices in the United States are in <u>Mountain View, California; New York City; and Seattle, Washington</u>. **Explanation:** Semicolons separate items in a series that contains internal commas.
	✔ The Google delegation includes <u>Jeff Huber, Senior Vice President of Engineering; Omid Kordestani, Senior Advisor in the Office of the CEO; and Rachel Whetstone, Vice President of Public Policy and Communications</u>. **Explanation:** Semicolons separate items in a series that contains internal commas.
S4. Use semicolons in a series of long dependent clauses.	✔ Google's excellent brand recognition is due to a variety of factors, <u>including that it accounts for 67 percent of the global search market; that it owns the popular online video service YouTube; and that, in spite of stiff competition, it maintains a dominant market share for webmail</u>. **Explanation:** Semicolons add clarity by separating long items in a series.

Semicolons

One major use for semicolons is to emphasize the relatedness between two independent clauses (see Table A.2). Semicolons also separate items in a series that contains internal commas or that is particularly long. Each rule in this section is identified with a letter (S, for semicolon) and a number.

Colons

Colons precede further explanations or elaborations. This rule is identified by letters (Co, for colon) and a number (see Table A.3).

TABLE A.3

Colons

Rule	Examples
Co1. Use a colon for further explanation or elaboration following an independent clause.	✔ Google faces <u>two major challenges</u>: It lacks product integration and its profitability is weakened by major currency fluctuations. **Explanation:** The colon separates a complete thought with an elaboration of *the two major challenges*.
	✔ Compared to other free webmail services, Gmail provides <u>several major benefits</u>: It provides more storage than any other major competitors, it contains a more efficient search-oriented interface, and it has a superior spam filter. **Explanation:** The colon separates a complete thought with elaboration of the *several major benefits*.
	✔ Google Sites has limited control of <u>various web design tools: For example</u>: you are restricted in using HTML, CSS, and JavaScript. **Explanation:** Independent clauses and related series are often separated by a colon and phrases such as *for example, such as*, and *namely*.
	✘ <u>Google's seven product groups are</u>: Google.com, applications, client, Google GEO, Android and Google Mobile, Google Checkout, and Google Labs. **Explanation:** The underlined introductory expression is not an independent clause, so a colon is inappropriate. It separates the verb from the object of the sentence (see C10, above).
	✔ <u>Google's seven product groups are the following</u>: Google.com, applications, client, Google GEO, Android and Google Mobile, Google Checkout, and Google Labs. **Explanation:** The underlined introductory expression is an independent clause, so a colon is appropriate.

TABLE A.4

Dashes and Hyphens

	Symbol	When to Use
Hyphen	-	To combine words (compound modifiers, some compounds)
En dash (also called figure dash)	–	To separate a range of values, such as years or page numbers
Dash (also called em dash)	—	To take the place of commas, semicolons, colons, or parentheses to add emphasis. Should be used sparingly. Consists of two hyphens with no space on either side.

Dashes and Hyphens

A dash is not the same as a hyphen; each has unique functions, and the two marks of punctuation should not be used in place of one another. A third, related mark is called an en dash. Table A.4 displays the widths and functions of hyphens, en dashes, and dashes.

The rules for dashes and hyphens are extensive, with many exceptions (see Table A.5). Consult a comprehensive style guidebook to ensure complete accuracy. Each rule in this table is identified with a letter (D, for dash; N, for en dash; and H, for hyphen) and a number.

TABLE A.5

Dash and Hyphen Rules

Rules	Examples
D1. Use dashes in place of commas for emphasis (often in pairs).	✔ Google Translate—which supports 59 languages—allows you to translate passages into nearly any language you can imagine. **Explanation:** Using dashes instead of commas highlights the additional information in a much stronger way.
D2. Use a dash in place of a semicolon for emphasis (but not between two independent clauses).	✔ Google Translate provides fairly good translation—that is, if you consider 70 to 75 percent accuracy as good. **Explanation:** Substituting a semicolon with a dash emphasizes the closely related afterthought.
D3. Use a dash in place of a colon for emphasis.	✔ Google Translate provides poor translation for most Asian languages—especially Chinese, Japanese, and Korean. **Explanation:** Substituting a dash for a colon highlights the elaboration in a much stronger way.
D4. Use dashes in place of parentheses for emphasis.	✔ WorldLingo—Google Translate's top competitor—provides the most accurate translation for most European languages. **Explanation:** Substituting dashes for parentheses highlights the additional information in a much stronger way.
D5. Use a dash to emphasize a single word.	✔ Innovation—that's what Google is all about. **Explanation:** This dash draws sharp attention to the term *innovation* and defines it as a central feature of Google culture.
D6. Use a dash for repetitions and restatements.	✔ Get a username now—before it's too late. **Explanation:** The dash restates *now* to reinforce urgency.
D7. Use a dash to summarize a preceding list.	✔ Brazil, Russia, India, China—these countries are the future for market growth. **Explanation:** This dash separates a series of items with a summary of what they are.
N1. Use an en dash to connect numbers or other items in a range.	✔ Google's headquarters are open for tours from 10 a.m.–3:30 p.m. Monday–Friday. **Explanation:** En dashes are used to separate a range of values, such as these ranges in hours and days.
H1. Use a hyphen to connect adjectives that modify a noun.	✔ Computer programmers have high-pressure jobs. **Explanation:** An adjective phrase or clause in front of a noun is hyphenated. ✘ Her computer programming job involves high-pressure. **Explanation:** An adjective phrase or clause that does not precede a noun is not hyphenated. ✔ Her computer programming job involves high pressure. **Explanation:** An adjective phrase or clause that does not precede a noun is not hyphenated. ✔ One of Google's long-term objectives is to rival Facebook with its social networking services. **Explanation:** An adjective + noun combination in front of a noun is hyphenated. ✔ Over the long term Google seeks to rival Facebook in the area of social networking. **Explanation:** An adjective + noun combination that does not precede a noun is not hyphenated. ✔ The one-way road in the Googleplex campus passes through three parks. **Explanation:** A compound that includes a number or letter in front of a noun is hyphenated. ✔ The road that passes through the Googleplex is one way. **Explanation:** A compound that includes a number or letter and does not precede a noun is not hyphenated. ✔ Larry Page is one of the most well-known business executives in the world. **Explanation:** An adverb + participle combination in front of a noun is hyphenated. ✔ Larry Page is well known around the world for his leadership in the technology business. **Explanation:** An adverb + participle combination that does not precede a noun is not hyphenated.

TABLE A.5

(*Continued*)

Rules	Examples
	✔ Google Docs provides an <u>easier-than-ever approach</u> to team writing. **Explanation:** A comparative phrase that includes the word *than* and that precedes a noun is hyphenated.
	✔ Google Docs makes team writing <u>easier than ever</u>. **Explanation:** A comparative phrase that includes the word *than* and that follows a noun is not hyphenated.
	✔ Larry and Sergey's <u>agreed-upon plan</u> was to sell off Google so that they could focus on their academic studies. **Explanation:** A participle + adverb combination in front of a noun is hyphenated.
	✔ Larry and Sergey had <u>agreed upon</u> a plan that would allow them to sell Google and continue their academic studies. **Explanation:** A participle + adverb combination that does not precede a noun is not hyphenated.
	✔ Google executives have adopted a <u>wait-and-see mentality</u> as far as developing a new social networking platform. **Explanation:** A verb + verb (often joined by *and* or *or*) combination in front of a noun is hyphenated.
	✔ Google executives will <u>wait and see</u> how the market emerges before committing more resources to developing a new social networking platform. **Explanation:** A verb + verb (often joined by *and* or *or*) combination that is not in front of a noun is not hyphenated.
	✔ The <u>break-even point</u> is around sales of $4.3 billion. **Explanation:** A verb + adverb combination in front of a noun is hyphenated.
	✔ We will <u>break even</u> when we reach sales of $4.3 billion. **Explanation:** A verb + adverb combination that does not precede a noun is not hyphenated.
	✔ She sent a <u>thank-you note</u> to each of the board members for their time and contributions. **Explanation:** A verb + noun combination in front of a noun is hyphenated.
	✔ I want to <u>thank you</u> for your time and contributions. **Explanation:** A verb + noun combination that does not precede a noun is not hyphenated.
	✔ Google has made <u>across-the-board cuts</u>. **Explanation:** Common phrases used to modify a noun are hyphenated.
	✔ Google will make cuts <u>across the board</u>. **Explanation:** Common phrases that do not precede a noun are not hyphenated.
H2. Use hyphens for particular kinds of compound adjectives as described here.	✔ We take a <u>research-based approach</u> to marketing. **Explanation:** A noun + participle combination is always hyphenated.
	✔ Our approach to marketing is <u>research-based</u>. **Explanation:** A noun + participle combination is always hyphenated.
	✔ We have a <u>long-standing commitment</u> to net neutrality. **Explanation:** An adjective + participle combination is always hyphenated.
	✔ Our commitment to net neutrality is <u>long-standing</u>. **Explanation:** An adjective + participle combination is always hyphenated.
	✔ <u>High-priced products</u> are not part of Google's business model. **Explanation:** An adjective + noun + *ed* combination is always hyphenated.
	✔ Google's business model does not involve any products that are <u>high-priced</u>. **Explanation:** An adjective + noun + *ed* combination is always hyphenated.
	✔ <u>Price-conscious customers</u> tend to use Google Docs rather than Microsoft Office. **Explanation:** A noun + adjective combination is always hyphenated.
	✔ Most customers who choose Google Docs over Microsoft Office are <u>price-conscious</u>. **Explanation:** A noun + adjective combination is always hyphenated.

TABLE A.6

Quotation Mark Rules

Rules	Examples
Q1. Use quotation marks to enclose direct quotations.	✔ As Larry Page stated, "I'm excited about our opportunities to make a big difference in people's lives through technology." **Explanation:** The quotation marks surround the *exact statement* made by Larry.
	✘ Larry Page stated that "he's excited about opportunities to make a difference in people's lives through technology." **Explanation:** Indirect statements typically begin with *that* and paraphrase a person's statements.
Q2. Use quotation marks to indicate the exact words of a source or speaker.	✔ Larry Page said that Google's technologies "make a big difference in people's lives." **Explanation:** The quotation marks indicate that these are exact words and not paraphrased.
	✔ Larry and Sergey often say that their ultimate goal is to create the "perfect search engine." **Explanation:** The quotation marks indicate that these are exact words and not paraphrased.
Q3. Use quotation marks to enclose titles of articles, presentations, and speeches.	✔ Randall Stross discussed the culture of education at Google in his recent article "What Is Google's Secret Weapon? An Army of Ph.D.'s." **Explanation:** Quotation marks surround the name of an article.
	✔ Larry Page's speech, "Don't Be Evil," at the annual convention revealed his basic philosophy about developing products and services for customers. **Explanation:** Quotation marks surround the name of a speech.

Quotation Marks

Quotation marks are used to display direct quotations, exact words, and some titles. Each rule in Table A.6 is identified by a letter (Q, for quotation) and a number.

Italics

Italics are used to emphasize words and phrases, highlight definitions, and set apart some titles. Alternatively, writers sometimes use underlining in place of italics. Each rule in Table A.7 is identified by a letter (I, for italic) and a number.

TABLE A.7

Rules for Italics

Case	Examples
I1. Use italics to emphasize a word or phrase.	✔ The misspelled term *googol* became the name of the company. **Explanation:** The word *googol* is emphasized by use of italics.
	✔ *To google it* has become part of everyday language much the way *to xerox it* was an everyday phrase in the 1980s. **Explanation:** *To google it* and *to xerox it* are italicized to highlight particular terms.
I2. Use italics for formal definition.	✔ The term *cloud computing* refers to using remote servers hosted on the Internet, rather than local servers or personal computers, to manage and process data. **Explanation:** Terms that are formally defined are typically italicized as is the case with *cloud computing*.
I3. Use italics for titles of books, newspapers, and magazines.	✔ Larry and Sergey are featured nearly once each month in *The Wall Street Journal*. **Explanation:** *The Wall Street Journal* is a newspaper, so it is italicized.
	✘ Reports that Larry Page would replace Eric Schmidt as CEO first surfaced in "Bloomberg Businessweek." **Explanation:** *Bloomberg Businessweek* is the name of a magazine and should be italicized.

TABLE A.8

Rules for Parentheses

Rules	Examples
P1. Use parentheses to enclose details and explanation.	✔ All correspondence can be sent to the CEO (Eric Schmidt), the global sales director (Nikesh Arora), or the vice president of public policy and communications (Rachel Whetstone). **Explanation:** By providing names in parentheses, additional details are provided for each position. The use of parentheses rather than dashes or commas emphasizes positions and de-emphasizes names.
	✔ Google has been identified as the most recognized brand in the world for three of the past five years (2009, 2011, 2012). **Explanation:** Provides additional information about the years.
	✔ Google's recent acquisitions (AdMob, On2 Technologies, ZAO Begun) show that it is aggressively pursuing new technologies. **Explanation:** Provides additional details about the acquisitions.
	✔ Please send your comments to Google's cloud computing team within two weeks (by May 29). **Explanation:** Clarifies the deadline.
P2. Use parentheses to enclose references and directions.	✔ Please read my report (attached to this email) about opportunities for Google in emerging markets in Africa. **Explanation:** Parentheses enclose directions to locate the report.
	✔ My last email to Larry (dated July 15) outlined a plan for Google opportunities in emerging markets in Africa. **Explanation:** Parentheses provide a date as a reference to a prior email.

Parentheses

Although people sometimes use parentheses and dashes interchangeably, they have opposite purposes. Dashes are intended to emphasize and draw attention to the phrase they set off, whereas parentheses are used to set off nonessential elements and are thus intended to de-emphasize the phrase that is contained within them. Each of the rules in Table A.8 is labeled with a letter (P, for parentheses) and a number.

Numbers, Dates, and Currency

Multiple rules apply to the treatment of numbers in a text. The following ones—in Table A.9—are identified by a letter (N, for number) and a number.

TABLE A.9

Rules for Numbers

Case	Examples
N1. Spell out numbers one through ten.	✔ Google's <u>two largest markets</u> are the United States and the United Kingdom. **Explanation:** The number is spelled out since it is ten or less.
	Exceptions: When related numbers within a sentence or paragraph are above ten.
	✔ In Google's senior management team, <u>3 of the 15 members</u> are former Microsoft employees. **Explanation:** Since a reference to 15 members is made, any other numbers referring to members should also be written in figure style.
	When referring to figures.
	✔ You can see Google's sales projections in <u>Figure 3</u>. **Explanation:** Any reference to a figure, table, or chart uses figure style.

TABLE A.9

(*Continued*)

Case	Examples
N2. Use numerals for numbers above ten.	✔ Google has <u>43 major product groups</u>. **Explanation:** Numbers over ten are generally written in figure style. ✔ My Gmail account has <u>8,028 messages</u>. **Explanation:** Numbers in thousands are generally written in numerals.
N3. Spell out numbers when they begin a sentence.	✔ <u>Eleven members</u> of Google's senior management team are former Microsoft employees. **Explanation:** Since the first word is a number, it is spelled out.
N4. Use a combination of numerals and words for large numbers (over a million).	✔ Revenues at Google topped <u>$2 billion</u> for the second consecutive year. **Explanation:** Large numbers typically include figures and words to avoid displaying too many zeroes. ✔ The mapping software project required nearly <u>3 million hours</u> of development. **Explanation:** Large numbers typically include figures and words to avoid displaying too many zeroes.
N5. Use numerals for dates.	✔ July 3, 2012 **Explanation:** Most dates are written with the month in word form to avoid confusion since some countries use a day-month-year format. **Alternatively:** 2012-07-03 **Explanation:** The *International Organization for Standardization* has adopted the YYYY-MM-DD format. **Avoid:** July 3rd, 2012 **Explanation:** Endings to numbers such as *nd* and *rd* are avoided in most business communication.
N6. Use numerals with currency symbols in text.	✔ On average Google software programmers make <u>$174 per hour</u>. **Explanation:** Currency amounts are written in figure form preceded by currency symbols. ✔ Many small businesses spend less than <u>$525 per month</u> on Google Adwords campaigns. **Explanation:** Currency amounts are written in figure form preceded by currency symbols.
N7. Spell out the word *percent* in text.	✔ The United States is Google's largest geographic market, accounting for approximately <u>47 percent of total revenues</u>. **Explanation:** The word *percent* is typically spelled out within sentences. **Exception:** Tables, forms, highly statistical documents.
N8. Use parentheses to indicate precise figures in text.	✔ Approximately half of Google's revenues (<u>47.3 percent</u>) came from the United States. **Explanation:** Precise figures are often placed in parentheses so that readers can process the information more easily. ✔ Nearly all of Google's revenues come from advertising (<u>$2.1 billion in advertising revenue out of $2.3 billion in total revenue</u>). **Explanation:** Precise figures are often placed in parentheses in text so that readers can process the information more easily.
N9. Spell out fractions in text.	✔ <u>One-fourth of all small businesses</u> in the United States use Google Adwords for advertising. **Explanation:** Fractions are spelled out in text. **Exception:** Mixed numbers (whole number plus fraction). ✔ Each year Google holds a <u>3½-day conference</u> for software developers. **Explanation:** Since the number is mixed (whole number, 3, plus fraction, 1/2), the fraction is written in figure form.
N10. Clearly differentiate adjacent numbers.	✔ In 2012, 89 percent of Gmail account holders accessed their email daily. **Explanation:** A comma is used to help readers quickly identify that these are two separate numbers. ✔ You can have up to twelve 100MB websites. **Explanation:** One of the adjacent numbers may be spelled out to help readers see that they are two separate numbers.

Grammar

Table A.10 presents only a few key rules of grammar among the many that guide written language. Each is identified with a letter (G, for grammar) and a number.

TABLE A.10

Grammar Rules

Case	Examples
G1. Ensure that pronouns agree with their antecedents in number, gender, and/or person.	✗ Google supports their employees by providing many professional development opportunities. **Explanation:** The antecedent, Google, is a singular thing. It should not be referred to as *they*, implying a plural.
	✔ Google supports its employees by providing many professional development opportunities. **Explanation:** The antecedent, Google, is a singular thing. Therefore, it is appropriately referred to as *it*.
	✗ Every employee at Google has their own health plan. **Explanation:** The antecedent, *employee*, is a singular person. Therefore, it should not be referred to as *they*, implying a plural. Writers sometimes do this incorrectly to avoid using sexist language.
	✔ Every employee at Google has his/her own health plan. **Explanation:** The antecedent, *employee*, is a singular person. Therefore, it is appropriately referred to as *he* or *she*.
	Alternatively: Employees at Google have their own health plans. **Explanation:** Changing the subject to a plural form avoids the necessity of using an awkward *he/she* expression.
	✗ Either Bill Gates or Steve Balmer will deliver their speech at the shareholders meeting. **Explanation:** Two singular nouns connected by *or* or *nor* are treated with singular pronouns.
	✔ Either Bill Gates or Steve Balmer will deliver his speech at the shareholders meeting. **Explanation:** Two singular nouns connected by *or* or *nor* are treated with singular pronouns.
	✗ I want to express our appreciation to you for your outstanding contributions over the past year. **Explanation:** The singular pronoun, *I*, should not be the antecedent for a plural possessive pronoun, *our*.
	✔ I want to express my appreciation to you for your outstanding contributions over the past year. **Explanation:** The singular pronoun, *I*, is an antecedent for the singular possessive pronoun, *my*.
	Alternatively: On behalf of all members of the senior management team, I want to express our appreciation to you for your outstanding contributions over the past year. **Explanation:** The antecedent for the plural possessive pronoun, *our*, is a plural noun, *members of the senior management team*.
G2. Ensure that subjects are paired with the correct verb form to achieve subject-verb agreement.	✗ Microsoft and each of its partners in the delegation is providing reports about upcoming developments in cloud computing. **Explanation:** The subject is plural (Microsoft *and* its partners), so the verb should not be in singular form (is).
	✔ Microsoft and each of its partners in the delegation are providing reports about upcoming developments in cloud computing. **Explanation:** The subject is plural (Microsoft *and* its partners), so the verb should be in plural form.
	✗ The handbook of employee benefits are online. **Explanation:** The subject is singular (handbook), so the verb should not be in plural form (are).
	✔ The handbook of employee benefits is online. **Explanation:** The subject is singular (handbook), so the verb should be in singular form (is).

TABLE A.10

(*Continued*)

Case	Examples
G3. Avoid comma splices.	✗ Sergey Brin is currently the President of Technology, Larry Page is currently the President of Products. **Explanation:** Two independent clauses should be separated by a period or a semicolon. They should never be separated by a comma unless a coordinating conjunction is inserted.
	✔ Sergey Brin is currently the President of Technology. Larry Page is currently the President of Products. **Explanation:** A period separates two independent clauses that are not separated by a coordinating conjunction.
	✔ Sergey Brin is currently the President of Technology, and Larry Page is currently the President of Products. **Explanation:** A coordinating conjunction *and* a comma can separate two independent clauses.
G4. Check for vague pronouns and replace them.	✗ Microsoft and Google are well known for attracting innovative, playful employees. They are also known for creating a work culture where playing practical jokes is common. They even play jokes on the public. **Explanation:** Some readers will be confused whether the *they* pronoun refers to *Microsoft and Google* or the *employees.*
	✔ Microsoft and Google are well known for attracting innovative, playful employees. The work culture allows employees to play practical jokes on one another. Sometimes the employees even play jokes on the public. **Explanation:** By removing so many references to *they,* the meaning becomes much clearer.
G5. Check for dangling expressions and misplaced modifiers and rewrite to eliminate them.	✗ Bill Gates spoke about his experience taking his SAT examination at the local university. **Explanation:** Dangling expressions create confusion because parts of the sentence are not in the correct order. In this sentence did Bill Gates talk at the local university or take the exam at the local university?
	✔ Bill Gates spoke at the local university about his experience taking his SAT examination. **Explanation:** This sentence is clear that Bill Gates spoke at the local university.
	✗ Scoring 1590 out of a possible 1600, the SAT exam didn't seem difficult. **Explanation:** Many dangling modifiers occur when an introductory participial phrase lacks a subject or does not clearly relate to the material that follows. This sentence is not clear because an SAT exam cannot score 1590 (rather, a person can score a 1590 on an SAT exam).
	✔ Scoring 1590 out of a possible 1600, Bill Gates thought the SAT exam didn't seem difficult. **Explanation:** This sentence is clearer—Bill Gates is the person who scored 1590 out of 1600.
	Alternatively: Because he scored 1590 out of a possible 1600, Bill Gates thought the SAT exam didn't seem difficult.

Commonly Misspelled and Confused Words

Spell-checking software is a good tool for identifying most, but not all, spelling errors. Table A.11 lists some commonly misspelled words. Most of the misspellings that are identified as incorrect in this table would not be detected by spell-checking software. For a comprehensive list, consult a guidebook such as the *Gregg Reference Manual.* An ✗ precedes **incorrect** examples, and a ✔ precedes **correct** examples. Parts of speech are noted where the two cases differ.

TABLE A.11

Commonly Misspelled and Confused Words

Case	Examples	Case	Examples
Accept: to receive (verb) *Except:* apart from; without (preposition or conjunction)	✗ We <u>except</u> all forms of payment. ✓ We <u>accept</u> all forms of payment. ✗ We take all forms of payment <u>accept</u> debit cards. ✓ We take all forms of payment <u>except</u> debit cards.	*Elicit:* to draw or bring out (verb) *Illicit:* illegal (adjective)	✗ We want to <u>illicit</u> their feedback. ✓ We want to <u>elicit</u> their feedback. ✗ We should avoid any <u>elicit</u> conduct. ✓ We should avoid any <u>illicit</u> conduct.
Advice: suggestions or recommendations (noun) *Advise:* to offer suggestions or to recommend (verb)	✗ Could you provide some <u>advise</u>? ✓ Could you provide some <u>advice</u>? ✗ Please <u>advice</u> whether to move forward with this plan. ✓ Please <u>advise</u> whether to move forward with this plan.	*Incite:* cause, give rise to (verb) *Insight:* novel idea (noun)	✗ His decisions have <u>insighted</u> a minor revolt among employees. ✓ His decisions have <u>incited</u> a minor revolt among employees. ✗ The business plan contains many <u>incites</u>. ✓ The business plan contains many <u>insights</u>.
All ready: complete; finished *Already:* previously; by this time	✗ The business plan is <u>already</u>. ✓ The business plan is <u>all ready</u>. ✗ She <u>all ready</u> wrote the business plan. ✓ She <u>already</u> wrote the business plan.	*Insure:* to provide compensation for damages *Ensure:* to make certain	✗ Let's <u>ensure</u> this against legal liabilities. ✓ Let's <u>insure</u> this against legal liabilities. ✗ Let's <u>insure</u> a smooth transition to the new executive team. ✓ Let's <u>ensure</u> a smooth transition to the new executive team.
Altogether: entirely *All together:* all in one place or in unison	✗ This report is <u>all together</u> confusing. ✓ This report is <u>altogether</u> confusing. ✗ Let's work on the report <u>altogether</u>. ✓ We should work on the report <u>all together</u>.	*Its:* possessive for *it* *It's:* contraction for *it is*	✗ The beauty of this plan is <u>it's</u> simplicity. ✓ The beauty of this plan is <u>its</u> simplicity. ✗ <u>Its</u> rare to have such a detailed plan. ✓ <u>It's</u> rare to have such a detailed plan.
Affect: to influence (verb) *Effect:* a result (noun)	✗ This <u>effects</u> our business plan. ✓ This <u>affects</u> our business plan. ✗ This has an <u>affect</u> on our business plan. ✓ This has an <u>effect</u> on our business plan.	*Lose:* to lose or to misplace (verb) *Loose:* not tight (adjective)	✗ We'll <u>loose</u> this opportunity if we do not act immediately. ✓ We'll <u>lose</u> this opportunity if we do not act immediately. ✗ There is a <u>lose</u> connection between your ideas. ✓ There is a <u>loose</u> connection between your ideas.

TABLE A.11

(Continued)

Case	Examples	Case	Examples
Apprise: to inform *Appraise: to assess*	✘ You need to <u>appraise</u> him of the situation. ✔ You need to <u>apprise</u> him of the situation. ✘ You should <u>apprise</u> his performance. ✔ You should <u>appraise</u> his performance.	*Moral: principles of rules of conduct* *Morale: cheerfulness, confidence, enthusiasm*	✘ Our company abides by high <u>morale</u> and ethical standards. ✔ Our company abides by high <u>moral</u> and ethical standards. ✘ Our company enjoys high employee <u>moral</u>. ✔ Our company enjoys high employee <u>morale</u>.
Capital: funds or resources; uppercase letters *Capitol: a government building where the legislature meets*	✘ We lack the <u>capitol</u> to make this investment. ✔ We lack the <u>capital</u> to make this investment. ✘ Our CEO testified at the <u>capital</u>. ✔ Our CEO testified at the <u>capitol</u>.	*Precede: to come beforehand* *Proceed: continue or move forward*	✘ Typically, the phone interview <u>proceeds</u> a face-to-face interview. ✔ Typically, the phone interview <u>precedes</u> a face-to-face interview. ✘ In some cases, you <u>precede</u> directly to a face-to-face interview. ✔ In some cases, you <u>proceed</u> directly to a face-to-face interview.
Complementary: something that fits well with or completes another person or object *Complimentary: free (as in a product or service); giving praise*	✘ We form teams with <u>complimentary</u> skill sets. ✔ We form teams with <u>complementary</u> skill sets. ✘ You will receive a <u>complementary</u> movie ticket as a show of thanks. ✔ You will receive a <u>complimentary</u> movie ticket as a show of thanks.	*Principal: primary; a person with authority* *Principle: a standard or guideline*	✘ My <u>principle</u> place of work is in my home office. ✔ My <u>principal</u> place of work is in my home office. ✘ One <u>principal</u> for working effectively at home is to limit distractions. ✔ One <u>principle</u> for working effectively at home is to limit distractions.
Council: a group that provides advice or recommendations (noun) *Counsel: to advise (verb), advice (noun), or legal representative/s (noun)*	✘ We will follow the recommendations of the <u>counsel</u>. ✔ We will follow the recommendations of the <u>council</u>. ✘ We received <u>council</u> not to provide this information publicly. ✔ We received <u>counsel</u> not to provide this information publicly.	*Than: used with comparisons* *Then: used to indicate a point in time*	✘ Gold values have grown faster <u>then</u> stock prices. ✔ Gold values have grown faster <u>than</u> stock prices. ✘ When gold values start falling, <u>than</u> you should move your funds into stocks. ✔ When gold values start falling, <u>then</u> you should move your funds into stocks.

Application Exercises

Directions: Place commas and other punctuation marks throughout these passages wherever needed, and name the rule that applies.

Example: To develop supply chain software and services Microsoft partnered with Infosys.

Answer: To develop supply chain software and services**,** Microsoft partnered with Infosys. (C7)

Comma Exercises

1. Bill Gates and Paul Allen who were childhood friends founded Microsoft in 1975. Bill met Steve who would later become the CEO of Microsoft at Stanford.
2. Bill Gates met the man who would later become the CEO of Microsoft at Stanford.
3. The two technology companies that consistently have the most brand value are Microsoft and Google.
4. In fact they consistently showed high profits during the recent recession.
5. Microsoft and Google the two companies that consistently have the most brand value showed high profits during the recession.
6. To hire Qi Lu as the new president of the Online Services Division was a masterful move by Microsoft.
7. Microsoft enjoys almost limitless advantages in terms of research and development budgets.
8. Steve Balmers took a smooth methodical approach to developing the five-year strategy.
9. Microsoft from my perspective gained its market dominance through anti-competitive practices.
10. Microsoft Word if you're looking for maximum functionality in your word processing far outperforms Google Docs.
11. Microsoft Word far outperforms Google Docs if you're looking for maximum functionality in your word processing.
12. Steve Balmers CEO since 2000 was a college classmate of Bill Gates.
13. MS-DOS an operating system developed initially for IBM personal computers became Microsoft's first major success.
14. As a result Bill Gates moved the headquarters to Washington.
15. Bill Gates gave up the CEO position in 2000 but he remained active at Microsoft by taking a position as chief software architect.
16. Since 2000 Steve Balmers has served as the Chief Executive Officer and Bill Gates has served as Chief Software Architect.
17. In the early years of Microsoft Bill Gates spent most of his time conducting business but also stayed involved in programming.
18. Microsoft's product categories include operating systems, server applications, information worker productivity applications, business solution applications,

high-performance computing applications and software development tools.
19. In 2008 Microsoft acquired Calista Technologies Kidaro Rapt Fast Search & Transfer Navic Networks and DATAllegro.
20. Most people who know Bill say that he is a stubborn determined executive.
21. After Bill moved to management roles he still read and approved most of the code developed for MS-DOS.
22. Under the new set of human resources guidelines all Microsoft employees must declare whether or not they are smokers.
23. Prior to joining the Microsoft team in 2009 Dr. Lu had worked at Yahoo! for 10 years.
24. By acquiring competitor companies Microsoft gains new customers new technology and new ideas.
25. Often Microsoft acquires competitor companies.
26. In July Bill Gates said that he would no longer focus on the day-to-day business activities at Microsoft.
27. In 1980 IBM agreed to let Microsoft develop an operating system for one of its lines of personal computers.
28. IBM agreed to let Microsoft starting in 1980 develop an operating system for one of its lines of personal computers.
29. The new Microsoft Office Suite will go on sale in July.
30. The new Microsoft Office Suite will go on sale in July 2012.
31. The new Microsoft Office Suite will go on sale on July 15 2012.
32. If you purchase the new Microsoft Office Suite between July 15 2012 and January 15 2013 you will receive a $100 rebate.
33. Microsoft employs more than 89000 employees.
34. The ED division develops and produces products such as the Xbox 360 third-party games and the Zune digital music and entertainment platform.
35. Steve Balmers is currently the CEO of Microsoft, Bill Gates continues to be the Chairman of the Board.

Semicolon, Colon, and Comma Exercises

36. Microsoft faces two major threats piracy and patent lawsuits.
37. Bill Gates focuses on product development and strategy Steve Balmers focuses on operations.
38. Bill Gates focuses on product development and strategy on the other hand Steve Balmers focuses on operations.
39. Microsoft's American offices are in Redmond Washington New York City San Francisco Birmingham Alabama and Phoenix Arizona.
40. Cloud computing involves three possible platforms software-as-a-service (SaaS) platform-as-a-service (PaaS) and infrastructure-as-a-service (IaaS).

Dash and Hyphen Exercises

41. Microsoft Office the leading business software for over two decades provides far more functionality than Google Docs.

42. Microsoft's spreadsheet software Excel is preferred by engineers, economists, and statisticians due to the highly specialized statistical functions.

43. The Microsoft cafeteria is open to visitors 11 a.m. 1:00 p.m. Monday Thursday.

44. Word, Excel, PowerPoint, Access these are the standard programs in the Microsoft Professional Suite.

45. In the short run Microsoft would like to increase its market share in the search engine market.

46. Microsoft has a short run goal to increase its market share in the search engine market.

47. Microsoft's investment based approach to research and development ensures that it produces highly applied results.

48. Because Microsoft has adopted an approach to R&D that is investment based it tends to produce results that are highly applied.

Directions: For each set of choices below (separated by slashes), choose the correct answer and name the rule that applies.

Example: Microsoft has a presence in over one hundred/100 countries.

Answer: 100 (N2)

Italics and Quotation Mark Exercises

49. The recent story about Microsoft in *The Wall Street Journal*/"The Wall Street Journal" was called Microsoft's Gamble on Cloud Computing/"Microsoft's Gamble on Cloud Computing."

50. Bill Gates said that he'd like to see the phrase *go bing it*/"go bing it" replace the phrase *go google it*/"go google it."

51. At the luncheon, his speech, titled *The Road to the Future*/"The Road to the Future," laid out his vision for cloud computing over the next decade.

Number Exercises

52. In 2013, 3/three Microsoft business divisions will be combined.

53. Revenues for the last fiscal year were $62,484 million/ $62,484,000,000.

54. Revenues rose 28 percent/28% over the past year.

55. Microsoft employs over 89 thousand/89,000 employees.

56. Microsoft has five/5 business divisions.

57. 5/Five Microsoft divisions make up the Microsoft corporation.

58. Microsoft lost money in 3/three of the 17/seventeen product groups.

59. Microsoft's largest division, Microsoft Business, accounts for approximately 31%/31 percent of its revenues.

60. In the search engine market, Google holds 63%/63 percent of the market share, compared to just 13%/13 percent for Microsoft.

61. Microsoft was fined $388 million/388 million dollars for infringing on Uniloc's anti-piracy software.

62. Bill Gates' Washington home is valued at approximately $125 million/$125,000,000, resulting in annual property taxes of roughly $990 thousand/$990,000.

Grammar Exercises

63. Microsoft joined with Accenture to create Avanade, an IT consultancy. They/It specialize/s in connecting to consumers through online platforms such as social networks.

64. Neither Yahoo! nor Microsoft has/have increased its/ their market share in the search engine market for the past five years.

65. Microsoft hold/s its/their annual shareholders meeting at the corporate headquarters.

66. Every new Microsoft employee should provide copies of his/her/their Social Security card/s at the orientation.

67. The manual about computer programming tips are/is on reserve at the corporate reading room.

68. Microsoft and its competitors in the technology industry is/are constantly changing.

Misspelled Words Exercises

69. Many of Google's HR policies are aimed at eliciting/ illiciting honest feedback.

70. The advice/advise on Microsoft's Help menu is not helpful.

71. All employees should ensure/insure that their LinkedIn pages do not contain any content contrary to the Code of Conduct.

72. This decision affects/effects every aspect of our marketing strategy.

73. Their next step is to identify how to raise enough capital/ capitol for the venture.

74. She told me that the two products contain complementary/complimentary features.

75. This search engine is much more reliable than/then Google's.

Formatting for Letters and Memos

Although most written business correspondence is sent electronically, memos and letters continue to be used in various business situations. When you do use memos and letters, you should use professional, standard formatting. This appendix contains three examples. You can find additional examples in the online resources, including formats for letters that aren't on letterhead and that are more than one page long.

Memos are most often used for formal announcements within organizations (see Figure B.1 for a sample memo). In most cases today, memos are distributed as attachments (usually in .pdf format) by email or other forms of electronic messages. Regardless of how memos are distributed, they contain fairly standard components and formatting. They begin with *To*, *From*, *Date*, and *Subject* lines. Then, they move to the body or message, without a salutation or closing. They end with special notations (see below for common types of notations in memos and letters). In most organizations, you can use standard memo templates, which are often created in-house and stored on corporate intranets. If your organization does not have a standard template, you can choose from dozens of professional ones that come with word processing software.

Business letters are written far less today than a few decades ago; however, they are still appropriate for various business situations. When you write a letter on behalf of your organization, use official letterhead and find out if your organization employs a standard format. If it doesn't, you can choose from several options, including block format and modified block format (see examples in Figures B.2 and B.3). Block format is the most common because it is very clean, with flush-left margins for the entire letter.

Memos and letters may contain various notations, including the following:

- *Carbon copy* (indicated by *c:* or *cc:*). This allows primary message recipients to see all individuals who have received a copy of the memo or letter.
- *Distribution list* (indicated by *Distribution:*). When you send a memo or letter to many individuals, you can use a distribution list to ensure everyone knows who received the document.
- *Preparer's initials.* When someone has written the letter on behalf of the sender, the preparer places his/her initials in lowercase text.
- *Enclosure or attachments* (indicated by *Enclosure*, *Enc.*, *Attachment*, or *Att.*). When you are including additional documents or materials, make reference to them with a notation.

Components of Memos

- To
- From
- Date
- Subject
- Body
- Notations (optional)

Components of Letters

- Letterhead
- Date
- Inside address
- Salutation
- Body
- Closing/Signature
- Notations (optional)

FIGURE B.1

Sample Memo

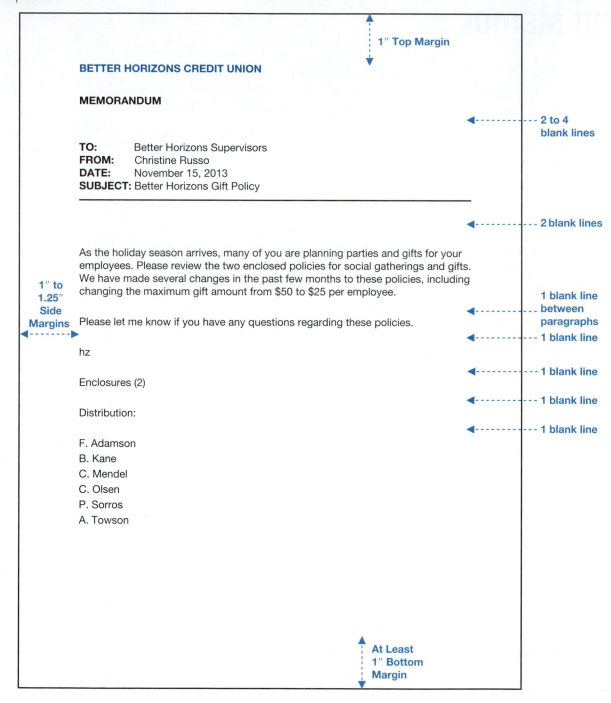

BETTER HORIZONS CREDIT UNION

MEMORANDUM

1″ Top Margin

2 to 4 blank lines

TO: Better Horizons Supervisors
FROM: Christine Russo
DATE: November 15, 2013
SUBJECT: Better Horizons Gift Policy

2 blank lines

As the holiday season arrives, many of you are planning parties and gifts for your employees. Please review the two enclosed policies for social gatherings and gifts. We have made several changes in the past few months to these policies, including changing the maximum gift amount from $50 to $25 per employee.

Please let me know if you have any questions regarding these policies.

hz

Enclosures (2)

Distribution:

F. Adamson
B. Kane
C. Mendel
C. Olsen
P. Sorros
A. Towson

1″ to 1.25″ Side Margins

1 blank line between paragraphs

1 blank line

1 blank line

1 blank line

1 blank line

At Least 1″ Bottom Margin

FIGURE B.2

Sample Letter in Block Format Style

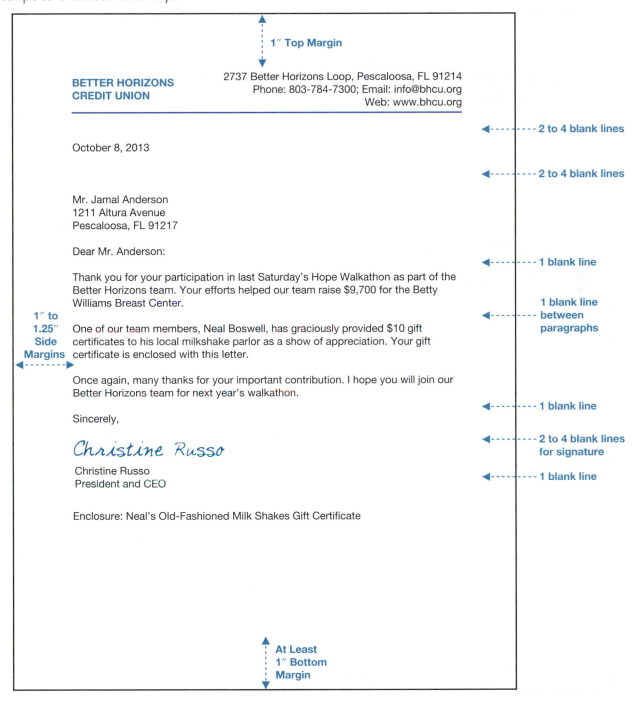

FIGURE B.3

Sample Letter in Modified Block Format Style

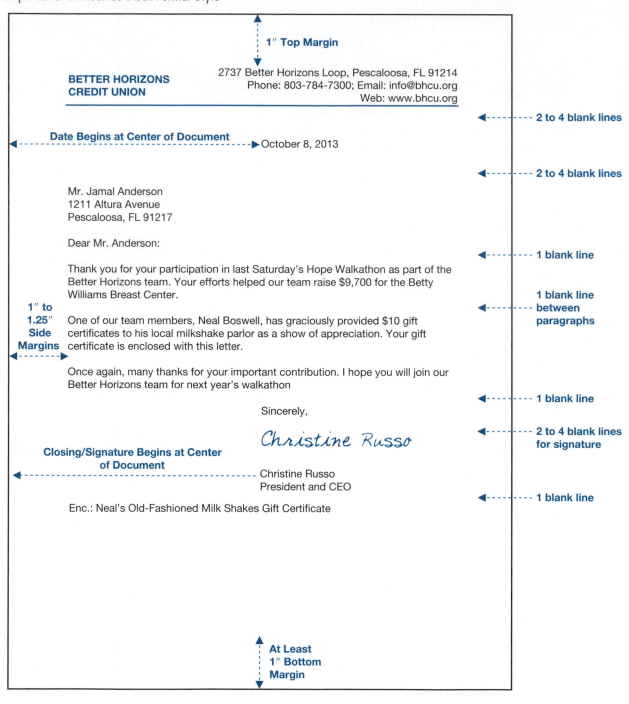

Creating Proposals and Business Plans

You will likely have many opportunities to write proposals and plans during your career. If you're good at it, you gain resources—financial resources and organizational support—to follow through on your business goals and objectives. Read the case, which is the basis for a business proposal (Figure C.1) and a business plan (Figure C.2).

Appendix Case: Conducting Local Market Research and Writing a Business Plan for Murphy's Heating and Cooling

Who's Involved

Shania Baker, owner of Baker Consulting
- Her business specializes in conducting local market research and helping local entrepreneurs write business plans.
- She started her consulting business about one year after graduating with a major in statistics and a minor in finance.

James Murphy, owner and president, Murphy's Heating and Cooling
- He has owned and run his HVAC business for the past 25 years.
- In the past five years, he has repositioned his business as an energy-efficient provider of heating and cooling solutions.

The Situation

James Murphy wants to expand his HVAC business to include solar energy installation. He already has an excellent reputation for installing energy-efficient solutions for local homeowners. His employees could rapidly develop the skills needed for solar installation. In order to expand, he needs to write a formal business plan as part of a loan application.

James's sense of the opportunity is primarily intuitive. He wants someone who can provide local market research that is reliable and quantitative. He also wants someone who can help him write the business plan.

James has approached Shania Baker of Baker Consulting. Several of his professional contacts have recommended her as someone who can help him conduct market research and write a well-formulated business plan.

Task 1
Shania wants to write a formal business proposal to James Murphy that will effectively gain him as a client.

Task 2
When James Murphy agrees to the proposal, Shania needs to write a business plan that meets his needs.

527

Many of the strategies and approaches to writing reports discussed in Chapters 12 and 13 apply to business proposals and business plans. Proposals and plans should be written to meet the needs of decision makers. They must be as precise, objective, and reliable as possible.

Most proposals and plans deal with decisions about how organizations will allocate resources for various business activities. In addition to providing technically sound, complete, and reliable information, proposals and plans should also tie the many complex pieces of data into a powerful, even inspiring, story line about how matching the requested resources to the larger ideas makes sense.

The Small Business Administration (SBA) has developed a simple set of recommendations for writing business plans:*

1. The business plan [or report] should tell a compelling story about your business, explaining who, what, when, where, how, and why.

2. Your plan should be focused and clear. It's not about the number of pages or style of the cover.

3. The plan should define specific business objectives and goals with general parameters to guide the organization.

4. Writing a business plan should force logic and discipline into a business.

5. A good business plan is a living document. It should be updated regularly.

Applying a story line approach to a business plan ties the many ideas into a simple, flowing narrative of how to address business problems (as emphasized in SBA's first recommendation). The appendix case offers a good example for applying a story line approach to reports. James Murphy and his management team intend to expand their heating and cooling business into solar energy installation. Their goal is to get a business loan. To get it, their business plan must present a plausible, simple story of how they will get from point A (heating and cooling business) to point B (a profitable solar installation business).

The data they present must be strong and sufficient while also supporting and reinforcing a simple story line. Conversely, the data cannot substitute for the story. James Murphy, his executive management team, Shania Baker, and the company's accountant have each spent a lot of time gathering information to develop the business plan. The data should emphasize and support the story line throughout the business plan. The story line should answer the basic questions of *what? who? when? where?* and *why?* while demonstrating how to get from point A to point B. It should explain a need and how people (you or employees from your organization) can meet that need.

If you look at the executive summaries for Shania's proposal to Murphy's (Figure C.1) and Murphy's final business plan (Figure C.2), you will notice that each one tells the story of how people will get from point A to point B. In particular, the executive summary in the business plan (Figure C.2) answers all the basic questions of the story line approach.

---

*Small Business Administration, "Write a Business Plan," retrieved September 15, 2010, from Small Business Administration website at www.sba.gov/smallbusinessplanner/plan/writeabusinessplan/index.html.

Components of a Business Proposal

- Cover Page
- Executive Summary
- Current Situation
- Specific Objectives
- Deliverables Overview
- Timeline
- Results Enhancers
- Pricing

Components of a Business Plan

- Cover Page
- Executive Summary
- Business Description
- Business Objectives
- Market Analysis
- Products and Services
- Organization/ Management
- Marketing and Sales Strategy
- Financial Management
- Appendixes

FIGURE C.1

Shania's Proposal to Murphy's Heating and Cooling

**Proposal to Conduct Local Market Analysis and
Develop a Business Plan for Murphy's Heating and Cooling**

Submitted by Shania Baker, Baker Consulting
July 1, 2013

Executive Summary

Baker Consulting proposes conducting a local market analysis and business plan for Murphy's Heating and Cooling to move into the residential solar energy business. Baker Consulting will provide the following: (1) a local market analysis and (2) a written business plan. Prior to writing the business plan, Murphy's Heating and Cooling will provide a five-year proforma income statement and other requested information. The proposed price is $13,000, which includes a $5,000 up-front fee prior to conducting the local market analysis and $8,000 final payment once the final business plan is completed and delivered.

> The *Executive Summary* provides the most essential points from the proposal.

Current Situation

Murphy's Heating and Cooling is seeking to expand into the solar installation business. The mission of Murphy's has been to provide energy-efficient heating and cooling solutions to King City area homeowners. Expanding into solar installations is a natural extension of Murphy's mission and is compatible with existing marketing and installation expertise among employees.

Murphy's is moving into an untested market, as few homes in this area have residential solar energy systems. A reliable local market analysis and business plan will help Murphy's obtain needed financing and expand into the residential solar energy business profitably.

> The *Current Situation* section describes the basic challenges that need to be addressed and solved.

Specific Objectives

> The *Specific Objectives* section provides clear statements about outcomes of the proposed work.

1. Conduct local market research for the following purposes:
   a. Understand how much King City homeowners know about solar energy options for their homes.
   b. Identify current interest levels among King City homeowners in solar energy systems for their homes.
   c. Identify what King City homeowners think are the primary benefits of residential solar energy systems.
   d. Identify the primary concerns King City homeowners have with residential solar energy systems.

2. Write a business plan for the following purposes:
   a. Obtain a five-year $375,000 loan.
   b. Create a five-year vision of business objectives that can serve as benchmarks for performance.

FIGURE C.1

(Continued)

Deliverables Overview

> The *Deliverables Overview* section describes the items and services that will be provided.

Baker Consulting will provide the following deliverables:

1. *A local market analysis for residential solar energy systems*. Baker Consulting will provide a written report, a two-hour presentation and discussion, and a digital file with raw data from 350 local homeowners.

2. *A written business plan*. The business plan will include all necessary information to apply for a business loan. Not including any appendixes, it will contain between 10 and 20 pages.

Murphy's Heating and Cooling will provide the following:

1. Three meetings between Baker Consulting and Murphy's Heating and Cooling to provide needed information for the business plan.

2. Current financial statements and a five-year pro forma income statement with clearly stated assumptions for the projections.

Timeline

> The *Timeline* section clearly states when key activities will occur and when deliverables are due.

Date to Complete	Activity
July 15	Kickoff meeting at Baker Consulting office with Murphy's Heating and Cooling Executive Management Team (estimate: two hours)
August 1	Local market analysis completed; presentation to Murphy's Heating and Cooling Executive Management Team (estimate: two hours)
August 15	Financial statement and proforma five-year income statements provided to Baker Consulting
September 1	Business plan draft provided to Murphy's Heating and Cooling
September 15	Final meeting to discuss any requests for final version of the business plan
October 1	Final business plan provided to Murphy's Heating and Cooling

Pricing and Payment Plan

The following table summarizes the price for this project based on my standard rates for soliciting survey responses and writing reports and plans.

Activity	Rate	Total
Collection of 350 surveys	$20 per survey	$ 7,000
Completing local market analysis	$120 per hour (20 hours)	$ 2,400
Writing business plan	$120 per hour (30 hours)	$ 3,600
		$13,000

The total pricing for conducting the local market analysis and writing a business plan is $13,000. This includes two payments: an up-front fee of $5,000 and a final payment of $8,000 when the business plan is delivered.

> The *Pricing and Payment Plan* section states the pricing for products and/or services and expectations for payment.

FIGURE C.2

A Business Plan for Murphy's Heating and Cooling's Expansion to Solar Energy Systems

**Expansion of Murphy's Heating and Cooling:
Becoming a Solar Dealer and Installer**

Title summarizes the story. In 11 words, the title captures the essence of the business plan.

October 2013

Prepared by

James Murphy
President/Owner

Jim Ellison
General Manager

Jada Hilton
Sales and Marketing

FIGURE C.2

(Continued)

Table of Contents

Table of Contents provides the road map.
Readers can quickly navigate to areas of interest.

FIGURE C.2

(*Continued*)

Executive Summary

We seek to expand Murphy's Heating and Cooling to become a solar dealer and installer. This is a natural move for our business. For nearly a decade, the mission of our company has been to provide energy-efficient solutions for heating and cooling homes. Installing residential solar energy systems fits this mission. For nearly a decade, our marketing model has been to promote the savings that homeowners can get from investing in new, energy-efficient HVAC systems. Marketing residential solar energy systems fits our marketing model, and we have thousands of existing, satisfied customers who trust us to help them save money. Installing residential solar energy systems requires skills and knowledge comparable and compatible with those of HVAC installation. We already have the employees who can apply their knowledge and skills to solar installation.

We will become a Polerus Solar dealer. Polerus is a widely respected wholesale distributor of solar energy products and services. It offers fast delivery of product, support for residential system designs, and full support for our customers with a customer service hotline and the best warranties in the business.

We will adopt a central selling theme that solar energy is a good investment. We will focus on the following key marketing ideas: a solar energy system can raise the resale value of your home, it pays for itself quickly, and it saves on monthly utility bills. We will also emphasize the reliability, affordability, and ease of purchase in our marketing campaigns.

We will use radio, direct mail, and our website to direct traffic to our showroom. Our marketing specialists will be trained to show potential customers the benefits of solar systems, make the purchase decisions less complex, and complete any paperwork necessary to maximize the amount of credits and rebates purchasers can receive. They will also set up home visits for our solar installers to provide price estimates.

Our initial solar team will be composed of seven employees and require several months of training and planning to be ready for installation and marketing. We have chosen our most reliable employees to lead this effort. These same employees effectively transitioned us to our focus on energy-efficient HVAC solutions during the past decade.

We seek a five-year $375,000 loan to start this new line of business. We expect high up-front costs but high profits within five years. In 2014, we expect losses of between $228,000 and $314,000. In 2015 and 2016, we estimate near break-even net profits. In 2017, we anticipate profits of between $178,000 and $209,000, and in 2018, we expect profits of between $285,000 and $749,000.

Executive Summary tells the story. What? Murphy's will expand into residential solar energy systems. *Who?* Key players from Murphy's, their expertise, and their roles are described. *How?* Murphy's organizational mission, marketing model and expertise, installation skills, and customer base can easily be adapted to a residential solar energy business. *When?* The transition to a solar energy dealer and installer will begin immediately. A plan covering five years is provided. *Why?* It fits the organizational mission and it will be profitable.

1

FIGURE C.2

(Continued)

> The *Business Description and Vision* explains how the key personnel, their history, their skills, their talents, and their passions naturally lead to their vision of installing residential solar energy systems in the King City area.

Business Description and Vision

Murphy's Heating and Cooling was founded by James Murphy in 1978. We have been the leading residential HVAC installer and servicer in the King City area for the past 20 years and have installed or serviced HVAC systems in approximately 5,000 homes during the past two decades.

We are an official Comfort HVAC Systems dealer. Comfort HVAC Systems is widely recognized as providing quality, energy-efficient systems. Each of the Comfort HVAC Systems has earned the ENERGY STAR rating. By relying on this well-known national vendor, we specialize in installing and servicing quality systems that are at the forefront of reducing energy requirements.

We have achieved consistent revenues and profits. During the past ten years, average annual profit has been approximately $250,000 on average annual revenue of roughly $1.6 million. The least profitable years over the past ten years were 2009 and 2010 during major downturns in the economy. However, in each of these years, we still achieved annual profits of between $50,000 and $60,000 and avoided laying off any of our employees.

Nearly 45 percent of new HVAC system installations are to previous Murphy's customers. This extensive level of repeat business shows how much customers trust us to install systems that meet their heating and cooling needs.

In 2002, James Murphy, President and Owner, and Jim Ellison, General Manager, began discussing ways to make the business more environmentally friendly. Within a few years, they chose to only install HVAC systems with exceptional energy efficiency ratings. In 2004, Murphy's formally created a mission statement to reflect this new focus:

> We install and service high-quality air heating and cooling systems that allow our customers to enjoy the comforts of their homes. We help our customers minimize energy use and expense by promoting the most energy-efficient systems. We provide practical heating and cooling solutions that reduce adverse impacts on the environment. Integrity, openness, and honesty are hallmarks of our approach.

Shortly after developing the mission statement, Murphy's employed several marketing strategies. First, we hired Jada Hilton to develop a formal marketing effort. Until her arrival, most marketing had occurred by word of mouth or radio ads. Jada helped create a showroom at the business office for customers to stop by and consider their options. She developed an expert understanding of how much money more efficient systems could save over time for customers. In so doing, she became intimately familiar with federal, state, local, and manufacturer credits and rebates available for upgrading to energy-efficient systems. She built an emphasis on savings due to energy-efficient systems into all of Murphy's marketing materials.

We intend to move into the residential solar installation business in the King City area. Moving into the solar installation is a natural extension of our current business for the following reasons: (a) it fits our mission to install energy-efficient systems into homes in the King City area; (b) it fits into our marketing model of emphasizing savings due to energy-efficient systems; (c) it fits our

2

FIGURE C.2

(Continued)

business model of becoming a local dealer for a national distributor with strong brand and distribution power; and (d) it fits our employees' abilities, since installing solar panels requires a similar knowledge base and skill set to installing HVAC systems.

We expect to become the most recognized solar installer and service provider (system maintenance) in the King City area. We will become an official Polerus Solar dealer within a few months and assemble an expert solar installation team (system designers and installers) that is certified by NABCEP (North American Board of Certified Energy Practitioners) from IREC/ISPQ (Interstate Renewable Energy Council/Institute for Sustainable Power Quality) accredited schools.

New Products and Services

Murphy's will install and service Polerus solar energy systems for homes in the King City area, including complete grid-tie, grid-tie with battery backup, and off-grid systems. We will also provide service to customers with existing solar energy systems at their homes.

Murphy's will become a Polerus Solar dealer. Polerus provides a comprehensive set of products and services to meet Murphy's needs. It provides a wide range of high-quality solar panels, modules, racking, inverters, and other parts for installation. Polerus also provides customer service hotlines for all of its products, which provide back-end support for any system that Murphy's installs. Polerus also provides systems to match dozens of home designs. It can deliver any large order to installation sites within two days. See appendix for additional information about Polerus products and services.

Marketing

> The *New Products and Services* section shows they are selecting the right external partners.

Our executive management team (James Murphy, Jim Ellison, and Jada Hilton) has gone through an extensive learning process about solar energy systems for homes. We began researching the solar installation business approximately 18 months ago. We have collectively attended three solar energy industry shows. We personally met and visited with representatives of four of the top solar wholesale distributors. Once we were comfortable with Polerus Solar, we asked them if we could meet with some of their current dealers who had worked with Polerus Solar for at least several years and who had succeeded in markets similar to our own. They referred us to five dealers. We talked to each by telephone. Two of the dealers graciously allowed us to visit them. Both were HVAC installers who had expanded into solar energy systems. Also, while developing our basic business plan, we hired Baker Consulting to conduct a local marketing study and integrate our ideas into a formal business plan.

Each stage of this learning process has reinforced the compelling reasons for expanding into this line of business. We are in an excellent position to use our existing customer base, marketing model, knowledge, skill set, and organizational mission to succeed in residential solar installation. In terms of marketing, we have considered the following areas that will impact our business: national market, barriers to adoption of solar energy, effective marketing for residential customers, and local market research.

FIGURE C.2

(Continued)

National Market for Residential Solar Energy

The U.S. solar market has expanded rapidly in recent years, and several factors and trends will lead to continued growth over the next two decades. Furthermore, with such small market penetration, the potential for new customers is extremely promising.

- *The U.S. solar market continues to grow despite the economic downturn.* In the last two years of economic recession, the U.S. solar market still grew tremendously, with 62 percent growth in 2008 and 36 percent growth in 2009. Industry analysts expect the total market for solar installations to grow by 30 percent per year over the next five years. By 2014, the market will be ten times the size of that in 2009.[1]

- *Price reductions and financial incentives for residential solar markets.* While residential energy prices from utilities continue to rise, the price of installing solar panels continues to fall. For example, solar modules have dropped in price by 40 to 50 percent in the last year. Furthermore, the many financial incentives provided by the federal and local governments further reduce the price of solar installations. Many of these incentives will be available for many years, and tax credits on solar systems can be carried forward through 2016. With a variety of federal, state, local, and utility incentives, as well as factory rebates, many homeowners can get systems at 50 to 60 percent off.[2]

- *Success in regional markets with extensive educational and marketing initiatives.* In locations where effective marketing and incentive systems have been put into place, solar installers have become extremely successful and profitable. For example, many solar installers have thrived in California, where active promotion from the state combined with the innovative marketing of wholesale distributors and local installers have resulted in incredible growth. Solar installations in California accounted for over half (53 percent) of solar installations in the U.S. during 2009. Fully functional photovoltaic marketplaces in states such as California show that a strong marketing model can result in many solar installations.[3]

- *Continued support from the federal government.* The Department of Energy has set a goal of generating 10 to 15 percent of the nation's energy from solar sources by 2030. Industry analysts anticipate continued strong support at the federal level for renewable energy sources.[4]

However, despite forecasts for strong growth, significant barriers to adoption still remain for residential solar systems. Industry analysts identify four major obstacles to purchase of residential solar systems: (1) high up-front costs; in one study of homeowners, 47 percent were most concerned about initial out-of-pocket costs; (2) perceived nonreliability; one-third of homeowners do not believe that solar technology has improved over the past 20 years; (3) perceived complexity of installation; and (4) lengthy decision-making process. Among homeowners who have purchased solar energy systems, one survey showed that nearly 40 percent take over two years to make a decision (see Figure 1 on the next page).[5]

> **Conclusions and other key points are set apart in bullets and/or italics throughout the document.** The use of bullets and other formatting features to set apart important ideas, assumptions, findings, and conclusions allows readers to gather the pertinent information rapidly. It also shows the detail-oriented, comprehensive approach of the writers.

4

FIGURE C.2

(*Continued*)

Figure 1. Decision-Making Time Needed

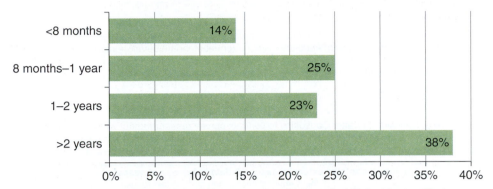

Decision-Making Time to Adopt Solar Systems for Homes
Most Homeowners Take Their Time Making Up Their Minds about Solar

Percentage of Homeowners with Installed Solar Energy Systems

Effective Approaches to Marketing to Residential Customers

Industry analysts and marketers have learned a lot about how to effectively market residential solar systems during the past two decades. While many early proponents and adopters were largely motivated by using environmentally friendly and renewable energy systems, promoting benefits to the environment as a central selling theme is not effective for the vast majority of homeowners. As leading industry group SmartPower concluded from over seven years of message research in the area of renewable energy and energy efficiency, "the 'environmental' message is not the answer to motivate consumers to purchase renewable energy technologies."[6] We intend to apply each of the following messaging strategies to our local marketing campaigns:

- *Market savings on energy bills over time*. Homeowners respond most positively to the message that solar energy systems are good investments that save money over time. In research of 75 focus group participants, SmartPower presented people with five messages to market solar power: (a) solar energy makes sense; (b) solar is a good investment; (c) solar is good for the health of future generations; (d) solar is good for the environment; and (e) solar creates energy independence. None of the respondents selected "good for the environment." The most chosen theme was "solar makes sense," and the second most chosen was "solar is a good investment." In surveys of existing homeowners in Arizona, saving on energy costs over time was the most frequently cited reason for adopting residential energy systems. The second most cited reason was saving money. Choosing solar energy systems to help the environment was far less common.

- *Market the affordability of installation costs*. Homeowners are particularly worried about high up-front costs. Studies have shown that consumers respond more positively to marketing based on specific amounts in monthly savings (i.e., seven-year $15,000 loan presented as a $125 monthly payment).

> **The report provides a balanced view of reasons for optimism and clear recognition of the marketing challenges.** As a result, readers will likely consider the perspectives in the report more credible.

5

FIGURE C.2

(Continued)

- *Minimize the complexity of the purchasing process.* Homeowners are often perplexed by the many solar installation options. They are even more overwhelmed with the paperwork and documentation needed to obtain various government and manufacturer tax credits and rebates.

- *Develop and establish partnerships with government and industry.* Successful solar installers establish relationships with state and local government, home developers, and real estate agents to raise the profile of solar energy in their communities, overcome misperceptions, and establish leads on installation projects.

Local Market Research

We commissioned Baker Consulting to conduct survey research about what homeowners in the King City area think about residential solar energy systems. They collected survey data from 382 homeowners. In the table below, we present findings from the survey. Then, we discuss broad conclusions.

> **The report contains extensive research data but does not overwhelm the reader.** Tables and charts contain most of the numerical information and the text focuses more on conclusions.

Survey Results from Homeowners in the King City Area regarding Solar Energy

How much do you know about solar energy options for your home?	Age Group					Total
	<30	31–40	41–50	51–65	>65	
Nothing at all	36.8%	26.7%	13.0%	13.2%	23.3%	19.9%
A little	31.6%	36.7%	50.0%	49.1%	37.2%	42.9%
Some	15.8%	20.0%	13.0%	9.4%	18.6%	14.7%
A lot	15.8%	16.7%	23.9%	28.3%	20.9%	2.0%
How interested are you in learning about installing solar energy for your home?						
Not interested	10.5%	13.3%	6.5%	26.4%	37.2%	20.4%
Slightly interested	10.5%	23.3%	26.1%	18.9%	18.6%	20.4%
Interested	63.2%	26.7%	26.1%	15.1%	16.3%	24.6%
Extremely interested	15.8%	36.7%	41.3%	39.6%	27.9%	34.6%
What would you consider the primary advantage of installing solar energy for your home? (Check one.)						
To save on energy costs over time	15.8%	33.3%	52.2%	52.8%	44.2%	44.0%
To help the environment	26.3%	23.3%	19.6%	20.8%	27.9%	23.0%
To save on my monthly energy bills	47.4%	26.7%	4.3%	1.9%	14.0%	13.6%
To reduce my carbon footprint	0.0%	6.7%	13.0%	20.8%	9.3%	12.0%
To increase the value of my home	10.5%	10.0%	10.9%	3.8%	4.7%	7.3%
What are your primary concerns about solar energy? (Check all that apply.)						
Impact on the value of my home	47.4%	70.0%	80.4%	73.6%	58.1%	68.6%
Appearance of solar panels on my home	36.8%	53.3%	47.8%	45.3%	44.2%	46.1%
Cost of installing solar panels on my home	26.3%	53.3%	69.6%	66.0%	53.5%	41.9%
Solar panels are not reliable enough	10.5%	26.7%	39.1%	49.1%	41.9%	37.7%
I don't know enough about solar panels	36.8%	13.3%	23.9%	28.3%	39.5%	28.3%
Installing solar panels is too complicated	10.5%	23.3%	23.9%	24.5%	30.2%	24.1%

Note: 382 homeowners (females, 44.5%, males, 55.5%; age: 30 and under, 9.9%; 31 to 40 years old, 15.7%; 41 to 50 years old, 24.1%; 51 to 65 years old, 27.7%; over 65 years old, 22.5%; income level: under $50,000, 20.9%; $50,000 to $75,000, 24.1%; $75,000 to $100,000, 28.3%; $100,000 to $150,000, 11.0%; over $150,000, 15.7%)

6

FIGURE C.2

(*Continued*)

Homeowners have strong interest but little knowledge of solar energy options. Approximately six in ten (59.2 percent) homeowners in the King City area say they are interested or extremely interested in learning more about solar energy options for their homes. Middle-aged homeowners (41 to 50) are the most interested; nearly 70 percent say they are interested. However, the majority of homeowners (62.8 percent) say they know nothing or little about solar energy options.

Homeowners identify financial benefits as the primary advantage of solar energy. Nearly half (44.0 percent) of homeowners identified the primary advantage of solar energy as saving on energy costs over time. Some homeowners (20.9 percent) perceived either saving on monthly energy bills or increasing the value of the home as the primary benefits. Altogether, about two in three (64.9 percent) viewed financial benefits as the primary benefits of solar energy. Roughly a third (35.0 percent) viewed environmental benefits (to help the environment, reducing carbon footprint) as most important. This is similar to national trends that show that financial benefits are a more compelling argument for using solar energy than environmental benefits. (See Figure 2 for breakdown by age group.)

Figure 2. Financial Considerations of King City Homeowners

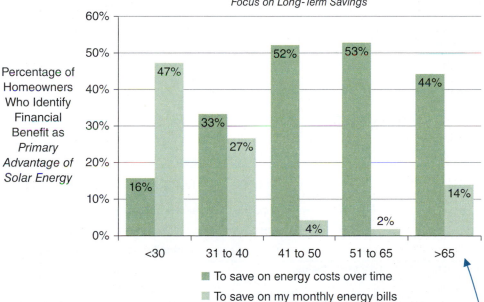

Focus on Short-Term versus Long-Term Financial Considerations
Younger Homeowners Focus on Monthly Savings; Older Homeowners Focus on Long-Term Savings

Percentage of Homeowners Who Identify Financial Benefit as *Primary Advantage of Solar Energy*

- To save on energy costs over time
- To save on my monthly energy bills

Impact on home value is the largest concern of homeowners. Nearly seven in ten (68.6 percent) homeowners are concerned that solar panels would hurt the value of their homes. Similarly, nearly half (46.1 percent) believe that solar panels would negatively impact the appearance of their homes. These concerns seem to be larger in our area compared to other locations. Perhaps the recent declines in real estate values have made homeowners particularly sensitive to issues related to home value. As we will describe in the next section, solar energy installation positively impacts home value. In our educational and promotional campaigns, we can inform homeowners about this misperception.

Statistics are segmented in a way that leads directly to recommendations. The primary way in which the statistics are grouped is in terms of age group. The distinctions in age group lead directly to related marketing strategies.

7

FIGURE C.2

(*Continued*)

The cost of installing solar panels is a major concern. Like those in nearly all nationwide markets, King City homeowners are concerned about the cost of installing solar panels: roughly four in ten (41.9 percent) cite this issue as an area of concern.

Middle-aged homeowners tend to be more informed of and interested in solar energy options but are also more skeptical. Middle-aged homeowners (41–50 years old and 51–65 years old) tend to know the most and be most interested in residential solar systems. Yet, they are also far more skeptical since more of them express concern about the impact on home value, system reliability, and up-front costs (see Figure 3 below).

Figure 3. Concerns about Solar Energy

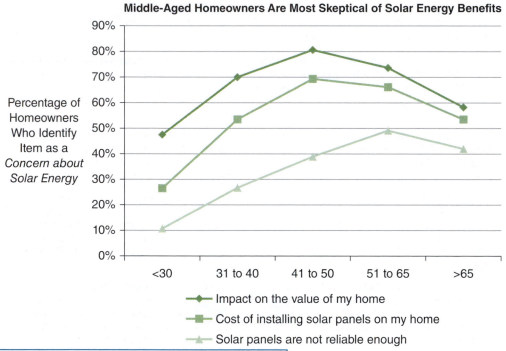

Middle-Aged Homeowners Are Most Skeptical of Solar Energy Benefits

Percentage of Homeowners Who Identify Item as a *Concern about Solar Energy*

Legend:
- Impact on the value of my home
- Cost of installing solar panels on my home
- Solar panels are not reliable enough

All of the data leads to a set of strategies.
The list of marketing strategies corresponds well with research findings and conclusions in the national and local markets sections.

Our Approach to Marketing

Based on the information we have collected from industry analyses, local surveys, and discussions with Polerus dealers, we are confident that we can apply the marketing model that we have been using for the past eight years with energy-efficient HVAC systems. Our marketing has been based on a central selling theme of savings over time, educating homeowners (reducing misperceptions) about energy-efficient options, reducing purchase complexity (creating a showroom and training marketing assistants to take care of paperwork for the many federal, local, and

FIGURE C.2

(Continued)

manufacturer credits and discounts available), and targeting the specific needs and preferences of various age groups. In particular, we will promote the following message campaigns, each of which is tied to the idea that residential energy systems are a good investment:

- Solar energy systems raise the resale value of your home by around $20,000 to $30,000.

- Solar energy systems pay for themselves within seven to ten years just from monthly savings in energy bills.

- Solar energy systems save the average homeowner about $70 to $85 per month on utility bills.

The marketing strategies are specific.

We will also emphasize reliability, affordability, and ease of purchase in our marketing. We will employ the following media for marketing:

Radio spots. We have used radio extensively over the past ten years and have concluded that it was instrumental in building our brand of savings through energy-efficient solutions. We can target various age groups quite effectively with radio. We will emphasize savings over time for radio stations that cater to middle-aged homeowners, and we will emphasize monthly savings more for radio stations that cater to younger homeowners.

Direct mail and phone call campaign. We will target approximately 15,000 households in a direct mail campaign. We will send two sets of mailings separated by three months. We will then target 500 top prospects in a direct call campaign. We followed a similar process when moving exclusively to energy-efficient HVAC systems and received excellent response.

Website development. We will revamp our website to focus on residential solar energy systems. The website will include an energy savings calculator so that users can get a quick estimate of savings they could receive based on the size of their homes. It will also contain extensive links to excellent publications developed by neutral authors, such as the U.S. Department of Energy's *A Consumer's Guide: Get Your Power from the Sun* and various resources on the Go Solar California website.

Showroom and site visits. The goal of marketing will be to create face-to-face contact with customers. Most often, this will occur for the first time with a visit to our showroom where our marketing specialists will illustrate and describe various options with Polerus solar energy systems. Marketing specialists will also demonstrate the financial gain from solar energy systems and the assistance that the marketing specialists will provide in the rebate and credit process. The next step will be for interested customers to have a site visit from a member of a solar installer team to answer any questions about the installation process and provide an exact estimate. We will expand the size of our current showroom to focus most heavily on residential solar energy systems. Since our building has approximately 2,000 square feet of unused space, we can easily accommodate this expansion with modest investments.

In all of our marketing efforts, we will adopt the many appealing and effective resources (logos, designs, content, etc.) available from Polerus as well as model efforts from successful government and industry initiatives. For example, we've identified a number of strategies used by successful solar installers in California, such as REC Solar, SolarCity, and Real Goods Solar.

9

FIGURE C.2

(Continued)

Organization and Management

Our current organization has 14 employees. We also regularly outsource work to an accountant and a lawyer. Murphy's has always ensured that our installers and technicians are trained properly to install and service the HVAC systems. All HVAC installers and service technicians are EPA and NATE certified. On average, they have eight years of experience.

Figure 4. Current Organization

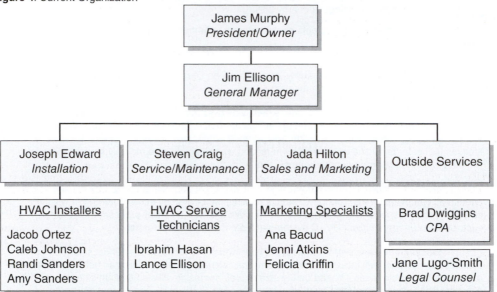

We expect to develop an expert solar team that is initially composed of seven employees. Jim Ellison will be in charge of overall business activities. Joseph Edward will move from his position as project manager for HVAC installation to the solar project manager. Two HVAC installers will join him: Caleb Johnson and Randi Sanders. Jada Hilton will continue to lead sales and marketing for the entire organization with a special focus on growing our solar installation business. Two of our marketing specialists will focus exclusively on residential solar energy systems: Ana Bacud and Jenni Atkins. Ana will be in charge of developing website content. Overall, we anticipate that 40 to 50 percent of marketing specialists' time will be used to manage incentive programs.

We will ensure that all of our solar installers and technicians receive proper training and accreditation. We will send our solar installation team for training at an IREC/ISPQ (Interstate Renewable Energy Council/Institute for Sustainable Power Quality) accredited school that provides NABCEP (North American Board of Certified Energy Practitioners) certification. Each individual will receive entry-level and advanced-level training in installation. Each course lasts approximately five days at costs of $1,100 to $1,600 per person. Also, Joseph Edward will receive an additional course in system design from Polerus.

> **Personnel charts quickly identify key roles.** Reports rarely inspire confidence in future performance without showing how key personnel will make things happen. This visual display of key players helps create the story of potential success in the solar energy business.

10

FIGURE C.2

(Continued)

Figure 5. New Solar Energy Business Team

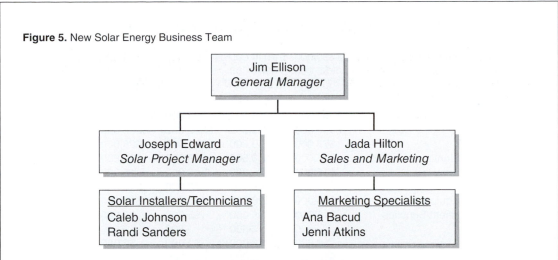

Financial Plan and Projections

We developed pro forma income statements for the next five years. We based our low-growth and high-growth projections on two current Polerus dealers who started their solar installation businesses in markets similar to ours. The low growth and high growth are based on sales forecasts achieved by each of these two businesses (number of installations for low-growth scenario: Year 1, 15; Year 2, 40; Year 3, 70; Year 4, 110; Year 5, 150; number of installations for high-growth scenario: Year 1, 20; Year 2, 50; Year 3, 80; Year 4, 150; Year 5, 300). While we consider the markets of those two installers similar to our own, we believe we have several advantages: we are already marketing energy-efficient and cost-saving solutions, and we have an existing customer base that is broader and more loyal.

Figure 6. Five-Year Estimates for Net Profits

> **Estimates of a low-growth and high-growth scenario show good planning.** Business-plan writers who provide various scenarios for sales, expenses, and other factors show that they are preparing carefully for the uncertainty of business.

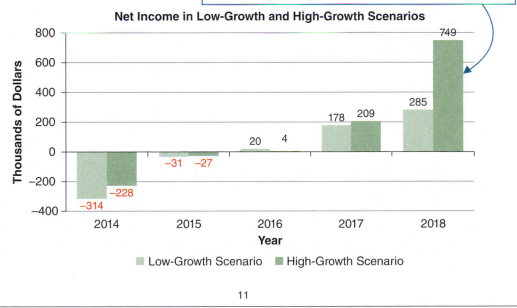

11

FIGURE C.2

(Continued)

Pro Forma 5-Year Income Statement in Low-Growth Scenario

Revenue

Revenue from Installations	$390,000	$1,040,000	$1,820,000	$2,860,000	$3,900,000
Revenue from Service Visits	$5,000	$10,000	$15,000	$20,000	$25,000
Total Revenue	$395,000	$1,050,000	$1,835,000	$2,880,000	$3,925,000

Expenses

COGS	$295,500	$786,000	$1,374,000	$2,157,000	$2,940,000
Payroll	$149,400	$153,882	$225,698	$270,869	$355,795
Advertising	$75,000	$50,000	$25,000	$25,000	$25,000
Legal & Accounting	$15,000	$10,500	$18,350	$28,800	$39,250
Training/Licensure	$15,000	$5,000	$15,000	$15,000	$15,000
Travel	$12,000	$8,000	$12,000	$12,000	$12,000
Installation Equipment	$85,000	$20,000	$65,000	$30,000	$30,000
Office Equipment/Supplies	$15,000	$5,000	$5,000	$5,000	$5,000
Utilities	$500	$500	$500	$500	$500
Insurance	$2,000	$2,000	$2,000	$2,000	$2,000
Interest	$18,000	$13,000	$7,000	$5,500	$3,500
Depreciation	$17,000	$17,000	$34,000	$34,000	$34,000
Miscellaneous Costs	$10,000	$10,000	$20,000	$20,000	$25,000
Income Before Taxes	($314,400)	($30,882)	$31,452	$274,331	$437,955
Income Taxes	$0	$0	$11,008	$96,016	$153,284
Net Income	($314,400)	($30,882)	$20,444	$178,315	$284,670

Pro Forma 5-Year Income Statement in High-Growth Scenario

Revenue

Revenue from Installations	$520,000	$1,300,000	$2,080,000	$3,900,000	$7,800,000
Revenue from Service Visits	$5,000	$12,000	$25,000	$40,000	$50,000
Total Revenue	$525,000	$1,312,000	$2,105,000	$3,940,000	$7,850,000

Expenses

COGS	$393,000	$982,200	$1,575,000	$2,949,000	$5,880,000
Payroll	$149,400	$192,282	$332,450	$419,224	$508,601
Advertising	$75,000	$50,000	$40,000	$40,000	$40,000
Legal & Accounting	$15,000	$13,120	$21,050	$39,400	$78,500
Training/Licensure	$15,000	$15,000	$20,000	$20,000	$20,000
Travel	$12,000	$12,000	$15,000	$15,000	$15,000
Installation Equipment	$30,000	$20,000	$20,000	$30,000	$40,000
Office Equipment/Supplies	$15,000	$5,000	$5,000	$5,000	$5,000
Utilities	$2,000	$2,200	$2,500	$3,000	$3,500
Insurance	$2,000	$2,000	$2,000	$2,000	$2,000
Interest	$18,000	$13,000	$7,000	$5,500	$3,500
Depreciation	$17,000	$17,000	$34,000	$51,000	$51,000
Miscellaneous Costs	$10,000	$15,000	$25,000	$40,000	$50,000
Income Before Taxes	($228,400)	($26,802)	$6,000	$320,876	$1,152,899
Income Taxes	$0	$0	$2,100	$112,307	$403,515
Net Income	($228,400)	($26,802)	$3,900	$208,569	$749,385

Business plans should provide financials. They should include current and projected balance sheet and income statements. Many business plans include other financial documents and calculations as well.

12

FIGURE C.2

(*Continued*)

With the sales projections in place, we worked with our CPA, Brad Dwiggins, to create the pro forma income statements for the solar installation portion of our business. We include specific assumptions about cost of goods sold, payroll, advertising, and other expenses in the appendix.

We seek a five-year $375,000 loan. We estimate high up-front costs as we get the solar installation business going. However, we expect high profitability within four years. In 2014, we expect losses of between $228,000 and $314,000. In 2015 and 2016, we estimate close to breaking even. In 2017, we anticipate profits of between $178,000 and $209,000, and in 2018, we expect profits of between $285,000 and $749,000.

Endnotes

1. Solar Buzz, *United States PV Market 2010; 2010-2014 Scenario Forecast* (San Francisco, CA: Author, June 2010).

2. Lyn Rosoff and Mark Sinclair, *Smart Solar Marketing Strategies: Clean Energy State Program Guide* (Washington, DC: Clean Energy Group and SmartPower, August 2009); Mark Sinclair and Steve Weisman, *Mainstreaming Solar Electricity: Strategies for States to Build Local Markets* (Washington, DC: Clean Energy Group and SmartPower, April 2008); Mark Sinclair, "Creating Demand – How to Market Solar," *Renewable Energy Focus* (October 2009): 18–21.

3. Environment California, *Rave Reviews for Solar Homes* (Sacramento, CA: State of California, March 2006). http://www.energy.ca.gov/2008publications/CEC-180-2008-004/CEC-180 -2008-004_MARKET_RESEARCH.PDF; U.S. Department of Energy, *A Consumer's Guide: Get Your Power from the Sun* (Washington, DC: Office of Energy Efficiency and Renewable Energy, December 2003) [Available at www.nrel.gov/docs/fy04osti/35297.pdf]; A Consumer's Guide to the California Solar Initiative: Statewide Incentives for Solar Energy Systems (Sacramento, CA: State of California, 2010) [Available at: http://www.cpuc.ca.gov/NR/rdonlyres/67C52E04-073C-4062-BDFD-BCB3C31F1AC6/0/SolarGuide.pdf]; Solar Buzz, *United States PV Market 2010; 2010–2014 Scenario Forecast* (San Francisco, CA: Author, June 2010).

4. Larry Sherwood, *US Solar Industry: Year in Review 2009* (Washington, DC: Solar Energy Industries Association, April 15, 2010).

5. Applied Materials, *Summer Solstice Survey* (Santa Clara, CA: Author, 2009); Mark Sinclair, "Creating Demand – How to Market Solar," *Renewable Energy Focus* (October 2009): 18–21; Adam Faiers and Charles Neame, "Consumer Attitudes towards Domestic Solar Power Systems," *Energy Policy* 34, no. 14 (2006): 1797–1806.

6. Lyn Rosoff and Mark Sinclair, *Smart Solar Marketing Strategies: Clean Energy State Program Guide* (Washington, DC: Clean Energy Group and SmartPower, August 2009): 2.

Reports that rely on secondary research include documentation. These endnotes provide the sources of secondary research used in the body of the business plan.

13

Photo Credits

Chapter 1
Opener: © Comstock/PunchStock; p. 3 (left): © Tony Cenicola/ The New York Times/Redux; p. 3 (middle): © Mark Samala/ZUMA Press/ Corbis; p. 3 (right): © David Paul Morris/Bloomberg via Getty Images; p. 16: Courtesy of Peter Cardon.

Chapter 2
Opener: © E. Audras/PhotoAlto; p. 25 (Jackson): © Jose Luis Pelaez Inc/ Blend Images LLC; p. 25 (Brody): © Dougal Waters/Digital Vision/Getty Images; p. 42: © BananaStock/Jupiterimages; p. 47: Courtesy of Peter Cardon.

Chapter 3
Opener: © Floresco Productions/Getty Images; p. 56 (Garcia): © Jose Luis Pelaez Inc/Blend Images LLC; p. 56 (Jeffreys): © Getty Images/Digital Vision; p. 56 (Brookshire): © image100/PunchStock; p. 56 (Yamada): © John A Rizzo/Pixtal/SuperStock; p. 56 (Garcia): © Jose Luis Pelaez Inc/Blend Images LLC; p. 56 (Brookshire): © image100/PunchStock; p. 57 (Jeffreys): © Getty Images/Digital Vision; p. 57 (Yamada): © John A Rizzo/Pixtal/SuperStock; p. 59 (Brookshire): © image100/PunchStock; p. 59 (Garcia): © Jose Luis Pelaez Inc/Blend Images LLC; p. 73: © Steve Cole/Getty Images; p. 77 (Jeffreys): © Getty Images/Digital Vision; p. 77 (Yamada): © John A Rizzo/Pixtal/SuperStock; p. 79: Courtesy of Peter Cardon.

Chapter 4
Opener: © Andersen Ross/Blend Images LLC; p. 88: © Alexandre Marchi/ PhotoPQR/L'Est Republicain/Newscom; p. 103: © Klaus Tiedge/Blend Images LLC; p. 107: Courtesy of Peter Cardon.

Chapter 5
Opener: © Digital Vision/Getty Images; p. 117 (Jackson): © Jose Luis Pelaez Inc/Blend Images LLC; p. 117 (Brody): © Dougal Waters/Digital Vision/ Getty Images; p. 117 (Johnson): © Polka Dot Images/Jupiterimages; p. 138: Courtesy of Peter Cardon.

Chapter 6
Opener: © Jon Feingersh/Blend Images LLC; p. 147 (Jorgenson): © Ariel Skelley/Blend Images LLC; p. 167: Courtesy of Peter Cardon.

Chapter 7
Opener: © Dimitri Vervitsiotis/Photographer's Choice/Getty Images; p. 178 (Garcia): © Jose Luis Pelaez Inc/Blend Images LLC; p. 178 (Jeffreys): © Getty Images/Digital Vision; p. 178 (Brookshire): © image100/ PunchStock; p. 178 (Anderton): © BananaStock; p. 178 (Yamada): © John A Rizzo/Pixtal/SuperStock; p. 178 (Brookshire): © image100/PunchStock; p. 178 (Jeffreys): © Getty Images/Digital Vision; p. 178 (Yamada): © John A Rizzo/Pixtal/SuperStock; p. 193 (Garcia): © Jose Luis Pelaez Inc/Blend Images LLC; p. 193 (Yamada): © John A Rizzo/Pixtal/SuperStock; p. 193 (Jeffreys): © Getty Images/Digital Vision; pp. 193, 195 (Brookshire): © image100/PunchStock; p. 195 (Garcia): © Jose Luis Pelaez Inc/Blend Images LLC; p. 195 (Jeffreys): © Getty Images/Digital Vision; p. 200 (arch): © Digital Vision/Getty Images; p. 200 (canyon): © Design Pics/Philippe Widling; p. 200 (skull): © Royalty-Free/Corbis; p. 200 (casino): © Brand X Pictures; p. 200 (hang gliding): © Brand X Pictures/Jupiterimages; p. 200 (road sign): © Image Source; p. 200 (Osborne): © John Dowland/Getty Images; p. 200 (cards): © Jamie Grill/Blend Images LLC; p. 201 (beach): © Royalty-Free/Corbis; p. 201 (Yamada): © John A Rizzo/Pixtal/SuperStock; p. 201 (empanadas): © Photodisc/Getty Images; p. 201 (dining): © Design Pics/Don Hammond; p. 201 (Yamada): © John A Rizzo/Pixtal/SuperStock; p. 201 (globe): © Dimitri Vervits/ImageState; p. 201 (vegetables): © Pixtal/ AGE Fotostock; p. 201 (boot): © C. Borland/PhotoLink/Getty Images; p. 201 (Tam): © Andersen Ross/Blend Images LLC; p. 201 (Yamada): © John A Rizzo/Pixtal/SuperStock; p. 201 (eclipse): © Tim Robberts/Photodisc/Getty Images; p. 203: Courtesy of Peter Cardon.

Chapter 8
Opener: © momentimages/Getty Images; p. 213 (Atkins): © Jose Luis Pelaez/Blend Images; p. 228: © Jose Luis Pelaez Inc/Blend Images LLC; p. 231 (flowers): © Burke/Triolo Productions/Getty Images; p. 231 (stamp): © Mark Steinmetz; p. 232: Courtesy of Peter Cardon.

Chapter 9
Opener: © E. Audras/PhotoAlto; p. 239 (Zogby): © Ingram Publishing; p. 239 (Russo): © BananaStock; p. 260: © Tom Grill/Corbis; p. 263: © Eric Audras/Getty Images; p. 264: Courtesy of Peter Cardon.

Chapter 10
Opener: © Tetra images RF/Getty Images; p. 271 (Hernandez): © Purestock/ Getty Images; p. 271 (Cooper): © Mike Powell/Getty Images; p. 271 (Adelman): © David Sacks/Digital Vision/Getty Images; p. 280 (Cooper): © Mike Powell/Getty Images; pp. 280, 290 (Hernandez): © Purestock/Getty Images; p. 290 (Adelman): © David Sacks/Digital Vision/Getty Images; p. 291 (Hernandez): © Purestock/Getty Images; p. 291 (Adelman): © David Sacks/Digital Vision/Getty Images; p. 294: Courtesy of James Sloan.

Chapter 11
Opener: © Joshua Hodge Photography; p. 302 (Russo): © BananaStock; p. 302 (Zogby): © Ingram Publishing; p. 310 (sunflower): © David Burton/ Beateworks/Corbis; p. 310 (children): © Design Pics/Don Hammond; p. 322 (sunflower): © David Burton/Beateworks/Corbis; p. 322 (family): © Ariel Skelley/Blend Images LLC; p. 322 (car): © Hannu Liivaar/Alamy; p. 322 (woman): © Caterina Bernardi/The Image Bank/Getty Images; p. 322 (Williams): © Fuse/Getty Images; p. 322 (house): © Peter Gridley/ Taxi/Getty Images; p. 322 (nest): © Stockbyte/Getty Images; p. 322 (QR Code): © Vincenzo Lombardo/Photographer's Choice/Getty Images; p. 322 (sunflower): © David Burton/Beateworks/Corbis; p. 322 (house): © Peter Gridley/Taxi/Getty Images; p. 322 (sunflower): © David Burton/Beateworks/ Corbis; p. 322 (coin bank): © Don Farrall/Getty Images; p. 322 (sunflower): © David Burton/Beateworks/Corbis; p. 322 (family): © Ariel Skelley/Blend Images LLC; p. 322 (charity event): © Dimitrios Kambouris/Getty Images for Avon; p. 322 (iPhone): © McGraw-Hill Companies, Inc; p. 322 (Zogby): © Ingram Publishing; p. 322 (Mitch): © S. Olsson/PhotoAlto; p. 322 (sunflower): © David Burton/Beateworks/Corbis; p. 322 (Zogby): © Ingram Publishing; p. 322 (presentation): © Robert Nicholas/OJO Images/Getty Images; p. 326 (sunflower): © David Burton/Beateworks/Corbis; p. 326 (family): © Ariel Skelley/Blend Images LLC; p. 327 (sunflower): © David Burton/Beateworks/Corbis; p. 327 (family): © Ariel Skelley/Blend Images LLC; p. 330: Courtesy of Steven Craig.

Chapter 12
Opener: © Juice Images/Getty Images; p. 343 (Anderton): © BananaStock; p. 343 (Garcia): © Jose Luis Pelaez Inc/Blend Images LLC; p. 370: Courtesy of John Phillip.

Chapter 13
Opener: © SelectStock/The Agency Collection/Getty Images; p. 379 (Anderton): © BananaStock; p. 379 (Garcia): © Jose Luis Pelaez Inc/Blend Images LLC; p. 410: Courtesy of Rich Harrill.

Chapter 14
Opener: © Abel Mitja Varela/Getty Images; p. 419 (Browne): © Take A Pix Media/Getty Images; p. 430: © DreamPictures/Blend Images LLC; p. 432 (people): © Willie B. Thomas; p. 432 (city): © Photodisc/Getty Images; p. 432 (factory both): © Zhang Lianxun/Dreamstime; p. 433 (hands): © Purestock/SuperStock; p. 433 (businesspeople): © Willie B. Thomas; p. 434: © Stockbyte/Getty Images; p. 438: Courtesy of James Robertson.

Chapter 15
Opener: © PhotoAlto/SuperStock; p. 445 (Browne): © Take A Pix Media/ Getty Images; p. 453 (top left): © Justin Horrocks/iStockphoto.com; p. 453 (top right): © Neustockimages/iStockphoto.com; p. 453 (middle left): © 4x6/iStockphoto.com; p. 453 (middle right): © drbimages/iStockphoto .com; p. 453 (bottom left): © g_studio/iStockphoto.com; p. 453 (bottom right): © Ann Marie Kurtz/iStockphoto.com; p. 459: Courtesy of James Robertson.

Chapter 16
Opener: © Eric Audras/PhotoAlto Agency RF Collections/Getty Images; p. 465 (Zogby), p. 481 (both): © Ingram Publishing; p. 497: Courtesy of Nancy Vaccaro.

Appendix C
P. 527 (Baker): © Jose Luis Pelaez Inc/Blend Images LLC; p. 527 (Murphy): © Dougal Waters/Digital Vision/Getty Images.

Index